VOLUME

COMPUTER AND ROBOT VISION

Robert M. Haralick
University of Washington

Linda G. Shapiro
University of Washington

 ADDISON-WESLEY PUBLISHING COMPANY

Reading, Massachusetts • Menlo Park, California • New York
Don Mills, Ontario • Wokingham, England • Amsterdam • Bonn
Sydney • Singapore • Tokyo • Madrid • San Juan • Milan • Paris

Library of Congress Cataloging-in-Publication Data

Haralick, Robert M.
      Computer and robot vision/Robert M. Haralick, Linda G. Shapiro.
        p.   cm.
      Includes bibliographical references and index.
      ISBN 0-201-10877-1 (v. 1)
        1. Computer vision. 2. Robot vision. 3. Image processing.
I. Shapiro, Linda G. II. Title.
TA1632.H37   1992
621.39'9--dc20   90-25550
                                                                                    CIP

1 2 3 4 5 6 7 8 9 10-HA-95949392

To Michael

PREFACE

This two-volume work is suitable for a full-year course on computer vision. The first volume covers low-level vision and with the exception of the section on shape from texture in the texture chapter, there is no reference to three dimension in the first-volume material. The entire discussion in the first volume is limited to image in and, image out or feature set out. Volume I covers the topics of binary machine vision, mathematical morphology, neighborhood operators, conditioning and labeling operations, the facet model for image processing, texture, region segmentation, and linear feature extraction. The second volume covers higher-level techniques, such as illumination, perspective projection, analytical photogrammetry, motion, image matching, consistent labeling, model matching, and knowledge-based vision systems. A glossary of computer vision terms occurring in Volume I and Volume II appears at the end of Volume II. For a course that covers only Volume I, professors may want to give the glossary out so that students may look up specific terms. The glossary is organized by concept as well as alphabetically and allows students a first compact overview of the field.

Volume I provides a complete course on low- and mid-level computer vision. The material is quite lengthy, even for a semester course. Some of the chapters have material that may be skipped depending on the emphases of the teacher and the background of the students. The computer vision overview chapter and the two binary machine vision chapters should be covered completely. The material in the statistical pattern recognition chapter may be omitted; its omission has no negative effect on the ability to cover the remaining chapters. If any kind of projects, however, are assigned using real images and requiring simple recognition, some kind of statistical pattern recognition is appropriate. Even if the theory of statistical pattern recognition is not part of the course, the professor should cover the decision tree construction procedure in the latter part of the statistical pattern recognition chapter.

The mathematical morphology chapter should be covered through the opening and closing operations, both binary and gray scale. The material on the morphological sampling theorem, bounding derivatives, and the relationship between morphology and median filtering may be skipped. Recursive morphology is important because of the computational efficiency, but if it is used only for the distance transform, then the professor should discuss the distance transform without the theoretical cover of the recursive morphology.

The conditioning and labeling chapter has a large variety of noise cleaning techniques, and it is probably not necessary to cover them all. The facet chapter should be covered through the edge and line (ridge and valley) detection techniques. The material on the topographic primal sketch may be omitted, unless of course some class projects are based on it. The texture chapter should be covered up to the shape from texture section. That section belongs in the second vision course. The image segmentation chapter and the arc extraction and segmentation chapter should be covered in full.

Some end-of-chapter problems are paper and pencil problems, and some are project problems that involve programming and experimenting under controlled conditions. These problems reflect the orientation that performance issues are important in computer vision. To help in doing experiments, Appendix C gives a short discussion of experimental protocol. Setting up experiments and making experimental comparisons under controlled conditions are important and perhaps have not been emphasized enough in the field. Computer vision solutions must satisfy requirements, such as experimentally determining under what conditions a particular computer vision algorithm meets the required performance. There is much to be learned from performance analyses that are crucial in putting together working machine vision systems.

The variety of language fluency required in computer vision is large and this two-volume work reflects it. The mathematics of linear algebra, probability, statistics, estimation theory, set theory, calculus, advanced calculus, optimization theory, and discrete mathematics are all used. Depending on the background of the students and the prerequisites of the class, the teacher may want to provide tutorial material to fill in the holes of the students' backgrounds. We have taught this material to graduate students in electrical engineering and computer science without requiring a specific prerequisite other than graduate standing. A strong undergraduate program covers most of the mathematics we use. When we teach high-level vision, we require a course in artificial intelligence.

Acknowledgements

Many people have contributed to the creation of this book. We are grateful for the comments of Dan Bloomberg, Dorothea Blostein, Gunilla Borgefors, Chinmoy Bose, Kevin Bowyer, Allen Hanson, Thomas Huang, Alireza Khontanzad, Stefano Levialdi, Murray Loew, George Nagy, L. F. Pau, Dragutin Petkovic, Azriel Rosenfeld, Jean Serra, Perry West, and Xinhua Zhuang on early versions of the text. All of our students and many former students and visitors to our lab have been involved in one way or another. In particular, we would like to thank Carsten Agerskov, Dilip Banerjee, Bhabatosh Chanda, Octavia Camps, Mauro

Costa, Ulrich Jacobi, Tapas Kanungo, Bharath Modayur, V. Ramesh, and Henrik Sloth for proofreading and Kevin Bowyer, Tapas Kanungo, Bharath Modayur, V. Ramesh, Larry Rystrom, Brett Thackray, Ken Thornton, and Hyonam Joo for providing figures and other material. Thanks also to our former program assistant, Bill Bertolas, for helping us to start the book and for lots of technical typing. Thanks most of all to our present program assistant, Stephen Graham, for providing a little of everything—typing, figures, proofreading, working with students, and managing the entire project.

We have tried to provide a balanced and thorough treatment of an expansive topic. Rather than covering everything to only survey depth, we tried to cover what we regarded as the most important topics in greater depth, in description, in theory, and, when possible, in algorithm. We have also tried to provide references to a good portion of the vision literature, even if the material referenced is not covered in the text. The project of writing these volumes has been a five-year effort. The field is very large and getting larger. For any one or two people to recognize the importance of or even read each published paper is indeed difficult. We hope that this book will help potential researchers and students of computer vision to become aware of the many different aspects of the field and will provide a firm foundation on which to build their own work.

Seattle, Washington

R. M. H.
L. G. S.

CONTENTS

3   Binary Machine Vision: Region Analysis   59

4   Statistical Pattern Recognition   95

7   Conditioning and Labeling   303

8   The Facet Model   371

9   Texture   453

A   Appendix   639

B   Appendix   659

C   Appendix   666

COMPUTER VISION
Overview

Introduction

Computer vision is the science that develops the theoretical and algorithmic basis by which useful information about the world can be automatically extracted and analyzed from an observed image, image set, or image sequence from computations made by special-purpose or general-purpose computers. Such information can be related to the recognition of a generic object, the three-dimensional description of an unknown object, the position and orientation of the observed object, or the measurement of any spatial property of an object, such as the distance between two of its distinguished points or the diameter of a circular section. Applications of the technology range from vision-guided robot assembly to inspection tasks involving mensuration, verification that all parts are present, or determination that surfaces have no defects.

An *image* is a spatial representation of an object, a two-dimensional or three-dimensional scene, or another image. It can be real or virtual, as in optics. In computer vision, image usually means recorded image, such as a video image, a digital image, or a picture. It may be abstractly thought of as a continuous function I of two variables defined on some bounded and usually rectangular region of a plane. The value of the image located at spatial coordinates (r,c) is denoted by $I(r,c)$. For optic or photographic sensors, $I(r,c)$ is typically proportional to the radiant energy received in the electromagnetic band to which the sensor or detector is sensitive in a small area around (r,c). In this case the image is called an *intensity image*. For range finder sensors, $I(r,c)$ is a function of the line-of-sight distance from (r,c) to an object in the three-dimensional world, and the image is called a *range* image. For tactile sensors, $I(r,c)$ is proportional to the amount by which the surface at and around (r,c) deforms the sensor. When the image is a map, $I(r,c)$ is an index or a symbol associated with some category such as color, thematic land use, soil type, or rock type. We refer to such an image as a *symbolic* image. A

1

recorded image may be in photographic, video signal, or digital format. In this text, when no particular image type or image format is specified, the default will be a digital intensity image. Such an image is represented by a matrix of numeric values each representing a quantized intensity value. When I is a matrix, then $I(r,c)$ is the intensity value at the position corresponding to row r and column c of the matrix.

The problems inherent in computer vision occur because the units of observation are not the units of analysis. The unit of the observed digital image is the *pixel*. A pixel has properties of position and value. By itself, knowledge of the position and value of any particular pixel almost always conveys no information related to the recognition of an object, the description of an object's shape, its position or orientation, the measurement of any distance on the object, or whether the object is defective.

To fully recognize an object means knowing that when it is viewed from a particular orientation, its sensor projection will agree with how it appears on the observed image. How it appears on the image has to do with the spatial configuration of pixel values and has little to do with any one particular value. Agreement between the observed spatial configuration and an expected sensor projection requires the capability to infer explicitly or implicitly an object position and orientation from the spatial configuration and then to confirm that the inference is correct.

The pixel values of intensity images are called *gray levels*. When 8–bit integers are used to store each pixel value, the gray levels range from 0 (black) to 255 (white), with everything in between representing some shade of gray. To infer object position, orientation, and category or class of object from the spatial configuration of gray levels requires the capability to infer which pixels are part of the object and which pixels are not. Then from among those pixels that are part of the object, it requires the capability to distinguish observed object features, such as special markings, lines, curves, or boundaries. These features themselves are organized in a spatial relationship on the image and on the object. Analytic inference of object shape and object position and orientation depends on matching the distinguished image features with corresponding object features and using the hypothesized match in conjunction with the known sensor projection geometry in a mathematical analysis.

To sum up the different units in this explanation, we have:

1. The unit of observation: the pixel;

2. The unit of three-dimensional object feature: a point, a line segment, an arc segment, a curved or planar surface;

3. The unit of two-dimensional image feature: a point, a line segment, or a region;

4. The unit of match or correspondence between object features and image features;

5. The unit of relation between object features;

6. The unit of relation between image features;

7. The unit of sensor position and orientation;

8. The unit of object position and orientation.

The kind of object, the way it is lit, its background, the kind of imaging sensor, and the viewpoint of the sensor all determine whether the computer vision problem is easy or difficult; that is, the transformation of the unit of pixel to the unit of object class with position and orientation may be either direct or involved. For example, suppose that the object is a white planar square on a uniform black background, as shown in the digital image of Fig. 1.1(a). A simple corner-feature extractor could identify the distinguishing corner points, as shown in the symbolic image of Fig. 1.1(b). The match between the image corner features and the object corner features is direct. Just relate the corners of the image square to the corners of the object square in, say, clockwise order, starting from any arbitrary correspondence. Then use the corresponding points to establish the sensor orientation relative to the plane of the square. If we know the size of the square, then we can completely and analytically determine the position and orientation of the square relative to the position and orientation of the camera. In this simple instance the unit of pixel is transformed into the unit of corner feature. The unit of corner feature on the image is transformed to the unit of match between image corners and object corners. Then the unit of match is transformed to the unit of object position and orientation relative to the natural coordinate system of the sensor. For confirmation of recognition, computer graphics means can be used to create an image of a square in the inferred square position and orientation. High similarity between the observed image and the graphics image or between the features of the observed image and the features of the simulated image provides evidence of confirmation.

On the other hand, the transformation process may be difficult. There may be a variety of complex objects that are imaged. Some objects may occlude parts of others. Shadows may occur. The object reflectances may be varied, and the background may be busy.

Figure 1.2(a) and (b) shows two different images of a three-dimensional industrial part, one on a plain white background and one simply lying on a table. While these images are far from the complexity that can arise in natural scenes, they are typical of images processed in robotic applications. Many different types of features can be extracted from such images to be used in algorithms for object recognition, pose determination, or inspection. The most commonly used features are edges, which are the locations where the intensity values change more than a predefined threshold value. Parts (c) and (d) of Fig. 1.2 show the edges extracted from parts (a) and (b), respectively. Notice that even in these fairly simple images not all of the three-dimensional edges between surfaces are detected by the edge detector. In Fig. 1.2(c) the edge between the top and side surfaces of the object is broken and more of it is missing than is present. In Fig. 1.2(d) the edge between the two side surfaces is missing entirely. In both cases the edge pixels are missing because of the lack of contrast between the surfaces in the image. Effects of highlights and shadows can cause some edges to disappear and extra edges to appear. Other types of features that may be extracted from intensity images include corners, holes, and topographic labelings of the gray tone intensity surface, such as peaks, pits, ridges, and valleys.

After simple atomic features have been detected, they may be merged into larger, composite features. Linear-feature pixels, such as edge or ridge pixels, are

0	0	0	0	0	0	0	0	0	0	0	0	0	0	0
0	0	0	0	0	0	0	0	0	0	0	0	0	0	0
0	0	0	0	0	0	0	0	0	0	0	0	0	0	0
0	0	0	0	0	0	0	0	0	0	0	0	0	0	0
0	0	0	0	0	0	0	0	0	0	0	0	0	0	0
0	0	0	0	0	255	255	255	255	255	0	0	0	0	0
0	0	0	0	0	255	255	255	255	255	0	0	0	0	0
0	0	0	0	0	255	255	255	255	255	0	0	0	0	0
0	0	0	0	0	255	255	255	255	255	0	0	0	0	0
0	0	0	0	0	255	255	255	255	255	0	0	0	0	0
0	0	0	0	0	0	0	0	0	0	0	0	0	0	0
0	0	0	0	0	0	0	0	0	0	0	0	0	0	0
0	0	0	0	0	0	0	0	0	0	0	0	0	0	0
0	0	0	0	0	0	0	0	0	0	0	0	0	0	0
0	0	0	0	0	0	0	0	0	0	0	0	0	0	0

(a)

N	N	N	N	N	N	N	N	N	N	N	N	N	N	N
N	N	N	N	N	N	N	N	N	N	N	N	N	N	N
N	N	N	N	N	N	N	N	N	N	N	N	N	N	N
N	N	N	N	N	N	N	N	N	N	N	N	N	N	N
N	N	N	N	N	N	N	N	N	N	N	N	N	N	N
N	N	N	N	N	C	N	N	N	C	N	N	N	N	N
N	N	N	N	N	N	N	N	N	N	N	N	N	N	N
N	N	N	N	N	N	N	N	N	N	N	N	N	N	N
N	N	N	N	N	N	N	N	N	N	N	N	N	N	N
N	N	N	N	N	C	N	N	N	C	N	N	N	N	N
N	N	N	N	N	N	N	N	N	N	N	N	N	N	N
N	N	N	N	N	N	N	N	N	N	N	N	N	N	N
N	N	N	N	N	N	N	N	N	N	N	N	N	N	N
N	N	N	N	N	N	N	N	N	N	N	N	N	N	N
N	N	N	N	N	N	N	N	N	N	N	N	N	N	N

(b)

Figure 1.1 Numeric digital intensity image (a) of a white (gray tone 255) square on a black (gray tone 0) background and symbolic image (b) of its corners. The symbol N means noncorner and C means corner.

linked together to form ordered sequences of pixels called *arcs,* which may be further transformed by fitting to straight lines or conics. Connected sets of pixels that have similar gray tones or other properties can be grouped together to form *regions.* The edge images of Fig. 1.2(c) and (d) can be converted into a set of straight and curved arcs. The intensity images of Fig. 1.2(a) and (b) can be *segmented* into regions whose pixels all have similar intensities. Example segmentations are shown in Fig. 1.2(e) and (f).

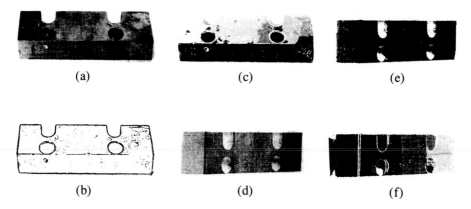

(a)   (c)   (e)

(b)   (d)   (f)

Figure 1.2 Two images of an industrial part (a) and (b), the corresponding (thinned and further processed) edge images (c) and (d), and the segmented images (e) and (f) from a region-growing operation.

The region units, arc units, and point units may then need to be transformed into units of spatial relation to describe interrelationships in the image such as adjacency of regions or proximity, collinearity, and parallelness of line segments. The transformation of the unit of relation to the unit of partial match may then be very complex because of the required combinatorial search over all possible matches. For each hypothesized partial match, the unit of partial match must be transformed to the unit of object position and orientation. Finally, confirming evidence must be established by determining the degree to which other feature units not involved in the partial match are located where expected and participate in the expected relationships among themselves and with the features that helped to determine the partial match.

Which kinds of unit transformation must be employed depends on the specific nature of the vision task, the complexity of the images, and the kind of prior information available.

1.2   Recognition Methodology

Computer recognition and inspection of objects is, in general, a complex procedure requiring a variety of steps that successively transform the iconic data to recognition information. Handling unconstrained environments is often difficult for today's computer vision and recognition technology because the existing algorithms are specialized and do not develop one or more of the necessary transformation steps to a high enough degree. Our thesis is that there are no shortcuts. A recognition methodology must pay substantial attention to each of the following six steps: image formation, conditioning, labeling, grouping, extracting, and matching. In this book we do not address the problem of image formation, although we do discuss modeling the brightness of surfaces as a function of illumination and the surface reflectivity function. And we do address the other five steps.

Conditioning, labeling, grouping, extracting, and matching constitute a canonical decomposition of the recognition problem, each step preparing and transforming the data in the right way for the next step. Depending on the computer vision application, we may have to apply this sequence of steps at one or more levels of the recognition and description process. As these steps work on any level in the unit transformation process, they prepare the data for the unit transformation, identify the first higher-level unit, and interpret it. The interpretation constitutes the second higher-level unit. Many vision algorithms incorporate these steps explicitly. Some algorithms embody one or more of the steps in an implicit way. Those that implicitly and explicitly miss a step will probably have an inherent weakness directly related to the missing step.

1.2.1   Conditioning

Conditioning is based on a model that suggests that the observed image is composed of an informative pattern modified by uninteresting variations that typically add to or multiply the informative pattern. Conditioning estimates the informative pattern on the basis of the observed image. Thus conditioning suppresses noise, which can be thought of as random unpatterned variations affecting all measurements. Conditioning can also perform background normalization by suppressing uninteresting systematic or patterned variations. Conditioning is typically applied uniformly and is context independent. The intensity images of Fig. 1.2(a) and (b) are the result of morphological conditioning algorithms applied to images obtained from a CCD camera. The original images had tiny bright spots due to illumination of the uneven metal surfaces. The bright spots were effectively removed by morphological opening and closing operations.

1.2.2   Labeling

Labeling is based on a model that suggests that the informative pattern has structure as a spatial arrangement of events, each spatial event being a set of connected pixels. Labeling determines in what kinds of spatial events each pixel participates. For example, if the interesting spatial events of the informative pattern are events only of high-valued and low-valued pixels, then the thresholding operation can be considered a labeling operation. Other kinds of labeling operations include edge detection, corner finding, and identification of pixels that participate in various shape primitives. The edge images of Fig. 1.2(c) and (d) are the result of applying a blur–minimum edge operator plus a thinning operation to the conditioned images.

1.2.3   Grouping

The labeling operation labels pixels with the kinds of primitive spatial events in which the pixel participates. The grouping operation identifies the events by collecting together or identifying maximal connected sets of pixels participating in the same kind of event. If the labels are symbolic, then the grouping is really a connected components operation. If the labels are the gray levels, then the grouping operation is what the vision literature calls a segmentation. If the labels are step edges, then the grouping operation constitutes edge linking, and so on. The segmented region images of Fig. 1.2(e) and (f) are the result of applying a region-growing segmentation algorithm to the conditioned images.

The grouping operation involves a change of logical data structure. The observed image, the conditioned image, and the labeled image are all digital image data structures. Depending on the implementation, the grouping operation can produce either an image data structure in which each pixel is given an index associated with the spatial event to which it belongs or a data structure that is a collection of sets. Each set corresponds to a spatial event and contains the pairs of (row, column) positions that participate in the event. In either case a change occurs in the logical data structure. The entities of interest before the grouping step are pixels. The entities of interest after the grouping step are sets of pixels.

1.2.4 Extracting

The grouping operation determines the new set of entities. But after the grouping step the new entities are naked. The only thing they possess is their identity. The extracting operation computes for each group of pixels a list of its properties. Example properties might include its centroid, its area, its orientation, its spatial moments, its gray tone moments, its spatial–gray tone moments, its circumscribing circle, its inscribing circle, and so on. Other properties might depend on whether the group is considered a region or an arc. If the group is a region, then number of holes might be a useful property. If the group is an arc, then average curvature might be a useful property.

Extracting also can measure topological or spatial relationships between two or more groupings. For example, an extracting operation may make explicit that two groupings touch or are spatially close or that one grouping is above another.

1.2.5 Matching

After the completion of the extracting operation, the events occurring on the image have been identified and measured. But the events in and of themselves have no meaning. The meaning of the observed spatial events emerges when a perceptual organization has occurred such that a specific set of spatial events in the observed spatial organization clearly constitutes an imaged instance of some previously known object, such as a chair or the letter A. Once an object or set of object parts has been recognized, then measurements such as the distance between two parts, the angle between two lines, or the area of an object part can be made and related to the allowed tolerance, for instance, in an inspection scenario.

It is the matching operation that determines the interpretation of some related set of image events, associating these events with some given three-dimensional object or two-dimensional shape. The association determined by matching establishes a correspondence between each spatial event in the related set of events on the image with some spatial event on the three-dimensional object or two-dimensional shape. The association is one that in some sense best matches both the character of the spatial events and their spatial relationships. Thus, after matching, two primitive image events that stand in some spatial relationship will have associated with them two object events that stand in a similar relationship.

A wide variety of image operations are matching operations. The classic one is template matching, which is effective only if the variety of instances expected to be encountered is limited. For example, rotation and size variations must be very small. The background must be nearly uniform. Random shape deformations must be minimal.

Simple shapes will correspond to a primitive spatial event, and the property measurement from the primitive spatial event will often be adequate to permit recognition of the shape. In this case the matching operation amounts to matching the vector of properties measured from the image spatial event with the vector of properties of a prototype representative. Such matching constitutes statistical pattern recognition.

Complex shapes will correspond to a set of primitive spatial events. Here, recognition must proceed by using the property vector of each observed spatial event as well as the spatial relationships between the events. In this case the matching amounts to determining a relational homomorphism with unary constraints established by the required matching of the property vectors of the observed image events with the property vectors of the prototype primitives. Such a matching is what constitutes structural pattern recognition.

1.3   Outline of Book

This text describes those aspects of computer vision that are needed in robotics and other real-world applications such as industrial-part inspection, medical diagnosis, aerial-image interpretation, and space station maintenance. Because the emphasis is on practical vision, those techniques that are most commonly used or will soon be used in real machine vision systems are emphasized, and those techniques that are of interest in studying perception, but not currently useful in practice, are only briefly mentioned or not mentioned at all. As important as they are, the issues of image formation and computer architectures particularly suited for vision are not addressed in this book.

This chapter has briefly introduced the concepts and terminology of computer vision. (A complete glossary of vision terms can be found in Chapter 21.)

Chapter 2 discusses some thresholding techniques to transform a gray scale image to a binary image where the binary-1 pixels are candidates for pixels that belong to the object of interest. Thresholding, as mentioned in Section 1.2, is a labeling operation. Connected component labeling, which transforms the binary pixel units to the region unit, is discussed next. Connected components labeling, as mentioned earlier, is a grouping operation. Chapter 2 also discusses signature segmentation, which is a competing operation but is weaker than connected components labeling.

Chapter 3 discusses the global shape and position features that may be computed from the region unit. This computation permits a two-dimensional feature vector unit to be associated with each region unit. This computation is the feature extraction step mentioned in Section 1.2.

Chapter 4 discusses the general concepts of statistical pattern recognition. It emphasizes the construction of decision trees to determine which regions and their feature vectors belong to objects of interest and whether those objects have no defects or are in the right orientation. Statistical pattern recognition provides the simplest techniques for accomplishing matching. It is the appropriate technology only in a restricted set of conditions.

Chapter 5 discusses the mathematical morphology algebraic approach to working with binary or gray scale images to extract objects on the basis of their shape characteristics even if the image is somewhat distorted or noisy or part of the object of interest is occluded. Because shape is the primary carrier of information in image data, the coherent set of nonlinear mathematical morphology techniques described in Chapter 5 constitutes one of the most important tools to be used in practical image analysis.

Chapter 6 discusses many low-level image analysis operations that can be done as neighborhood operations. Emphasis is placed on the general form of the neighborhood operator. The linear shift invariant operator plays an important role, but there are other recursive and nonrecursive operators that operate on numeric or symbolic images. This chapter gives a variety of examples for such operators.

Chapter 7 discusses different kinds of neighborhood operators to accomplish the conditioning and labeling operations identified in Section 1.2. In this chapter conditioning relates mainly to noise cleaning, and labeling to edge detection.

Chapter 8 discusses the facet model for image processing. Emphasis here is on setting up the appropriate image models so that estimates of partial derivatives may be obtained and used in diverse labeling applications whose defining characteristics are given in terms of local spatial derivatives.

Chapter 9 discusses a variety of approaches to image texture analysis and characterization. These approaches are suitable for determining texture feature vectors associated either with given regions or with a pixel's local neighborhood.

Chapter 10 surveys several image segmentation techniques to accomplish the transformation of the gray scale image, where the pixel is the unit, to a symbolic image in which each pixel's value is an index of the region to which it belongs. Here, the new higher-level unit is the region, a unit that can have a rich variety of shape, geometric, topological, and gray scale properties associated with it.

Chapters 1 through 10 work with the image data structure to produce points, regions, or point sequences associated with region boundaries or lines on the image. Chapter 11 discusses the segmentation of point sequences and the extraction of features for each segment. These techniques are important in representing boundary information in a structural form to permit shape-matching algorithms to work.

The chief vision sensor is the optic camera sensor. The main issues involved with this sensor are what determines the brightness of any point in a scene (its radiometry) and what determines where it appears on the image (its perspective projection geometry). Chapter 12 examines radiometry, the bidirectional reflection distribution function, and polarization. The inverse radiometry techniques considered in Chapter 12 include photometric stereo and shape from shading. Chapter 13 discusses the mathematics of the perspective projection and a variety of direct techniques for using object model features and their two-dimensional perspective projections to infer the position of the object with respect to the camera reference frame. Chapter 13 focuses on inverse perspective geometry.

The problem of determining where an object is relative to a camera, or equivalently of determining where the camera is relative to the world, is one of the basic problems of analytic photogrammetry. Chapter 14 reviews the contemporary methods used by photogrammetrists. The techniques are mainly applicable when prior knowledge of the position of the camera lens is correct to within 10% and prior knowledge of orientation of the optic axis is correct to within 15°.

Chapter 15 discusses the inference of surface structure and shape from a time sequence of imagery. The time sequence can be due to camera motion, object motion, or both.

Chapter 16 explores the theory of image matching. It emphasizes differential matching and matching using interest operators. All the techniques discussed estimate not only the spatial transformation by which one image can be made to correspond to another but also the accuracy of the match.

The basis of structured matching is the relational homomorphism. Chapter 17 discusses such matching from the general point of view of consistent labeling. It emphasizes both the theory behind the matching and the algorithms for accomplishing the matching. Chapter 18 investigates object recognition, both two-dimensional and three-dimensional, and covers object models and representations and several general matching techniques. Chapter 19 discusses the concepts involved in knowledge-based vision and the systems that different groups have implemented for accomplishing this task. Such systems are highly model and domain knowledge driven.

Chapter 20 discusses the issues of accuracy and performance assessment, matters that are most important for practical vision systems. Accuracy is handled first from the point of view of the spatial quantization inherent in all digital processing systems, then in terms of the experimental protocol and required statistical analysis to determine repeatability, accuracy, and error rate of vision systems.

Chapter 21 is a glossary of computer vision terms. It is organized by concept so that a reading of the glossary from beginning to end provides a compact review of the field. Associated with the glossary is an index organized alphabetically so that specific terms can be looked up quickly.

Various general books or edited books on computer vision are listed in the bibliography section. Journals that publish articles on vision include *IEEE Transactions on Pattern Analysis and Machine Intelligence; IEEE Transactions on Robotics and Automation; IEEE Transactions on Systems, Man, and Cybernetics; Computer Vision, Graphics, and Image Processing (now published as two separate journals, CVGIP: Image Understanding and CVGIP: Graphical Models and Image Processing); Computer Vision; Pattern Recognition; Pattern Recognition Letters; Image and Vision Computing;* and *Machine Vision and Applications*. Conferences that publish articles on vision include: Computer Vision and Pattern Recognition; International Conference on Computer Vision; International Conference on Pattern Recognition; Scandinavian Conference on Image Analysis; the Image Understanding Workshop; and many of the SPIE Conferences.

■ Bibliography

Ballard, D. H., and C. M. Brown, *Computer Vision,* Prentice-Hall, Englewood Cliffs, NJ, 1982.

Batchelor, B. G., D. A. Hill, and D. C. Hodgson, *Automated Visual Inspection,* IFS, Bedford, United Kingdom, 1985.

Boyle, R. D., and R. C. Thomas, *Computer Vision: A First Course,* Blackwell Scientific, Oxford, 1988.

Brown, C. M. (ed.), *Advances in Computer Vision,* Vols. 1 and 2, Lawrence Erlbaum, Hillsdale, NJ, 1988.

Fischler, M. A., and O. Firschein, *Intelligence: The Eye, the Brain and the Computer,* Addison-Wesley, Reading, MA, 1987.

Freeman, H. (ed.), *Machine Vision for Inspection and Measurement,* Academic Press, New York, 1989.

Gonzalez, R. C., and P. Wintz, *Digital Image Processing,* 2d ed., Addison-Wesley, Reading, MA, 1987.

Horn, B. K. P., *Robot Vision,* MIT Press, Cambridge, MA, 1986.

Kanade, T., *Three Dimensional Vision,* Kluwer, Boston, 1987.

Levine, A. D., *Vision in Man and Machine,* McGraw-Hill, New York, 1985.

Marr, D., *Vision,* W.H. Freeman, San Francisco, 1982.

Nevatia, R., *Machine Perception,* Prentice-Hall, Englewood Cliffs, NJ, 1982.

Pau, L. F., *Computer Vision for Electronic Manufacturing,* Plenum Press, New York, 1990.

Pentland, A. P., *From Pixels to Predicates,* Ablex, Norwood, NJ, 1986.

Pugh, A. (ed.), *Robot Vision,* IFS, Bedford, United Kingdom, 1983.

Rosenfeld, A., and A. Kak, *Digital Picture Processing,* 2d ed., Vols. 1 and 2, Computer Science and Applied Mathematics, Academic Press, Orlando, FL, 1982.

Schalkoff, R. J., *Digital Image Processing and Computer Vision: An Introduction to Theory and Implementations,* Wiley, New York, 1989.

Shirai, Y., *Three-Dimensional Computer Vision,* Symbolic Computation, Springer-Verlag, Berlin, 1987.

2 BINARY MACHINE VISION

Thresholding and Segmentation

2.1 Introduction

In the detection and recognition of two-dimensional or three-dimensional objects or object defects by a computer vision system, the input image is often simplified by generating an output image whose pixels tend to have high values if they are part of an object of interest and low values if they are not part of any object of interest. To actually recognize an object, regions on the image that have the potential for being some part of the object first need to be identified. The simplest, although not necessarily the best, way to identify these object regions is to perform a threshold-labeling operation in which each pixel that has a high enough value is given the value binary 1. The value binary 1 here designates that the pixel has some possibility of being part of an object of interest. Each pixel that does not have a high enough value is given the value binary 0. This designates that it has little possibility of being part of any object of interest. The generation and analysis of such a binary image is called *binary machine vision.*

The first step of binary machine vision is to threshold a gray scale image, thereby labeling each pixel as a binary 0 or a binary 1. The binary-1 label designates a pixel that is considered to be part of an object of interest. The binary-0 label designates a background pixel. Thresholding is a labeling operation.

Depending on the complexity of the objects and the nature of the shapes to be identified and their binary expected relative positions, the next stage of processing could be one of two midlevel vision grouping techniques: connected components labeling or signature segmentation. Both these techniques make a transformation on the kind of units being processed. The units of the image are the pixels. The units after the transformation are more complex; they are called regions or segments and are composed of groupings of pixels. After the regions are defined, a variety of measurements can be made on them. This constitutes an attribute labeling or property measurement step that we call *feature extraction.* The regions are finally assigned an object class or an object defect class or category through a pattern recognition technique. This constitutes the matching and inferring steps.

The operation sequence of thresholding, connected components labeling, region property measurement, and statistical pattern recognition is called *connected components analysis*. This was the basis of what has come to be known as the SRI algorithm (Gleason and Agin, 1979; Agin, 1980). The operation sequence of thresholding, signature segmentation, region property measurement, and statistical pattern recognition is called *signature analysis*. This chapter covers the topics of thresholding and segmentation. Thresholding is discussed in Section 2.2; segmentation by connected components labeling, in Section 2.3; and signature segmentation and analysis, in Section 2.4.

2.2   Thresholding

Thresholding is a labeling operation on a gray scale image. Thresholding distinguishes pixels that have higher gray values from pixels that have lower gray values. Pixels whose gray values are high enough are given the binary value 1. Pixels whose gray values are not high enough are given the binary value 0. Figure 2.1 illustrates a simple gray scale image. Figure 2.2 illustrates a thresholded image obtained by making all pixels having a value greater than 1 a binary 1 and all other pixels a binary 0.

The question of thresholding is a question of the automatic determination of the threshold value. What basis can be used? Since the threshold value separates the dark background from the bright object (or vice versa), the separation could ideally be done if the distribution of dark pixels were known and the distribution of bright pixels were known. The threshold value could then be determined as that separation value for which the fraction of dark pixels labeled binary 1 equals the fraction of bright pixels labeled binary 0. Such a threshold value would equalize the probability of the two kinds of errors: the error of assigning a pixel belonging to the background as a binary 1 and the error of assigning a pixel belonging to the object as a binary 0. The difficulty here is that the independent distributions of dark and bright pixels are often not known ahead of time. What is known is the image histogram, which tells how many pixels are associated with any gray value in the mixture distribution.

The *histogram h* of a digital image I is defined by $h(m) = \#\{(r,c) \mid I(r,c) = m\}$, where m spans each gray level value and $\#$ is the operator that counts the number of elements in a set. A histogram can be computed by using an array data structure and a very simple procedure. Let H be a vector array dimensioned from 0 to MAX, where 0 is the value of the smallest possible gray level value and MAX is the value of the largest. Let I be a two-dimensional array, dimensioned 1 to ROWSIZE by 1 to COLSIZE that holds a gray level image. The histogram procedure is given by

procedure Histogram(I,H);
"Initialize histogram to zero."

								5	8	9			
									9	8	9		
		5								7	9	8	
		3									6	9	9
		5				7							
	2					6							
	8						5			1	1		
3							6			1	1	1	
							7						
	4	3						3	2	6	2		
	2	4						3	8	4	3		
	5	9						7	2	3	9		

Figure 2.1 Original gray scale image. Pixels having no numbers have value of 0.

```
for i := 0 to MAX do
    H(i) := 0;
    "Compute values by accumulation."
    for r := 1 to ROWSIZE do
        for c := 1 to COLSIZE do
            begin
                grayval := I(r,c);
                H(grayval) := H(grayval) + 1
            end
        end for
    end for
end Histogram
```

If the distributions of dark pixels and bright pixels are widely separated, then the image histogram will be bimodal, one mode corresponding to the dark pixels and one mode corresponding to the bright pixels. With little distribution overlap, the threshold value is easily chosen as a value in the valley between the two dominant histogram modes. This is illustrated in Figs. 2.3 through 2.5. However, as the

							1	1	1			
								1	1	1		
		1						1	1	1		
		1							1	1	1	
		1			1							
	1				1							
	1					1		1	1			
1						1		1	1	1		
						1						
	1	1						1	1	1	1	
	1	1						1	1	1	1	
	1	1						1	1	1	1	

Figure 2.2 Thresholded gray scale image. All pixels greater than 0 are marked with a binary 1.

distributions for the bright and dark pixels become more and more overlapped, the choice of threshold value as the valley between the two histogram modes becomes more difficult, because the valley begins to disappear as the two distributions begin to merge together. Furthermore, when there is substantial overlap, the choice of threshold as the valley point is less optimal in the sense of minimizing classification error.

To make this point, we consider an example. Figure 2.6 illustrates an image of a BNC T-connector on a dark textured background. In such a simple image one might hope for a pixel to be either a part of the background or a part of the object of interest based purely on its gray value. But things are not so simple. Figure 2.7 shows a histogram of the BNC T-connector image of Fig. 2.6. For this image the histogram of the combination of the bright object on the dark background is not bimodal. The placement of the threshold is not so easy to determine.

Figure 2.8 illustrates different thresholds applied to the image of Fig. 2.6. Some are too low. Some are too high. Thresholds that are too low incorrectly label more pixels as bright (and therefore as part of the object of interest) than appropriate. Thresholds that are too high incorrectly label more pixels as dark (and therefore as not part of the object of interest) than appropriate.

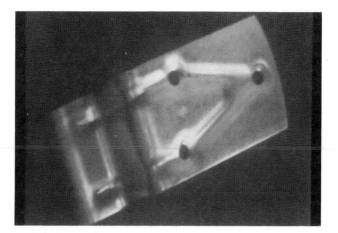

Figure 2.3 Image of a metal part.

Simple thresholding schemes such as that employed on the image of Fig. 2.6 and shown as the images of Fig. 2.8 compare each pixel's gray value with the same global threshold and make the distinction on the basis of whether the pixel's gray value is higher than the threshold. More complex thresholding schemes use a spatially varying threshold. Such techniques can compensate for a variety of local spatial context effects. Some of the more complex thresholding algorithms can be decomposed into two algorithms; the first algorithm produces the spatially varying threshold image, and the second subtracts the spatially varying threshold image from the original image and then performs a simple thresholding on the difference image. Such a spatially varying threshold image can be thought of as a means of performing

Figure 2.4 Histogram of the image of Fig. 2.3. The histogram shows two dominant modes. The small mode on the left tail is not significant.

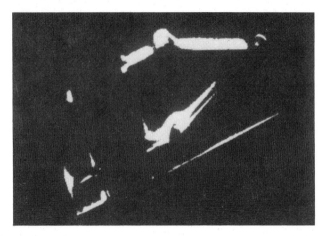

Figure 2.5 Metal-part image of Fig. 2.3 thresholded at gray level 148, which is in the valley between the two dominant modes.

background normalization. The technique of constructing a spatially varying threshold image arises naturally in the opening and closing residue operations, which are discussed in Chapter 5 on mathematical morphology.

In this section we give an introductory discussion of two methods for simple thresholding. The key issue is how to select the most appropriate threshold value. Since all pixels will be compared with the same global threshold, and no further information is available, it is natural to base the selection of the threshold on the image histogram.

The two techniques we discuss are based on finding a threshold that minimizes a criterion function. The first method minimizes the within-group variance. The second method minimizes the Kullback information measure (Kullback, 1959).

Figure 2.6 BNC T-connector against a dark background.

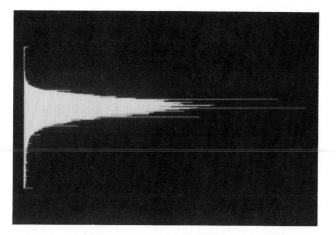

Figure 2.7 Histogram of the BNC T-connector image of Fig. 2.6.

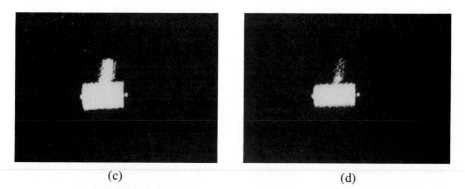

(a)   (b)

(c)   (d)

Figure 2.8 Image of the BNC T-connector thresholded at four levels: (a) 110, (b) 130, (c) 150, and (d) 170.

2.2.1   Minimizing Within-Group Variance

Let $P(1),\ldots,P(I)$ represent the histogram probabilities of the observed gray values $1,\ldots,I;P(i) = \#\{(r,c) \mid Image(r,c) = i\}/\#R \times C$, where $R \times C$ is the spatial domain of the image. If the histogram is bimodal, the histogram thresholding problem is to determine a best threshold t separating the two modes of the histogram from each other. Each threshold t determines a variance for the group of values that are less than or equal to t and a variance for the group of values greater than t. The definition for best threshold suggested by Otsu (1979) is that threshold for which the weighted sum of group variances is minimized. The weights are the probabilities of the respective groups.

We motivate the within-group variance criterion by considering the situation that sometimes happens in a schoolroom. An exam is given and the histogram of the resulting scores is bimodal. There are the better students and the worse students. Lectures that are aimed at the better students go too fast for the others, and lectures that are aimed at the level of the worse students are boring to the better students. To fix this situation, the teacher decides to divide the class into two mutually exclusive and homogeneous groups based on the test score. The question is to determine which test score to use as the dividing criterion. Ideally each group should have test scores that have a unimodal bell-shaped histogram, one around a lower mean and one around a higher mean. This would indicate that each group is homogeneous within itself and different from the other.

A measure of group homogeneity is variance. A group with high homogeneity will have low variance. A group with low homogeneity will have high variance. One possible way to choose a dividing criterion is to choose a dividing score such that the resulting weighted sum of the within-group variances is minimized. This criterion emphasizes high group homogeneity. A second way to choose the dividing criterion is to choose a dividing score that maximizes the resulting squared difference between the group means. This difference is related to the between-group variance. Both dividing criteria lead to the same dividing score because the sum of the within-group variances and the between-group variances is a constant.

Let σ_W^2 be the weighted sum of group variances, that is, the *within-group variance*. Let $\sigma_1^2(t)$ be the variance for the group with values less than or equal to t and $\sigma_2^2(t)$ be the variance for the group with values greater than t. Let $q_1(t)$ be the probability for the group with values less than or equal to t and $q_2(t)$ be the probability for the group with values greater than t. Let $\mu_1(t)$ be the mean for the first group and $\mu_2(t)$ the mean for the second group. Then the within-group variance σ_W^2 is defined by

$$\sigma_W^2(t) = q_1(t)\,\sigma_1^2(t) + q_2(t)\,\sigma_2^2(t)$$

where

$$q_1(t) = \sum_{i=1}^{t} P(i)$$

$$q_2(t) = \sum_{i=t+1}^{I} P(i) \tag{2.1}$$

$$\mu_1(t) = \sum_{i=1}^{t} i\, P(i)/q_1(t)$$

$$\mu_2(t) = \sum_{i=t+1}^{I} i\, P(i)/q_2(t) \tag{2.2}$$

$$\sigma_1^2(t) = \sum_{i=1}^{t} [i - \mu_1(t)]^2\, P(i)/q_1(t)$$

$$\sigma_2^2(t) = \sum_{i=t+1}^{I} [i - \mu_2(t)]^2\, P(i)/q_2(t) \tag{2.3}$$

The best threshold t can then be determined by a simple sequential search through all possible values of t to locate the threshold t that minimizes $\sigma_W^2(t)$. In many situations this can be reduced to a search between the two modes. However, identification of the modes is really equivalent to the identification of separating values between the modes.

There is a relationship between the within-group variance $\sigma_W^2(t)$ and the total variance σ^2 that does not depend on the threshold. The total variance is defined by

$$\sigma^2 = \sum_{i=1}^{I} (i - \mu)^2 P(i)$$

where

$$\mu = \sum_{i=1}^{I} i\, P(i)$$

The relationship between the total variance and the within-group variance can make the calculation of the best threshold less computationally complex. By rewriting σ^2, we have

$$\sigma^2 = \sum_{i=1}^{t} [i - \mu_1(t) + \mu_1(t) - \mu]^2\, P(i) + \sum_{i=t+1}^{I} [i - \mu_2(t) + \mu_2(t) - \mu]^2\, P(i)$$

$$= \sum_{i=1}^{t} \{[i - \mu_1(t)]^2 + 2[i - \mu_1(t)][\mu_1(t) - \mu] + [\mu_1(t) - \mu]^2\} P(i)$$

$$+ \sum_{i=t+1}^{I} \{[i - \mu_2(t)]^2 + 2[i - \mu_2(t)][\mu_2(t) - \mu] + [\mu_2(t) - \mu]^2\} P(i)$$

But

$$\sum_{i=1}^{t} [i - \mu_1(t)][\mu_1(t) - \mu] P(i) = 0 \quad \text{and}$$

$$\sum_{i=t+1}^{I} [i - \mu_2(t)][\mu_2(t) - \mu)] P(i) = 0$$

Since

$$q_1(t) = \sum_{i=1}^{t} P(i) \quad \text{and} \quad q_2(t) = \sum_{i=t+1}^{I} P(i)$$

$$\sigma^2 = \sum_{i=1}^{t} [i - \mu_1(t)]^2 P(i) + [\mu_1(t) - \mu]^2 q_1(t)$$

$$+ \sum_{i=t+1}^{I} [i - \mu_2(t)]^2 P(i) + [\mu_2(t) - \mu]^2 q_2(t)$$

$$= [q_1(t) \sigma_1^2(t) + q_2(t) \sigma_2^2(t)]$$
$$+ \{q_1(t) [\mu_1(t) - \mu]^2 + q_2(t) [\mu_2(t) - \mu]^2\} \qquad (2.4)$$

The first bracketed term is called the within-group variance σ_W^2. It is just the sum of the weighted variances of each of the two groups. The second bracketed term is called the between-group variance σ_B^2. It is just the sum of the weighted squared distances between the means of each group and the grand mean. The between-group variance can be further simplified. Note that the grand mean μ can be written as

$$\mu = q_1(t) \mu_1(t) + q_2(t) \mu_2(t) \qquad (2.5)$$

Using Eq. (2.5) to eliminate μ in Eq. (2.4), substituting $1 - q_1(t)$ for $q_2(t)$, and simplifying, we obtain

$$\sigma^2 = \sigma_W^2(t) + q_1(t)[1 - q_1(t)] [\mu_1(t) - \mu_2(t)]^2$$

Since the total variance σ^2 does not depend on t, the t minimizing $\sigma_W^2(t)$ will be the t maximizing the between-group variance $\sigma_B^2(t)$,

$$\sigma_B^2(t) = q_1(t) [1 - q_1(t)] [\mu_1(t) - \mu_2(t)]^2 \qquad (2.6)$$

To determine the maximizing t for $\sigma_B^2(t)$, the quantities determined by Eqs. (2.1) to (2.3) all have to be determined. However, this need not be done independently for each t. There is a relationship between the value computed for t and that computed for the next $t : t + 1$. We have directly from Eq. (2.1) the recursive relationship

$$q_1(t + 1) = q_1(t) + P(t + 1) \qquad (2.7)$$

with initial value $q_1(1) = P(1)$.

From Eq. (2.2) we obtain the recursive relation

$$\mu_1(t + 1) = \frac{q_1(t) \mu_1(t) + (t + 1)P(t + 1)}{q_1(t + 1)} \qquad (2.8)$$

with the initial value $\mu_1(0) = 0$. Finally, from Eq. (2.5) we have

$$\mu_2(t + 1) = \frac{\mu - q_1(t + 1) \mu_1(t + 1)}{1 - q_1(t + 1)} \qquad (2.9)$$

Figure 2.9 illustrates the binary image produced by the Otsu threshold. Kittler and Illingworth (1985) note that the between group variance σ_B^2 is not necessarily a unimodal criterion, even though Otsu had hypothesized it was. Also, when the fractions

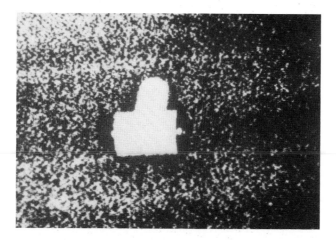

Figure 2.9 Binary image produced by thresholding the T-connector image of Fig. 2.6 with the Otsu threshold.

of pixels in each mode are far from being approximately equal, the minimization of σ_W^2 or the equivalent maximization of σ_B^2 will not necessarily produce the correct answer.

2.2.2 Minimizing Kullback Information Distance

Kittler and Illingworth (1985) suggest a different criterion from Otsu's. They assume that the observations come from a mixture of two Gaussian distributions having respective means and variances (μ_1, σ_1^2) and (μ_2, σ_2^2) and respective proportions q_1 and q_2. They determine the threshold T that results in q_1, q_2, μ_1, μ_2, σ_1, σ_2, which minimize the Kullback (1959) directed divergence J from the observed histogram $P(1), \ldots, P(I)$ to the unknown mixture distribution f. J is defined by

$$J = \sum_{i=1}^{I} P(i) \log \left[\frac{P(i)}{f(i)} \right]$$

A mixture distribution f having fraction q_1 of distribution h_1 and fraction q_2 of distribution h_2 can be represented as

$$f(i) = q_1 h_1(i) + q_2 h_2(i)$$

The mixture distribution of the two Gaussians reflected in the histogram therefore takes the form

$$f(i) = \frac{q_1}{\sqrt{2\pi}\sigma_1} e^{-\frac{1}{2}\left(\frac{i-\mu_1}{\sigma_1}\right)^2} + \frac{q_2}{\sqrt{2\pi}\sigma_2} e^{-\frac{1}{2}\left(\frac{i-\mu_2}{\sigma_2}\right)^2}$$

The meaning of J can be understood in the following way. Let H be the hypothesis that the observed outcomes follow probability distribution P. Let H' be the hypothesis that the observed outcomes follow probability distribution f. Let i

designate a value of an outcome. Then $Prob(i|H) = P(i)$ and $Prob(i|H') = f(i)$. Denote the prior probability of H by $Prob(H)$ and the prior probability of H' by $Prob(H')$.

By definition of conditional probability,

$$Prob(H|i) = \frac{Prob(i|H)Prob(H)}{Prob(i|H)Prob(H) + Prob(i|H')Prob(H')}$$

$$= \frac{P(i)Prob(H)}{P(i)Prob(H) + f(i)Prob(H')}$$

Similarly,

$$Prob(H'|i) = \frac{f(i)Prob(H')}{P(i)Prob(h) + f(i)Prob(H')}$$

Dividing the two equations and rearranging them yields:

$$\frac{Prob(H|i)Prob(H')}{Prob(H'|i)Prob(H)} = \frac{P(i)}{f(i)}$$

Hence

$$\log \frac{P(i)}{f(i)} = \log \frac{Prob(H|i)}{Prob(H'|i)} - \log \frac{Prob(H)}{Prob(H')} \tag{2.10}$$

The right-hand side of Eq. (2.10) is the difference between the logarithm of the odds in favor of H after observing outcome i and the logarithm of the odds in favor of H before observing outcome i. Therefore $\log P(i)/f(i)$ has the interpretation of the information in the outcome i for discrimination in favor of H against H'. Under the hypothesis H, the mean information in favor of H against H' is then

$$J(P;f) = \sum_{i=1}^{I} P(i) \log \frac{P(i)}{f(i)}$$

$J(P;f)$ has the property that (1) $J(P;f) \geq 0$ for all probability distributions P and f, and (2) $J(P;f) = 0$ if and only if $P = f$ (Kullback, 1959). However, J is not symmetric and does not satisfy the triangle inequality and is therefore not a metric.

The parameters of the mixture distribution can be estimated by minimizing J. Now J can be rewritten

$$J = \sum_{i=1}^{I} P(i) \log P(i) - \sum_{i=1}^{I} P(i) \log f(i)$$

Clearly the first term does not depend on the unknown parameters. The minimization can be done by minimizing the second term. Hence we take the information measure H to be minimized where

$$H = - \sum_{i=1}^{I} P(i) \log f(i)$$

To carry out the minimization, we assume that the modes are well separated. Hence for some threshold t that separates the two modes

$$f(i) \approx \begin{cases} q_1 \Big/ \left(\sqrt{2\pi}\sigma_1\right) e^{-\frac{1}{2}\left(\frac{i-\mu_1}{\sigma_1}\right)^2}, & i \leq t \\[2ex] q_2 \Big/ \left(\sqrt{2\pi}\sigma_2\right) e^{-\frac{1}{2}\left(\frac{i-\mu_2}{\sigma_2}\right)^2}, & i > t \end{cases}$$

Now

$$H(t) = -\sum_{i=1}^{t} P(i) \log \frac{q_1}{\sqrt{2\pi}\sigma_1} e^{-\frac{1}{2}\left(\frac{i-\mu_1}{\sigma_1}\right)^2}$$

$$- \sum_{i=t+1}^{I} P(i) \log \frac{q_2}{\sqrt{2\pi}\sigma_2} e^{-\frac{1}{2}\left(\frac{i-\mu_2}{\sigma_2}\right)^2}$$

Upon simplifying we obtain

$$H = \frac{1 + \log 2\pi}{2} - q_1 \log q_1 - q_2 \log q_2 + \frac{1}{2}\left(q_1 \log \sigma_1^2 + q_2 \log \sigma_2^2\right) \tag{2.11}$$

The assumption of well separated modes means that if t is the threshold that separates the modes, the mean and variance estimated from $P(1), \ldots, P(t)$ will be close to the true mean and variance μ_1 and σ_1. Likewise, the mean and variance estimated from $P(t+1), \ldots, P(I)$ will be close to the true mean and variance μ_2 and σ_2. Hence, using the estimated quantities for the unknown quantities, $H(t)$ can be evaluated for each threshold t. The value t that minimizes $H(t)$ is then the best threshold. Figure 2.10 illustrates the binary image of the BNC T-connector image produced by the Kittler-Illingworth technique. Figure 2.11 shows the histogram of the T-connector image and the places where the Otsu technique and the Kittler-Illingworth technique determine the threshold. The difference is substantial. In this case the Otsu technique detected all the pixels belonging to the connecter but at the

Figure 2.10 Binary image produced by thresholding the T-connector image of Fig. 2.6 with the Kittler-Illingworth threshold.

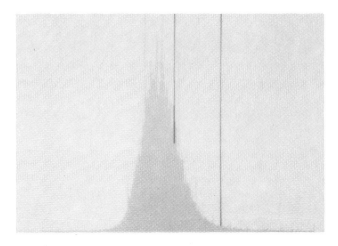

Figure 2.11 Histogram of the image of Fig. 2.6 showing where the Otsu and Kittler-Illingworth techniques choose the threshold value. The leftmost dark line is the Otsu threshold. The rightmost dark line is the Kittler-Illingworth threshold.

expense of many background pixels being falsely detected. In the case of the Kittler-Illingworth technique, no background pixels were falsely detected, but not quite all the connector pixels were detected. On balance, for gray scale images having bimodal histograms, machine vision techniques will have an easier job working with the binary images produced by the Kittler-Illingworth threshold than with the images produced by the Otsu threshold.

The evaluation of the best Kittler-Illingworth threshold t can be simplified by using the results of the previous t. From Eqs. (2.1) and (2.3), we can develop the recursive equations

$$\sigma_1^2(t+1) = \frac{q_1(t)\left\{\sigma_1^2(t) + [\mu_1(t) - \mu_1(t+1)]^2\right\} + P(t+1)[(t+1) - \mu_1(t+1)]^2}{q_1(t+1)}$$

$$\sigma_2^2(t+1) = \frac{[1 - q_1(t)]\left\{\sigma_2^2(t) + [\mu_2(t) - \mu_2(t+1)]^2\right\} - P(t+1)[(t+1) - \mu_2(t+1)]^2}{1 - q_1(t+1)}$$

which can be used in evaluating the $H(t)$ of Eq. (2.10). Then $\mu_1(t)$, $\mu_2(t)$, and $q_1(t)$ can be recursively computed using Eqs. (2.7), (2.8), and (2.9).

Instead of using the criterion of Kittler and Illingworth, we can use the more theoretically powerful criterion of probability of correct classification $P_c(t)$ that would be obtained by a threshold classifier under the assumption of class conditional Gaussian distributions. If we assume, without loss of generality, that $\mu_1 < \mu_2$, the probability of correct classification with threshold value t is given by

$$P_c(t) = q_1(t)\phi\left(\frac{t - \mu_1}{\sigma_1}\right) + q_2(t)\left[1 - \phi\left(\frac{t - \mu_2}{\sigma_2}\right)\right]$$

where

$$\phi(x) = \frac{1}{\sqrt{2\pi}} \int_{-\infty}^{x} e^{-\frac{1}{2}u^2} du$$

This is illustrated in Fig. 2.12.

In using the criterion of probability of correct classification, the means μ_1 and μ_2 are each computed by using a distribution; one of whose tails has been truncated. The smaller-valued mean comes from a distribution whose right tail has been truncated, and the larger-valued mean comes from a distribution whose left tail has been truncated. Thus the smaller mean is biased too small and the larger mean is biased too high. It is possible to correct for these biases.

If μ denotes the mean of a normal distribution having variance σ^2, with a truncated right tail, and μ^* denotes the mean of the same normal distribution without its right tail, then it is easy to derive

$$\mu^* = \mu - \frac{\sigma}{\phi\left(\frac{t-\mu^*}{\sigma}\right)} \frac{1}{\sqrt{2\pi}} e^{-\frac{1}{2}\left(\frac{t-\mu^*}{\sigma}\right)^2}$$

where t is the truncation point.

As a first order correction to μ, we can estimate the mean of the normal without a truncated right tail by

$$\hat{\mu} = \mu + \frac{\sigma}{\phi\left(\frac{t-\mu}{\sigma}\right)} \frac{1}{\sqrt{2\pi}} e^{-\frac{1}{2}\left(\frac{t-\mu}{\sigma}\right)^2}$$

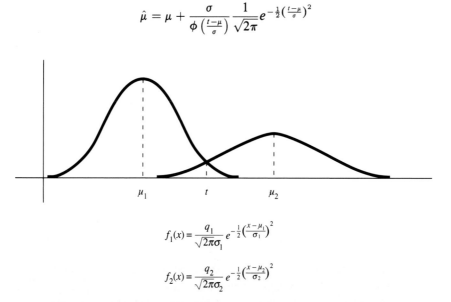

$$f_1(x) = \frac{q_1}{\sqrt{2\pi}\sigma_1} e^{-\frac{1}{2}\left(\frac{x-\mu_1}{\sigma_1}\right)^2}$$

$$f_2(x) = \frac{q_2}{\sqrt{2\pi}\sigma_2} e^{-\frac{1}{2}\left(\frac{x-\mu_2}{\sigma_2}\right)^2}$$

Figure 2.12 Mixture of two Gaussians. If an assignment is made to background pixel whenever $x < t$ and an assignment is made to foreground pixel whenever $x > t$, the probability of observing an $x < t$ and classifying it as background will be the area under f_1 to the left of t. The probability of observing an $x > t$ and classifying it as foreground will be the area under f_2 to the right of t.

Similarly, if μ denotes the mean of a normal distribution with a truncated left tail, we can obtain

$$\hat{\mu} = \mu + \frac{\sigma}{1 - \phi\left(\frac{t-\mu^*}{\sigma}\right)} \frac{1}{\sqrt{2\pi}} \, e^{-\frac{1}{2}\left(\frac{t-\mu}{\sigma}\right)^2}$$

Cho, Haralick, and Yi (1989) demonstrate how the use of these corrections can improve the performance of the Kittler-Illingworth technique.

Several other thresholding techniques are discussed in the vision literature. Some of them do not work as well as the Kullback information we do discuss. Unfortunately, there seems to be no uniform solution to the thresholding problem without simplifying the assumptions such as mixture of Gaussians.

Weszka and Rosenfeld (1978) discuss a variety of ways to evaluate thresholding techniques. Weszka (1978) and Sahoo et al. (1988) survey thresholding techniques. Tsai (1985) suggests thresholding based on preserving values of moments. Wu, Hong, and Rosenfeld (1982) suggest using a quadtree segmentation procedure. There, the histogram of the resulting larger near piecewise constant regions will be highly peaked, the various peaks corresponding to the modes.

A few papers have suggested combining histogram information with edge and gradient information: Weszka, Nagel, and Rosenfeld (1974); Weszka and Rosenfeld (1979); Milgram and Herman (1979); and Kittler, Illingworth, and Föglein (1985). Kirby and Rosenfeld (1979) combine gray level and local neighborhood gray level. Abutaleb (1989) uses the same combination along with an entropy criterion. Ahuja and Rosenfeld (1978) suggest using the distribution of spatially neighboring gray tones. Kohler (1981) selects a threshold to maximize the resulting contrast between the gray value coming from binary-1 pixels adjacent to binary-0 pixels.

2.3   Connected Components Labeling

Connected components analysis of a binary image consists of the connected components labeling of the binary-1 pixels followed by property measurement of the component regions and decision making. The connected components labeling operation performs the unit change from pixel to region or segment. All pixels that have value binary 1 and are connected to each other by a path of pixels all with value binary 1 are given the same identifying label. The label is a unique name or index of the region to which the pixels belong. The label is the identifier for a potential object region. Connected components labeling is a grouping operation.

The units of the image are pixels, and the filtering techniques of image processing transform pixels to pixels. Connected components labeling is one image-processing technique that can make a unit change from pixel to region. The region is a more complex unit than the pixel. The only properties a pixel has are its position and its gray level or brightness level. A region has a much richer set of properties. A region has shape and position properties as well as statistical properties of the gray levels of the pixels in the region.

To each region, therefore, we can construct an N-tuple or vector of its measurement properties. One way to recognize different objects, object defects, or characters is to distinguish between the regions on the basis of their measurement properties. This is the role of statistical pattern recognition, which is discussed in Chapter 4. This section examines connected components labeling algorithms, which in essence group together all pixels belonging to the same region and give them the same label. Software for performing connected components labeling can be found in Ronse and Divijver (1984) and in Cunningham (1981). An APL-based strategy for the extraction of binary image structures is given in Mussio and Padula (1985).

2.3.1 Connected Components Operators

Once a gray level image has been processed to remove noise and thresholded to produce a binary image, a connected components labeling operator can be employed to group the binary-1 pixels into maximal connected regions. These regions are called the *connected components* of the binary image, and the associated operator is called the *connected components operator*. Its input is a binary image and its output is a symbolic image in which the label assigned to each pixel is an integer uniquely identifying the connected component to which that pixel belongs. Figure 2.13 illustrates the connected components operator as applied to the 1-pixels of a binary image. The same operator can, of course, be applied to the 0-pixels.

Two 1-pixels p and q belong to the same connected component C if there is a sequence of 1-pixels $(p_0, p_1, \ldots, p_n)$ of C where $p_0 = p$, $p_n = q$, and p_i is a neighbor of p_{i-1} for $i = 1, \ldots, n$. Thus the definition of a connected component depends on the definition of neighbor. When only the north, south, east, and west neighbors of a pixel are considered part of its neighborhood, then the resulting regions are called *4-connected*. When the north, south, east, west, northeast, northwest, southeast, and southwest neighbors of a pixel are considered part of its neighborhood, the resulting regions are called *8-connected*. This is illustrated in Fig. 2.14. Whichever definition is used, the neighbors of a pixel are said to be *adjacent* to that pixel. The *border* of a connected component of 1-pixels is the subset of pixels belonging to the component that are also adjacent to 0-pixels. Similarly,

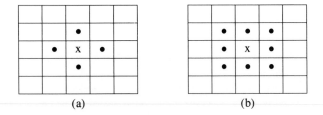

(a)   (b)

Figure 2.13 (a) Function of the connected components operator on a binary image; (b) Symbolic image produced from (a) by the connected components operator.

0	1	1	0	1	0	0
0	1	1	0	1	0	1
1	1	1	0	1	0	1
0	0	0	0	1	1	1
0	1	0	0	0	0	0
0	1	1	1	1	1	0
0	1	1	1	0	0	0

(a)

0	1	1	0	2	0	0
0	1	1	0	2	0	2
1	1	1	0	2	0	2
0	0	0	0	2	2	2
0	3	0	0	0	0	0
0	3	3	3	3	3	0
0	3	3	3	0	0	0

(b)

Figure 2.14 (a) Pixels, •, that are 4-connected to the center pixel x; (b) pixels, •, that are 8-connected to the center pixel x.

the border of a connected component of 0-pixels is the subset of pixels of that component that are also adjacent to 1-pixels.

Rosenfeld (1970) has shown that if C is a component of 1s and D is an adjacent component of 0s, and if 4-connectedness is used for 1-pixels and 8-connectedness is used for 0-pixels, then either C surrounds D (D is a hole in C) or D surrounds C (C is a hole in D). This is also true when 8-connectedness is used for 1-pixels and 4-connectedness for 0-pixels, but not when 4-connectedness is used for both 1-pixels and 0-pixels and not when 8-connectedness is used for both 1-pixels and 0-pixels. Figure 2.15 illustrates this phenomenon. The surroundedness property is desirable because it allows borders to be treated as closed curves. Because of this, it is common to use one type of connectedness for 1-pixels and the other for 0-pixels.

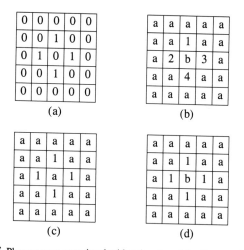

0	0	0	0	0
0	0	1	0	0
0	1	0	1	0
0	0	1	0	0
0	0	0	0	0

(a)

a	a	a	a	a
a	a	1	a	a
a	2	b	3	a
a	a	4	a	a
a	a	a	a	a

(b)

a	a	a	a	a
a	a	1	a	a
a	1	a	1	a
a	a	1	a	a
a	a	a	a	a

(c)

a	a	a	a	a
a	a	1	a	a
a	1	b	1	a
a	a	1	a	a
a	a	a	a	a

(d)

Figure 2.15 Phenomenon associated with using 4- and 8-adjacency in connected components analyses. Numeric labels are used for components of 1-pixels and letter labels for 0-pixels. (a) Binary image; (b) connected components labeling with 4-adjacency used for both 1-pixels and 0-pixels; (c) connected components labeling with 8-adjacency used for both 1-pixels and 0-pixels; and (d) connected components labeling with 8-adjacency used for 1-pixels and 4-adjacency used for 0-pixels.

2.3.2 Connected Components Algorithms

The connected components operator is widely used in industrial applications where an image often consists of a small number of objects against a contrasting background. Examples include finding scratches and dents on newly painted cars, finding the electronic components on surface-mounted device boards, and finding the characters of serial numbers on tires. The speed of the algorithm that performs the connected components operation is often critical to the feasibility of the application. In this section we discuss several algorithms, from a very slow one that requires no storage to several very fast ones that can be used for industrial applications. For the sake of brevity we omit discussion of connected components algorithms based on border finding techniques such as those of Mason and Clemens (1968), Danielsson (1982), and Bartneck (1989).

All the algorithms process a row of the image at a time. Modifications to process a subimage rectangular window at a time are straightforward. All the algorithms assign new labels to the first pixel of each component and attempt to propagate the label of a pixel to its neighbors to the right or below it. Consider the image shown in Fig. 2.16; assume 4-adjacency with a left-to-right, top-to-bottom scan order. In the first row, two 1-pixels separated by three 0-pixels are encountered. The first is assigned label 1; the second, label 2. In row 2 the first 1-pixel is assigned label 1 because it is a 4-neighbor of the already-labeled pixel above it. The second 1-pixel of row 2 is also assigned label 1 because it is a 4-neighbor of the already-labeled pixel on its left. This process continues until the pixel marked A in row 4 is encountered. Pixel A has a pixel labeled 2 above it, and it connects regions 1 and 2. Thus all the pixels labeled 1 and all the pixels labeled 2 really belong to the same component; in other words, labels 1 and 2 are equivalent. The differences among the algorithms are of three types, as reflected in the following questions.

1. What label should be assigned to pixel A?

2. How does the algorithm keep track of the equivalence of two (or more) labels?

3. How does the algorithm use the equivalence information to complete the processing?

0	0	1	0	0	0	1
0	0	1	1	0	0	1
0	0	1	1	1	0	1
0	0	1	1	1	1	1

(a)

0	0	1	0	0	0	2
0	0	1	1	0	0	2
0	0	1	1	1	0	2
0	0	1	1	1	1	A

(b)

Figure 2.16 Propagation process. Label 1 has been propagated from the left to reach pixel A. Label 2 has been propagated down to reach pixel A. The connected components algorithm must assign a label to A and make labels 1 and 2 equivalent. Part (a) shows the original binary image, and (b) the partially processed image.

2.3.3   An Iterative Algorithm

The iterative algorithm (Haralick, 1981) uses no auxillary storage to produce the labeled image from the binary image. It would be useful in environments whose storage is severely limited or on SIMD hardware. It consists of an initialization step plus a sequence of top-down label propagation followed by bottom-up label propagation iterated until no label changes occur. Figure 2.17 illustrates the iterative algorithm on a simple image.

This algorithm and the others will be expressed in pseudocode for an NLINES by NPIXELS binary image I and label image LABEL. The function NEWLABEL generates a new integer label each time it is called. The function NEIGHBORS returns the set of already-labeled neighbors of a given pixel on its own line or the previous line. The function LABELS, when given such a set of already-labeled pixels, returns the set of their labels. Finally, the function MIN, when given a set of labels, returns the minimum label.

> **procedure** Iterate;
> "Initialization of each 1-pixel to a unique label"
> **for** L := 1 to NLINES **do**
>   **for** P := 1 to NPIXELS **do**
>   **if** I(L,P) = 1
>   **then** LABEL (L,P) := NEWLABEL( )
>   **else** LABEL(L,P) := 0
>   **end for**
> **end for**;
> "Iteration of top-down followed by bottom-up passes"
> **repeat**

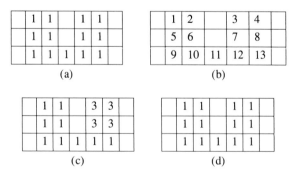

(a)   (b)

(c)   (d)

Figure 2.17 Iterative algorithm for connected components labeling. Part (a) shows the original binary image; (b) the results after initialization of each 1-pixel to a unique label; (c) the results after the first top-down pass, in which the value of each nonzero pixel is replaced by the minimum value of its nonzero neighbors in a recursive manner going from left to right and top to bottom; and (d) the results after the first bottom-up pass.

"Top-down pass"

```
CHANGE := false;
for L := 1 to NLINES do
   for P := 1 to NPIXELS do
      if LABEL(L,P) <> 0 then
         begin
            M := MIN(LABELS(NEIGHBORS((L,P)) ∪ (L,P)));
            if M <> LABEL(L,P)
            then CHANGE := true;
            LABEL(L,P) := M
         end
      end for
   end for;
```

"Bottom-up pass"

```
for L := NLINES to 1 by -1 do
   for P := NPIXELS to 1 by -1 do
      if LABEL(L,P) <> 0 then
         begin
            M := MIN(LABELS(NEIGHBORS((L,P)) ∪ (L,P)));
            if M <> LABEL(L,P)
            then CHANGE := true;
            LABEL(L,P) := M
         end
      end for
   end for
until CHANGE := false
end Iterate
```

This algorithm selects the minimum label of its neighbors to assign to pixel A. It does not directly keep track of equivalences but instead uses a number of passes through the image to complete the labeling. It alternates top-down, left-to-right passes with bottom-up, right-to-left passes so that labels near the bottom or right margins of the image will propagate sooner than if all passes were top-down, left-to-right. This is an attempt to reduce the number of passes. The algorithm has a natural extension for SIMD parallel processing (Manohar and Ramapriyan, 1989).

2.3.4 The Classical Algorithm

The classical algorithm, deemed so because it is based on the classical connected components algorithm for graphs, was described in Rosenfeld and Pfaltz (1966). This algorithm makes only two passes through the image but requires a large global table for recording equivalences. The first pass performs label propagation, much as described above. Whenever a situation arises in which two different labels can propagate to the same pixel, the smaller label propagates and each such equivalence found is entered in an equivalence table. Each entry in the equivalence table consists of an ordered pair, the values of its components being the labels found to be equivalent. After the first pass, the equivalence classes are found by taking the transitive closure of the set of equivalences recorded in the equivalence table. In the algorithm we call this the "Resolve" function. It is a standard algorithm discussed in many books on algorithms, such as Aho, Hopcroft, and Ullman (1983). Each equivalence class is assigned a unique label, usually the minimum (or oldest) label in the class. Finally, a second pass through the image performs a translation, assigning to each pixel the label of the equivalence class of its pass-1 label. This process is illustrated in Fig. 2.18, and the algorithm is given below.

```
procedure Classical
"Initialize global equivalence table."
EQTABLE := CREATE( );
"Top-down pass 1"
for L := 1 to NLINES do
   "Initialize all labels on line L to zero."
   for P := 1 to NPIXELS do
      LABEL(L,P) := 0
   end for;
   "Process the line."
   for P := 1 to NPIXELS do
      if F(L,P) := 1 then
         begin
            A := NEIGHBORS((L,P));
            if ISEMPTY(A)
            then M := NEWLABEL( )
            else M := MIN(LABELS(A));
            LABEL(L,P) := M;
            for X in LABELS(A) and X <> M
               ADD(X, M, EQTABLE)
            end for;
         end
   end for
end for;
"Find equivalence classes."
EQCLASSES := Resolve(EQTABLE);
for E in EQCLASSES
   EQLABEL(E) := min(LABELS(E))
end for;
"Top-down pass 2"
for L := 1 to NLINES do
   for P := 1 to NPIXELS do
```

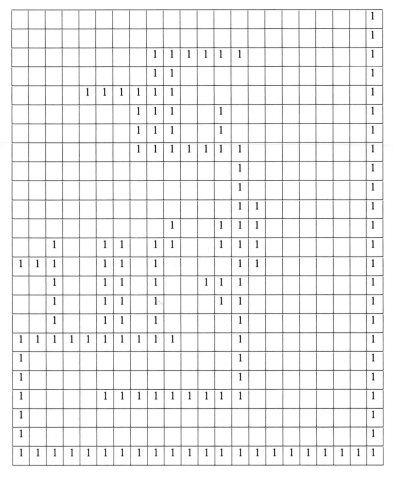

(a)

Figure 2.18 Classical connected components labeling algorithm: Part (a) shows the initial binary image, and (b) the labeling after the first top-down pass of the algorithm. The equivalence classes found are 1: { 1,12,7,8,9,10,5 } and 2: { 2,3,4,6,11,13 }.

```
        if I(L,P) = 1
        then LABEL(L,P) := EQLABEL(CLASS(LABEL(L,P)))
      end for
    end for
  end Classical
```

The algorithm referred to as RESOLVE is simply the algorithm for finding the connected components of the graph structure defined by the set of equivalences (EQTABLE) defined in pass 1. The nodes of the graph are region labels, and the edges are pairs of labels that have been declared equivalent. The procedure, which

																	1	1	1	1
																				1
							2	2	2	2	2	2								1
							2	2												1
			3	3	3	3	2	2												1
						3	2	2				4								1
						3	2	2				4								1
						3	2	2	2	2	2	2								1
												2								1
												2								1
												2	2							1
									5		6	2	2							1
		7			8	8		9	5		6	2	2							1
10	10	7			8	8		9				2	2							1
		7			8	8		9		11	11	2								1
		7			8	8		9			11	2								1
		7			8	8		9				2								1
12	12	7	7	7	7	7	7	7	7			2								1
12												2								1
12												2								1
12				13	13	13	13	13	13	13	13	2								1
12																				1
12																				1
12	12	12	12	12	12	12	12	12	12	12	12	12	12	12	12	12	12	12	12	1

(b)

Figure 2.18 *Continued.*

uses a standard depth-first search algorithm, can be stated as follows:

procedure RESOLVE(EQTABLE);
    list_of_components := nil;
    for each unmarked node N in EQTABLE
      current_component := DFS(N,EQTABLE);
      add_to_list(list_of_components,current_component)
    end for
end RESOLVE

In this procedure, *list_of_components* is a list that will contain the final resultant equivalence classes. The function DFS performs a depth-first search of the graph beginning at the given node *N* and returns a list of all the nodes it has visited in the process. It also marks each node as it is visited. A standard depth-first search algorithm is given in Horowitz and Sahni (1982) and in most other data structures texts.

The main problem with the classical algorithm is the global equivalence table. For large images with many regions, the equivalence table can become very large. On some machines there is not enough memory to hold the table. On other machines that use paging, the table gets paged in and out of memory frequently. For example, on a VAX 11/780 system, the classical algorithm ran (including I/O) in 8.4 seconds with 1791 page faults on one 6000-pixel image but took 5021.0 seconds with 23,674 page faults on one 920,000-pixel image. This motivates algorithms that avoid the use of the large global equivalence table for computers employing virtual memory.

2.3.5 A Space-Efficient Two-Pass Algorithm That Uses a Local Equivalence Table

One solution to the space problem is the use of a small local equivalence table that stores only the equivalences detected from the current line of the image and the line that precedes it. Thus the maximum number of equivalences is the number of pixels per line. These equivalences are then used in the propagation step to the next line. In this case not all the equivalencing is done by the end of the first top-down pass, and a second pass is required for both the remainder of the equivalence finding and for assigning the final labels. The algorithm is illustrated in Fig. 2.19. As in the iterative algorithm, the second pass is bottom-up. This is not required but is done this way for consistency with other algorithms that do require a bottom-up pass, and will be discussed in a later chapter. We will state the general algorithm (Lumia, Shapiro, and Zuniga, 1983) in the same pseudocode we have been using and then describe, in more detail, an efficient run-length implementation.

```
procedure Local_Table_Method
"Top-down pass"
for L := 1 to NLINES do
   begin
       "Initialize local equivalence table for line L."
       EQTABLE := CREATE( );
       "Initialize all labels on line L to zero."
       for P := 1 to NPIXELS do
          LABEL(L,P) := 0
       end for;
       "Process the line."
       for P := 1 to NPIXELS do
          if I(L,P) := 1 then
              begin
                 A := NEIGHBORS((L,P));
                 if ISEMPTY(A)
                 then M := NEWLABEL( )
```

1	2	3	4	5	6	7	8	9	10	11	12	13	14	15	16	17	18	19	20	21	22	23	24
																				1	1	1	1
																							1
									2	2	2	2	2	2									1
									2	2													1
			2	2	2	2	2	2															1
						2	2	2					4										1
						2	2	2					4										1
						2	2	2	2	2	2	2											1
														2									1
														2									1
														2	2								1
								5						2	2	2							1
	7				8	8		5	5					2	2	2							1
7	7	7			8	8		5						2	2								1
	7				8	8		5					2	2	2								1
	7				8	8		5						2	2								1
	7				8	8		5						2									1
5	5	5	5	5	5	5	5	5	5					2									1
5														2									1
5														2									1
5					2	2	2	2	2	2	2	2											1
5																							1
5																							1
1	1	1	1	1	1	1	1	1	1	1	1	1	1	1	1	1	1	1	1	1	1	1	1

Figure 2.19 Results after the top-down pass of the local table method on the binary image of Fig. 2.18(a). Note that on the lines where equivalences were detected, the pixels have different labels from those they had after pass 1 of the classical algorithm. For example, on line 5 the four leading 3s were changed to 2s on the second scan of that line, after the equivalence of labels 2 and 3 was detected. The bottom up pass will now propagate the label 1 to all pixels of the single connected component.

```
        else M := MIN(LABELS(A) );
        LABEL(L,P) := M;
        for X in LABELS(A) and X <> M
            ADD (X,M, EQTABLE)
        end for
    end
end for;
```

"Find equivalence classes detected on this line."

EQCLASSES := Resolve(EQTABLE);

```
    for E in EQCLASSES do
       EQLABEL(E) := MIN(LABELS(E))
    end for;
```

"Relabel the parts of line L with their equivalence class labels."

```
    for P := 1 to NPIXELS do
       if I(L,P) := 1
       then LABEL(L,P) := EQLABEL(CLASS(LABEL(L,P)))
    end for
  end
end for;
```

"Bottom-up pass"

```
for L := NLINES to 1 by -1 do
  begin
```

"Initialize local equivalence table for line L."

```
    EQTABLE := CREATE( );
```

"Process the line."

```
    for P := 1 to NPIXELS do
      if LABEL(L,P) <>0 then
         begin
           LA := LABELS(NEIGHBORS(L,P));
           for X in LA and X <> LABEL(L,P)
              ADD (X,LABEL(L,P), EQTABLE)
           end for
         end
      end for
  end
end for
```

"Find equivalence classes."

```
EQCLASSES := Resolve(EQTABLE);
for E in EQCLASSES do
   EQLABEL(E) := MIN(LABELS(E))
end for ;
```

"Relabel the pixels of line L one last time."

```
for P := 1 to NPIXELS do
   if LABEL(L,P) <> 0
   then LABEL(L,P) := EQLABEL(CLASS(LABEL(L,P)))
end for
end Local_Table_Method
```

In comparison with the classical algorithm, the local table method took 8.8 seconds with 1763 page faults on the 6000-pixel image, but only 626.83 seconds with 15,391 page faults on the 920,000-pixel image, which is 8 times faster. For an even larger 5,120,000-pixel image, the local table method ran 31 times faster than the classical method.

2.3.6   An Efficient Run-Length Implementation of the Local Table Method

In many industrial applications the image used is from a television camera and thus is roughly 512×512 pixels, or 260K, in size. On an image half this size, the local table method as implemented on the VAX 11/780 took 116 seconds to execute, including I/O time. But industrial applications often require times of less than one second. To achieve this kind of efficiency, the algorithm can be implemented on a machine with some special hardware capabilities. The hardware is used to rapidly extract a run-length encoding of the image, and the software implementation can then work on the more compact run-length data. Ronse and Devijver (1984) advocate this approach.

A *run-length encoding* of a binary image is a list of contiguous typically horizontal runs of 1-pixels. For each run, the location of the starting pixel of the run and either its length or the location of its ending pixel must be recorded. Figure 2.20 shows the run-length data structure used in our implementation. Each run in the image is encoded by its starting- and ending-pixel locations. (ROW, START_COL) is the location of the starting pixel, and (ROW, END_COL) is the location of the ending pixel, PERM_LABEL is the field in which the label of the connected component to which this run belongs will be stored. It is initialized to zero and assigned temporary values in pass 1 of the algorithm. At the end of pass 2, the PERM_LABEL field contains the final, permanent label of the run. This structure can then be used to output the labels back to the corresponding pixels of the output image.

Consider a run P of 1-pixels. During pass 1, when the run has not yet been fully processed, PERM_LABEL(P) will be zero. After run P has been processed and determined to be adjacent to some other run Q on the previous row, it will be assigned the current label of Q, PERM_LABEL(Q). If it is determined to be adjacent to other runs $Q_1, Q_2, \ldots, Q_K$ also on the previous row, then the equivalence of PERM_LABEL(Q), PERM_LABEL(Q_1), PERM_LABEL(Q_2), $\ldots$, PERM_LABEL(Q_K) must be recorded. The data structures used for recording the equivalences are shown in Fig. 2.21. For a given run P, PERM_LABEL(P) may be zero or nonzero. If it is nonzero, then LABEL(PERM_LABEL(P)) may be zero or nonzero. If it is zero, then PERM_LABEL(P) is the current label of the run and there is no equivalence class. If it is nonzero, then there is an equivalence class and the value of LABEL(PERM_LABEL(P)) is the label assigned to that class. All the labels that have been merged to form this class will have the same class label; that is, if run P and run P′ are in the same class, LABEL(PERM_LABEL(P)) = LABEL(PERM_LABEL(P′)). When such an equivalence is determined, if each run was already a member of a class and the two classes were different, the two classes are merged. This is accomplished by linking together each prior label belonging

	ROW_START	ROW_END
1	1	2
2	3	4
3	5	6
4	0	0
5	7	7

(a)   (b)

	ROW	START_COL	END_COL	PERM_LABEL
1	1	1	2	0
2	1	4	5	0
3	2	1	2	0
4	2	5	5	0
5	3	1	3	0
6	3	5	5	0
7	5	2	5	0

(c)

Figure 2.20 Binary image (a) and its run-length encoding (b) and (c). Each run of 1-pixels is encoded by its row (ROW) and the columns of its starting and ending pixels (START_COL and END_COL). In addition, for each row of the image, ROW_START points to the first run of the row and ROW_END points to the last run of the row. The PERM_LABEL field will hold the component label of the run; it is initialized to zero.

to a single class in a linked list pointed to by EQ_CLASS(L) for class label L and linked together using the NEXT field of the LABEL/NEXT structure. To merge two classes, the last cell of one is made to point to the first cell of the second, and the LABEL field of each cell of the second is changed to reflect the new label of the class.

In this implementation the value of the minimum label does not always become the label of the equivalence class. Instead, a single-member class is always merged into and assigned the label of a multimember class. This allows the algorithm to avoid traversing the linked list of the larger class to change all its labels when only one element is being added. Only when both classes are multimember is one of the labels selected. In this case the first label of the two being merged is selected as the equivalence class field. The equivalencing procedure, make_equivalent, is given below.

procedure make_equivalent (I1, I2);

"I1 is the value of PERM_LABEL(R1) and I2 is the value of PERM_LABEL(R2) for two different runs R1 and R2. They have been detected to be

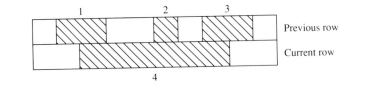

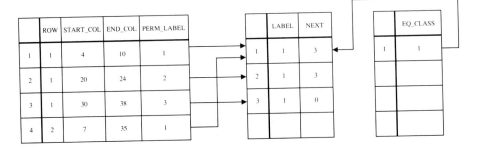

Figure 2.21 Data structures used for keeping track of equivalence classes. In this example, run 4 has PERM_LABEL 1, which is an index into the LABEL array, that gives the equivalence class label for each possible PERM_LABEL value. In the example, PERM_LABELS 1,2, and 3 have all been determined to be equivalent, so LABEL(1), LABEL(2), and LABEL(3) all contain the equivalence class label, which is 1. Furthermore, the equivalence class label is an index into the EQ_CLASS array that contains pointers to the beginnings of the equivalence classes that are linked lists in the LABEL/NEXT structure. In this example there is only one equivalence class, class 1, and three elements of the LABEL/NEXT array are linked together to form this class.

equivalent. The purpose of this routine is to make them equivalent in the data structures.''

case

LABEL(I1) = 0 and LABEL(I2) = 0:

"Both classes have only one member. Create a new class with I1 as the label."

> **begin**
>   LABEL(I1) := I1;
>   LABEL(I2) := I1;
>   NEXT(I1) := I2;
>   NEXT(I2) := 0;
>   EQ_CLASS(I1) := I1
> **end**;

LABEL(I1) = LABEL(I2):

"Both labels already belong to the same class."

> **return**;

LABEL(I1) <> 0 and LABEL(I2) = 0:

"There is more than one member in the class with label I1,
but only one in the class with label I2. So add the
smaller class to the larger."

   begin
     BEGINNING := LABEL(I1);
     LABEL(I2) := BEGINNING;
     NEXT(I2) := EQ_CLASS(BEGINNING);
     EQ_CLASS(BEGINNING) := I2
   end;

LABEL(I1) = 0 and LABEL(I2) <> 0:

"There is more than one member in the class with label I2,
but only one in the class with label I1. Add the smaller class
to the larger."

   begin
     BEGINNING := LABEL(I2);
     LABEL(I1) := BEGINNING;
     NEXT(I1) := EQ_CLASS(BEGINNING);
     EQ_CLASS(BEGINNING) := I1
   end;

LABEL (I1) <> 0 and LABEL (I2) <> 0:

"Both classes are multimember. Merge them by linking the first
onto the end of the second, and assign label I1."

   begin
     BEGINNING := LABEL(I2);
     MEMBER := EQ_CLASS(BEGINNING);
     EQ_LABEL := LABEL(I1);
     while NEXT(MEMBER) <> 0 **do**
       LABEL(MEMBER) := EQ_LABEL;
       MEMBER := NEXT(MEMBER)
     end while;
     LABEL(MEMBER) := EQ_LABEL;
     NEXT(MEMBER) := EQ_CLASS(EQ_LABEL);
     EQ_CLASS(EQ_LABEL) := EQ_CLASS(BEGINNING);
     EQ_CLASS(BEGINNING) := 0
   end
end case;
return
end make_equivalent

With this procedure, the run length implementation is as follows:

procedure Run_Length_Implementation
"Initialize PERM_LABEL array."
for R := 1 to NRUNS **do**

```
        PERM_LABEL(R) := 0
end for;
```

"Top-down pass"

```
for L := 1 to NLINES do
    begin
        P := ROW_START(L);
        PLAST := ROW_END(L);
        if L = 1
        then begin Q := 0; QLAST := 0 end
        else begin Q := ROW_START(L-1); QLAST := ROW_END(L-1) end;
        if P <> 0 and Q <> 0
        then INITIALIZE_EQUIV( );
```

"SCAN 1"

"Either a given run is connected to a run on the previous row or
it is not. If it is, assign it the label of the first run to which it
is connected. For each subsequent run of the previous
row to which it is connected and whose label is different from its
own, equivalence its label with that run's label."

```
    while P<= PLAST and Q <= QLAST do
```

"Check whether runs P and Q overlap."

```
        case
            END_COL(P) < START_COL(Q):
```

"Current run ends before start of run on previous row."

```
                P := P +1;
            END_COL(Q) < START_COL(P):
```

"Current run begins after end of run on previous row."

```
                Q := Q + 1;
            else :
```

"There is some overlap between run P and run Q."

```
                begin
                    PLABEL := PERM_LABEL(P);
                    case
                        PLABEL = 0:
```

"There is no permanent label yet; assign Q's label."

```
                            PERM_LABEL(P) := PERM_LABEL(Q);
                        PLABEL <> 0 and PERM_LABEL(Q) <> PLABEL;
```

"There is a permanent label that is different from the
label of run Q; make them equivalent."

```
                            make_equivalent(LABEL, PERM_LABEL(Q));
                    end case;
```

"Increment P or Q or both as necessary."

```
                    case
                       END_COL(P) > END_COL(Q):
                          Q := Q+1;
                       END_COL(Q) > END_COL(P);
                          P := P + 1;
                       END_COL(Q) = END_COL(P):
                          begin Q := Q+1; P := P+1 end;
                    end case
                 end
              end case
           end while;
```

"SCAN 2"

"Make a second scan through the runs of the current row. Assign new labels to isolated runs and the labels of their equivalence classes to all the rest."

```
P := ROWSTART(L);
while P <= PLAST do
   begin
      PLABEL := PERM_LABEL(P);
      case
         PLABEL = 0:
```

"No permanent label exists yet, so assign one."

```
            PERM_LABEL(P) := NEW_LABEL( );
         PLABEL <> 0 and LABEL(PLABEL) <> 0:
```

"Permanent label and equivalence class; assign the equivalence class label."

```
            PERM_LABEL(P):=LABEL(PLABEL);
      end case;
      P := P + 1
   end
end while
```

"Bottom-up pass"

```
for L := NLINES to 1 by -1 do
   begin
      P := ROW_START(L);
      PLAST := ROW_END(L);
      if L = NLINES
      then begin Q := 0; QLAST := 0 end
      else begin Q := ROW_START(L+1); QLAST := ROW_END(L+1) end
      if P <> 0 and Q <> 0
      then INITIALIZE_EQUIV( );
```

"SCAN 1"

```
      while P <= PLAST and Q <= QLAST do
```

```
    case
      END_COL(P) < START_COL(Q):
        P := P+1;
      END_COL(Q) < START_COL(P):
        Q := Q+1
    else :
```

"There is some overlap; if the two adjacent runs have different labels, then assign Q's label to run P."

```
      begin
        if PERM_LABEL(P) <> PERM_LABEL(Q) then
          begin
            LABEL(PERM_LABEL(P)) := PERM_LABEL(Q);
            PERM_LABEL(P) := PERM_LABEL(Q)
          end;
```

"Increment P or Q or both as necessary."

```
        case
          END_COL(P) > END_COL(Q):
            Q := Q + 1
          END_COL(Q) > END_COL(P):
            P := P+1
          END_COL(Q) = END_COL(P):
            begin Q := Q+1; P := P+1 end
        end case;
      end
    end case
  end while
```

"SCAN 2"

```
  P := ROW_START(L);
  while P ≤ PLAST do
```

"Replace P's label by its class label."

```
    if LABEL(PERM_LABEL(P)) <> 0
    then PERM_LABEL(P) := LABEL(PERM_LABEL(P));
  end while
end
end Run_Length_Implementation
```

There is one other significant difference between procedure Run_Length_Implementation and procedure Local_Table_Method besides the data structures. Procedure Local_Table_Method computed equivalence classes using Resolve both in the top-down pass and in the bottom-up pass. Procedure Run_Length_Implementation updates equivalence classes in the top-down pass using make_equivalent, but it only propagates and replaces labels in the bottom-up pass. This gives correct results not only in procedure Run_Length_Implementation but also back in procedure Local_Table_Method. To prove this, note that the last row of the image is labeled correctly by the two algorithms. That is, after the top-down pass, each pixel in the last row has its final label. (This was proved in Lumia, Shapiro, and Zuniga, 1983.)

Now consider the bottom-up pass. The bottom row is already correctly labeled. Suppose k rows have been correctly labeled and the algorithm proceeds with row $k+1$ (from the bottom). Further suppose there are two pixels p and q on row $k+1$ that are part of the same connected component but have different labels from the top-down pass. Then the bridge between p and q that connects them must certainly be below them, since if it were above them, they would have the same label from the propagation and equivalencing efforts of the top-down pass. Since the bridge is below, there must be pixels on row k that form part of the bridge and whose labels will propagate to p and q. But row k is correctly labeled. So these bridge pixels all have the same final label, and that one label will become the label of both p and q. Therefore only propagation is necessary on the bottom-up pass in both algorithms to take care of this situation.

A second situation occurs when row $k+1$ has two pixels p and q that are part of the same connected component and, although they have the same label from the top-down pass, it is not the final label because of some bridging that occurs for the component segment from below. In this case at least one of the pixels p or q must bridge to a correctly labeled neighboring pixel on row k from the bottom. Then one

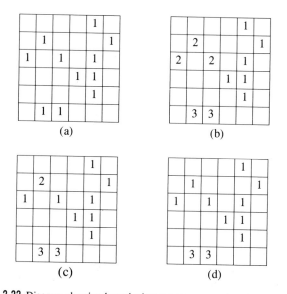

Figure 2.22 Diagram showing how the bottom-up pass needs only to propagate and replace the label 1 to the two pixels having label 2 on the fourth row from bottom. Note that one of these label-2 pixels is not connected to a label-1 pixel. This means that the neighborhood propagate only will not work for the bottom-up pass. After the 1-labeled pixel of row 4, column 4, propagates its label to the 2-labeled pixel of row 3, column 3, the replace operation must replace the label of the 1-labeled pixel of row 3, column 1, to label 1. (a) Binary image; (b) labeling after top-down pass; (c) labeling after processing the first four bottom rows; (d) final labeling after bottom-up pass.

pixel, say p, will get a correct label from the neighborhood propagate operation. In order for q to get the correct label, the replace operation must be performed in which each pixel on row $k + 1$ from the bottom that has the same label as q gets its label replaced by the label that the neighborhood propagate operation gave pixel p. This situation is illustrated in Fig. 2.22.

2.4   Signature Segmentation and Analysis

Signature analysis, like connected components analysis, performs a unit change from the pixel to the region or segment. Signature segmentation consists of taking one or more projections of a binary image or a subimage of a binary image, segmenting each projection to form the new higher-level unit, and taking property measurements of each projection segment. Signature analysis consists of generating the binary image by a thresholding technique, taking projections, and finally making decisions about the objects on the basis of properties of the projections. Projections can be vertical, horizontal, diagonal, circular, radial, spiral, or general projections. Signature analysis was first used in character recognition. It is important for binary vision because it can easily be computed in real time. Sanz, Hinkle, and Dinstein (1985) and Sanz and Dinstein (1987) discuss one kind of a pipeline architecture to compute projections and projection-based geometric features.

A general projection of a given binary image can be produced by masking a projection index image with the given binary image. Each pixel of the resulting image has a value of 0 if the corresponding pixel on the binary image is a 0. And if the pixel of the binary image is a 1, then the pixel will take the value of the corresponding pixel of the projection index image. The *signature*, which is a projection, is the histogram of the nonzero pixels of the resulting masked image. To produce a vertical projection, the projection index image contains the value c in every pixel having column coordinate c. Thus a vertical projection is a one-dimensional function that for each column has a value given by the number of pixels in the binary image in the column having value binary 1. Figure 2.23 illustrates a $45°$ diagonal projection.

In signature analysis the binary image must be processed in such a way that the clutter of all noninteresting object entities is eliminated before projections are taken. This could be done partly by the gray scale processing preceding the thresholding operation, partly by binary morphological operations (discussed in Chapter 5) after thresholding, and partly by simple masking.

If the clutter has been successfully eliminated and the objects are known to be separated horizontally, then a vertical projection will be most useful. If the objects are known to be separated vertically, then a horizontal projection will be most useful. If a window, called a bounding box, can be found that is guaranteed to contain one and only one object, then all projections relative to this window would have potential use. O'Gorman and Sanderson (1986) discuss a converging squares projection technique to locate centroids and bounding boxes of image regions.

The next stage of signature segmentation is a projection segmentation. The segmentation accomplishes a transformation of the pixel as a unit to the projection segment as a unit. Successive mutually exclusive segments can be determined by

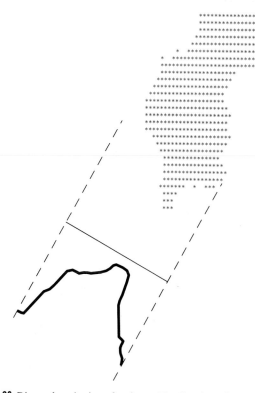

Figure 2.23 Diagonal projection of a shape. The direction of the projection is 45° counterclockwise from the column axis.

locating places where the projection values are relatively small. For example, those locations having a vertical projection with sufficiently or relatively small values are indicative of columns that have a very small number of pixels with binary 1. Hence they are likely to arise from the projection of object ends. A similar statement can be made about horizontal, diagonal, or arbitrary projections. These locations constitute endpoints of intervals that mark the projected boundary of objects of interest. Thus the segmentation process produces projection segments bounded by zero or low-valued projection counts and whose projection counts within the segment tend to be unimodal. These projection segments constitute the new units for the next step of the analysis.

Projection segmentation induces a segmentation of the image in the following way. Suppose that one segment determined from the vertical projection is given by $\{c | s \leq c \leq t\}$ and that one segment determined from the horizontal projection is given by $\{r | u \leq r \leq v\}$. These vertical and horizontal segments naturally define a segment R of the image by

$$R = \{(r, c) \mid u \leq r \leq v \text{ and } s \leq c \leq t\}$$

If there are N_H segments of the horizontal projection and N_V segments of the vertical projection, then $N_H N_V$ mutually exclusive segments will be induced on the image, each segment being a rectangular subimage.

This induction of a segmentation on the image from its vertical and horizontal projection segmentations leads to an iterative way of refining the initial segmentation of the image. The iterative refinement technique works as follows: Segment the vertical and horizontal projections of the image. Induce a segmentation on the image from these segmentations. Now treat each rectangular subimage as the image was treated. Determine its vertical and horizontal projections, segment the projections, and induce the segmentation back onto the subimage. The refinement process can continue in this way until each resulting rectangular subimage has a vertical and horizontal projection that consists of precisely one segment and therefore cannot be further divided.

■ EXAMPLE 2.1

In the example we consider the binary image shown in Fig. 2.24, which also shows the vertical and horizontal projections of the image. The horizontal projection mask image associated with the horizontal projection is shown in Fig. 2.25. The binary image masked by the horizontal projection mask is shown in Fig. 2.26. The horizontal projection shown in Fig. 2.24 is the histogram of

1	1	1	1	1	1	1	1	1	1	1	1	1	1
2	2	2	2	2	2	2	2	2	2	2	2	2	2
3	3	3	3	3	3	3	3	3	3	3	3	3	3
4	4	4	4	4	4	4	4	4	4	4	4	4	4
5	5	5	5	5	5	5	5	5	5	5	5	5	5
6	6	6	6	6	6	6	6	6	6	6	6	6	6
7	7	7	7	7	7	7	7	7	7	7	7	7	7
8	8	8	8	8	8	8	8	8	8	8	8	8	8
9	9	9	9	9	9	9	9	9	9	9	9	9	9
10	10	10	10	10	10	10	10	10	10	10	10	10	10
11	11	11	11	11	11	11	11	11	11	11	11	11	11
12	12	12	12	12	12	12	12	12	12	12	12	12	12
13	13	13	13	13	13	13	13	13	13	13	13	13	13

Figure 2.24 Binary image and its vertical and horizontal projections. The horizontal projection is the histogram of the binary image masked by the horizontal projection mask of Fig. 2.25. The masked image is shown in Fig. 2.26.

								1	1	1				3
									1	1	1			3
		1								1	1	1		4
		1									1	1	1	4
		1				1								2
	1					1								2
	1						1							2
1							1							2
								1						1
														0
	1	1							1	1	1	1		6
	1	1							1	1	1	1		6
	1	1							1	1	1	1		6
1	5	6	0	0	0	2	2	2	5	6	6	5	1	

Figure 2.25 Horizontal projection mask.

								1	1	1			
									2	2	2		
		3								3	3	3	
		4									4	4	4
		5				5							
	6					6							
	7						7						
8							8						
								9					
	11	11							11	11	11	11	
	12	12							12	12	12	12	
	13	13							13	13	13	13	

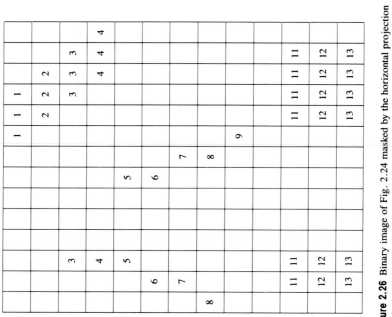

Figure 2.26 Binary image of Fig. 2.24 masked by the horizontal projection mask shown in Fig. 2.25.

the nonzero pixels of the horizontally masked image. The vertical projection can be understood in a similar manner.

Each projection of Fig. 2.24 has one segment with zero value surrounded by nonzero-value segments. This permits the image to be segmented once vertically and once horizontally. This segmentation is shown in Fig. 2.27.

Figure 2.27 also shows the vertical and horizontal projections for each of the four image regions arising from the initial segmentation. Only the horizon-

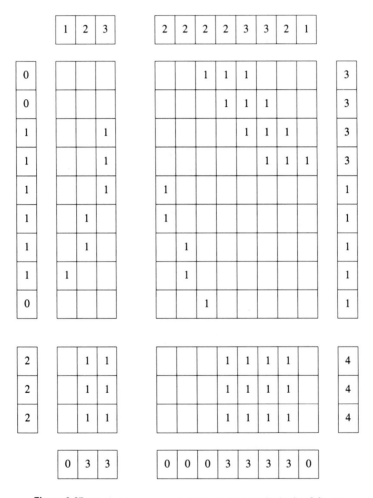

Figure 2.27 Binary image segmented into regions on the basis of the segmentation of the initial vertical and horizontal projections. Also shown are the vertical and horizontal projections of each region.

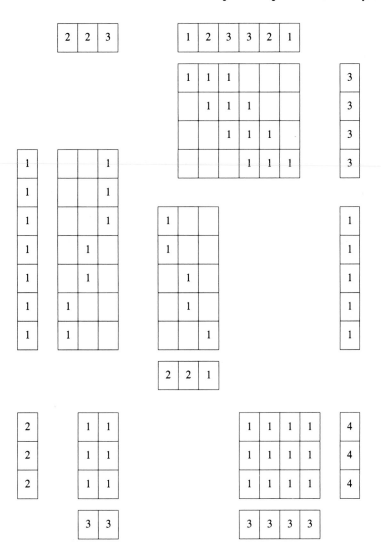

Figure 2.28 Binary image segmented into regions on the basis of the segmentation of Fig. 2.27. Also shown are the vertical and horizontal projections of each region.

tal projection for the upper right region has a zero value area surrounded by nonzero values. This suggests that the upper right region can be further divided horizontally into two pieces. But all the other regions cannot be divided any further. The final segmentation and its vertical and horizontal projections are shown in Fig. 2.28.

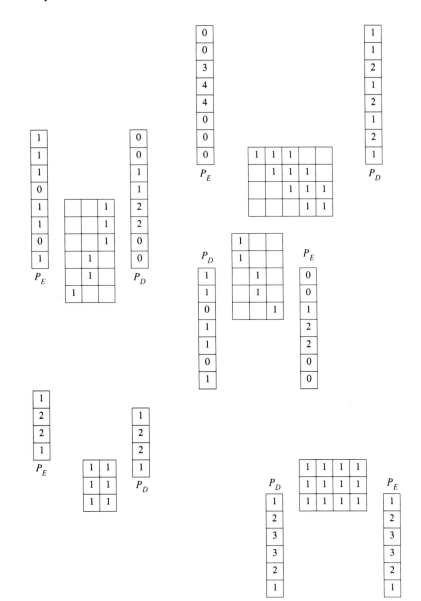

Figure 2.29 Diagonal projections P_D and P_E for each of the five image regions of Fig. 2.28. P_D is the diagonal projection taken 45° clockwise from the horizontal. P_E is the diagonal projection taken 135° clockwise from the horizontal.

Figure 2.29 shows the diagonal projections for each of the five image regions. From the vertical, horizontal, and diagonal projections, the centroids, second central moments, and bounding rectangle can be easily computed. Such computations are described in Chapter 3.

The final phase of signature analysis measures features of each of the projection segments. One feature can consist of the sum of all the projection values in the segment. This feature gives object area. Another is the weighted sum of all projection positions in the segment, weighted by the projection value. This produces a central projected position. Others can include numbers and heights of peaks and numbers and depths of valleys. If the shape of the projection is known to be sufficiently simple, a fit of a suitable functional form to the segment projection values can be made. A feature vector can be constructed from the computed parameters of the fit. Finally, the projection segment can be normalized to have a prespecified length, and the normalized projection values can constitute a projection measurement vector. Computation of signature properties is described in Chapter 3.

Thus after signature analysis, to each projection segment we have an N-tuple or vector of its measurement properties. To recognize different objects, object defects, or characters is to distinguish between their projected segments on the basis of their measurement properties. This is the role of statistical pattern recognition, which is discussed in Chapter 4.

2.5   Summary

When the component segmentation is done in a simple situation—simple meaning that the components are spaced away from each other and there are relatively few components—then signature segmentation is the technique of choice because it has a faster implementation than the connected components analysis techniques, both in special pipeline hardware and in standard computer hardware. However, when there are many components and they are near one another, with protrusions that wiggle into another component's bays, signature segmentation will not work. In this case connected component analysis must be used.

Exercises

2.1.   Use a pseudorandom-number generator to generate 1000 numbers from a Gaussian distribution having mean 100 and standard deviation 10. Then generate another 1000 numbers from a Gaussian distribution having mean 150 and standard deviation 10. Round the resulting 2000 numbers to integers. Determine their histogram.

2.2. Write a program that inputs a histogram and evaluates the location of a threshold by using the Otsu technique. Execute this program on the histogram generated in Exercise 2.1.

2.3. Write a program that inputs a histogram and outputs the location of a threshold by using the Kittler-Illingworth technique. Execute this program on the histogram generated in Exercise 2.1.

2.4. Use a pseudorandom-number generator to generate 1000 numbers from a Gaussian distribution having mean 100 and standard deviation 10. Then generate 5000 numbers from a Gaussian distribution having mean 150 and standard deviation 10. Round the resulting 6000 numbers to integers. Determine their histogram.

2.5. Compare the locations where the Otsu and the Kittler-Illingworth techniques locate the threshold. Which produces the better threshold value, and why is it better?

2.6. Write a program to determine the connected components of a binary image by using the classical algorithm. Perform some experiments to determine how long the algorithm takes to execute as a function of image size and the fraction of binary-1 pixels the image has.

2.7. Write a program to determine the connected component of a binary image by using the algorithm of Section 2.3.5. Determine how long the algorithm takes to execute as a function of image size and the fraction of binary-1 pixels the image has.

2.8. Write a program to determine the connected components of a binary image by first run-length encoding the binary image and then using the run-length algorithm of Section 2.3.5. Determine how long the algorithm takes to execute as a function of image size and the fraction of binary-1 pixels the image has.

2.9. Write a program that can take the horizontal, vertical, and diagonal projections of a binary image.

2.10. Write a program that uses the horizontal, vertical, and diagonal projections to perform a signature segmentation. Apply this segmentation procedure to binary images that you create having rectangular, square, and circular objects. How many and how large do the objects have to be before the signature segmentation procedure is not able to fully segment the image?

■ Bibliography

Abutaleb, A. S., "Automatic Thresholding of Gray-Level Pictures Using Two-Dimensional Entropy," *Computer Vision, Graphics, and Image Processing,* Vol. 47, 1989, pp. 22–32.

Agin, G., "Computer Vision System for Industrial Inspection and Assembly," *IEEE Transactions on Computers,* Vol. 13, 1980, pp. 11–20.

Aho, A. V., J. E. Hopcroft, and J.D. Ullman, *Data Structures and Algorithms,* Addison-Wesley, Reading, MA, 1983.

Ahuja, N., and A. Rosenfeld, "A Note on the Use of Second-Order Gray-Level Statistics for Threshold Selection," *IEEE Transactions on Systems, Man, and Cybernetics,* Vol. SMC-8, 1978, pp. 895–898.

Bartneck, N., "A General Data Structure for Image Analysis Based on a Description of Connected Components," *Computing,* Vol. 42, 1989, pp. 17–34.

Carlotto, M. J., "Histogram Analysis Using a Scale-Space Approach," *IEEE Transactions on Pattern Analysis and Machine Intelligence,* Vol. PAMI-9, 1987, pp. 121–129.

Cho, S., R. M. Haralick, and S. Yi, "Improvement of Kittler and Illingworth's Minimum Error Thresholding," *Pattern Recognition,* Vol. 22, 1989, pp. 609–617.

Cunningham, R., "Segmenting Binary Images," *Robotics Age,* July 1981, pp. 4–19.

Danielsson, P. E., "An Improved Segmentation and Coding Algorithm for Binary and Non-Binary Images," *IBM Journal of Research and Development,* Vol. 26, 1982, pp. 698–707.

Derin, H., "Estimating Components of Univariate Gaussian Mixtures using Prony's Method," *IEEE Transactions on Pattern Analysis and Machine Intelligence,* Vol. PAMI-9, 1987, pp. 142–148.

Dunn, S. M., D. Harwood, and L. S. Davis, "Local Estimation of the Uniform Error Threshold," *IEEE Transactions on Pattern Analysis and Machine Intelligence,* Vol. PAMI-6, 1984, pp. 742–747.

Gleason, G. J., and G. J. Agin, "A Modular Vision System for Sensor Controlled Manipulation and Inspection," *Proceedings of the Ninth International Symposium on Industrial Robots,* Washington, DC, 1979, pp. 57–70.

Haralick, R. M., "Some Neighborhood Operators," *Real-Time Parallel Computing Image Analysis,* M. Onoe, K. Preston, Jr., and A. Rosenfeld (eds.), Plenum, New York, 1981.

Horowitz, E., and Sahni, *Fundamentals of Data Structures,* Computer Science Press, Rockville, MD, 1982.

Kapur, J. N., P. K. Sahoo, and A.K.C. Wong, "A New Method for Gray-Level Picture Thresholding Using the Entropy of the Histogram," *Computer Vision, Graphics, and Image Processing,* Vol. 29, 1985, pp. 273–285.

Kirby, R. L., and A. Rosenfeld, "A Note on the use of (Gray Level, Local Average Gray Level) Space as an Aid in Threshold Selection," *IEEE Transactions on Systems, Man, and Cybernetics,* Vol. SMC-9, 1979, pp. 860–864.

Kittler, J., and J. Illingworth, "On Threshold Selection Using Clustering Criteria," *IEEE Transactions on Systems, Man, and Cybernetics,* Vol. SMC-15, 1985, pp. 652–655.

Kittler, J., and J. Illingworth, "Minimum Error Thresholding," *Pattern Recognition,* Vol. 19, 1986, pp. 41–47.

Kittler, J., J. Illingworth, and J. Föglein, "Threshold Selection Based on a Simple Image Statistic," *Computer Vision, Graphics, and Image Processing,* Vol. 30, 1985, pp. 125–147.

Kohler, R., "A Segmentation System Based on Thresholding," *Computer Graphics and Image Processing,* Vol. 15, 1981, pp. 319–338.

Kullback, S., *Information Theory and Statistics,* Wiley, New York, 1959.

Lee, J. S., and M. C. K. Yang, "Threshold Selection Using Estimates from Truncated Normal Distribution," *IEEE Transactions on Systems, Man, and Cybernetics,* Vol. SMC-19, 1989, pp. 422–429.

Lumia, R., L. G. Shapiro, and O. Zuniga, "A New Connected Components Algorithm for Virtual Memory Computers," *Computer Vision, Graphics, and Image Processing,* Vol. 22, 1983, pp. 287–300.

Manohar, M., and H. K. Ramapriyan, "Connected Component Labeling of Binary Images on a Mesh Connected Massively Parallel Processor," *Computer Vision, Graphics, and Image Processing,* Vol. 45, 1989, pp. 133–149.

Mardia, K. V., and T. J. Hainsworth, "A Spatial Thresholding Method for Image Segmentation," *IEEE Transactions on Pattern Analysis and Machine Intelligence,* Vol. PAMI-10, 1988, pp. 919–927.

Mason, S. J. and J. K. Clemens, "Character Recognition in an Experimental Reading Machine for the Blind," *Recognizing Patterns,* S. Kolers and M. Eden (eds.), MIT Press, Cambridge, MA, 1968, pp. 156–167.

Milgram, D. L., and M. Herman, "Clustering Edge Values for Threshold Selection," *Computer Graphics and Image Processing,* Vol. 10, 1979, pp. 272–280.

Mussio, P., and M. Padula, "An Approach to the Definition, Description, and Extraction of Structures in Binary Digital Images," *Computer Vision, Graphics, and Image Processing,* Vol. 31, 1985, pp. 19–49.

O'Gorman, L., and A. C. Sanderson, "Some Extensions of the Converging Squares Algorithm for Image Feature Analysis," *IEEE Transactions on Pattern Analysis and Machine Intelligence,* Vol. PAMI-8, 1986, pp. 520–524.

Otsu, N., "A Threshold Selection Method from Gray-Level Histograms," *IEEE Transactions on Systems, Man, and Cybernetics,* Vol. SMC-9, 1979, pp. 62–66.

Pérez, A., and R. C. Gonzalez, "An Iterative Thresholding Algorithm for Image Segmentation," *IEEE Transactions on Pattern Analysis and Machine Intelligence,* Vol. PAMI-9, 1987, pp. 742–751.

Pun, T., "Entropic Thresholding, A New Approach," *Computer Vision, Graphics, and Image Processing,* Vol. 16, 1981, pp. 210–239.

Ronse, C., and P. A. Devijver, *Connected Components in Binary Images: The Detection Problem,* Research Studies, Letchworth, Herts, England, 1984.

Rosenfeld, A., "Connectivity in Digital Pictures," *Journal of the Association for Computing Machinery,* Vol. 17, 1970, pp. 146–160.

Rosenfeld, A., and J. L. Pfaltz, "Sequential Operations in Digital Picture Processing," *Journal of the Association for Computing Machinery,* Vol. 13, 1966, pp. 471–494.

Sahoo, P. K., *et al.,* "A Survey of Thresholding Techniques," *Computer Vision, Graphics, and Image Processing,* Vol. 41, 1988, pp. 233–260.

Sanz, J., and I. Dinstein, "Projection-Based Geometrical Feature Extraction for Computer Vision: Algorithms in Pipeline Architectures," *IEEE Transactions on Pattern Analysis and Machine Intelligence,* Vol. PAMI-9, 1987, pp. 160–168.

Sanz, J., E. B. Hinkle, and I. Dinstein, "Computing Geometric Features of Digital Objects in General Purpose Image Processing Pipeline Architectures," *Proceedings of the Conference on Computer Vision and Pattern Recognition,* San Francisco, 1985, pp. 265–270.

Tsai, W. H., "Moment-Preserving Thresholding: A New Approach," *Computer Vision, Graphics, and Image Processing,* Vol. 29, 1985, pp. 377–393.

Weszka, J. S., "A Survey of Threshold Selection Techniques," *Computer Graphics and Image Processing,* Vol. 7, 1978, pp. 259–265.

Weszka, J. S., R. N. Nagel, and A. Rosenfeld, "A Threshold Selection Technique," *IEEE Transactions on Computers,* December, 1974, pp. 1322–26.

Weszka, J. S., and A. Rosenfeld, "Threshold Evaluation Techniques," *IEEE Transactions on Systems, Man, and Cybernetics,* Vol. SMC-8, 1978, pp. 622–628.

———, "Histogram Modification for Threshold Selection," *IEEE Transactions on Systems, Man, and Cybernetics,* Vol. SMC-9, 1979, pp. 38–52.

Wu, A. Y., T. H. Hong, and A. Rosenfeld, "Threshold Selection Using Quadtrees," *IEEE Transactions on Pattern Analysis and Machine Intelligence,* Vol. PAMI-4, 1982, pp. 90–94.

CHAPTER

3 BINARY MACHINE VISION
Region Analysis

3.1 Introduction

The analysis phase of binary machine vision consists of computing global properties for each region produced by the connected components labeling algorithm or each segment produced by the signature segmentation. The properties of each region or segment are stored as a measurement vector that is the input to a classifier. This chapter describes the computation of properties from regions and segments. The next chapter provides an introduction to the classification of these property vectors by statistical pattern recognition. Structural matching, another classification technique, is described in Chapter 17.

3.2 Region Properties

The connected components labeling operator produces regions. A variety of property measurements can be made on each region on the basis of the region's shape and the gray level values for those pixels that participate in the region. The gray level values for all pixels in a region give rise to a histogram of the gray level values of the region, just as all the pixels in an image give rise to the histogram of the image. Mean gray level value is only one summary statistic of the histogram. Variance, skewness, and kurtosis are other statistics of the region's gray levels. Co-occurrence measures of the region's spatial distribution of gray levels constitute summary statistics about a region's microtexture.

Other properties include its gray level spatial second moments, its area, its bounding rectangle, its extremal points, its second central moments, and its orientation. The gray level spatial second moments can measure the degree to which a region is shaded, with one side slightly brighter than the other. It can also measure the orientation of the shading. The bounding rectangle of a region is the smallest

59

rectangle—with sides oriented parallel to the row and column axes of the image—that contains or circumscribes the region. The region has eight extremal points: leftmost bottom, leftmost top, rightmost bottom, rightmost top, topmost left, topmost right, bottommost left, and bottommost right. A region has shape properties, such as area, number of holes, length of perimeter, length of major and minor axes of best fitting ellipse, and orientation of major axis.

In the discussion that follows, we denote the set of pixels in a region by R. Simple global properties include the region's area A and centroid $(\bar{r}, \bar{c})$. Assuming square pixels, we define these properties by

Area:

$$A = \sum_{(r,c) \in R} 1$$

Centroid:

$$\bar{r} = \frac{1}{A} \sum_{(r,c) \in R} r$$

$$\bar{c} = \frac{1}{A} \sum_{(r,c) \in R} c$$

Note that even though each $(r,c) \in R$ is a pair of integers, $(\bar{r}, \bar{c})$ is generally not a pair of integers.

The length of the perimeter P of a region is another global property. A simple definition of the perimeter of a region without holes is the sequence of its interior border pixels. A pixel of a region is a border pixel if it has some neighboring pixel that is outside the region. When 8-connectivity is used to determine whether a pixel inside the region is connected to a pixel outside the region, the resulting set of perimeter pixels is 4-connected. When 4-connectivity is used to determine whether a pixel inside the region is connected to a pixel outside the region, the resulting set of perimeter pixels is 8-connected. This motivates the following definition for the 4-connected perimeter P_4 and the 8-connected perimeter P_8 of a region R.

$$P_4 = \{(r,c) \in R | N_8(r,c) - R \neq \emptyset\}$$
$$P_8 = \{(r,c) \in R | N_4(r,c) - R \neq \emptyset\}$$

To compute length $|P|$ of perimeter P, the pixels in P must be ordered in a sequence $P = <(r_o,c_o), \ldots, (r_{K-1}, c_{K-1})>$, each pair of successive pixels in the sequence being neighbors, including the first and last pixels. Then

$$|P| = \#\{k | (r_{k+1}c_{k+1}) \in N_4(r_k, c_k)\}$$
$$+ \sqrt{2}\#\{k | (r_{k+1}, c_{k+1}) \in N_8(r_k, c_k) - N_4(r_k, c_k)\}$$

where $k+1$ is computed modulo K.

The length of the perimeter $\|P\|$ squared divided by the area (A) is sometimes used as a measure of a shape's compactness or circularity. However, Rosenfeld (1974) shows that for digital shapes, $\|P\|^2/A$ assumes its smallest value not for digital circles, as it would for continuous planar shapes, but for digital octagons or diamonds, depending on whether the perimeter is computed as the number of its 4-neighboring border pixels or as the length of its border, counting 1 for vertical or horizontal moves and $\sqrt{2}$ for diagonal moves. Other common properties computed for a shape include the radius of its circumscribing circle, the radius of its maximal inscribed circle, the mean distance μ_R from the centroid to the shape boundary, and the standard deviation σ_R of the distances from the centroid to the shape boundary. The properties μ_R and σ_R can be defined in terms of the pixels (r_k, c_k), $k = 0, \ldots, K - 1$ in the perimeter P.

$$\mu_R = \frac{1}{K} \sum_{k=0}^{K-1} \| (r_k, c_k) - (\bar{r}, \bar{c}) \|$$

$$\sigma_R^2 = \frac{1}{K} \sum_{k=0}^{K-1} [\| (r_k, c_k) - (\bar{r}, \bar{c}) \| - \mu_R]^2$$

Haralick (1974) shows that μ_R / σ_R has the following properties:

1. As the digital shape becomes more circular, the measure μ_R / σ_R increases monotonically.

2. The values of μ_R / σ_R for similar digital and continuous shapes are similar.

3. It is orientation and area independent.

Furthermore, the number N of sides to a regular digital polygon can be estimated from the circularity measure μ_R / σ_R by the relation

$$N = 1.4111 \left(\frac{\mu_R}{\sigma_R} \right)^{.4724}$$

We can determine for each region R its gray level mean μ and its gray level variance σ^2. The gray level mean is a first-order property. The gray level variance is a second-order property. Average gray level:

$$\mu = \frac{1}{A} \sum_{(r, c) \in R} I(r, c)$$

Gray level variance:

$$\sigma^2 = \frac{1}{A} \sum_{(r, c) \in R} [I(r, c) - \mu]^2 = \left[\frac{1}{A} \sum_{(r, c) \in R} I(r, c)^2 \right] - \mu^2$$

We can determine for each region R some microtexture properties that are a function of the region's co-occurrence matrix. Let S be a set of all pairs of pixels in the region R that are in a designated spatial relationship. For example, S could be the set of all pairs of pixels in R that are 4-neighbors. Define the region's co-occurrence matrix P by

$$P(g_1, g_2) = \frac{\#\{[(r_1, c_1), (r_2, c_2)] \in S \mid I(r_1, c_1) = g_1 \text{ and } I(r_2, c_2) = g_2\}}{\#S}$$

Common texture features include the texture second moment M, the entropy E, the correlation ρ, the contrast C, and the homogeneity H (Haralick, Shanmugam, and Dinstein, 1973). They can all be defined in terms of the co-occurrence P:

$$M = \sum_{g_1, g_2} P^2(g_1, g_2)$$

$$E = -\sum_{g_1, g_2} P(g_1, g_2) \log P(g_1, g_2)$$

$$\rho = \sum_{g_1, g_2} (g_1 - \mu)(g_2 - \mu) P(g_1, g_2) / \sigma^2$$

where

$$\mu = \frac{1}{2} \left[\sum_{g_1} \sum_{g_2} g_1 P(g_1, g_2) + \sum_{g_1} \sum_{g_2} g_2 P(g_1, g_2) \right]$$

$$\sigma^2 = \frac{1}{2} \left[\sum_{g_1} \sum_{g_2} (g_1 - \mu)^2 P(g_1, g_2) + \sum_{g_1} \sum_{g_2} (g_2 - \mu)^2 P(g_1, g_2) \right]$$

$$C = \sum_{g_1} \sum_{g_2} |g_1 - g_2| P(g_1, g_2)$$

$$H = \sum_{g_1} \sum_{g_2} \frac{P(g_1, g_2)}{k + |g_1 - g_2|} \qquad \text{where } k \text{ is some small constant}$$

Other features can be found in Gleason and Agin (1979) and Pavlidis (1977).

For each region, we can determine properties that relate to its shape and orientation. The first-order measurements that relate to shape and orientation can be derived from the region's extremal pixels. Second-order measurements that relate to shape and orientation can be obtained from the second order spatial moments. First we will discuss a region's extremal pixels and some shape properties computable from them. Then we will discuss a region's second order spatial moments and the properties computable from them.

3.2.1 Extremal Points

As shown in Fig. 3.1, there can be as many as eight distinct extremal pixels to a region: topmost right, rightmost top, rightmost bottom, bottommost right, bottommost left, leftmost bottom, leftmost top, and topmost left. Each extremal point has an extremal coordinate value in either its row or column coordinate position. Each extremal point lies on the normally oriented bounding rectangle of the region. This too is shown in Fig. 3.1. Figure 3.2 shows two simple regions in which different extremal points may be coincident. For example, in the rectangle the topmost right extremal point and the rightmost top extremal point are coincident. In the elongated diamond the topmost right and the topmost left extremal points are coincident.

To help discuss and mathematically define the extremal points of a region, we use the associations given in Table 3.1.

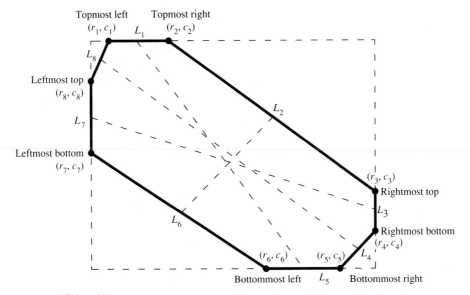

Figure 3.1 The eight extremal points a region can have and the normally oriented bounding rectangle that encloses the region. The interior dotted lines pair together opposite sides.

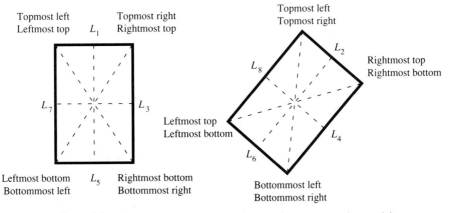

Figure 3.2 Two regions in which the extremal points are not unique and in which they pair differently. The interior dotted lines pair together opposite sides. Because some extremal points are coincident, some opposite sides have zero length.

Table 3.1   Association of the name of the eight extremal points with their coordinate representation.

Name of Extremal Point	Coordinate Representation
Topmost left	(r_1, c_1)
Topmost right	(r_2, c_2)
Rightmost top	(r_3, c_3)
Rightmost bottom	(r_4, c_4)
Bottommost right	(r_5, c_5)
Bottommost left	(r_6, c_6)
Leftmost bottom	(r_7, c_7)
Leftmost top	(r_8, c_8)

Let R be the given region. The extremal points of R can be defined in terms of the topmost row, *rmin,* of R; the bottommost row, *rmax,* of R; the leftmost column, *cmin,* of R; and the rightmost column, *cmax,* of R. The definitions for these extremal coordinates are given in Table 3.2.

Now we can directly define the coordinates of the extremal points:

$$r_1 = r_2 = rmin \qquad\qquad r_5 = r_6 = rmax$$
$$c_1 = \min\{c\,|(rmin, c) \in R\} \qquad c_5 = \max\{c\,|(rmax, c) \in R\}$$
$$c_2 = \max\{c\,|(rmin, c) \in R\} \qquad c_6 = \min\{c\,|(rmax, c) \in R\}$$
$$r_3 = \min\{r\,|(r, cmax) \in R\} \qquad r_7 = \max\{r\,|(r, cmin) \in R\}$$
$$r_4 = \max\{r\,|(r, cmax) \in R\} \qquad r_8 = \min\{r\,|(r, cmin) \in R\}$$
$$c_3 = c_4 = cmax \qquad\qquad c_7 = c_8 = cmin$$

Table 3.2   Association of the name of an extremal coordinate with its definition.

Name of Extremal Coordinate	Coordinate Representation and Definition
Topmost row	$rmin = \min\{r\,|(r, c) \in R\}$
Bottommost row	$rmax = \max\{r\,|(r, c) \in R\}$
Leftmost column	$cmin = \min\{c\,|(r, c) \in R\}$
Rightmost column	$cmax = \max\{c\,|(r, c) \in R\}$

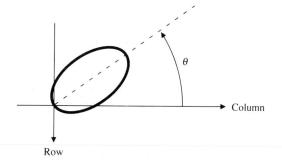

Figure 3.3 The eight extremal points a region can have and the normally oriented bounding rectangle that encloses the region. The interior dotted lines pair together opposite extremal points. They constitute the axes M_1, M_2, M_3, and M_4.

Extremal points occur in opposite pairs: topmost left with bottommost right; topmost right with bottommost left; rightmost top with leftmost bottom; and rightmost bottom with leftmost top. Each pair of opposite extremal points defines an axis. Useful properties of the axis include its axis length and orientation. Because the extremal points come from a spatial digitization or quantization, the standard Euclidean distance formula will provide distances that are biased slightly low. (Consider, for example, the length covered by two pixels horizontally adjacent. From the left edge of the left pixel to the right edge of the right pixel is a length of 2, but the distance between the pixel centers is only 1.) The appropriate calculation for distance adds a small increment to the Euclidean distance to account for this. The increment depends on the orientation angle of the axis. Letting these respective axes be M_1, M_2, M_3, and M_4, where M_1 is the axis between extremal points (r_1, c_1) and (r_5, c_5), M_2 is the axis between extremal points (r_2, c_2) and (r_6, c_6), M_3 is the axis between extremal points (r_3, c_3) and (r_7, c_7), and M_8 is the axis between extremal points (r_4, c_4) and (r_8, c_8) (Fig. 3.3), we have

$$M_1 = \sqrt{(r_1 - r_5)^2 + (c_1 - c_5)^2} + Q(\phi_1)$$

$$M_2 = \sqrt{(r_2 - r_6)^2 + (c_2 - c_6)^2} + Q(\phi_2)$$

$$M_3 = \sqrt{(r_3 - r_7)^2 + (c_3 - c_7)^2} + Q(\phi_3) \qquad (3.1)$$

$$M_4 = \sqrt{(r_4 - r_8)^2 + (c_4 - c_8)^2} + Q(\phi_4)$$

The axes M_1, M_2, M_3, and M_4 have orientations ϕ_1, ϕ_2, ϕ_3, and ϕ_4, where the orientation of a line segment taken counterclockwise with respect to the column (horizontal) axis as shown in Fig. 3.4 is defined by

$$\phi_1 = \tan^{-1} \frac{r_1 - r_5}{-(c_1 - c_5)}$$

$$\phi_2 = \tan^{-1} \frac{r_2 - r_6}{-(c_2 - c_6)}$$

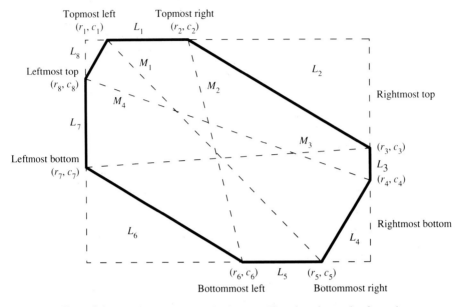

Figure 3.4 Orientation convention for the axes. The orientation angle of an axis is measured counterclockwise from the column axis.

$$\phi_3 = \tan^{-1} \frac{r_3 - r_7}{-(c_3 - c_7)} \tag{3.2}$$

$$\phi_4 = \tan^{-1} \frac{r_4 - r_8}{-(c_4 - c_8)}$$

The exact value for $Q(\theta)$ as shown in Fig. 3.5 is given by

$$Q(\theta) = \begin{cases} \frac{1}{|\cos \theta|} & \text{if } |\theta| < 45° \\ \frac{1}{|\sin \theta|} & \text{if } |\theta| > 45° \end{cases} \tag{3.3}$$

If a quick calculation for distance needs to be done, the average value 1.12 can be used for $Q(\theta)$. The largest error incurred for this approximation is .294.

The axes are also paired: M_1 with its mate M_3, and M_2 with its mate M_4. Major and minor axes of thin elongated or linelike regions can be determined from M_1, M_2, M_3, and M_4. The major axis will be the one having length $\max\{M_1, M_2, M_3, M_4\}$. The minor axis will be its mate. When the major axis is not unique, the minor axis will be the shortest among the axes mating to the longest-length axis. An example is shown in Fig. 3.6. There the major axis is $M_1 = M_2 = M_3$. The minor axis is M_4, and it will, in general, be longer than the width of the region since it is not necessarily orthogonal to the major axis. The width of the region can, however, be estimated by multiplying the minor axis by the absolute value of the size of the difference in the orientation of the major and minor axes.

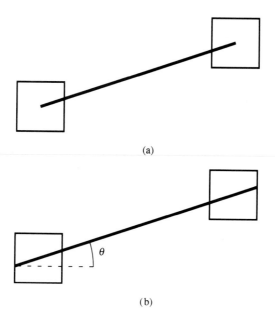

(a)

(b)

Figure 3.5 Diagram showing why the distance between two pixels must be increased if it is to count length going from the left edge of the left pixel to the right edge of the right pixel. Part (a) shows the distance between pixel centers; (b) shows the left edge to right edge distance. Each pixel must add a length that is the length of the hypotenuse of a right triangle having base 1/2. For $|\theta| < 45°$, this length is $1/2 \cos \theta$ for each pixel.

To characterize elongated triangular shapes, the distances between all pairs of extremal points must be computed. The extremal point having the greatest sum of its two largest distances to other extremal points can be selected as the apex of the triangle. The two other extremal points then constitute the vertices at the base of the triangle. To be more precise, define the distance between the ith and jth extremal point by

$$M_{ij} = \sqrt{(r_i - r_j)^2 + (c_i - c_j)^2} + 1.12$$

Let k_1, k_2, and k_3 be any indices maximizing $M_{k_1 k_2} + M_{k_1 k_3}$. Then the vertices of the triangle are (r_{k_1}, c_{k_1}), (r_{k_2}, c_{k_2}), and (r_{k_3}, c_{k_3}).

For a triangle known to be an isosceles triangle, the length L of the long sides can be estimated by $L = (M_{k_1 k_2} + M_{k_1 k_2})/2$, and the length B of the base can be estimated by $B = M_{k_2 k_3}$. From the geometry of the isosceles triangle, the height of altitude h is given by

$$h = \sqrt{L^2 - \left(\frac{B}{2}\right)^2}$$

The orientation of the isosceles triangle can be estimated as the orientation ϕ_h of its

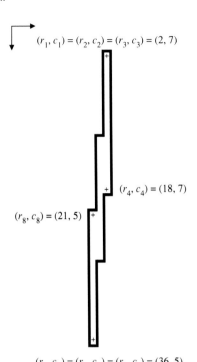

$$M_1 = M_2 = M_3 = \sqrt{(2-36)^2 + (7-5)^2)} + 1.12 = 35.18$$
$$M_4 = \sqrt{(18-21)^2 + (7-5)^2} + 1.12 = 4.73$$
$$\phi_1 = \phi_2 = \phi_3 = \tan^{-1}\frac{-34}{-(2)} = -93.37°$$

Figure 3.6 Calculation of the axis length and orientation of a linelike shape.

altitude, which is given by

$$\phi_h = \tan^{-1}\frac{\frac{1}{2}(r_{k_2}+r_{k_3})-r_{k_1}}{-[\frac{1}{2}(c_{k_2}+c_{k_3})-c_{k_1}]}$$

Figure 3.7 illustrates these calculations for an example isosceles triangle.

The orientation for square and rectangular shapes can also be determined from M_1, M_2, M_3, M_4 and ϕ_1, ϕ_2, ϕ_3, ϕ_4. From the geometry of Fig. 3.8 it is apparent that the two longest axes of M_1, M_2, M_3, and M_4 are the diagonals of the square or rectangle and that these two longest axes are mates. Denote the length of the longest axis by $M_{(1)}$. Let the length of its mate be $M_{m(1)}$. Denote the orientation of the longest axis by $\phi_{(1)}$. Let the orientation of its mate be $\phi_{m(1)}$. From Fig. 3.8,

$$\phi_1 = 180 + \theta_R + \alpha \quad \phi_2 = 180 + \theta_R + \alpha$$
$$\phi_3 = 180 + \theta_R - \alpha \quad \phi_4 = 180 + \theta_R - \alpha \tag{3.4}$$

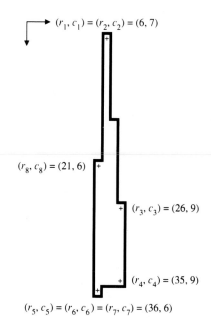

$(r_1, c_1) = (r_2, c_2) = (6, 7)$

$(r_8, c_8) = (21, 6)$

$(r_3, c_3) = (26, 9)$

$(r_4, c_4) = (35, 9)$

$(r_5, c_5) = (r_6, c_6) = (r_7, c_7) = (36, 6)$

$M_{13} = M_{23} = \sqrt{(6 - 26)^2 + (7 - 9)^2} + 1.12 = 21.22$

$M_{14} = M_{24} = \sqrt{(6 - 35)^2 + (7 - 9)^2} + 1.12 = 30.19$

$M_{15} = M_{25} = M_{16} = M_{26} = M_{17} = M_{27} =$
$\sqrt{(6 - 36)^2 + (7 - 6)^2} + 1.12 = 31.14$

$M_{18} = M_{28} = \sqrt{(6 - 21)^2 + (7 - 6)^2} + 1.12 = 16.15$

$M_{34} = \sqrt{(26 - 35)^2 + (9 - 9)^2} + 1.12 = 10.12$

$M_{35} = M_{36} = M_{37} = \sqrt{(26 - 36)^2 + (9 - 6)^2} + 1.12 = 11.56$

$M_{38} = \sqrt{(26 - 21)^2 + (9 - 6)^2} + 1.12 = 6.95$

$M_{45} = M_{46} = M_{47} = \sqrt{(35 - 36)^2 + (9 - 6)^2} + 1.12 = 4.28$

$M_{48} = \sqrt{(35 - 21)^2 + (9 - 6)^2} + 1.12 = 15.44$

$M_{58} = M_{68} = M_{78} = \sqrt{(36 - 21)^2 + (6 - 6)^2} + 1.12 = 16.42$

$k_1 = 1, \quad k_2 = 4, \quad k_3 = 5$

$L = 30.67$

$B = 4.28$

$h = 30.60$

$\phi_h = \tan^{-1} \frac{\frac{1}{2}(35+36)-6}{-(\frac{1}{2}(9+6)-7)}$

$= \tan^{-1} \frac{29.5}{-.5}$

$= 90.97°$

Figure 3.7 Calculations for length of sides, base, and altitude for an example isosceles triangle.

Hence, regardless who the mates are, the orientation θ_R of the rectangle is given by

$$\theta_R = \frac{\phi_1 + \phi_{m1}}{2} - 180 \tag{3.5}$$

where θ_R is the counterclockwise angle to the first side encountered from the horizontal axis and $0° \leq \theta_R \leq 90°$.

Care must be used in the computation of ϕ_1 and ϕ_3, which are defined by Eq. (3.4). The topmost, bottommost, leftmost, and rightmost vertices must be associated with coordinates exactly as shown in Fig. 3.8 and used in Eq. (3.1). The

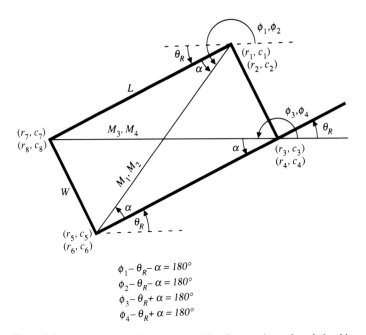

$$\phi_1 - \theta_R - \alpha = 180°$$
$$\phi_2 - \theta_R - \alpha = 180°$$
$$\phi_3 - \theta_R + \alpha = 180°$$
$$\phi_4 - \theta_R + \alpha = 180°$$

Figure 3.8 Geometry of the tilted rectangle. The diagram shows the relationship between the angular orientation θ_R and the angles of the axes joining opposite pairs of extremal points. Here (r_1, c_1) is the topmost vertex; (r_3, c_3) the rightmost vertex; (r_5, c_5) the bottommost vertex; and (r_7, c_7) the leftmost vertex.

relationship given in Eq. (3.5) is the relation when $\phi_1 > 0$ and $\phi_3 > 0$. Should ϕ_1 or ϕ_3 be computed as a negative value from the arctangent function, 360° must be added to it to make it positive before it can be used in Eq. (3.5). Shown in Fig. 3.9 is an example calculation.

Also from Eq. (3.4), the included angle α between the rectangle side and the diagonal is given by

$$\alpha = \min\left\{ \frac{|\phi_{(1)} - \phi_{m(1)}|}{2}, 180 - \frac{|\phi_1 - \phi_{m1}|}{2} \right\}$$

The length L and width W of the rectangle are functions of α :

$$L = \frac{M_{(1)} + M_{m(1)}}{2} \cos \alpha$$

$$W = \frac{M_{(1)} + M_{m(1)}}{2} \sin \alpha$$

We can define the line segment lengths $L_1, \ldots, L_8$ between successive pairs of extremal points as shown in Fig. 3.10. These lengths can form the basis of the description of octagonal shapes in terms of their axes. There are four possible axes for octagonal-shaped regions. Each axis has a length and an orientation. The dominant axis will be taken to be the major axis of the region, and its orientation

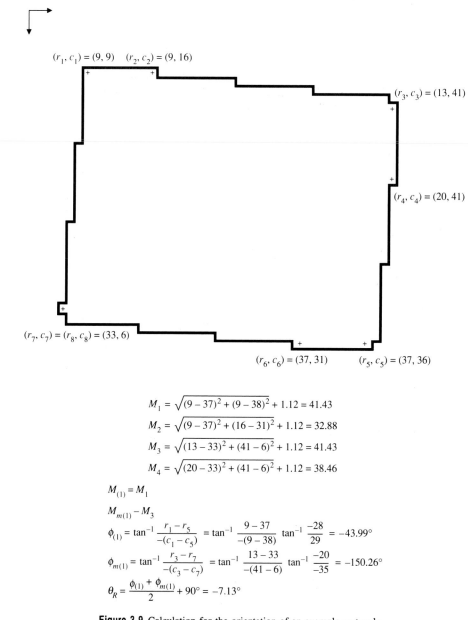

$$M_1 = \sqrt{(9-37)^2 + (9-38)^2} + 1.12 = 41.43$$

$$M_2 = \sqrt{(9-37)^2 + (16-31)^2} + 1.12 = 32.88$$

$$M_3 = \sqrt{(13-33)^2 + (41-6)^2} + 1.12 = 41.43$$

$$M_4 = \sqrt{(20-33)^2 + (41-6)^2} + 1.12 = 38.46$$

$$M_{(1)} = M_1$$

$$M_{m(1)} - M_3$$

$$\phi_{(1)} = \tan^{-1} \frac{r_1 - r_5}{-(c_1 - c_5)} = \tan^{-1} \frac{9-37}{-(9-38)} \quad \tan^{-1} \frac{-28}{29} = -43.99°$$

$$\phi_{m(1)} = \tan^{-1} \frac{r_3 - r_7}{-(c_3 - c_7)} = \tan^{-1} \frac{13-33}{-(41-6)} \quad \tan^{-1} \frac{-20}{-35} = -150.26°$$

$$\theta_R = \frac{\phi_{(1)} + \phi_{m(1)}}{2} + 90° = -7.13°$$

Figure 3.9 Calculation for the orientation of an example rectangle.

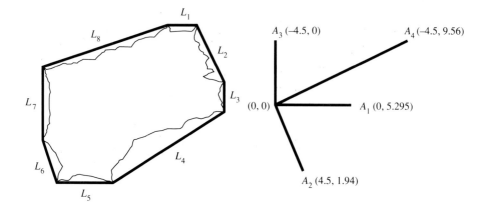

Side length	Extremal point	Axis length	Axis orientation
$L_1 = 3$	$(r_1, c_1) = (2, 13)$	$A_1 : 5.295$	$0°$
$L_2 = 5.51$	$(r_2, c_2) = (2, 15)$	$A_2 : 4.935$	$-66.9°$
$L_3 = 3$	$(r_3, c_3) = (6, 17)$	$A_3 : 4.5$	$90°$
$L_4 = 10.55$	$(r_4, c_4) = (8, 17)$	$A_4 : 10.575$	$25.2°$
$L_5 = 5$	$(r_5, c_5) = (13, 9)$		
$L_6 = 4.28$	$(r_6, c_6) = (13, 5)$		
$L_7 = 6$	$(r_7, c_7) = (10, 4)$		
$L_8 = 10.6$	$(r_8, c_8) = (5, 4)$		

Figure 3.10 Axes and their mates that arise from octagonal-shaped regions and their extremal points.

will be the orientation of the region. The line segment lengths are defined by:

$$L_1 = |c_1 - c_2| + 1$$
$$L_2 = \sqrt{(r_2 - r_3)^2 + (c_2 - c_3)^2} + Q(\theta_2)$$
$$L_3 = |r_3 - r_4| + 1$$
$$L_4 = \sqrt{(r_4 - r_5)^2 + (c_4 - c_5)^2} + Q(\theta_4)$$
$$L_5 = |c_5 - c_6| + 1$$
$$L_6 = \sqrt{(r_6 - r_7)^2 + (c_6 - c_7)^2} + Q(\theta_2)$$
$$L_7 = |r_7 - r_8| + 1$$
$$L_8 = \sqrt{(r_8 - r_1)^2 + (c_8 - c_1)^2} + Q(\theta_4)$$

The lengths of the four axes are denoted by A_1, A_2, A_3, and A_4. They are determined by

$$A_1 = \frac{(L_1 + L_5)}{2}$$

$$A_2 = \frac{(L_2 + L_6)}{2}$$

$$A_3 = \frac{(L_3 + L_7)}{2}$$

$$A_4 = \frac{(L_4 + L_8)}{2}$$

Axes for each region occur in mating pairs: A_1 with A_3, and A_2 with A_4. The major axis is the one having the largest length. The minor axis is its axis mate. These axes are different from M_1, M_2, M_3, and M_4.

The orientation angle for A_1 is always $0°$, since the line segments that define it are horizontal, and the orientation angle for A_3 is always $90°$, since the line segments that define it are always vertical. The counterclockwise orientation angle for A_2 is given by

$$\theta_2 = \frac{1}{2A_2}\left[L_2 \tan^{-1}\frac{r_2 - r_3}{-(c_2 - c_3)} + L_6 \tan^{-1}\frac{r_7 - r_6}{-(c_7 - c_6)}\right]$$

The orientation angle for A_4 is given by

$$\theta_4 = \frac{1}{2A_4}\left[L_4 \tan^{-1}\frac{r_4 - r_5}{-(c_4 - c_5)} + L_8 \tan^{-1}\frac{r_1 - r_8}{-(c_1 - c_8)}\right]$$

3.2.2 Spatial Moments

There are three second-order spatial moments of a region. They are denoted by μ_{rr}, μ_{rc}, and μ_{cc} and are defined as follows:

Second-order row moment: $\qquad \mu_{rr} = \frac{1}{A}\sum_{(r,\,c)\in R}(r - \bar{r})^2$

Second-order mixed moment: $\qquad \mu_{rc} = \frac{1}{A}\sum_{(r,\,c)\in R}(r - \bar{r})(c - \bar{c})$

Second-order column moment: $\qquad \mu_{cc} = \frac{1}{A}\sum_{(r,\,c)\in R}(c - \bar{c})^2$

The second spatial moments have value and meaning for a region of any shape, the same way that the covariance matrix has value and meaning for any two-dimensional probability distribution. If the region is an ellipse, an algebraic meaning can be given to the second spatial moments.

If a region R is an ellipse whose center is the origin, then R can be expressed as

$$R = \{(r, c) \mid dr^2 + 2erc + fc^2 \leq 1\}$$

A relationship exists between the coefficients d, e, and f of the equation of the ellipse and the second moments μ_{rr}, μ_{rc}, and μ_{cc}, as shown in Appendix A. It is given by

$$\begin{pmatrix} d & e \\ e & f \end{pmatrix} = \frac{1}{4(\mu_{rr}\mu_{cc} - \mu_{rc}^2)} \begin{pmatrix} \mu_{cc} & -\mu_{rc} \\ -\mu_{rc} & \mu_{rr} \end{pmatrix}$$

Since the coefficients d, e, and f determine the lengths of the major and minor axes and the orientation of the ellipse, this relationship means that the second moments μ_{rr}, μ_{rc}, and μ_{cc} also determine the lengths of the major and minor axes and the orientation of the ellipse.

To determine the lengths of the major and minor axes and their orientations from the second-order moments, we must consider four cases. These are discussed in Appendix A and are summarized here:

1. $\mu_{rc} = 0$ and $\mu_{rr} > \mu_{cc}$

The major axis is oriented at an angle of $-90°$ counterclockwise from the column axis and has a length of $4\mu_{rr}^{1/2}$. The minor axis is oriented at an angle of $0°$ counterclockwise from the column axis and has a length of $4\mu_{cc}^{1/2}$.

2. $\mu_{rc} = 0$ and $\mu_{rr} \leq \mu_{cc}$

The major axis is oriented at an angle of $0°$ counterclockwise from the column axis and has a length of $4\mu_{cc}^{1/2}$. The minor axis is oriented at an angle of $-90°$ counterclockwise from the column axis and has a length of $4\mu_{rr}^{1/2}$.

3. $\mu_{rc} \neq 0$ and $\mu_{rr} \leq \mu_{cc}$

The major axis is oriented at an angle of

$$\tan^{-1}\left\{ \frac{-2\mu_{rc}}{\mu_{rr} - \mu_{cc} + \left[(\mu_{rr} - \mu_{cc})^2 + 4\mu_{rc}^2\right]^{1/2}} \right\}$$

counterclockwise with respect to the column axis and has a length of

$$\left[8\left\{ \mu_{rr} + \mu_{cc} + \left[(\mu_{rr} - \mu_{cc})^2 + 4\mu_{rc}^2\right]^{1/2} \right\} \right]^{1/2}$$

The minor axis is oriented at an angle $90°$ counterclockwise from the major axis and has a length of

$$\left[8\left\{ \mu_{rr} + \mu_{cc} - \left[(\mu_{rr} - \mu_{cc})^2 + 4\mu_{rc}^2\right]^{1/2} \right\} \right]^{1/2}$$

4. $\mu_{rc} \neq 0$ and $\mu_{rr} > \mu_{cc}$

The major axis is oriented at an angle of

$$\tan^{-1} \frac{\left[\left\{ \mu_{cc} + \mu_{rr} + \left[(\mu_{cc} - \mu_{rr})^2 + 4\mu_{rc}^2\right]^{1/2} \right\} \right]^{1/2}}{-2\mu_{rc}}$$

counterclockwise with respect to the column axis and has a length of

$$\left[8\left\{\mu_{rr} + \mu_{cc} + \left[(\mu_{rr} - \mu_{cc})^2 + 4\mu_{rc}^2\right]^{1/2}\right\}\right]^{1/2}$$

The minor axis is oriented at an angle of 90° counterclockwise from the major axis and has a length of

$$\left[8\left\{\mu_{rr} + \mu_{cc} - \left[(\mu_{rr} - \mu_{cc})^2 + 4\mu_{rc}^2\right]^{1/2}\right\}\right]^{1/2}$$

3.2.3 Mixed Spatial Gray Level Moments

Region properties include properties about the region's position, extent, and shape as well as properties about the gray levels of pixels that participate in the region. Simple gray level properties include gray level mean and variance. Other gray level properties include the mixed spatial gray level moments we discuss here.

There are two second-order mixed gray level spatial moments. They are defined by

$$\mu_{rg} = \frac{1}{A} \sum_{(r,c)\in R} (r - \bar{r})[I(r, c) - \mu]$$

$$\mu_{cg} = \frac{1}{A} \sum_{(r,c)\in R} (c - \bar{c})[I(r, c) - \mu]$$

The mixed gray level spatial moments can be used to determine the least-squares, best-fit gray level intensity planes to the observed gray level spatial pattern of the region R. The least-squares fit to the observed $I(r,c)$ is the gray level intensity plane $\alpha(r - \bar{r}) + \beta(c - \bar{c}) + \gamma$ determined from the α, β, and γ that minimizes

$$\epsilon^2 = \sum_{(r,c)\in R} \left[\alpha(r - \bar{r}) + \beta(c - \bar{c}) + \gamma - I(r,c)\right]^2$$

Taking partial derivatives of ϵ^2 with respect to α, β, and γ and setting these partial derivatives to zero leads to the normal regression equation that in this instance is

$$\begin{pmatrix} \sum_{(r,c)\in R} (r - \bar{r})^2 & \sum_{(r,c)\in R} (r - \bar{r})(c - \bar{c}) & \sum_{(r,c)\in R} (r - \bar{r}) \\ \sum_{(r,c)\in R} (r - \bar{r})(c - \bar{c}) & \sum_{(r,c)\in R} (c - \bar{c})^2 & \sum_{(r,c)\in R} (c - \bar{c}) \\ \sum_{(r,c)\in R} (r - \bar{r}) & \sum_{(r,c)\in R} (c - \bar{c}) & \sum_{(r,c)\in R} 1 \end{pmatrix} \begin{pmatrix} \alpha \\ \beta \\ \gamma \end{pmatrix} =$$

$$\begin{pmatrix} \sum_{(r,c)\in R} (r - \bar{r})I(r,c) \\ \sum_{(r,c)\in R} (c - \bar{c})I(r,c) \\ \sum_{(r,c)\in R} I(r,c) \end{pmatrix}$$

Since $\sum_{(r,c)\in R} (r - \bar{r}) = 0$ and $\sum_{(r,c)\in R} (c - \bar{c}) = 0$, this system of three equations simplifies to

$$
\begin{pmatrix}
\sum_{(r,c)\in R} (r - \bar{r})^2 & \sum_{(r,c)\in R} (r - \bar{r})(c - \bar{c}) & 0 \\
\sum_{(r,c)\in R} (r - \bar{r})(c - \bar{c}) & \sum_{(r,c)\in R} (c - \bar{c})^2 & 0 \\
0 & 0 & \sum_{(r,c)\in R} 1
\end{pmatrix}
\begin{pmatrix} \alpha \\ \beta \\ \gamma \end{pmatrix}
=
$$

$$
\begin{pmatrix}
\sum_{(r,c)\in R} (r - \bar{r})(I(r,c) - \gamma) \\
\sum_{(r,c)\in R} (c - \bar{c})(I(r,c) - \gamma) \\
\sum_{(r,c)\in R} I(r,c)
\end{pmatrix}
$$

Hence

$$
\gamma = \frac{1}{A} \sum_{(r,c)\in R} I(r,c) = \mu
$$

Recalling that

$$
\mu_{rr} = \frac{1}{A} \sum_{(r,c)\in R} (r - \bar{r})^2
$$

$$
\mu_{rc} = \frac{1}{A} \sum_{(r,c)\in R} (r - \bar{r})(c - \bar{c})
$$

$$
\mu_{cc} = \frac{1}{A} \sum_{(r,c)\in R} (c - \bar{c})^2
$$

we know that the unknown parameters α and β must satisfy

$$
\begin{pmatrix} \mu_{rr} & \mu_{rc} \\ \mu_{rc} & \mu_{cc} \end{pmatrix}
\begin{pmatrix} \alpha \\ \beta \end{pmatrix}
=
\begin{pmatrix} \mu_{rg} \\ \mu_{cg} \end{pmatrix}
$$

Now by Kramer's rule we can solve for α and β, obtaining

$$
\alpha = \frac{\begin{vmatrix} \mu_{rg} & \mu_{rc} \\ \mu_{cg} & \mu_{cc} \end{vmatrix}}{\begin{vmatrix} \mu_{rr} & \mu_{rc} \\ \mu_{rc} & \mu_{cc} \end{vmatrix}}
$$

and

$$
\beta = \frac{\begin{vmatrix} \mu_{rr} & \mu_{rg} \\ \mu_{rc} & \mu_{cg} \end{vmatrix}}{\begin{vmatrix} \mu_{rr} & \mu_{rc} \\ \mu_{rc} & \mu_{cc} \end{vmatrix}}
$$

Therefore the equation of the fitted plane is given by

$$
\hat{I}(r, c) = \alpha(r - \bar{r}) + \beta(c - \bar{c}) + \mu, \qquad (r, c) \in R
$$

■ EXAMPLE 3.1

To illustrate what connected components analysis does, consider the gray scale image shown in Fig. 2.1. It contains a background of 0. There are two line objects and three blob objects. The purpose of the image processing task is to determine the position, size, and orientation of each

- bright line,
- dark line,
- bright blob,
- dark blob.

We use the convention that dark means a low-valued gray level (less than 6 in our example) and bright means a high-valued gray level (6 or greater in our example). Notice that the processing must analyze units that are not pixels. The units of analysis are lines and blobs. The properties of these units are location, shape, and gray level. The properties of these higher level units are not the corresponding properties of pixels. However, the gray level properties of an object's pixels will determine the gray level properties of the objects to which they belong. The spatial arrangement of an object's pixels will determine the shape of the higher level unit to which they belong. The positions of the pixels will determine the positions of the higher-level unit to which they belong.

The connected components grouping operation on a binary image is a unit transformation operation. It changes the unit of analysis. The binary image for our example is shown in Fig. 2.2. All pixels greater than 0 on the original gray scale image are marked binary-1 on the thresholded image. The unit on the thresholded image is the pixel. The unit on the labeled image is the region. The regions are the maximal-sized connected groups of pixels all having the value binary 1 on the thresholded image. The connected components labeling operation assigns to each binary-1 pixel the unique label of the connected component to which it belongs. Operations that follow the connected components labeling treat the region as a unit, measuring a variety of gray level and shape properties for each region.

The connected components labeled image in Fig. 3.11 has five regions, whose names or labels are 1 through 5. Each of the five regions can be measured on the basis of several properties. Most of the properties discussed in Section 3.3 for the example are tabulated in Table 3.3. For the example problem, we use the criterion that a mean gray level less than 6 signifies a dark region and a mean gray level greater than or equal to 6 signifies a bright region. Also, we use the criterion that a major-to-minor axis ratio greater than 3 signifies a line object and a ratio less than or equal to 3 signifies a blob object. By these analysis criteria, we find that region 1 is a bright blob, region 2 is a dark line, region 3 is a bright line, region 4 is a dark blob, and region 5 is also a dark blob.

■

								1	1	1			
									1	1	1		
	2									1	1	1	
	2										1	1	1
	2					3							
2						3							
2							3						
2							3						
								3					
	4	4							5	5	5	5	
	4	4							5	5	5	5	
	4	4							5	5	5	5	

Figure 3.11 Connected components labeling of the image in Fig. 2.2.

Table 3.3   All the properties measured from each of the regions determined by the connected components labeling.

Property	1	2	3	4	5
Topmost left (r_1, c_1)	(1,9)	(3,3)	(5,7)	(11,2)	(11,10)
Topmost right (r_2, c_2)	(1,11)	(3,3)	(5,7)	(11,3)	(11,13)
Rightmost top (r_3, c_3)	(4,14)	(3,3)	(9,9)	(11,3)	(11,13)
Rightmost bottom (r_4, c_4)	(4,14)	(5,3)	(9,9)	(13,3)	(13,13)
Bottommost right (r_5, c_5)	(4,14)	(8,1)	(9,9)	(13,3)	(13,13)
Bottommost left (r_6, c_6)	(4,12)	(8,1)	(9,9)	(13,2)	(13,10)

Table 3.3 *Continued.*

Property	1	2	3	4	5
Leftmost bottom (r_7, c_7)	(1,9)	(8,1)	(6,7)	(13,2)	(13,10)
Leftmost top (r_8, c_8)	(1,9)	(8,1)	(5,7)	(11,2)	(11,10)
L_1	2	0	0	1	3
L_2	4.24	0	4.47	0	0
L_3	0	2	1	2	2
L_4	0	3.61	0	0	0
L_5	2	0	0	1	3
L_6	4.24	0	4.47	0	0
L_7	0	0	1	2	2
L_8	0	5.39	0	0	0
A_1	2	0	0	1	3
A_2	4.24	0	4.47	0	0
A_3	0	1	1	2	2
A_4	0	4.50	0	0	0
Major axis orientation	$-45°$	$61.43°$	$-63.43°$	$90°$	$0°$
Major axis length	4.24	4.50	4.47	2	3
Area a	12	6	6	6	12
Row centroid $\bar{r}$	2.5	5.5	7.5	1.83	12
Column centroid $\bar{c}$	11.5	2.33	8.0	2.5	12.5
Gray level mean μ	8.0	4.0	6.33	3.83	3.42
Gray level variance σ^2	1.82	6.4	.82	7.77	6.45
Minor axis orientation	$0°$	$90°$	$90°$	$0°$	$90°$
Minor axis length	2	1	1	1	2

3.3   Signature Properties

We assume here that we are able to obtain, as discussed in Chapter 2, the required projections for any designated region R of an image. The projections are easily obtainable in pipeline hardware (Sanz, 1985; Sanz and Dinstein, 1987). The projections have been used in diverse applications, including character recognition (Breuer and Vajta, 1975; Spinrad, 1965; Pavlidis, 1968; Nakimoto et al., 1973; Yamamoto and Mori, 1978; Fujita, Nakanishi, and Miyata, 1976), shape analysis and recognition (Ma and Kusic, 1979; Wang, 1975; Pavlidis, 1978; Wong and Steppe, 1969), corner detection (Wu and Rosenfeld, 1983), chromosome recognition (Rutovitz, 1970; Klinger, Koehman, and Alexandridis, 1971), and cytology (Preston, 1976), to name a few. We will show how properties obtainable from vertical, horizontal, and diagonal projections include area, centroid of the region, second moments, and bounding rectangle. Then we will illustrate the use of signature analysis to determine the orientation and position of a rectangle and the position of a circle.

First we recall the definition of projections and show how to compute the properties just mentioned from the projections. The vertical projection P_V is defined by

$$P_V(c) = \#\{r \,|\, (r,\, c) \in R\}$$

The horizontal projection P_H is defined by

$$P_H(r) = \#\{c \,|\, (r,\, c) \in R\}$$

There are two diagonal projections: one going from lower left to upper right and one going from upper left to lower right. The diagonal projection P_D goes from lower left to upper right and is defined by

$$P_D(d) = \#\{(r,\, c) \in R \,|\, r + c = d\}$$

The diagonal projection P_E goes from upper left to lower right and is defined by

$$P_E(e) = \#\{(r,\, c) \in R \,|\, r - c = e\}$$

The area A can be obtained from any projection. For example,

$$A = \sum_{(r,\, c)\in R} 1 = \sum_r \sum_{\{c\,|\,(r,\,c)\in R\}} 1$$
$$= \sum_r P_H(r)$$

The top row, rmin, of the bounding rectangle is given by

$$\mathrm{rmin} = \min\{r\,|\,(r,\, c) \in R\}$$
$$= \min\{r\,|\,P_H(r) \neq 0\}$$

The bottom row, rmax, of the bounding rectangle is given by

$$\mathrm{rmax} = \max\{r\,|\,(r,\, c) \in R\}$$
$$= \max\{r\,|\,P_H(r) \neq 0\}$$

The leftmost column, cmin, of the bounding rectangle is given by

$$\text{cmin} = \min\{c\,|(r,\ c) \in R\}$$
$$= \min\{c\,|P_V(c) \neq 0\}$$

The rightmost column, cmax, of the bounding rectangle is given by

$$\text{cmax} = \max\{c\,|(r,\ c) \in R\}$$
$$= \max\{c\,|P_V(c) \neq 0\}$$

The row centroid $\bar{r}$ can be obtained from the horizontal projection P_H, as shown by the following straightforward calculation.

$$\bar{r} = \frac{1}{A} \sum_{(r,\,c)\in R} r$$

$$= \frac{1}{A} \sum_r \sum_{\{c\,|(r,\,c)\in R\}} r$$

$$= \frac{1}{A} \sum_r r \sum_{\{c\,|(r,\,c)\in R\}} 1$$

$$= \frac{1}{A} \sum_r r P_H(r)$$

The column centroid $\bar{c}$ can be obtained from the vertical projection P_V as follows:

$$\bar{c} = \frac{1}{A} \sum_{(r,\,c)\in R} c$$

$$= \frac{1}{A} \sum_c \sum_{\{r\,|(r,\,c)\in R\}} c$$

$$= \frac{1}{A} \sum_c c \sum_{\{c\,|(r,\,c)\in R\}} 1$$

$$= \frac{1}{A} \sum_c c\, P_V(c)$$

The diagonal centroid $\bar{d}$ can be obtained from the diagonal projection P_D.

$$\bar{d} = \frac{1}{A} \sum_d d\, P_D(d)$$

The diagonal centroid $\bar{e}$ can be obtained from the diagonal projection P_E.

$$\bar{e} = \frac{1}{A} \sum_e e\, P_E(e)$$

The diagonal centroid $\bar{d}$ is related to the row and column centroid

$$\bar{d} = \frac{1}{A} \sum_{d} d \sum_{\{(r,c) \in R | r+c=d\}} 1$$

$$= \frac{1}{A} \sum_{d} \sum_{\{(r,c) \in R | r+c=d\}} (r+c)$$

$$= \frac{1}{A} \sum_{d} \sum_{\{(r,c) \in R | r+c=d\}} r + \frac{1}{A} \sum_{d} \sum_{\{(r,c) \in R | r+c=d\}} c$$

$$= \frac{1}{A} \sum_{(r,c) \in R} r + \frac{1}{A} \sum_{(r,c) \in R} c$$

$$= \bar{r} + \bar{c}$$

Similarly, the diagonal centroid $\bar{e}$ is related to the row and column centroid

$$\bar{e} = \bar{r} - \bar{c}$$

The second row moment μ_{rr} can be obtained from the horizontal projection P_H.

$$\mu_{rr} = \frac{1}{A} \sum_{(r,c) \in R} (r - \bar{r})^2$$

$$= \frac{1}{A} \sum_{r} \sum_{\{c | (r,c) \in R\}} (r - \bar{r})^2$$

$$= \frac{1}{A} \sum_{r} (r - \bar{r})^2 \sum_{\{c | (r,c) \in R\}} 1$$

$$= \frac{1}{A} \sum_{r} (r - \bar{r})^2 P_H(r)$$

Likewise, the second column moment μ_{cc} can be obtained from the vertical projection P_V.

$$\mu_{cc} = \frac{1}{A} \sum_{(r,c) \in R} (c - \bar{c})^2$$

$$= \frac{1}{A} \sum_{c} \sum_{\{r | (r,c) \in R\}} (c - \bar{c})^2$$

$$= \frac{1}{A} \sum_{c} (c - \bar{c})^2 \sum_{\{r | (r,c) \in R\}} 1$$

$$= \frac{1}{A} \sum_{c} (c - \bar{c})^2 P_V(c)$$

The second diagonal moment μ_{dd} can be obtained from the diagonal projection P_D.

$$\mu_{dd} = \frac{1}{A} \sum_{d} (d - \bar{d})^2 P_D(d)$$

The second diagonal moment μ_{dd} is related to μ_{rc}, μ_{rr}, and μ_{cc}.

$$\mu_{dd} = \frac{1}{A} \sum_d \sum_{\{(r,c) \in R | r+c=d\}} (r + c - \bar{r} - \bar{c})^2$$

$$= \frac{1}{A} \sum_{(r,c) \in R} [(r - \bar{r}) + (c - \bar{c})]^2$$

$$= \frac{1}{A} \sum_{(r,c) \in R} (r - \bar{r})^2 + 2(r - \bar{r})(c - \bar{c}) + (c - \bar{c})^2$$

$$= \mu_{rr} + 2\mu_{rc} + \mu_{cc}$$

Hence the second mixed moment can be obtained from the second diagonal moment μ_{dd} by

$$\mu_{rc} = \frac{\mu_{dd} - \mu_{rr} - \mu_{cc}}{2}$$

The second diagonal moment μ_{ee} is also related to μ_{rc}, μ_{rr}, and μ_{cc}.

$$\mu_{ee} = \frac{1}{A} \sum_e \sum_{\{(r,c) \in R | r-c=e\}} (r - c - \bar{r} + \bar{c})^2$$

$$= \frac{1}{A} \sum_{(r,c) \in R} [(r - \bar{r}) - (c - \bar{c})]^2$$

$$= \frac{1}{A} \sum_{(r,c) \in R} (r - \bar{r})^2 - 2(r - \bar{r})(c - \bar{c}) + (c - \bar{c})^2$$

$$= \mu_{rr} - 2\mu_{rc} + \mu_{cc}$$

Hence the second mixed moment can also be obtained from the second diagonal moment μ_{ee} by

$$\mu_{rc} = \frac{\mu_{rr} + \mu_{cc} - \mu_{ee}}{2}$$

The relationship between the two diagonal moments μ_{dd} and μ_{ee} implies that the mixed moment μ_{rc} can be obtained directly from μ_{dd} and μ_{ee}.

$$\mu_{rc} = \frac{\mu_{dd} - \mu_{ee}}{4}$$

3.3.1 Using Signature Analysis to Determine the Center and Orientation of a Rectangle

Signature analysis is important because of its easy, fast implementation. Many problems in industrial application can be solved with signature analysis. In SMD circuit board inspection, one inspection task is concerned with the position and orientation of rectangular parts and the position of circular parts. If 16 parts, for example, can be in one image frame, then in one frame time, video-rate hardware may com-

may compute the signatures for 16 parts. In this section we show how signature analysis can be used for rectangular parts. In the next section we show how it can be used for circular parts.

To determine the center and orientation of a rectangular region of known size by signature analysis, such as in Fig. 3.12, we can partition the rectangle into six regions formed by two vertical lines, a known distance g apart, and one horizontal line, as shown in Figure 3.13. This partition constitutes the projection index image. We assume that the corners of the rectangle are guaranteed to be in the extreme sextants of the partition. That is, the upper left-hand corner is in the sextant labeled A in Fig. 3.14, the lower left-hand corner, in the sextant labeled B; the upper right-hand corner, in the sextant labeled C; and the lower right-hand corner, in the sextant labeled D. Consistent with the model-based approach, the height h and width w of the rectangle are assumed known. The sextant partition constitutes the projection index image. The area of intersection of the rectangle with each sextant is determined by masking the projection index image with the binary image of the rectangle, as discussed in Section 2.4. A histogram of the masked projection image (the signature) then provides the area of intersection of each sextant with the rectangle. The problem is how to use the six area numbers to determine the units and orientation of the rectangle.

To solve the problem, set up a local x-,y-coordinate system whose origin is in the center of the six-celled partition. In actual practice there might be many

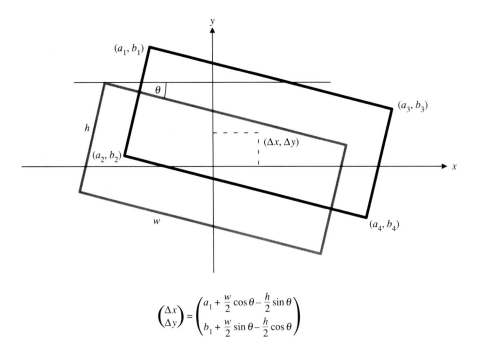

$$\begin{pmatrix} \Delta x \\ \Delta y \end{pmatrix} = \begin{pmatrix} a_1 + \dfrac{w}{2}\cos\theta - \dfrac{h}{2}\sin\theta \\ b_1 + \dfrac{w}{2}\sin\theta - \dfrac{h}{2}\cos\theta \end{pmatrix}$$

Figure 3.12 Geometry for determining the translation of the center of a rectangle in terms of the location of one corner, the length of its sides, and its orientation angle.

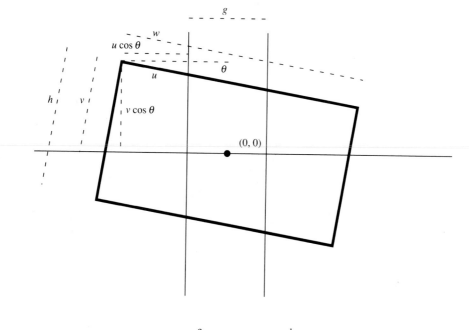

$$\begin{pmatrix} \Delta x \\ \Delta y \end{pmatrix} = \begin{pmatrix} \frac{-g}{2} - u\cos\theta + \frac{w}{2}\cos\theta - \frac{h}{2}\sin\theta \\ v\cos\theta - \frac{w}{2}\sin\theta - \frac{h}{2}\cos\theta \end{pmatrix}$$

Figure 3.13 Geometry for determining the translation of the center of a rectangle in terms of the lengths u and v.

partitions on the image, one for the determination of each part in the image. We first suppose that the coordinates (a_1, b_1) of the upper left-most corner are known and that the orientation angle θ that the side of length w makes with the horizontal line is known. We solve for the coordinates $(\Delta x, \Delta y)$ of the center of the rectangle as follows.

First we determine the coordinate $(\Delta x, \Delta y)$ of the center of the rectangle in terms of the line segment length v from the upper left corner of the rectangle to the horizontal line and the line segment length u from the upper left corner of the rectangle to the left-most vertical line. From the geometry shown in Figure 3.13, we immediately have the results.

For a clockwise rotation of θ, a point (x, y) is rotated to the point (x_{rot}, y_{rot}), where

$$\begin{pmatrix} x_{rot} \\ y_{rot} \end{pmatrix} = \begin{pmatrix} \cos\theta & \sin\theta \\ -\sin\theta & \cos\theta \end{pmatrix} \begin{pmatrix} x \\ y \end{pmatrix}$$

For a rotation and shift of $(\Delta x, \Delta y)$, the point (x, y) becomes the point (x_{new}, y_{new}), where

$$\begin{pmatrix} x_{new} \\ y_{new} \end{pmatrix} = \begin{pmatrix} x_{rot} \\ y_{rot} \end{pmatrix} + \begin{pmatrix} \Delta x \\ \Delta y \end{pmatrix}$$

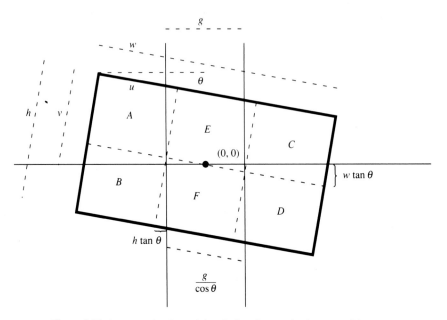

Figure 3.14 Geometry for determining the lengths u and v in terms of the measured areas A, B, C, D, E, and F.

For the case of the corner (a_1, b_1), we have from Figure 3.12

$$\begin{pmatrix} a_1 \\ b_1 \end{pmatrix} = \begin{pmatrix} \cos\theta & \sin\theta \\ -\sin\theta & \cos\theta \end{pmatrix} \begin{pmatrix} \frac{-w}{2} \\ \frac{h}{2} \end{pmatrix} + \begin{pmatrix} \Delta x \\ \Delta y \end{pmatrix}$$

$$= \begin{pmatrix} \frac{-w}{2}\cos\theta + \frac{h}{2}\sin\theta \\ \frac{w}{2}\sin\theta + \frac{h}{2}\cos\theta \end{pmatrix} + \begin{pmatrix} \Delta x \\ \Delta y \end{pmatrix}$$

from which it immediately follows that

$$\begin{pmatrix} \Delta x \\ \Delta y \end{pmatrix} = \begin{pmatrix} a_1 + \frac{w}{2}\cos\theta - \frac{h}{2}\sin\theta \\ b_1 - \frac{w}{2}\sin\theta - \frac{h}{2}\cos\theta \end{pmatrix}$$

Upon substituting $-g/2 - u\cos\theta$ for a_1 and $v\cos\theta$ for b_1, we obtain

$$\begin{pmatrix} \Delta x \\ \Delta y \end{pmatrix} = \begin{pmatrix} \frac{-g}{2} - u\cos\theta + \frac{w}{2}\cos\theta - \frac{h}{2}\sin\theta \\ v\cos\theta - \frac{w}{2}\sin\theta - \frac{h}{2}\cos\theta \end{pmatrix} \tag{3.6}$$

Next we determine the lengths u and v in terms of the measured areas A, B, C, D, E, and F as shown in Figure 3.14. From the geometry we can directly derive the appropriate equations.

From Fig. 3.14 we have

$$A + B = uh + \frac{1}{2}h^2\tan\theta$$

$$C + D = \left(w - \frac{g}{\cos\theta} - u\right)h - \frac{1}{2}h^2\tan\theta$$

We use both equations to maintain symmetry and numerical stability to determine an expression for u. Subtracting the first from the second,

$$(C + D) - (A + B) = \left(w - \frac{g}{\cos\theta}\right)h - 2uh - h^2\tan\theta$$

Bringing the $2uh$ term as the sole term on one side of the equation, yields

$$2uh = -(C + D) + (A + B) + \left(w - \frac{g}{\cos\theta}\right)h - h^2\tan\theta$$

Hence

$$u = \frac{(A + B) - (C + D)}{2h} + \frac{1}{2}\left(w - \frac{g}{\cos\theta}\right) - \frac{1}{2}h\tan\theta \qquad (3.7)$$

Also from Figure 3.14 we have

$$A + E + C = vw - \frac{1}{2}w^2\tan\theta$$

$$B + F + D = (h - v)w + \frac{1}{2}w^2\tan\theta$$

Again we use both equations to maintain symmetry and numerical stability to determine an expression for v. Subtracting one from the other, we obtain

$$(A + E + C) - (B + F + D) = vw - \frac{1}{2}w^2\tan\theta - hw + vw - \frac{1}{2}\tan\theta$$

$$= 2vw - hw - w^2\tan\theta$$

Solving for v yields

$$2vw = (A + E + C) - (B + F + D) + hw + w^2\tan\theta$$

$$v = \frac{(A + E + C) - (B + F + D)}{2w} + \frac{h}{2} + \frac{w}{2}\tan\theta \qquad (3.8)$$

Substituting the derived values of u and v from Eqs. (3.7) and (3.8) in terms of the measured area A, B, C, D, E, and F into Eq. (3.6) for the rectangle center, we have for Δx

$$\Delta x = \frac{g}{2} - u\cos\theta + \frac{w}{2}\cos\theta - \frac{h}{2}\sin\theta$$

$$\Delta x = \frac{g}{2} - \left[\frac{(A + B) - (C + D)}{2h} + \frac{1}{2}\left(w + \frac{g}{\cos\theta}\right) - \frac{1}{2}h\tan\theta\right]\cos\theta$$

$$+ \frac{w}{2}\cos\theta - \frac{h}{2}\sin\theta$$

$$\Delta x = \frac{(C + D) - (A + B)}{2h}\cos\theta$$

And for Δy

$$\Delta y = v \cos\theta - \frac{w}{2}\sin\theta - \frac{h}{2}\cos\theta$$

$$= \left[\frac{(A + E + C) - (B + F + D)}{2w} + \frac{h}{2} + \frac{w}{2}\tan\theta\right]\cos\theta - \frac{w}{2}\sin\theta - \frac{h}{2}\cos\theta$$

$$= \frac{(A + E + C) - (B + F + D)}{2w}\cos\theta + \frac{h}{2}\cos\theta + \frac{w}{2}\sin\theta - \frac{w}{2}\sin\theta - \frac{h}{2}\cos\theta$$

$$= \frac{(A + E + C) - (B + F + D)}{2w}\cos\theta$$

Finally, it is easy to determine the rotation angle θ in terms of the areas E and F, which constitute a parallelogram. From the geometry it is obvious that

$$E + F = \frac{hg}{\cos\theta}$$

from which

$$\cos\theta = \frac{hg}{E + F}$$

3.3.2   Using Signature Analysis to Determine the Center of a Circle

To determine the center position of a circular region from signature analysis, we first partition the circle into four quadrants formed by two orthogonal lines guaranteed to meet inside the circle; then we measure the area in each quadrant from the histogram of the masked projection index image that consists of the four quadrants of a circle. To understand how to convert the area measurements into position information, consider the situation resulting when a chord partitions a circle into two regions A and B. Suppose the chord is a distance d from the circle center and that the radius of the circle is r.

Let θ be the angle between the perpendicular bisector of the chord and a line segment from the chord to the circle center (Fig. 3.15). Then the total area of the two right triangles is $d\sqrt{r^2 - d^2}$ and the area of the sector with central angle 2θ and radius r is $r^2\theta$. The angle θ is given by $\theta = \cos^{-1}\frac{d}{r}$. Therefore the area of the segment determined by the chord and the circle circumference is

$$A = r^2 \cos^{-1}\frac{d}{r} - d\sqrt{r^2 - d^2}$$

$$= r^2 \left[\cos^{-1}\frac{d}{r} - \frac{d}{r}\sqrt{1 - \left(\frac{d}{r}\right)^2}\right]$$

Noting that $\theta = \cos^{-1}\frac{d}{r}$, we can rewrite the segment area.

$$A = \frac{r^2}{2}[2\theta - \sin 2\theta]$$

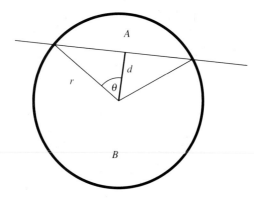

Figure 3.15 Geometry for the circle, its center, and a chord.

The total area of the circle is

$$A + B = \pi r^2$$

Hence the radius of the circle can be determined by

$$r = \sqrt{\frac{A + B}{\pi}}$$

Using this in the expression for the segment area, we obtain

$$\frac{2\pi A}{A + B} = 2\theta - \sin 2\theta$$

This transcendental equation has no closed-form solution for θ. It can be approximately solved for θ by a table–look-up technique. Then once θ has been computed, the offset d is determined by

$$d = \sqrt{\frac{A + B}{\pi}} \cos \theta$$

Now we are ready to consider the original problem of determining the center of a circle in unknown position. Measure the areas $A, B, C,$ and D (Fig. 3.16).

If $A + B > C + D$, then the y-coordinate of the circle's center is positive; otherwise it is negative. If $B + D > A + C$, then the x-coordinate of the circle's center is positive; otherwise it is negative.

The magnitude of the y-coordinate is given by

$$|\Delta y| = \sqrt{\frac{A + B + C + D}{\pi}} \cos \theta_y$$

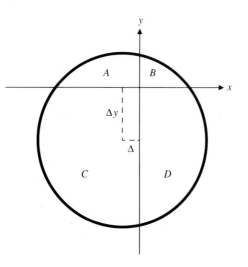

Figure 3.16 Circle projected onto the four quadrants of the projection index image.

where θ_y satisfies

$$\frac{2\pi(A + B)}{A + B + C + D} = 2\theta_y - \sin 2\theta_y$$

The magnitude of the x-coordinate is given by

$$|\Delta x| = \sqrt{\frac{A + B + C + D}{\pi}} \cos \theta_x$$

where θ_x satisfies

$$\frac{2\pi(B + D)}{A + B + C + D} = 2\theta_x - \sin 2\theta_x$$

 3.4   **Summary**

In this chapter we have discussed a set of important properties of regions obtained from connected components or signature analysis. The properties have included spatial moments and mixed spatial gray level moments as well as extremal points. We have illustrated how it is possible to infer from the extremal points the sizes and orientation of linelike, trianglelike, rectanglelike, and octagonlike regions. Finally, we have shown how signature analysis can be used to determine the center and orientation of a rectangle and the center of a circle.

Exercises

3.1. Consider an elongated region whose extremal points are given by

$$
\begin{array}{llll}
(r_1,c_1) & (24,137) & (r_5,c_5) & (39,155) \\
(r_2,c_2) & (24,163) & (r_6,c_6) & (39,145) \\
(r_3,c_3) & (30,181) & (r_7,c_7) & (32,119) \\
(r_4,c_4) & (32,181) & (r_8,c_8) & (30,119)
\end{array}
$$

Determine $M_1, M_2, M_3, M_4, \phi_1, \phi_2, \phi_3$ and ϕ_4. If this region is considered to be a rectangle, what would the computed orientation, length, and width of the rectangle be? What is the problem with assuming a rectangle model for a region whose shape does not satisfy the assumed model?

3.2. Determine the value of $\|P\|^2/A$ for a regular planar polygon having N sides and show that it is always greater than the value of $\|P\|^2/A$ for a circle.

3.3. Show that for a regular polygon of N sides the mean radii between the centroid and the boundary is given by

$$
\mu_R = \frac{Nb}{\pi} \log \left(\frac{1 + \sin \, \pi/N}{\cos \, \pi/N} \right)
$$

where b is the perpendicular distance between the polygon centroid and one of its sides.

3.4. Show that for a regular polygon of N sides the standard deviation of the radii between the centroid and the boundary is given by

$$
\sigma_R = \frac{Nb}{\pi} \left[\frac{\pi}{N} \tan \frac{\pi}{N} - \log^2 \left(\frac{1 + \sin \, \pi/N}{\cos \, \pi/N} \right) \right]^{\frac{1}{2}}
$$

3.5. Write a computer program to construct binary digital images of a digital circle or a digital diamond. Digital circles are specified by their radius and digital diamonds by the length of their sides. For any generated figure determine the value of $\|P\|^2/A$ where the length of the perimeter is the number of interior border pixels that are 4–adjacent to the background. Compare the values of $\|P\|^2/A$ for digital circles and digital diamonds by graphing each as a function of A.

3.6. A rectangle of width W and length L has an unknown orientation θ, where θ is the angle between the horizontal axis and the side of length L. A connected component analysis of an image of the rectangle measures the width W_B and length L_B of the bounding rectangle. Show that the orientation of the rotated rectangle satisfies

$$
\sin 2\theta = \frac{2(W_B L_B - WL)}{W^2 + L^2}
$$

3.7. Perform the following experiment to determine the accuracy of the signature analysis technique of Section 3.3.1 for determining the center and orientation of a rectangle as a function of noise and scale. Fix the rectangle to be L pixels in length by W pixels in width and the sextant partition to have a middle sextant of length $\frac{L}{3}$ pixels. Orient the rectangle so that the length L side is horizontal. Then choose a random rotation θ between $-45°$ and $45°$ and a random translation (r,c) for row and column between $\frac{-L}{6}$ and $\frac{L}{6}$ pixels. Finally, with probability p, change a 0-pixel to a 1-pixel or a 1-pixel to a 0-pixel. With the noisy rectangle use the signature analysis technique to estimate the position of the center $(\hat{r}, \hat{c})$ of the rectangle and its orientation $\hat{\theta}$. Repeat the experiment 100 times observing $(\hat{r}_i, \hat{c}_i, \hat{\theta}_i), i = 1, \ldots, 100$. Define

$$d_t = \sqrt{\frac{1}{100} \sum_{i=1}^{100} (r_i - \hat{r}_i)^2 + (c_i - \hat{c}_i)^2} \quad \text{and} \quad d_\theta = \frac{1}{100} \sum_{i=1}^{100} |\hat{\theta}_i - \theta_i|,$$

where (r_i, c_i) is the true position of the ith rectangle. Plot d_t and d_θ as a function of noise parameter p. Change L and W and repeat the experiments. Compare the results.

3.8. Perform the following experiment to determine the accuracy of the signature analysis techniques of Section 3.3.2 for determining the center of a circular region. Generate circular regions having radius r. With probability p, change a 0-pixel to a 1-pixel or a 1-pixel to a 0-pixel. With the noisy circle, use the signature analysis technique to estimate the position of the center $(\hat{r}, \hat{c})$ of the circle. Repeat this experiment 100 times observing $(\hat{r}_i, \hat{c}_i), i = 1, \ldots, 100$. Define

$$d_t = \sqrt{\frac{1}{100} \sum_{i=1}^{100} (r_i - \hat{r}_i)^2 + (c_i - \hat{c}_i)^2}$$

Plot d_t as a function of noise parameter p and radius r.

3.9. Determine the extremal points of the ellipse $(x - x_c)'A(x - x_c) = 1$, where $x_c = \binom{5}{7}$ and

$$A = \frac{1}{146} \begin{pmatrix} 10 & -2 \\ -2 & 15 \end{pmatrix}$$

3.10. Consider an ellipse defined by $x'Ax = 1$, where

$$A = \begin{pmatrix} d & e \\ e & f \end{pmatrix}.$$

Show that the major axis length can be given by

$$\frac{\sqrt{2}\sqrt{d + f + \sqrt{(d - f)^2 + 4e^2}}}{\sqrt{df - e^2}}$$

and the minor axis length can be given by

$$\frac{\sqrt{2}\sqrt{d + f - \sqrt{(d - f)^2 + 4e^2}}}{\sqrt{df - e^2}}$$

3.11. Write a program that inputs a connected component image and outputs a property vector for each connected component. The property vector should have components of area, perimeter, centroid, orientation of fitted ellipse, length of major axis, length of minor axis, extremal points, standard deviation of the distance between centroid and boundary, and mean distance between centroid and boundary.

3.12. Write a program that generates binary images having nontouching squares and circles. Make the squares have random orientation. Make a histogram of the values for each property for the square regions and for the circle regions. What property looks most promising to distinguish circles from squares? How large do the squares and circles have to be before it becomes easy to distinguish a square from a circle by using the standard deviation of the distance between the centroid and boundary and the mean distance between centroid and boundary?

Bibliography

Breuer, P., and M. Vajta, "Structural Chracter Recognition by Forming Projections," *Problems in Control Information Theory,* Vol. 4, 1975, pp. 339-352.

Fujita, T., M. Nakanishi, and K. Miyata, "The Recognition of Chinese Characters (Kanji) Using Time Variation of Peripheral Belt Patterns," *Proceedings of the Third International Joint Conference on Pattern Recognition,* Coronado, CA, 1976, pp. 119-121.

Gleason, G. J., and G. J. Agin, "A Modular Vision System for Sensor Controlled Manipulation and Inspection," *Proceedings of the Ninth International Symposium on Industrial Robots,* Washington, DC, March, 1979, pp. 57-70.

Haralick, R. M., "A Measure of Circularity of Digital Figures," *IEEE Transactions on Systems, Man, and Cybernetics,* Vol. SMC-4, 1974, pp. 394-396.

Haralick, R. M., K. Shanmugam, and I. Dinstein, "Textural Features for Image Classification," *IEEE Transactions on Systems, Man, and Cybernetics,* Vol. SMC-3, 1973, pp. 610-621.

Klinger, A., "Pattern Width at a Given Angle," *Communications of the ACM,* Vol. 14, 1971, pp. 21-25.

Klinger, A., A. Koehman, and N. Alexandridis, "Computing Analysis of Chromosome Patterns: Feature-Encoding for Flexible Decision Making," *IEEE Transactions on Computers,* Vol. C-20, 1971, pp. 1014-22.

Ma, K., and G. Kusic, "An Algorithm for Distortion Analysis in Two-Dimensional Patterns Using Its Projections," *Proceedings of the Seventh New England Bioengineering Conference,* Troy, NY, 1979, pp.177-180.

Nakimoto, Y., et al., "Improvement of Chinese Character Recognition Using Projection Profiles," *Proceedings of the First International Joint Conference on Pattern Recognition,* Washington, D.C., 1973, pp. 172-178.

Pavlidis, T., "Computer Recognition of Figures through Decomposition," *Information and Control,* Vol. 14, 1968, pp. 526-537.

———, *Structural Pattern Recognition,* Springer-Verlag, New York, 1977.

———, "Algorithms for Shape Analysis of Contours and Wave-Forms," *Proceedings of the Fourth International Conference on Pattern Recogntion,* Kyoto, Japan, 1978, pp. 70-85.

Preston, K., "Digital Picture Analysis in Cytology," *Digital Picture Analysis,* A. Rosenfeld (ed.), Springer-Verlag, New York, 1976, pp. 209-294.

Rosenfeld, A., "Compact Figures in Digital Pictures," *IEEE Transactions on Systems, Man, and Cybernetics,* Vol. SMC-4, 1974, pp. 221-223.

Rutovitz, D., "Centromere Finding: Some Shape Descriptors for Small Chromosome Outlines," *Machine Intelligence,* Vol. 5, 1970, pp. 435-462.

Sanz, J. L. C., "A New Method for Computing Polygonal Masks in Image Processing Pipeline Architectures," *Pattern Recognition,* Vol. 18, 1985, pp. 241-247.

Sanz, J. L. C., and I. Dinstein, "Projection-Based Geometrical Feature Extraction for Computer Vision: Algorithms in Pipeline Architectures," *IEEE Transactions on Pattern Analysis and Machine Intelligence,* Vol. PAMI-9, 1987, pp. 160-168.

Spinrad, R. J., "Machine Recognition of Hand Printing," *Information and Control,* Vol. 8, 1965, pp. 124–142.

Wang, Y. R., "Characterization of Binary Patterns and Their Projections," *IEEE Transactions on Computers,* Vol. C–24, 1985, pp. 1032–35.

Wong, E., and J. A. Steppe, "Invariant Recognition of Geometric Shapes," *Methodologies of Pattern Recognition,* S. Watanabe (ed.), Academic Press, New York, 1969, pp. 535–546.

Wu, Z. Q., and A. Rosenfeld, "Filtered Projections as an Aid in Corner Detection," *Pattern Recognition,* Vol. 16, 1983, pp. 31–38.

Yamamoto, K., and S. Mori, "Recognition of Handprinted Characters by Outermost Point Methods," *Proceedings of the Fourth International Conference on Pattern Recognition,* Kyoto, Japan, 1978, pp. 794–796.

4 STATISTICAL PATTERN RECOGNITION

4.1 Introduction

Statistical pattern recognition begins with units, such as image regions or projected segments, on which a variety of measurements have been made. Each unit has an associated measurement vector. The purpose of statistical pattern recognition is to classify each unit on the basis of its measurement vector. The classification matches the unit with its feature vector to the "closest" category. It does so by means of a decision rule. The decision rule is designed optimally to assign each unit to a class or category on the basis of its measurement vector. Optimally can mean, for example, with the smallest classification error for a given set of measurements and for a given computational complexity of decision rule. Hence statistical pattern recognition techniques include:

1. Feature selection and extraction techniques either to reduce the number of measurements to be made or to reduce the dimensionality of the vectors representing the measurements made to the decision rule,

2. Decision rule construction techniques,

3. Techniques for the estimation of decision rule error.

4.2 Bayes Decision Rules: Maximum Utility Model for Pattern Discrimination

In the simple pattern discrimination or pattern identification process, a unit is observed or measured and a category assignment is made that names or classifies the unit as a type of object. The unit's category assignment is made solely on the basis of the observed measurement, which is sometimes called the pattern. We may discuss this event of classifying the observed unit by referring to the distinct facts characterizing the situation.

1. There is a set of categories C from which the class assignment must come. When referring to an assigned category, we will usually use the symbol a.
2. The observed unit has a true category identification that is also a member of the set C. When referring to a true category identification, we will usually use the symbol t.
3. There is a set of measurements D from which the observed measurement d must come. Each element of D may be a number, a value, or an N-tuple of values.

We denote this event of classifying the observed unit by the triple (t,a,d).

Some events occur more frequently than others, and it is natural to use the concept of probability to measure these differences in frequencies of occurrence. We will write $P(t,a,d)$ to denote the probability of the event (t,a,d).

4.2.1 Economic Gain Matrix

We assume that the act of making category assignments carries consequences (t,a,d) economically or in terms of utility. These consequences have solely to do with the use to which the automatic discrimination is put. They are specified ahead of time by the user of the pattern discrimination system, and they may depend only on which category is the true category identification for the observed unit and which category is the assigned category identification for the unit. The consequences cannot depend on which unit is being observed or what measurement has been taken of the observed unit. Hence the cause of the consequence is the true-assigned category identification pair (t,a). We will write $e(t,a)$ to denote the economic gain or the utility that results from observing a unit whose true category identification is t and whose assigned category identificaton is a. The economic gain matrix captures within it all the information that relates the classification produced by a decision rule to the utility of the resulting classification to a user. We will see that it provides the accounting mechanism for optimally balancing the errors made by a decision rule so that the resulting expected utility of the automatic classification is highest.

To illustrate the meaning of the economic gain matrix, we will consider a few examples. For our first example, we take the person for whom it is important to be right the largest possible fraction of the time. Such a person would choose an economic gain matrix defined by

$$e(t,a) = \begin{cases} 1 & \text{if } t = a \\ 0 & \text{otherwise} \end{cases}$$

Such a gain matrix is called the identity gain matrix.

Contrast this situation with the person having to decide on the basis of an image of a jet fan blade whether or not the observed unit has a crack. The investigation test costs 10 dollars. If the person decides it does have a crack, then the finely machined fan blade will be discarded, and this will cost 500 dollars for the cracked blade plus 10 dollars for the test. However, if he decides that the fan blade does not have a crack, but it really does, there is an expected loss of 50 million dollars due to a potential airplane crash. The economic gain matrix in this situation is shown in Table 4.1. Optimizing a decision rule using this matrix rather than the identity matrix will lead to a very different kind of decision rule.

For our second example, we consider the case of an automatic defect-inspection machine. Such a machine classifies objects in its environment as being correctly made (good) or incorrectly made (bad). Its performance is characterized by the fraction of objects it classifies as good or bad and that are really good or bad. Thus there are two possible true states and two possible detected states for the object. We denote by P(true good, assigned good) the fraction of objects that are truly good and are also classified as assigned good. For P(true good, assigned good) we use the shorthand notation $P(g, g)$. We denote by P(true good, assigned bad) the fraction of objects that are truly good but are assigned bad. For P(true good, assigned bad) we use the shorthand notation $P(g, b)$. We denote by P(true bad, assigned good) $= P(b, g)$ the fraction of objects that are truly bad but are assigned good. We denote by P(true bad, assigned bad) $= P(b, b)$ the fraction of objects that are truly bad and are assigned bad. All the performance information for a machine performing classification in a given object environment can be captured in a 2×2 table, as shown in Table 4.2.

For each possible true and detected state combination, there is an economic consequence, e. In printed circuit board inspection, for example, a board that is good and is detected as good will yield its manufacturer a profit. A board that is detected as bad whether or not it is actually good or bad may have to be thrown away if there is no rework station. In this case the manufacturer loses the cost of the board. A board that is bad but is detected as good is very costly because components will be mounted on the board and, when it is discovered that the board will not work, the cost of the board and components may be lost. Since there are four possible performance states, there are four possible economic consequences:

Table 4.1   Economic gain matrix for the inspection of a jet fan blade.

		Assigned State	
		Crack	No Crack
True State	Crack	−$510	−$50,000,000
	No Crack	−$510	$10

Table 4.2 2×2 contingency table of fraction of objects in each possible true- and detected-state combination.

		Detected State	
		Good	Bad
True State	Good	$P(g,g)$	$P(g,b)$
	Bad	$P(b,g)$	$P(b,b)$

$e(g, g)$, $e(g, b)$, $e(b, g)$, and $e(b, b)$. When e is positive, it designates a profit consequence. When e is negative, it designates a loss consequence. These economic consequences can also be summarized in a 2×2 table (Table 4.3).

The expected profit per object manufactured can then be computed from the tables by performing an average of the economic consequences weighted by the probabilities of their occurrences:
Expected profit per object $= E =$

$$P(g,g)\, e(g,g) + P(g,b)\, e(g,b) + P(b,g)\, e(b,g) + P(b,b)\, e(b,b)$$

The information in Table 4.2 summarizes the performance of the machine in a given environment. If the environment changes, such as when a different etching solution is used for printed circuit boards, then Table 4.2 can change. This kind of change is due not to a change in the detection machine but to a change in the fraction of good objects manufactured, $P(g) = P(g,g) + P(g,b)$, and the fraction of bad objects manufactured, $P(b) = P(b,g) + P(b,b)$.

Table 4.3 2×2 contingency table of resulting economic consequences (profits) for each possible true- and detected-state combination.

		Detected State	
		Good	Bad
True State	Good	$e(g,g)$	$e(g,b)$
	Bad	$e(b,g)$	$e(b,b)$

The machine performance somewhat more isolated from its operating environment can be specified by the conditional probabilities: Given that an object is good, the probability that it is detected as good,

$$P(g|g) = \frac{P(g,g)}{P(g,g) + P(g,b)}$$

given that an object is good, the probability that it is detected as bad,

$$P(b|g) = \frac{P(g,b)}{P(g,g) + P(g,b)}$$

given that an object is bad, the probability that it is detected as good,

$$P(g|b) = \frac{P(b,g)}{P(b,g) + P(b,b)}$$

and given that an object is bad, the probability that it is detected as bad,

$$P(b|b) = \frac{P(b,b)}{P(b,g) + P(b,b)}$$

The conditional probability $P(b|g)$ is called the false-detection or false-alarm rate, and the conditional probability $P(g|b)$ is called the misdetection rate. From $P(b|g)$ and $P(g|b)$ the two other conditional probabilities $P(g|g)$ and $P(b|b)$ can be readily computed:

$$P(g|g) = 1 - P(b|g)$$
$$P(b|b) = 1 - P(g|b)$$

In summary, the manufacturing environment is characterized by the fraction $P(g)$ of good objects manufactured. The machine's performance is characterized by the false-alarm rate $P(b|g)$ and misdetection rate $P(g|b)$. The economic consequences are specified by the four numbers $e(g,g)$, $e(g,b)$, $e(b,g)$, and $e(b,b)$. The expected profit per object manufactured is given by the weighted average:

$$E = \{[1 - P(b|g)]e(g,g) + P(b|g)e(g,b)\}P(g)$$
$$+ \{P(g|b)e(b,g) + [1 - P(g|b)]e(b,b)\}[1 - P(g)]$$

Discussion

Any automatic defect-detection machine has parameters that can be varied in its hardware and in its software or algorithms. As these parameters vary, the false-alarm and misdetection rates will inevitably change. In fact, it is always possible to trade a higher false-alarm rate for a somewhat lower misdetection rate just by making it more likely for the machine to call an object bad. Likewise, it is always possible to trade a higher misdetection rate for a somewhat lower false-alarm rate just by making it more likely for the machine to call an object good.

Every automated defect-detection machine can be completely characterized in its operating environment by the curve of its false-alarm rate versus its misdetection rate, a function that is called its operating curve. Maximizing profit over different manufacturing runs involving different objects will require different trade-offs between false-alarm and misdetection rates for the different objects. Therefore the businessperson who seeks to maximize profits will want to use an automated defect-detection machine in which the operating point on the curve of the false-detection rate versus the misdetection rate can be appropriately set. This suggests that the machine algorithm parameters affecting false-alarm and misdetection rates must be easily varied in the field.

We now illustrate by examples how a small trade-off between misdetection and false-alarm rates can have a significant profit impact. In the examples there are two alternative operating points: (misdetection rate, false-alarm rate) = (.2, .1) or (.15, .12). The operating point in Example 4.1 yields a profit of $1446.50, and the operating point in Example 4.2 yields a profit of $1536.35.

■ EXAMPLE 4.1

Table 4.4 gives the conditional probabilities for operating point (.2, .1) (misdetection rate, false-alarm rate). Table 4.5 lists the economic consequence for each possible outcome. The expected profit per object manufactured that results from this situation is $1446.50.
Manufacturing environment:

$$f(g) = .95 \text{ prior probability of an object being good}$$
$$f(b) = .05 \text{ prior probability of an object being bad}$$

Expected profit per object manufactured

$$= [.8 \times 2000 - .2 \times 100].95 + [-.1 \times 10,000 - .9 \times 100].05$$
$$= 1580 \times .95 - 1090 \times .05$$
$$= \$1446.50$$

Table 4.4   Machine performance.

		Detected State	
		Good	Bad
True State	Good	$P(g|g) = .8$	$P(b|g) = .2$
	Bad	$P(g|b) = .1$	$P(b|b) = .9$

Table 4.5   Economic consequence.

		Detected State	
		Good	Bad
True State	Good	$e(g,g) = \$2000$	$e(g,b) = \$100$
	Bad	$e(b,g) = -\$10,000$	$e(b,b) = -\$100$

EXAMPLE 4.2

Table 4.6 gives the conditional probabilities for operating point (misdetection rate, false-alarm rate) (.15, .12). Table 4.7 lists the economic consequence for each possible outcome (the same consequences as in Example 4.1). The expected profit per object manufactured from this situation is $1536.35. Manufacturing environment

$$f(g) = .95 \text{ prior probability of an object being good}$$
$$f(b) = .05 \text{ prior probability of an object being bad}$$

Expected profit per object manufactured

$$= [.85 \times 2000 - .15 \times 100].95 + [-.12 \times 10,000 - .88 \times 100].05$$
$$= 1685 \times .95 - 1288 \times .05$$
$$= \$1536.35$$

Table 4.6   Machine performance.

		Detected State	
		Good	Bad
True State	Good	$P(g|g) = .85$	$P(b|g) = .15$
	Bad	$P(g|b) = .12$	$P(b|b) = .88$

Table 4.7   Economic consequence.

		Detected State	
		Good	Bad
True State	Good	$e(g,g) = \$2000$	$e(g,b) = \$100$
	Bad	$e(b,g) = -\$10,000$	$e(b,b) = -\$100$

4.2.2 Decision Rule Construction

Our next task is to understand how to compute average or expected gain. Since $P(t,a,d)$ is the probability of observing a unit whose true category identification is t, whose assigned category identification is a, and whose measurement is d, we may determine the probability of the consequence (t,a) by summing $P(t,a,d)$ on d, its third argument.

$$P(t,a) = \sum_{d \in D} P(t,a,d)$$

The notation $d \in D$ means that the measurement d belongs to the measurement set D. The notation $\sum_{d \in D}$ means that a summation is to take place in which there will be one term in the summation for each measurement d in the set D. Since exactly one measurement is associated with each unit, and since the measurement must come from the set D, summing $P(t,a,d)$ over all $d \in D$ will yield the probability of the consequence (t,a).

Now the probability of the consequence (t,a) is $P(t,a)$, and the utility of the consequence is $e(t,a)$. The fraction of the time that economic gain $e(t,a)$ results from making a classification is $P(t,a)$. Therefore we may compute the expected value or average value of the gain e as the weighted average of the economic gain $e(t,a)$, where the weight associated with $e(t,a)$ is $P(t,a)$. We denote this average economic gain by $E[e]$.

$$E[e] = \sum_{t \in C} \sum_{a \in C} e(t,a)P(t,a)$$

Figure 4.1 illustrates graphically what information is used to compute $E[e]$.

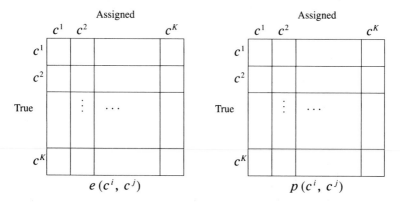

Figure 4.1 Calculations of $E[e]$. Overlay the economic gain matrix on top of the table of probabilities for time and assigned classification. $E[e]$ is the sum of the products of the corresponding entries.

Note that when the economic gain matrix is the identity matrix, the expected gain is precisely the probability of correct assignment.

$$E[e] = \sum_{t \in C} \sum_{a \in C} e(t,a)P(t,a) = \sum_{t \in C} P(t,t) = P(\text{correct assignment})$$

The reason for examining the expected gain is that the use of different decision rules, which assign a category to an observed unit, will change the expected gain. A best decision rule will make its assignments in a way that maximizes the expected gain. Thus our next task is to discover the explicit effect a decision rule has on the resulting expected gain so that we can construct a decision rule having maximum gain.

Let us review the processes that lead to the occurrence of event (t,a,d) :

1. There is an observed unit that has measurements d and whose true category identification is t.

2. Using only measurements d, the decision rule makes the assignment to category a.

It is clear that in making the category assignment, the decision rule can use only the measurement data. For it to use the unit's true category identification would make a joke of the entire pattern identification process. The assumption that the decision rule may use only the measurement data in making a category assignment is called the *fair game assumption*. If we think of nature as determining the true category identification of a unit and the decision rule as determining the assigned category identification, then the fair game assumption means that nature and the decision rule are not in collusion.

The fair game assumption amounts to a conditional independence assumption that can be precisely stated once we define the required conditionals. By $P(a \mid t,d)$ we denote the conditional probability of making an assignment to a category a given that the observed unit has true category identification t and observed measurement

d. From the definition of conditional probability,

$$P(a \mid t,d) = \frac{P(t,a,d)}{P(t,d)}$$

By $P(a \mid d)$ we denote the conditional probability of making assignment to category a given that the observed unit has measurement d. From the definition of conditional probability,

$$P(a \mid d) = \frac{P(a,d)}{P(d)}$$

The fair game assumption states

$$P(a \mid t,d) = P(a \mid d)$$

The fair game assumption immediately leads to the fact that conditioned on measurement d, the true category and the assigned category are independent. We can see this easily. By definition,

$$P(t,a \mid d) = \frac{P(t,a,d)}{P(d)}$$

But

$$P(t,a,d) = P(a \mid t,d)P(t,d)$$

and by the fair game assumption, $P(a \mid t,d) = P(a \mid d)$. Hence

$$P(t,a \mid d) = \frac{P(a \mid d)P(t,d)}{P(d)}$$

Now by definition of conditional probability,

$$\frac{P(t,d)}{P(d)} = P(t \mid d)$$

Therefore

$$P(t,a \mid d) = P(a \mid d)P(t \mid d)$$

In order to help us distinguish between the conditional probability $P(t \mid d)$ of a unit having true category identification t, given that it has measurement d, a conditional probability that nature determines, and the conditional probability $P(a \mid d)$ of a decision rule assigning category a to an observed unit having measurement d, we will use the notation $f(a \mid d)$ for the conditional probability associated with the decision rule.

The decision rule is completely defined by the conditional probability $f(a \mid d)$. If the decision rule is deterministic, then for some assigned category $a, f(a \mid d) = 1$ and for all other categories $a', a' \neq a, f(a' \mid d) = 0$. Decision rules that are not deterministic are called probabilistic, nondeterministic, or stochastic decision rules.

The consideration of decision rules that are probabilistic may seem counterintuitive. After all, a decision rule that, when given measurement d, randomly assigns to category a_1, say, two-thirds of the time and to category a_2 one-third of the time, is a rule that, when measurement d are given, in effect simply spins the roulette wheel. If the 30-position wheel stops at a number between 1 and 20, then an assignment is made to category a_1. If the wheel stops at a number between 21 and 30, then an assignment is made to category a_2.

We have adopted a notation allowing decision rules to be probabilistic because probabilistic rules are more general, covering the deterministic decision rules as well as the nondeterministic ones. In this section we explore some of the properties that probabilistic decision rules have. In Section 4.5 we will discuss some of the special optimal properties that they can have.

At this point we are ready to show the explicit dependence that the decision rule has on the expected gain. Recall that

$$E[e] = \sum_{t \in C} \sum_{a \in C} e(t,a)P(t,a)$$

$$= \sum_{t \in C} \sum_{a \in C} e(t,a) \sum_{d \in D} P(t,a,d)$$

Now by definition of conditional probability, $P(t,a,d) = P(t,a \mid d)P(d)$, and by the fair game assumption $P(t,a \mid d) = f(t \mid d)f(a \mid d)$. Hence

$$E[e] = \sum_{t \in C} \sum_{a \in C} e(t,a) \sum_{d \in D} P(t \mid d)f(a \mid d)P(d)$$

$$= \sum_{t \in C} \sum_{a \in C} e(t,a) \sum_{d \in D} f(a \mid d)P(t,d)$$

To analyze the dependence $f(a \mid d)$ has on $E[e]$, we need to rearrange the summation separating the effect of $f(a \mid d)$ from $P(t,d)$ and $e(t,a)$. The best we can do is regroup $P(t,d)$ and $e(t,a)$ together and perform the sum over all $t \in C$ first. This yields

$$E[e;f] = \sum_{d \in D} \left\{ \sum_{a \in C} f(a \mid d) \left[\sum_{t \in C} e(t,a)P(t,d) \right] \right\}$$

Notice that we have explicitly represented the fact that the decision rule f influences the expected value of economic gain. The term in square brackets depends only on the measurement d and assigned category a. The decision rule f can distribute its probability differently over the assigned categories for each measurement d. With a little thought, it is clear that if the decision rule $f(a \mid d)$ were to put any nonzero probability on a category a that did not maximize

$$\sum_{t \in C} e(t,a)P(t,d)$$

then the decision rule would not maximize $E[e;f]$. Hence a decision rule f that maximizes $E[e;f]$ must satisfy the condition that, if for some category $a \in C$

$$\sum_{t \in C} e(t,a)P(t,d) < \max_{b \in C} \sum_{t \in C} e(t,b)P(t,d)$$

then $f(a \mid d) = 0$. If there is more than one category a that maximizes

$$\sum_{t \in C} e(t,a)P(t,d)$$

then the decision rule can be probabilistic and can distribute its probability in any arbitrary way over all categories that achieve the maximum. If the category that achieves the maximum for each d is unique, then the decision rule is necessarily deterministic.

Therefore we have discovered how to construct the optimal decision rule f. Let a measurement d be given for an observed unit. Then

$$f(a \mid d) = 0 \ \text{if} \ \sum_{t \in C} e(t,a)P(t,d) < \max_{b \in C} \sum_{t \in C} e(t,b)P(t,d)$$

and the probability is divided in any arbitrary way among the categories a that maximize

$$\sum_{t \in C} e(t,a)P(t,d)$$

Decision rules that maximize the expected economic gain are called *Bayes decision rules*. A Bayes decision rule f satisfies $E[e; f] \geq E[e; g]$ for any decision rule g. Since for any measurement d, a Bayes decision rule must put all its probability on categories that maximize

$$\sum_{t \in C} e(t,a)P(t,d)$$

and since it may do so in any arbitrary way, we may construct a deterministic Bayes rule that puts all of its probability on some category a that maximizes

$$\sum_{t \in C} e(t,a)P(t,d)$$

Thus we see that in any situation we can find a deterministic Bayes rule.

We can now illustrate the mechanics of constructing a Bayes rule. Let the economic gain matrix have its rows labeled by true category identification and its columns labeled by assigned category identification. Suppose measurement $d \in D$ is made of the observed unit. Append a column of the joint probabilities of true category measurement $P(t_1, d), \ldots, P(t_K, d)$ alongside the last column of the economic gain matrix. Then successively overlay the probability column on each column of the economic gain matrix and compute the sum of products. For the ath column the sum of products is

$$\sum_{t \in C} e(t,a)P(t,d)$$

Now find the column yielding the largest sum of products. A deterministic Bayes rule may then assign the unit having measurements d to the first category having the largest sum of products. The economic gain achieved by the decision rule will then be the sum over all measurements d of the highest sum of products.

Figure 4.2 illustrates this technique on an example problem. Consider what category assignment must be made for a unit having measurement d_1. Placing the column of probabilities for d_1 alongside column 1 and column 2 of the economic gain matrix and computing the sums of the products, we obtain .12 for column 1 and .2 for column 2. Since column 2 yields the largest result, a Bayes rule must put all the probability on the assignment to category c_2.

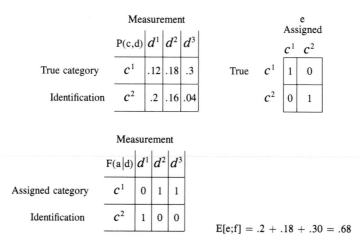

Figure 4.2 Calculation of the Bayes decision rule and calculation of the expected gain.

Not all of the time will a unit having measurements d_1 be assigned the correct assignment. For the .2 fraction of the time that a unit is observed having measurement d_1 and true category identification c_2, the unit will be assigned its correct category identification. For the .12 fraction of the time that a unit is observed having measurement d_1 and true category identification c_1, the unit will be assigned to incorrect category c_2.

For each true-assigned category identification pair (t,a), the probability $P(t,a)$ can be computed from

$$P(t,a) = \sum_{d \in D} P(t,d)f(a \mid d)$$

Continuing from the example of Fig. 4.2, we may overlay the first row of the joint probability table $P(t,d)$ onto the first row of the decision rule probability table $f(a \mid d)$ and take the sum of the products. The result is $.12 \times 0 + .18 \times 1 + .3 \times 1 = .48$. Hence the probability is .48 of encountering a unit whose true category identification is c^1 and whose assigned category identification is c^1. Overlaying the first row of the joint probability table $P(t,d)$ onto the second row of the division rule probability table $f(a|d)$ and taking the sum of products yields $.12 \times 1 + .18 \times 0 + .3 \times 0 = .12$. Hence the probability is .12 of encountering a unit whose true category identification is c^1 but whose incorrect assigned identification is c^2. In a similar manner by successively overlaying the second row of the joint probability table $P(t,d)$ onto the decision rule probability table $f(a|d)$, we can obtain $P(c_2,c_1) = .2$ and $P(c_2,c_2) = .2$. This is illustrated in Fig. 4.3.

Therefore we have discovered how to construct the optimal decision rule f. Let a measurement d be given for an observed unit. Then

$$f(a|d) = 0 \quad \text{if} \quad \sum_{t \in C} e(t,a)P(t,d) < \max_{b \in C} \sum_{t \in C} e(t,b)P(t,d)$$

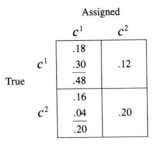

Figure 4.3 Calculation of the decision rule error for the decision rule constructed in Fig. 4.2.

and the probability is divided in any arbitrary way among the categories a that maximize $\sum_{t \in C} e(t,a)P(t,d)$.

Our second example problem differs from the last one in that measurement space here is considered to be continuous rather than discrete. So in the places where we had to use summation on terms involving probability functions, we must instead use integration on terms involving probability density functions.

For this example, possible measurements lie in the closed interval $[0, 1]$. The conditional density of a measurement having value x given category t_1 is $3x^2$, and the conditional density of a measurement having value x given category t_2 is $3(1-x^2)/2$. It is easy to verify that $3x^2$ and $3(1-x^2)/2$ are indeed density functions over the interval $[0, 1]$ because on that interval they are both nonnegative and they both integrate to 1.

$$\int_0^1 3x^2\, dx = 1$$

$$\int_0^1 \frac{3(1-x^2)}{2}\, dx = 1$$

Let us suppose that the prior probability of category t_1 is $\frac{1}{3}$ and the prior probability of category t_2 is $\frac{2}{3}$. In this case the joint probability of true category identification t_1 and measurement x is $P(t_1,x) = 3(1-x^2)/2 \cdot \frac{2}{3} = (1-x^2)$. Using an identity gain matrix, a Bayes decision rule will assign an observed unit to category t_1 when

$$P(t_1,x) \geq P(t_2,x)$$

and will assign an observed unit to category t_2 when $P(t_2,x) > P(t_1,x)$. Now $P(t_1,x) \geq P(t_2,x)$ implies $x^2 \geq (1-x^2)$. Upon taking square roots and rearranging, we obtain $x \geq \frac{\sqrt{2}}{2} = .707$. Thus where x is greater than .707, we assign to category t_1; otherwise we assign to category t_2:

$$f(t_1 \mid x) = \begin{cases} 1 & \text{when } x \geq .707 \\ 0 & \text{otherwise} \end{cases} \quad \text{and} \quad f(t_2 \mid x) = \begin{cases} 1 & \text{when } x < .707 \\ 0 & \text{otherwise} \end{cases}$$

Next we compute the expected economic gain obtained by using this decision rule. By definition,

$$E[e;f] = \sum_{t \in D} \sum_{a \in C} e(t,a) \int_{x=0}^{1} f(t \mid x) P(t,x) dx$$

Since we are using an identity gain matrix, only the terms where $t = a$ count. Hence

$$E[e;f] = \sum_{t \in C} \int_{x=0}^{1} f(t \mid x) P(t,x) dx$$

Expanding the summation, we have

$$E[e;f] = \int_{x=0}^{1} f(t_1 \mid x) P(t,x) dx + \int_{x=0}^{1} f(t_2 \mid x) P(t,x) dx$$

Now substituting the Bayes decision rule for f results in

$$E[e;f] = \int_{\frac{\sqrt{2}}{2}}^{1} x^2 dx + \int_{0}^{\frac{\sqrt{2}}{2}} (1 - x^2) dx$$

$$= \frac{x^3}{3} \Big|_{\frac{\sqrt{2}}{2}}^{1} + \left(x - \frac{x^3}{3} \right) \Big|_{0}^{\frac{\sqrt{2}}{2}}$$

$$= \frac{1}{3} - \frac{(\frac{\sqrt{2}}{2})^3}{3} + \frac{\sqrt{2}}{2} - \frac{(\frac{\sqrt{2}}{2})^3}{3}$$

$$= .805$$

4.3   Prior Probability

The Bayes rule f is given by

$$f(a \mid d) = \begin{cases} 1 & \text{if } \sum_{t \in C} e(t,a) P(t,d) = \max_{b \in C} \sum_{t \in C} e(t,b) P(t,d) \\ 0 & \text{otherwise} \end{cases}$$

where we assume here that the maximizing category is unique. Notice that $P(t,d) = P(d \mid t) P(t)$, where $P(d \mid t)$ is the conditional probability of observing measurement d given that the unit's true category identification is t and $P(t)$ is the prior probability of observing a unit whose true category identification is t. Therefore a Bayes rule can be determined by assigning any category that maximizes

$$\sum_{t \in C} e(t,a) P(d \mid t) P(t)$$

This form is useful because often the probability $P(d \mid t)$ is the probability that is estimated, and it is often represented parametrically as some function of the mean, of the covariance, and of d. The prior probability $P(t)$ is the probability with which we expect to find a unit whose true category identification is t before we observe the unit's measurements. If we have no expectations about how frequently we expect to find each category, then we can invoke the equal-probability-of-ignorance assumption and choose all the category prior probabilities to be equal. If the economic gain matrix is the identity matrix, then the resulting decision rule is called a maximum likelihood decision rule.

Because the investigator is free to choose the category prior probabilities in accordance with prior expectations, a Bayes rule that assigns to that category a maximizing

$$\sum_{t \in C} e(t,a)P(d \mid t)P(t)$$

when observing a unit having measurement d is said to be a Bayes rule with respect to true prior probability function $P(t)$.

4.4   Economic Gain Matrix and the Decision Rule

Now that we have seen how the probabilities and economic gain matrix determine a decision rule, we can ask in what way the resulting decision rule is sensitive or not sensitive to the choice of economic gain matrix. In this section we show that decision rules determined by economic gain matrices that differ by some additive constant and a positive multiplicative constant are the same decision rule. Thus economic gain matrices really only have to be known up to an additive and multiplicative constant.

To understand why this happens, suppose $e_1(t,a)$ and $e_2(t,a)$ are two different economic gain functions and $e_2(t,a) = k_1 e_1(t,a) + k_2$ where $k_1 > 0$. Then the decision rule determined by economic gain e_2 will assign an observed unit with measurement d to category a when

$$\sum_{t \in C} e_2(t,a)P(t,d) \geq \sum_{t \in C} e_2(t,a')P(t,d) \quad \text{for every } a' \in C$$

Since $e_2(t,a) = k_1 e_1(t,a) + k_2$, this inequality is equivalent to

$$\sum_{t \in C} [k_1 e_1(t,a) + k_2]P(t,d) \geq \sum_{t \in C} [k_1 e(t,a') + k_2]P(t,d) \quad \text{for every } a' \in C$$

Breaking each summation into two pieces, one involving the $k_1 e_1(t,a)P(t,d)$ term and the other involving the $k_2 P(t,d)$ term, we discover that both sides of the inequality have the summation $\sum_{t \in C} k_2 p(t,d)$. Subtracting this from both sides of the inequality leaves

$$k_1 \sum_{t \in C} e_1(t,a)P(t,d) \geq k_1 \sum_{t \in C} e(t,a')P(t,d) \quad \text{for every } a' \in C$$

Since the constant k_1 is positive, we can divide both sides of the inequality and obtain

$$\sum_{t \in C} e_1(t,a)P(t,d) \geq \sum_{t \in C} e_1(t,a')P(t,d) \quad \text{for every } a' \in C$$

This is, of course, precisely the test that the decision rule based on economic gain e_1 would use when assigning an observed unit having measurements d. Thus the two decision rules are identical.

We close this section by illustrating a few interesting kinds of economic gain matrices that yield the same decision rule. For the sake of simplicity we assume that there are three categories. We have already seen that the identity economic gain matrix

$$\begin{pmatrix} 1 & 0 & 0 \\ 0 & 1 & 0 \\ 0 & 0 & 1 \end{pmatrix}$$

maximizes the probability of correct classification. For this economic gain, every correct decision gains 1 and every incorrect decision gains 0. The dual of this situation is one in which every correct decision gains 0 and every incorrect decision loses 1 (gains -1). The corresponding economic gain matrix is

$$\begin{pmatrix} 0 & -1 & -1 \\ -1 & 0 & -1 \\ -1 & -1 & 0 \end{pmatrix}$$

Since this matrix can be obtained by adding the constant -1 to every term of the identity gain matrix, these matrices must generate the same optimal rule.

A more balanced situation is one in which 1 is gained for every correct assignment and 1 is lost for every incorrect assignment. The following gain matrix corresponds to this situation.

$$\begin{pmatrix} 1 & -1 & -1 \\ -1 & 1 & -1 \\ -1 & -1 & 1 \end{pmatrix}$$

Notice that it is obtainable from the identity gain matrix by multiplying every entry of the identity matrix by the positive constant 2 and then subtracting 1 from each entry. Hence the more balanced situation in which we gain when we are correct and lose when we are not yields the same decision rule as the one that maximizes probability of correct identification.

We might think that this equivalence of economic gain matrices has been due to the fact that the amount gained or lost upon correct or incorrect assignments was the same. This is not the case. Consider what happens when upon a correct assignment we gain a positive amount x and upon an incorrect assignment we lose a positive amount y. The economic gain matrix then takes the form

$$\begin{pmatrix} x & -y & -y \\ -y & x & -y \\ -y & -y & x \end{pmatrix}$$

But this matrix too is obtainable from the identity matrix by multiplying it by the positive amount $(x + y)$ and then subtracting y from every entry.

Bayes decision rules that do not maximize probability of correct identification are obtained by using economic gain matrices in which the diagonal terms are not equal or in which the off-diagonal terms are not equal, The economic gain matrix

$$\begin{pmatrix} 1 & -20 & -1 \\ -2 & 5 & -1 \\ -3 & -30 & 10 \end{pmatrix}$$

would lead to a decision rule that might tend to make many assignments to category 3, because if the assignment is correct, there is a lot (10) to gain, and if the assignment is incorrect, there is not much to lose (-1). On the other hand, few assignments would be made to category 2 because of the stiff losses $(-20$ or $-30)$ that would result from the decision rule being wrong. Assignments to category 2 would be made only if the probability of the assignment being correct was very high.

Let us now rework the second example in which the conditional density of x given category t_1 is $3x^2$ and the conditional density of x given category t_2 is $3(1 - x^2)/2$. The prior probability of category t_1 is $\frac{1}{3}$ and the prior probability of category t_2 is $\frac{2}{3}$. We use an arbitrary economic gain matrix

$$\begin{pmatrix} a & b \\ c & d \end{pmatrix}$$

where we naturally assume $a > b$ and $d > c$. In this case the Bayes decision rule will assign to category t_1 when

$$aP(t_1, x) + cP(t_2, x) \geq bP(t_1, x) + dP(t_2, x)$$

Upon substituting the densities for $P(t_1, x)$ and $P(t_2, x)$, we obtain

$$ax^2 + c(1 - x^2) \geq bx^2 + d(1 - x^2)$$

This inequality is equivalent to

$$x^2 \geq \frac{d - c}{(a - b) + (d - c)}$$

Hence, since $x \in [0, 1]$, the Bayes decision rule will assign to category t_1 when

$$x \geq \frac{\sqrt{d - c}}{\sqrt{(a - b) + (d - c)}}$$

4.5   Maximin Decision Rule

In order to determine a Bayes decision rule, we have to know the joint probability function $P(c, d)$ or at least the conditional probability function $P(c|d)$. But this means that to use the conditional probability function $P(d|c)$ to determine $P(c|d)$, we must also know the prior probability function. This leads us to constructing decision rules that are Bayes decision rules with respect to a prior probability function $P(c)$.

All is well when something definite is known about the prior probability function. But when a situation exists in which the prior probabilities cannot be known and it is unreasonable to assume that they are equal (equal-probability-of-ignorance assumption), and when we want to be particularly careful about not incurring large losses, the Bayes decision rule is not appropriate. In these circumstances an appropriate decision rule is one that maximizes the average gain over the worst prior probability functions. Such a conservative decision rule is called a *maximin decision rule*.

A decision rule f is called a maximin decision rule if and only if

$$\min_{P(c^1),\ldots,P(c^K)} \sum_{j=1}^{K} E[e \mid c^j; f]P(c^j) \geq \min_{P(c^1),\ldots,P(c^K)} \sum_{j=1}^{K} E[e \mid c^j; g]P(c^j)$$

for any decision rule g, where

$$E[e \mid c^j; f] = \sum_{d \in D} \sum_{k=1}^{K} e(c^k, c^j)P(d \mid c^j)f(c^k \mid d)$$

Thus the expected gain of a maximin rule is the same as the expected gain of the Bayes rule under the worst possible prior probability function. When the maximization is done only over all deterministic decision rules g instead of over all decision rules randomized or deterministic, then the rule is called a *deterministic maximin rule*.

Because $\sum_{j=1}^{K} P(c^j) = 1$ and $P(c^j) \geq 0$, the minimum economic gain under all prior probability functions certainly can be achieved when, for a category c^k having smallest conditional gain, $P(c^k) = 1$, and for all other categories, the prior probability is zero. Hence a decision rule f is a maximin decision rule if and only if

$$\min_{j=1,\ldots,K} E[e \mid c^j; f] \geq \min_{j=1,\ldots,K} E[e \mid c^j; g]$$

for any decision rule g.

Finding a maximin decision rule is generally difficult. (It is easy to illustrate that the problem of finding one is equivalent to a large linear programming problem.) Unlike the Bayes rule, which can always have a deterministic form, the maximin decision rule is generally probabilistic. Under certain circumstances the maximin decision rule is deterministic and is therefore the same as the deterministic Bayes rule with respect to the worst possible priors. Under other circumstances the deterministic maximin rule yields the same expected gain as the deterministic Bayes rule only under the worst possible prior probability function. In general, however, the three rules are distinct. We will illustrate these properties by a few examples.

■ **EXAMPLE 4.3**

Consider the case where there are two categories c^1 and c^2; three possible measurements d^1, d^2, and d^3; and a conditional probability function $P(d \mid c)$ given by

$P(d \mid c)$	d^1	d^2	d^3
c^1	.2	.3	.5
c^2	.5	.4	.1

There are eight possible decision rules. When the gain matrix e has 0s off the diagonal and 1s on the diagonal, the conditional gains of e given c for the decision rule can be computed as

				Measurements			Conditional gains	
				d^1	d^2	d^3	$E[e\|c^1;f]$	$E[e\|c^2;f]$
		f_1		c^1	c^1	c^1	1	0
		f_2		c^1	c^1	c^2	.5	.1
		f_3		c^1	c^2	c^1	.7	.4
Decision		f_4		c^1	c^2	c^2	.2	.5
rule		f_5		c^2	c^1	c^1	.8	.5
		f_6		c^2	c^1	c^2	.3	.6
		f_7		c^2	c^2	c^1	.5	.9
		f_8		c^2	c^2	c^2	0	1

Clearly, of the deterministic decision rules, f_5 and f_7 will maximize the minimum expected conditional gain, each yielding a minimum expected conditional gain of .5; f_5 and f_7 are then deterministic maximin rules.

Figure 4.4 graphs the expected gains for each of the possible deterministic decision rules as a function of the prior probability $P(c^1)$. Notice that (1) as the prior probability changes, the expected gain for each decision rule changes; (2) no one decision rule will do the best in all circumstances; (3) and the lowest expected Bayes gain is obtained with decision rules f_5 and f_7. The Bayes gain for f_5 as a function of $P(c^1)$ is

$$E[e;f_5] = .3P(c^1) + .5$$

The Bayes gain for f_7 as a function of $P(c^1)$ is

$$E[e;f_7] = -.4P(c^1) + .9$$

The lowest possible Bayes gain is achieved for decision rules f_5 and f_7 when $P(c^1) = \frac{4}{7}$ and $P(c^2) = \frac{3}{7}$. For this worst-case prior probability, the Bayes gain is .6714; the deterministic maximin decision rule and the Bayes decision rule under this worst possible prior probability function yield the same expected gain only for this prior. There are other prior probability functions under which the deterministic decision rules f_5 and f_7 yield lower expected gains than .6714, the worst possible Bayes gain. Consider, for example, the prior $P(c^1) = 0$ and $P(c^2) = 1$. Under these conditions deterministic decision rule f_5 yields .5 expected gain. Consider, for another example, the prior $P(c^1) = 1$ and $P(c^2) = 0$. Under these conditions deterministic decision rule f_7 also yields .5 expected gain.

The general maximin decision rule is a probabilistic one and is guaranteed to achieve the worst possible Bayes gain of .6714 regardless of the values of the prior probability functions. Fig. 4.5 illustrates the expected gains given category c^1 or c^2 for each of the eight deterministic decision rules, which each appear in the figure as a point. The area within the smallest polygon containing the eight

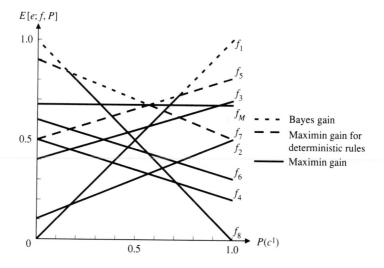

Figure 4.4 Expected gain that the eight possible decision rules yield $E[e \mid c^2; f]$ under specified prior probability functions.

deterministic decision rules represents the set of possible expected conditional gains for all possible decision rules—deterministic and probabilistic. This is because any probabilistic decision rule can be represented as a linear convex combination of deterministic ones and the area within the polygon represents the set of all linear convex combinations of the decision rule points.

Now to determine a decision rule f that maximizes

$$\min_{\substack{j \\ j=1,\dots,K}} E[e \mid c^j; f]$$

We draw a dashed line representing the equation $E[e \mid c^1; f] = E[e \mid c^2; f]$. The point where this line meets the boundary of the polygon farthest from the origin represents the probabilistic maximin decision rule that has a minimum expected gain of .6714. Using the facts that the distance between f_5 and f_7 is .5, that the distance between f_7 and $(.6714, .6714)$ is .2857, and that the distance between f_5 and $(.6714, .6714)$ is .2143, we see that the probabilistic maximin decision rule is one that is f_5 with probability $\frac{.2857}{.5} = \frac{4}{7}$ and f_7 with probability $\frac{.2143}{.5} = \frac{3}{7}$.

Let f_M be the probabilistic maximin decision rule just computed.

$$f_M = \begin{cases} f_5 & \text{with probability } \frac{4}{7} \\ f_7 & \text{with probability } \frac{3}{7} \end{cases}$$

The expected gain for the probabilistic decision rule f_M can be determined by

$$E[e; f_m] = \frac{4}{7} E[e; f_5] + \frac{3}{7} E[e; f_7]$$

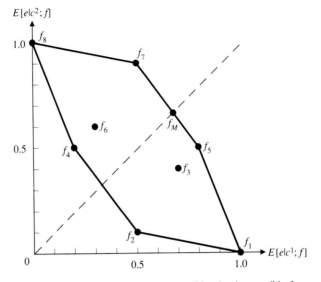

Figure 4.5 Convex set of the expected conditional gains possible for any decision rule. The decision rule f_M is the maximum decision rule and is probabilistic.

Since

$$E[e; f_5] = .3P(c^1) + .5, \quad \text{and} \quad E[e; f_7] = -0.4P(c^1) + .9$$

then

$$E[e; f_M] = \frac{4}{7}[.3P(c^1) + .5] + \frac{3}{7}[-.4P(c^1) + .9]$$

$$= \frac{4.7}{7} = .6714$$

Notice how the expected gain for the probabilistic maximin decision rule is not dependent on the prior probability function. No matter what the prior probability function, the expected gain for the probabilistic maximin decision rule is the same number, the expected gain of a Bayes rule under the worst possible prior probability function.

<hr>

EXAMPLE 4.4

In our next example we illustrate how the maximin decision rule can be deterministic and therefore the same as the Bayes rule with respect to the most unfavorable prior probability function. We consider the case where there are two

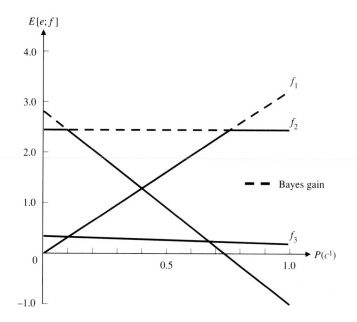

Figure 4.6 Expected gains as a function of prior probability for a variety of decision rules. Notice that f_2, which is the maximin rule, is the Bayes rule under a large range of prior probabilities.

categories c^1 and c^2, and two measurements d^1 and d^2, where the conditional probability function $P(d|c)$ is given by

$P(d\|c)$	d^1	d^2
c^1	$\frac{3}{4}$	$\frac{1}{4}$
c^2	$\frac{1}{8}$	$\frac{7}{8}$

and where the economic gain matrix e is given by

e	c^1	c^2
c^1	$3\frac{2}{3}$	-1
c^2	0	$\frac{20}{7}$

There are four possible decision rules. The conditional gains given by each category for the decision rules are

	d^1	d^2	$E[e\|c^1;f]$	$E[e\|c^2;f]$
f_1	c^1	c^1	$3\frac{2}{3}$	0
f_2	c^1	c^2	$2\frac{1}{2}$	$2\frac{1}{2}$
f_3	c^2	c^1	$\frac{1}{6}$	$\frac{5}{14}$
f_4	c^2	c^2	-1	$\frac{20}{7}$

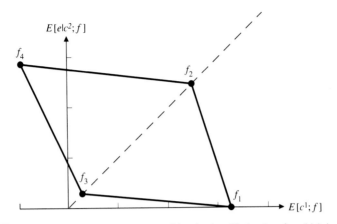

Figure 4.7 Convex set of expected conditional gains. Notice that f_2, which is a deterministic decision rule, is the maximin decision rule in this case.

Clearly, of the deterministic decision rules, f_2 will maximize the minimum expected gain yielding a minimum expected gain of $2\frac{1}{2}$. Figure 4.6 graphs the expected gains for each of the possible deterministic decision rules as a function of the prior probability $P(c^1)$. The lowest possible Bayes gain of $2\frac{1}{2}$ occurs over a large middle range of values for prior probability $P(c^1)$. Figure 4.7 illustrates the expected gains given category c^1 or c^2 for each of the four possible deterministic decision rules. The area within the polygon represents the set of conditional gains possible for all possible decision rules—deterministic and probabilistic. Notice that f_2 lies on the line $E[e \mid c^1; f] = E[e \mid c^2; f]$ and is on the boundary of the polygon farthest away from the origin. Hence the deterministic rule f_2 is the maximin decision rule.

■

EXAMPLE 4.5

Our third example illustrates a situation in which

1. The deterministic maximin rule will perform better than the general maximin rule for some priors and worse for other priors and yet never better than a Bayes rule;

2. The general maximin rule has the same conditional gain given any category, and this conditional gain equals the gain obtained with the Bayes rules under the worst possible prior probability function;

3. The general maximin rule is not deterministic and not equal to the Bayes rule under the worst possible prior probability function.

There are two categories c^1 and c^2, three possible measurements d^1, d^2, and d^3; and a conditional probability function $P(d|c)$ given by

$P(d|c)$	c^1	c^2	f_1	f_2	f_3	f_4	f_5	f_6	f_7	f_8
d_1	.3	.25	c^1	c^1	c^1	c^1	c^2	c^2	c^2	c^2
d_2	.4	.45	c^1	c^2	c^2	c^2	c^1	c^1	c^2	c^2
d_3	.3	.3	c^1	c^2	c^1	c^2	c^1	c^2	c^1	c^2

There are eight possible decision rules, and when the gain matrix e has 0s off the diagonal and 1s on the diagonal, the conditional gains given a category for each decision rule is given by

$P(c|d)$	c^1	c^2	f_1	f_2	f_3	f_4	f_5	f_6	f_7	f_8
c^1			.1	.7	.6	.3	.7	.4	.3	0
c^2			0	.3	.45	.75	.25	.55	.7	1

Clearly, of the deterministic decision rules, f_3 and f_6 will maximize the minimum expected conditional gains, each yielding a minimum expected conditional gain of .45 and .4, respectively, which is less than the minimum Bayes gain. Notice also that for some priors f_3 can yield an expected gain as high as .6 and that for others f_6 can yield an expected gain as high as .55, either one of which is greater than the minimum Bayes gain. Thus f_3 and f_6 are the deterministic maximin decision rules. Examination of Fig. 4.8 shows that the lowest expected Bayes gain is obtained with decision rules f_1 and f_4. The Bayes gain for f_1 as a function of $P(c^1)$ is $E[e;f_1] = P(c^1)$. The Bayes gain for f_4 as a function of $P(c^1)$ is $E[e;f_4] = -.45P(c^1) + .75$. The lowest possible Bayes gain is achieved for decision rules f_1 and f_4 when the prior probability function is $P(c^1) = \frac{15}{29}$ and $P(c^2) = \frac{14}{29}$. For this worst-case prior probability function, the Bayes gain is $\frac{15}{29} = .5172$. Here the deterministic Bayes rules and the deterministic maximin rules are different. Furthermore, the deterministic maximin rule and the general maximin rule are not the same.

Since the expected gain of the general maximin rule does not change with prior probability function and since Figs. 4.8 and 4.9 show that the general maximin rule will be to use f_1 with some probability p and use f_2 with probability $(1 - p)$, the maximin rule f can be computed from the formulas for its expected gain.

$$E[e;f] = pE[e;f_1] + (1 - p)E[e;f_4]$$
$$= pP(c^1) + (1 - p)[-.45P(c^1) + .75]$$
$$= P(c^1)[1.45p - .45] + .75(1 - p)$$

To guarantee that $E[e,f]$ has no dependence on the prior probability function

$P_c(d)$	c^1	c^2	f_1	f_2	f_3	f_4	f_5	f_6	f_7	f_8
d_1	.3	.25	c^1	c^1	c^1	c^1	c^2	c^2	c^2	c^2
d_2	.4	.45	c^1	c^2	c^2	c^2	c^1	c^1	c^2	c^2
d_3	.3	.3	c^1	c^2	c^1	c^2	c^1	c^2	c^1	c^2
		c^1	1	.7	.6	.3	.7	.4	.3	0
		c^2	0	.3	.45	.75	.25	.55	.7	1

$E[e|c^j; f]$

$f_d(c)$	c^1	c^2
d_1	1	0
d_2	.3103	.6897
d_3	.3103	.6897

$E[e; f]$

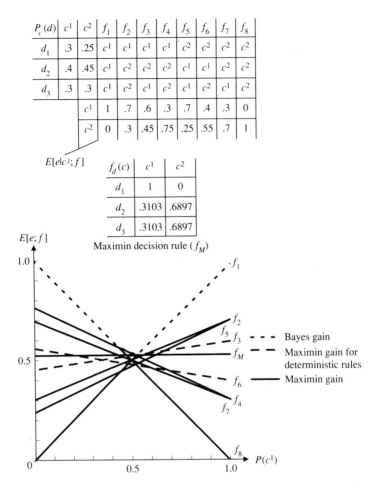

Figure 4.8 Expected gain as a function of prior probability for a variety of decision rules. The decision rule f_M is the maximin decision rule, and it is probabilistic.

$P(c)$, we must obtain $p = \frac{.45}{1.45} = .3103$. For the maximin decision rule f defined by

$$f(c|d) = \begin{cases} f(d|1) & \text{with probability } .3103 \\ f(d|4) & \text{with probability } .6897 \end{cases}$$

the expected gain $E[e; f]$ is $.75(1 - .3103) = .5172$, the same as the Bayes gain for the worst possible prior probability. Also notice that, depending on the prior probability, the deterministic maximin rule can perform better or worse than the general maximin rule. We conclude this section by a more formal statement and demonstration of the properties of a maximin decision rule.

The first proposition states that the maximin decision rule achieves the Bayes gain under the worst possible prior probability. The second proposition states that if the expected gain of a Bayes decision rule with respect to a given prior probability

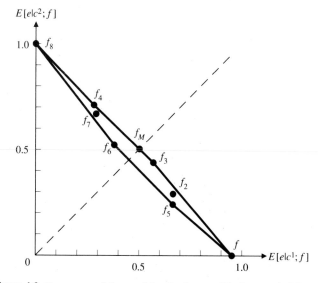

Figure 4.9 Convex set of the conditional gains possible for any decision rule. The decision rule f_M is the maximin decision rule, and it is probabilistic.

is equal to the minimum of its class conditional expected gain then the decision rule is also a maximin decision rule. The third proposition states that if the expected gain of a decision rule with respect to a prior probability with nonzero support for all categories is equal to the minimum of the expected class conditional gains, then the expected conditional gains are all equal. The fourth proposition states that the Bayes gain is a convex function of the prior probability function. The fifth proposition states that convex functions over closed convex sets are unimodal. The last proposition states that the expected gain of any decision rule must be less than the Bayes gain.

Proposition 4.1: The maximin decision rule achieves the gain of a Bayes rule under the worst possible prior probability function.

Proof:

Suppose that f is a maximin decision rule. Then

$$\min_{P(c)} \sum_{j=1}^{K} E[e \mid c^j; f]P(c^j) \geq \min_{P(c)} \sum_{j=1}^{K} E[e \mid c^j; g]P(c^j)$$

for any decision rule g.

Now notice that

$$\sum_{j=1}^{K} E[e \mid c^j; g]P(c^j)$$

is the expected gain of the decision rule g under the prior probability function P.

$$\sum_{j=1}^{K} E[e \mid c^j; g] P(c^j) = \sum_{j=1}^{K} \sum_{d \in D} \sum_{k=1}^{K} e(c^k, c^j) P(d \mid c^j) g(c^k \mid d) P(c^j)$$

$$= \sum_{d \in D} \sum_{j=1}^{K} \sum_{k=1}^{K} e(c^k, c^j) g(c^k \mid d) P(d, c^j)$$

$$= E[e; g, P]$$

Hence

$$\min_{P} E[e; f, P] \geq \min_{P} E[e; g, P]$$

for any decision rule g.

Now corresponding to each prior probability function P there exists a Bayes rule g_P that maximizes the expected gain under P. Hence

$$\min_{P} E[e; f, P] \geq \min_{P} E[e; g_P, P] \geq \min_{P} E[e; g, P]$$

for any decision rule g.

But for each P, $E[e; g_P, P] \geq E[e, g, P]$ for any decision rule g since g_P is a Bayes rule with respect to P. In particular, this is true for decision rule f. Hence

$$\min_{P} E[e; g_P, P] \geq \min_{P} E[e; f, P]$$

This implies that

$$\min_{P} E[e; f, P] = \min_{P} E[e; g_P, P]$$

The expected gain of a maximin decision rule equals the Bayes gain under the worst prior probability function. The maximin decision rule therefore achieves the gain of a Bayes rule under the most unfavorable prior probability function.

Proposition 4.2: Let f be a Bayes decision rule satisfying for some prior probability function P

$$E[e; f, P] = \min_{\substack{j \\ j=1,\ldots,K}} E[e \mid c^j; f]$$

Then f is a maximin decision rule and P is the most unfavorable prior probability function.

Proof:

Since f is a Bayes decision rule, $E[e; f, P] \geq E[e; g, P]$ for any decision rule g.

Since

$$E[e;f,P] = \min_{\substack{j \\ j=1,2,\ldots,K}} E[e \mid c^j;f]$$

we must obtain that

$$\min_{\substack{j \\ j=1,\ldots,K}} E[e \mid c^j;f] \geq E[e;g,P]$$

for any decision rule g.

But for any decision rule g,

$$E[e;g,P] \geq \min_{\substack{j \\ j=1,\ldots,K}} E[e \mid c^j;g]$$

so that

$$\min_{\substack{j \\ j=1,\ldots,K}} E[e \mid c^j;f] \geq \min_{\substack{j \\ j=1,\ldots,K}} E[e \mid c^j;g]$$

for any decision rule g.

Thus f is a maximin decision rule.

Since the gain of f under any prior probability P' satisfies

$$E[e;f,P'] \geq \min_{\substack{j \\ j=1,\ldots,K}} E[e \mid c^j;f] = E[e;f,P]$$

and since f is a Bayes rule, then P is the most unfavorable prior probability function for the Bayes rule f.

Proposition 4.3: If $E[e;f,P] = \min_j E[e \mid c^j;f]$ for a decision rule f and prior probability P satisfying $P(c^j) > 0$ for every category c^j, then $E[e \mid c^j;f] = E[e;f,P]$ for every category c^j.

Proof:

Let category c^k satisfy $E[e \mid c^k;f] = \min_j E[e \mid c^j;f]$. Then

$$E[e \mid c^k;f] = E[e;f,P] = \sum_{j=1}^{K} E[e \mid c^j;f]P(c^j)$$

Now suppose that for some category c^n, $E[e \mid c^n;f] > E[e \mid c^k;f]$.

$$\sum_{j=1}^{K} E[c^j;f]P(c^j) = \sum_{\substack{j=1 \\ j\neq n}}^{K} E[e \mid c^j;f]P(c^j) + E[e \mid c^n;f]P(c^n)$$

$$> \sum_{\substack{j=1 \\ j\neq n}}^{K} E[e \mid c^j;f]P(c^j) + E[e \mid c^k;f]P(c^n)$$

since $P(c^n) > 0$. Certainly

$$\sum_{\substack{j=1 \\ j \neq n}}^{K} E[e \mid c^j; f] P(c^j) \geq \sum_{\substack{j=1 \\ j \neq n}}^{K} E[e \mid c^k; f] P(c^j)$$

so that

$$E[e \mid c^k; f] > \sum_{\substack{j=1 \\ j \neq n}}^{K} E[e \mid c^k; f] P(c^j) + E[e \mid c^k; f] P(c^n) = E[e \mid c^k; f]$$

This is a contradiction. Thus for no category c^n must $E[e \mid c^n; f] > E[e \mid c^k; f]$. But $E[e \mid c^n; f] = \min_j E[e \mid c^j; f]$. Therefore for every category c^n, $E[e \mid c^n; f] = E[e \mid c^k; f]$, and $E[e; f, P] = \min_j E[e \mid c^j; f] = E[e \mid c^n; f]$ for every category c^n.

Proposition 4.4:   The Bayes gain as a function of the prior probability function is convex.

Proof:

The Bayes gain curve as a function of P is $\max_f E[e; f, P]$. Let θ satisfying $1 \geq \theta \geq 0$ be given. Let P_1 and P_2 be two prior probability functions. Consider

$$\max_f E[e; f, \theta P_1 + (1 - \theta) P_2] = \max_f \{\theta E[e; f, P_1] + (1 - \theta) E[e; f, P_2]\}$$

$$\leq \theta \max_f E[e; f, P_1] + (1 - \theta) \max_f E[e; f, P_2]$$

Hence the Bayes gain for a convex combination of P_1 and P_2 is less than the convex combination of the Bayes gain for P_1 and P_2. Thus the Bayes gain is a convex function.

Proposition 4.5:   Let I be a closed convex set and f be a convex function over I. Then f is unimodal.

Proof:

Let x^* satisfy $f(x^*) \leq f(x)$ for all $x \in I$. Suppose z, y, and x^* all lie along a line in I with y between z and x^*. Since I is convex, there exists a θ, $0 \geq \theta \geq 1$, such that $y = \theta z + (1 - \theta) x^*$. Now $f(\theta z + (1 - \theta) x^*) \leq \theta f(z) + (1 - \theta) f(x^*)$, since f is convex.

But $f(x^*) \leq f(z)$, so that

$$\theta f(z) + (1 - \theta) f(x^*) \leq \theta f(z) + (1 - \theta) f(z) = f(z)$$

Hence $f(z) \geq f(y) \geq f(x^*)$, so that f is unimodal.

Proposition 4.6: $E[e;f] \leq \sum_{d \in D} \max_k \sum_{j=1}^{K} e(c^k, c^j)P(d;c^j)$ and $E[e;f^*] \geq E[e;f]$ for any f if and only if $f^*(c^n|d) = 0$ when

$$\sum_{j-1}^{K} e(c^n, c^j)P(d, c^j) < \max_k \sum_{j=1}^{K} e(c^k, c^j)P(d, c^j)$$

for each n.

Proof:

$$\max_k \sum_{j=1}^{K} e(c^k, c^j)P(d, c^j) \geq \sum_{j=1}^{K} e(c^n, c^j)P(d, c^j)$$

for each n.

Since $f_d(c^i) \geq 0$,

$$f(c^i|d) \left\{ \max_k \sum_{j=1}^{K} e(c^k, c^j)P(d, c^j) \right\} \geq f(c^i|d) \sum_{j=1}^{K} e(c^n, c^j)P(d, c^j)$$

This equation holds for each c^i and for each d. Hence by summing c^i over and d, we obtain

$$\sum_{d \in D} \sum_{i=1}^{K} f(c^i|d) \left\{ \max_k \sum_{j=1}^{K} e(c^k, c^j)P(d, c^j) \right\}$$

$$\geq \sum_{d \in D} \sum_{i=1}^{K} f(c^i|d) \sum_{j=1}^{K} e(c^n, c^j)P(d, c^j)$$

Notice that

$$\sum_{d \in D} \sum_{i=1}^{K} f(c^i|d) \left\{ \max_k \sum_{j=1}^{K} e(c^k, c^j)P(d, c^j) \right\}$$

$$= \sum_{d \in D} \left\{ \max_k \sum e(c^k, c^j)P(d, c^j) \right\} \left\{ \sum_{i=1}^{K} f(c^i|d) \right\}$$

Because $f_d(c^i)$ is a conditional probability function, $\sum_{j=1}^{K} f_d(c^i) = 1$. Thus

$$\sum_{d \in D} \left\{ \max_k \sum e(c^k, c^j)P(d, c^j) \right\}$$

$$\geq \sum_{d \in D} \sum_{i=1}^{K} f(c^i|d) \sum_{j=1}^{K} e(c^n, c^j)P(d, c^j) = E[e;f]$$

The upper bound can be achieved by any conditional probability $f^*(c^i|d)$ satisfying $f^*(c^n|d) = 0$ when

$$\sum_{j=1}^{K} e(c^n, c^j)P(d, c^j) < \max_{k} \sum_{j=1}^{K} e(c^k, c^j)P(d, c^j)$$

4.6   Decision Rule Error: Misidentification/False Identification

Making decisions necessarily includes the possibility of making errors. For each category there are two types of error: an error of misidentification and an error of false-identification. A *misidentification error* for category c^k occurs when a decision rule assigns a unit whose true category is c^k to some category c^j, $c^j \neq c^k$. A misidentification error for c^k is also called a type I error or an error of omission for category c^k. The misidentification error rate for category c^k is defined by the conditional probability of a misidentification error occurring for an unit given that the unit's true category is c^k. When there are only two categories, the false-identification error for the one category of interest is called a false-alarm error. We denote the misidentification error rate for category c^k by α_k.

$$\alpha_k = P \text{ (unit not assigned to } c^k | \text{true category of unit is } c^k)$$

$$= \frac{\displaystyle\sum_{\substack{j=1 \\ j \neq k}}^{K} \sum_{d \in D} f(c^j|d)P(d, c^k)}{P(c^k)}$$

A *false-identification error* for category c^k occurs when the decision rule assigns a unit to category c^k, but the true category identification is c^j, $c^j \neq c^k$. A false-identification error for c^k is also called a type II error or an error of commission for category c^k. We denote the false-identification error rate for category c^k by β_k.

$$\beta_k = P(\text{unit assigned to } c^k | \text{true category of unit is } c^j, \; c^j \neq c^k)$$

$$= \frac{\displaystyle\sum_{\substack{j=1 \\ j \neq k}}^{K} \sum_{d \in D} f(c^k|d)P(d, c^j)}{1 - P(c^k)}$$

If a wrong category c^j is assigned to a unit whose true category is c^k, then this constitutes a misidentification error for category c^k and a false-identification error for category c^j. Thus it becomes apparent that the total number of misidentification errors equals the total number of false-identification errors. Likewise, the total error rate is the weighted average of the misidentification error rates as well as the weighted average of the false-identification error rates. To see this, let P_c denote the probability of correct classification. Then

$$P_c = \sum_{k=1}^{K} \sum_{d \in D} f(c^k|d)P(d, c^k)$$

Let P_e be the total error rate. Then $P_e = 1 - P_c$. Hence

$$P_e = 1 - \sum_{k=1}^{K} \sum_{d \in D} f(c^k|d)P(d,c^k)$$

$$= \sum_{j=1}^{K} \sum_{k=1}^{K} \sum_{d \in D} f(c^j|d)P(d,c^k) - \sum_{k=1}^{K} \sum_{d \in D} f(c^k|d)P(d,c^k)$$

$$= \sum_{j=1}^{K} \sum_{\substack{k=1 \\ k \neq j}}^{K} \sum_{d \in D} f(c^j|d)P(d,c^k) \tag{4.1}$$

$$= \sum_{k=1}^{K} \sum_{\substack{j=1 \\ j \neq k}}^{K} \sum_{d \in D} f(c^j|d)P(d,c^k)$$

$$= \sum_{k=1}^{k} \alpha_k P(c^k)$$

Making a change of variables in Eq. (4.1), we replace j by k and k by j.

$$P_e = \sum_{k=1}^{K} \sum_{\substack{j=1 \\ j \neq k}}^{K} \sum_{d \in D} f(c^k|d)P(d,c^j)$$

$$= \sum_{k=1}^{K} \beta_k[1 - P(c^k)]$$

There is a relationship between the misidentification error rate for a given category and the false-identification error rate for the category. If a decision rule g has, for a given category, a lower misidentification error rate than a decision rule f, then the decision rule g will have a higher false-identification rate than the decision rule f for the given category, provided the probability that both rules assign to category c_k is the same.

Let $\alpha_k(f)$ be the misidentification error rate of decision rule f for category c^k and $\alpha_k(g)$ be the misidentification error rate of decision rule g for category c^k. Suppose $\alpha_k(f) \leq \alpha_k(g)$ and

$$\sum_{j=1}^{K} \sum_{d \in D} f(c^k|d)P(d,c^j) \geq \sum_{j=1}^{K} \sum_{d \in D} g(c^k|d)P(d,c^j).$$

Then

$$\alpha_k(f) = \frac{\sum_{d \in D} P(d,c^k)[1 - f(c^k|d)]}{P(c^k)}$$

$$\leq \frac{\sum_{d \in D} P(d,c^k)[1 - g(c^k|d)]}{P(c^k)} = \alpha_k(g)$$

Therefore

$$\sum_{d \in D} P(d,c^k)f(c^k|d) \geq \sum_{d} P(d,c^k)g(c^k|d) \tag{4.2}$$

Next consider the false-identification error rate $\beta_k(f)$ for category c^k.

$$\beta_k(f) = \frac{\displaystyle\sum_{\substack{j=1 \\ j \neq k}}^{K} \sum_{d \in D} f(c^k|d)P(d,c^j)}{1 - P(c^k)}$$

$$= \frac{\displaystyle\sum_{j=1}^{K} \sum_{d \in D} f(c^k|d)P(d,c^j) - \sum_{d \in D} f(c^k|d)P(d,c^k)}{1 - P(c^k)}$$

Now

$$\sum_{j=1}^{K} \sum_{d} f(c^k|d)P(d,c^j) = f(c^k)$$

the probability that decision rule f makes an assignment to category c^k. Using the assumption $f(c^k) = g(c^k)$ and the relation of Eq. (4.2), we obtain $\beta_k(f) \geq \beta_k(g)$.

Let f be a decision rule whose misidentification error rate for category c^k is $\alpha_k(f)$. In order to reduce the misidentification rate for category c^k, we want to construct another decision rule g that is related to f by the following properties: Whatever the measurement d, the probability with which decision rule g assigns d to category c^k is larger than or equal to the probability with which decision rule f assigns to category c^k. That is, $g(c^k|d) \geq f(c^k|d)$. It is easy to see that the misidentification error rate for category c^k of decision rule g is smaller than the misidentification error rate for category c^k of decision rule f.

$$\alpha_k(g) = \frac{\displaystyle\sum_{\substack{j=1 \\ j \neq k}}^{K} \sum_{d \in D} g(c^j|d)P(d,c^k)}{P(c^k)}$$

$$= \frac{\displaystyle\sum_{d \in D} [1 - g(c^k|d)]P(d,c^k)}{P(c^k)}$$

$$\leq \frac{\displaystyle\sum_{d \in D} [1 - f(c^k|d)]P(d,c^k)}{P(c^k)} = \alpha_k(f)$$

However, the false-identification error rate of category c^k for decision rule g must be larger than the false-identification error rate of category c^k for decision rule f.

$$\beta_k(g) = \frac{\displaystyle\sum_{\substack{j=1 \\ j \neq k}}^{K} \sum_{d \in D} g(c^k|d)P(d,c^j)}{1 - P(c^k)}$$

$$\geq \frac{\displaystyle\sum_{\substack{j=1 \\ j \neq k}}^{K} \sum_{d \in D} f(c^k|d)P(d,c^j)}{1 - P(c^k)} = \beta_k(f)$$

It does not follow that, just because a decision rule f has a misidentification error rate for category c^k that is less than the misidentification error rate of decision rule g for category c^k, the false-alarm rate for category c^k of decision rule f must be greater than the false-alarm rate for category c^k of decision rule g. To see this, consider the following two category example.

$P(d,c)$	c^1	c^2		f	c^1	c^2		g	c^1	c^2
d_1	.2	.05		d_1	1	0		d_1	0	1
d_2	.1	.05		d_2	0	1		d_2	0	1
d_3	.05	.1		d_3	0	1		d_3	0	1
d_4	.05	.1		d_4	0	1		d_4	0	1
d_5	.05	.15		d_5	0	1		d_5	1	0
d_6	.05	.05		d_6	1	0		d_6	1	0

For this example, $\alpha_1(f) = 0.5$ and $\beta_1(f) = 0.2$, whereas $\alpha_1(g) = 0.8$ and $\beta_1(g) = 0.4$. With respect to category c^k, decision rule g is worse on both misidentification and false-alarm rates.

4.7   Reserving Judgment

An important technique that can be used to control error rate is reserved judgment. Reserved judgment gives the decision rule one more option. Instead of giving assignments for every measurement d, the decision rule may opt to withhold judgment for some measurements. The decision rule is then characterized by the fraction of time it withholds judgment and the error rate for those measurements it does assign. Chow (1970) introduced the idea of reserved judgment to pattern recognition and worked out the relationship between the reject threshold and the error rate.

To see how this works, we let α_k^o be the maximum misidentification rate we can tolerate for category c^k, and we let β_k^o be the maximum false-alarm error rate we can tolerate for category c^k. The subset of measurements D^* that are not rejected we define by

$$D^* = \{d \in D | \quad (1) \; P(d,c^k) \geq P(d,c^j), j \neq k \;\; \text{implies}$$

$$P(d,c^k) \geq P(d) - \beta_k^o [1 - P(c^k)] P(d)$$

$$\text{and (2) } P(d,c^k) < P(d,c^j) \;\; \text{for some } j \;\; \text{implies}$$

$$P(d,c^k) \leq \alpha_k^o P(d) P(c^k)$$

The set D^* is called the acceptance region. The smaller we make α_k^o and β_k^o, the fewer the measurements that can qualify into the set D^*. The set $D - D^*$ is the reject region. Let $\alpha_k(f)$ be the misidentification rate of category c^k for decision rule f and $\beta_k(f)$ be the false-alarm rate of category c^k for decision rule f. Then

$$\alpha_k(f) = \sum_{d \in D^*} \sum_{\substack{j=1 \\ j \neq k}}^{K} f(c^j|d)P(d,c^k)/P(c^k)$$

$$\sum_{d \in D^*} P(d,c^k)[1 - f(c^k|d)]/P(c^k)$$

$$\sum_{\substack{d \in D^* \\ f(c^k|d)=0}} P(d,c^k)/P(c^k)$$

But $P(d,c^k) \leq \alpha_k^o P(d)P(c^k)$. Hence

$$\alpha_k(f) \leq \sum_{\substack{d \in D^* \\ f(c^k|d)=0}} \alpha_k^o P(d)P(c^k)/P(c^k) \leq \alpha_k^o$$

A similar calculation for $\beta_k(f)$ produces

$$\beta_k(f) = \sum_{d \in D^*} \sum_{\substack{j=1 \\ j \neq k}}^{K} f(c^k|d)P(d,c^j)/[1 - P(c^k)]$$

$$\sum_{d \in D^*} f(c^k|d)[P(d) - P(d,c^k)]/[1 - P(c^k)]$$

$$\sum_{\substack{d \in D^* \\ f(c^k|d)=1}} [P(d) - P(d,c^k)]/[1 - P(c^k)]$$

But $P(d,c^k) \geq P(d) - \beta_k^o[1 - P(c^k)]P(d)$, so that $P(d) - P(d,c^k) \leq \beta_k^o[1 - P(c^k)]P(d)$. Hence

$$\beta_k(f) \leq \sum_{\substack{d \in D^* \\ f(c^k|d)=1}} \beta_k^o[1 - P(c^k)]P(d)/[1 - P(c^k)]$$

$$\leq \beta_k^o$$

4.8   Nearest Neighbor Rule

One of the important kinds of decision rule is the nearest neighbor rule. Rather than estimating the class conditional probabilities and making an assignment on the basis of the class conditioned probabilities, the nearest neighbor rule assigns a pattern vector x to the class of the closest vector in the training set to x. That is, if $x_1, \ldots, x_N$ are the N pattern vectors of the training set and have true class identification $c^1, \ldots, c^N$, respectively, then a pattern x is assigned to class c^n, where

$$\rho(x,x^n) \leq \rho(x,x^i) \quad i = 1, \ldots, N$$

and ρ is a metric or measurement space. Cover and Hart (1967) discuss the nearest neighbor rule and give bounds that relate the error rate of the nearest neighbor rule to a Bayes rule. They show that the nearest neighbor rule will not have an error rate worse than twice the Bayes error rate.

The chief difficulty with the nearest neighbor rule is that a brute-force nearest neighbor algorithm will have a computational complexity in proportion to the number of patterns in the training set. Attention then must focus on how to edit the training set by removing from it pattern vectors that have little or no influence on the class assignment of an arbitrary pattern vector x. It is easy to understand qualitatively which patterns these are. They are the ones located in the middle rather than the boundaries of a class region. Hart (1968) introduced the condensed nearest neighbor rule. Fischer and Patrick (1970), Chang (1974), Gates (1972), Wagner (1973), Ullman (1974), Penrod and Wagner (1977), Koplowitz and Brown (1981), and Voisin and Devijver (1987) all discuss techniques for editing out training set vectors that will not make a difference. Fukunaga and Narendra (1975) discuss a branch-and-bound approach to the computation of the k nearest neighbors. They reported results suggesting that only 61 distance computations had to be made on a training data set having 1000 samples. Friedman, Baskett, and Shuster (1975) discuss a methodology by which to order the patterns in the training set to reduce the number of calculations.

Another variation on the nearest neighbor technique is to assign a pattern vector to the class of the majority of its k nearest neighboring patterns from the training set. For discussion on these variations, see Goldstein (1972), Tomek (1976), Bailey and Jain (1978), Dudani (1976), Goin (1984), Kim and Park (1986), Krzyzak (1986), and Macleod, Luck, and Titterington (1987).

4.9   A Binary Decision Tree Classifier

A simple single-stage classifier tests an unknown unit against each class and assigns the unknown unit to one of the classes by an exhaustive search procedure. By contrast, a decision tree classifier makes the assignment through a hierarchical decision procedure. The classification process can be described by means of a tree, in which at least one terminal node is associated with each pattern class, and the interior nodes represent various collections of mixed classes. In particular, the root node represents the entire collection of classes into which a unit may be classified. Instead of one decision rule for each pattern class, there is one decision tree that handles all the classes together.

Figure 4.10 shows a typical binary decision tree classifier. When an unknown unit enters the decision tree at the root node, a decision rule associated with the root node is applied to the unit's measurement vector to determine the descendant path that the unit will follow. This process is repeated until a terminal node is reached. Every terminal node has an associated class to which the unit is finally assigned.

The binary decision tree classifier has been studied by many researchers (Landeweerd, Timmers, and Gelsema, 1983; Lin and Fu, 1983; Mui and Fu, 1983; Shi and Fu, 1980; and Miyakawa, 1989), who discuss methods of selecting optimal fea-

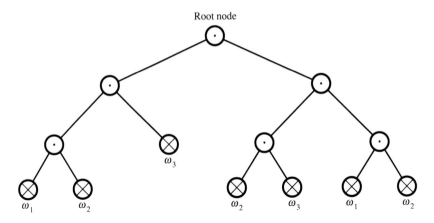

Root node

Figure 4.10 A binary decision tree: $\odot$ represents a nonterminal node, and $\otimes$ represents a terminal node. The ω_i's are the labels associated with the terminal nodes.

tures at each nonterminal node and give decision rules associated with the selected feature sets. But most of them assume that complete probabilistic information is given in their derivation of the optimal strategy. The decision tree construction process described here is similar to that discussed in Breiman et al. (1984) and makes no such assumption; it has the advantage that it simultaneously performs feature extraction as part of the decision tree construction process.

There are three major problems in constructing a decision tree classifier: choosing a tree structure, choosing features to be used at each nonterminal node, and choosing the decision rule to be used at each nonterminal node. In this section we present a method of designing a binary decision tree classifier that uses a simple discriminant function as a decision rule at each nonterminal node. This method is similar to Talmon's (1985), who describes a nonparametric partitioning procedure for generating a binary decision tree. For a decision rule at each nonterminal node, he selects a measurement component and thresholds it. In our decision tree construction procedure, in addition to thresholding a measurement component, we allow more complex decision rules, such as linear or quadratic rules. To help decide the value of the threshold required at each node, we use, as Talmon does, the entropy function. An alternative procedure (Kurzynski, 1983), is to use the probability of misclassification in place of entropy.

Section 4.9.1 describes the decision tree construction process, and Section 4.9.2 discusses the various types of decision rules that can be used at each nonterminal node.

4.9.1 Decision Tree Construction

The decision trees considered here are binary trees with simple discriminant functions; thus every nonterminal node has exactly two children. During classification, if the node's discriminant function is less than a threshold, the left child is taken; if it is greater than the threshold, the right child is taken. This section describes the design process of the binary tree classifier using a simple discriminant function. We first present two methods of expanding a nonterminal node according to the selection of a decision rule for the node. We show how to use an entropy purity function to decide what the threshold value should be, and we discuss the relationship of the purity function to the χ^2 test statistic. We discuss the criteria for deciding when to stop expanding a node and for assigning a class. We also discuss an alternative purity function that uses the probability of misclassification in place of entropy.

We begin by presenting some notational conventions. Let $U = \{u_k : k = 1, \ldots, N\}$ be the unit-training set to be used to design the binary tree classifier. Each unit u_k in the training set has an associated measurement X_k with known true class. At any nonterminal node n, let Ω^n be the set of M^n classes still possible for a unit at node n. Let $U^n = \{u_k^n : k = 1, \ldots, N^n\}$ be the subset of N^n training units associated with node n. Let N_c^n be the number of units (training samples) for class c in node n. Since N^n is the total number of training samples in node n, we must have $N^n = \sum_{c=1}^{M^n} N_c^n$.

There are two ways to construct a decision rule at node n. For those decision rules that need prior statistical information, the set Ω^n is successively partitioned into all possible partitions having two nonempty groups of classes, Ω_{LEFT}^n and Ω_{RIGHT}^n. For each partition $\{\Omega_{LEFT}^n, \Omega_{RIGHT}^n\}$, the best discriminant function f is computed by using the set of training samples contained in that node. The decision rule selected for node n is that function corresponding to the partition whose discriminant function has the greatest purity, a quality we will precisely define later. The Bayes quadratic decision rule is an example of one that requires prior statistical information. For decision rules that do not need prior statistical information, a node can be expanded without a prior partition of the set Ω^n. An example of this kind of rule is thresholding a measurement component.

Now we define how the decision rule works at node n. Consider unit u_k^n, which has measurement vector x_k^n. If the discriminant function $f(x_k^n)$ is less than or equal to the threshold, then u_k^n is assigned to class Ω_{LEFT}^n, otherwise it is assigned to class Ω_{RIGHT}^n. An assignment to Ω_{LEFT}^n means that a unit descends to the left child node. An assignment to Ω_{RIGHT}^n means that a unit descends to the right child node.

Given a discriminant function f, we sort the units in the set U^n in an ascending order according to their discriminant function value. Let x_k^n, for $k = 1, \ldots, N^n$, be the measurement vectors sorted in such a way that $f(x_k^n) \leq f(x_{k+1}^n)$ for $k = 1, \ldots, N^n - 1$, and let w_k^n be the true classes associated with the measurement vectors x_k^n. Then a set of candidate thresholds T^n for the decision rules that do not need a prior partition of the set Ω^n is defined by

$$T^n = \left\{ \frac{f(x_{k+1}^n) - f(x_k^n)}{2} \middle| w_{k+1}^n \neq w_k^n \right\}$$

For the decision rules that need a prior partition of the set Ω^n, the set of candidate thresholds T^n is defined by

$$T^n = \left\{ \frac{f(x^n_{k+1}) - f(x^n_k)}{2} \middle| w^n_{k+1} \in \Omega^n_{LEFT}, w^n_k \in \Omega^n_{RIGHT} \quad \text{or} \right.$$

$$\left. w^n_{k+1} \in \Omega^n_{RIGHT}, w^n_k \in \Omega^n_{LEFT} \right\}$$

For each threshold value, unit u^n_k is classified by using the decision rule specified above. We count the number of samples n^t_{Lc} assigned to Ω^n_{LEFT} whose true class is c, and we count the number of samples n^t_{Rc} assigned to Ω^n_{RIGHT} whose true class is c.

$$n^t_{Lc} = \# \left\{ u^n_k \middle| f(x^n_k) \leq t \text{ and } w^n_k = c \right\}$$

$$n^t_{Rc} = \# \left\{ u^n_k \middle| f(x^n_k) > t \text{ and } w^n_k = c \right\}$$

Let n^t_L be the total number of samples assigned to Ω^n_{LEFT} and n^t_R be the total number of samples assigned to Ω^n_{RIGHT}, that is,

$$n^t_L = \sum_{c=1}^{M^n} n^t_{Lc}$$

$$n^t_R = \sum_{c=1}^{M^n} n^t_{Rc}$$

We define the purity PR^t_n of such an assignment made by node n to be

$$PR_n = \sum_{c=1}^{M^n} (n^t_{Lc} \ln p^t_{Lc} + n^t_{Rc} \log p^t_{Rc})$$

where

$$p^t_{Lc} = \frac{n^t_{Lc}}{n_L}$$

$$p^t_{Rc} = \frac{n^t_{Rc}}{n_R}$$

The discriminant threshold selected is the threshold t that maximizes the purity value PR^t_n. The purity is such that it gives maximum value when the training samples are completely separable. For example, consider a nonterminal node having m units in each of three classes in the training sample. If the selected decision rule separates the training samples such that the *LEFT* child contains all units in one class and the *RIGHT* child contains all units in the other two classes, the purity is $0 - 2(m \ln \frac{1}{2}) = -2m \ln 2$. In the worst case, when both the *LEFT* and the *RIGHT* children contain the same number of units for each class, the purity is $-3(\frac{m}{2} \ln \frac{1}{3}) - 3(\frac{m}{2} \ln \frac{1}{3}) = -3m \ln 3$. Thus we can easily see that the purity value of the former case, where the training samples are completely separable, is greater than the purity value of the latter case, where the training samples are not separable.

The maximization of the purity can also be explained in terms of the χ^2 test of goodness of fit. If a decision node is effective, the distribution of classes for the children nodes will be significantly different from each other. A statistical test of significance can be used to verify this. One test statistic that measures the significance of the difference of the distributions is defined by

$$\chi^2 = \sum_{c=1}^{M^n} \left(n_{Lc}^t \ln p_{Lc}^t + n_{Rc}^t \ln p_{Rc}^t - N_c^n \ln \frac{N_c^n}{N^n} \right)$$

It has a χ^2 distribution with $M - 1$ degree of freedom. Comparing this equation with PR_n^t, we find that the χ^2 value is just the sum of the purity PR_n^t and some constant value.

When we use the decision rule that needs a prior partition of the set Ω^n for every possible partition of the set Ω^n the discriminant function is computed together with the threshold value that maximizes the purity of the resulting assignment. Among all partitions of the set Ω^n, the one yielding an assignment with the maximum purity is selected, and the corresponding discriminant function with its associated threshold is chosen as a decision rule at that node. But for the decision rules in which the discriminant function can be obtained without a prior partition, we simply select the threshold that gives the greatest purity of the resulting assignment.

Now we discuss the problem of when to stop the node expanding process and how to assign a class to the terminal node. First, it is not reasonable to generate a decision tree that has more terminal nodes than the total number of training samples. Using this consideration as a starting point, we set the maximum level of the decision tree to be $\log_2 N^1 - 1$, which makes the number of terminal nodes less than $\frac{N^1}{2}$, where N^1 is the number of training samples in node 1, the root node. Next, if the χ^2 value is small, the distributions of classes for the children nodes are not significantly different from each other, and the parent node need not be further divided. Finally, when the number N^n of units at node n becomes small, the χ^2 test cannot give a reliable result, and also some parametric decision rules cannot be designed on small training sets. Therefore we stop expanding node n when N^n is less than some lower limit. If one of these conditions is detected, then the node n becomes a terminal node.

When a node becomes terminal, an assignment of a label to the node is made. For the trivial case when the set U^n consists of units of only one class, that class is assigned to the node. For other cases the terminal nodes are assigned a class that is the most probable one for its associated training samples.

An alternative decision tree construction procedure uses the probability of misclassification in place of entropy. In this procedure the decision rule selected for the nonterminal node is the one that yields the minimum probability of misclassification of the resulting assignment. To describe the termination condition of a node expansion, we first define type I and type II errors as follows: Let type I error be the probability that a unit whose true class is in Ω_{LEFT}^n is classified as Ω_{RIGHT}^n, and type II error be the probability that a unit whose true class is in Ω_{RIGHT}^n is classified as Ω_{LEFT}^n. Then, if the sample space is completely separable, we would get zero for both type I and type II errors. Since this is not always the case, we control these errors by considering only those thresholds in the process of threshold selection that give type I error less than ϵ_I and type II error less than ϵ_{II}, where ϵ_I and ϵ_{II} are values determined before we start constructing the decision tree. Next, in the process of expanding a nonterminal node, if we cannot find a decision rule that gives type I error less than ϵ_I and type II error less than ϵ_{II}, which means that the sample space is not separable at a ϵ_I and ϵ_{II} level, we stop expanding this nonterminal node. This process of decision tree construction is repeated until there is no nonterminal node left or the level of the decision tree reaches the maximum level. Assignment of a class to a nonterminal node is done in the same way as in the previous procedure.

We can use any one of the following five decision rules at each nonterminal node:

- Thresholding the measurement component,
- Fisher's linear decision rule,
- Bayes quadratic decision rule,
- Bayes linear decision rule,
- Linear decision rule from the first principal component.

In the next section we describe each of these rules.

4.9.2 Decision Rules

As just described, there are two groups of classes at each nonterminal node in the binary decision tree. For the purpose of discussion, we denote all the classes in one group as Ω_{LEFT} and all the classes in the other group as Ω_{RIGHT}. The job of the decision rules discussed here is to separate the left class Ω_{LEFT} from the right class Ω_{RIGHT}. We will employ the same notational conventions used previously. The superscript n denoting the node number will be dropped from the expression if it is clear from the context that we are dealing with one particular node n.

Thresholding the Measurement Component

The simplest form for a linear decision rule is a comparison of one measurement component to a threshold. This is called a *threshold decision* rule. If the selected measurement component is less than or equal to the threshold value, then we assign class Ω_{LEFT} to the unit u_k; otherwise we assign class Ω_{RIGHT} to it. This decision rule requires a measurement component index and a threshold. It can be designed nonparametrically without a prior partition of the set of possible categories as follows: One measurement component is selected, and the set of threshold candidates T of that component is computed. For each threshold in the set T, all units in the training set U^n are classified into either class Ω_{LEFT} or class Ω_{RIGHT} according to their value of the selected measurement component. The number of units for each class assigned to class Ω_{LEFT} and to class Ω_{RIGHT} is counted, and the entropy purity is computed from the resulting classification. A threshold is selected from the set of threshold candidates T such that, when the set U^n is classified with that threshold, a maximum purity in the assignment results. This process is repeated for all possible measurement components, and the component and threshold that yield an assignment with the maximum purity are selected.

Fisher's Linear Decision Rule

Let x_k be the d-dimensional feature vector associated with a unit u_k to be classified. Then the linear discriminant function is a linear function of the form

$$f(x_k) = V^t x_k + v_{d+1}$$

where V is a weighting vector and v_{d+1} is called the threshold. This form of linear discriminant function uses a hyperplane to separate the feature space into two regions. The decision rule assigns u_k to one region if $f(x_k) > 0$ and to the other region if $f(x_k) < 0$. If $f(x_k) = 0$, the indeterminacy may be resolved arbitrarily. It is easy to see that using a linear discriminant function is equivalent to projecting a pattern vector x_k onto a line in the direction of vector V and comparing the position of the projection with that of the threshold v_{d+1}. Fisher's linear discriminant function is obtained by maximizing the Fisher's discriminant ratio, which, as described below, is the ratio of the projected between-class scatter to the projected within-class scatter.

First, this decision rule needs a prior partition of the set of categories. This partition induces a partition on the unit training set U^n. Let v the unknown weighting vector and $z_k = v^t x_k$ the projected point associated with unit u_k. For $i = 1$ or 2 (designating class Ω_{LEFT} and class Ω_{RIGHT}) let the estimated class conditional mean vector μ_i and the mean vector of the mixture distribution μ be defined as

$$\mu_i = \frac{1}{N_i} \sum_{u_k \in i} x_k$$

$$\mu = \sum_{i=1}^{2} P_i \mu_i$$

where N_i and P_i represent the number of samples and the probability of the class i in the training sample associated with the node, respectively. Then the between-class scatter matrix S_b for a two-class case is given by

$$S_b = \sum_{i=1}^{2} P_i (\mu_i - \mu)(\mu_i - \mu)^t$$

$$= P_1 P_2 (\mu_1 - \mu_2)(\mu_1 - \mu_2)^t$$

If we let S_i be the class conditional scatter matrix of class i, then

$$S_i = \frac{1}{N_i} \sum_{u_k \in i} [(x_k - \mu_i)(x_k - \mu_i)^t], \quad i = 1, 2$$

and if we let S_w be the average class conditional scatter matrix, then

$$S_w = \sum_{i=1}^{2} P_i S_i$$

Finally, if we let S designate the scatter matrix of the mixture distribution,

$$S = \frac{1}{N_1 + N_2} \sum_{k=1}^{N^n} [(x_k - \mu)(x_k - \mu)']$$

then

$$S = S_w + S_b$$

In the one-dimensional projected space of $z_k = v'x_k$, one can easily show that the projected between-class scatter s_b and the projected within-class scatter s_w are expressed as

$$s_b = v'S_b v$$

$$s_w = v'S_w v$$

Then the Fisher discriminant ratio is defined as

$$F(v) = \frac{s_b}{s_w} = \frac{v'S_b v}{v'S_w v}$$

When using the Fisher discriminant ratio, we seek to compute an optimum direction v, such that orthogonally projected samples are maximally discriminated. The optimum direction v can be found by taking the derivative of $F(v)$ and setting it to zero, as

$$\nabla F(v) = (v'S_w v)^{-2}(2S_b v v'S_w v - 2v'S_b v S_w v) = 0$$

From this equation it follows that

$$v'S_b v S_w v = S_b v v'S_w v$$

If we divide both sides by the quadratic term $v'S_b v$, then

$$S_w v = \left(\frac{v'S_w v}{v'S_b v}\right) S_b v$$

$$= \lambda S_b v$$

$$= \lambda P_1 P_2 (\mu_1 - \mu_2)(\mu_1 - \mu_2)' v$$

$$= \lambda \kappa (\mu_1 - \mu_2)$$

where λ and κ are some scalar values defined as

$$\lambda = \frac{v'S_w v}{v'S_b v}$$

$$\kappa = P_1 P_2 (\mu_1 - \mu_2)' v$$

Thus we have the weighting vector v as

$$v = K S_w^{-1}(\mu_1 - \mu_2)$$

where $K = \lambda \kappa$ is a multiplicative constant. The threshold v_{d+1} is the value that maximally discriminates between two classes.

Bayes Quadratic Decision Rule

The Bayes quadratic decision rule assumes that the class conditional distribution of the measurements is multivariate normal, that is,

$$p(x_k|\omega_i) = (2\pi)^{-\frac{M}{2}} |\Sigma_i|^{-\frac{1}{2}} \exp\left[-\frac{1}{2}(x_k - \mu_i)^t \Sigma_i^{-1}(x_k - \mu_i)\right]$$

The Bayes quadratic decision rule assigns class ω_c to an unknown unit u_k if

$$p(x_k|\omega_c)P_c = \max_i p(x_k|\omega_i)P_i$$

If we substitute the multivariate normal function for the class conditional probabilities and take the logarithm of the resultant equation, we have

$$\frac{P_c}{|\Sigma_c|^{-\frac{1}{2}}} - \frac{1}{2}(x_k - \mu_c)^t \Sigma_c^{-1}(x_k - \mu_c) =$$

$$\max_i \left\{ \ln \frac{P_i}{|\Sigma_i|^{-\frac{1}{2}}} - \frac{1}{2}(x_k - \mu_i)^t \Sigma_i^{-1}(x_k - \mu_i) \right\}$$

For a multiclass problem it is too costly to compute all class conditional density functions $p(x_k|\omega_i)$. Feiveson (1983) derives an algorithm that obviates the need for evaluating all conditional density functions for each category, thus resulting in a substantial reduction in processing time. He computes an array of branch-and-bound thresholds in the design stage of the decision rule and uses this array in the application stage to speed up the process. We describe his algorithm here.

For each (i,j), $i > j$, threshold values γ_{ij} with the following properties are computed.

$$p(x_k|\omega_i)P_i > \gamma_{ij} \Rightarrow p(x_k|\omega_i)P_i > p(x_k|\omega_j)P_j$$

$$p(x_k|\omega_j)P_j > \gamma_{ij} \Rightarrow p(x_k|\omega_j)P_j > p(x_k|\omega_i)P_i$$

The algorithm to find these thresholds is given below.

Define function g and h by

$$h(\lambda) = \left[(1 - \lambda)\Sigma_i^{-1} + \lambda\Sigma_j^{-1}\right]^{-1} \cdot \left[(1 - \lambda)\Sigma_i^{-1}\mu_i + \lambda\Sigma_j^{-1}\mu_j\right]$$

$$g(\lambda) = c_j - c_i - [h(\lambda) - \mu_j]^t \Sigma_j^{-1} [h(\lambda) - \mu_j]$$
$$+ [h(\lambda) - \mu_i]^t \Sigma_i^{-1} [h(\lambda) - \mu_i]$$

where

$$c_i = 2 \ln P_i - \ln |\Sigma_i|$$

Step 1: Find λ^* in $[0,1]$ such that $g(\lambda^*) = 0$.
Step 2: Let $y_0 = h(\lambda^*)$.
Step 3: Compute $\gamma_{ij} = f_i(y_0)$, where

$$f_i(y) = c_i - (y - \mu_i)^t \Sigma_i^{-1}(y - \mu_i)$$

This computation is done in the design process of the decision rule to speed up the actual classification process later. The following algorithm explains the classification process that uses these threshold values.

Step 1: Obtain a new vector x_k, let $i = 1$, and evaluate $f_1(x_k)$. Make E an empty set. (At later stages, E will contain the indexes of eliminated categories.)

Step 2: Let $A = \{j | j > i, j \notin E\}$. (This set contains the indexes of categories still to be tested.) For $j \in A$, put $j \in E$ and remove j from A if $f_i(x_k) > \gamma_{ij}$. If $f_i(x_k) > \gamma_{ij}$ for every $j \in A$ or if $A = \phi$, classify u_k into category i and return to step 1.

Step 3: For $j \in A$ such that $f_i(x_k) < \gamma_{ij}$, first evaluate $f_j(x_k)$.

    a. If $f_j(x_k) < f_i(x_k)$, put j in E and remove j from A. For each $l \in A$, put $l \in E$ and remove l from A if $f_j(x_k) > \gamma_{jl}$. Go back to step 2.

    b. If $f_j(x_k) > f_i(x_k)$, let the new value of i be equal to j and go back to step 2.

Since we deal with the two class problem in the binary decision tree, only one threshold γ_{12} is computed for each possible partition of the set U^n.

Bayes Linear Decision Rule

If we assume that the covariance matrices for all categories are the same, the Bayes quadratic decision rule becomes a linear decision rule for the two class problem. For this case the Bayes quadratic rule can be rewritten as follows:

Assign class 1 (1 and 2 designate class Ω_{LEFT} and class Ω_{RIGHT}, respectively) to an unknown unit u_k if

$$p(x_k|1)P_1 \geq p(x_k|2)P_2$$

otherwise assign class 2 to it. If we substitute the multivariate normal function for the class conditional probabilities and take the logarithm of the resultant equation, we have

$$\ln \frac{P_1}{|\Sigma|^{-\frac{1}{2}}} - \frac{1}{2}(x_k - \mu_1)^t \, \Sigma^{-1}(x_k - \mu_1) \geq$$

$$\ln \frac{P_2}{|\Sigma|^{-\frac{1}{2}}} - \frac{1}{2}(x_k - \mu_2)^t \, \Sigma^{-1}(x_k - \mu)$$

where Σ is the common covariance matrix and μ_i is the mean vector for class i. Rearranging it, we have the Bayes linear decision rule as follows:

Assign u_k to class 1 if

$$(\mu_1 - \mu_2)^t \Sigma^{-1} \left(x_k - \frac{\mu_1 + \mu_2}{2} \right) + \ln \frac{P_1}{P_2} \geq 0$$

otherwise assign it to class 2. Thus the weighting vector V and the threshold v_{d+1} are defined by

$$v = \Sigma^{-1}(\mu_1 - \mu_2)$$

$$v_{d+1} = \ln \frac{P_1}{P_2} - v^t \left(\frac{\mu_1 + \mu_2}{2} \right)$$

Since the fixed threshold value is computed for each partition of the set Ω^n, there is no need to go through the process of finding the threshold that gives the maximum purity. Instead, the decision rule produced for each partition is applied to the set Ω^n, and the purity of the resulting assignment is computed. The decision rule associated with the partition that gives the maximum purity will be selected.

Linear Decision Rule from the First Principal Component

The first principal component is the one-dimensional subspace for which the projected variance is larger than for any other one-dimensional subspace. Thus, if the measurement vectors $x_k's$ are projected on the axis that spans the first principal component, the coordinates of the projected vectors have the largest variance. Since the coordinates of the projected vectors are widely spread on this axis, if the projected coordinates are used as values for the discriminant function, it is expected, but not guaranteed, to have significant discriminatory information. Therefore we are interested in finding an axis v such that the variance of the projected coordinates $z_k = v'x_k$ on this axis is maximum. It turns out that the axis v is the eigenvector associated with the largest eigenvalue of the covariance matrix of the measurement vectors associated with the units in the unit training set U^n.

Let μ and Σ be the estimated mean vector and the estimated covariance matrix of the measurement vectors x_k. Then the variance of the projected coordinates, σ_z^2, can be expressed as follows:

$$\sigma_z^2 = \frac{1}{N} \sum_{k=1}^{N} v'(x_k - \mu)(x_k - \mu)'v$$

$$= v'\left[\frac{1}{N} \sum_{k=1}^{N} (x_k - \mu)(x_k - \mu)'\right] v$$

$$= v'\Sigma v$$

where the covariance matrix Σ is a positive, semidefinite, real symmetric matrix.

To maximize the projected variance, we must find a v such that $v'\Sigma v$ is maximized subject to the constraint $v'v = 1$. Using Lagrange multiplier λ, we set the following derivative to 0.

$$\frac{\partial}{\partial v}\left[v'\Sigma v - \lambda(v'v - 1)\right] = 0$$

Taking the required derivation results in

$$\Sigma v = \lambda v$$

Hence v must be an eigenvector of Σ with corresponding eigenvalue λ. To determine which eigenvector maximizes $v'\Sigma v$, notice that

$$v'\Sigma v = v'(\lambda v) = \lambda v'v = \lambda$$

since $v'v$ is constrained to have unit norm. Therefore v is the eigenvector of Σ having the largest eigenvalue.

Since the category grouping information is not used in computing the principal component, a prior partition of the set of categories Ω^n is not needed in the process of expanding a nonterminal node. Therefore the weighting vector v is computed as the eigenvector associated with the maximum eigenvalue of the covariance matrix

Σ of the measurement vectors of units in the unit training set U^n, and the threshold that gives the maximum purity value is selected for the decision rule.

4.10   Decision Rule Error Estimation

Once a decision rule is constructed, it is important to characterize its performance in terms of its errors. To test the decision rule, the first technique that people often think of is to use the data set on which the rule was trained. This technique, called the resubstitution method, has a fundamental problem having to do with an important methodological point: The data set used to train or to construct the decision rule must be independent of the data set used to test the decision rule. If this methodology of independent training and test sets is not followed, the error estimate for the decision rule will be biased low. How low depends on the number of samples in the training set, the dimensionality of the pattern vectors, the number of classes, and the complexity of the decision rule (Fukunaga and Hayes, 1989).

The qualitative reason for the bias when the test and training sets are identical is easy to explain. It is possible for the constructed decision rule to memorize the training set data rather than generalize from it. This happens when the degrees of freedom in the decision rule (the number of its free parameters) become similar to the degrees of freedom in the training data set (number of samples × dimensionality of each sample). Relationships among accuracy, sample size, and dimensionality were first discussed by Hughes (1968), Abend and Harley (1968), Chandrasekaran (1971), and Chandrasekaran and Jain (1975).

One common error estimation technique, called the hold-out method, is to divide the total data set in half. Use one half to construct the decision rule and the other half to test it. Then use the second half to construct the rule and the first half to test it. The error rates for both halves are then combined to establish the error estimate. The natural generalization on this idea is to divide the data set into N parts, train on the first $N-1$ parts, and then test on the Nth part. Then train on the $N-1$ parts, omitting the $N-1$st part, and test on the $N-1$st part. Continue the training and testing, each time omitting one part from the decision rule construction procedure and then testing on the omitted part. Then combine the results of the N tests together to establish an estimate of the error rate. Fukunaga and Hayes (1989) discuss the estimation of classifier performance using the resubstitution and hold-out methods.

The natural technique to estimate error rates is to count. Suppose there are N patterns in the test set $x_1, \ldots, x_n$, and each pattern x_n has true class c^n. The decision rule assigns pattern x_n to class ξ^n. The probability that the true class is c and the assigned class is ξ can then be estimated by

$$\hat{P}(c, \xi) = \#\{n | c^n = c \text{ and } \xi^n = \xi\}/N$$

Lachenbruck and Mickey (1968) and McLachlan (1976) discuss the optimistic error bias of this estimator when the test set is identical to the training set. It is therefore important to use the hold-out method when employing the counting technique to estimate error rates if the bias is to be avoided. Glick (1978) discusses a smooth modification of the counting estimator to reduce its variance.

4.11   Neural Networks

The use of neural networks for pattern recognition dates from the pioneering work done by Rosenblatt (1962) and Block (1962). Nilson (1965) is a good general reference. A neural network is a set of units each of which takes a linear combination of values from either an input vector or the output of other units. The linear combination then goes through a nonlinear function, such as a threshold or a sigmoid. Associated with the neural network is a training algorithm by which the pattern measurement vectors may be presented, one by one; the responses of the neural network observed; and then a reinforcement algorithm or back propagation algorithm applied to the network to change the weights so that the network's total response becomes closer to the desired response.

The simplest neural network is the linear decision rule. Here the network is single layered and the nonlinear function is a threshold. The neural network divides the measurement space by hyperplanes. More complex neural networks would add additional layers whose inputs might be the outputs of previous layers or the pattern measurement vectors. Those units whose inputs are only the outputs of previous layers are called hidden units. When the nonlinear function is a threshold, the hidden units permit a division of measurement space to be made by piecewise hyperplanes; thereby arbitrarily shaped decision regions may be approximated.

For reasons of brevity we do not give a detailed discussion of neural networks. We only mention that owing to the anthropomorphic name, it is easy for people to assume that neural networks do more than they actually do. The limitations of the networks that Rosenblatt and Block discussed were explored by Minsky and Papert (1969). After the publication of their book, interest in perceptrons and neural networks decreased. Kohonen (1984) showed how to use the neural network paradigm for associated memories. Hopfield (1984) gave a generalization of the simple neural network. A back propagation algorithm for the updating of the weights in a general neural network was published by Rumelhart (1987). The new back propagation algorithm has revived interest in the general neural networks.

4.12   Summary

We have reviewed the Bayesian approach to decision rule construction and have shown how to construct decision rules that maximize an expected utility. Our discussion has had elements of a game theoretic perspective. We discussed maximin decision rules that maximize the worst possible gain. Then we illustrated how the misidentification and false-alarm error rates are related and how a decision rule with reserved judgment can help keep these error rates as low as desired at the expense, of course, of not making decisions. We reviewed the nearest neighbor rule and discussed the construction of decision trees having a variety of possible simple decision rules at each node. Then we discussed the estimation of decision rule error and made a brief mention of neural networks.

The pattern recognition literature is extensive, and we have not done more in this chapter than briefly touch on some of the basic concepts.

Table 4.8 provides a listing of selected books on statistical pattern recognition. Kanal (1974) provides a good review of some of the classic research literature.

Table 4.8   Selected books on statistical pattern recognition.

Author	Title and Review Source
Satosi Watanabe (ed.)	**Methodologies of Pattern Recognition,** Academic Press, New York, 1969, 579 pages. *IEEE Transactions on Information Theory,* Vol IT–17, 1971, pp. 633–634. *Pattern Recognition—Human and Mechanical,* Wiley, New York, 1985.
Harry Andrews	**Introduction to Mathematical Techniques in Pattern Recognition,** Prentice-Hall, Englewood Cliffs, NJ, 1972, 504 pages. *IEEE Transactions on Information Theory,* Vol. IT–19, 1973, p. 831.
Keinosuke Fukunaga	**Introduction to Statistical Pattern Recognition** Academic Press, New York, 1972, 382 pages. *IEEE Transactions on System, Man, and Cybernetics,* Vol. SMC–6, 1976, p. 238. *IEEE Transactions on Information Theory,* Vol. IT–19, 1973, pp. 829–830.
William Meisel	**Computer—Oriented Approaches to Pattern Recognition** Academic Press, New York, 1972, 262 pages.

Table 4.8   *Continued.*

Author	Title and Review Source
	IEEE Transactions on Systems, Man, and Cybernetics, Vol. SMC–5, 1975, p. 209.
	IEEE Transactions on Computers, Vol. C–23, 1974, p. 112.
	IEEE Transactions on Computers, Vol. C–27, 1978, p. 429.
	IEEE Transactions on Information Theory, Vol. IT–19, 1973, pp. 832–833.
Edward Patrick	**Fundamentals of Pattern Recognition** Prentice-Hall, Englewood Cliffs, NJ, 1972, 528 pages.
	IEEE Transactions on Systems, Man, and Cybernetics, Vol. SMC–3, 1973, p. 528.
	IEEE Transactions on Information Theory, Vol. IT–19, 1973, pp. 830–831.
Richard Duda and Peter Hart	**Pattern Classification and Scene Analysis** Wiley, New York, 1973, 482 pages.
	IEEE Transactions on Computers, Vol. C–23 1974, p. 223.
	IEEE Transactions on Information Theory, Vol. IT–19, 1973, pp. 827–829.
Julian Ullman	**Pattern Recognition Techniques** Crane-Russak, New York, 1973, 412 pages.
	IEEE Transactions on Computers, Vol. C–23, 1974, pp. 220–222.
	IEEE Transactions on Information Theory, Vol. IT–20, 1974, p. 400.
Bruce Batchelor	**Practical Approach to Pattern Classification** Plenum Press, London, 1974, 243 pages.

Table 4.8   *Continued.*

Author	Title and Review Source
King–Sun Fu	**Syntactic Methods in Pattern Recognition** Academic Press, New York, 1974, 397 pages. *IEEE Transactions on Systems, Man, and Cybernetics,* Vol. SMC–6, 1976, p. 590.
Julius Ton and Rafael Gonzales	**Pattern Recognition Principles** Addison-Wesley, Reading, MA, 1974, 377 pages. *IEEE Transactions on Systems, Man, and Cybernetics,* Vol SMC–6, 1974, pp. 332–333.
Pierre Devijver and Josef Kittler	**Pattern Recognition: A Statistical Approach** Prentice-Hall International, London, 1982, 448 pages.
Leo Breiman J. Friedman, R. Olshen, and C. Stone	**Classification and Regression Trees** Wadsworth and Brooks, Monterey, CA, 1984, 358 pages.
Mike James	**Classification Algorithms** Collins, London, 1985, 209 pages.
Mike James	**Pattern Recognition** Wiley, New York, 1988, 142 pages.
Monique Pavel	**Fundamentals of Pattern Recognition** Marcel-Dekker, New York, 1989, 183 pages.

■ Exercises

4.1. Suppose that there are two classes each distributed as Gaussians with

$$\mu_1 = \begin{pmatrix} 1 \\ 1 \end{pmatrix} \text{ and } \Sigma_1 = \begin{pmatrix} 1 & 0 \\ 0 & 2 \end{pmatrix}$$

for the first class and

$$\mu_2 = \begin{pmatrix} 3 \\ 7 \end{pmatrix} \text{ and } \Sigma_2 = \begin{pmatrix} 1 & 0 \\ 0 & 2 \end{pmatrix}$$

for the second class. Assume that the prior probabilities are equal and the gain matrix is the identity. Sketch the Bayesian boundary.

4.2.   Repeat Exercise 4.1 with prior probability for the first class being P and the second class being $1 - P$. Show in your sketch how that Bayesian boundary changes as a function of P.

4.3.   Repeat Exercise 4.1 with covariance matrix $\Sigma_2 = \begin{pmatrix} 3 & 0 \\ 0 & 1 \end{pmatrix}$.

4.4.   Repeat Exercise 4.1 with the gain matrix being $\begin{pmatrix} 1 & -10 \\ 0 & 1 \end{pmatrix}$.

4.5.   Repeat Exercise 4.1 with the gain matrix being

$$\begin{pmatrix} 1 & c \\ 0 & 1 \end{pmatrix}$$

Show in your sketch how the Bayesian boundary changes as a function of c. (Make c take negative values.)

4.6.   a. Write a subroutine to generate N dimensional vectors in an unit hypercube.
   b. Write a subroutine to generate a hyperplane boundary that roughly passes through the middle of the unit hypercube.
   c. Write a subroutine to label the generated vector according to which side of the hyperplane it is on.
   d. Using (a), (b), and (c), generate a two-class labeled data set.

4.7.   a. Write a subroutine to calculate the mean and covariance matrix of the generated data set of Exercise 4.6.
   b. Write a subroutine using the calculated mean and covariance matrix of (a) to assign each vector to one of the classes assuming the class conditional distributions are Gaussian.
   c. Using (a) and (b) assign each vector of the generated data set to a class.
   d. Compare the assigned labels to the generated labels, and compute an error rate.

4.8.   a. Write a subroutine to perform a nearest neighbor decision rule.
   b. Using the data generated in Exercise 4.6 and the subroutine written in (a), assign each data vector to a class.
   c. Compute the error rate.

4.9.   a. Write a subroutine to perform a Fisher's linear discriminant decision rule.
   b. Apply this rule to the data generated in Exercise 4.6.
   c. Compute the error rate.

4.10. Exercises 4.7, 4.8, and 4.9 employed the same data set for designing the decision rule and testing the decision rule. Now repeat Exercise 4.7, but use an independently generated data set labeled according to the same decision boundary as the generating mechanism used in the initial labeling. Now determine the error rate as a function of the number of vectors in the training set, the number of vectors in the test set, and the dimensionality of the vector.

4.11. Repeat Exercise 4.10 using the nearest neighbor rule.

4.12. Repeat Exercise 4.10 using Fisher's linear discriminant rule.

4.13. Write a program to generate class conditional Gaussian vectors given class mean and covariance matrices.

4.14. Repeat Exercise 4.7 using the data generated in Exercise 4.13.

4.15. Repeat Exercise 4.8 using the data generated in Exercise 4.13.

4.16. Repeat Exercise 4.9 using the data generated in Exercise 4.13.

4.17. Repeat Exercise 4.10 using the data generated in Exercise 4.13.

4.18. Repeat Exercise 4.11 using the data generated in Exercise 4.13.

4.19. Repeat Exercise 4.12 using the data generated in Exercise 4.13.

■ Bibliography

Abend, K., and T. J. Harley, "Comments on the Mean Accuracy of Statistical Pattern Recognizers," *IEEE Transactions on Information Theory,* Vol. IT–14, 1968, pp. 420–421.

Allais, D. C., "The Problem of Too Many Measurements in Pattern Recognition and Prediction," *IEEE International Convention Record,* Vol. 14, 1966, pp. 124–130.

Anderson, J., and E. Rosenfeld, *Neurocomputing,* MIT Press, Cambridge, MA, 1988.

Andrews, H., *Introduction to Mathematical Techniques in Pattern Recognition,* Prentice-Hall, Englewood Cliffs, NJ, 1972.

Argentiero, P., R. Chin, and P. Beaudet, "An Automated Approach to the Design of Decision Tree Classifiers," *IEEE Transactions on Pattern Analysis and Machine Intelligence,* Vol. PAMI-4, 1982, pp. 51–57.

Babu, C. C., "On Divergence and Probability of Error in Pattern Recognition," *Proceedings of the IEEE,* 1973, pp. 798–799.

Bailey, T., and A. K. Jain, "A Note on Distance–Weighted k-Nearest Neighbor Rules," *IEEE Transactions on Systems, Man, and Cybernetics,* Vol. SMC-8, 1978, pp. 311–313.

Batchelor, B. G., *Practical Approach to Pattern Classification,* Plenum Press, London, 1974.

———, (ed.), *Pattern Recognition: Ideas in Practice,* Plenum Press, New York, 1978.

Bianchini, R., and C. Freima, "On the Size of Weights Required for Linear–Input Switching Functions," *IRE Transactions on Electronic Computers,* 1961, pp. 288–289.

Block, H. D., "The Perceptron: A Model for Brain Functioning, I," *Reviews of Modern Physiçs,* Vol. 34, 1962, pp. 123–135.

Bobrowski, L., "Linear Discrimination with Symmetrical Models," *Pattern Recognition,* Vol. 19, 1986, pp. 101–109.

Bobrowski, L., and W. Niemiro, "A Method of Synthesis of Linear Discriminant Function in the Case of Nonseparability," *Pattern Recognition,* Vol. 17, 1984, pp. 205–210.

Bow, S. T., *Pattern Recognition: Applications to Large Data-Set Problems,* Electrical Engineering and Electronics, Marcel Dekker, New York, 1984.

Brailovsky, V., "On the Influence of Sample Set Structure on Devision Rule Quality for the Case of a Linear Discriminant Function," *IEEE Transactions on Pattern Analysis and Machine Intelligence,* Vol. PAMI-3, 1981, pp. 454–458.

Breiman, L., et al., *Classification and Regression Trees,* Wadsworth and Brooks, Monterey, CA, 1984.

Chandrasekaran, B., "Independence of Measurements and the Mean Recognition Accuracy," *IEEE Transactions on Information Theory,* Vol. IT-17, 1971, pp. 452–456.

Chandrasekaran, B., and T. J. Harley, "Comments on the Mean Accuracy of Statistical Pattern Recognizers," *IEEE Transactions on Information Theory,* Vol. IT-14, 1968, pp. 421–423.

Chandrasekaran, B., and A. K. Jain, "Quantization Complexity and Independent Measurements," *IEEE Transactions on Computers,* Vol C-23, 1974, pp. 102–106.

Chandrasekaran, B., and A. K. Jain, "Independence, Measurement Complexity, and Classification Performance," *IEEE Transactions on Systems, Man, and Cybernetics,* Vol. SMC-5, 1975, pp. 240-244.

———, "Independence, Measurement Complexity, and Classification Performance: An Emendation," *IEEE Transactions on Systems, Man, and Cybernetics,* Vol. SMC-7, 1977, pp. 564-566.

Chang, C. L., "Pattern Recognition by Piecewise Linear Discriminant Functions," *IEEE Transactions on Computers,* Vol. C-22, 1973, pp. 859-862.

———, "Finding Prototypes for Nearest Neighbor Classifiers," *IEEE Transactions on Computers,* Vol. C-23, 1974, pp. 1179-1184.

Chen, C. H., *Statistical Pattern Recognition,* Spartan Books, Rochelle Park, NJ, 1973.

Chittineni, C. B., "On the Estimation of the Probability of Error," *Pattern Recognition,* Vol. 9, 1977, pp. 191-196.

Chow, C. K., "On Optimum Recognition Error and Reject Tradeoff," *IEEE Transactions on Information Theory,* Vol. IT-16, 1970, pp. 41-46.

Chu, J. T., "Optimal Decision Functions for Computer Character Recognition," *Journal of the Association for Computing Machines,* Vol. 12, 1965, pp. 213-226.

Chu, J. T., and J. C. Chueh, "Error Probability in Decision Functions for Character Recognition," *Journal of the Association for Computing Machines,* Vol. 14, 1967, pp. 273-280.

Cockett, J. R. B., and Y. Zhu, "A New Incremental Learning Technique for Decision Trees with Thresholds," *SPIE Applications of Artificial Intelligence VII,* Vol. 1095, 1989, pp. 804-811.

Cover, T. M., "Geometrical and Statistical Properties of Systems of Linear Inequalities with Applications in Pattern Recognition," *IEEE Transactions on Electronic Computers,* Vol. EC-14, 1965, pp. 326-334.

Cover, T. M., and P. E. Hart, "Nearest Neighbor Pattern Classification," *IEEE Transactions on Information Theory,* Vol. IT-13, 1967, pp. 21-27.

Das, S. K., and D. F. Stanat, "A Modified Training Procedure for Linear Threshold Devices," *IEEE Transactions on Computers,* Vol. C-21, 1972, pp. 396-397.

Dasarathy, B. V., "Nosing Around the Neighborhood: A New System Structure and Classification Rule for Recognition in Partially Exposed Environments," *IEEE Transactions on Pattern Analysis and Machine Intelligence,* Vol. PAMI-2, 1980, pp. 67-71.

Davis, L., *Genetic Algorithms and Simulated Annealing,* Pitman, London, 1987.

Day, N. E., "Linear and Quadratic Discrimination in Pattern Recognition," *IEEE Transactions on Information Theory,* Vol. IT-15, 1969, pp. 419-420.

Devijver, P., "Error-Reject Relationships in Nearest Neighbor Decision Rules," *Proceedings of the Third International Joint Conference on Pattern Recognition,* 1976, pp. 255-259.

Devijver, P., and J. Kittler, *Pattern Recognition: A Statistical Approach,* Prentice Hall International, London, 1982.

Devroye, L., "The Uniform Convergence of Nearest Neighbor Regression Function Estimators and Their Application in Optimization," *IEEE Transactions on Information Theory,* Vol. IT-24, 1978, pp. 142-151.

———, "On the Inequality of Cover and Hart in Nearest Neighbor Discrimination," *IEEE Transactions on Pattern Analysis and Machine Intelligence,* Vol. PAMI-3, 1981, pp. 75-78.

Devroye, L., "Any Discrimination Rule Can Have an Arbitrarily Bad Probability of Error for Finite Sample Size," *IEEE Transactions on Pattern Analysis and Machine Intelligence,* Vol. PAMI-4, 1982, pp. 154–157.

——, "Automatic Pattern Recognition: A Study of the Probability of Error," *IEEE Transactions on Pattern Analysis and Machine Intelligence,* Vol. 10, 1988, pp. 530–543.

Devroye, L., and T. J. Wagner, "A Distribution–Free Performance Bound in Error Estimation," *IEEE Transactions on Information Theory,* Vol. IT-22, 1976, pp. 586–587.

Du, H. C., and R. C. T. Lee, "Symbolic Gray Code as a Multikey Hashing Function," *IEEE Transactions on Pattern Analysis and Machine Intelligence,* Vol. PAMI-2, 1980, pp. 83–90.

Duda, R. O., and H. Fossum, "Pattern Classification by Iteratively Determined Linear and Piecewise Linear Discriminant Functions," *IEEE Transactions on Electronic Computers,* Vol. EC-15, 1966, pp. 220–232.

Duda, R. O., and P. E. Hart, *Pattern Classification and Scene Analysis,* Wiley, New York, 1973.

Dudani, S. A., "The Distance-Weighted k-Nearest-Neighbor Rule," *IEEE Transactions on Systems, Man, and Cybernetics,* Vol. SMC-6, 1976, pp. 325–327.

Duin, R. P. W., "Comments on Independence, Measurement Complexity, and Classification Performance," *IEEE Transactions on Systems, Man, and Cybernetics,* Vol. SMC-7, 1977, pp. 559–564.

El-Sheikh, T. S., and A. G. Wacker, "Effect of Dimensionality and Estimation on the Performance of Gaussian Classifiers," *Pattern Recognition,* Vol. 12, 1980, pp. 115–126.

Feiveson, A. H., "Classification by Thresholding," *IEEE Transactions on Pattern Analysis and Machine Intelligence*, Vol. PAMI-5, 1983, pp. 48–54.

Fischer, F. P., and E. A. Patrick, "A Preprocessing Algorithm for Nearest Neighbor Decision Rules," *Proceedings of the National Electronics Conference,* Vol. 26, 1970, pp. 481–485.

Flick, T. E., and L. K. Jones, "Efficient Error Estimation for Gaussian Classifiers," *Seventh International Conference on Pattern Recognition,* Montreal, 1984, pp. 1347–50.

Foley, D. H., "Considerations of Sample and Feature Size," *IEEE Transactions on Information Theory,* Vol. IT-18, 1972, pp. 618–626.

Friedman, J. H., F. Baskett, and L. J. Shuster, "An Algorithm for Finding Nearest Neighbors," *IEEE Transactions on Computers,* Vol. C-24, 1975, pp. 1000–6.

Friedman, J. H., J. L. Bentley, and R. A. Finkel, "An Algorithm for Finding Best Matches in Logarithmic Expected Time," *ACM Transactions on Mathematical Software,* Vol. 3, 1977, pp. 2–9, 226.

Fu, K. S., *Syntatic Methods in Pattern Recognition,* Academic Press, New York, 1974.

Fukunaga, K., *Introduction to Statistical Pattern Recognition,* Academic Press, New York, 1972.

Fukunaga, K., and T. E. Flick, "An Optimal Global Nearest Neighbor Metric," *IEEE Transactions on Pattern Analysis and Machine Intelligence,* Vol. PAMI-6, 1984a, pp. 314–318.

——, "Classification Error for a Very Large Number of Classes," *IEEE Transactions on Pattern Analysis and Machine Intelligence,* Vol. PAMI-6, 1984b, pp. 779–788.

Fukunaga, K., and R. R. Hayes, "Effects of Sample Size in Classifier Design," *IEEE Transactions on Pattern Analysis and Machine Intelligence,* Vol. 11, 1989a, pp. 873–885.

Fukunaga, K., and R. R. Hayes, "Estimation of Classifier Performance," *IEEE Transactions on Pattern Analysis and Machine Intelligence,* Vol. 11, 1989b, pp. 1087–1101.

Fukunaga, K., and L. D. Hostetler, " k–Nearest–Neighbor Bayes–Risk Estimation," *IEEE Transactions on Information Theory,* Vol. IT–21, 1975, pp. 285–293.

Fukunaga, K., and D. M. Hummels, "Bias of Nearest Neighbor Estimates," *IEEE Transactions on Pattern Analysis and Machine Intelligence,* Vol. PAMI–9, 1987a, pp. 103–112.

———, "Bayes Error Estimation Using Parzen and k-NN Procedures," *IEEE Transactions on Pattern Analysis and Machine Intelligence,* Vol. PAMI–9, 1987b, pp. 634–643.

———, "Leave–One–Out Procedures for Nonparametric Error Estimates," *IEEE Transactions on Pattern Analysis and Machine Intelligence,* Vol. 11, 1989, pp. 421–425.

Fukunaga, K., and D. L. Kessell, "Estimation of Classification Error," *IEEE Transactions on Computers,* Vol. C–20, 1971, pp. 1521–27.

———, "Application of Optimum Error–Reject Functions," *IEEE Transactions on Information Theory,* Vol. IT–18, 1972, pp. 814–817.

———, "Nonparametric Bayes Error Estimation Using Unclassified Samples," *IEEE Transactions on Information Theory,* Vol. IT–19, 1973, pp. 434–440.

Fukunaga, K., and J. M. Mantock, "A Nonparametric Two–Dimensional Display for Classification," *IEEE Transactions on Pattern Analysis and Machine Intelligence,* Vol. PAMI–4, 1982, pp. 427–436.

Fukunaga, K., and P. T. Narendra, "A Branch and Bound Algorithm for Computing k–Nearest Neighbors," *IEEE Transactions on Computers,* Vol. C–24, 1975, pp. 750–754.

Fukunaga, K., and R. D. Short, "A Class of Feature Extraction Criteria and Its Relation to the Bayes Risk Estimate," *IEEE Transactions on Information Theory,* Vol. IT–26, 1980, pp. 59–65.

Fukushima, K., "A Neural Network for Visual Pattern Recognition," *IEEE Transactions on Computers,* Vol. 21, 1988, pp. 65–74.

Ganesalingam, S., and G. J. MacLachlan, "Error Rate Estimation on the Basis of Posterior Probabilities," *Pattern Recognition,* Vol. 12, 1980, pp. 405–413.

Garber, F. D., and A. Djouadi, "Bounds on the Bayes Classification Error Rate Based on Pairwise Risk Functions," *IEEE Transactions on Pattern Analysis and Machine Intelligence,* Vol. 10, 1988, pp. 281–288.

Gates, G. W., "The Reduced Nearest Neighbor Rule," *IEEE Transactions on Information Theory,* Vol. IT–18, 1972, pp. 431–433.

Glick, N., "Additive Estimators for Probabilities of Correct Classification," *Pattern Recognition,* Vol. 10, 1978, pp. 211–222.

Goin, J. E., "Classification Bias of the k-Nearest Neighbor Algorithm," *IEEE Transactions on Pattern Analysis and Machine Intelligence,* Vol. 6, 1984, pp. 379–381.

Goldstein, M., "k_n-Nearest Neighbor Classification," *IEEE Transactions on Information Theory,* Vol. IT–18, 1972, pp. 627–629.

Györfi, L., Z. Györfi, and I. Vajda, "Bayesian Decision with Rejection," *Problems of Control and Information Theory,* Vol. 8, 1979, pp. 445–452.

Haralick, R. M., "Glossary and Index to Remotely Sensed Image Pattern Recognition Concepts," *Pattern Recognition,* Vol. 5, 1973, pp. 391–403.

———, "Pattern Discrimination Using Ellipsoidally Symmetric Multivariate Density Functions," *Pattern Recognition,* Vol. 9, 1977, pp. 89–94.

———, "Decision Making in Context," *IEEE Transaction on Pattern Analysis and Machine Intelligence,* Vol. PAMI–5, 1983, pp. 417–428.

Hart, P. E., "The Condensed Nearest Neighbor Rule," *IEEE Transactions on Information Theory,* Vol. IT-14, 1968, pp. 515-516.

Highleyman, W. H., "A Note on Optimum Pattern Recognition Systems," *IRE Transactions on Electronic Computers,* Vol. EC-10, 1961, pp. 287-288.

——, "Linear Decision Functions, with Application to Pattern Recognition," *Proceedings of the IRE,* 1962, pp. 1501-14.

Hopfield, J. J., "Neural Networks and Physical Systems with Emergent Collective Computational Abilities," *Proceedings of the National Academy of Sciences, USA,* Vol. 81, 1984, pp. 3088-92.

Hughes, G. F., "On the Mean Accuracy of Statistical Pattern Recognizers," *IEEE Transactions on Information Theory,* Vol. IT-14, 1968, pp. 55-63.

——, "Number of Pattern Classifier Design Samples per Class," *IEEE Transactions on Information Theory,* Vol. IT-15, 1969, pp. 615-619.

Jain, A. K., R. C Dubes, and C. C. Chen, "Bootstrap Techniques for Error Estimation," *IEEE Transactions on Pattern Analysis and Machine Intelligence,* Vol. PAMI-9, 1987, pp. 628-633.

Jain, A. K., and W. G. Waller, "On the Optimal Number of Features in the Classification of Multivariate Gaussian Data," *Pattern Recognition,* Vol. 10, 1978, pp. 365-374; Also in *Proceedings of the Fourth International Joint Conference on Pattern Recognition,* Kyoto, Japan, 1978, pp. 265-269.

James, M., *Classification Algorithms,* Collins, London, 1985.

——, *Pattern Recognition,* Wiley, 1988.

Kain, R. Y., "The Mean Accuracy of Pattern Recognizers with Many Pattern Classes," *IEEE Transactions on Information Theory,* Vol. IT-15, 1969, pp. 424-425.

Kalayeh, H. M., and D. A. Landgrebe, "Predicting the Required Number of Training Samples," *IEEE Transactions on Pattern Analysis and Machine Intelligence,* Vol. PAMI-5, 1983, pp. 664-667.

Kanal, L., "Patterns in Pattern Recognition: 1968-1974," *IEEE Transactions on Information Theory,* Vol. IT-20, 1974, pp. 697-722.

Kanal, L., and B. Chandrasekaran, "On Dimensionality and Sample Size in Statistical Pattern Classification," *Pattern Recognition,* Vol. 3, 1971, pp. 225-234.

Kazakos, D., "Quantization Complexity and Training Sample Size in Detection," *IEEE Transactions on Information Theory,* Vol. IT-24, 1978, pp. 229-237.

Kim, B. S., and S. B. Park, "A Fast *k* Nearest Neighbor Finding Algorithm Based on the Ordered Partition," *IEEE Transactions on Pattern Analysis and Machine Intelligence,* Vol. PAMI-8, 1986, pp. 761-766.

Kittler, J., "On the Efficiency of Data Utilization in System Error Estimation," *Proceedings of the Sixth International Conference on Pattern Recognition,* Münich, 1982, pp. 868-871.

Kittler, J., and P. A. Devijver, "An Efficient Estimator of Pattern Recognition System Error Probability," *Pattern Recognition,* Vol. 13, 1981, pp. 245-249.

——, "Statistical Properties of Error Estimators in Performance Assessment of Recognition Systems," *IEEE Transactions on Pattern Analysis and Machine Intelligence,* Vol. PAMI-4, 1982, pp. 215-220.

Kittler, J., and L. F. Pau, "Automatic Inspection by Lots in the Presence of Classification Errors," *Pattern Recognition,* Vol. 12, 1980, pp. 237-241.

Kohonen, T., *Self-Organization and Associative Memory,* Springer-Verlag, Berlin, 1984.

Koplowitz, J., and T. A. Brown, "On the Relation of Performance to Editing in Nearest Neighbor Rules," *Pattern Recognition,* Vol. 13, 1981, pp. 251-255.

Krzyzak, A., "The Rates of Convergence of k-NN Classification Rules," *Proceedings of the Conference on Computer Vision and Pattern Recognition,* 1986, pp. 524–526.

Kulkarni, A. V., "On the Mean Accuracy of Hierarchical Classifiers," *IEEE Transactions on Computers,* Vol. C–27, 1978, pp. 771–776.

Kurzynski, M. W., "The Optimal Strategy of a Tree Classifier," *Pattern Recognition,* Vol. 16, 1983, pp. 81–87.

Lachenbruck, P. A., and M. R. Mickey, "Estimation of Error Rates in Discrimination Analysis," *Technometrics,* Vol. 10, 1968, pp. 1–11.

Landeweerd, G. H., T. Timmers, and E. S. Gelsema, "Binary Tree versus Single Level Tree Classification of White Blood Cells," *Pattern Recognition,* Vol. 16, 1983, pp. 571–577.

Lapsa, P. M., "Some Statistical Bounds for the Accuracy of Distance–Based Pattern Classification," *Pattern Recognition,* Vol. 11, 1979, pp. 95–108.

Levine, A., L. Lustick, and B. Saltzberg, "The Nearest-Neighbor Rule for Small Samples Drawn from Uniform Distributions," *IEEE Transactions on Information Theory,* Vol. IT–17, 1973, pp. 697–699.

Lin, Y. K., and K. S. Fu, "Automatic Classification of Cervical Cells Using a Binary Tree Classifier," *Pattern Recognition,* Vol. 16, 1983, pp. 69–80.

Longstaff, I. D., "On Extensions to Fisher's Linear Discriminant Function," *IEEE Transactions on Pattern Analysis and Machine Intelligence,* Vol. PAMI–9, 1987, pp. 321–325.

Macleod, J. E. S., A. Luk, and D. M. Titterington, "A Re-Examination of the Distance-Weighted k-Nearest Neighbor Classification Rule," *IEEE Transactions on Systems, Man, and Cybernetics,* Vol. SMC–17, 1987, pp. 689–707.

Martin, W. C., "On Obtaining Separating Hyperplanes via Linear Programming," *IEEE Transactions on Systems, Man, and Cybernetics,* Vol. SMC–1, 1971, pp. 87–88.

McCulloch, W. S., and W. H. Pitts, "A Logical Calculus of Ideas Immanent in Nervous Activity," *Bulletin of Mathematical Biophysics,* Vol. 5, 1943, pp. 115–133; reprinted in W.S. McCulloch, *Embodiments of Mind,* MIT Press, Cambridge, MA, 1965, pp. 19–39.

McLachlan, G. J., "The Basis of the Apparent Error Rate in Discriminant Analysis," *Biometrika,* Vol. 3, 1976, pp. 239–244.

Meisel, W., *Computer-Oriented Approaches to Pattern Recognition,* Academic Press, New York, 1972.

Minsky, M., and S. Papert, *Perceptrons: An Introduction to Computational Geometry,* MIT Press, Cambridge, MA, 1969.

Miyakawa, M., "Criteria for Selecting a Variable in the Construction of Efficient Decision Trees," *IEEE Transactions on Computers,* Vol. 38, 1989, pp. 130–141.

Mui, J. K., and K. S. Fu, "Automated Classification of Nucleated Blood Cells Using a Binary Tree Classifier," *IEEE Transactions on Pattern Analysis and Machine Intelligence* Vol. PAMI–2, 1980, pp. 429–443.

Nilson, J. N., *Learning Machines,* McGraw-Hill, New York, 1965.

Patrick, E., *Fundamentals of Pattern Recognition,* Prentice Hall, Englewood Cliffs, NJ, 1972.

Pau, L. F., "Game Theoretical Pattern Recognition," *IEEE Transactions on Pattern Analysis and Machine Intelligence,* Vol. PAMI–6, 1984, pp. 118–122.

Pavel, M., *Fundamentals of Pattern Recognition,* Marcel Dekker, New York, 1989.

Pearl, J., "Capacity and Error Estimates for Boolean Classifiers with Limited Complexity," *IEEE Transactions on Pattern Analysis and Machine Intelligence,* Vol. PAMI-1, 1979, pp. 350-356.

Penrod, C. S., and T. J. Wagner, "Another Look at the Edited Nearest Neighbor Rule," *IEEE Transactions on Systems, Man, and Cybernetics,* Vol. SMC-7, 1977, pp. 92-94.

Peterson, D. W., "Some Convergence Properties of a Nearest Neighbor Decision Rule," *IEEE Transactions on Information Theory,* Vol. IT-16, 1970, pp. 26-31.

Raudya, S., "On Dimensionality, Learning Sample Size and Complexity of Classification Algorithms," *Proceedings of the Third International Joint Conference on Pattern Recognition,* Coronado, CA, 1976, pp. 166-169.

——, "Determination of Optimal Dimensionality in Statistical Pattern Classification," *Pattern Recognition,* Vol. 11, 1979, pp. 263-270.

Rey, W. J. J., "On the Upper Bound of the Probability of Error, Based on Chebyshev's Inequality, in Two-Class Linear Discrimination," *Proceedings of the IEEE, Letters,* 1976, pp. 361-362.

Rosenblatt, F., *Principles of Neurodynamics,* Spartan Books, Washington, DC, 1962.

Rumelhart, D. E., J. L. McClelland, and the PDP Research Group, *Parallel Distributed Processing,* Vol. 1: *Foundations,* MIT Press, Cambridge, MA, 1987.

Shi, Q. Y., and K. S. Fu, "A Method for the Design of Binary Tree Classifiers," *Pattern Recognition,* Vol. 16, 1983, pp. 593-603.

Sklansky, J., and L. Michelotti, "Locally Trained Piecewise Linear Classifiers," *IEEE Transactions on Pattern Analysis and Machine Intelligence,* Vol. PAMI-2, 1980, pp. 101-111.

Sklansky, J., and G. Wassel, *Pattern Classifiers and Trainable Machines,* Springer-Verlag, New York, 1981.

Smith, F. W., "Pattern Classifier Design by Linear Programming," *IEEE Transactions on Computers,* Vol. C-17, 1968, pp. 367-372.

Smith, F. W., "Small-Sample Optimality of Design Techniques for Linear Classifiers of Gaussian Patterns," *IEEE Transactions on Information Theory,* Vol. IT-18, 1972, pp. 118-126.

Spivak, S., "A Multisurface Method for Pattern Classification," *Pattern Recognition,* Vol. 22, 1989, pp. 587-591.

Srihari, S. N., T. Snabb, and L. E. White, "An Algorithm for Determining Identity of Nearest-Neighbor and Potential Function Decision Rules," *Pattern Recognition,* Vol. 12, 1980, pp. 293-299.

Talmon, J. L., "A Multiclass Nonparametric Partitioning Algorithm," Department of Medical Informatics, Free University, Amsterdam, 1985.

Tank, D., and J. Hopfield, "Collective Computation in Neuron-Like Circuits," *Scientific American,* December 1987, pp. 104-114.

Tomek, I., "A Generalization of the $k - NN$ Rule," *IEEE Transactions on Systems, Man, and Cybernetics,* Vol. SMC-6, 1976, pp. 121-126.

Ton, J., and R. Gonzales, *Pattern Recognition Principles,* Addison-Wesley, Reading, MA, 1974.

Toussaint, G. T., "On the Divergence Between Two Distributions and the Probability of Misclassification of Several Decision Rules," *Proceedings of the Second International Conference on Pattern Recognition,* Copenhagen, 1974, pp. 27-34.

——, "Bibliography on Estimation of Misclassification," *IEEE Transactions on Information Theory,* Vol. IT-20, 1976, pp. 472-479.

Trank, G. V., "A Problem of Dimensionality: A Simple Example," *IEEE Transactions on Pattern Analysis and Machine Intelligence,* Vol. PAMI-9, 1979, pp. 306-307.

Ullman, J., *Pattern Recognition,* Crane-Russak, New York, 1973.

Ullman, J., "Automatic Selection of Reference Data for Use in a Nearest-Neighbor Method of Pattern Classification," *IEEE Transactions on Information Theory,* Vol. IT-18, 1974, pp. 541-543.

Van Ness, J. W., "Dimensionality and Classification Performance with Independent Coordinates," *IEEE Transactions on Systems, Man, and Cybernetics,* Vol. SMC-7, 1977, pp. 560-564.

Voisin, J., and P. A. Devijver, "An Application of the Multiedit-Condensing Technique to the Reference Selection Problem in a Print Recognition System," *Pattern Recognition,* Vol. 20, 1987, pp. 465-474.

Wagner, T. J., "Convergence of the Edited Nearest Neighbor," *IEEE Transactions on Information Theory,* Vol. IT-17, 1973a, pp. 696-697.

——, "Strong Consistency of a Nonparametric Estimate of a Density Function," *IEEE Transactions on Systems, Man, and Cybernetics,* Vol. SMC-3, 1973b, pp. 289-290.

——, "Nonparametric Estimates of Probability Densities," *IEEE Transactions on Information Theory,* Vol. IT-21, 1975, pp. 438-440.

Watanabe, S., (ed.), *Methodologies of Pattern Recognition,* Academic Press, New York, 1969.

Whitney, A. W., and S. J. Dwyer, "Performance and Implementation of the k-Nearest Neighbor Decision Rule with Incorrectly Identified Training Samples," *Proceedings of the Fourth Annual Allerton Conference on Circuits and Systems Theory,* Allerton, CA, 1966, pp. 96-106.

Widrow, B., and R. Winter, "Neural Nets for Adaptive Filtering and Adaptive Pattern Recognition," *IEEE Computer,* Vol. 21, 1988, pp. 25-39.

Wilson, D. L., "Asymptotic Projection of Nearest Neighbor Rule Using Edited Data," *IEEE Transactions on Systems, Man, and Cybernetics,* Vol. SMC-2, 1972, pp. 408-420.

Wu, C., D. Landgrebe, and P. Swain, "The Decision Tree Approach to Classification," School of Electrical Engineering, Purdue University, TR-EE 75-17, May 1975.

 MATHEMATICAL MORPHOLOGY

5.1 Introduction

An algebraic system of operators, such as those of mathematical morphology, is useful because compositions of its operators can be formed that, when acting on complex shapes, are able to decompose them into their meaningful parts and separate them from their extraneous parts. Such a system of operators and their compositions permit the underlying shapes to be identified and optimally reconstructed from their distorted, noisy forms. Furthermore, they permit each shape to be understood in terms of a decomposition, each entity of the decomposition being some suitably simple shape.

A familiar example of a nonmorphological algebraic system is the algebraic system of convolution and its frequency domain representation. Here any finite duration function f can be represented as a sum of sinusoids. Distorting f can be modeled by adding to it sinusoids some of which may not have been part of its original representation, or f can be modeled by convolving it with some kernel k. Whatever the distortion, understanding what happens in terms of the sinusoidal (frequency domain) representation permits one to develop procedures to undo optimally the undesired distortion or the undesired transformation and to estimate, reconstruct, extract, or recognize the underlying f on the basis of observing its distorted form.

What the algebra of convolution does for linear systems, the algebra of mathematical morphology does for shape. Since shape is a prime carrier of information in machine vision, the importance of mathematical morphology is evident. Morphological operations can simplify image data, preserving their essential shape characteristics, and can eliminate irrelevancies. As the identification and decomposition of objects, object features, object surface defects, and assembly defects correlate directly with shape, mathematical morphology clearly has an essential structural role to play in machine vision (Crimmins and Brown, 1985; Haralick, Sternberg, and Zhuang, 1987; Serra, 1986a, b). Discussions of processor architecture for near real time morphological operations can be found in Sternberg (1981, 1982, 1983, 1985), Gerritsen and Verbeek (1984), Kimmel et al. (1985), Lougheed and McCubbrey (1980), Abbott, Haralick, and Zhuang (1988), and Huang, Jenkins, and Sawchuk (1989). The initial theoretical work in mathematical morphology was done by Hadwiger (1957). Matheron (1975) developed it in conjunction with integral geometry and size measurement, Kirsch (1957) first showed its utility in image processing, and Serra (1982) produced the first systematic theoretical treatment of the subject.

We begin our study with a discussion of binary morphology. We will give examples illustrating how to use the algebra of binary morphology for shape primitive extraction. Then we will conclude with a discussion of gray scale morphology.

5.2   Binary Morphology

The language of binary mathematical morphology is that of set theory. Sets in mathematical morphology represent the shapes that are manifested on binary or gray scale images. The set of all the black pixels in a black and white image (a binary image) constitutes a complete description of the binary image. Sets in Euclidean 2-space denote foreground regions in such binary images. Sets in Euclidean 3-space may denote time-varying binary imagery or static gray scale imagery as well as binary solids. Sets in higher-dimensional spaces may incorporate additional image information, such as color or multiple perspective imagery. Mathematical morphological transformations apply to sets of any dimensions, those like Euclidean N-space or like its discrete or digitized equivalent, the set of N-tuples of integers, Z^N. For the sake of simplicity we will refer to either of these sets as E^N. When $N = 2$, morphology can be done on a hexagonal grid rather than on a square grid. Golay (1969) was the first to introduce binary morphology on a hexagonal grid.

Those points in a set being morphologically transformed are considered to be the selected set of points, and those in the complement set are considered to be not selected. In binary images the selected set of points is the foreground and the set of points not selected is the background.

The primary morphological operations are dilation and erosion. From dilation and erosion the morphological operations of opening and closing can be composed. It is these latter two operations that have a close connection to shape representation, decomposition, and primitive extraction.

5.2.1   Binary Dilation

Dilation is the morphological transformation that combines two sets by using vector addition of set elements. Binary dilation was first used by Minkowski, and in the mathematics literature it is called *Minkowski addition*. If A and B are sets in N-space (E^N) with elements a and b respectively, $a = (a_1, \ldots, a_N)$ and $b = (b_1, \ldots, b_N)$ being N-tuples of element coordinates, then the dilation of A by B is the set of all possible vector sums of pairs of elements, one coming from A and one coming from B.

More formally, the *dilation* of A by B is denoted by $A \oplus B$ and is defined by

$$A \oplus B = \{c \in E^N \mid c = a + b \text{ for some } a \in A \text{ and } b \in B\}$$

Because addition is commutative, dilation is commutative: $A \oplus B = B \oplus A$.

In practice the sets A and B are not thought of symmetrically. The first set A of the dilation $A \oplus B$ is associated with the image underlying morphological processing, and the second set B is referred to as the *structuring element,* the shape that acts on A through the dilation operation to produce the result $A \oplus B$. We will refer to A as a set or an image.

Dilation by disk structuring elements corresponds to isotropic swelling or expansion algorithms common to binary image processing. Dilation by small squares (3×3) is a neighborhood operation easily implemented by adjacency connected array architectures and is the one that many image-processing people know by the name "fill," "expand," or "grow." Some example dilation transformations are illustrated in Figs. 5.1 and 5.2. The coordinate system we use for all the examples in the next few sections is (row, column).

Dilation can be used for noise removal. Consider the image $\dot{J}$ created by $J = I \cap (I \oplus N_4)$, where N_4 is the set of four 4-neighbors belonging to the pixel $(0,0)$. Then any time a pixel has a 4-neighbor, it will not be in $I \oplus N_4$. Therefore J consists of only those points in I that have at least one of its 4-neighbors. All 4-isolated pixels have been removed. Note that pixels on a diagonal line of one pixel width will also be eliminated in J because pixels that are diagonal neighbors are not 4-connected.

To characterize the dilation operation, we need a notation for the translation of a set. Let A be a subset of E^N and t be an N-tuple of E^N. We denote the translation of A by the point t by A_t.

$$A_t = \{c \in E^N \mid c = a + t \text{ for some } a \in A\}$$

$$A = \{(0,1),(1,1),(2,1),(2,2),(3,0)\}$$

$$B = \{(0,0),(0,1)\}$$

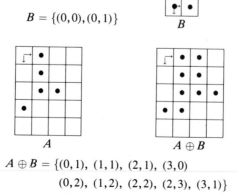

$$A \oplus B = \{(0,1),\ (1,1),\ (2,1),\ (3,0)$$
$$(0,2),\ (1,2),\ (2,2),\ (2,3),\ (3,1)\}$$

Figure 5.1 Dilation operation represented in terms of sets, and their corresponding binary images.

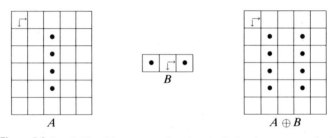

Figure 5.2 Set A dilated by a structuring element B that does not contain the origin. As a result, the dilated set is not even guaranteed to have a single point in common with A. However, there are always translations of $A \oplus B$ that can contain A.

The dilation operation can be represented as a union of translates of the structuring element: $A \oplus B = \bigcup_{a \in A} B_a$. This union can be thought of as a neighborhood operator. The structuring element B is swept over the image. Each time the origin of the structuring element B touches a binary-1 pixel, the entire translated structuring-element shape is ORed to the output image where the initial output image has only zero-valued pixels.

Because dilation is commutative, the dilation of A by B can also be represented as the union of the translates of the image A taken over all the points of B : $A \oplus B = \bigcup_{b \in B} A_b$. This representation is definitely not like a neighborhood operator. Rather, it corresponds to how pipeline architectures implement dilation in near real time. Neglecting, for the moment, boundary effects, translating the image corresponds to delaying the image by some amount in its raster scan order. The representation $A \oplus B = \bigcup_{b \in B} A_b$ indicates that the dilation of the image A by B can be accomplished by delaying the raster scan of the image A by amounts corresponding to the points in structuring element B and then ORing the delayed raster scans to produce the dilation.

Because addition is associative, dilation is also associative: $(A \oplus B) \oplus C = A \oplus (B \oplus C)$. The associative property of dilation is called the *chain rule* or the *iterative rule* and has important practical significance. Consider how the dilation of an $N \times N$ image by a $2^K \times 2^K$ square structuring element can be accomplished in a pipeline architecture. By using the straightforward representation, the dilation can be accomplished with $(2^K)^2$ stages, each stage consisting of a shift of the image and an OR of the shifted image into the previous result. The time complexity is the time required for one raster scan of the image, and the computational complexity is 2^{2K} operations.

Now a structuring element such as a $2^K \times 2^K$ square is highly decomposable. It can be represented in separable form as a row L^r of 2^K pixel positions dilated by a column L^c of 2^K pixel positions, where each pixel position is represented as a column vector; $L^r = \{\binom{0}{0}, \binom{1}{0}, \ldots, \binom{2^K-1}{0}\}$ and $L^c = \{\binom{0}{0}, \binom{0}{1}, \ldots, \binom{0}{2^K-1}\}$. Furthermore, a linear sequence of 2^K pixels on a row itself can be represented as a composition of K dilations of two point sets $L_0^r, \ldots, L_{K-1}^r$. For example, $L^r = L_0^r \oplus$

$L_0^r \oplus L_1^r \oplus \ldots \oplus L_{K-1}^r$, where $L_k^r = \{\binom{0}{0}, \binom{2^k}{0}\}$. Similarly, $L^c = L_0^c \oplus L_1^c \oplus \ldots \oplus L_{K-1}^c$, where $L_k^c = \{\binom{0}{0}, \binom{0}{2^k}\}$. By the associative law for dilation, dilating by a structuring element decomposable as a composition of $2K$ dilations can be accomplished iteratively by $2K$ successive dilations; that is, $A \oplus (K_1 \oplus K_2 \oplus \ldots \oplus K_N) = \{\ldots[(A \oplus K_1) \oplus K_2] \oplus \ldots\} \oplus K_N$. The pipeline time complexity using this representation is still the time required for one raster scan, but the computational complexity is $2K$ stages. The transformation of 2^{2K} to $2K$ in computational complexity is very signficant when K is over 5.

Other properties of dilation include that of dilating by a translated structuring element. This produces the translation of the dilation: $A \oplus B_t = (A \oplus B)_t$. Because dilation is commutative, the dilation of A by B is the dilation of B by A. Because dilation distributes over union, dilating a union of two sets is also the union of dilations: $(B \cup C) \oplus A = (B \oplus A) \cup (C \oplus A)$. The distribution of dilation over union is to mathematical morphology what the distribution of convolution over sums is to linear operator theory.

Dilating by a structuring element that is representable as a union of two sets is the union of the dilation, $A \oplus (B \cup C) = (A \oplus B) \cup (A \oplus C)$. Dilating a set A by a structuring element containing the origin produces a result guaranteed to contain A. Operators whose output contains their inputs are called *extensive*. Thus dilation is extensive when the structuring element contains the origin. As shown in Fig. 5.2, however, when the origin is not in the structuring element, the resulting dilation may have nothing in common with the set being dilated.

Finally, dilation preserves order. If $A \subseteq B$, then $A \oplus K \subseteq B \oplus K$. Operators that have this property are called *increasing*.

5.2.2 Binary Erosion

Erosion is the morphological dual of dilation. It is the morphological transformation that combines two sets by using containment as its basis set. If A and B are sets in Euclidean N-space, then the erosion of A by B is the set of all elements x for which $x + b \in A$ for every $b \in B$. Some image-processing people use the word *shrink* or *reduce* for erosion. Minkowski subtraction is a close relative to morphological erosion.

The erosion of A by B is denoted by $A \ominus B$ and is defined by

$$A \ominus B = \{x \in E^N \mid x + b \in A \text{ for every } b \in B\}$$

Erosion is illustrated in Fig. 5.3.

The utility of the erosion transformation is better appreciated when the erosion is expressed in a different form. The erosion of an image A by a structuring element B is the set of all elements x of E^N for which B translated to x is contained in A. In fact, this was the definition that Matheron (1967) used for erosion. The proof is immediate from the definitions of erosion and translation.

$$A \ominus B = \{x \in E^N \mid B_x \subseteq A\}$$

$$A = \{(1,0),\ (1,1),\ (1,2),\ (1,3),\ (1,4),\ (1,5),$$
$$(2,1),\ (3,1),\ (4,1),\ (5,1),\}$$
$$B = \{(0,0),\ (0,1)\}$$
$$A \ominus B = \{(1,0),\ (1,1),\ (1,2),\ (1,3),\ (1,4)\}$$

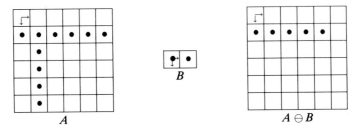

Figure 5.3 Erosion of a set, and its corresponding binary image.

Thus the structuring element B may be visualized as a probe that slides across the image A, testing the spatial nature of A at every point. Where B translated to x can be contained in A (by placing the origin of B at x), then x belongs to the erosion $A \ominus B$.

Erosion can be viewed as a morphological transformation that combines two sets by using vector subtraction of set elements. Expressed as a difference of elements a and b, erosion becomes

$$A \ominus B = \{x \in E^N \mid \text{for every } b \in B, \text{ there exists an}$$
$$a \in A \text{ such that } x = a - b\}$$

This is the definition that Hadwiger (1957) used for erosion.

Whereas dilation can be represented as a union of translates, erosion can be represented as an intersection of the negative translates:

$$A \ominus B = \bigcap_{b \in B} A_{-b}$$

Hence the same architecture that accomplishes dilation can accomplish erosion by changing the OR function to an AND function and by using the image translated by the negated points of the structuring element instead of the image translated by its points. Figure 5.4 illustrates how erosion can be computed as an intersection of translates of A.

The erosion transformation is popularly conceived of as a shrinking of the original image. In set terms, the eroded set is often thought of as being contained in the original set. A transformation that has this property is called *antiextensive*. However, the erosion transformation is necessarily antiextensive when the origin belongs to the structuring element. That is, if $0 \in B$, then $A \ominus B \subseteq A$. To see this, let $x \in A \ominus B$. Then, by definition of erosion, $x + b \in A$ for every $b \in B$. Since $0 \in B$, $x = x + 0 \in A$.

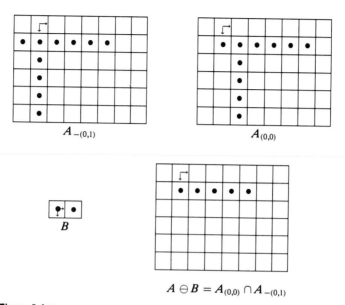

$$A \ominus B = A_{(0,0)} \cap A_{-(0,1)}$$

Figure 5.4 Erosion operation represented as the intersection of translated sets.

Figure 5.5 illustrates how eroding by a structuring element that does not contain the origin can lead to a result that has nothing in common with the set being eroded. It is possible, however, for an erosion of A by B to be a subset of A and for B also not to contain the origin. To see this, let $A = \{1,2,3,4\}$ and $B = \{-1,1\}$. Then $A \ominus B = \{2,3\} \subseteq A$, and yet $0 \notin B$.

Dilating a translated set results in a translated dilation. That is, $A_t \oplus B = (A \oplus B)_t$. But, eroding by a translated structuring element results in a translated erosion where the translation is negated; $A \ominus B_t = (A \ominus B)_{-t}$. Like dilation, erosion is increasing; if $A \subseteq B$, then $A \ominus K \subseteq B \ominus K$. Further, eroding by a larger structuring element produces a smaller result; if $K \subseteq L$, then $A \ominus L \subseteq A \ominus K$.

The dilation and erosion transformations bear a marked similarity in that what one does to the image foreground the other does to the image background. Indeed, their similarity can be formalized as a duality relationship. Two operators are dual

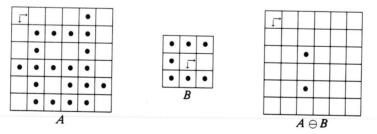

Figure 5.5 Erosion of a set A by a structuring element B that does not contain the origin. As a result, no point of the erosion is guaranteed to be in common with A. However, some translations of $A \ominus B$ are contained in A.

when the negation of a formulation employing the first operator is equal to the same formulation employing the second operator on the negated variables. An example is DeMorgan's law, which states the duality between set union and intersection, $(A \cup B)^c = A^c \cap B^c$. Here the negation of a set A is its complement, $A^c = \{x \in E^n \mid x \notin A\}$. In morphology, negation of a set can occur in two possible ways: in a logical sense, whereby the negation is set complement, or in a geometric sense, whereby it is a reversing of the orientation of the set with respect to its coordinate axes. Such reversing is called reflection.

Let $B \subseteq E^N$. The reflection of B is denoted by $\check{B}$ and is defined by

$$\check{B} = \{x \mid \text{ for some } b \in B, \ x = -b\}$$

The reflection occurs about the origin. Matheron (1975) refers to $\check{B}$ as "the symmetrical set of B with respect to the origin." Serra (1982) refers to $\check{B}$ as "B transpose."

As given in the following theorem, the complement of an erosion is the dilation of the complement by the reflection. The duality of dilation and erosion employs both logical and geometric negation because of the different roles played by the image and the structuring element in an expression employing these morphological operators.

Theorem 5.1: Erosion Dilation Duality

$$(A \ominus B)^c = A^c \oplus \check{B}$$

Proof:
$x \in (A \ominus B)^c$ if and only if $x \notin A \ominus B$. $x \notin A \ominus B$ if and only if there exists $b \in B$ such that $x + b \notin A$. There exists $b \in B$ such that $x + b \in A^c$ if and only if there exists $b \in B$ such that $x \in (A^c)_{-b}$. There exists $b \in B$ such that $x \in (A^c)_{-b}$ if and only if $x \in \bigcup_{b \in B}(A^c)_{-b}$. Now $x \in \bigcup_{b \in B}(A^c)_{-b}$ if and only if $x \in \bigcup_{b \in \check{B}}(A^c)_b$; and $x \in \bigcup_{b \in \check{B}}(A^c)_b$ if and only if $x \in A^c \oplus \check{B}$.

Corollary 5.1:

$$(A \oplus B)^c = A^c \ominus \check{B}$$

Figure 5.6 illustrates an instance of the duality relationship $(A \ominus B)^c = A^c \oplus \check{B}$.

The erosion of a set that itself has a decomposition as the intersection of two sets is the intersection of the erosions, $(A \cap B) \ominus K = (A \ominus K) \cap (B \ominus K)$, as shown in Fig. 5.7. The erosion of a set by a structuring element that has a decomposition as the union of two sets is the intersection of the erosions; $A \ominus (K \cup L) = (A \ominus K) \cap (A \ominus L)$. However, the erosion of a set by a structuring element that has a decomposition as the intersection of two sets is guaranteed only to contain the union of the erosion of the set with each of the sets of the intersection decomposition; $A \ominus (B \cap C) \supseteq (A \ominus B) \cup (A \ominus C)$. Figure 5.8 shows that this relationship cannot be made stronger.

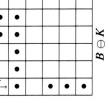

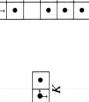

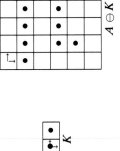

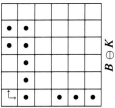

$$(A \cap B) \ominus K = (A \ominus K) \cap (B \ominus K)$$

Figure 5.7 An instance of the relationship $(A \cap B) \ominus K = (A \ominus K) \cap (B \ominus K)$.

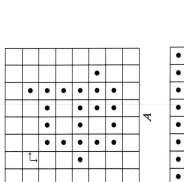

Figure 5.6 Duality relation between erosion and dilation. The set A eroded by B is the complement of the set A^c dilated by $\breve{B}$. By convention, we understand that for the complemented set A^c or $A^c \oplus \breve{B}$, all pixels outside the area illustrated are binary-1 pixels.

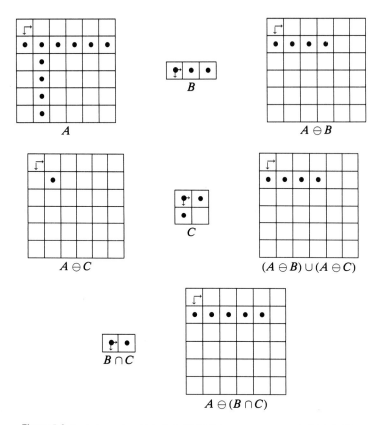

Figure 5.8 An instance in which $A \ominus (B \cap C)$ is a proper superset of $(A \ominus B) \cup (A \ominus C)$, thereby showing that the general relation $A \ominus (B \cap C) \supseteq (A \ominus B) \cup (A \ominus C)$ cannot be made any stronger.

Finally, with respect to structuring element decomposition, a chain rule for erosion holds when the structuring element is decomposable through dilation,

$$A \ominus (B \oplus C) = (A \ominus B) \ominus C$$

This relation is as important as the chain rule relation (associativity) for dilation because it permits a large erosion to be computed more efficiently by two or more successive smaller erosions.

Although dilation and erosion are dual, this does not imply that we can freely perform cancellation on morphological equalities. For example, if $A = B \ominus C$, then dilating both sides of the expression by C results in $A \oplus C = (B \ominus C) \oplus C \neq B$. However, a containment relationship does hold: $A \subseteq B \ominus C$ if and only if $B \supseteq A \oplus C$.

Binary erosion is related to Minkowski subtraction. The *Minkowski subtraction* of B from A is given by $\bigcap_{b \in B} A_b$. Hadwiger (1957) discusses binary morphology using the operations of Minkowski addition and subtraction.

Erosion can be used to determine the genus of a binary image I. The genus $g(I)$ is the number of connected components of I minus the number of holes of

I. A hole is a connected component of the binary-0 pixels that does not connect with the border frame of the image. If 4-connectedness is used for the binary-1 pixels, then 8-connectedness must be used for the binary-0 pixels, and vice versa. When 4-connectedness is used for the binary-1 pixels (Minsky and Papert, 1969) and 8-connectedness for the binary-0 pixels, the genus can be computed by using the structuring elements shown in Fig. 5.9 by

$$g_4(I) = \#I - \#I \ominus V - \#I \ominus H + \#I \ominus B \qquad (5.1)$$

When 8-connectedness is used for the binary-1 pixels and 4-connectedness for the binary-0 pixels, the genus can be computed by

$$g_8(I) = \#I - \#I \ominus V - \#I \ominus H - \#I \ominus D_1 - \#I \ominus D_2 +$$
$$\#I \ominus C_1 + \#I \ominus C_2 + \#I \ominus C_3 + \#I \ominus C_4 - \#I \ominus B \qquad (5.2)$$

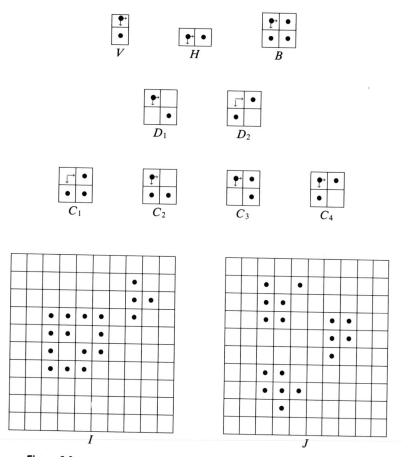

Figure 5.9 Structuring elements that can be used to determine the genus of a binary image, and two examples with this genus computed according to Eqs. (5.1) and (5.2); $g_4(I) = 1$, $g_4(J) = 4$, $g_8(I) = 0$, $g_8(J) = 3$.

5.2.3   Hit-and-Miss Transform

The hit-and-miss morphological transform (Serra, 1982) is a natural operation to select out pixels that have certain geometric properties, such as corner points, isolated
points, or border points, and that performs template matching, thinning, thickening,
and centering. This transform is accomplished by using intersections of erosions.

Let J and K be two structuring elements that satisfy $J \cap K = \phi$. The hit-and-
miss transformation of set A by (J, K) is denoted by $A \otimes (J, K)$ and is defined by

$$A \otimes (J, K) = (A \ominus J) \cap (A^c \ominus K)$$

The hit-and-miss transform can be used to locate particular spatial patterns. For
example, if $J = \{(0,0)\}$ and $K = \{(0,1), (0,-1), (1,0), (-1,0)\}$, then $I \otimes (J, K)$
is the set of all 4-isolated pixels of I.

Gray (1971) was the first to give a hit-and-miss transform approach to the
computation of the genus of a binary image. We follow Serra (1982), who uses the
structuring elements shown in Fig. 5.10. The calculation is given by

$$g_4(I) = \#I \otimes (J_1, K_1) + \#I \otimes (J_2, K_2) - \#I \otimes (J_3, K_3)$$
$$g_8(I) = \#I \otimes (J_1, K_1) - \#I \otimes (J_4, K_4)$$

We next describe the hit-and-miss transform used to find upper right-hand corner
points of a set A. Figure 5.11 shows the J and K structuring elements. J locates all
pixels of A that have south and west neighbors that are also a part of A. These can
be thought of as all pixels of A that are candidates for being corner pixels, because
having south and west neighbors in A is a necessary condition for a corner pixel. K
locates all pixels of A^c that have south and west neighbors in A^c. Notice that J and
K are displaced from one another. K is J translated by one pixel to the northeast.
The pixels that K locates can be thought of as all pixels of A^c that are candidates
for being an exterior border pixel to a corner pixel of A. They are those that have
north, east, and northeast binary-1 neighbors in A^c.

Levialdi (1967, 1968, 1971, 1972), Arcelli and Levialdi (1971a,b, 1972), Arcelli, Cordella, and Levialdi (1973, 1980), and Sklansky, Cordella, and Levialdi
(1976) discuss varieties of thickening, thinning, and concavity extraction algorithms,
all of which can be described in terms of the morphological operations of erosion,

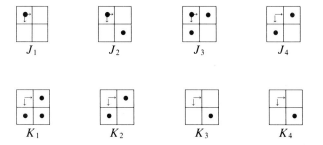

Figure 5.10 Structuring element by which genus can be computed via a hit-and-
miss transform.

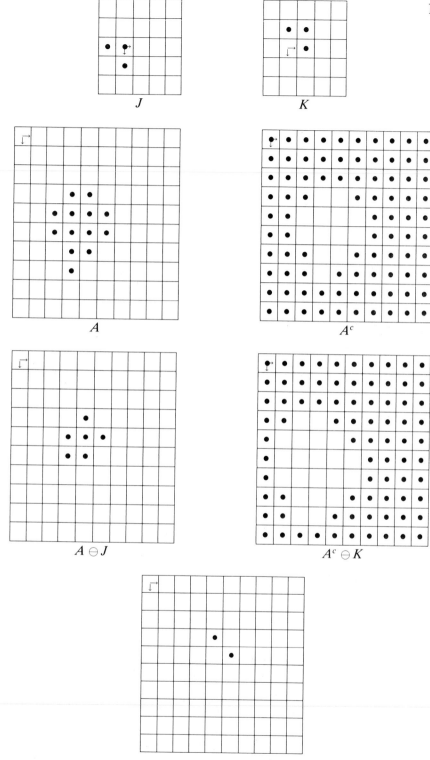

$$A \otimes (J,K) = (A \ominus J) \cap (A^c \ominus K)$$

Figure 5.11 Location of upper right-hand corner points by the hit-and-miss transform.

dilation, and hit-and-miss transformation. Their work often emphasizes architectures for accomplishing the operations in parallel.

Thickening and Thinning

The *thickening* of A by structuring-element pair (J,K) is denoted by $A \odot (J,K)$ and is defined by $A \odot (J,K) = A \cup A \otimes (J,K)$. To get a thickening that properly contains A, $0 \notin J$ and $J \cap K = \phi$. The *thinning* of A by structuring-element pair (J,K) is denoted by $A \oslash (J,K)$ and is defined by $A \oslash (J,K) = A - A \otimes (J,K)$.

Iterations of thickenings can be used to determine convex hulls. For example, we define the 45° digital convex hull of a set A to be the intersection of all half-planes whose normal is a multiple of 45° and that contain A.

Using the sequence of eight structuring-element pairs shown in Fig. 5.12, we let $A_o = A$ and

$$A_{n+1} = \left(\ldots \left\{ [A_n \odot (J_1, K_1)] \odot (J_2, K_2) \right\} \odot \ldots \odot (J_8, K_8) \right).$$

Then an approximate 45° convex hull is A_N for any N for which $A_N = A_{N+1}$.

Iterations of the thinning operation can be employed to determine skeletons. For example, we define the octagonal skeleton of A to be the set of all pixels of

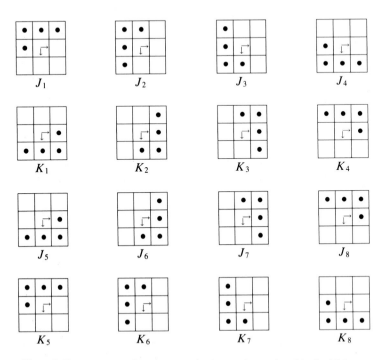

Figure 5.12 Eight structuring-element pairs that can be employed in the thickening operation to determine a 45° convex hull.

A that are the centers of maximal octagons contained in A. Using the sequence of eight structuring-element pairs shown in Fig. 5.13, we let $A_o = A$ and

$$A_{n+1} = \left(\dots \left\{ [A_n \oslash (J_1, K_1)] \oslash (J_2, K_2) \right\} \oslash \dots \oslash (J_8, K_8) \right)$$

Then the octagonal skeleton is A_N for any N for which $A_N = A_{N+1}$.

Counting

The combination of erosions and a hit-and-miss transform can be used to help count the number of 8-connected regions in a binary image. Levialdi (1972) gives an algorithm whose essence is the following:

Let I be the initial binary image and K_1, K_2, K_3, K_4, L_1, and L_2 be the structuring elements shown in Fig. 5.14. Define $I_0 = I$ and the count $c_0 = \#I_0 \otimes (L_1, L_2)$, which is the number of isolated binary-1 pixels on the initial image. Suppose iteration n has completed. Define

$$I_{n+1} = \bigcup_{i=1}^{4} I_n \ominus K_i$$

Each successive iteration erodes the spatial pattern toward the top right without

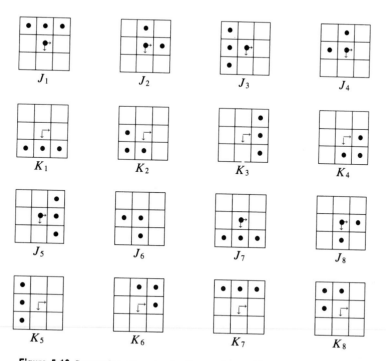

Figure 5.13 Structuring-element pairs that can be used iteratively to determine an octagonal skeleton.

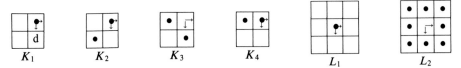

Figure 5.14 Structuring elements involved in Levialdi's counting algorithm for 8-connected regions.

altering the connectivity structure of the region to which the pixels belong. Whenever an isolated binary-1 pattern is found, it is counted.

$$c_{n+1} = c_n + \#I_{n+1} \otimes (L_1, L_2)$$

The final count is given by c_N, where N is the smallest integer for which $I_N = \phi$.

Counting 4-connected regions can proceed in a similar fashion. The required structuring elements K_1, K_2, K_3, L_1, and L_2 are shown in Fig. 5.15. The algorithm is given by

$$c_0 = \#I_0 \otimes (L_1, L_2)$$

$$I_{n+1} = \bigcup_{i=1}^{3} I_n \ominus K_i$$

$$c_{n+1} = c_n + \#I_{n+1} \otimes (L_1, L_2)$$

The final count is given by c_N, where N is the smallest integer for which $I_N = \phi$.

Template Matching

The hit-and-miss transform can be employed to do template matching. Suppose the template pattern is given by the set T, and the window within which the template T is situated is given by the set W, $W \supseteq T$. A point x from image I is said to match the template exactly if T translated to x is contained in I and if what is not in T, to the extent of W, is contained in I^c. Or more compactly,

$$T_x \subseteq I \quad \text{and} \quad (W - T)_x \subseteq I^c$$

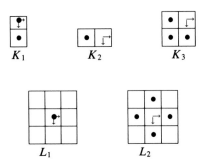

Figure 5.15 Structuring elements involved in Levialdi's counting algorithm for 4-connected regions.

From this form, it is quickly apparent that the set of match points is given by $I \otimes (T, W - T)$. This is essentially the template-matching idea in Crimmins and Brown (1985), who use the equivalent condition $I \cap W_x = T_x$ to define when a point x exactly matches the template T.

A natural way to loosen the exact-matching idea to K-tolerance matching is to define the set of K-tolerance matching points of I to the template T in window W by

$$\{x | (T \ominus K)_x \subseteq I \text{ and } (T \oplus K)^c_x \cap W_x \subseteq I^c\}$$

where K can be thought of as a small disklike structuring element containing the origin. In this case $T \ominus K \subseteq T$ and $(T \oplus K)^c \subseteq T^c$, which immediately implies that any exactly matching point must be a K-tolerance matching point. Expressed as a hit-and-miss transform, the set of K-tolerance matching points of I to the template T in window W is given by

$$I \otimes [T \ominus K, W - (T \oplus K)]$$

5.2.4 Dilation and Erosion Summary

The following list summarizes the algebraic relations among dilation, erosion, set union, and set intersection. The proofs for these relations are fairly direct and are left for the exercises.

$$(A \oplus B) \oplus C = A \oplus (B \oplus C)$$
$$(A \cup B) \oplus C = (A \oplus C) \cup (B \oplus C)$$
$$A \oplus B = \bigcup_{b \in B} A_b$$
$$A \subseteq B \Rightarrow A \oplus C \subseteq B \oplus C$$
$$(A \cap B) \oplus C \subseteq (A \oplus C) \cap (B \oplus C)$$
$$A \oplus (B \cup C) = (A \oplus B) \cup (A \oplus C)$$
$$(A \oplus B)^c = A^c \ominus \check{B}$$
$$A \oplus B_t = (A \oplus B)_t$$
$$A \oplus B = B \oplus A$$
$$(A \ominus B) \ominus C = A \ominus (B \oplus C)$$
$$(A \cap B) \ominus C = (A \ominus C) \cap (B \ominus C)$$
$$A \ominus B = \bigcap_{b \in B} A_{-b}$$
$$A \subseteq B \Rightarrow A \ominus C \subseteq B \ominus C$$
$$(A \cup B) \ominus C \supseteq (A \ominus C) \cup (B \ominus C)$$
$$A \ominus (B \cap C) \supseteq (A \ominus B) \cup (A \ominus C)$$
$$A \ominus (B \cup C) = (A \ominus B) \cap (A \ominus C)$$
$$A \ominus B_t = (A \ominus B)_{-t}$$

5.2.5 Opening and Closing

Now we are ready to understand another reason why dilation and erosion have an essential connection to shape. Dilations and erosions are usually employed in pairs, either dilation of an image followed by the erosion of the dilated result, or erosion of an image followed by the dilation of the eroded result. In either case the result of successively applied dilations and erosions is an elimination of specific image detail smaller than the structuring element without the global geometric distortion of unsuppressed features.

Of particular significance is that image transformations employing successively applied dilations and erosions are idempotent, that is, their reapplication effects no further changes to the previously transformed result. The practical importance of idempotent transformations is that they comprise complete and closed stages of image analysis algorithms because shapes can be naturally described in terms of the structuring elements under which they can be opened or closed and yet remain the same.

Opening and closing stand to morphology exactly as the orthogonal projection operator stands to linear algebra. An orthogonal projection operator is idempotent and selects the part of a vector that lies in a given subspace. Likewise, opening and closing provide the means by which given subshapes and supershapes of a complex shape can be selected.

The functionality of opening and closing corresponds closely to the specification of a filter by its bandwidth. Morphologically filtering an image by an opening or closing operation corresponds to the ideal nonrealizable bandpass filters of conventional linear filtering. Once an image is ideal-bandpassed filtered, further ideal-bandpass filtering does not alter the result.

The *opening* of image B by structuring element K is denoted by $B \circ K$ and defined by $B \circ K = (B \ominus K) \oplus K$. The *closing* of image B by structuring element K is denoted by $B \bullet K$ and defined by $B \bullet K = (B \oplus K) \ominus K$. If B is unchanged by opening it with K, we say that B is *open* with respect to K or B is open under K, whereas if B is unchanged by closing it with K, we say that B is *closed* with respect to K or B is closed under K. Morphological opening and closing have no relation to topologically open or closed sets.

The ability of an opening to select from a set the subset that matches the structuring element of the opening is immediate from the opening characterization theorem, which states

$$A \circ K = \{x \in A \mid \text{ for some } t \in A \ominus K, \ x \in K_t \text{ and } K_t \subseteq A\}$$

The opening of A by K selects precisely those points of A that match K in the sense that the points can be covered by some translation of the structuring element K that itself is entirely contained in A. Opening an image with a disk structuring element smooths the contour, breaks narrow isthmuses, and eliminates small islands and sharp peaks or capes. Closing an image with a disk structuring element smooths the contours; fuses narrow breaks and long, thin gulfs; eliminates small holes; and fills gaps on the contours.

It is not difficult to understand how this characterization of opening arises. After all, by definition a point x is in the opening $A \circ K$ if and only if $x \in (A \ominus K) \oplus K$. And this happens if and only if for some $t \in A \ominus K$, $x \in \{t\} \oplus K = K_t$. But $t \in A \ominus K$ if and only if $K_t \subseteq A$.

The characterization theorem makes clear that unlike erosion and dilation, opening is invariant to the translation of the structuring element. That is, $A \circ K = A \circ K_x$ for any x. It is also easy to see from the opening characterization theorem that opening is an antiextensive transformation. Like erosion and dilation, opening is also an increasing transformation.

Reorganizing the information in the opening characterization theorem, we can write

$$A \circ K = \bigcup_{y \in A \ominus K} K_y$$
$$= \bigcup_{K_y \subseteq A} K_y$$

which gives a vivid picture of the primitive matching that a morphological opening accomplishes. The points in the opening $A \circ K$ are precisely those obtained by sweeping the structuring element all over the inside of A, never permitting any part of the structuring element K to be outside A. The set of all points covered by the sweep is precisely the opening of A by K.

Figure 5.16 illustrates how this primitive geometric shape-matching property of the morphological opening can be used to decompose objects. The figure shows a shape F that consists of a disklike body and an elongated ellipselike handle. To decompose this shape into its parts, we open it with a small disk structuring element L. The radius of L is just larger than the width of the ellipse. Opening F with L produces $F \circ L$, which is the disk body of F. The residue $F - F \circ L$ of the opening is the ellipse handle.

In extracting the primitive parts of F, the order of the operations is important. The larger primitives must be obtained first and the smaller ones second. To see this, consider what happens if we open F with an ellipselike structuring element K

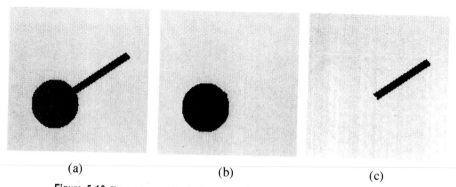

(a)   (b)   (c)

Figure 5.16 Extraction of the body and handle of a shape F by opening with L for the body and taking the residue of the opening for the handle; (a) F, (b) $F \circ L$, and (c) $F - F \circ L$.

in an attempt to extract the handle of F first. $F \circ K$ consists of the elliptical handle in addition to most of the disklike body of F. What has been eliminated from F by the opening with K is only a pair of small sliver areas from the disk body of F in which the ellipse K does not fit.

Figure 5.17 illustrates a shape F that has a vertical trunklike body and two horizontal arms. In this case the arms and the trunk can be extracted independently. To extract the trunk, we open with a smaller trunklike structuring element L whose vertical length is larger than the width of each of the horizontal arms. To extract the arms, we open with a smaller horizontally oriented structuring element K whose length is just larger than the width of the trunk.

Figure 5.18(a) illustrates a shape F that has a base, a trunk, a horizontal arm, and a small vertical arm attached to the horizontal arm. In adition, F is perturbed by salt-and-pepper noise. Opening with a disk structuring element K_1, whose radius is just larger than the largest noise spot, will eliminate the background noise and round the corners of F (Fig. 5.18b). Then closing with a disk K_2 eliminates the inside salt-and-peper noise (Fig. 5.18c). To eliminate small peninsulas, we open with a disk K_3 just smaller than the disk used for closing. This produces the image $G = [(F \circ K_1) \bullet K_2] \circ K_3$ of Fig. 5.18(d). To extract the base of F, we open with a smaller baselike structuring element K_4 (Fig. 5.18e). Then from the residue $H = G - G \circ K_4$ (Fig. 5.18f) we open with a small vertically oriented structuring element K_5 to extract the trunk (Fig. 5.18g). The horizontal area can then be extracted from the residue $H - H \circ K_5$ by opening the residue with a small horizontally oriented structuring element K_6. The residue of this last opening is the small remaining vertically oriented area.

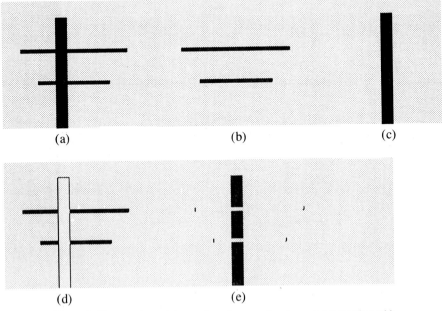

Figure 5.17 Extraction of the trunk and arms of a shape F by opening with vertically and horizontally oriented structuring elements.

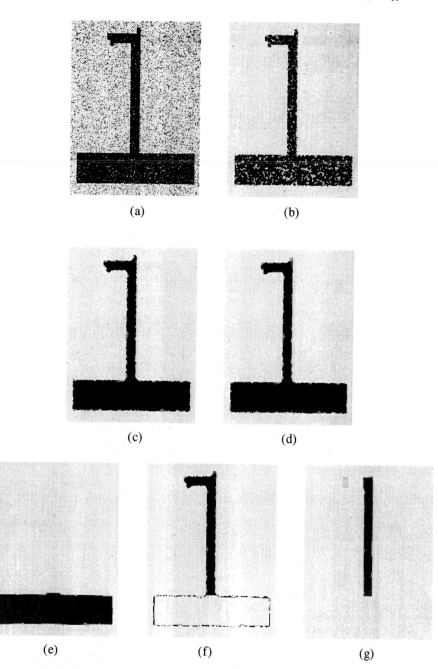

Figure 5.18 Extraction of the base, trunk, and horizontal and vertical areas of a shape F immersed in salt-and-pepper background noise by conditioning and then opening; (a) original image, (b) opening with a disk of radius 1, (c) closing with a disk of radius 4, (d) opening with a disk of radius 3, (e) opening with a rectangle of size 21×20, (f) residue of the opening, and (g) opening residue of opening with a vertical structuring element.

Figure 5.19(a) shows a binary image of disks with average diameter of 35 pixels in a dense background of short line segments. To eliminate the line segments, we can perform an opening. Opening the image of Fig. 5.19(a) with a disk structuring element having diameter 13 produces the image of Fig. 5.19(b), a surprising almost perfect result.

For a final example, Fig. 5.20 shows the operations required for a complete opening sequence tree decomposition. Figure 5.21 illustrates this decomposition for the image shown in Fig. 5.20.

The duality between dilation and erosion implies a duality between opening and closing. The complement of an opening with K is the closing of A complement with the reflection of K.

$$(A \circ K)^c = [(A \ominus K) \oplus K]^c = (A \ominus K)^c \ominus \check{K} = (A^c \oplus \check{K}) \ominus \check{K}$$
$$= A^c \bullet \check{K}$$

The opening characterization theorem and the duality between opening and closing lead to a closing characterization that states

$$A \bullet K = \{x \mid x \in \check{K}_t \text{ implies } \check{K}_t \cap A \neq \phi\}$$

The closing of A includes all points satisfying the condition that anytime the point can be covered by a translation of the reflected structuring element, there must be some point in common between the reflected translated structuring element and A. It is obvious from the closing characterization theorem that, like opening, closing is invariant to the translation of the structuring element. That is, $A \bullet K_x = A \bullet K$ for any x.

From the opening characterization theorem, it follows that the opening of A is contained in A. Set operators with this property are said to be *antiextensive*. Opening is antiextensive. From the closing characterization theorem, it follows that A is contained in the closing of A. Set operators with this property are said to be

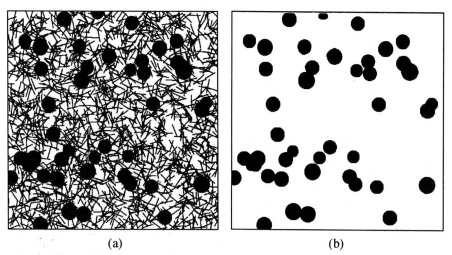

(a)   (b)

Figure 5.19 (a) A binary image. (b) Opening of (a) with a disk structuring element.

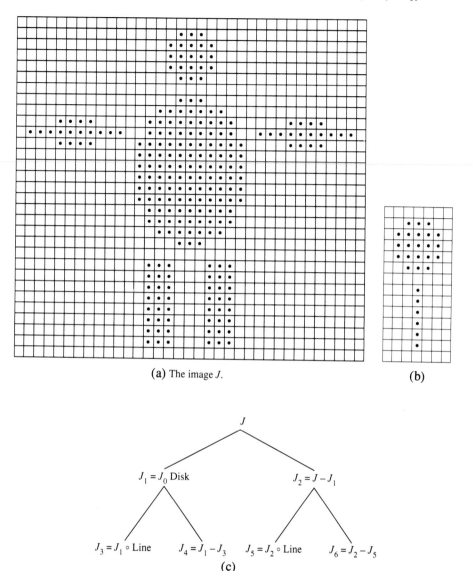

(a) The image J.

(b)

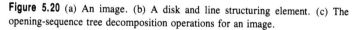

(c)

Figure 5.20 (a) An image. (b) A disk and line structuring element. (c) The opening-sequence tree decomposition operations for an image.

extensive. Hence closing is an extensive transformation. Since dilation and erosion are increasing operations, compositions of dilation and erosion will be increasing. In particular then, closing, like opening, is an increasing operation.

Sets dilated by K remain invariant under an opening with K. That is,

$$A \oplus K = (A \oplus K) \circ K$$

This comes about because $A \bullet K \supseteq A$, and since dilation is increasing, $(A \bullet K) \oplus K \supseteq A \oplus K$. But $(A \bullet K) \oplus K = [(A \oplus K) \ominus K] \oplus K = (A \oplus K) \circ K$ and

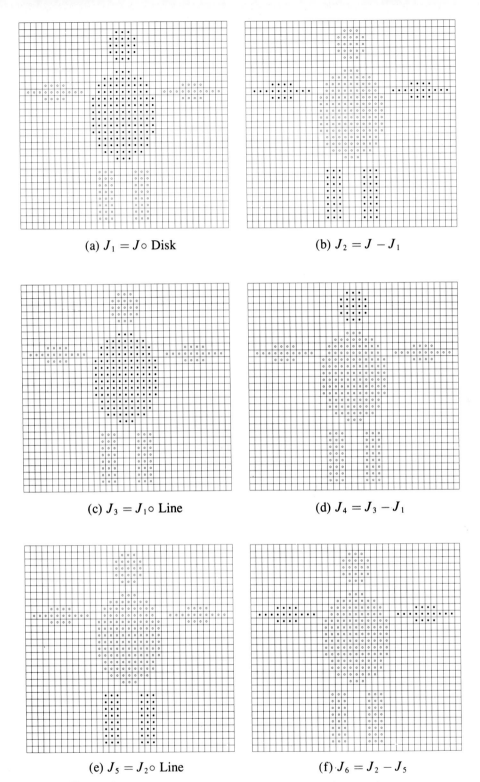

(a) $J_1 = J \circ$ Disk

(b) $J_2 = J - J_1$

(c) $J_3 = J_1 \circ$ Line

(d) $J_4 = J_3 - J_1$

(e) $J_5 = J_2 \circ$ Line

(f) $J_6 = J_2 - J_5$

Figure 5.21 Results of the opening-sequence tree decomposition operations applied to image J of Fig. 5.20(a). The o designates a point in J that is not in the illustrated set. A • designates a point in the illustrated set.

$(A \oplus K) \circ K \subseteq A \oplus K$. Now from $(A \oplus K) \subseteq (A \bullet K) \oplus K = (A \oplus K) \circ K \subseteq A \oplus K$, we can infer that $A \oplus K = (A \oplus K) \circ K$. By duality, eroded sets remain invariant under closing;

$$A \ominus K = (A \ominus K) \bullet K$$

The idempotency of the opening operation quickly follows from the opening representation theorem and the invariance of eroded sets to closing. Just note that

$$(A \circ K) \circ K = \bigcup_{y \in (A \circ K) \ominus K} K_y$$

$$= \bigcup_{y \in (A \ominus K) \bullet K} K_y$$

$$= \bigcup_{y \in A \ominus K} K_y$$

$$= A \circ K$$

By duality, closing is also idempotent.

The increasing and idempotency properties of opening and closing imply fairly directly that any set between the opening of A and A will have the same opening as A, and any set between A and the closing of A will have the same closing as A. That is, $A \circ K \subseteq B \subseteq A$ implies $B \circ K = A \circ K$, and $A \subseteq B \subseteq A \bullet K$ implies $B \bullet K = A \bullet K$.

Open sets are the smallest sets that have a given erosion. To see this, suppose that the erosions of two sets A and B are identical; $A \ominus K = B \ominus K$. Further, suppose that B purports to be a subset of the opening $A \circ K; B \subseteq A \circ K$. Then dilating each side of $A \ominus K = B \ominus K$ by K results in $A \circ K = B \circ K$. Since $B \circ K \subseteq B$ and $A \circ K = B \circ K$, we have $A \circ K \subseteq B$. But $B \subseteq A \circ K$ and $B \supseteq A \circ K$ imply $B = A \circ K$. Hence B cannot be any smaller than $A \circ K$. Similarly, closed sets are the largest sets that have a given dilation. Opening the residue of an opening must always produce an empty set: $(A - A \circ K) \circ K = \phi$. This means that we can consider the opening residue $A - A \circ K$ as consisting of all those points of A that cannot match K. Meyer (1986) calls the opening residue the *top hat transformation*.

The fact that sets dilated by a structuring element K are open under K and sets eroded by a structuring element K are closed under K has some important consequences in terms of constructing other idempotent morphological operators. Consider, for example, the operator defined by first opening with one structuring element and then closing with another. Since opening and closing are increasing, this open-close composition is, of course, increasing. But it is also idempotent. Consider

$$\left(\left[(A \circ K) \bullet L \right] \circ K \right) \bullet L = \left[\left([(A \ominus K) \oplus (K \oplus L)] \ominus (K \oplus L) \right) \right.$$

$$\left. \oplus (K \oplus L) \right] \ominus L$$

$$= \left([(A \ominus K) \oplus (K \oplus L)] \circ (K \oplus L) \right) \ominus L$$

And since a set dilated by $K \oplus L$ must be open under $K \oplus L$,

$$\left(\left[(A \circ K) \bullet L \right] \circ K \right) = \left[(A \ominus K) \oplus (K \oplus L) \right] \ominus L$$

$$= \left(\left[(A \ominus K) \oplus K \right] \oplus L \right) \ominus L$$

$$= (A \circ K) \bullet L$$

In an exactly similar manner, the close-open composition is idempotent:

$$\left(\left[(A \bullet L) \circ K \right] \bullet L \right) \circ K = (A \bullet L) \circ K$$

Opening with a structuring element such as a disk of radius r smooths the shape from the inside. The opened shape has an inside curvature less than or equal to $\frac{1}{r}$ everywhere. Closing with a disk of radius r smooths the shape from the outside. The closed shape has an outside curvature less than or equal to $\frac{1}{r}$ everywhere. An idempotent morphological sequence such as opening with disk (radius= r_i) and then closing the result with disk (radius= r_0) will generate a shape whose outside curvature is everywhere less than or equal to $\frac{1}{r_0}$ and whose inside curvature will have a high probability of being less than or equal to $\frac{1}{r_i}$ everywhere.

It is straightforward to verify that A is open under K if and only if A can be represented as the dilation of some set by K. Likewise, A is closed under K if and only if A can be represented as the erosion of some set by K.

In general, the opening of a union of two sets contains the union of the openings. Likewise, the closing of an intersection of two sets is contained in the intersection of the closing. However, unions of sets morphologically open with respect to K are morphologically open with respect to K, and intersections of sets morphologically closed with respect to K are morphologically closed with respect to K. The opening of an intersection of two sets is contained in the intersection of the openings. The closing of a union of two sets is contained in the union of the closings. Open sets that are dilated by any structuring element remain open. Closed sets that are eroded by any structuring element remain closed.

If $L \subseteq K$, it does not necessarily follow that $A \circ L \supseteq A \circ K$, which might be expected. This is illustrated in Fig. 5.22, where it can be seen that $L \subseteq K$, yet $A \circ L$ is a strict subset of $A \circ K$. However, opening with a structuring element K that can be expressed as a dilation decomposition $K = K_1 \oplus K_2$ does produce the relationship $A \circ (K_1 \oplus K_2) \subseteq A \circ K_1$. This is easily derived by using the fact that opening is antiextensive.

$$A \circ (K_1 \oplus K_2) = \left[A \ominus (K_1 \oplus K_2) \right] \oplus (K_1 \oplus K_2)$$

$$= \left\{ \left[(A \ominus K_1) \ominus K_2 \right] \oplus K_1 \right\} \oplus K_2$$

$$= \left\{ \left[(A \ominus K_1) \ominus K_2 \right] \oplus K_2 \right\} \oplus K_1$$

$$= \left\{ (A \ominus K_1) \circ K_2 \right\} \oplus K_1$$

$$\subseteq (A \ominus K_1) \oplus K_1 = A \circ K_1$$

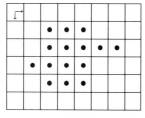

A

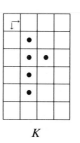

K

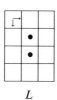

L

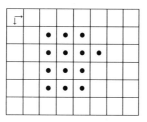

$A \circ K$

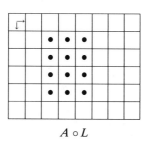

$A \circ L$

Figure 5.22 Two structuring elements K and L, where $L \subseteq K$. The set A is opened by K and by L. In this instance the opening by the large structuring element produces the larger result.

Similarly, closing with a structuring element $K_1 \oplus K_2$ must produce a superset of closing with K_1.

There is a theorem that establishes that if $K \circ L = K$, then opening with the larger structuring element does indeed result in a smaller opening, $A \circ K \subseteq A \circ L$, and also the larger closing $A \bullet K \supseteq A \bullet L$. There is also a sieve theorem that under the condition $K \circ L = K$ provides that $(A \circ K) \circ L = A \circ K$. Here opening can be thought of as sieving. Opening with the larger structuring element K corresponds to sieving with the smaller sieve. Opening with the smaller structuring element L corresponds to sieving with the larger sieve. The operation $(A \circ K) \circ L$ then corresponds to taking the material that has successfully passed through the holes of the smaller sieve and then passing it through the sieve with the larger holes. Obviously everything that passed through the smaller holes will also pass through the larger holes. Hence the second sieving removes nothing, so that $(A \circ K) \circ L = A \circ K$. It is similar with closing, $K \circ L = K$ implies $(A \bullet K) \bullet L = A \bullet K$.

Closings may be used to detect spatial clusters of points. Suppose a set A of points has spatial point clusters separated from each other by a distance greater than $2\rho_0$, and each spatial cluster C is a subset of points of A having the following partition property with distance ρ_0. For any two-celled partition $\{\Pi_1, \Pi_2\}$ of a spatial cluster C, there exist three points p_1, p_2, and $p_3 \in C$ such that:

1. The distance between each pair of points is greater than $\frac{1}{2}\rho_0$ and less than ρ_0;

2. Each cell of the partition contains at least one of the three points — that is, $\Pi_1 \cap \{p_1, p_2, p_3\} \neq \emptyset, \quad \Pi_2 \cap \{p_1, p_2, p_3\} \neq \emptyset$.

In this case a closing operation with a disk structuring element having radius $2\rho_0$ will change each spatial point cluster to a connected set. Each spatial cluster can then be identified by determining what points of A are in each connected component. This idea is illustrated in Fig. 5.23.

Openings and closings may be used to select all pixels that belong to line

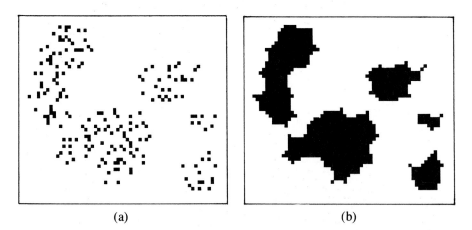

(a)	(b)

Figure 5.23 (a) A binary image with five clusters of points. Points within each cluster satisfy the partition property with distance ρ_0, and the clusters are farther from each other than $2\rho_0$ pixels. (b) The image of (a) closed by a disk with a radius just greater than $2\rho_0$.

segments in a given direction θ and that have a length greater than L and possible gaps no bigger than length K. We begin with a binary image I all of whose binary-1 pixels are participating in lines. Each line in which a 1-pixel participates has a width of at least $w, w > 1$. Since lines are thin, no 1-pixel participates in a line whose width at the pixel is greater than d_1. The two assumptions can be morphologically stated as

$$I \circ \text{disk (diameter} = w) = I$$
$$I \ominus \text{disk (diameter} = d_1) = \phi$$

To select only binary-1 pixels that participate in segments of at least length d_2 in direction θ, we can open the image I by a line segment oriented in direction θ and having length d_2.

$$I_1 = I \circ \text{line (direction} = \theta, \text{ length} = d_2)$$

Then to eliminate all gaps whose lengths are smaller than K, we can perform a closing with a line segment oriented in direction θ and having length K. Because of the raster grid discretization, the closing will not guarantee closing the gaps unless the line segments on the image have at least width 2.

$$I_2 = I_1 \bullet \text{line (direction} = \theta, \text{ length} = K)$$

Finally, to select only those line segments with lengths greater than L, we do an opening.

$$I_3 = I_2 \circ \text{line (direction} = \theta, \text{ length} = L)$$

EXAMPLE 5.1

This example describes a morphologically based algorithm for the identification of leads coming from a SMD component. The algorithm was developed by C. Archibald (1985), and the analysis we give is based on Joo and Haralick (1989).

The analysis is divided into four parts: input image, description, goal, morphological procedure, and reasoning and knowledge. The input image that the algorithm is expecting and the goal image that the algorithm is supposed to produce are described in plain English. The morphological procedure that accomplishes the task is presented in a step-by-step fashion, each step corresponding to a single meaningful primitive morphological operation. In each step i, G_i, or B_i represents the gray scale or the binary image produced, and G_0 designates the original input image.

Input Image:

- The image shown in Fig. 5.24 consists of one very dark component mounted on a medium-bright background.

- The background can have both dark and bright stripes.

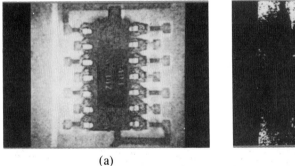

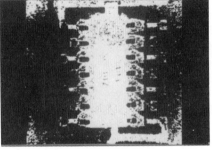

(a)   (b)

(c)   (d)

(e)   (f)

Figure 5.24 (a) G_0, (b) B_1, (c) B_2, (d) B_3, (e) G_4, (f) G_5, (g) G_6, (h) B_7, (i) B_8, (j) B_9.

- The component is rectangular shaped and located in the middle of the image. It is the largest dark object in the image. The leads are horizontally oriented in a vertical column and connected to the two vertical boundaries of the component. The body of the rectangle may contain medium-bright or bright objects that are smaller or thinner than the leads.

- The leads are very bright and small rectangular-shaped objects. The distance between a pair of leads next to each other is longer than the

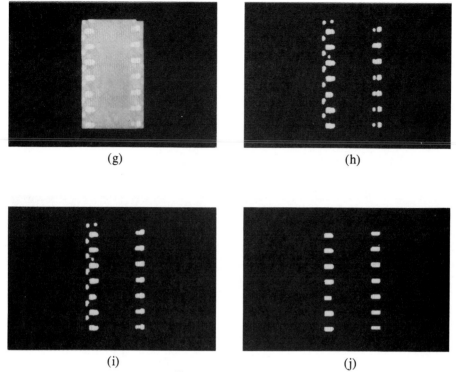

Figure 5.24 *Continued.*

height of one lead. The leads themselves may contain some small, dark areas.

Goal:

- Detect only the bright, almost-rectangular-shaped blobs with known size, the leads, which are located inside the very dark, large, rectangular-shaped component in the middle of the image. The small, dark areas that may exist inside the lead should also be detected as being a part of the lead. Thus each detected lead should be convex shaped with no holes.

Morphological Procedure:

1. $B_1 = G_0 < 200$:
   Extract the dark region (Fig. 5.24a).

2. $B_2 = B_1 \oplus \text{box}(5,5)$:
   Improve connectivity. This will fill holes caused by the medium-bright objects inside the component, but not the leads (Fig. 5.24b).

3. $B_3 = B_2 \ominus \text{box}(80,100)$:
   Erode to isolate the interior of the IC component. The component is the only blob larger than a box that is 80 pixels in column and 100 pixels in

row. An erosion with a large box removes all blobs smaller than the size of the box (Fig. 5.24c).

4. $G_4 = B_3 \oplus box(160, 90)$:
   Generate a mask that covers the component and its leads. The width of the box is bigger than that of the box used in the previous erosion (Fig. 5.24d).

5. $G_5 = G_0 \wedge G_4$:
   Extract the part of the image that contains the area of interest, the component with leads (Fig. 5.24e).

6. $G_6 = G_5 \circ rod(4)$:
   Remove small, noisy, relatively bright areas within the dark extracted area (Fig. 5.24f).

7. $B_7 = G_6 > 174$:
   Extract the bright leads (Fig. 5.24g).

8. $B_8 = B_7 \bullet box(8, 2)$:
   Improve connectivity of the detected leads (Fig. 5.24h).

9. $B_9 = B_8 \circ box(20, 3)$:
   Remove noisy blobs smaller than the leads (Fig. 5.24i).

Reasoning and Knowledge:

- We need to distinguish the bright blobs in the component from the ones in the background. Using the fact that the leads are *inside* the dark component, try to find the dark component including the leads. Use the detected component as a mask to select only the leads (steps 1 to 5).

- To distinguish the darker component from the leads, use a thresholding for absolute darkness (step 1). We can predict that the thresholding will produce an image consisting of the component with many holes because of the leads and the smaller bright objects inside the component. It could also have dark blobs in the background.

- Remove holes inside the component by a dilation operation (step 2).

- Remove the dark objects in the background by an opening operation (steps 3 and 4). These two operations should be applied in the order mentioned above.

- We need to find ony the connected convex blobs (leads) with certain size and shape (steps 6 and 9).

- A gray scale opening operation can be used to remove small, noisy peaks (step 6).

- To detect bright leads, use thresholding for absolute brightness (step 7).

- Fill in the holes inside the detected leads by a closing operation (step 8). This step also connects small but clustered pixels. Step 6 helped to prevent some of this from happening, but it does not guarantee that none of it will happen.

- Select only the leads by an opening operation by a proper structuring element that can benefit inside the leads but not inside other noisy blobs (step 9).

5.2.6 Morphological Shape Feature Extraction

There are a few ways in which morphological operations can capture essential information about the shape of a set. They involve eroding or opening the set with successive structuring elements that are related to one another by a linear ordering. The simplest among these uses a sequence of two-point structuring elements. Let $h \in R^N$, $h \neq 0$, and let the set $A \subseteq R^N$. Define the structuring elements $K(m)$ by $K(m) = \{0, mh\}$, $m = 1, \ldots, M$. The covariance function of A with respect to h is then given by

$$C(A; h)(m) = \#A \ominus K(m)$$

where $\#A$ denotes number of elements in A.

A second approach is to begin with a given structuring element K containing at least one other element in addition to the zero element. Define $K(0) = \{0\}$, $K(m) = K(m-1) \oplus K$. This determines the linear ordering of related structuring elements. Then define the interior erosion function I of the set A with respect to structuring element K by

$$I(A; K)(m) = \#A \ominus K(m)$$

A third approach is to use openings instead of erosions. In this case we define the interior opening function J of the set A with respect to the structuring element K by

$$J(A; K)(m) = \#A \circ K(m)$$

A fourth approach, which Maragos (1987) calls the *morphological pattern spectrum,* is to use the difference between the successive openings from I. The spectrum S of the set A with respect to the structuring element K is defined by

$$S(A; K)(m) = \#A \circ K(m) - \#A \circ K(m-1), \ m \geq 1$$

5.2.7 Fast Dilations and Erosions

In video rate hardware that performs morphological operations, the operation is typically performed on every pixel. So if an $L \times L$ binary image I having N binary-1 pixels is dilated by a structuring element having 2^M pixels, the total number of operations performed in a brute force manipulation is $L \times L \times 2^M$. But if the structuring element has a dilation decomposition of M two-element sets, then when the dilation is implemented by using the decomposition, the total number of operations will be $L \times L \times 2 \times M$. In this section we discuss how to determine structuring-element dilation decomposition (Zhuang and Haralick, 1986).

The structuring-element decomposition problem is given a structuring element S. Determine the smallest N and corresponding structuring elements $H_1, H_2, \ldots, H_N$ such that

$$S = H_1 \oplus H_2 \oplus \ldots \oplus H_N$$

Here we illustate the decomposition techniques for the case when each H_n can have only two elements. Without loss of generality, we may assume that one of the two elements in each H_n is the origin.

If a structuring element $H = \{0, h\}$, then

$$A \oplus H = A \cup A_h \text{ and } A \ominus H = A \cap A_{-h}$$

Dilation with H is accomplished by a shift to produce A_h followed by a union with A. Erosion with H is accomplished by a shift to produce A_{-h} followed by an intersection with A.

To compute a dilation of A with a canonical two-point decomposition $H_1 \oplus \ldots \oplus H_N$, the computation proceeds in the form

$$\left(\cdots \left[(A \oplus H_1) \oplus H_2 \right] \cdots \right) \cdots H_N$$

where each successive dilation is accomplished by taking the previous result, shifting it, and ORing the shifted result with the previous result to produce the next result. That is, if $H_n = \{0, h_n\}, n = 1, \ldots, N$,

$$B^1 = A \oplus H_1 = A \cup A_{h_1}$$

and

$$B^n = B^{n-1} \oplus H_{n-1} = B^{n-1} \cup (B^{n-1})_{h_{n-1}}, \quad n = 2, \ldots, N$$

then the desired result $A \oplus H_1 \oplus \cdots \oplus H_N = B^N$.

Similarly, to compute an erosion of A with a canonical two-point decomposition $H_1 \oplus \cdots \oplus H_N$, the computation proceeds in the form

$$\left(\cdots \left[(A \ominus H_1) \ominus H_2 \right] \cdots \right) \ominus \cdots H_N$$

where each successive erosion is accomplished by taking the previous result, shifting it, and ANDing the shifted result with the previous result to produce the next result. That is, if

$$B^1 = A \ominus H_n = A \cap A_{-h_1}$$

and

$$B^n = B^{n-1} \ominus H_{n-1} = B^{n-1} \cap (B^{n-1})_{-h_{n-1}}, \quad n = 2, \ldots, N$$

then the desired result $A \ominus (H_1 \oplus \cdots \oplus H_N) = B^N$.

The basis for understanding how to determine the decomposition

$$S = H_1 \oplus H_2 \oplus \cdots \oplus H_N$$

is to recognize that if $S = H_1 \oplus H_2 \oplus \cdots \oplus H_N$, then

$$S = S \circ H_n, \quad n = 1, \ldots, N$$

Now if $S = S \circ H_n$ and if $0 \in H_n$, then $h \in H_n$ implies that there exist a $p_1 \in S$ and a $p_2 \in S$ such that $h = p_1 - p_2$. This can be seen from the following argument. If $S = S \circ H_n$, then by the opening characterization theorem there exists a p_1 such that for every $h \in H_n$ there exists a $p_2 \in S$ such that $h + p_1 = p_2$. Since

$0 \in H_n$, $p_1 + 0 = p_2$, so that $p_1 \in S$. Hence it is certainly true that for every $h \in H$ there exist a $p_1 \in S$ and a $p_2 \in S$ such that $h = p_1 - p_2$.

Therefore the first step in determining the decomposition of S is to search among pairs of points p_1 and p_2 of S and test to see if $S = S \circ \{0, \ p_1 - p_2\}$. If a pair of such points is found, then reduce S by

$$S' = S \ominus \{0, \ p_1 - p_2\}$$

and recursively repeat the process. If no such pair of points can be found, then search among quadruples of points p_1, p_2, p_3, and p_4 of S and test to see if $S = S \circ \{0, \ p_1 - p_2, \ p_3 - p_4\}$, and so on. A dilation composition of S is then given as the dilation of each of the sets used in reducing S.

5.3   Connectivity

There is a close relation between morphology and connectivity. In this section we discuss and describe a formal approach to connectivity through the notion of the separation relation and then give the basic relations between some of the morphological operations and connectivity. Then we discuss a relationship between binary image noise cleaning and connectivity.

5.3.1 Separation Relation

We begin with definitions for some kinds of binary relations in which each component of an ordered pair belonging to the relation is a set.

Let S be a binary relation in which each component of an ordered pair belonging to S is a set. We say that:

1. S is *symmetric* if and only if $(X, Y) \in S$ implies $(Y, X) \in S$;
2. S is *exclusive* if and only if $(X, Y) \in S$ implies $X \cap Y = \phi$;
3. S is *hereditary* if and only if $(X, Y) \in S$ implies $(X', Y') \in S$ for each $X' \subseteq X$ and $Y' \subseteq Y$;
4. S is *extensive* if and only if $(\{x\}, \{y\}) \in S$ for every $x \in X$ and $y \in Y$ implies $(X, Y) \in S$.

Let S be a binary relation in which each component of an ordered pair belonging to S is a set. S is called a *separation* if and only if S is symmetric, exclusive, hereditary, and extensive. If $(A, B) \in S$, we say that A and B are *separated* or that A and B are not connected together. If $(A, B) \notin S$, we say that with respect to S, A and B are *connected* together. We now give two examples of separation relations. The first example defines a separation in terms of a metric function. The second example defines a separation in terms of a morpological dilation.

EXAMPLE 5.2

Let S be a binary relation on a metric space with distance function d. Take $S = \{(A, B) \mid d(A, B) > \theta\}$ for some $\theta > 0$, where $d(A, B) = \min_{a \in A} \min_{b \in B} d(a, b)$.

Then S is a separation. Why? Consider:

1. S is symmetric since $(A,B) \in S$ implies $d(A,B) > \theta$. And $d(A,B) > \theta$ implies $d(B,A) > \theta$, which implies $(B,A) \in S$.
2. S is exclusive since $(A,B) \in S$ implies $d(A,B) > \theta > 0$, which implies $d(a,b) > \theta$ for every $a \in A, b \in B$. Let $a \in A$ be given. Since d is a metric, $d(a,b) > \theta$ for every $b \in B$. Hence $a \notin B$. Therefore $A \cap B = \phi$.
3. S is hereditary. Let $(A,B) \in S$ and $A' \subseteq A, B' \subseteq B$. Since $(A,B) \in S$, $d(A,B) > \theta$. But $d(A,B) = \min_{\substack{a \in A \\ b \in B}} d(a,b) \leq \min_{\substack{a \in A' \\ b \in B'}} d(a,b)$.

   Thus $d(A',B') > d(A,B) > \theta$ that by definition of S implies $(A',B') \in S$.
4. S is extensive. Suppose for all $a \in A$ and $b \in B, (\{a\},\{b\}) \in S$. Then $d(a,b) > \theta$. But $d(a,b) > \theta$ for all $a \in A$ and $b \in B$ implies $d(A,B) > \theta$, so we must have $(A,B) \in S$.

■

EXAMPLE 5.3

Let D be any structuring element containing the origin. Define the binary relation S by $S = \{(A,B) \mid (A \oplus D) \cap (B \oplus D) = \phi\}$ Then S is a separation. Why? Consider:

1. S is symmetric since $(A \oplus D) \cap (B \oplus D) = (B \oplus D) \cap (A \oplus D)$.
2. S is exclusive. Suppose $(A,B) \in S$. Then $(A \oplus D) \cap (B \oplus D) = \phi$. But since $0 \in D, A \subseteq A \oplus D$ and $B \subseteq B \oplus D$. Hence $A \cap B \subseteq (A \oplus D) \cap (B \oplus D)$, so that $A \cap B = \phi$.
3. A is hereditary. Suppose $(A,B) \in S$. Let $A' \subseteq A$ and $B' \subseteq B$. Since dilation is increasing, $A' \oplus D \subseteq A \oplus D$ and $B' \oplus D \subseteq B \oplus D$. Then it follows that $(A' \oplus D) \cap (B' \oplus D) \subseteq (A \oplus D) \cap (B \oplus D) = \phi$ since $(A,B) \in S$. But this implies that $(A' \oplus D) \cap (B' \oplus D) = \phi$, which by definition of S means that $(A',B') \in S$.
4. S is extensive. Let A and B be any sets satisfying $(\{a\},\{b\}) \in S$ for every $a \in A$ and $b \in B$. Then by definition of $S, (\{a\} \oplus D) \cap (\{b\} \oplus D) = \phi$ for every $a \in A$ and $b \in B$. This implies

$$\bigcup_{a \in A} \bigcup_{b \in B} (\{a\} \oplus D) \cap (\{b\} \oplus D) = \phi$$

By the distributivity of intersections and unions,

$$\bigcup_{a \in A} \bigcup_{b \in B} (\{a\} \oplus D) \cap (\{b\} \oplus D)$$

$$= \bigcup_{a \in A} \left[(\{a\} \oplus D) \cap \bigcup_{b \in B} (\{b\} \oplus D) \right]$$

Since the dilation of a union is the union of the dilation,

$$\bigcup_{a \in A} \left[(\{a\} \oplus D) \bigcap \bigcup_{b \in B} (\{b\} \oplus D) \right] = \bigcup_{a \in A} \left[(\{a\} \oplus D) \bigcap (B \oplus D) \right]$$

Again by the distributivity of intersections and unions,

$$\bigcup_{a \in A} \left[(\{a\} \oplus D) \bigcap (B \oplus D) \right] = \left[\bigcup_{a \in A} (\{a\} \oplus D) \right] \bigcap (B \oplus D)$$

Finally, since the dilation of a union is the union of the dilation,

$$\left[\bigcup_{a \in A} (\{a\} \oplus D) \right] \bigcap (B \oplus D) = (A \oplus D) \bigcap (B \oplus D)$$

Therefore $(A \oplus D) \cap (B \oplus D) = \phi$, so that by definition of S, $(A, B) \in S$. ∎

Certain properties of hereditary and extensive binary relations are easy to establish and are needed to prove some of the assertions we make later in this section. If R is a hereditary extensive binary relation, then $(A, B) \in R$ and $(C, D) \in R$ implies $(A \cup C, B \cap D) \in R$ and $(A \cap C, B \cup D) \in R$. Since separation is both hereditary and extensive, if S is a separation and if A and B are separated and C and D are separated, then $A \cup C$ is separated from $B \cap D$ and $A \cap C$ is separated from $B \cup D$.

Let S be a separation. A set A is called *not connected* or *disconnected* with respect to the separation S if and only if there exists a two-celled partition $\pi = \{\pi_1, \pi_2\}$ of A, $\pi_1 \neq \phi$ and $\pi_2 \neq \phi$ such that $(\pi_1, \pi_2) \in S$. A set A is called *connected* with respect to the separation S if and only if every two-celled partition $\pi = \{\pi_1, \pi_2\}$ of A satisfying $\pi_1 \neq \phi$ and $\pi_2 \neq \phi$ also satisfies $(\pi_1, \pi_2) \notin S$. A point x is *connected to a point y* in A if and only if there exists some connected subset $B \subseteq A$ such that $x, y \in B$. Point connectedness is obviously a symmetric and reflexive relation.

From these definitions it follows that A is connected with respect to a separation S if and only if for every $x, y \in A$, x is connected to y in A. To see this, suppose A is connected. Let $x, y \in A$. Then since A is connected and $x, y \in A$, by definition of point connectivity, x is connected to y in A.

Now suppose for every $x, y \in A$, x is connected to y in A. Suppose A is not connected. Then there exists a partition $\pi = \{\pi_1, \pi_2\}$ of A satisfying $\pi_1 \neq \phi$, $\pi_2 \neq \phi$ and $(\pi_1, \pi_2) \in S$. Since $\pi_1 \neq \phi$ and $\pi_2 \neq \phi$, there exist a $p \in \pi_1$ and a $q \in \pi_2$. But $p, q \in A$ implies p is connected to q in A. Hence there exists $B \subseteq A$ such that $p, q \in B$ and B is connected. But $\pi_1 \cap B \neq \phi$ since $p \in \pi_1 \cap B$, and $\pi_2 \cap B \neq \phi$ since $q \in \pi_2 \cap B$. Since B is connected, $(\pi_1 \cap B, \pi_2 \cap B) \notin S$. Now $(\pi_1, \pi_2) \in S$ and S being a separation implies $(\pi_1 \cap B, \pi_2 \cap B) \in S$ since separations are hereditary. This establishes a contradiction to the supposition that A is not connected. Therefore A is connected.

The definitions for connectivity and separation lead to a variety of properties that are all part of what we expect connectivity to mean. If A and B are two connected sets that are connected together with respect to a separation S, then $A \cup B$ is also connected with respect to S. If A and B are two connected sets with respect to a separation S, then $A \cup B$ disconnected implies that A and B are separated, that is, $(A, B) \in S$. If A is a connected set and B is a connected set with respect to a separation S, then $A \cap B \neq \phi$ implies $A \cup B$ is connected with respect to S. If A, B, and C are nonempty connected sets, then A not separated from B and B not separated from C implies $A \cup B \cup C$ is connected. If A and B are separated and D is connected, then $D \subseteq A \cup B$ implies $D \subseteq A$ or $D \subseteq B$. Finally, connectivity is transitive: If a point x is connected to y in A and y is connected to z in A, then x is connected to z in A. Since a reflexive, symmetric, transitive relation is an equivalence relation, and since connectivity is reflexive, symmetric, and transitive, connectivity induces a partition on any set. The cells of the partition are the maximal connected subsets (the connected components) of the given set.

The essential relationships between connectivity and morphological operations are given in the following theorem.

Theorem 5.2: (1.) If A and B are each connected, then the dilation $A \oplus B$ is connected; and (2.) if A is separated from B and the structuring element K is connected, then the erosion of the union of A and B by K is the union of the erosions, $(A \cup B) \ominus K = (A \ominus K) \cup (B \ominus K)$.

Proof:

1. Let $x, y \in A \oplus B$. Then there exist $x_a, y_a \in A$ and $x_b, y_b \in B$ such that $x = x_a + x_b$ and $y = y_a + y_b$. Since B is connected, any translate of B is connected. Hence B_{x_a} is connected. Now $x = x_a + x_b \in B_{x_a}$ and $x_a + y_b \in B_{x_a}$, since x_b and y_b belong to B. Then x is connected to $x_a + y_b$ in $A \oplus B$, since $B_{x_a} \subseteq A \oplus B$ is connected. Since A is connected, the translate A_{y_b} is connected. But $x_a + y_b \in A_{y_b}$ and $y = y_a + y_b \in A_{y_b}$, since x_a and y_a belong to A. Then $x_a + y_b$ is connected to y in $A \oplus B$, since $A_{y_b} \subseteq A \oplus B$ is connected. Finally, x is connected to $x_a + y_b$ in $A \oplus B$, and $x_a + y_b$ connected to y in $A \oplus B$ implies x is connected to y in $A \oplus B$.

2. We already have $(A \cup B) \ominus K \supseteq (A \ominus K) \cup (B \ominus K)$, which holds for all A, B, and K. So we just need to establish that $(A \cup B) \ominus K \subseteq (A \ominus K) \cup (B \ominus K)$. Let $x \in (A \cup B) \ominus K$. Then $K_x \subseteq A \cup B$. A separated from B and K_x and K_x connected implies $K_x \subseteq A$ or $K_x \subseteq B$. Hence $x \in (A \ominus K) \cup (B \ominus K)$.

Corollary 5.2: If A is separated from B and K is connected, then the opening of the union of A and B is the union of the openings, $(A \cup B) \circ K = (A \circ K) \cup (B \circ K)$.

Proof:

$$
\begin{aligned}
(A \cup B) \circ K &= \Big((A \cup B) \ominus K\Big) \oplus K \\
&= \Big((A \ominus K) \cup (B \ominus K)\Big) \oplus K \\
&= \Big((A \ominus K) \oplus K\Big) \cup \Big((B \ominus K) \oplus K\Big) \\
&= (A \circ K) \cup (B \circ K)
\end{aligned}
$$

5.3.2 Morphological Noise Cleaning and Connectivity

The concept of separation is an important one when it comes to understanding how images that have been perturbed by noise can be morphologically filtered to remove some of the noise. We illustrate this fact in a situation of dropout noise. Suppose that random noise N removes points from an ideal image A to produce the observed image B. That is, $B = A \cap N^c = A - N$. When the noise N is separated from A^c, it may be possible to recover the ideal A, without error, from the observed B.

Before stating the conditions under which this is possible, let us first understand what it means for N to be separated from A^c. When N is separated from A^c, no point of N is connected to A^c. Hence all the points of N must be interior to A. The noise N produces one or moreholes in A, none of which perturbs the boundary of A.

The conditions required under which A can be recovered without error from B require that A be closed under a symmetric structuring element K that can annihilate the noise N. That is, $A \bullet K = A$, $N \circ K = \phi$, and $K = \check{K}$. In this case the morphological noise-removal algorithm is simple. Estimate A by $B \bullet K$. Under all the above conditions, $A = B \bullet K$.

The proof that $(A - N) \bullet K = A$ is direct. Notice that $[(A - N) \bullet K]^c = (A^c \cup N) \circ K$. Since K is connected and N is separated from A^c, then $(A^c \cup N) \circ K = (A^c \circ K) \cup (N \circ K)$. But $N \circ K = \phi$. Hence $(A^c \cup N) \circ K = A^c \circ K$. Complementing both sides of this equality, $[(A^c \cup N) \circ K]^c = (A^c \circ K)^c$. By the duality between opening and closing and the fact that K is symmetric, $(A^c \circ K)^c = A \bullet K$. Since A is closed under K, $A \bullet K = A$. Therefore $(A - N) \bullet K = A$.

5.3.3 Openings, Holes, and Connectivity

Openings can create holes in a connected set that is being opened. To see this, consider a set $A = \{1,2,3,4,5\}$ being opened by a structuring element $K = \{-2,2\}$. Then $A \circ K = \{1,5\}$. In terms of two-dimensional shapes, consider opening a disk A by an annulus K whose outside diameter is the diameter of A. In this case $A \circ K = K$. The disk A and the annulus K are obviously connected, and the opening that is equal to K has a hole that is the hole of the annulus.

Likewise, it is possible for a closing to create additional connected components. To see this, let two points be connected if their absolute difference is no greater than 1. Consider a set $A = \{-2, -1, 0, 1, 2, 8, 9, 10, 11, 12\}$ that has two connected components being closed by a set $K = \{-3, 3\}$. Then by direct calculation $A \bullet K = (A \oplus K) \ominus K = \{-2, -1, 0, 1, 2, 4, 5, 6, 8, 9, 10, 11, 12\}$. Notice that a new connected component $\{4, 5, 6\}$ is part of the closing.

Opening a connected set having no holes with a connected structuring element having no holes can produce a connected set with holes. Consider the set shown in Fig. 5.25. The boundary of the shape can be thought of as the perimeter of three disks centered at the vertices of an equilateral triangle. The disks have the same radius equal to any length between 50% and 55% of the side length of the equilateral triangle. The union of three such disks has a hole in the center. The shape of Fig. 5.25, however, has this hole filled. Now if the shape is opened by a disk structuring element whose radius is also between 50% and 55% of the length of the triangle side, the result is, as shown, a connected set with a hole. By the duality between opening and closing, it is apparent that closing can introduce new connected components.

5.3.4 Conditional Dilation

Sometimes it is desirable to select those connected components of an image I that have a nonempty area after some morphological processing that might have been erosion, for example. The morphological operation of conditional dilation facilitates the selection of the entire component.

Let D be a small disk structuring element. The conditional dilation of an image J by D with respect to an image I is denoted by $J \oplus |_I D$ and is defined in an iterative manner.

Let $J_0 = J$ and $J_n = (J_{n-1} \oplus D) \cap I$. The set D used in conditional dilation relates to the meaning of separation described in Example 5.3. Then the conditional dilation of J by D with respect to I is defined by $J \oplus |_I D = \bigcup_{m=0}^{\infty} J_m$. For discretized

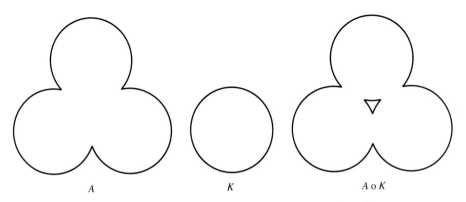

A K $A \circ K$

Figure 5.25 Introduction of holes by an opening. The connected set A has no holes. After being opened by a disk structuring element K, the opened set has a hole.

sets arising from digital images, this definition reduces to $J \oplus |_I D = J_m$, where the index m is the smallest index satisfying $J_m = J_{m-1}$.

To illustrate this operation, consider parts (a) and (b) of Fig. 5.26, which show a set A and a structuring element K. Figure 5.26(c) shows the image, which is A opened by K. Notice that some components of A have been eliminated, and those that remain have been reduced by the opening. To regain the entirety of the two selected components, a conditional dilation is performed with a disk structuring element (Fig. 5.26d).

Conditional dilation is used in a variety of applications at machine vision companies such as Applied Intelligent Systems, Inc., which has provided this idea for noise removal in a thresholded image. The image J arises from thresholding a gray scale image with a high conservative threshold. This guarantees that the pixels that are binary-1 are almost certainly part of an object of interest. Now a low false-alarm rate is concomitant with a high misdetection rate, so there are many pixels that are part of an object of interest and are not labeled binary-1 in J.

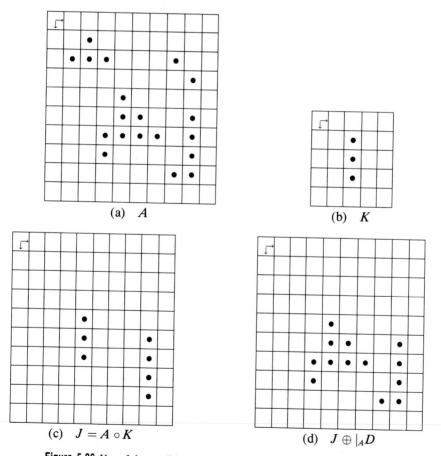

(a) A

(b) K

(c) $J = A \circ K$

(d) $J \oplus |_A D$

Figure 5.26 Use of the conditional dilation to select components having a particular property.

The image I arises from thresholding the gray scale image with a lower threshold. This creates a binary image in which almost all the pixels that are part of objects of interest are labeled binary-1. Since the misdetection rate is low, the false-alarm rate will be high. The image I will have many binary-1 pixels that are not part of any object of interest.

Since objects are usually spatially simple and connected compared to noise, conditionally dilating J with respect to I can fill out the incompleteness of J to the bounds allowed by I and not pick up in the conditionally dilated image $J \oplus |_I D$ any of the noise in I that is not connected to a binary-1 pixel in J.

5.4   Generalized Openings and Closings

Many of the properties of morphological openings and closings arise from the fact that morphological openings are increasing, antiextensive, and idempotent, and morphological closings are increasing, extensive, and idempotent. In this section we introduce the concept of *generalized opening,* which is any operation that has the increasing, antiextensive, and idempotent properties. The *generalized closing* is any operation that has increasing, extensive, and idempotent properties.

We can see fairly directly that unions of generalized openings are generalized openings. Let γ_1 and γ_2 be generalized openings. For any set A, define γ by $\gamma(A) = \gamma_1(A) \cup \gamma_2(A)$. Let $A \subseteq B$. Then

$$\gamma(A) = \gamma_1(A) \cup \gamma_2(A)$$

Since γ_1 and γ_2 are increasing, $\gamma_1(A) \subseteq \gamma_1(B)$ and $\gamma_2(A) \subseteq \gamma_2(B)$. Thus

$$\gamma(A) \subseteq \gamma_1(B) \cup \gamma_2(B) = \gamma(B)$$

so that γ is increasing. From the antiextensivity of γ_1 and γ_2, it follows that γ is also antiextensive.

$$\gamma(A) = \gamma_1(A) \cup \gamma_2(A) \subseteq A \cup A = A$$

Finally, γ is idempotent. To see this, notice that

$$\gamma[\gamma(A)] = \gamma[\gamma_1(A) \cup \gamma_2(A)]$$
$$= \gamma_1[\gamma_1(A) \cup \gamma_2(A)] \cup \gamma_2[\gamma_1(A) \cup \gamma_2(A)]$$

Since

$$\gamma_1(A) \subseteq \gamma_1(A) \cup \gamma_2(A)$$

then

$$\gamma_1[\gamma_1(A)] \subseteq \gamma_1(A) \cup \gamma_2(A)$$

Hence

$$\gamma[\gamma(A)] \supseteq \gamma_1[\gamma_1(A)] \cup \gamma_2[\gamma_2(A)] = \gamma_1(A) \cup \gamma_2(A) = \gamma(A)$$

Also, since γ is antiextensive, $\gamma[\gamma(A)] \subseteq \gamma(A)$. Then $\gamma[\gamma(A)] \supseteq \gamma(A)$ and $\gamma[\gamma(A)] \subseteq \gamma(A)$ imply $\gamma[\gamma(A)] = \gamma(A)$.

There are examples of generalized openings and closings that are not constructed from morphological openings and closings. The operator $\gamma(A) = (A \oplus K) \cap A$ for any symmetric K is a generalized opening. Since $A \oplus K = \{x \mid \check{K}_x \cap A \neq \phi\}$ and $K = \check{K}$, the operator $\gamma(A)$ selects all those points x of A such that K_x has a near-empty intersection with A. That γ is increasing and antiextensive is direct. To see that γ is idempotent, consider

$$\gamma[\gamma(A)] = \{[(A \oplus K) \cap A] \oplus K\} \cap A$$

$$= \left\{ \left[\left(\bigcup_{k' \in K} A_{k'} \right) \cap A \right] \oplus K \right\} \cap A$$

$$= \left\{ \left[\bigcup_{k' \in K} (A_{k'} \cap A) \right] \oplus K \right\} \cap A$$

$$= \left\{ \bigcup_{k \in K} \bigcup_{k' \in K} (A_{k'} \cap A)_k \right\} \cap A$$

$$= \left\{ \bigcup_{k \in K} \bigcup_{k' \in K} (A_{k'+k} \cap A_k) \right\} \cap A$$

Since $K = \check{K}$, for every $k \in K$ there exists a $k' \in K$ such that $k' + k = 0$. Hence

$$\bigcup_{k \in K} \bigcup_{k' \in K} (A_{k'+k} \cap A_k) \supseteq \bigcup_{k \in K} (A \cap A_k)$$

Therefore,

$$\gamma[\gamma(A)] \supseteq \left\{ \bigcup_{k \in K} (A \cap A_k) \right\} \cap A = \bigcup_{k \in K} (A \cap A_k) = \gamma(A)$$

Finally, since γ is antiextensive, $\gamma[\gamma(A)] \subseteq \gamma(A)$, which with $\gamma[\gamma(A)] \supseteq \gamma(A)$ implies $\gamma[\gamma(A)] = \gamma(A)$.

Corresponding to any generalized opening γ there is a corresponding generalized closing ϕ defined by

$$\phi(A) = \left[\check{\gamma}(\check{A}^c) \right]^c$$

The closing ϕ so defined is increasing, extensive, and idempotent. To see the increasing property, suppose $A \subseteq B$. Then $A^c \supseteq B^c$, and since γ is increasing, $\gamma(\check{A}^c) \supseteq \gamma(\check{B}^c)$. Hence $\phi(A) = \check{\gamma}(\check{A}^c)^c \subseteq \check{\gamma}(\check{B}^c)^c = \phi(B)$. Because γ is antiextensive, ϕ is extensive. That is, for any set A^c, $\gamma(\check{A}^c) \subseteq \check{A}^c$. Hence $\gamma(\check{A}^c)^c \supseteq (\check{A}^c)^c = \check{A}$. Therefore $\phi(A) = \check{\gamma}(\check{A}^c)^c \supseteq [(\check{A})]\check{} = A$. Finally, ϕ is idempotent because γ is idempotent.

$$\phi[\phi(A)] = \phi\left[\check{\gamma}(\check{A}^c)^c \right]$$

$$= \left(\check{\gamma} \left[\check{\gamma}(\check{A}^c)^c \right]^c \right)^c$$

$$= (\check{\gamma}[\gamma(\check{A}^c)])^c$$

$$= [(\gamma[\gamma(\check{A}^c)])^c]\check{}$$

$$= \check{\gamma}(\check{A}^c)^c = \phi(A)$$

For example, corresponding to the generalized opening $\gamma(A) = (A \oplus K) \cap A$, where $K = \check{K}$, there is a generalized closing defined by

$$
\begin{aligned}
\phi(A) &= \left[\check{\gamma}(\check{A}^c)\right]^c \\
&= \left(\left[(\check{A}^c \oplus K) \cap \check{A}^c\right]\check{\,}\right)^c \\
&= \left[(\check{A}^c \oplus K)^c \cup \check{A}\right]\check{\,} \\
&= \left[(\check{A} \ominus \check{K}) \cup \check{A}\right]\check{\,} \\
&= (A \ominus K) \cup A
\end{aligned}
$$

As unions of generalized openings are generalized openings, intersections of generalized closings are generalized closings.

5.5   Gray Scale Morphology

The binary morphological operations of dilation, erosion, opening, and closing are all naturally extended to gray scale imagery by the use of a min or max operation (Sternberg, 1982, 1983, 1985, 1986; Haralick, Sternberg, and Zhuang, 1986, 1987; Dougherty and Giardina, 1988).

We will develop the extension in the following way. First we introduce the concept of the top surface of a set and the related concept of the umbra of a surface. Then we define gray scale dilation as the surface of the dilation of the umbras. From this definition we proceed to the representation that indicates that gray scale dilation can be computed in terms of a maximum operation and a set of addition operations. A similar plan is followed for erosion, which can be evaluated in terms of a minimum operation and a set of subtraction operations.

Of course, having a definition and a means of evaluating the defined operations does not imply that the properties of gray scale dilation and erosion are the same as binary dilation and erosion. To establish that the relationships are identical, we explore some of the relationships between the umbra and surface operations. Our explanation shows that umbra and surface operations are in one direction inverses of each other. Then we illustrate how the umbra operation is a homomorphism from the gray scale morphology to the binary morphology. Once we have the homomorphism in hand, all the interesting relationships follow by appropriately unwrapping and wrapping the involved sets or functions.

5.5.1 Gray Scale Dilation and Erosion

We begin with the concepts of the surface of a set and the umbra of a surface. Suppose a set A in Euclidean N-space is given. We adopt the convention that the first $(N - 1)$ coordinates of the N-tuples of A constitute the spatial domain of A, and the Nth coordinate is for the surface. For ordinary gray scale imagery, $N = 3$. The *top* or *top surface* of A is a function defined on the projection of A onto its first $(N - 1)$ coordinates. For each $(N - 1)$-tuple x, the top surface of A at x is the highest value y such that the N-tuple $(x, y) \in A$, as shown in Fig. 5.27. If

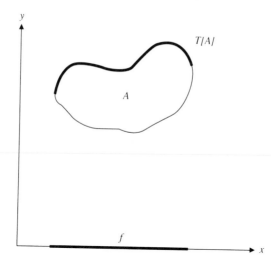

Figure 5.27 Concept of top or top surface of a set.

the space we work in is Euclidean, we can express this relationship by using the concept of supremum. If the space is discrete, we use the more familiar concept of maximum. Since we have suppressed the underlying space in what follows, we use maximum throughout. The careful reader will want to translate maximum to supremum under the appropriate circumstances.

Let $A \subseteq E^N$ and $F = \{x \in E^{N-1} \mid \text{for some } y \in E, (x, y) \in A\}$. The *top* or *top surface* of A, denoted by $T[A] : F \rightarrow E$, is defined by

$$T[A](x) = \max \{y \mid (x, y) \in A\}$$

A set $A \subseteq E^{N-1} \times E$ is an *umbra* if and only if $(x,y) \in A$ implies that $(x,z) \in A$ for every $z \leq y$.

For any function f defined on some subset F of Euclidean $(N-1)$-space, the umbra of f is a set consisting of the surface f and everything below the surface.

Let $F \subseteq E^{N-1}$ and $f : F \rightarrow E$. The *umbra* of f, denoted by $U[f]$, $U[f] \subseteq F \times E$, is defined by

$$U[f] = \{(x, y) \in F \times E \mid y \leq f(x)\}$$

Obviously the umbra of f is an umbra.

Figure 5.28 illustrates a discretized one-dimensional function f defined as a domain consisting of seven successive column positions and a finite portion of its umbra that lies on or below the function f. The actual umbra has infinite extent below f. Note that because the gray scale morphology so closely involves functions defined on the real line or plane, our example illustrations use the ordinary (x, y) coordinate frame instead of the row-column coordinate frame employed in the examples of the binary morphology.

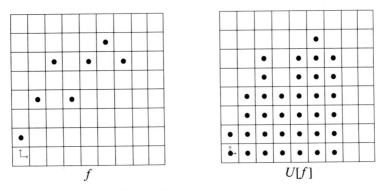

Figure 5.28 A function and its umbra.

Having defined the operations of taking a top surface of a set and the umbra of a surface, we can define gray scale dilation. The gray scale dilation of two functions is defined as the surface of the dilation of their umbras.

Let F, $K \subseteq E^{N-1}$ and let $f : F \rightarrow E$ and $k : K \rightarrow E$. The dilation of f by k is denoted by $f \oplus k$, $f \oplus k : F \oplus K \rightarrow E$, and is defined by

$$f \oplus k = T \{U[f] \oplus U[k]\}$$

Figure 5.29 illustrates a second discretized one-dimensional function k defined on a domain consisting of three successive column positions and a finite portion of its umbra that lies on or below the function k. In Fig. 5.30 the dilation of the umbra of f (from the previous example) by the umbra of k is shown, as well as the surface of the dilation of the umbras of f and k.

The definition of gray scale dilation tells us conceptually how to compute the gray scale dilation, but this is not a reasonable way to compute it in hardware. The following theorem establishes that gray scale dilation can be accomplished by taking the maximum of a set of sums. Hence gray scale dilation has the same complexity as convolution. However, instead of doing the summation of products as in convolution, we do a maximum of sums.

Let $f : F \rightarrow E$ and $k : K \rightarrow E$. Then $f \oplus k : F \oplus K \rightarrow E$ can be computed by using

$$(f \oplus k)(x) = \max \{f(x - z) + k(z) \mid z \in K, x - z \in F\}$$

These calculations for a sample f are shown in Fig. 5.31.

$$k \qquad\qquad U[k]$$

Figure 5.29 A small structuring element k and its umbra $U[k]$.

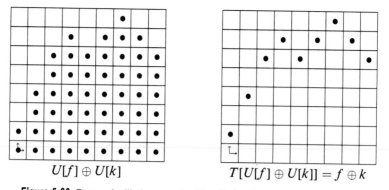

$$U[f] \oplus U[k] \qquad\qquad T[U[f] \oplus U[k]] = f \oplus k$$

Figure 5.30 Gray scale dilation conceived by dilating the umbras and then taking the gray scale dilation to be the resulting top surface.

	K		
y	-1	0	1
$k(y)$	-36	0	36

	F				
x	4	5	6	7	8
$f(x)$	19	23	9	29	-12

y	1	0	-1
$f(3-y)$	—	—	19
$k(y)$	36	0	-36
$f(3-y)+k(y)$	—	—	-17
$(f \oplus k)(3) = \max\limits_{\substack{y \in K \\ 3-y \in F}} f(3-y)+k(y)$			-17

y	1	0	-1
$f(4-y)$	—	19	23
$k(y)$	36	0	-36
$f(4-y)+k(y)$	—	19	-13
$(f \oplus k)(4) = \max\limits_{\substack{y \in K \\ 4-y \in F}} f(4-y)+k(y)$			19

y	1	0	-1
$f(5-y)$	19	23	9
$k(y)$	36	0	-36
$f(5-y)+k(y)$	55	23	-25
$(f \oplus k)(5) = \max\limits_{\substack{y \in K \\ 5-y \in F}} f(5-y)+k(y)$			55

Figure 5.31 Calculations for a gray scale dilation.

y	1	0	-1
$f(6-y)$	23	9	29
$k(y)$	36	0	-36
$f(6-y)+k(y)$	59	9	-7
$(f \oplus k)(6) = \max_{\substack{y \in K \\ 6-y \in F}} f(6-y)+k(y)$			59

y	1	0	-1
$f(7-y)$	9	29	-12
$k(y)$	36	0	-36
$f(7-y)+k(y)$	45	29	-48
$(f \oplus k)(7) = \max_{\substack{y \in K \\ 7-y \in F}} f(7-y)+k(y)$			45

y	1	0	-1
$f(8-y)$	29	-12	—
$k(y)$	36	0	-36
$f(8-y)+k(y)$	65	-12	—
$(f \oplus k)(8) = \max_{\substack{y \in K \\ 8-y \in F}} f(8-y)+k(y)$			65

y	1	0	-1
$f(9-y)$	-12	—	—
$k(y)$	36	0	-36
$f(9-y)+k(y)$	24	—	—
$(f \oplus k)(9) = \max_{\substack{y \in K \\ 9-y \in F}} f(9-y)+k(y)$			24

x	3	4	5	6	7	8	9
$f(x)$	—	19	23	9	29	-12	—
$(f \oplus k)(x)$	-17	19	55	59	45	-65	24

Figure 5.31 *Continued.*

The definition of gray scale erosion is similar to the definition of gray scale dilation. The gray scale erosion of one function by another is the surface of the binary erosions of the umbra of one by the umbra of the other.

Let $F \subseteq E^{N-1}$ and $K \subseteq E^{N-1}$. Let $f : F \rightarrow E$ and $k : K \rightarrow E$. The erosion of f by k is denoted by $f \ominus k$, $f \ominus k : F \ominus K \rightarrow E$, and is defined by $f \ominus k = T \{U[f] \ominus U[k]\}$.

Figure 5.32 uses the same functions f and k of the previous example to show the erosion of f by k by taking the surface of the erosion of the umbra of f by the umbra of k.

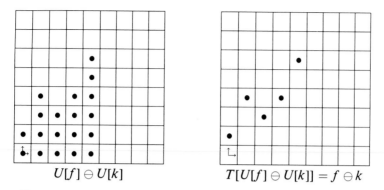

$$U[f] \ominus U[k] \qquad\qquad T[U[f] \ominus U[k]] = f \ominus k$$

Figure 5.32 Gray scale erosion conceived by eroding the umbra of f by the umbra of k and then taking the gray scale erosion to be the resulting top.

Computing a gray scale erosion is accomplished not by performing the operation indicated in its definition but by taking the minimum of a set of differences. Hence its complexity is the same as that of dilation. Its form is like correlation with the summation of correlation replaced by the minimum operation and the product of correlation replaced by the subtraction operation.

Let $f : F \to E$ and $k : K \to E$. Then $f \ominus k : F \ominus K \to E$ can be computed by using

$$(f \ominus k)(x) = \min_{z \in K}\{f(x + z) - k(z)\}$$

Figure 5.33 illustrates these calculations for a sample f. Figure 5.34 illustrates an example of gray scale dilation and erosion.

5.5.2 Umbra Homomorphism Theorems

The basic relationship between surface and umbra operations is that they are, in a certain sense, inverses of each other. More precisely, the surface operation will always undo the umbra operation. That is, the surface operation is a left inverse of the umbra operation as given: $T\{U[f]\} = f$.

The umbra operation, however, is not an inverse of the surface operation. Without any constraints on the set A, the strongest statement that can be made is that the umbra of the surface of A contains A (Fig. 5.35). When the set A is an umbra, then the umbra of the surface of A is itself A. In this case the umbra operation is an inverse of the surface operation.

Having established that the surface operation is always an inverse of the umbra operation and that the umbra operation is the inverse of the surface operation when the set being operated on is itself an umbra, we next need to note that the dilation of one umbra by another is an umbra and that the erosion of one umbra by another is also an umbra.

Now we are ready for the umbra homomorphism theorem, which states that the operation of taking an umbra is a homomorphism from the gray scale morphology to the binary morphology.

y	-1	0	1
$k(y)$	-36	0	36

x	3	4	5	6	7	8	9
$f(x)$	-12	31	55	59	45	7	-48

y	-1	0	1
$f(4+y)$	-12	31	55
$k(y)$	-36	0	36
$f(4+y)-k(y)$	24	31	19
$(f \ominus k)(4) = \min\limits_{y \in K} f(4+y) - k(y)$			19

y	-1	0	1
$f(5+y)$	31	55	59
$k(y)$	-36	0	36
$f(5+y)-k(y)$	67	55	23
$(f \ominus k)(5) = \min\limits_{y \in K} f(5+y) - k(y)$			23

y	-1	0	1
$f(6+y)$	55	59	45
$k(y)$	-36	0	36
$f(6+y)-k(y)$	91	59	9
$(f \ominus k)(6) = \min\limits_{y \in K} f(6+y) - k(y)$			9

y	-1	0	1
$f(7+y)$	59	45	7
$k(y)$	-36	0	36
$f(7+y)-k(y)$	95	45	-29
$(f \ominus k)(7) = \min\limits_{y \in K} f(7+y) - k(y)$			-29

y	-1	0	1
$f(8+y)$	45	7	-48
$k(y)$	-36	0	36
$f(8+y)-k(y)$	81	7	-84
$(f \ominus k)(8) = \min\limits_{y \in K} f(8+y) - k(y)$			-84

x	3	4	5	6	7	8	9
$f(x)$	-12	31	55	59	45	7	-48
$(f \ominus k)(x)$	—	19	23	9	-29	-84	—

Figure 5.33 Calculations for a gray scale erosion.

(a)

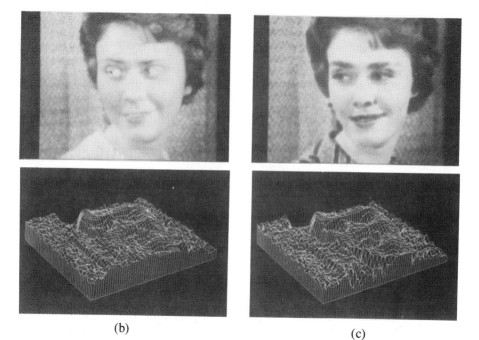

(b)   (c)

Figure 5.34 (a) A woman's face in an image form and in a perspective projection surface plot form. This image is morphologically processed with a paraboloid structuring element given by $6(8 - r^2 - c^2)$, $-2 \le r \le 2$, $-2 \le c \le 2$. (b) Erosion of the woman's face in image form and perspective projection surface plot form. (c) Dilation of her face in image form and perspective projection surface plot form.

Theorem 5.3: Umbra Homomorphism Theorem

Let F, $K \subseteq E^{N-1}$ and let $f : F \to E$ and $k : K \to E$. Then

1. $U[f \oplus k] = U[f] \oplus U[k]$
2. $U[f \ominus k] = U[f] \ominus U[k]$

Proof:

1. $f \oplus k = T\{U[f] \oplus U[k]\}$ so that $U[f \oplus k] = U[T\{U[f] \oplus U[k]\}]$.
   But $U[f] \oplus U[k]$ is an umbra, and for sets that are umbras, the umbra

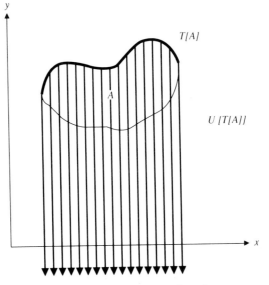

Figure 5.35 Umbra of the top surface of a set.

operation undoes the surface operation. Hence

$$U[f \oplus k] = U\big[T\{U[f] \oplus U[k]\}\big] = U[f] \oplus U[k]$$

2. $f \ominus k = T\{U[f] \ominus U[k]\}$ so that $U[f \ominus k] = U\big[T\{U[f] \ominus U[k]\}\big]$. But $U[f] \ominus U[k]$ is an umbra, and for sets that are umbras, the umbra operation undoes the surface operation. Hence

$$U[f \ominus k] = U\big[T\{U[f] \ominus U[k]\}\big] = U[f] \ominus U[k]$$

The umbra homomorphism property is used to prove relationships by first wrapping the relationship (reexpressing it in terms of umbra and top surface operations), then transforming it through the umbra homomorphism property, and finally unwrapping it by using the definitions of gray scale dilation and erosion. To illustrate this method, we state and prove the commutivity and associativity of gray scale dilation and the chain rule for gray scale erosion.

Proposition 5.1: $f \oplus k = k \oplus f$

Proof:

By definition of gray scale dilation,

$$f \oplus k = T\{U[f] \oplus U[k]\}$$

by the commutivity of binary dilation,

$$= T\{U[k] \oplus U[f]\}$$

and by definition of gray scale dilation,

$$= k \oplus f$$

Proposition 5.2: $k_1 \oplus (k_2 \oplus k_3) = (k_1 \oplus k_2) \oplus k_3$

Proof:

By definition of gray scale dilation,

$$k_1 \oplus (k_2 \oplus k_3) = T \{U[k_1] \oplus U[k_2 \oplus k_3]\}$$

by the umbra homomorphism theorem,

$$= T \{U[k_1] \oplus (U[k_2] \oplus U[k_3])\}$$

by the associativity of binary dilation,

$$= T \{(U[k_1] \oplus U[k_2]) \; U[k_3]\}$$

by the umbra homomorphism theorem for dilation,

$$= T \{U[k_1 \oplus k_2] \oplus U[k_3]\}$$

and by definition of gray scale dilation,

$$= (k_1 \oplus k_2) \oplus k_3$$

Proposition 5.3: $(f \ominus k_1) \ominus k_2 = f \ominus (k_1 \oplus k_2)$

Proof:

By definition of gray scale erosion,

$$(f \ominus k_1) \ominus k_2 = T \{U[f \ominus k_1] \ominus U[k_2]\}$$

by the umbra homomorphism theorem for erosion,

$$= T \{(U[f] \ominus U[k_1]) \ominus U[k_2]\}$$

by the iterative law for erosion,

$$= T \{U[f] \ominus (U[k_1] \oplus U[k_2])\}$$

by the umbra homomorphism theorem for dilation,

$$= T \{U[f] \ominus U[k_1 \oplus k_2]\}$$

and by definition of gray scale dilation,

$$= f \ominus (k_1 \oplus k_2)$$

There is a duality relationship between gray scale dilation and erosion just as there is a duality relation between binary dilation and erosion. For any function $k : K \rightarrow E$, define the reflection of k by $\check{k} : \check{K} \rightarrow E$, where $\check{k}(x) = k(-x)$. Then for any $x \in (F \ominus \check{K}) \cap (F \oplus K)$

$$-(f \oplus k)(x) = - \max_{\substack{z \in K \\ x-z \in F}} [f(x-z) + k(z)]$$

$$= \min_{\substack{z \in K \\ x-z \in F}} [-f(x-z) - k(z)]$$

$$= \min\{-f(x+z) - \check{k}(z) | z \in \check{K}, x+z \in F\}$$

$$= \min\{-f(x+z) - \check{k}(z) | z \in \check{K}\}$$

$$= \left[(-f) \ominus \check{k}\right](x)$$

5.5.3 Gray Scale Opening and Closing

Gray scale opening and closing are defined in an analogous way to opening and closing in binary morphology, and they have similar properties.

Let $f : F \to E$ and $k : K \to E$. The gray scale *opening* of f by structuring element k is denoted by $f \circ k$ and is defined by $f \circ k = (f \ominus k) \oplus k$.

Let $f : F \to E$ and $k : K \to E$. The gray scale *closing* of f by structuring element k is denoted by $f \bullet k$ and is defined by $f \bullet k = (f \oplus k) \ominus k$.

The duality between gray scale dilation and gray scale erosion leads to a duality between gray scale opening and gray scale closing.

$$-(f \circ k)(x) = \left[(-f) \bullet \check{k}\right](x)$$

It follows from the umbra homomorphism theorem that

$$U[f \circ k] = U[f] \circ U[k]$$
$$U[f \bullet k] = U[f] \bullet U[k]$$
$$f \circ k = f \quad \text{if and only if} \quad U[f \circ k] = U[f]$$
$$f \bullet k = f \quad \text{if and only if} \quad U[f \bullet k] = U[f]$$

A gray scale geometric representation for gray scale opening can be quickly determined by using the above relation. Certainly it is the case that $(f \circ k)(x) = T\{U[f \circ k]\}(x)$. But $U[f \circ k] = U[f] \circ U[k]$, and by the opening representation theorem

$$U[f] \circ U[k] = \bigcup_{v \in U[f] \ominus U[k]} U[k]_v = \bigcup_{U[k]_v \subseteq U[f]} U[k]_v$$

Hence

$$(f \circ k)(x) = T\left[\bigcup_{U[k]_v \subseteq U[f]} U[k]_v\right](x)$$

This relation states that the gray scale opening of f by k can be visualized by sliding the k under f. The locus of all the highest points reached by some part of k during the slide then constitutes the opening.

A geometric representation for closing can also be obtained. To set this up, notice that $(f \bullet k)(x) = T\{U[f \bullet k]\}(x) = T\{U[f] \bullet U[k]\}(x)$ by the umbra homomorphism theorem. Now by the duality between opening and closing, $(f \bullet k)(x) = T\{(U[f]^c \circ U[\check{k}]^c)\}(x)$. Using the convention that the top of a set A is a function whose domain consists of only those x for which $\max\{y \mid (x,y) \in A\} < \infty$, we can give a concrete interpretation to the top of the complement of a set. It is simply the bottom of the set. We denote the bottom or bottom surface of a set A by $B[A]$, $B[A](x) = \min\{y \mid (x,y) \in A\}$, where we use the convention that the domain for the function $B[A]$ is precisely that set of all x such that $\min\{y \mid (x,y) \in A\} > -\infty$. Then we can represent the gray scale closing by

$$(f \bullet k)(x) = B\{U[f]^c \circ U[\check{k}]\}(x)$$
$$= B\left\{\bigcup_{\check{U}[k]_v \subseteq U[f]^c} \check{U}[k]_v\right\}(x)$$

This relation provides an interpretation for gray scale closing. The interpretation of the gray scale closing of f with k is to take the structuring element k, reflect it left-right, turn it upside-down, and sweep the result above the top of f. The locus of all the lowest points reached by some part of the reflected upside-down structuring element during its sweep is the closing of f by k.

From these representation theorems for gray scale opening and closing, it is apparent that $f \circ k \leq f$ and $f \geq f \bullet k$. Also, since gray scale dilation and erosion are increasing, gray scale opening and closing are increasing. That is, $f < g$ implies $f \circ k < g \circ k$ and $f \bullet k < g \bullet k$.

The important idempotency property of the opening and closing operations in binary morphology extends to gray scale morphology. The proof proceeds by expressing the opening or closing as the top of its umbra. Then it unwraps the umbra of the opening or closing, using the umbra homomorphism theorem. The idempotency of the opening or closing in binary morphology reduces the inside expression of umbras. Finally, the umbra homomorphism theorem rewraps the resulting expression as the umbra of a gray scale dilation or erosion. Therefore $(f \circ k) \circ k = f \circ k$ and $(f \bullet k) \bullet k = f \bullet k$.

Some important equalities and inequalities relate umbras, tops, minima, and maxima. They can all be verified directly. The umbra of the minimum of two functions is the intersection of their umbras. The top of a union of two sets is the maximum of their tops. The top of an intersection of two sets is not greater than the minimum of the tops. To see why the last relation must be an inequality, consider the example sets $A = \{(1,4),(1,5),(2,3),(2,4)\}$ and $B = \{(1,4),(1,6),(2,3),(2,5)\}$. Then $A \cap B = \{(1,4),(2,3)\}$, so that $T[A \cap B](1) = 4$ and $T[A \cap B](2) = 3$. But $T[A](1) = 5$, $T[A](2) = 4$, $T[B](1) = 6$, and $T[B](2) = 5$. Hence $\min\{T[A],T[B]\}(1) = 5$ and $\min\{T[A], T[B]\}(2) = 5$, thereby illustrating a case in which $T[A \cap B] < \min\{T[A],T[B]\}$.

When A and B are umbras, however, $T[A \cap B] = \min\{T[A],T[B]\}$.

Proposition 5.4: $T[A \cap B] \leq \min\{T[A],T[B]\}$ with equality when A and B are umbras.

Proof:

Let $y = T[A \cap B](x)$. Then $y = \max\{z \mid (x,z) \in A \cap B\}$. Since $A \cap B \subseteq A, y \leq \max\{z \mid (x,z) \in A\} = T[A](x)$. Since $A \cap B \subseteq B$, $y \leq \max\{z \mid (x,z) \in B\} = T[B](x)$. Hence $y \leq \min\{T[A](x),T[B](x)\}$. Therefore $T[A \cap B] \leq \min\{T[A],T[B]\}$.

Now suppose that A and B are umbras. Let $y_A = T[A](x)$, $y_B = T[B](x)$, and $y = \min\{y_A, y_B\}$. Then $y \leq y_A$. But since A is an umbra, $y \leq y_A$ implies $(x,y) \in A$. Similarly $y \leq y_B$, and since B is an umbra, $y \leq y_B$ implies $(x,y) \in B$. Now $(x,y) \in A$ and $(x,y) \in B$ imply $(x,y) \in A \cap B$. But $T[A \cap B](x) = \max\{z \mid (x,z) \in A \cap B\} \geq y$, since $(x,y) \in A \cap B$. Hence when A and B are umbras, $\min\{T[A],T[B]\} = T[A \cap B]$.

If we use the relations

$$U[\min\{f,g\}] = U[f] \cap U[g]$$
$$U[\max\{f,g\}] = U[f] \cup U[g]$$
$$T[A \cup B] = \max\{T[A],\ T[B]\}$$
$$T[A \cap B] \leq \min\{T[A],\ T[B]\}$$

with equality when A and B are umbras, as well as the umbra homomorphism theorems as well as the duality relations, there follow

$$\max\{f,g\} \oplus k = \max\{f \oplus k, g \oplus k\}$$
$$\min\{f,g\} \oplus k \leq \min\{f \oplus k, g \oplus k\}$$
$$\max\{f,g\} \ominus k \geq \max\{f \ominus k, g \ominus k\}$$
$$\min\{f,g\} \ominus k = \min\{f \ominus k, g \ominus k\}$$
$$k \ominus \max\{f,g\} = \min\{k \ominus f, k \ominus g\}$$
$$k \ominus \min\{f,g\} \geq \max\{k \ominus f, k \ominus g\}$$
$$\max\{f,g\} \circ k \geq \max\{f \circ k, g \circ k\}$$
$$\min\{f,g\} \circ k \leq \min\{f \circ k, g \circ k\}$$
$$\max\{f,g\} \bullet k \geq \max\{f \bullet k, g \bullet k\}$$
$$\min\{f,g\} \bullet k \leq \min\{f \bullet k, g \bullet k\}$$

The proofs for these relationships all follow a similar pattern. Consider, for example, $\max\{f,g\} \oplus h$. By definition of gray scale dilation, $\max\{f,g\} \oplus k = T\left[U[\max\{f,g\}] \oplus U[k]\right]$. But $U[\max\{f,g\}] = U[f] \cup U[g]$. Hence

$$\max\{f,g\} \oplus k = T\left[(U[f] \cup U[g]) \oplus U[k]\right]$$

If we use the fact that binary dilation distributes over set union, $\max\{f,g\} \oplus k = T\left[(U[f] \oplus U[k]) \cup (U[g] \oplus U[k])\right]$. If we use the fact that $T[A \cup B] = \max\{T[A], T[B]\}$, there follows $\max\{f,g\} \oplus k = \max\{T(U[f] \oplus U[k]), T(U[g] \oplus U[k])\}$. Now by the umbra homomorphism theorem for gray scale dilation,

$$\max\{f,g\} \oplus k = \max\left\{T\left[U(f \oplus k)\right], T\left[U(g \oplus k)\right]\right\}$$

And finally by definition of gray scale dilation, $\max\{f,g\} \oplus k = \max\{f \oplus k, g \oplus k\}$.
Next consider $\min\{f,g\} \ominus k$.

$$\min\{f,g\} \ominus k = T\left[U[\min\{f,g\}] \ominus U[k]\right]$$
$$= T\left[\left(U[f] \cap U[g]\right) \ominus U[k]\right]$$
$$= T\left[(U[f] \ominus U[k]) \cap (U[g] \ominus U[k])\right]$$
$$= T\left[U[f \ominus k] \cap U[g \ominus k]\right]$$

But since $U[f \ominus k]$ and $U[g \ominus k]$ are umbras,

$$T(U[f \ominus k] \cap U[g \ominus k]) = \min\{T(U[f \ominus k]), T(U[g \ominus k])\}$$
$$= \min\{f \ominus k, g \ominus k\}$$

Hence $\min\{f, g\} \ominus k = \min\{f \ominus k, g \ominus k\}$.

If $f \circ k = f$ and $g \circ k = g$, then $\max\{f, g\} \circ k = \max\{f, g\}$. If $f \bullet k = f$ and $g \bullet k = g$, then $\min\{f, g\} \bullet k = \min\{f, g\}$.

It is easy to use gray scale openings and closings to extract that part of a gray scale image having a given shape and gray scale structure. For example, consider a surface-defect inspection problem. Defects in surfaces that are highly finished or highly polished will often tend to scatter the light more than does the rest of the surface. Such defects will appear as small, dark areas. Let us suppose for this example that dark means dark in both an absolute and a relative sense. Relative means that the contrast of a defect area relative to its surroundings must be significant. To extract all relatively dark areas smaller than a disk of radius R_1, we can first close the image with a rodlike structuring element of radius R_1. The defect areas will have high values in the residue of this closing. To detect the defect areas then amounts to ANDing together a threshold of the original image with a threshold of the closing residue image. An alternative approach is to select the bright regions and then mask the original image with the threshold image to produce a gray scale image of only the bright regions. This image can then be closed and the residue of the closing obtained. A thresholding of the residue then produces the defect area. Figure 5.36 illustrates such a processing sequence.

Now suppose that the defect areas are not entirely defective. That is, suppose that the defects can have small bright areas contained within them. In this case these brighter areas within the defect can act like pedestals on which the closed surface must stand. The contrast of these areas in the residue of the closing will be much smaller, thereby making these areas more difficult to detect by thresholding. Such a situation can be handled by conditioning the image by first opening the image with a small rodlike structuring element. Bright areas smaller than the radius of the rod will then be changed to the darker values of their nearby surroundings. The initial algorithm for defect detection will then work on this conditioned image.

As in the binary case, generalized gray scale openings and closings can be defined. The maximum of a set of gray scale openings constitutes a generalized gray scale opening. The minimum of a set of gray scale closings constitutes a generalized gray scale closing.

Figure 5.37 illustrates a use of generalized opening. Part (a) shows a scanning electron microscope image of a vascular casting of the capillaries of the gut of a mouse. Part (b) illustrates the image sharpened by the unsharp mask technique. The image of Part (b) was then opened by line segments of length 25 in each of eight orientations: $0°$, $27°$, $45°$, $63°$, $90°$, $117°$, $135°$, and $153°$. The generalized opening was obtained by taking the maximum of these eight opened images. Values on the generalized open image above a threshold of 150 are shown in Fig. 5.37(c). Only the large and straight vessels remain. The difference between sharpened image and the masked generalized open image is shown in Fig. 5.37(d). There only the smallest capillaries remain.

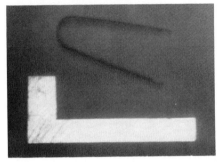

(a)

(b)

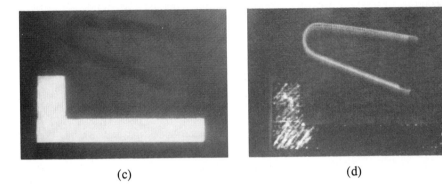

(c)

(d)

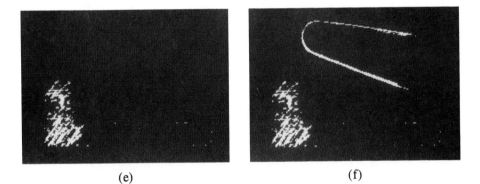

(e)

(f)

Figure 5.36 Defect detection of a polished surface. (a) Original image f_0; (b) thresholding of the original image; (c) original image masked by the thresholded image and then closed with a rod structuring element R; (d) closing residue; (e) thresholding of the closing residue; and (f) ANDing of the two thresholded images. The algorithm can be compactly written by $\{[f_0 \wedge (f_0 > t_1)] \bullet R - f_0 \wedge (f_0 > t_2)\} > t_2 \wedge (f_0 \bullet t_1)$.

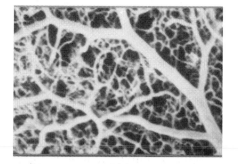
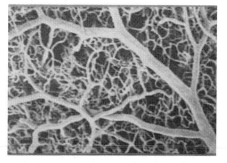

(a)   (b)

(c)   (d)

Figure 5.37 Example of how the generalized opening can be used. (a) Original image f; (b) sharpened image g; (c) $h = k \wedge m$, where $k = \max\{g \circ l_1, \ldots, g \circ l_8\}$, $m = k > t$, and $l_1, \ldots, l_8$ are line structuring elements in direction $0°$, $27°$, $45°$, $63°$, $90°$, $117°$, $135°$, $153°$; and (d) $g - h$.

5.6   Openings, Closings, and Medians

One of the most common nonlinear noise-smoothing filters in image processing is the median filter. Its advantages are that it is a high-efficiency estimator of local mean when the noise is fat-tailed, it is robust to outlier pixel values, and it leaves edges sharp. Images that remain unchanged after being median filtered are special. They are called *median root images*. To obtain the "closest" median root image of a given input image merely requires repeatedly median filtering the given image until there is no change. A relationship exists between openings, closings, and median roots: An image that is both opened and closed with respect to a constant-valued structuring element is a median root image.

To understand how this comes about, first notice that if K is any subset of E^{N-1} and k is a constant-valued structuring element defined on K, then the opening and closing of an image f have a simple form:

$$(f \circ k)(x) = \max_{z \in K} \min_{y \in K} f(x - z + y)$$
$$(f \bullet k)(x) = \min_{z \in K} \max_{y \in K} f(x + z - y)$$

Because of this, the actual value of a constant-valued structuring element does not influence the results of an opening or a closing taken with respect to it.

From the expression of an opening or a closing in terms of min and max, it is apparent that the effective neighborhood used in an opening or a closing with a structuring element whose domain is K is $K \oplus \check{K}$. As we will be comparing an opening and a closing with a median filtering, we will use $K \oplus \check{K}$ as the neighborhood for the median filtering. We denote the median value around the point x of all points in the neighborhood $K \oplus \check{K}$ by $\operatorname*{med}_{w \in K \oplus \check{K}} f(x + w)$. Since the opening at a point x of f with respect to a constant-valued structuring element k is given by $\max_{z \in K} \min_{y \in K} f(x - z + y)$, we focus our attention on the highest possible value of $\min_{y \in K} f(x - z + y)$ as z is allowed to vary over K. Suppose $\#K = M$. Now regardless of the value of z, the highest possible value will occur when the list of M values $< f(x - z + y) : y \in K >$ contains the M-highest values of the list $< f(x + w) : w \in K \oplus \check{K} >$, which is guaranteed to contain every value of the list $< f(x - z + y) : y \in \check{K} >$ when $0 \in K$. If the number of points in $K \oplus \check{K}$ is less than or equal to $2M - 1$, then the smallest among these M-highest values must be less than or equal to $\operatorname*{med}_{w \in K \oplus \check{K}} f(x + w)$, since the list $< f(x + w) : w \in K \oplus \check{K} >$ has no more than $2M - 1$ values. Then $(f \circ k)(x) \leq \operatorname*{med}_{w \in K \oplus \check{K}} [f(x + w)]$. A parallel argument leads to the fact that $\operatorname*{med}_{w \in K \oplus \check{K}} f(x + w) \leq (f \bullet k)(x)$.

From these two inequalities it immediately follows that if f is both opened and closed with respect to k,

$$(f \circ k)(x) = f(x) = (f \bullet k)(x)$$

then

$$f(x) = \operatorname*{med}_{w \in K \oplus \check{K}} f(x + w)$$

Hence functions that are both opened and closed with respect to a constant-valued structuring element defined on a domain K containing the origin and satisfying $\#K \oplus \check{K} \leq 2\#K - 1$ must be their own median roots.

Some properties of opening and closing suggest a morphological way of approximating a median filtering. We provide this motivation by considering functions defined on a one-dimensional domain. We fix a point x and consider the conditions under which it is the case, for a particular x, that $f(x)$ might equal $(f \circ k)(x)$ or $(f \bullet k)(x)$, where k is a constant-valued structuring element.

From the geometric meaning of opening and closing, it is obvious that if $f(x)$ is monotonically increasing or monotonically decreasing over a large enough interval around x, then $f(x) = (f \circ k)(x) = (f \bullet k)(x)$. How large is large enough? If the constant-valued structuring element has domain K, then large enough is $K \oplus \check{K}$. To see this, suppose the domain K is some small interval. In this case, if f is monotonically increasing, the left endpoint of the constant-valued structuring element will be able to touch $f(x)$, with the entire structuring element able to stay at or below f for its entire length. If f is monotonically decreasing, the right endpoint of the constant-valued structuring element will be able to touch $f(x)$, with the entire structuring element able to stay at or below f. Now it is clear from the geometric meaning of opening that $f(x) = (f \circ k)(x)$ when f is monotone at x. A similar argument establishes that $f(x) = (f \bullet k)(x)$ when f is monotone at x.

Monotonicity is not the only sufficient cause of the value of f at a given point being the value of its closing or opening at that given point. If $f(x)$ is the global minimum in a neighborhood of sufficient size around x, then $f(x) = (f \circ k)(x)$. Here sufficient size again means size of $(K \oplus \check{K})_x$. Note that the condition is global minimum and not relative or local minimum. As illustrated in Fig. 5.38, if a relative minimum occurs between two other relative minima whose distance apart is less than the size of the structuring-element domain, then the opened value at the middle relative minimum will be the algebraically lowest of the surrounding relative minima. Similarly, if $f(x)$ is the global maximum in a neighborhood of sufficient size around x, then $f(x) = (f \bullet k)(x)$.

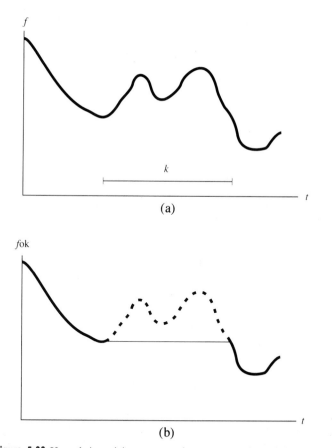

Figure 5.38 If a relative minimum occurs between two other relative minima within the span of the structuring element, then the opened value at the middle relative minimum will be the greater of the surrounding relative minima thereby showing that at local minima it is not necessarily the case that $f(x) = (f \circ k)(x)$. (a) f and k; (b) $f \circ k$, with the part of f that differs from $f \circ k$ depicted in dotted lines.

Finally, if f is monotone in a neighborhood of $K \oplus \check{K}$ around x, note that $f(x) = \underset{w \in K \oplus \check{K}}{\text{med}} f(x + w)$.

These properties involving openings, closings, and medians suggest the following morphological approximation g to a median filtering: Define g by

$$g(x) = \begin{cases} (f \circ k)(x) & \text{if } | (f \circ k)(x) - f(x) | \geq | (f \bullet k)(x) - f(x) | \\ (f \bullet k)(x) & \text{otherwise} \end{cases}$$

Consider the relationship of g to the median-filtered value. If f is monotone at x, $\underset{w \in K \oplus \check{K}}{\text{med}} f(x + w) = f(x) = (f \circ k)(x) = (f \bullet k)(x)$, so that $g(x) = \underset{w \in K \oplus \check{K}}{\text{med}} f(x + w)$. If f is not monotone at x and f has a global neighborhood minimum at x, then $(f \circ k)(x) = f(x) \leq \underset{w \in K \oplus \check{K}}{\text{med}} f(x + w)$, which implies that $g(x) = (f \bullet k)(x) \geq \underset{w \in K \oplus \check{K}}{\text{med}} f(x + w)$. Hence the values of such minimum points are changed to values that are higher than the neighborhood median. However, the new value is not the neighborhood maximum since $f(x)$ cannot simultaneously be a neighborhood minimum, a neighborhood maximum, and not monotone at x. Thus a change has been made from the extreme value to something that is not an extreme value.

Likewise, if f is not monotone at x and has a global neighborhood maximum at x, then $(f \bullet k)(x) = f(x) \geq \underset{w \in K \oplus \check{K}}{\text{med}} f(x + w)$, which implies that $g(x) = (f \circ k)(x) \leq \underset{w \in K \oplus \check{K}}{\text{med}} f(x + w)$. Hence the values of such maximum points are changed to values that are lower than the neighborhood median. However, the new value is not the neighborhood minimum. Thus again a change has been made from an extreme value to something that is not an extreme value.

5.7   Bounding Second Derivatives

Opening or closing a gray scale image simplifies the image complexity. When the structuring element of the opening or closing is parabolic, this simplification can be understood in terms of the way the Laplacian of the opened or closed images is bounded. In this manner opening and closing can be viewed as morphological filters that eliminate all points on the image that have excessively high values of second partial derivatives. Actually, this elimination occurs only for pixels at which the first partial derivatives are suitably small. Opening bounds the Laplacian of the image from below, and closing bounds it from above.

A precise statement of the bounding effect can be given as follows: Let the neighborhood support of the structuring element k be a square $2K \times 2K$ neighborhood, and let the parabolic structuring element k be defined by $k(x, y) = \frac{c}{2}(K^2 - x^2 - y^2)$. Let the image be denoted by f. Suppose the bound B satisfies

$$\max_{\substack{x \\ -K \leq x \leq K}} \max_{\substack{y \\ -K \leq y \leq K}} \max_{\substack{s \\ |s| = 1}} \max_{\substack{t \\ |t| = 1}} | R(x, y, s, t) | = B$$

where

$$f(x+s,y+t) = f(x,y) + s\frac{\partial f}{\partial x}(x,y) + t\frac{\partial f}{\partial y}(x,y)$$

$$+ \frac{s^2}{2}\frac{\partial^2 f}{\partial x^2}(x,y) + \frac{t^2}{2}\frac{\partial^2 f}{\partial y^2}(x,y) + R(x,y,s,t)$$

If the first partial derivatives of f are bounded by

$$-KC \le \frac{\partial f}{\partial x}(x,y) \le KC$$

and

$$-KC \le \frac{\partial f}{\partial y}(x,y) \le KC$$

and $f = f \circ k$, then the Laplacian is bounded below by

$$-2C - 2B \le \frac{\partial^2 f}{\partial x^2}(x,y) + \frac{\partial^2 f}{\partial y^2}(x,y)$$

To understand how this arises, we first need to demonstrate the validity of the following proposition:

If $-KC \le W \le KC$, then for every z_0, $-K \le z_0 \le K$, there exists a y_0, $|y_0 - z_0| = 1$ and $-K \le y_0 \le K$ such that $(z_0 - y_0)(W + z_0 C) \ge 0$.

This relation is proved by a straightforward case analysis.

Case 1: $z_0 = K$. In this case take $y_0 = K - 1$. Then $(z_0 - y_0)(W + z_0 C) = [K - (K-1)](W + KC)$. Since $-KC \le W$, then $W + KC \ge 0$.

Case 2: $z_0 = -K$. In this case take $y_0 = -K + 1$. Then $(z_0 - y_0)(W + z_0 C) = [-K - (-K+1)](W - KC)$. Since $W \le KC$, then $-(W - KC) \ge 0$.

Case 3: $-K < z_0 < K$. In this case examine $W + z_0 C$. Either $W + z_0 C \ge 0$ or $W + z_0 C < 0$. If $W + z_0 C \ge 0$, take $y_0 = z_0 - 1$. If $W + z_0 C < 0$, take $y_0 = z_0 + 1$.

With this preliminary relation proved, we can proceed with the derivation of the main bounding relation. Since $f = (f \ominus k) \oplus k$,

$$f(x,y) = \max_{\substack{(u_1,u_2) \\ -K \le u_1 \le K \\ -K \le u_2 \le K}} \min_{\substack{(v_1,v_2) \\ -K \le v_1 \le K \\ -K \le v_2 \le K}} [f(x + v_1 - u_1, y + v_2 - u_2)$$

$$- k(v_1,v_2) + k(u_1,u_2)]$$

But

$$f(x + v_1 - u_1, y + v_2 - u_2) = f(x,y) + (v_1 - u_1)\frac{\partial f}{\partial x}(x,y)$$

$$+ (v_2 - u_2)\frac{\partial f}{\partial y}(x,y) + \frac{(v_1 - u_1)^2}{2}\frac{\partial^2 f}{\partial x^2}(x,y)$$

$$+ \frac{(v_2 - u_2)^2}{2}\frac{\partial^2 f}{\partial y^2}(x,y)$$

$$+ R(x,y,v_1 - u_1, v_2 - u_2)$$

and

$$k(v_1, v_2) = k(u_1, u_2) + (v_1 - u_1)\frac{\partial k}{\partial x}(u_1, u_2) + (v_2 - u_2)\frac{\partial k}{\partial y}(u_1, u_2)$$
$$+ \frac{(v_1 - u_1)^2}{2}\frac{\partial^2 k}{\partial x^2}(u_1, u_2) + (v_2 - u_2)^2\frac{\partial^2 k}{\partial y^2}(u_1, u_2)$$

Upon substituting, canceling, and rearranging,

$$0 = \max_{(u_1, u_2)}\min_{(v_1, v_2)}\left\{(v_1 - u_1)\left[\frac{\partial f}{\partial x}(x, y) - \frac{\partial k}{\partial x}(u_1, u_2)\right]\right.$$
$$+ (v_2 - u_2)\left[\frac{\partial f}{\partial y}(x, y) - \frac{\partial k}{\partial y}(u_1, u_2)\right]$$
$$+ \frac{(v_1 - u_1)^2}{2}\left[\frac{\partial^2 f}{\partial x^2}(x, y) - \frac{\partial^2 k}{\partial x^2}(u_1, u_2)\right]$$
$$+ \frac{(v_2 - u_2)^2}{2}\left[\frac{\partial^2 f}{\partial y^2}(x, y) - \frac{\partial^2 k}{\partial y^2}(u_1, u_2)\right]$$
$$\left. + R(x, y, v_1 - u_1, v_2 - u_2)\right\}$$

Upon substituting the values of the partial derivatives of k, unfolding the minimum and maximum operations, and reorganizing these results, there exist a u_1^0 and u_2^0, $-K \le u_1^0 \le K$ and $-K \le u_2^0 \le K$, such that

$$(u_1^0 - v_1)\left[\frac{\partial f}{\partial x}(x, y) + Cu_1^0\right] + (u_2^0 - v_2)\left[\frac{\partial f}{\partial y}(x, y) + Cu_2^0\right]$$
$$\le \frac{(v_1 - u_1^0)^2}{2}\left[\frac{\partial^2 f}{\partial x^2}(x, y) + C\right]$$
$$+ \frac{(v_2 - u_2^0)^2}{2}\left[\frac{\partial^2 f}{\partial y^2}(x, y) + C\right]$$
$$+ R(x, y, v_1 - u_1^0, v_2 - u_2^0)$$

But since

$$-KC \le \frac{\partial f}{\partial x}(x, y) \le KC$$

for every u_1^0, there exists a v_1^0, $|v_1^0 - u_1^0| = 1$ and $-K \le v_1^0 \le K$, such that

$$0 \le (u_1^0 - v_1^0)\left[\frac{\partial f}{\partial x}(x, y) + Cu_1^0\right]$$

and since

$$-KC \le \frac{\partial f}{\partial y}(x, y) \le KC$$

for every u_2^0, there exists a v_2^0, $|v_2^0 - u_2^0| = 1$ and $-K \le v_2^0 \le K$, such that

$$0 \le (u_2^0 - v_2^0)\left[\frac{\partial f}{\partial y}(x, y) + Cu_2^0\right]$$

Hence

$$0 \leq \frac{1}{2}\left[\frac{\partial^2 f}{\partial x^2}(x,y)+C\right]+\frac{1}{2}\left[\frac{\partial^2 f}{\partial y^2}(x,y)+C\right]+R(x,y,v_1^0-u_1^0,v_2^0-u_2^0)$$

Finally, since $B \geq |R(x,y,v_1^0-u_1^0,v_2^0-u_2^0)|$,

$$-2B-2C \leq \frac{\partial^2 f}{\partial x^2}(x,y)+\frac{\partial^2 f}{\partial y^2}(x,y)$$

5.8   Distance Transform and Recursive Morphology

In everything we have discussed so far, the morphological operation is applied to the input image and produces an output image. The order in which the morphological operator is applied to the input pixels is irrelevant. Indeed the operator could be applied simultaneously in parallel to all input positions, and the results would be identical to the operator applied in any sequential order.

Recursive morphology is a departure from this state of affairs. Associated with a particular recursive morphological operator will be a particular scan order of input positions. This scan order governs the order in which the operation is to be applied. The scan order is a sequence of input positions in which each input position occurs exactly once. The output of the recursive morphological operator depends not only on the input pixels associated with each input location but also on one or more previously computed output values. Hence each output value can be made to depend on all the input pixel values at positions prior to the current position, according to the associated scan order. In this manner global information can be accumulated with fixed-size operators, thereby making the computation of the global information less computationally intensive than if it were to be computed by more straightforward procedure.

We motivate our discussion of recursive morphology with the distance transform. To each point in a given set A, the distance transform assigns a number that is the distance between the point and A^c. When the distance is the city block (L_1, distance), then the distance transform of a digital M-row by an N-column image I can be computed recursively by a two-pass procedure (Rosenfeld and Pfaltz, 1968).

The first pass requires a standard left-right top-bottom raster scan order, and the second pass requires a reverse right-left bottom-top scan order. At each pixel position (r,c), the output $J(r,c)$ is defined in terms of the binary input image I and the values at previously computed positions of J by

$$J(r,c) = \begin{cases} \min\{J(r,c-1),J(r-1,c)\}+1, & \text{if } I(r,c)=1 \\ 0, & \text{if } I(r,c)=0 \end{cases}$$

We use the convention that $J(r,-1) = J(-1,c) = 0$. Note that $(r,c-1)$ is the position just prior to (r,c) in the standard raster scan order, and $(r-1, c)$ is the position N pixels prior to position (r,c) in the standard raster scan order, where N is the number of columns in image I.

The second pass produces the distance transform image D, which is defined for

$$(r,c) \in \{0,1,\ldots,M-1\} \times \{0,1,\ldots,N-1\}$$

by

$$D(r,c) = \min\{J(r,c), D(r,c+1)+1, D(r+1,c)+1\}$$

where we use the convention that $D(r,N) = D(M,c) = 0$. Note that $(r,c+1)$ is the positon just prior to (r,c) in the reverse raster scan order, and $(r+1,c)$ is the position N pixels prior to position (r,c) in the reverse raster scan order. Figure 5.39 illustrates this operation.

The number of operations per pixel for the forward scan is one comparison, one addition, and one minimum of two values. The number of operations for the backward scan is two additions and two minima, each of two values. Not distinguishing between the different operations, we find a total of seven operations per pixel.

Now consider how we could accomplish this city-block distance transform image by standard morphological operations. Consider successively eroding the input image I with a cross-structuring element $K = \{(0,0),(0,1),(1,0),(-1,0),(0,-1)\}$. Define $I_n = I_{n-1} \ominus K$, where we take $I_0 = I$. It is clear that each erosion changes to zero those binary-1 pixels that are 4-adjacent to some binary-0 pixel. The city-block distance of a pixel to its nearest binary-0 pixel is then just the number of images for which it retains the value binary-1. If the image is $N \times N$, then after $\lceil N/2 \rceil$ successive erosions the resulting image must be all binary-0. Hence by this brute-force

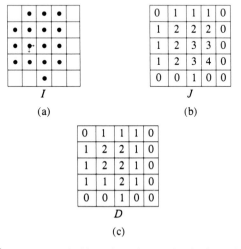

Figure 5.39 (a) An example binary input image; (b) the forward scan output image J produced by a recursive morphological operation with the structuring element $F = \{(0,-1),(-1,0)\}$; and (c) the city-block distance transform of image I produced by a recursive morphological operation on image J with the structuring element $B = \{(0,0),(0,1),(1,0)\}$.

technique the distance transform image D can be obtained as

$$D(r,c) = \sum_{n=0}^{\lceil N/2 \rceil} I_n(r,c)$$

Equivalently $D(r,c) = \max\{n \mid I_{n-1}(r,c) \neq 0\}$. The number of operations per pixel required to perform the calculation this way is $5N/2$, since each erosion involves five operations. Obviously the computational savings gained by the recursive operation are very significant.

Since each pass of the recursively computed city-block transform involves a minimum operation, we can associate it with a recursive gray scale erosion operation. Having been thus motivated, we are ready to provide the formal notational conventions for the recursive morphological operation. Then we reexpress the two-pass city-block transform in terms of the recursive notation.

Let $F \subseteq E^{N-1}$ and let $f : F \rightarrow E$ be the function to be recursively eroded. Let k_1 and k_2 be structuring elements having respective domains $K_1, K_2 \subseteq E^{N-1}$. In recursive morphology, k_1 will be the structuring element associated with the nonrecursive part of the operation, and k_2 will be the structuring element associated with the recursive part. For the recursive computations to be well defined, they must be capable of being done in an order such that the computation for the current value depends only on input values or on previously computed output values. If S is a sequence denoting the order in which the outputs are to be computed, a relationship must exist between K_2, the domain of the structuring element associated with the recursive part of the computation, and S. This relationship requires that if at any time in the computation for the current input position a value is needed for the recursive morphologically defined function, then this value must be one that in fact had been previously computed. Otherwise the computation could not proceed.

The *recursive morphological erosion* with respect to scan order S of a function f by a structuring element $k = (k_1, k_2)$ is denoted by $f \ominus_S k$. It is a function whose domain is $(F \ominus K_1) \oplus K_2$, and it is defined by

$$(f \ominus_S k)(x) = \begin{cases} \min\{(f \ominus k_1)(x), [(f \ominus_S k) \ominus k_2](x)\}, x \in F \ominus K_1 \\ h(x), \qquad\qquad x \in (F \ominus K_1) \oplus K_2 - F \ominus K_1 \end{cases}$$

The function h that appears in the definition provides the initial values to get the recursive computation going. It does exactly what the statement $J(r, -1) = J(-1, c) = 0$ did in the recursive computation of the city-block distance transform.

Thus the recursive erosion of f is produced by eroding f by k_1, the non-recursive component of the structuring element, then eroding the previously computed recursive erosion $f \ominus_S k$ by the recursive component k_2 of the structuring element and taking the minimum of the two results.

As mentioned earlier, in order for this computation to proceed sequentially, a relationship must exist between K_2 and S. This relationship can now be stated precisely. Any time a value for $f \ominus_S k$ is required at a point $x + z$, where $z \in K_2$ — so that the value for $\{(f \ominus_S k) \ominus k_2\}(x) = \min_{z \in K_2}\{(f \ominus_S k)(x + z) - k_2(z)\}$ can be computed — then if $x + z$ is a value in $S, x + z$ must occur prior to where x occurs in S. That is, if $S = < x_1, x_2, \ldots, x_n, \ldots >$, a complete ordering of the members of $F \ominus K_1$ and $z \in K_2$, then $x_n + z \in S$ implies that for some m, $1 \le m < n$, $x_n + z = x_m$.

With respect to the city-block distance transform example, the domain K_1 of the structuring element for the nonrecursive component of the erosion is simply the origin: $K_1 = \{(0,0)\}$. The structuring element k_1 is defined by $k_1(0,0) = 0$. The domain K_2 of the structuring element k_2 associated with the recursive part of the computation is the set $\{(0,-1),(-1,0)\}$, and the structuring element k_2 is defined by

$$k_2(0,-1) = -1$$
$$k_2(-1,0) = -1$$

If the input image F has spatial domain $F = \{0,1,\ldots,M-1\} \times \{0,1,\ldots,N-1\}$, then $F \ominus K_1 = F \ominus \{(0,0)\} = F$. The scan order $\mathcal{F}$ must then be a complete ordering of $\{0,1,\ldots,M-1\} \times \{0,1,\ldots,N-1\}$, and it is given by

$$\mathcal{F} =< (0,0),(0,1),\ldots,(0,N-1),(1,0),(1,1),\ldots,(1,N-1),\ldots,$$
$$(M-1,0),(M-1,1),(M-1,N-1) >$$

The initial value function h is defined by $h(r,c) = 0, (r,c) \in [(F \ominus K_1) \oplus K_2] - F \ominus K_1$. Then by definition

$$(f \ominus_{\mathcal{F}} k)(r,c) = \begin{cases} \min\{(f \ominus k_1)(r,c),[(f \ominus_{\mathcal{F}} k) \ominus k_2](r,c)\}, & (r,c) \in F \ominus K_1; \\ 0, & (r,c) \in (F \ominus K_1) \oplus K_2 - F \ominus K_1 \end{cases}$$

Since $K_1 = \{(0,0)\}$ and $k_1(0,0) = 0, F \ominus K_1 = F$ and $(f \ominus k_1)(r,c) = f(r,c)$. Hence

$$(f \ominus_{\mathcal{F}} k)(r,c) \begin{cases} \min\{f(r,c),[(f \ominus_{\mathcal{F}} k) \ominus k_2](r,c)\}, & (r,c) \in F \\ 0, & (r,c) \in F \oplus K_2 - F \end{cases}$$

If $f(r,c) = \infty$, then

$$\min\{f(r,c),[(f \ominus_{\mathcal{F}} k) \ominus k_2](r,c)\}$$
$$= \min\{\infty, \min[(f \ominus_{\mathcal{F}} k)(r,c-1)+1,(f \ominus_{\mathcal{F}} k)(r-1,c)+1]\}$$
$$= \min\{(f \ominus_{\mathcal{F}} k)(r,c-1),(f \ominus_{\mathcal{F}} k)(r-1,c)\}+1$$

If $f(r,c) = 0$, then

$$\min\{f(r,c),[(f \ominus_{\mathcal{F}} k) \ominus k_2](r,c)\}$$
$$= \min\{0, \min[(f \ominus_{\mathcal{F}} k)(r,c-1)+1,(f \ominus_{\mathcal{F}} k)(r-1,c)+1]\}$$
$$= 0$$

Therefore, in the case when f takes only a value 0 or ∞,

$$(f \ominus_{\mathcal{F}} k)(r,c)$$
$$= \begin{cases} \min\{(f \ominus_{\mathcal{F}} k)(r,c-1),(f \ominus_{\mathcal{F}} k)(r-1,c)\}+1, & \text{if } f(r,c) = \infty \\ 0, & \text{if } f(r,c) = 0 \\ 0, & (r,c) \in F \oplus K_2 - F \end{cases}$$
$$= \begin{cases} \min\{(f \ominus_{\mathcal{F}} k)(r,c-1),(f \ominus_{\mathcal{F}} k)(r-1,c)\}+1, & \text{if } f(r,c) = \infty \\ 0, & \text{if } f(r,c) = 0 \end{cases}$$

where we take $(f \ominus_{\mathcal{F}} k)(r, -1) = (f \ominus_{\mathcal{F}} k)(-1, c) = 0$. Obviously this is in exactly the same form as the definition given for the distance transform image J.

For the second pass k_1, the nonrecursive component of the structuring element k has domain $K_1 = \{(0,0)\}$, and it is defined by $k_1(0,0) = 0$. The recursive component of the structuring element k has domain $K_2 = \{(1,0),(0,1)\}$, and k_2 is defined by $k_2(1,0) = k_2(0,1) = -1$. The scan order sequence $\mathcal{B}$ is the reverse or backward raster scan order.

$$\mathcal{B} = \Big\langle (M-1, N-1), (M-1, N-2), \dots, (M-1, 0),$$
$$(M-2, N-1), (M-2, N-2), \dots, (M-2, 0), \dots,$$
$$(0, N-1), (0, N-2), \dots, (0,0) \Big\rangle$$

Then by definition

$$(f \ominus_{\mathcal{B}} k)(r,c)$$
$$= \begin{cases} \min\{(f \ominus k_1)(r,c), [(f \ominus_{\mathcal{B}} k) \ominus k_2](r,c)\}, (r,c) \in F \ominus K_1 \\ 0, \qquad\qquad\qquad (r,c) \in (F \ominus K_1) \oplus K_2 - F \ominus K_1 \end{cases}$$

Since $K_1 = \{(0,0)\}$ and $k_1(0,0) = 0, F \ominus K_1 = F$ and $(f \ominus k_1)(r,c) = f(r,c)$. Since

$$K_2 = \{(0,1),(1,0)\} \text{ and } k_2(0,1) = k_2(1,0) = -1,$$
$$F \oplus K_2 - F = \{(M,0),(M,1),\dots,(M,N-1),(0,N),(1,N),\dots,(M-1,N)\}$$
$$(f \ominus_{\mathcal{B}} k)(r,c) = \begin{cases} \min\{f(r,c), \min[(f \ominus_{\mathcal{B}} k)(r,c+1) + 1, (f \ominus_{\mathcal{B}} k)(r+1,c) + 1]\}, \\ \qquad\qquad\qquad (r,c) \in F(r,c) \in F \oplus K_2 - F \\ 0, \end{cases}$$
$$= \min\{f(r,c), (f \ominus_{\mathcal{B}} k)(r,c+1) + 1,$$
$$(f \ominus_{\mathcal{B}} k)(r+1,c) + 1\}, (r,c) \in F$$

where we use the convention that $(f \ominus_{\mathcal{B}} k)(M,c) = (f \ominus_{\mathcal{B}} k)(r,N) = 0, c = 0, 1, \dots, N-1$, and $r = 0, 1, \dots, M-1$. Clearly this is exactly the form for the city-block distance function d.

Before going on, we give the following theorem, which establishes that the definition given for the recursive erosion must always result in a sequentially computable function.

Theorem 5.4: Let $F, K_1, K_2 \subseteq E^{N-1}$, $f : F \rightarrow E$, $k_1 : K_1 \rightarrow E$, $k_2 : K_2 \rightarrow E$, $h : (F \ominus K_1) \oplus K_2 - F \ominus K_1 \rightarrow E$, and $d : (F \ominus K_1) \oplus K_2 \rightarrow E$. Suppose d satisfies

$$d(x) = \begin{cases} \min\{(f \ominus k_1)(x), (d \ominus k_2)(x)\}, & x \in F \ominus K_1 \\ h(x), & x \in (F \ominus K_1) \oplus K_2 - F \ominus K_1 \end{cases}$$

Let $S = <x_1, \dots, x_n, \dots, >$ be a complete ordering of the elements of $F \ominus K_1$ satisfying the condition that for every $z \in K_2$ such that $x_n + z \in F \ominus K_1$, there exists an index $m, 1 \leq m < n$, such that $x_n + z = x_m$. Then d is unique and sequentially computable according to the ordering S.

Proof:

If $x \in (F \ominus K_1) \oplus K_2 - F \ominus K_1$, then $d(x) = h(x)$, and there is nothing to prove. If $x \in F \ominus K_1$, then $d(x) = \min\{(f \ominus k_1)(x), (d \ominus k_2)(x)\}$. For the minimum to be well defined, both $(f \ominus k_1)(x)$ and $(d \ominus k_2)(x)$ need to be well defined. Since $x \in F \ominus K_1$, from the definition of gray scale erosion, $(f \ominus k_1)(x)$ is indeed well defined. The only question is whether $(d \ominus k_2)(x)$ is a well-defined, unique value. We show inductively that $(d \ominus k_2)(x)$ is always well defined and has a unique value.

Base case. Consider the computation for $(d \ominus k_2)(x_1)$. By definition $(d \ominus k_2)(x_1) = \min_{z \in K_2} d(x_1 + z) - k_2(z)$. For any $z \in K_2$ there are two cases. Either $x_1 + z \in F \ominus K_1$ or not. If $x_1 + z \in F \ominus K_1$, then by hypothesis there exists an index $m, 1 \leq m < 1$ such that $x_1 + z = x_m$. Clearly no number m can satisfy $1 \leq m < 1$, so this case cannot occur. If $x_1 + z \notin F \ominus K_1$, then by definition of $d, d(x_1 + z) = h(x_1 + z)$. Hence $(d \ominus k_2)(x_1) = \min_{z \in K_2} h(x_1 + z) - k_2(z)$, a well-defined computation that produces a unique result.

Inductive step. Suppose $d(x_1), \ldots, d(x_n), n > 1$, have been computed. Consider the computation for $(d \ominus k_2)(x_{n+1})$. By definition $(d \ominus k_2)(x_{n+1}) = \min_{z \in K_2} d(x_{n+1} + z) - k(z)$. If $x_{n+1} + z \in F \ominus K_1$, then by hypothesis there exists an index $m, 1 \leq m < n$ such that $x_{n+1} + z = x_m$. Hence $d(x_{n+1} + z) = d(x_m)$, a previously computed value. If $x_{n+1} + z \notin F \ominus K_1$, then by definition of d, $d(x_{n+1} + z) = h(x_{n+1} + z)$. Therefore in either case the computation $\min_{z \in K_2} d(x_{n+1} + z) - k_2(z)$ is well defined so that $(d \ominus k_2)(x_{n+1})$ has a direct computable value.

5.9   Generalized Distance Transform

In the previous section we showed how the recursive morphological erosion could be used to compute efficiently the L_1 distance transform of any set by making the correspondence between the calculations that the Rosenfeld and Pfaltz (1968) algorithm performs and the calculations that an appropriately defined morphological erosion performs. In this section we define a generalized distance transform and prove that an appropriately defined recursive morphological erosion could be used to compute efficiently the generalized distance transform (Wang and Bertrand, 1988).

We begin with the definition of the generalized distance transform. Let $A \subseteq E^N$ be the set whose generalized distance transform is to be computed. Let $K \subseteq E^N$ be the structuring element with respect to which the generalized distance transform is going to be computed. We require $0 \in K$. For each $x \in A$, the generalized distance transform of A with respect to K is denoted by $d[A, K](x)$, and its value is one more than the largest integer n such that $x \in \{\ldots[(A \ominus K) \ominus K] \ominus \ldots \ominus K\}$, A eroded by K n successive times.

We define $\underset{m}{\oplus} K$ by $\underset{0}{\oplus} K = \{0\}$ and $\underset{m+1}{\oplus} K = (\underset{m}{\oplus} K) \oplus K$. Hence $A \oplus (\underset{m}{\oplus} K) = \{\ldots[(A \oplus K) \oplus K] \oplus \ldots \oplus K\}$, A dilated by K m successive times. Similarly, by the chain rule for erosion, $A \ominus (\oplus K) = \{ \ldots [(A \ominus K) \ominus K] \ominus \ldots \ominus K \}, A$ eroded by K m successive times. This can be written even more compactly by $A \ominus_m K$, whose definition is $A \ominus \left(\oplus_m K \right)$. With this notation we can compactly define

$$d[A,K](x) = \max\{n \mid x \in A \ominus_{n-1} K\} \quad \text{for} \quad x \in A$$

For $x \notin A$, we define $d[A,K](x) = 0$. If $K = \{(0,0), (0,-1), (-1,0), (0,1), (1,0)\}$, the generalized distance transform of any set A with respect to K is just the city-block transform we discussed earlier.

To determine under what conditions a recursive morphological erosion can be designed to compute $d[A,K]$, we first note that the following proposition establishes that $d[A,K]$ must satisfy the recursive relation

$$d[A,K](x) = 1 + \min_{z \in \dot{K}} d[A,K](x+z) \quad \text{for any} \quad x \in A$$

where $\dot{K} = K - \{0\}$. And therefore

$$d[A,K](x) = \begin{cases} 1 + \min_{z \in \dot{K}} d[A,K](x+z), & \text{for any} \quad x \in A; \\ 0, & x \notin A \end{cases}$$

This relation will quickly lead to a recursive morphological erosion for computing $d[A,K]$ for a restricted kind of structuring element K. Then we will generalize the result and show how a two-pass morphological erosion can perform the calculation of the disance transform for any K.

Proposition 5.5: Let $A \subseteq E^N$ and $K \subseteq E^N$ with $0 \in K$. For any $x \in E^N$ define

$$d[A,K](x) = \begin{cases} \max\{n \mid x \in A \ominus_{n-1} K\}, & \text{if } x \in A \\ 0, & \text{if } x \notin A \end{cases}$$

Then for any $x \in A, d[A,K](x) = 1 + \min_{z \in \dot{K}} d[A,K](x+z)$, where $\dot{K} = K - \{0\}$.

Proof:
Let $m = \min_{z \in \dot{K}} d[A,K](x+z)$ and $x \in A$. Hence $m = \min_{z \in \dot{K}} \max\{n \mid x+z \in A \ominus_{n-1} K\}$. Since $0 \in K$ and $x \in A$, the condition that for every $z \in \dot{K}$ there exists a $j \geq 1$ such that $x+z \in A \ominus_j K$ and the condition that $x \in A \ominus K$ are equivalent. Hence

$$m = \begin{cases} \min_{z \in \dot{K}} \max\{n \mid x+z \in A \ominus_{n-1} K\}, & \text{if } x \in A \ominus K \\ 0, & \text{if } x \notin A \ominus K \end{cases}$$

Case 1: $x \notin A \ominus K$. In this case since $x \in A$ and $x \notin A \ominus K$, by definition of $d[A,K], d[A,K](x) = 1$. Since in this case $m = 0, 1 + m = 1$, so that $d[A,K](x) = 1 + \min_{z \in \dot{K}} d[A,K](x+z)$.

Case 2: $x \in A \ominus K$. In this case $\max\{n \mid x \in A \underset{n-1}{\ominus} K\}$ is certainly defined.

Let $m = \min_{z \in \dot{K}} \max\{n \mid x + z \in A \underset{n-1}{\ominus} K\}$. Hence for every $z \in \dot{K}, m \le$

$\max\{n \mid x + z \in A \underset{n-1}{\ominus} K\}$, and this implies $x + z \in A \underset{m-1}{\ominus} K$. Now

$x + z \in A \underset{m-1}{\ominus} K$ for every $z \in \dot{K}$ implies $x \in (A \underset{m-1}{\ominus} K) \ominus \dot{K}$. By the

chain rule for erosion, $x \in A \ominus [(\underset{m-1}{\oplus} K) \oplus \dot{K}]$.

Now $x \in A = A \ominus \{0\}$ and $x \in A \ominus [(\underset{m-1}{\oplus} K) \oplus \dot{K}]$ implies $x \in \{A \ominus$

$[(\underset{m-1}{\oplus} K) \oplus \dot{K}]\} \cap [A \ominus \{0\}]$. But $\{A \ominus [(\underset{m-1}{\oplus} K) \oplus \dot{K}]\} \cap [A \ominus \{0\}] = A \ominus$

$\left([(\underset{m-1}{\oplus} K) \oplus \dot{K}] \cup \{0\}\right)$. Since $0 \in K$, a direct inductive proof establishes

$[(\underset{m-1}{\oplus} K) \oplus \dot{K}] \cup \{0\} = \underset{m}{\oplus} K$. Hence $x \in \underset{m}{\oplus} K$, and this certainly implies $1 + m \le$

$\max\{n \mid x \in A \underset{n-1}{\ominus} (\underset{}{\oplus} K)\} = d[A, K](x)$. Now we show that $d[A, K](x) <$

$2 + m$; thus we have the inequality $1 + m \le d[A, K](x) < 2 + m$, which will

imply $1 + m = d[A, K](x)$. By definition of $m, m = \min_{z \in \dot{K}} \max\{n \mid x + z \in$

$A \underset{n-1}{\ominus} (\underset{}{\oplus} K)\}$. Hence for some $z \in \dot{K}$, $x + z \notin A \underset{(m+1)-1}{\ominus} (\underset{}{\oplus} K) = A \ominus (\underset{m}{\oplus} K)$,

so that $x \notin A \ominus (\underset{m+1}{\oplus} K)$. Now $x \notin A \underset{m+1}{\ominus} K$ implies $d[A, K](x) = \max\{n \mid x \in$

$A \underset{n-1}{\ominus} K\} < m + 2$.

Corollary 5.3:

$$d[A, K](x) = \begin{cases} 1 + \min_{z \in \dot{K}} d[A, K](x + z), & x \in A \\ 0, & x \notin A \end{cases}$$

Having established that if $d[A, K]$ is the generalized distance transform of A with respect to K, then we obtain

$$d[A, K](x) = \begin{cases} 1 + \min_{z \in \dot{K}} d[A, K](x + z), & x \in A \\ 0, & x \notin A \end{cases}$$

We are now ready to see under what conditions this relation can be used to calculate d recursively. We must be able to order the elements in A such that for any $x \in A$, if $z \in \dot{K}$ and if $x + z \in A$, then $x + z$ is a value that has been previously computed. If such an ordering exists, then for any $x \in A$, the computation $\min_{z \in \dot{K}} d[A, K](x + z)$ can be directly done by using the previously computed values of $d[A, K](x + z)$ if $x + z \in A$ and by using the base value of 0 if $x + z \notin A$. Thus if the ordering is the forward raster scan ordering $\mathcal{F}$ and if K satifies $K \subseteq \{(r, c) \mid (c \le 0 \text{ when } r = 0) \text{ or } (r < 0)\}$, then for any $(i, j) \in K, (r + i, c + j)$ will be a value that occurs prior to (r, c) in $\mathcal{F}$, and $d[A, K](x)$ will be able to be recursively computed according to the ordering $\mathcal{F}$. Expressing $d[A,K]$ as a recursive morphological erosion is direct. Define $f : F \rightarrow E, F \supseteq A$, by

$$f(x) = \begin{cases} 1, & x \in A \\ 0, & x \notin A \end{cases}$$

Let $K_1 = \{0\}, K_2 = \dot{K}, k_1(0) = 0$, and $k_2(z) = -1$ for any $z \in K_2$. Finally, let $k = (k_1, k_2)$. Then $d[A,K](x) = (f \ominus_{\mathcal{F}} k)(x)$.

The next proposition establishes that for any K_1, K_2 with $0 \in K_1$ satisfying $K = K_1 \cup K_2$, the generalized distance transform of a set A with respect to K satisfies $d[A,K](x) = \min\{d[A,K_1](x), \min_{z \in K_2} d[A,K](x + z) + 1\}$. This relation leads to a two-pass procedure for the computation of $d[A,K](x)$ in the case that A and K are two-dimensional. In the first pass, forward ordering $\mathcal{F}$ is used and K_1 is selected to be the subset of K such that for every $(r,c) \in \mathcal{F}, (i,j) \in K_1$ implies that $(r+i, c+j)$ occurs before (r,c) does in $\mathcal{F}$. Hence $K_1 = K \cap \{(r,c) \mid (c \leq 0$ and $r = 0)$ or $(r < 0)\}$. In the second pass, a complementary backward ordering $\mathcal{B}$ is used and $K_2 = K \cap \{(r,c) \mid (c > 0$ and $r = 0)$ or $r > 0\}$. Since $\{(r,c) \mid (c \leq 0$ and $r = 0)$ or $r < 0\} = \{(r,c) \mid (c > 0$ and $r = 0)$ or $r > 0\}^c$, K_1 and K_2 constitute a partition of K so that $K = K_1 \cup K_2$.

Proposition 5.6: Let $A, K_1, K_2 \subseteq E^N$ with $0 \in K_1$. Let $K = K_1 \cup K_2$. Then

$$d[A,K](x) = \min\{d[A,K_1](x), \min_{z \in K_2} d[A,K](x + z) + 1\}$$

Proof:
Either $x \in A$ or $x \notin A$. If $x \notin A, d[A,K_1](x) = 0$ and $d[A,K] = 0$ by definition, so it is indeed the case that

$$0 = d[A,K] = \min\{0, \min_{z \in K_2} d[A,K](x + z) + 1\}$$

If $x \in A$, let $n_1 = d[A,K_1](x)$ and $m_1 = \min_{z \in K_2} d[A,K](x + z)$. Then $x \in A \ominus (\underset{n_1-1}{\oplus} K_1)$ and $x \in A \ominus [(\underset{m_1-1}{\oplus} K) \oplus K_2]$. Hence $x \in [A \ominus (\underset{n_1-1}{\oplus} K_1)] \cap \{A \ominus [(\underset{m_1-1}{\oplus} K) \oplus K_2]\}$, so that $x \in A \ominus \{(\underset{n_1-1}{\oplus} K_1) \cup [(\underset{m_1-1}{\oplus} K) \oplus K_2]\}$. Let $m = \min\{n_1, m_1 + 1\}$. Then

$$(\underset{n_1-1}{\oplus} K_1) \cup [(\underset{m_1-1}{\oplus} K) \oplus K_2] \supseteq (\underset{m-1}{\oplus} K_1) \cup [(\underset{m-2}{\oplus} K) \oplus K_2]$$

$$\supseteq (\underset{m-1}{\oplus} K_1) \cup [(\underset{m-2}{\oplus} K_2) \oplus K_2]$$

$$\supseteq (\underset{m-1}{\oplus} K_1) \cup [(\underset{m-1}{\oplus} K_2)]$$

$$\supseteq \underset{m-1}{\oplus} (K_1 \cup K_2) = \underset{m-1}{\oplus} K$$

Hence $A \ominus [(\underset{n_1-1}{\oplus} K_1) \cup (\underset{m_1-1}{\oplus} K) \oplus K_2] \subseteq A \ominus (\underset{m-1}{\oplus} K)$. Therefore $x \in A \ominus (\underset{m-1}{\oplus} K)$, so that $m \leq \max\{n \mid x \in A \ominus (\underset{n-1}{\oplus} K)\}$. Now either $m = d[A,K_1](x)$ or $m = 1 + \min_{z \in K_2} d[A,K](x + z)$. If $m = d[A,K_1](x)$, then $x \in A \ominus (\underset{m-1}{\oplus} K_1)$

and $x \notin A \ominus (\bigoplus K_1)$. In this case $\max\{n \mid x \in A \ominus (\underset{n-1}{\bigoplus} K)\} < m + 1$.

Now $m \leq \max\{n \mid x \in A \ominus (\underset{n-1}{\bigoplus} K)\} < m + 1$ implies $m = \max\{n \mid x \in A \ominus (\underset{n-1}{\bigoplus} K)\}$. If $m = 1 + \underset{z \in K_2}{\min} d[A, K](x + z)$, then $x \in A \ominus [(\underset{m-2}{\bigoplus} K) \oplus K_2]$

and $x \notin A \ominus [(\underset{m-1}{\bigoplus} K) \oplus K_2]$. Now $(\underset{m-1}{\bigoplus} K) \oplus K_2 \subseteq (\underset{m-1}{\bigoplus} K) \oplus K = \underset{m}{\bigoplus} K$. Hence

$A \ominus [(\underset{m-1}{\bigoplus} K) \oplus K_2] \supseteq A \ominus (\underset{m}{\bigoplus} K)$. Since $x \notin A \ominus [(\underset{m-1}{\bigoplus} K) \oplus K_2], x \notin A \ominus (\underset{m}{\bigoplus} K)$.

Now $x \notin A \ominus (\underset{m}{\bigoplus} K)$ implies $\max\{n \mid x \in A \ominus (\underset{n-1}{\bigoplus} K)\} < m + 1$, and

$m \leq \max\{n \mid x \in A \ominus (\underset{n-1}{\bigoplus} K)\} < m + 1$ implies that $m = \max\{n \mid x \in A \ominus (\underset{n-1}{\bigoplus} K)\} = d[A, K](x)$.

5.10   Medial Axis

Blum (1962, 1967) introduced a new method of shape description. He initially called it the *medial axis,* and later (Blum, 1973; Blum and Nagel, 1978) the *symmetric axis.* To understand the medial axis, consider the following visualization for a two-dimensional shape. Let the shape be a region of grass surrounded by bare soil. Simultaneously at all boundary points of the grass region light a fire that burns uniformly from the border of the grass region to its interior. Eventually the fire burning from one part of the border will meet the fire burning from another part of the border. Since all the grass will have been burned at the meeting place, the fire will quench and be extinguished. The locus of points on the arc of fire extinction is the medial axis. Each point on the medial axis has an associated value that is the distance between it and the boundary. For a uniform burn rate, this distance is proportional to the time it took for the fire to reach the given point from the time the grass fire was set. The medial axis with its medial axis distance function is called the *medial axis transform.*

The medial axis transform is an information preserving representation of shape. To see this, just consider running the grass fire backward. With time running in reverse, set a grass fire on each point of the medial axis exactly at the time the original grass fire is extinguished at that point. The boundary of the fire at time $t = 0$ would be the boundary of the original given shape.

When started at a point, a fire burning at a uniform rate will spread out in a circular fashion. Hence the medial axis representation can be understood as the decomposition of the shape in terms of maximal disks. Each point on the medial axis is a center of a maximal-sized disk that is contained within the shape. The radius of the disk is the distance value associated with the medial axis point. It should then come as no surprise that the medial axis is related to the generalized distance transform.

Montanari (1969) describes an algorithm for the determination of the medial axis for a shape whose boundary can be piecewise approximated by straight-line segments and circular arcs. Rosenfeld and Pfaltz (1966) describe an algorithm for the determination of the medial axis that they call a skeleton for digital shapes.

Unlike the medial axis of a shape in a continuous domain, the medial axis of a connected digital shape may not be connected and it may not be invariant to rotation and rescaling of the original shape. Hilditch (1968) and Hilditch and Rutovitz (1969) were among the first to develop algorithms that gave connected medial axes to connected shapes. Others include Arcelli and Sanniti di Baja (1978), Arcelli, Cordella, and Levialdi (1973, 1974, 1981), Bertrand (1984), Naccache and Shinghal (1984), Rearick (1985), and Arcelli and Sanniti di Baja (1989). Mott-Smith (1970) and Meyer (1986) provided a general theory for the discrete medial axis transform. Lantuejoule (1980) was able to characterize Blum's medial axis in terms of morphological operations. Gong and Bertrand (1988) give a four-pass algorithm using a grid that is the union of the original and dual grids.

We begin our treatment of the digital medial axis or skeleton by considering the axis as the locus of the centers of maximal digital disks that are contained within the shape. But we will be a little more general in that, instead of being restricted only to maximal digital disks, we will handle any arbitrary maximal-sized elementary shape. Throughout our discussion we assume that the sets we work with are discrete digital sets. Serra (1982) discusses continuous sets in Euclidean space where the medial axis and the morphological skeletons are close but not exactly the same. Prewitt (1970) calls the digital medial axis the endoskeleton and the medial axis of the background the exoskeleton.

Let K denote the basic elementary structuring element with respect to which we will determine the medial axis. K morphologically homothetic shapes of size n are easily generated by dilating $\{0\}$ with K n times: $\underset{n}{\oplus} K$. Our only requirements for K will be that K contain the origin and be bounded. The *medial axis* of a set A with respect to a structuring element K is denoted by $MA(A,K)$ and is defined by

$$MA(A,K) = \{x \mid x \in K_y \text{ and } (\underset{d[A,K](y)-1}{\oplus} K)_y \supseteq (\underset{d[A,K](x)-1}{\oplus} K)_x \text{ imply } x = y\}$$

where $d[A,K]$ is the generalized distance transform of A with respect to K. To understand this definition, recall that

$$d[A,K](x) = \max\{m \mid x \in A \underset{m-1}{\ominus} K\}$$
$$= \max\{m \mid x \in A \ominus (\underset{m-1}{\oplus} K)\}$$
$$= \max\{m \mid (\underset{m-1}{\oplus} K)_x \subseteq A\}$$

Hence the largest morphologically homothetic set of K that can be contained in a shape A and centered at a point x in the shape is

$$(\underset{d[A,K](x)-1}{\oplus} K)$$

The medial axis definition states that if x lies in the K-neigborhood of any point y whose associated maximal K-homothetic set centered at y can contain the maximal-sized K-homothetic set at x, then $x = y$. In other words, the medial axis of a set A with respect to a structuring element K contains the centers of all K-homothetic sets that are maximal with respect to the property of containment. A point x cannot be a medial axis point if it has a neighbor y whose largest K-homothetic set that is contained in A and centered at y can contain the largest K-homothetic set that is contained in A and centered at x.

If the set A is nonempty, then the medial axis of A is nonempty. Suppose $MA[A,K] = \phi$. Then $A \neq \phi$ and $x \in K_y$, and

$$(\underset{d[A,K](y)-1}{\oplus} K)_y \supseteq (\underset{d[A,K](x)-1}{\oplus} K)_x$$

implies $x \neq y$. But $0 \in K$, so that $x \in K_x$. Now $x \in K_x$ and

$$(\underset{d[A,K](x)-1}{\oplus} K)_x \supseteq (\underset{d[A,K](x)-1}{\oplus} K)_x$$

holds, and since $MA[A,K] = \phi$, $x \neq x$, clearly a contradiction.

It should be obvious that since $0 \in K$, if $x \in K_y$ and m and n are integers with $m < n$, then

$$(\underset{m}{\oplus} K)_x \subseteq (\underset{n}{\oplus} K)_y$$

Just consider that with $x \in K_y$, $0 \in K$, and $m < n$

$$(\underset{m}{\oplus} K)_{x-y} \subseteq (\underset{m}{\oplus} K) \oplus K = \underset{m+1}{\oplus} K \subseteq \underset{n}{\oplus} K$$

On a sequential computer, the most rapid way to compute the medial axis transform is in terms of the generalized distance transform. The medial axis contains exactly those points that are relative extrema for the generalized distance transform (Rosenfeld and Pfaltz, 1966; Arcelli and Sanniti di Baja, 1984; Borgefors and Sanniti di Baja, 1988).

Let $Ext(A,K)$ denote the set of extremal points of the generalized distance transform of a set A with respect to structuring element K. Then

$$Ext(A,K) = \{x \in A \mid d[A,K](x) \geq d[A,K](y) \text{ for every } y \in K_x\}$$

It follows from this definition that every point of the medial axis must be a relative extremum. That is, $MA(A,K) \subseteq Ext(A,K)$. To see this, let $x \in MA(A,K)$ and suppose that $x \notin Ext(A,K)$. In this case there must exist a y, $x \in K_y$ such that $d[A,K](x) < d[A,K](y)$. Now $0 \in K$, $x \in K_y$, and $d[A,K](x) < d[A,K](y)$ imply

$$(\underset{d[A,K](x)-1}{\oplus} K)_x \subseteq (\underset{d[A,K](y)-1}{\oplus} K)_y$$

But by definition of medial axis, this set of conditions implies $x = y$. And $x = y$ is a contradiction of $d[A,K](x) < d[A,K](y)$.

Proving that every relative extremum of the distance transform is a point in the medial axis involves the boundedness of the structuring element K. A set K is said to be *bounded* if and only if for every point $k \in K$ and $x \neq 0$ there exists some integer M such that $k + mx \notin K$ for $m > M$.

If K is bounded, then $K_x \subseteq K$ must imply $x = 0$. To see this, note that if $K_x \subseteq K$ and $k \in K$, then it must follow that $k + mx \in K$ for every positive integer m. Now if K is bounded, $K_x \subseteq K, x \neq 0$, and $k \in K$, then it must be that $k + mx \in K$ for every positive integer m. This contradicts the boundedness of k. Hence it must be that $x = 0$.

Now we are ready to establish that any relative extremum of the generalized distance transform of A with respect to K must be a point of the medial axis of A with respect to K. So we let $x \in Ext(A,K)$. Then $d[A,k](x) > d[A,K](y)$ for $x \in K_y$.

Now suppose $x \in K_y$ and $\left(\bigoplus_{d[A,K](y)-1} K \right)_y \supseteq \left(\bigoplus_{d[A,K](x)-1} K \right)_x$. Then

$$\left(\bigoplus_{d[A,K](y)-1} K \right)_{y-x} \supseteq \bigoplus_{d[A,K](x)-1} K$$

Since $0 \in K$ and $d[A,K](x) \geq d[A,K](y)$,

$$\bigoplus_{d[A,K](x)-1} K \supseteq \bigoplus_{d[A,K](y)-1} K$$

Since K is bounded,

$$\bigoplus_{d[A,K](y)-1} K$$

is bounded. But $\left(\bigoplus_{d[A,K](y)-1} K \right)$ bounded with

$$\left(\bigoplus_{d[A,K](y)-1} K \right)_{y-x} \supseteq \bigoplus_{d[A,K](y)-1} K \text{ implies } y - x = 0.$$

And $x = y$ implies $x \in MA(A,K)$. We have therefore established the medial axis characterization theorem.

Theorem 5.5: Medial Axis Characterization Theorem
Let $0 \in K$ and K be bounded. Then $Ext(A,K) = MA(A,K)$.

The medial axis transform of a set A is determined by the medial axis of A and the medial axis distance function f defined on the medial axis of A. The medial axis function is directly related to the generalized distance. Indeed, for any $x \in MA(A,K), f(x) = d[A,K](x) - 1$, as shown in Fig. 5.40.

5.10.1 Medial Axis and Morphological Skeleton

Serra (1982) credits Lantuejoule (1978) for the following definition of the morphological skeleton of a set A with respect to a structuring element K by the sets

$$S_0, \ldots, S_N, \text{ where } S_n = A \ominus_n K - (A \ominus_n K) \circ K \text{ and } A \ominus_0 K = A$$

The skeleton of A is then given by $\bigcup_{n=0}^{N} S_n$. Figure 5.41 illustrates this definition.

It follows that if $x \in S_n$, then (1) $d[A,K](x) = n+1$ and (2) $x \in MA(A,K)$. To show (1), consider $(A \ominus_n K) \circ K$. Since $0 \in K$,

$$A \underset{n+1}{\ominus} K \subseteq (A \underset{n+1}{\ominus} K) \oplus K = (A \underset{n}{\ominus} K) \circ K$$

Hence

$$A \underset{n}{\ominus} K - (A \underset{n+1}{\ominus} K) \oplus K \subseteq A \underset{n}{\ominus} K - A \underset{n+1}{\ominus} K$$

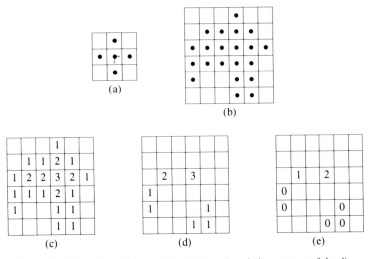

Figure 5.40 Generation of the medial axis from the relative extrema of the distance transform. (a) Structuring element K; (b) A; (c) $d[A,K](x)$ for $x \in A$; (d) $Ext[A,K]$ and associated $d[A,K](x)$ for $x \in Ext[A,K]$; and (e) $MA[A,K]$ and associated medial axis function. Only those pixels with values shown are part of the medial axis.

So if $x \in S_n$,

$$x \in A \ominus_n K \text{ and } x \notin A \ominus_{n+1} K$$

which by definition of $d[A,K](x)$ implies $d[A,K](x) = n + 1$.

To show that $x \in S_n$ implies $x \in MA(A,K)$ involves a little more work. Let $x \in K_y$. Now $x \in S_n$ implies $x \notin (A \ominus_n K) \circ K$. By the opening characterization theorem, it is not the case that there exists a t such that $x \in K_t$ and $K_t \subseteq A \ominus_n K$. But this means that for every $t, x \notin K_t$ or $K_t \not\subseteq A \ominus_n K$. Since $x \in K_y$, it must be that $K_y \not\subseteq A \ominus_n K$. By definition of erosion, $y \notin (A \ominus_n K) \ominus K = A \ominus_{n+1} K$. Therefore $d[A,K](y) - 1 \le n$, so that $d[A,K](y) \le n + 1 = d[A,K](x)$. Now we have established that $x \in K_y$ implies $d[A,K](y) \le d[A,K](x)$, so that by the medial axis characterization theorem, $x \in MA(A,K)$.

Conversely, it also holds that if $x \in MA(A,K)$ and $d[A,K](x) = n + 1$, then $x \in S_n$. To show that $x \in S_n$ we must show that

$$x \in A \ominus_n K \quad \text{and} \quad x \notin (A \ominus_n K) \circ K$$

It is easy to establish that $x \in A \ominus_n K$. Since

$$d[A,K](x) = n + 1, (\oplus_n K)_x \subseteq A$$

Hence by definition of erosion, $x \in A \ominus_n K$.

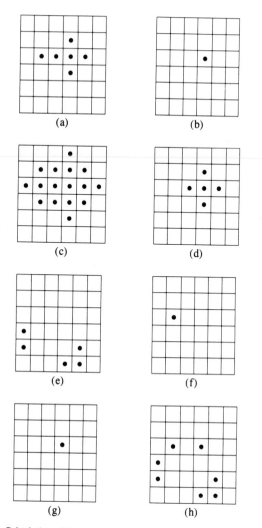

Figure 5.41 Calculation of the morphological skeleton for the set A with respect to structuring element K. (a) $A \ominus K$; (b) $A \ominus K$; (c) $A \circ K$; (d) $(A \ominus K) \circ K$; (e) $S_0 = A - A \circ K$; (f) $S_1 = A \ominus K - (A \ominus K) \circ K$; (g) $S_2 = A \underset{2}{\ominus} K - (A \ominus K) \circ K$; and (h) $S = S_0 \cup S_1 \cup S_2$. Both A and K are shown in Fig. 5.40.

To show $x \notin (A \underset{n}{\ominus} K) \circ K$, we suppose this is not the case and show a contradiction. Suppose $x \in (A \underset{n}{\ominus} K) \circ K$. Then $x \in (A \ominus K) \oplus K$. Hence there exist a $z \in A \underset{n+1}{\ominus} K$ and a $y \in K$ such that $x = z + y$. Thus $x \in K_z$. Now $x \in K_z$ and $x \in MA(A,K)$ imply $d[A,K](z) \leq d[A,K](x) = n + 1$. But $z \in A \underset{n+1}{\ominus} K$ implies $d[A,K](z) \geq n + 2$, a contradiction. Therefore $x \notin (A \underset{n}{\ominus} K) \circ K$, so that

$$x \in A \ominus_{n} K - (A \ominus_{n} K) \circ K = S_n$$

We close our discussion by showing that the medial axis permits a perfect reconstruction of the given shape. The reconstruction is given by the relation

$$A = \bigcup_{n=0}^{N} S_n \oplus_{n} K$$

where N is the largest integer such that $S_N \neq \phi$.

Note that

$$\bigcup_{n=0}^{N} S_n \oplus_{n} K = \bigcup_{n=0}^{N} \left[A \ominus_{n} K - (A \ominus_{n} K) \circ K \right] \oplus_{n} K$$

$$\subseteq \bigcup_{n=0}^{N} [A \ominus_{n} K] \oplus_{n} K$$

$$\subseteq \bigcup_{n=0}^{N} A \circ (\oplus_{n} K) \subseteq \bigcup_{n=0}^{N} A = A$$

Also if $x \in A$, then there exists a $y \in MA(A,K)$ such that

$$x \in (\bigoplus_{d[A,K](y)-1} K)_y$$

For if not, then for every $y \in MA(A,K)$

$$x \notin (\bigoplus_{d[A,K](y)-1} K)_y$$

But in this case x would have to be in $MA[A,K]$. Since

$$x \in (\bigoplus_{d[A,K](x)-1} K)_x$$

we have a contradiction. So there must exist a $y \in MA(A,K)$ such that

$$x \in (\bigoplus_{d[A,K](y)-1} K)_y \subseteq A$$

But we have just proved that $y \in MA(A,K)$ implies $y \in S_n$, where $n = d[A,K](y) - 1$. Hence

$$x \in S_n \oplus_{n} K \subseteq \bigcup_{n=1}^{N} S_n \oplus_{n} K$$

Skiz

Lantuejoul (1980) defines a skeleton of the background based on zones of influence. Serra (1982) calls this skeleton the skiz. To define the zones of influence, we begin with a representation of the given set A as the union of its connected components $C_1, \ldots, C_N$:

$$A = \bigcup_{n=1}^{N} C_n$$

The zone of influence Z_n associated with component C_n is the set of all points that are closer to C_n than to any other component:

$$Z_n = \{x \mid \rho(x, C_n) < \rho(x, C_m), \quad m \neq n\}$$

where $\rho(x, C)$ denotes the distance from the point x to the set C. The points that do not belong to any Z_n are the points that are equidistant between two different components. These points are the points of the skiz of A^c :

$$S_z(A^c) = \left(\bigcup_{n=1}^{N} Z_n \right)^c$$

There is a small difficulty with this definition when working in a discrete digital domain where the possibility exists that a straight line between two connected components might be an even number of pixels in length. In this case there is no pixel on this line that is not in a zone of influence, and the important connectivity property of the skiz is lost. One way to handle this situation is to define the digital skiz of A^c as those positions x of the digital medial axis A^c for which there exist two distinct connected components of A that have nonempty intersections with a structuring element one size greater than the maximal-sized structuring element that can be positioned at x and remain inside A^c. That is,

$$S_z(A^c) = \{x \in MA(A^c, K) \mid \text{ for some } m, n, \quad m \neq n,$$

$$\left(\bigoplus_{d[A^c, K](x)} K \right)_x \cap C_n \neq \phi \text{ and}$$

$$\left(\bigoplus_{d[A^c, K](x)} K \right)_x \cap C_m \neq \phi\}$$

5.11   Morphological Sampling Theorem

Before sets are sampled for morphological processing, they must be morphologically simplified by an opening or a closing (Haralick et al., 1989). Such sampled sets can be reconstructed in two ways: by either a closing or a dilation. In both reconstructions the sampled reconstructed sets are equal to the sampled sets. A set contains its closing reconstruction and is contained in its dilation reconstruction; indeed, these are extremal bounding sets. That is, the largest set that downsamples to a given set is its reconstruction by dilation; the smallest is its reconstruction by closing. Furthermore, the distance from the maximal to the minimal reconstruction is no more than the diameter of the reconstruction structuring element. Morphological sampling thus provides reconstructions positioned only to within some spatial tolerance that depends on the sampling interval. This spatial limitation contrasts with the sampling reconstruction process in signal processing from which only those frequencies below the Nyquist frequency can be reconstructed.

It is exactly the presence of small details such as small objects, object protrusions, object intrusions, and holes before sampling that causes the sampled result to be unrepresentative of the original, just as in signal processing the presence of frequencies higher than the Nyquist frequency causes the sampled signal to be unrepresentative of the original signal. In communications this "aliasing" means that signals must be low-pass filtered before sampling. Likewise in morphology, the sets must be morphologically filtered and simplified before sampling. Small objects and object protrusions can be eliminated by a suitable opening operation. Small object intrusions and holes can be eliminated by a suitable closing. Since opening and closing are duals, we develop our motivation by considering just the opening operation.

Opening a set F by a structuring element K in order to eliminate small details of F raises, in turn, the issue of how K should relate to the sampling set S. If the sample points of S are too finely spaced, little will be accomplished by the reduction in resolution. On the other hand, if S is too coarse relative to K, objects preserved in the opening may be missed by the sampling. S and K can be coordinated by demanding that there be a way to reconstruct the opened image from the sampled opened image. Of course, details smaller than K are removed by the opening and cannot be reconstructed.

One natural way to reconstruct a sampled opening is by dilation. If S and K were coordinated to make the reconstructed image (first opened, then sampled, and then dilated) the same as the opened image, we would have a morphological sampling theorem nearly identical to the standard sampling theorem of signal processing. However, morphology cannot provide a perfect reconstruction, as illustrated by the following one-dimensional continuous-domain example.

Let the image F be the union of three topologically open intervals

$$F = (3.1, \ 7.4) \cup (11.5, \ 11.6) \cup (18.9, \ 19.8)$$

where (x, y) denotes the topologically open interval between x and y. We can remove all details less than length 2 by opening with the structuring element $K = (-1, \ 1)$ consisting of the topologically open interval from -1 to 1. Then the opened image $F \circ K = (3.1, \ 7.4)$. What should the corresponding sample set be? Consider a sampling set $S = \{x \mid x \text{ an integer}\}$, with a sample spacing of unity; other spacings such as .2, .5, or .7 could illustrate the same sampling concept as well. The sampled opened image $(F \circ K) \cap S = \{4, 5, 6, 7\}$. Dilating by K to reconstruct the image produces $[(F \circ K) \cap S] \oplus K = (3, 8)$, an interval that properly contains $F \circ K$. The dilation fills in between the sample points but cannot "know" to expand on the left end by a length of .9 and yet expand by .4 on the right end. However, the reconstruction is the largest one for which the sampled reconstruction $\{[(F \circ K) \cap S] \oplus K\} \cap S$ produces the sampled opening $(F \circ K) \cap S = \{4, 5, 6, 7\}$. This is easily seen in the example because substituting the closed interval $[3, 8]$ for the open interval $(3, 8)$ produces the sampled closed interval $[3, 8] \cap S = \{3, 4, 5, 6, 7, 8\}$ that properly contains $(F \circ K) \cap S = \{4, 5, 6, 7\}$.

In the remainder of this section we give a complete derivation of the results illustrated in the example. First, note that to use a structuring element K as a "reconstruction kernel," K must be large enough to ensure that the dilation of the sampling set S by K covers the entire space E^N. For technical reasons apparent in the derivations, we also require that K be symmetric, $K = \check{K}$. In the standard sampling theorem, the period of the highest frequency present must be sampled at least twice in order to reconstruct properly the signal from its sampled form. In mathematical morphology there is an analogous requirement. The sample spacing must be small enough so that the diameter of K is just smaller than these two sample intervals. Hence the diameter of K is large enough to contain two, but not three, sample points. We express this relationship by requiring that

$$x \in K_y \Rightarrow K_x \cap K_y \cap S \neq \emptyset$$
$$\text{and } K \cap S = \{0\}$$

The first condition implies that the dilation of sample points fills the whole space; that is, $S \oplus K = E^N$ when K is not empty. If the points in the sampling set S are spaced no father apart than d, then the corresponding reconstructing kernel K could be the topologically open ball of radius d. In this case $x \in K_y \Rightarrow K_x \cap K_y \cap S \neq \emptyset$. Notice that two points that are d apart can lie on the diameter of $2d$. But since the ball is topologically open, the diameter cannot contain three points spaced d apart. Hence the radius of K is just smaller than the sampling interval. Also notice that if a sample point falls in the center of K, K will not contain another sample point.

The morphological sampling theorem we develop here pertains mainly to the digital domain. Consider the two-dimensional continuous case in which there is a regular square grid sampling, and the sample interval in each direction has length L. To guarantee that $K \cap S = \{0\}$, the biggest possible disk K is the open disk with radius L.

The difficulty occurs with the condition $x \in K_y \Rightarrow K_x \cap K_y \cap S \neq \emptyset$. Figure 5.42 shows a square whose length-L side is the sampling interval. It also shows several translates of K and a disk of the radius L. Select two points that are no farther apart than distance L in the following way. Take one point x to be in the interior of one shaded region of Fig. 5.42. Take the other point y to be opposite it interior to

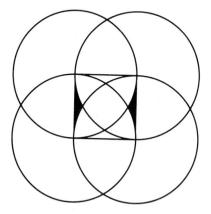

Figure 5.42 Example of how two points can be chosen no farther apart than the sample distance, yet no sample point is simultaneously less distant than the sample distance to each of them. Take the two points to be opposite each other, each interior to one of the shaded regions. Consider the sample points to be the corners of the square.

the other shaded region. With this selection the distance between the two points is guaranteed to be less than L. Yet it is apparent from the geometry that since none of the four open disks of diameter L can contain the two points that are distance L apart, the condition $x \in K_y \Rightarrow K_x \cap K_y \cap S \neq \emptyset$ cannot be satisfied. This is because each open disk represents exactly the set of points each having the property that, if an open disk were centered at the point, the open disk would contain a sample point. Hence, with the disk K being defined by the L_2 norm, there can be no morphological sampling theorem in the continuous case. In fact the only norm by which K can be defined that yields a morphological sampling theorem in the continuous case is the L_∞ norm.

Because the shaded region in Fig. 5.42 is so narrow, this difficulty does not arise in the digital case. Suppose that the original domain is discrete, with nearest points at distance 1 from each other. Then the condition $x \in K_y \Rightarrow K_x \cap K_y \cap S \neq \emptyset$ is easily satisfied for any $L \in \{2,3,4,5,6,7\}$ since in this case $L(1 - \frac{\sqrt{3}}{2}) < 1$. Figure 5.43 illustrates the case in which the sample interval L is 6. Notice that the distance between any pair of digital points, one from a region corresponding to one of the shaded regions of Fig. 5.42 and the other from the region opposite it, must be greater than L. Hence for any two such points x and y, it is not the case that $x \in K_y$. So the difficulty with $x \in K_y$ and $K_x \cap K_y \cap S = \emptyset$ cannot arise.

We now develop the binary morphological sampling theorem. In what follows, the set $F \subseteq E^N$, the reconstruction structuring element will be denoted by $K \subseteq E^N$, and the sampling set will be denoted by $S \subseteq E^N$. Although not necessary for every proposition, we assume that S and K obey the following five conditions:

1. $S = S \oplus S$
2. $S = \check{S}$

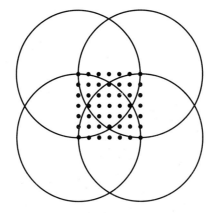

Figure 5.43 Satisfying the condition $x \in K_y \Rightarrow K_x \cap K_y \cap S \neq \emptyset$ in the digital case in which K is a circular disk. Notice that for any pair of digital points in the regions corresponding to the shaded region of Fig. 5.42, the distance between them is not less than the radius of the open disk K. Hence the difficulty illustrated in Fig. 5.42 cannot arise.

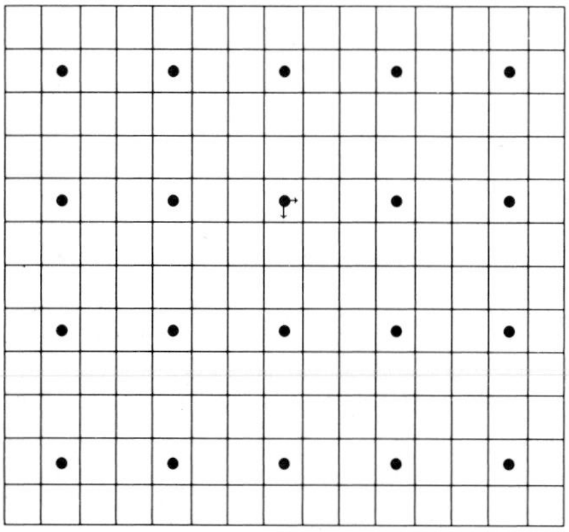

Figure 5.44 Sampling every third pixel by row and by column. The sampling set
S is represented by all points shown as •.

3. $K \cap S = \{0\}$
4. $K = \check{K}$
5. $a \in K_b \Rightarrow K_a \cap K_b \cap S \neq \emptyset$

Figure 5.44 illustrates the S associated with a 3-to-1 downsampling. Figure 5.45 illustrates a structuring element K satisfying conditions 3, 4, and 5. Conditions 1 through 3 imply that if $x \in S$, then $S_x = S$, and also since $K \cap S = \{0\}$, $x \in S$ implies $K_x \cap S = \{x\}$. Both these facts are utilized in several proofs for the relationships that follow.

5.11.1 Set-Bounding Relationships

It is obvious that since $0 \in K$, the reconstruction of a sampled set $F \cap S$ by dilation with K produces a superset of the sampled set $F \cap S$. That is, $F \cap S \subseteq (F \cap S) \oplus K$. The reconstruction by dilation is open so that $[(F \cap S) \oplus K] \circ K = (F \cap S) \oplus K$. Moreover, the erosion and dilation of the original image F by K bound the reconstructed sampled image in the following set relationships.

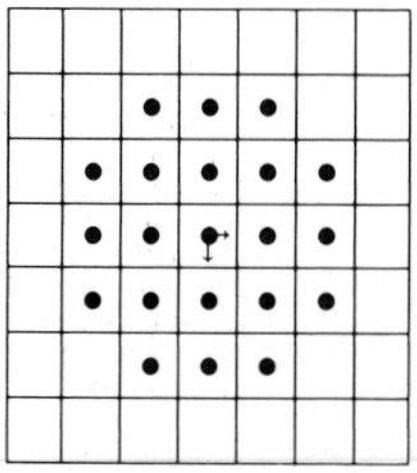

Figure 5.45 A symmetric structuring element K that is a digital disk of radius $\sqrt{5}$. For the sampling set S of Fig. 5.44, $K \cap S = \{0\}$, and $x \in K_y$ implies $K_x \cap K_y \cap S \neq \emptyset$.

$$F \ominus K \subseteq (F \cap S) \oplus K \subseteq F \oplus K$$

This relation shows that the reconstruction by dilation cannot be too far away from F since the reconstruction is constrained to lie between F eroded by K and F dilated by K. This closeness between F and the dilation reconstruction $(F \cap S) \oplus K$ is strengthened when we realize that sampling F and sampling the dilation reconstruction of F produce identical results.

$$F \cap S = [(F \cap S) \oplus K] \cap S$$

That this is true can be seen from the following derivation.

From this result it rapidly follows that sampling followed by a dilation reconstruction is an idempotent operation. That is, $\left([(F \cap S) \oplus K] \cap S \right) \oplus K = (F \cap S) \oplus K$.

Considering sampling followed by reconstruction as an operation, we discover that it is an increasing operation, distributing over union but not over intersection.

The dilation reconstruction of a sampled F is always a superset of F opened by the reconstruction structuring element K. Hence if F is open under K, then F is contained in its dilation reconstruction.

$$F \circ K \subseteq (F \cap S) \oplus K$$

From the idempotency of the operation, it then follows that the reconstruction of the opened sampled image F is bounded by $F \circ K$ on the low side and $F \circ K$ dilated by K on the high side.

$$F \circ K \subseteq \left[(F \circ K) \cap S \right] \oplus K \subseteq (F \circ K) \oplus K$$

If F is morphologically simplified and filtered so that $F = F \circ K$, then the previous bounds reduce to

$$F \subseteq (F \cap S) \oplus K \subseteq F \oplus K$$

By reconsidering our example $F = (3.1, \ 7.4) \cup (11.5, \ 11.6) \cup (18.9, \ 19.8)$, which is not open under $K = (-1, 1)$, we can see that such an F is not necessarily a lower bound for the reconstruction. In this case $F \cap S = \{4, 5, 6, 7, 19\}$ and the reconstruction $(F \cap S) \oplus K = (3, 8) \cup (18, 20)$, which does not contain F. This suggests that the condition that F be open under K is essential in order to have $F \subseteq (F \cap S) \oplus K$.

Finally, we mention that the reconstruction $(F \cap S) \oplus K$ is the largest open set that when sampled produces $F \cap S$.

Proposition 5.7: Let $A \subseteq E^N$ satisfy $A \cap S = F \cap S$ and $A = A \circ K$. Then $A \supseteq (F \cap S) \oplus K$ implies $A = (F \cap S) \oplus K$.

Proof:
Suppose $A \supseteq (F \cap S) \oplus K$, $A \cap S = F \cap S$, and $A = A \circ K$. Since $A \cap S = F \cap S$, $(A \cap S) \oplus K = (F \cap S) \oplus K$. But $A = A \circ K$ implies $A \subseteq (A \cap S) \oplus$

$K = (F \cap S) \oplus K$. Now $A \subseteq (F \cap S) \oplus K$, together with the supposition $A \supseteq (F \cap S) \oplus K$, implies $A = (F \cap S) \oplus K$.

Thus we have established the maximality of the reconstruction $(F \cap S) \oplus K$ with respect to the two properties of being open and downsampling to $F \cap S$. What about a minimal reconstruction? Certainly we would expect a minimal reconstruction to be contained in the maximal reconstruction and to contain the sampled image. Since closing is extensive, we immediately have $F \cap S \subseteq (F \cap S) \bullet K$. Since $0 \in K$, erosion is an antiextensive operation. Hence $(F \cap S) \bullet K = [(F \cap S) \oplus K] \ominus K \subseteq (F \cap S) \oplus K$. These relations suggest the possibility of a reconstruction by closing. Indeed it is the case that under the conditions specified by the sampling theorem,

$$F \ominus K \subseteq (F \cap S) \bullet K \subseteq (F \cap S) \oplus K \subseteq F \oplus K$$

This bounding relationship can be derived from the following argument. Let $x \in F \ominus K$. Then $K_x \subseteq F$. To show that $x \in (F \cap S) \bullet K$, we will show that $x + k \in (F \cap S) \oplus K$ for every $k \in K$. So let $k \in K$. Then $x + k \in K_x$. But $x + k \in K_x$ implies $K_x \cap K_{x+k} \cap S \neq \emptyset$. Hence there exists $s \in K_x \cap K_{x+k} \cap S$. Now $s \in K_x$ and $K_x \subseteq F$ imply $s \in F$. Hence $s \in F \cap S$. Furthermore, $s \in K_{x+k}$ implies there exists $k' \in K$ such that $s = x + k + k'$. Rearranging, we have $s - k' = x + k$. But $K = \check{K}$, so $k' \in K$ implies $-k' \in K$. Now $s \in F \cap S$ and $-k' \in K$ imply $s - k' \in (F \cap S) \oplus K$. Therefore $F \ominus K \subseteq (F \cap S) \bullet K$. Since $0 \in K, (F \cap S) \bullet K \subseteq (F \cap S) \oplus K$. Since $F \cap S \subseteq F, (F \cap S) \oplus K \subseteq F \oplus K$.

As with the dilation reconstruction, the sampled closing reconstruction is identical to the sampled image.

$$[(F \cap S) \bullet K] \cap S = F \cap S$$

Consider our example $F = (3.1, \ 7.4) \cup (11.5, \ 11.6) \cup (18.9, \ 19.8)$, which is closed under $K = (-1, \ 1)$. If the sampling set S is the integers, then $F \cap S = \{4, 5, 6, 7, 19\}$. Closing $F \cap S$ with K can be visualized via the opening/closing duality $(F \cap S) \bullet K = [(F \cap S)^c \circ \check{K}]^c$. Opening the set $(F \cap S)^c$ with $\check{K} = K$ produces $(F \cap S)^c \circ K = \{ x \neq 19 \mid x < 4 \ \text{or} \ > 7 \}$. Hence $(F \cap S) \bullet K = [(F \cap S)^c \circ K]^c = \{x \mid x = 19 \ \text{or} \ 4 \leq x \leq 7\}$, and sampling produces $[(F \cap S) \bullet K] \cap S = \{4, 5, 6, 7, 19\} = F \cap S$.

Finally, we note that the closing reconstruction $(F \cap S) \bullet K$ is the smallest closed set that when sampled produces $F \cap S$.

Proposition 5.8: Let $A \subseteq E^N$ satisfy $A \cap S = F \cap S$ and $A = A \bullet K$. Then $A \subseteq (F \cap S) \bullet K$ implies $A = (F \cap S) \bullet K$.

Proof:

Suppose $A \subseteq (F \cap S) \bullet K$. Now $A \cap S = F \cap S$ implies $(A \cap S) \bullet K = (F \cap S) \bullet K$. Since $(A \cap S) \bullet K \subseteq A \bullet K$ and $A \bullet K = A$, we obtain $(F \cap S) \bullet K \subseteq A$. But $A \subseteq (F \cap S) \bullet K$ and $A \supseteq (F \cap S) \bullet K$ imply $A = (F \cap S) \bullet K$.

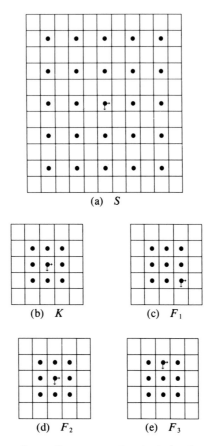

Figure 5.46 A sampling set S, a reconstruction structuring element K, and three sets F_1, F_2, and F_3, each of which is open under K.

5.11.2 Examples

To illustrate more clearly the bounding relationships developed in the previous section between a set and its sample reconstructions, we give three simple examples. The domain of these examples is defined as $E \times E$, where E is the set of integers. The sample set S is chosen as the set of even numbers in both row and column directions. Thus

$$S = \{(r,c)|r \in E \text{ and is even}; \quad c \in E \text{ and is even}\}$$

K is chosen as a box of size 3×3 whose center is defined as the origin. The sets S and K and the three example sets F_1, F_2, and F_3 are shown in Fig. 5.46. The sets F_1, F_2, and F_3 are 3×3 boxes with different origins, and the condition $F = F \circ K$ holds for all these example sets.

The results of $F \ominus K$, $F \cap S$, $(F \cap S) \bullet K$, $(F \cap S) \oplus K$, and $F \oplus K$ for sets F_1, F_2, and F_3 are shown in Figs. 5.47–5.49.

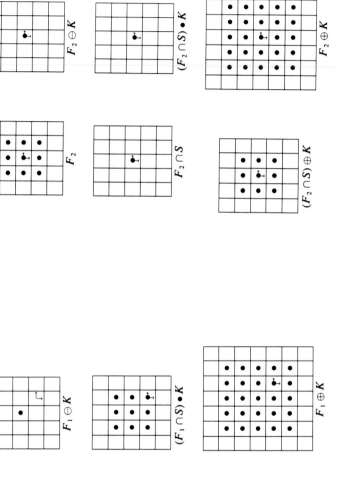

Figure 5.48 A second example of how the erosion and dilation of F_2 bound the minimal reconstruction $(F \cap S) \bullet K$ and the maximal reconstruction $(F_2 \cap S) \oplus K$, respectively, which in turn bound F_2.

Figure 5.47 Example of how the erosion and dilation of F_1 bound the minimal reconstruction $(F_1 \cap S) \bullet K$ and the maximal reconstruction $(F_1 \cap S) \oplus K$, respectively, that in turn bound F_1 because F_1 is both open and closed under K.

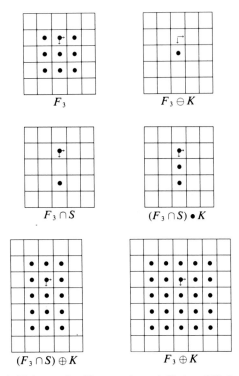

Figure 5.49 A third example of how erosion and dilation of F_2 bound (in this case properly) the minimal reconstruction $(F_3 \cap S) \bullet K$ and the maximal reconstruction $(F_3 \cap S) \oplus K$, respectively, which in turn bound (in this case properly) F_3.

EXAMPLE 5.4

All the pixels contained in the vertical boundaries of F_1 have even column coordinates, and those in the horizontal boundaries of F_1 have even row coordinates. Since the sample set S consists of pairs of even numbers and F_1 is a 3×3 box, the set $F_1 \cap S$ consists of the four corner points of F_1 and is contained in the boundary set of F_1. Hence the closing reconstruction of $F_1 \cap S$ recovers F_1, and the dilation reconstruction of $F_1 \cap S$ is equivalent to $F \oplus K$. In fact the following two equalities hold only when (1) the sampling is every other row and column, (2) a set's vertical boundaries have even column coordinates, and (3) its horizontal boundaries have even row coordinates.

$$(F \cap S) \bullet K = F \quad \text{and} \quad (F \cap S) \oplus K = F \oplus K$$

The bounding relationships for F_1, illustrated in Fig. 5.47, are

$$F_1 \ominus K \subseteq (F_1 \cap S) \bullet K = F_1 \subseteq (F_1 \cap S) \oplus K = F_1 \oplus K$$

EXAMPLE 5.5

Since all pixels contained in the vertical boundaries of F_2 have odd column coordinates, those in the horizontal boundaries of F_2 have odd row coordinates, and F_2 is a small 3×3 box, the set $F_2 \cap S$ does not contain any part of the boundary of F_2. Thus the closing reconstruction of $F_2 \cap S$ equals $F_2 \ominus K$, and the dilation reconstruction of $F_2 \cap S$ is equivalent to F_2. Similar to Example 5.4, the following equalities hold only when the sampling is every other row and column and has its odd column coordinates in its vertical boundaries and its odd row coordinates in its horizontal boundaries.

$$F \ominus K = (F \cap S) \bullet K \quad \text{and} \quad F = (F \cap S) \oplus K$$

The bounding relationships for F_2, illustrated in Fig. 5.48, are

$$F_2 \ominus K = (F_2 \cap S) \bullet K \subseteq F_2 = (F_2 \cap S) \oplus K \subseteq F_2 \oplus K$$

EXAMPLE 5.6

The pixels contained in the vertical boundaries of F_3 have odd column co-ordinates, and the pixels in the horizontal boundaries of F_3 have even row coordinates. Hence no equalities should exist in the bounding relationship as shown in Fig. 5.49. The bounding relationships for F_3 are

$$F_3 \ominus K \subseteq (F_3 \cap S) \bullet K \subseteq F_3 \subseteq (F_3 \cap S) \oplus K \subseteq 3 \oplus K$$

To explain why the opening condition $F = F \circ K$ is needed for the bounding relationships involving F, we show an example set F_4 that deviates from the set F_3 by adding six extra points to it (see Fig. 5.50). The sample and reconstruction results of $F_4, F_4 \cap S, (F_4 \cap S) \bullet K$, and $(F_4 \cap S) \oplus K$ are exactly the same as the results for F_3. However, no bounding relationships between F_4 and its sample reconstructions are applicable. If we open F_4 by K, the bounding relationships exist because $F_4 \circ K = F_3$.

5.11.3 Distance Relationships

We have established the maximality of the reconstruction $(F \cap S) \oplus K$ with respect to the property of being open and downsampling to $F \cap S$, and the minimality of

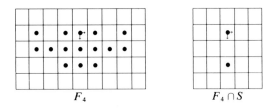

Figure 5.50 A set F_4 that is not open under K. Its sampling $F_4 \cap S$ is identical to the sampling of F_3, yet the maximal reconstruction $(F_4 \cap S) \oplus K$ does not constitute an upper bound for F_4 as in the previous examples.

the reconstruction $(F \cap S) \bullet K$ with respect to the property of being closed and downsampling to $F \cap S$. In this section we define more precisely how far $F \ominus K$ is from $F \bullet K$, how far $F \circ K$ is from $F \oplus K$, and how far $(F \cap S) \bullet K$ is from $(F \cap S) \oplus K$. This is important to know because $F \ominus K \subseteq (F \cap S) \bullet K \subseteq F$ when $F = F \bullet K$; $F \subseteq (F \cap S) \oplus K \subseteq F \oplus K$ when $F = F \circ K$; and $(F \cap S) \bullet K \subseteq F \subseteq (F \cap S) \oplus K$ when $F = F \circ K = F \bullet K$. Notice that in all three cases the difference between the lower- and the upper-set bound is at most a dilation by K. This motivates us to define a distance function to measure the distance between two sets and to work out the relation of the distance between a set and its dilation by K to the size of the set K. In this section we show that with a suitable definition of distance, all these distances are less than the radius of K. Since K is related to the sampling distance, all the above-mentioned distances are less than the sampling interval.

For the size of a set B, denoted by $r(B)$, we use the radius of its circumscribing disk whose origin is in B. Thus $r(B) = \min_{x \in B} \max_{y \in B} \|x - y\|$. The more mathematically correct forms of inf for min and sup for max may be substituted when the space E is the real line. In this case the proofs in this section require similar modifications. For a set A that contains a set B, a natural pseudodistance from A to B is defined by $\rho(A, B) = \max_{x \in A} \min_{y \in B} \|x - y\|$. It is easy to verify that (1) $\rho(A, B) \geq 0$, (2) $\rho(A, B) = 0$ implies $A \subseteq B$, and (3) $\rho(A, C) \leq \rho(A, B) + \rho(B, C) + r(B)$. The asymmetric relation (2) is weaker than the corresponding metric requirement that $\rho(A, B) = 0$ if and only if $A = B$, and relation (3) is weaker than the metric triangle inequality.

The pseudodistance ρ has a very direct interpretation: $\rho(A, B)$ is the radius of the smallest disk that, when used as a structuring element to dilate B, produces a result that contains A.

Proposition 5.9:

Let $disk(r) = \{x \mid \|x\| \leq r\}$ and $A, B \subseteq F^N$. Then $\max_{a \in A} \min_{b \in B} \|a - b\| = inf\{r \mid A \subseteq B \oplus disk(r)\}$.

Proof:

Let $\rho_0 = \max_{a \in A} \min_{b \in B} \|a - b\|$ and $r_0 = inf\{r \mid A \subseteq B \oplus disk(r)\}$. Let $a \in A$ be given. Let $b_0 \in B$ satisfy $\|a - b_0\| = \min_{b \in B} \|a - b\|$. Now $\rho_0 = \max_{x \in A} \min_{y \in B} \|x - y\| \geq \min_{b \in B} \|a - b\|$. Hence $\rho_0 \geq \|a - b_0\|$, so that $a - b_0 \in disk(\rho_0)$. Now

$b_0 \in B$ and $a - b_0 \in disk(\rho_0)$ imply $a = b_0 + (a - b_0) \in B \oplus disk(\rho_0)$. Hence $A \subseteq B \oplus disk(\rho_0)$. Since $r_0 = inf \{r | A \subseteq B \oplus disk(r)\}$, $r_0 \leq \rho_0$. Suppose $A \subseteq B \oplus disk(r_0)$. Then $\max_{a \in A} \min_{b \in B \oplus disk(r_0)} ||a - b|| = 0$. Hence $\max_{a \in A} \min_{b \in B} \min_{y \in disk(r_0)} ||a - b - y|| = 0$. But $||(a - b) - y|| \geq ||a - b|| - ||y||$. Therefore

$$0 \geq \max_{a \in A} \min_{b \in B} \min_{y \in disk(r_0)} ||a - b|| - ||y||$$

$$\geq \max_{a \in A} \min_{b \in B} ||a - b|| + \min_{y \in disk(r_0)} -||y||$$

$$\geq \max_{a \in A} \min_{b \in B} ||a - b|| - \max_{y \in disk(r_0)} ||y||$$

Now $\rho_0 = \max_{a \in A} \min_{b \in B} ||a - b||$ and $r_0 = \max_{y \in disk(r_0)} ||y||$ imply $0 \geq \rho_0 - r_0$, so that $r_0 \geq \rho_0$. Finally, $r_0 \leq \rho_0$ and $r_0 \geq \rho_0$ imply $r_0 = \rho_0$.

The pseudodistance ρ can be used as the basis for a true set metric by making it symmetric. We define the set metric $\rho_M(A, B) = \max\{\rho(A, B), \rho(B, A)\}$, also called the Hausdorf metric. Before we actually prove that ρ_M is indeed a metric, we note that $\rho_M(A, B) = inf \{r | A \subseteq B \oplus disk(r)$ and $B \subseteq A \oplus disk(r)\}$. This happens since

$$\rho_M(A, B) = \max\{\rho(A, B), \rho(B, A)\}$$

$$= \max\left\{inf \{r | A \subseteq B \oplus disk(r)\}, inf \{r | B \subseteq A \oplus disk(r)\}\right\}$$

$$= inf \{r | A \subseteq B \oplus disk(r) \text{ and } B \subseteq A \oplus disk(r)\}$$

Proposition 5.10:

1. $\rho_M(A, B) \geq 0$

2. $\rho_M(A, B) = 0$ if and only if $A = B$

3. $\rho_M(A, B) = \rho_M(B, A)$

4. $\rho_M(A, C) \leq \rho_M(A, B) + \rho_M(B, C)$

Proof:

1. $\rho_M(A, B) \geq 0$ since $\rho(A, B) \geq 0$ and $\rho(B, A) \geq 0$.

2. Suppose $\rho_M(A, B) = 0$. Then $\max\{\rho(A, B), \rho(B, A)\} = 0$. Since $\rho(A, B) \geq 0$ and $\rho(B, A) \geq 0$, we must have $\rho(A, B) = 0$ and $\rho(B, A) = 0$. But $\rho(A, B) = 0$ implies $A \subseteq B$, and $\rho(B, A) = 0$ implies $B \subseteq A$. Now $A \subseteq B$ and $B \subseteq A$ imply $A = B$. Also $\rho_M(A, A) = \max\{\rho(A, A), \rho(A, A)\} = \rho(A, A)$. Since $A \subseteq A$, $\rho(A, A) = 0$.

3. Immediate from symmetry of max.

4. Let $\rho_{12} = \rho_M(A, B)$ and $\rho_{23} = \rho_M(B, C)$. Then $A \subseteq B \oplus disk(\rho_{12}), B \subseteq C \oplus disk(\rho_{23}), B \subseteq A \oplus disk(\rho_{12}), C \subseteq B \oplus disk(\rho_{23})$. Hence $A \subseteq C \oplus disk(\rho_{23}) \oplus disk(\rho_{12}) \subseteq C \oplus disk(\rho_{12} + \rho_{23})$ and $C \subseteq A \oplus disk(\rho_{12}) \oplus disk(\rho_{23}) \subseteq A \oplus disk(\rho_{12} + \rho_{23})$. Now $A \subseteq C \oplus disk(\rho_{12} + \rho_{23})$ and

$C \subseteq A \oplus disk(\rho_{12} + \rho_{23})$ imply $\rho_{12} + \rho_{23} \geq inf \{r | A \subseteq C \oplus disk(r), C \subseteq A \oplus disk(r)\}$. Therefore

$$\rho_M(A, B) + \rho_M(B, C) \geq \rho_M(A, C).$$

A strong relationship between the set distance and the dilation of sets must be developed to translate set bounding relationships to distance bounding relationships. We show that $\rho(A \oplus B, C \oplus D) \leq \rho(A, C) + \rho(B, D)$ and then quickly extend the result to $\rho_M(A \oplus B, C \oplus D) \leq \rho_M(A, C) + \rho_M(B, D)$.

Proposition 5.11:

1. $\rho(A \oplus B, C \oplus D) \leq \rho(A, C) + \rho(B, D)$

2. $\rho_M(A \oplus B, C \oplus D) \leq \rho_M(A, C) + \rho_M(B, D)$

Proof:

1. $\rho(A \oplus B, C \oplus D) = \max\limits_{x \in A \oplus B} \min\limits_{y \in C \oplus D} \|x - y\|$

$= \max\limits_{a \in A} \max\limits_{b \in B} \min\limits_{c \in C} \min\limits_{d \in D} \|a + b - c - d\|$

$\leq \max\limits_{a \in A} \max\limits_{b \in B} \min\limits_{d \in D} \min\limits_{c \in C} [\|a - c\| + \|b - d\|]$

$\leq \max\limits_{a \in A} \max\limits_{b \in B} \min\limits_{d \in D} [(\min\limits_{c \in C} \|a - c\|) + \|b - d\|]$

$\leq \max\limits_{a \in A} \min\limits_{c \in C} \|a - c\| + \max\limits_{b \in B} \min\limits_{d \in D} \|b - d\|$

$\leq \rho(A, C) + \rho(B, D)$

2. $\rho_M(A \oplus B, C \oplus D) = \max\{\rho(A \oplus B, C \oplus D), \rho(C \oplus D, A \oplus B)\}$

$\leq \max\{\rho(A, C) + \rho(B, D), \rho(C, A) + \rho(D, B)\}$

$\leq \max\{\rho(A, C), \rho(C, A)\} + \max\{\rho(B, D), \rho(D, B)\}$

$\leq \rho_M(A, C) + \rho_M(B, D)$

From the last result it is apparent that dilating two sets with the same structuring element cannot increase the distance between the sets. Dilation tends to suppress differences between sets, making them more similar. More precisely, if $B = D = K$, then $\rho_M(A \oplus K, C \oplus K) \leq \rho_M(A, C)$. It is also apparent that $\rho_M(A, A \oplus K) = \rho_M(A \oplus \{0\}, A \oplus K) \leq \rho_M(A, A) + \rho_M(\{0\}, K) = \rho_M(\{0\}, K) \leq \max\limits_{k \in K} \|k\|$. Indeed, since the reconstruction structuring element $K = \check{K}$ and $0 \in K$, the radius of the circumscribing disk is precisely $\max\limits_{k \in K} \|k\|$. Hence the distance between A and $A \oplus K$ is no more than the radius of the circumscribing disk of K.

Proposition 5.12: If $K = \check{K}$ and $0 \in K$, then $r(K) = \max\limits_{k \in K} \|k\|$.

Proof:

$$r(K) = \min_{x \in K} \max_{y \in K} ||x - y|| \le \max_{y \in K} ||0 - y|| = \max_{y \in K} ||y|| \quad \text{and}$$

$$\max_{y \in K} ||y|| = \frac{1}{2} \max_{y \in K} ||y - x + x + y|| \text{ for } x \in K$$

$$\le \frac{1}{2} \{ \max_{y \in K} ||y - x|| + \max_{y \in K} ||x + y|| \} \text{ for } x \in K$$

$$\le \frac{1}{2} \{ \max_{y \in K} ||x - y|| + \max_{y \in K} ||x - y|| \} \text{ for } x \in K$$

$$\le \max_{y \in K} ||x - y|| \text{ for } x \in K$$

$$\le \min_{x \in K} \max_{y \in K} ||x - y|| = r(K)$$

Since $\rho_M(A, A \oplus K) \le \max_{k \in K} ||k||$ and $\max_{k \in K} ||k|| = r(K)$, we have $\rho_M(A, A \oplus K) \le r(K)$. Also, since $A \bullet K \supseteq A$, $\rho_M(A \bullet K, A) = \rho(A \bullet K, A)$. Since $0 \in K$, $A \bullet K \subseteq A \oplus K$. Hence $\rho_M(A \bullet K, A) = \rho(A \bullet K, A) \le \rho \left[(A \bullet K) \oplus K, A \right] = \rho(A \oplus K, A) \le r(K)$.

It immediately follows that the distance between the minimal and maximal reconstructions, which differ only by a dilation by K, is no greater than the size of the reconstruction structuring element; that is, $\rho_M \left[(F \cap S) \bullet K, (F \cap S) \oplus K \right] \le r(K)$. When $F = F \circ K = F \bullet K, (F \cap S) \bullet K \subseteq F \subseteq (F \cap S) \oplus K$. Since the distance between the minimal and maximal reconstructions is no greater than $r(K)$, it is unsurprising that the distance between F and either of the reconstructions is no greater than $r(K)$. We can reason the following way:

It is readily verified that if $A \subseteq B \subseteq C$, then (1) $\rho_M(A, B) \le \rho_M(A, C)$ and (2) $\rho_M(B, C) \le \rho_M(A, C)$.

Now it immediately follows that if $F = F \circ K = F \bullet K$, $\rho_M \left[F, (F \cap S) \oplus K \right] \le r(K)$ and $\rho_M \left[F, (F \cap S) \bullet K \right] \le r(K)$.

When the image F is open under K, the distance between F and its sampling $F \cap S$ can be no greater than $r(K)$. Why? It is certainly the case that $F \cap S \subseteq F \subseteq (F \cap S) \oplus K$. Hence $\rho_M(F, F \cap S) \le \rho_M[F \cap S, (F \cap S) \oplus K] \le r(K)$.

If two sets are both open under the reconstruction structuring element K, then the distance between the sets must be no greater than the distance between their samplings plus the size of K.

Proposition 5.13: If $A = A \circ K$ and $B = B \circ K$, then $\rho_M(A, B) \le \rho_M(A \cap S, B \cap S) + r(K)$.

Proof:
Consider $\rho(A, B)$. $\rho(A, B) \le \rho(A, B \cap S)$. Since $A = A \circ K$, $A \subseteq (A \cap S) \oplus K$. Hence $\rho(A, B) \le \rho(A, B \cap S) \le \rho \left[(A \cap S) \oplus K, B \cap S \right] \le \rho(A \cap S, B \cap S) + r(K)$.
Similarly, since $B = B \circ K, \rho(B, A) \le \rho(B \cap S, A \cap S) + r(K)$.

Now

$$\rho_M(A,B) = \max\{\rho(A,B),\rho(B,A)\}$$
$$\leq \max\{\rho(A \cap S, B \cap S) + r(K), \rho(B \cap S, A \cap S) + r(K)\}$$
$$\leq r(K) + \max\{\rho(A \cap S, B \cap S), \rho(B \cap S, A \cap S)\}$$
$$\leq r(K) + \rho_M(A \cap S, B \cap S)$$

From the last result it is easy to see that if F is closed under K, then the distance between F and its minimal reconstruction $(F \cap S) \bullet K$ is no greater than $r(K)$. Consider

$$\rho_M\left[F, (F \cap S) \bullet K\right] \leq \rho_M\left[F \cap S, \left((F \cap S) \bullet K\right) \cap S\right] + r(K)$$

$$\leq \rho_M(F \cap S, F \cap S) + r(K) = r(K)$$

These distance relationships mean that just as the standard sampling theorem cannot produce a reconstruction with frequencies higher than the Nyquist frequency, the morphological sampling theorem cannot produce a reconstruction whose positional accuracy is better than the radius of the circumscribing disk of the reconstruction structuring element K. Since the diameter of this disk is just short of being large enough to contain two sample intervals, the morphological sampling theorem cannot produce a reconstruction whose positional accuracy is better than the sampling interval.

■ **EXAMPLE 5.7**

We use the example sets F_1, F_2, F_3, and F_4 in computing the distance between the original images and the sample reconstruction images. The values $\max_{y \in K} \|x - y\|$ for each $x \in K$ are shown in Fig. 5.51. The minimum value among them, $\sqrt{2}$, is the radius $r(K)$, since $r(K) = \min_{x \in K} \max_{y \in K} \|x - y\|$.

We now measure the distance between two sample reconstructions for all the example sets. To compute $\rho_M((F_1 \cap S) \bullet K, (F_1 \cap S) \oplus K)$, we first compute $\rho[(F_1 \cap S) \oplus K, (F_1 \cap S) \bullet K]$ and $\rho[(F_1 \cap S) \bullet K, (F_1 \cap S) \oplus K]$. The values $\min_{y \in (F_1 \cap S) \bullet K} \|x - y\|$ for all $x \in (F_1 \cap S) \oplus K$ are shown in Fig. 5.52. The maximum value among them, $\sqrt{2}$, is the distance $\rho[(F_1 \cap S) \oplus K, (F_1 \cap S) \bullet K]$.

	$\sqrt{2}$	$\sqrt{5}$	$\sqrt{2}$	
	$\sqrt{5}$	$\sqrt{2}$	$\sqrt{5}$	
	$\sqrt{2}$	$\sqrt{5}$	$\sqrt{2}$	

Figure 5.51 The $\max_{y \in K} \|x - y\|$ values for all $x \in K$ where K is the digital disk having radius $\sqrt{2}$.

	$\sqrt{2}$	1	1	1	$\sqrt{2}$	
	1	0	0	0	1	
	1	0	0	0	1	
	1	0	0	0	1	
	$\sqrt{2}$	1	1	1	$\sqrt{2}$	

Figure 5.52 The $\min\limits_{y\in(F_1\cap S)\bullet K} \|x-y\|$ for all $x \in (F_1\cap S)\oplus K$.

Similarly, we can compute $\rho[(F_1\cap S)\bullet K, (F_1\cap S)\oplus K]$, which equals 0. Thus $\rho_M[(F_1\cap S)\bullet K, (F_1\cap S)\oplus K]$ equals $\sqrt{2}$, which is exactly the radius $r(K)$. Similarly, the distance between two reconstructions for sets F_2, F_3, and F_4 can be measured, and they are all equal to $r(K)$.

5.12   Summary

We have discussed both binary and gray scale morphology and have shown the geometric-shape meaning of the erosion, dilation, opening, and closing operations. We have discussed the primary shape-matching properties of opening and closing and related this shape-matching property to the idempotency of opening and closing. We have illustrated morphological processing operations for a variety of shape extraction, noise cleaning, thickening, thinning, and skeletonizing applications. We have shown how to extend the standard morphological operations to recursive morphology and discussed its application to generalized distance transform. Finally, we have discussed the morphological sampling theorem.

Because mathematical morphology constitutes a highly nonlinear algebra, the mathematics of morphology is not part of the typical engineering or computer science curriculum as might be, for example, the mathematics of convolution. Therefore many people in image processing and computer vision do not routinely use mathematical morphology in the design of their processing algorithms. By providing evidence of the power of the techniques of mathematical morphology, as well as the detail of the exposition in this chapter, we hope that mathematical morphology has been made more accessible and will find its way into the toolbox of image-processing and computer vision algorithm designers and researchers.

Exercises

5.1.   Show
   a. $A \oplus B_x = (A \oplus B)_x$
   b. $A \ominus B_x = (A \ominus B)_{-x}$
   c. $A_x \ominus B = (A \ominus B)_x$

5.2. Prove that $(A \oplus B)^c = A^c \ominus \check{B}$.

5.3. Suppose $A = A \circ B$. Show

   a. $A^c = A^c \bullet \check{B}$

   b. $F \circ A \subseteq F \circ B$

   c. $F \bullet B \subseteq F \bullet A$

   d. $(F \circ B) \circ A = F \circ A$

   e. $(F \circ A) \circ B = F \circ A$

   f. $(F \bullet B) \bullet A = F \bullet A$

   g. $(F \bullet A) \bullet B = F \bullet A$

5.4. Show that if A and B are separated and D is connected, then $D \subseteq A \cup B$ implies $D \subseteq A$ or $D \subseteq B$.

5.5. Show that if $T \subseteq W$, then $T_x \subseteq F$ and $(W - T)_x \subseteq F^c$ if and ony if $F \cap W_x = T_x$.

5.6. Show that if $B \neq \emptyset$, then there always exists an x such that $A_x \subseteq A \oplus B$.

5.7. Show that if $B \neq \emptyset$, then there always exists an x such that $A \ominus B \subseteq A_x$.

5.8. Suppose $S = T \oplus B$. Show that $S = S \circ B$.

5.9. Suppose $S = S \circ B \neq \emptyset$. Show that there exists a $T \neq \emptyset$ such that $T = S \ominus B$.

5.10. Show that the operation of taking the residue of an opening is idempotent.

5.11. Show that a set $T = \{(1,1),(2,3),(3,-1)\}$ closed by a structuring element $K = \{(r,c) \mid -2 \le r \le 2, -2 \le c \le 2\ r,c$ integer$\}$ produces a filled-in triangle, but that a set $L = \{(1,1),(2,3)\}$ closed by K does not fill in the pixels separating $(1,1)$ from $(2,3)$.

5.12. Show that to connect together the three vertices of an equilateral triangle by a closing operator with a disk structuring element, the radius of the disk must be larger than the side length of the triangle.

5.13. a. Show that to connect together the three vertices of an isosceles triangle with included angle θ and leg length h, the radius of the disk structuring element must be larger than $h/[2 \sin(\theta/2)]$.

   b. Show that to connect together the three vertices of an arbitrary triangle whose smallest angle is θ and largest side is h, the radius of the disk structuring element must be larger than $h/[2\ sin(\theta/2)]$.

   c. Show that to connect together the three vertices of an arbitrary triangle whose largest side ρ_L is smaller than $2\rho_s$, where ρ_s is the length of the smallest side, the radius of the disk structuring element for the closing operation must be greater than $2\rho_L$.

5.14. Show $I \otimes (J,K) = I^c \otimes (K,J)$.

5.15. Show $J \cap K \neq \emptyset$ implies $F \otimes (J,K) = \emptyset$.

5.16. Suppose $J_1 \subseteq J_2$ and $K_1 \subseteq K_2$. Show

   a. $F \otimes (J_1,K_1) \supseteq F \otimes (J_2,K_2)$

   b. $F \odot (J_1,K_1) \supseteq F \odot (J_2,K_2)$

   c. $F \oslash (J_1,K_1) \subseteq F \oslash (J_2,K_2)$

5.17. The isocontours of $d[A,K]$ are rings within A. The nth isocontour is defined by $R_n = \{x \mid d[A,K](x) = n\}$. Show

   a. $R_n = A \underset{n-1}{\ominus} K - A \underset{n}{\ominus} K$

   b. $R_n \underset{n-1-m}{\oplus} K \subseteq A \underset{m}{\ominus} K$

5.18. Let $d(x,A)$ denote the Euclidean distance between the point x and the set A and let disk (ρ) denote a disk of radius ρ, $\rho > 0$. Show that $d(x,A) < \rho$ implies $x \in A \oplus$ disk (ρ).

5.19. Show that $\overline{A \oplus \overline{A}} = \{0\}$ and for any R, $\overline{\overline{A} \oplus R} = \{0\}$ when $A \neq \emptyset$.

5.20. For any set A and nonnegative integer m, define $N_4(A,m) = \{a \in A \,|\, |\#N_4(a)| = m\}$, where $N_4(a)$ designates the four elements in the 4-neighborhood of the element a. For a given set F, write a morphological expression for

a. $N_4(F,0)$

b. $N_4(F,1)$

c. $N_4(F,2)$

d. $N_4(F,3)$

e. $N_4(F,4)$

5.21. Let N_4 be defined as in Exercise 5.22. What geometric pattern from the set F is selected by

a. $A = N_4(F,2)$

b. $B = N_4(A,0)$

c. $C = N_4(A,1)$

d. $D = N_4(C,1)$

e. $E = B \cup C \cup D$

5.22. Show that $A = (A \circ K_1) \circ K_2$ if and only if $A = A \circ K_1$ and $A = A \circ K_2$.

5.23. Show that $(A \circ K_1) \circ K_2 = (A \circ K_2) \circ K_1$ when $A = (A \circ K_1) \circ K_2$.

5.24. Show that $\big([(A \circ K_1) \circ K_2] \circ K_1\big) \circ K_2 = (A \circ K_1) \circ K_2$ when $A = (A \circ K_1) \circ K_2$.

5.25. Suppose that B is a maximal subset of A satisfying $B = B \circ K_1$ and $B = B \circ K_2$. Suppose that C is a maximal subset of A also satisfying $C = C \circ K_1$ and $C = C \circ K_2$. Show that $B = C$. (A subset B of A satisfying property P is maximal if and only if for any set D, $B \subseteq D \subseteq A$, and D satisfying property P implies $B = D$.)

5.26. Assume K and S obey the required sampling relationships. Show

$$F_1 \subseteq F_2 \text{ implies } (F_1 \cap S) \oplus K \subseteq (F_2 \cap S) \oplus K$$

$$\Big[(F_1 \cup F_2) \cap S\Big] \oplus K = \Big[(F_1 \cap S) \oplus K\Big] \cup \Big[(F_2 \cap S) \oplus K\Big]$$

$$\Big[(F_1 \cap F_2) \cap S\Big] \oplus K \subseteq \Big[(F_1 \cap S) \oplus K\Big] \cap \Big[(F_2 \cap S) \oplus K\Big]$$

5.27. Assume K and S obey the required sampling relationships. Show

$$F_1 \subseteq F_2 \text{ implies } (F_1 \cap S) \bullet K \subseteq (F_2 \cap S) \bullet K$$

$$[(F_1 \cup F_2) \cap S] \bullet K \supseteq [(F_1 \cap S) \bullet K] \cup [(F_2 \cap S) \bullet K]$$

$$[(F_1 \cap F_2) \cap S] \bullet K \subseteq [(F_1 \cap S) \bullet K] \cap [(F_2 \cap S) \bullet K]$$

▪ Bibliography

Abbott, L., R. M. Haralick, and X. Zhuang, "Pipeline Architectures for Morphological Image Analysis," *Machine Vision and Applications,* Vol. 1, 1988, pp. 23–40.

Acharya, R. S., and R. Laurette, "Mathematical Morphology for 3D Image Analysis," *Proceedings of the ICASSP-88,* New York, 1988.

Arcelli, C., L. Cordella, and S. Levialdi, "Parallel Thinning of Binary Pictures," *Electronics Letters,* Vol. 2, 1973, pp. 22–38.

Arcelli, C., L. Cordella, and S. Levialdi, "A Grassfire Transformation for Binary Digital Pictures," *Proceedings of the Second International Conference on Pattern Recognition*, Copenhagen, 1974, pp. 152–154.

———, "More about a Thinning Algorithm," *Electronics Letters*, Vol. 16, 1980, pp. 51–53.

———, "From Local Maxima to Connected Skeletons," *IEEE Transactions on Pattern Analysis and Machine Intelligence*, Vol. PAMI-3, 1981, pp. 134–143.

Arcelli, C., and S. Levialdi, "Concavity Extraction by Parallel Processing," *IEEE Transactions on Systems, Man, and Cybernetics*, Vol. SMC-1, 1971a, pp. 394–396.

———, "Picture Processing and Overlapping Blobs," *IEEE Transactions on Computers*, Vol. C-20, 1971b, pp. 1111–15.

———, "Parallel Shrinking in Three Dimensions," *Computer Graphics and Image Processing*, Vol. 1, 1972, pp. 21–29.

———, "On Blob Reconstruction," *Computer Graphics and Image Processing*, Vol. 2, 1973, pp. 22–38.

Arcelli, C., and G. Sanniti di Baja, "On the Sequential Approach to Medial Line Transformation," *IEEE Transactions on Systems, Man, and Cybernetics*, Vol. SMC-8, 1978, pp. 139–144.

———, "Quenching Points in Distance Labeled Pictures," *Proceedings of the Seventh International Conference on Pattern Recognition*, Montreal, 1984, pp. 344–346.

———, "Finding Local Maxima in a Pseudo-Euclidean Distance Transform," *Computer Vision, Graphics, and Image Processing*, Vol. 43, 1988, pp. 361–367.

———, "A One-Pass Two-Operation Process to Detect the Skeletal Pixels on the 4-Distance Transform," *IEEE Transactions on Pattern Analysis and Machine Intelligence*, Vol. 11, 1989, pp. 411–414.

Archibald, C., "Identify Leads Coming from a SMD Component," *Machine Vision International Report*, Ann Abor, 1985.

Bertrand, G., "Skeletons in Derived Grids," *Proceedings of the Seventh International Conference on Pattern Recognition*, Montreal, 1984, pp. 326–329.

Blum, H., "An Associative Machine for Dealing with the Visual Field and Some of its Biological Implications," in E. E. Bernard and M. R. Kare (eds.), *Biological Prototypes and Synthetic Systems*, Vol. 1, Plenum Press, New York, 1962.

———, "A Transformation for Extracting New Descriptors of Shape," in W. Wathen-Dunn (ed.), *Models for the Perception of Speech and Visual Form*, MIT Press, Cambridge, MA, 1967.

———, "Biological Shape and Visual Science (Part I)," *Journal of Theoretical Biology*, Vol. 38, 1973, pp. 205–287.

Blum, H., and R. N. Nagel, "Shape Description Using Weighted Symmetric Axis Features," *Pattern Recognition*, Vol. 10, 1978, pp. 167–180.

Borgefors, G., and G. Sanniti di Baja, "Skeletonizing the Distance Transform on the Hexagonal Grid," *Proceedings of the Ninth International Conference on Pattern Recognition*, Rome, 1988, pp. 504–507.

Calabi, L., and W. E. Hartnett, "A Motzkin-Type Theorem for Closed, Convex Sets," *Proceedings of the American Mathematical Society*, Vol. 19, 1968a, pp. 1495–98.

———, "Shape Recogition, Prairie Fires, Convex Deficiencies and Skeletons," *American Mathematics Monthly*, Vol. 75, 1968b, pp. 335–342.

Chen, M. H., and P. F. Yan, "A Multiscaling Approach Based on Morphological Filtering," *IEEE Transactions on Pattern Analysis and Machine Intelligence*, Vol. 11, 1989, pp. 694–700.

Coleman, E. N., Jr., and R. E. Simpson, "Acquisition of Randomly Oriented Workpieces through Structure Mating," *Proceedings of the Conference on Computer Vision and Pattern Recognition,* San Francisco, 1985, pp. 350–357.

Coyle, E. J., and J. H. Lin, "Stack Filters and the Mean Absolute Error Criterion," *IEEE ASSP,* Vol. 36, 1988, pp. 1244–54.

Crimmins, T. R., "Geometric Filter for Speckle Reduction," *Applied Optics,* Vol. 24, 1985, pp. 1438–43.

Crimmins, T. R., and W. R. Brown, "Image Algebra and Automatic Shape Recognition," *IEEE Transactions on Aerospace and Electronic Systems,* Vol. AES-21, 1985, pp. 60–69.

Dougherty, E. R., and C. R. Giardina, "Error Bounds for Morphologically Derived Measurements," *SIAM Journal of Applied Mathematics,* Vol. 47, 1987a, pp. 425–440.

——, "Image Algebra-Induced Operators and Induced Subalgebras," *Proceedings of the SPIE 845: Visual Communications and Image Processing II,* 1987b, pp. 270–275.

——, "Morphology on Umbra Matrices," *International Journal of Pattern Recognition and Artificial Intelligence,* Vol. 2, 1988, pp. 367–385.

Feehs, R. J., and G. R. Arce, "Multidimensional Morphological Edge Detection," *Proceedings of the SPIE 845: Visual Communications and Image Procesing II,* 1987, pp. 285–292.

Gerritsen, F. A., and P. W. Verbeek, "Implementaton of Cellular-Logic Operators Using 3 * 3 Convolution and Table Lookup Hardware," *Computer Vision, Graphics, and Image Processing,* Vol. 27, 1984, pp. 115–123.

Ghosh, P. K., "A Mathematical Model for Shape Description Using Minkowski Operators," *Computer Vision, Graphics, and Image Processing,* Vol. 44, 1988, pp. 239–269.

Giordina, C. R. and E. R. Dougherty, *Morphological Methods in Image and Signal Processing,* Prentice Hall, Englewood Cliffs, NJ, 1988.

Golay, M. J. E., "Hexagonal Parallel Pattern Transformation," *IEEE Transactions on Computers,* Vol. C-18, 1969, pp. 733–740.

Gong, W. X., and G. Bertrand, "A Fast Skeletonization Algorithm Using Derived Grids," *Proceedings of the Ninth International Conference on Pattern Recognition,* Rome, 1988, pp. 776–778.

Gray, S. B., "Local Properties of Binary Images in Two Dimensions," *IEEE Transactions on Computers,* Vol. C-20, 1971, pp. 551–561.

Hadwiger, H., *Vorlesungen über inhalt, oberfläche, und isoperimetrie,* Springer-Verlag, Berlin, 1957.

Haralick, R. M., et al., "Multiresolution Morphology," *Proceedings of the First International Conference on Computer Vision,* London, 1987, pp. 516–520.

——, "The Digital Morphological Sampling Theorem," *IEEE Transactions on Acoustics, Speech, and Signal Processing,* Vol. ASSP-37, 1989, pp. 2067–90.

Haralick, R. M., S. R. Sternberg, and X. Zhuang, "Grayscale Morphology," *Proceedings of the IEEE Computer Society Conference on Computer Vision and Pattern Recognition,* Miami Beach, 1986, 543–550.

——, "Image Analysis Using Mathematical Morphology," *IEEE Transactions on Pattern Analysis and Machine Intelligence,* Vol. PAMI-9, 1987, pp. 523–550.

Hilditch, J., "An Application of Graph Theory in Pattern Recognition," in D. Michie (ed.), *Machine Intelligence,* Vol. 3, Edinburgh University Press, Edinburgh, 1968, pp. 325–347.

——, "Linear Skeletons from Square Cupboards," in B. Meltzer and D. Michie (eds.), *Machine Intelligence,* Vol. 4, Edinburgh University Press, Edinburgh, 1969, pp. 403–420.

Hilditch, J., and J. Rutovitz, "Chromosome Recognition." *Annals of the New York Academy of Science,* Vol. 157, 1969, pp. 339–364.

Huang, K. S., B. K. Jenkins, and A. A. Sawchuk, "Binary Image Algebra and Optical Cellular Logic Processor Design," *Computer Vision, Graphics, and Image Processing,* Vol. 45, 1989, pp. 295–345.

Joo, H., and R. M. Haralick, "A Compendium of Morphological Image Processing Algorithms," *Proceedings of the DAGM Symposium,* Hamburg, 1989, pp. 1–27.

Kimmel, M. J., et al., "MITE: Morphic Image Transform Engine, An Architecture for Reconfigurable Pipelines of Neighborhood Processes," *Proceedings of the IEEE Computer Society Workshop on Pattern Analysis and Image Database Management,* Miami Beach, 1985, pp. 493–500.

Kirsch, R. A., et al., "Experiments in Processing Pictorial Information with a Digital Computer," *Proceedings of the Eastern Joint Computer Conference,* 1957, pp. 221–229.

Lantuejoul, C., "La squelettisation et son application aux mésures topologiques des mosaiques polycristallines," Ph.D. thesis, Paris School of Mines, 1978.

———, "Skeletonization in Quantitative Metallography," *Issues of Digital Image Processing,* R. M. Haralick and J. C. Simon (eds.), Sijthoff and Noordhoff, Groningen, The Netherlands, 1980.

Lee, J. S. J., R. M. Haralick, and L. G. Shapiro, "Morphologic Edge Detection," *IEEE Transactions on Robotics and Automation,* Vol. RA-3, 1987, pp. 142–156.

Levialdi, S., "Incremental Ratio by Parallel Logic," *Electronics Letters, IEE,* Vol. 13, 1967, p. 554.

———, "Clopan: A Closedness Pattern Analyzer," *Proceedings of the IEE,* Vol. 115, 1968, pp. 879–880.

———, "Parallel Pattern Processing," *IEEE Transactions on Systems, Man, and Cybernetics,* Vol. SMC-1, 1971, pp. 292–296.

———, "On Shrinking Binary Picture Patterns," *Communications of the ACM,* Vol. 15, 1972, pp. 7–10.

Lougheed, R. M., and D. L. McCubbrey, "The Cytocomputer: A Practical Pipelined Image Processor," *Proceedings of the Seventh Annual Symposium on Computer Architecture,* 1980, LaBaule, France, pp. 271–277.

Maragos, P., "Pattern Spectrum of Images and Morphological Shape-Size Complexity," *Proceedings of the 1987 International Conference on Acoustics, Speech, and Signal Processing,* Dallas, 1987, pp. 241–244.

———, "Morphology-Based Symbolic Image Modeling, Multi-Scale Nonlinear Smoothing, and Pattern Spectrum," *Proceedings of the IEEE CVPR-88,* Ann Arbor, 1988a, pp. 766–773.

———, "Optimal Morphological Approaches for Image Matching and Object Detection," *Proceedings of the Second International Conference on Computer Vision,* Tarpon Springs, FL, 1988b, pp. 695–699.

———, "A Representation Theory for Morphological Image and Signal Processing," *IEEE Transactions on Pattern Analysis and Machine Intelligence,* Vol. PAMI-11, 1989a, pp. 586–599.

———, "A Representation Theory for Morphological Image and Signal Processing," *IEEE Transactions on Pattern Analysis and Machine Intelligence,* Vol. 11, 1989b, pp. 586–599.

———, "Pattern Spectrum and Multi-Scale Shape Representation," *IEEE Transactions on Pattern Analysis and Machine Intelligence,* Vol. PAMI-11, 1989c, pp. 701–716.

Maragos, P., and R. W. Shafer, "Applications of Morphological Filtering to Image Analysis and Processing," *Proceedings of the IEEE International Conference on Acoustics, Speech, and Signal Processing,* Tokyo, 1986a, pp. 2067–70.

Maragos, P., and R. W. Shafer, "Morphological Skeleton Representation and Coding of Binary Images," *IEEE Transactions on Acoustics, Speech, and Signal Processing,* Vol. ASSP-34, 1986b, pp. 1228–44.

———, "Morphological Filters—Part I: Their Set-Theoretic Analysis and Relations to Linear Shift-Invariant Filters," *IEEE Transactions on Acoustics, Speech, and Signal Processing,* Vol. ASSP-35, 1987a, pp. 1153–69.

———, "Morphological Filters—Part II: Their Relations to Median, Order-Statistic, and Stack Filters," *IEEE Transactions on Acoustics, Speech, and Signal Processing,* Vol. ASSP-35, 1987b, pp. 1170–84.

Maragos, P., and R. Ziff, "Threshold Parallelism in Morphological Feature Extraction, Skeletonization, and Pattern Spectrum," *Proceedings of the SPIE 1001: Visual Communications and Image Processing,* 1988.

Matheron, G., *Random Sets and Integral Geometry,* Wiley, New York, 1975.

Meyer, F., "Iterative Image Transformations for an Automatic Screening of Cervical Smears," *Journal of Histochemistry and Cytochemistry,* Vol. 27, 1979, pp. 128–135.

———, "Automatic Screening of Cytological Specimens," *Computer Vision, Graphics, and Image Processing,* Vol. 35, 1986, pp. 356–369.

Minsky, M., and S. Papert, *Perceptions,* MIT Press, Cambridge, MA, 1969.

Montanari, U., "A Method of Obtaining Skeletons Using a Quasi-Euclidean Distance," *Journal of the Association of Computing Machinery,* Vol. 15, 1968, pp. 600–624.

———, "Continuous Skeletons from Digitized Images," *Journal of the Association for Computing Machinery,* Vol. 16, 1969, pp. 534–549.

Mott-Smith, C., "Medial Axis Transformation," in *Picture Processing and Psychopictorics,* B. S. Lipkin and A. Rosenfeld (eds.), Academic Press, New York, 1970.

Naccache, N. J., and R. Shinghal, "An Investigation into the Skeletonization Approach of Hilditch," *Pattern Recognition,* Vol. 17, 1984, pp. 279–284.

Nakagawa, Y., and A. Rosenfeld, "A Note on the Use of Local Min an Max Operations in Digital Picture Processing," *IEEE Transactions on Systems, Man, and Cybernetics,* Vol. SMC-8, 1978, pp. 899–901.

Noble, J. A., "Morphological Feature Detectors," in *Proceedings of the Second International Conference on Computer Vision,* Tarpon Springs, FL, 1988, pp. 112–116.

Peleg, S., and A. Rosenfeld, "A Min-Max Medial Axis Transformation," *IEEE Transactions on Pattern Analysis and Machine Intelligence,* Vol. PAMI-3, 1981, pp. 208–210.

Pfaltz, J., and L. Rosenfeld, "A Computer Representation of Planar Regions by their Skeletons," *Communications of the Association for Computing Machinery,* Vol. 10, 1967, pp. 119–127.

Philbrick, O., "Shape Description with the Medial Axis Transformation," G. C. Cheng et al. (eds.), *Pictorial Pattern Recognition,* Thompson, Washington, D.C., 1968, pp. 395–407.

Pitas, I., and A. N. Venetsanopoulos, "Shape Decomposition by Mathematical Morphology," *Proceedings of the First International Conference on Computer Vision,* London, 1987, pp. 621–625.

Preston, Jr., K., "Cellular Logic Computers for Pattern Recognition," *Computer,* Vol. 16, 1983, pp. 36–47.

Prewitt, J. M. S., "Object Enhancement and Extraction," *Picture Processing and Psychopictorics,* B. S. Lipkin and A. Rosenfeld (eds.), Academic Press, New York, 1970.

Rearick, T. C., "Syntactical Methods for Improvement of the Medial Axis Transformation," *SPIE Applications of Artificial Intelligence II,* Vol. 548, 1985, pp. 110–115.

Richardson, C. H., and R. W. Schafer, "Application of Mathematical Morphology to FLIR Images," *Proceedings of the SPIE 845: Visual Communications and Image Processing II*, 1987, pp. 249–252.

Ritter, G. X., J. L. Davidson, and J. N. Wilson, "Beyond Mathematical Morphology," *Proceedings of the SPIE 845: Visual Communications and Image Processing II*, 1987, pp. 260–269.

Ritter, G. X., and J. N. Wilson, "Image Algebra in a Nutshell," *Proceedings of the First International Conference on Computer Vision*, London, 1987, pp. 641–645.

Rodenacker, K., et al., "Mathematical Morphology in Grey Images," *Proceedings of the 1983 European Signal Processing Conference*.

Rosenfeld, A., and J. L. Pfaltz, "Sequential Operations in Digital Picture Processing," *Journal of the Association for Computing Machinery*, Vol. 13, 1966, pp. 471–494.

——, "Distance Functions in Digital Pictures," *Pattern Recognition*, Vol. 1, 1968, pp. 33–61.

Serra, J., *Image Analysis and Mathematical Morphology*, Academic Press, New York, 1982.

——, "From Mathematical Morphology to Artificial Intelligence," *Proceedings of the International Conference on Pattern Recognition*, Munich, 1986a, pp. 1336–43.

——, "An Introduction to Mathematical Morphology," *Computer Vision, Graphics, and Image Processing*, Vol. 35, 1986b, pp. 283–305.

—— (ed.), *Image Analysis and Mathematical Morphology*, Vol. 2: *Theoretical Advances*, Academic Press, New York, 1988.

Shih, F. Y. C., and O. R. Mitchell, "Threshold Decomposition of Gray-Scale Morphology into Binary Morphology, *IEEE Transactions on Pattern Analysis and Machine Intelligence*, Vol. PAMI-11, 1989, pp. 31–42.

Sklansky, J., L. P. Cordella, and S. Levialdi, "Parallel Detection of Concavities in Cellular Blobs," *IEEE Transactions on Computers*, Vol. C–25, 1976, pp. 187–196.

Skolnick, M. M., "Application of Morphological Transformations to the Analysis of Two-Dimensional Electrophoretic Gels of Biological Materials," *Computer Vision, Graphics, and Image Proessing*, Vol. 35, 1986, pp. 306–332.

Skolnick, M. M., S. Kim, and R. O'Bara, "Morphological Algorithms for Computing Non-Planar Point Neighborhoods on Cellular Automata," *Proceedings of the Second International Conference on Computer Vision*, Tampa, 1988, pp. 106-111.

Sternberg, S. R., "Parallel Architectures for Image Processing," in *Real-Time/Parallel Computing*, M. Onoe, K. Preston, and A. Rosenfeld (eds.), Plenum Press, New York, 1981, pp. 347–359.

——, "Cellular Computers and Biomedical Image Processing," *Biomedical Images and Computers*, J. Sklansky and J. C. Bisconte (eds.), Springer-Verlag, Berlin, 1982, pp. 294–319.

——, "Biomedical Image Processing," *Computer*, Vol. 16, 1983, pp. 23–34.

——, "An Overview of Image Algebra and Related Architectures," *Integrated Technology for Parallel Image Processing*, Academic Press, London, 1985, pp. 79–100.

——, "Grayscale Morphology," *Computer Vision, Graphics, and Image Processing*, Vol. 35, 1986, pp. 333–355.

Sternberg, S. R., and E. S. Sternberg, "Industrial Inspection by Morphological Virtual Gauging," *IEEE Workshop on Computer Architecture, Pattern Analysis, and Image Database Management*, Pasadena, CA, 1983.

Stevenson, R. L., and G. R. Arce, "Morphological Filters: Statistics and Further Syntactic Properties," *IEEE Transactions on Circuits and Systems,* Vol. CAS-34, 1987, pp. 1292–1305.

Sun, F. K., and S. L. Rubin, "Algorithm Development for Autonomous Image Analysis Based on Mathematical Morphology," *Proceedings of the SPIE 845: Visual Communications and Image Processing,* 1987, pp. 216–226.

Vogt, R. C., "Morphological Operator Distributions Based on Monotonicity and the Problem Posed by Digital Disk-Shaped Structuring Elements," *Proceedings of the SPIE 938: Digital and Optical Shape Representation and Pattern Recognition,* 1988, pp. 384–392.

Wang, X., and G. Bertrand, "An Algorithm for a Generalized Distance Transformation Based on Minkowski Operators," *Proceedings of Ninth International Conference on Pattern Recognition,* Rome, 1988, pp. 1164–68.

Yamada, H., and T. Kasvand, "Transparent Object Extraction from Regular Textured Backgrounds by Using Binary Parallel Operations," *Computer Vision, Graphics, and Image Processing,* Vol. 40, 1987, pp. 41–53.

Yokoi, S., J. I. Toriwaki, and T. Fukumura, "On Generalized Distance Transformation of Digitized Pictures," *IEEE Transactions on Pattern Analysis and Machine Intelligence,* Vol. PAMI-3, 1981, pp. 424–443.

Zhou, Z., and A. N. Venetsanopoulos, "Morphological Skeleton Representation and Shape Recognition," *Proceedings of the IEEE ICASSP-88,* New York, 1988, pp. 948–951.

Zhuang, X., and R. M. Haralick, "Morphological Structuring Element Decomposition," *Computer Vision, Graphics, and Image Processing,* Vol. 35, 1986, pp. 370–382.

NEIGHBORHOOD OPERATORS

6.1 Introduction

The workhorse of low-level vision is the *neighborhood operator*. It can perform the jobs of conditioning, labeling, and grouping. In this chapter we describe how and why the neighborhood operator works. We begin with its definition.

The output of a neighborhood operator at a given pixel position is a function of the position, of the input pixel value at the given position, of the values of the input pixels in some neighborhood around the given input position, and possibly of some values of previously generated output pixels. Neighborhood operators can be classified according to type of domain, type of neighborhood, and whether or not they are recursive. The two types of domain consist of numeric or symbolic data. Operators that have a numeric domain are usually defined in terms of arithmetic operations, such as addition, subtraction, or computation of minima or maxima. Operators that have a symbolic domain are defined in terms of Boolean operations, such as AND, OR, or NOT, or table–look-up operations.

Neighborhood operators whose output is only a function of an input image neighborhood related to the output pixel position are called *nonrecursive neighborhood operators*. Neighborhood operators whose output depends in part on previously generated output values are called *recursive neighborhood operators*. We begin our discussion with nonrecursive neighborhood operators.

A neighborhood might be so small and asymmetric as to contain only one nearest neighbor, such as a pixel's north or east neighbor, or it may be large enough to contain all the pixels in some symmetric $N \times N$ neighborhood centered around the given position. N, for example, could be five pixels (Fig. 6.1).

For a pixel whose (row, column) position is (r,c), we let $N(r,c)$ designate the set of the neighboring pixel positions around position (r,c). For example, depending on the neighborhood operator, $N(r,c)$ could include only one neighbor; it could include the nearest four neighbors; it might consist of an $M \times M$ square of neighbors

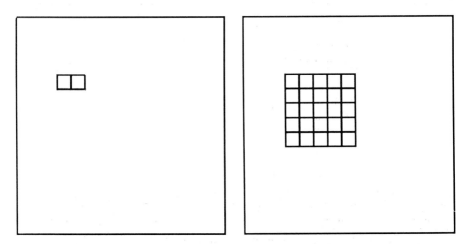

Figure 6.1 A small and a large square neighborhood that might be used in a neighborhood operator.

centered around (r,c), the set of all neighboring pixel positions whose Euclidean distance to pixel (r,c) is less than or equal to $\rho_0(r,c)$, the distance ρ_0 depending on (r,c); or it might consist of the set of all neighboring pixel positions whose Euclidean distance to pixel (r,c) is less than or equal to ρ_0 and whose row index is less than or equal to r, and so on.

Letting f designate the input image and g the output image, we can write the action of a general nonrecursive neighborhood operator ϕ as

$$g(r,c) = \phi\big[r,c,f(r',c') : (r',c') \in N(r,c)\big]$$

the notation $f(r',c') : (r',c') \in N(r,c)$ meaning a list of the values $f(r',c')$ for each of the $(r',c') \in N(r,c)$ in a preagreed-upon order that the notation itself suppresses.

One common nonrecursive neighborhood operator is the *linear operator*. The output value at pixel position (r,c) of a linear operator is given as a possibly position-dependent linear combination of all the input pixel values at positions in the neighborhood of (r,c).

$$g(r,c) = \sum_{(r',c') \in N(r,c)} f(r',c')w(r',c',r,c)$$

The most common nonrecursive neighborhood operator is the kind that is employed uniformly on the image. Its action on identical neighborhood spatial configurations is the same regardless of where on the image the neighborhood is located. This kind of neighborhood operator is called *shift-invariant* or *position invariant*.

The action for a shift-invariant nonrecursive neighborhood operator can be written as

$$g(r,c) = \phi\big[f(r',c') : (r',c') \in N(r,c)\big]$$

where the neighborhood N itself satisfies a shift invariance:

$$(r',c') \in N(r,c) \quad \text{implies} \quad (r'-u,c'-v) \in N(r-u,c-v) \quad \text{for all} \quad (u,v).$$

It should be obvious that shift-invariant operators commute with translation operators. That is, the result of a shift-invariant operator on a translated image is the same as translating the result of the shift-invariant operator on the given image. To see this, suppose the translation is by (r_0, c_0). Then the translation of the given image $f(r,c)$ is $f(r - r_0, c - c_0)$, and the translation of the result $g(r,c)$ is $g(r - r_0, c - c_0)$, where

$$g(r,c) = \phi\big[f(r',c') : (r',c') \in N(r,c)\big]$$

Consider the translation of the result: $g(r - r_0, c - c_0)$.

$$g(r - r_0, c - c_0) = \phi\big[f(r',c') : (r',c') \in N(r - r_0, c - c_0)\big]$$

Make a change of dummy variables. Let $u = r' + r_0$ and $v = c' + c_0$. Then

$$g(r - r_0, c - c_0) = \phi\big[f(u - r_0, v - c_0) : (u - r_0, v - c_0) \in N(r - r_0, c - c_0)\big]$$
$$= \phi\big[f(u - r_0, v - c_0) : (u,v) \in N(r,c)\big]$$

since the neighborhood N is shift-invariant. Now $\phi\big[f(u - r_0, v - c_0) : (u,v) \in N(r,c)\big]$ is the result of the neighborhood operator acting on the translated input image, and $g(r - r_0, c - c_0)$ is the translation of the neighborhood operator acting on the given image. Their equality states that the result of a shift-invariant operator on a translated image is the same as translating the result of the shift-invariant operator on the given image.

Compositions of shift-invariant operators are also shift-invariant. More precisely, suppose

$$g(r,c) = \phi_1\big[f(r',c') : (r',c') \in N_1(r,c)\big]$$

and

$$h(r,c) = \phi_2\big[g(r',c') : (r',c') \in N_2(r,c)\big]$$

Then the composition $\phi_2\phi_1$, first applying ϕ_1 and then ϕ_2, is shift-invariant. To see this, note that

$$h(r - r_0, c - c_0) = \phi_2\big[g(r' - r_0, c' - c_0) : (r',c') \in N_2(r,c)\big]$$

and

$$g(r' - r_0, c' - c_0) = \phi_1\big[f(r'' - r_0, c'' - c_0) : (r'',c'') \in N_1(r',c')\big]$$

Shifting f by (r_0, c_0) produces a g shifted by (r_0, c_0), and the g shifted by (r_0, c_0) produces an h shifted by (r_0, c_0). So shifting f by (r_0, c_0) and then applying ϕ_1 followed by ϕ_2 results in an h that has been shifted by (r_0, c_0).

An important kind of shift-invariant neighborhood operator is the linear shift-invariant operator. The output value at pixel position (r,c) of a linear shift-invariant operator is given as a fixed linear combination of all input pixel values at positions in the neighborhood of (r,c). The neighborhood itself is shift invariant, and the weights of the linear combination are the same from neighborhood to neighborhood. If we designate by W the neighborhood of all pixel positions around $(0,0)$, then the action of the linear shift-invariant operator on an image f having domain F can be written

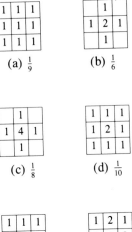

Figure 6.2 Common 3×3 masks used for noise cleaning. The mask in (a) is called the 3×3 box filter.

as

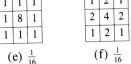

$$g(r,c) = \sum_{\substack{(r',c') \in W \\ (r+r',c+c') \in F}} f(r+r',c+c')w(r',c')$$

The weight function w is called the kernel or the mask of weights, W is the domain of w, and the operation itself is called the cross-correlation of f with w. We write

$$g = f \otimes w$$

Figures 6.2 and 6.3 illustrate common linear shift-invariant operators for noise cleaning. Figure 6.4 shows the indexing of the mask, the indexing of the image, and the application of the mask to the image. Figure 6.5 shows the application of a mask with weights to an image.

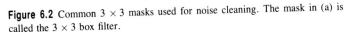

Figure 6.3 Common 5×5 masks used for noise cleaning. The mask in (a) comes from a repeated application of a 3×3 box filter; in (b) from the function $8 - (r^2 + c^2)$; in (c) from $\binom{4}{r+2}\binom{4}{c+2}$, where r and c range between -2 and $+2$ and $\binom{u}{v}$ designates the binomial coefficient $\binom{u}{v} = \frac{u!}{(u-v)!v!}$.

W (rows **r**, columns **c**)

	-1,-1	-1,0	-1,1
r	0,-1	**0,0**	0,1
	1,-1	1,0	1,1

Image (rows **r**, columns **c**)

	(1,1)	(1,2)	(1,3)		
	(2,1)	**(2,2)**	(2,3)		
r	(3,1)	(3,2)	(3,3)		

Assume $w(r',c') = 1$ for all (r',c').

$$
\begin{aligned}
g(2,2) = {} & f(2+(-1),2+(-1)) + f(2+(-1),2+0) + f(2+(-1),2+1) \\
& + f(2+0,2+(-1)) + f(2+0,2+0) + f(2+0,2+1) \\
& + f(2+1,2+(-1)) + f(2+1,2+0) + f(2+1,2+1)
\end{aligned}
$$

$$
\begin{aligned}
= {} & f(1,1) + f(1,2) + f(1,3) \\
& + f(2,1) + f(2,2) + f(2,3) \\
& + f(3,1) + f(3,2) + f(3,3)
\end{aligned}
$$

Figure 6.4 Indexing of the mask (left), and of the image (right), and the computation of the cross-correlation for pixel (2,2) of the image.

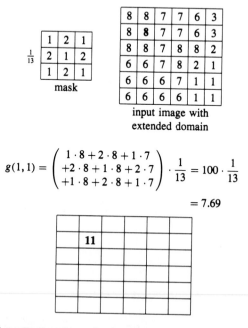

mask ($\frac{1}{13}$ ·)

1	2	1
2	1	2
1	2	1

input image with extended domain

8	8	7	7	6	3
8	**8**	7	7	6	3
8	8	7	8	8	2
6	6	7	8	2	1
6	6	6	7	1	1
6	6	6	6	1	1

$$
g(1,1) = \begin{pmatrix} 1\cdot 8 + 2\cdot 8 + 1\cdot 7 \\ +2\cdot 8 + 1\cdot 8 + 2\cdot 7 \\ +1\cdot 8 + 2\cdot 8 + 1\cdot 7 \end{pmatrix} \cdot \frac{1}{13} = 100 \cdot \frac{1}{13}
$$

$$
= 7.69
$$

	11				

Figure 6.5 Application of a mask of weights to pixel (2,2) of an image for the cross-correlation operation.

1,1	1,2	1,3	1,4
2,1	2,2	2,3	2,4
3,1	3,2	3,3	3,4
4,1	4,2	4,3	4,4

-1,0	
0,0	0,1

(Assume all weights are 1)

Figure 6.6 A nonsymmetric L-shaped mask and the application of the convolution operator to an image using this mask. The effect is like applying a cross-correlation operator with the L-shaped mask flipped.

The cross-correlation has a close relative, a linear shift-invariant operation called convolution. The convolution of f with w is denoted by $f * w$ and is defined by

$$(f * w)(r,c) = \sum_{\substack{(r',c') \in W \\ (r-r',c-c') \in F}} f(r - r', c - c')w(r',c')$$

The convolution has the same form as the cross-correlation, but it indexes differently over the pixels of the image. If the mask is symmetric, convolution and correlation are the same; otherwise the convolution operation flips the mask. Figure 6.6 illustrates the indexing of a nonsymmetric mask and an image and the operation of the convolution operator. A more detailed discussion of linear shift-invariant operators is given in Section 6.4.

Another example of a shift-invariant operator includes the gray scale morphological operators of dilation and erosion, whose action can be written as

$$d(r,c) = \max_{(r',c') \in W} [f(r - r', c - c') + w(r',c')]$$

and

$$e(r,c) = \min_{(r',c') \in W} [f(r + r', c + c') - w(r',c')]$$

respectively. Finally, for our last example we take the multiplicative maximum and minimum shift-invariant operator

$$m_1(r,c) = \max_{(r',c') \in W} [f(r - r', c - c')w(r',c')]$$

$$m_2(r,c) = \min_{(r',c') \in W} [f(r + r', c + c')w(r',c')]$$

defined by Ritter, Shrader-Frechette, and Wilson (1987), Ritter and Wilson (1987), and Wilson and Ritter (1987).

6.2   Symbolic Neighborhood Operators

In this section we discuss a variety of symbolic and symbolic-related neighborhood operators in a way that emphasizes their common form (Haralick, 1981). Gray

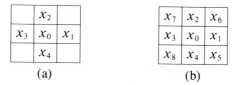

Figure 6.7 Indexing of the pixels in (a) 4-connected and (b) 8-connected neighborhoods of x_0.

(1971) examines symbolic-related neighborhood operators that compute local properties, most of which we do not address here. The symbolic operators are useful for image segmentation tasks as well as for the labeling of primitives involved in structural image analysis. The common form of the operators suggests the possibility of a large-scale integration hardware implementation in the VLSI device technology.

The simple operators discussed here may use two basic neighborhoods: a 4-connected neighborhood and an 8-connected neighborhood. As illustrated in Fig. 6.7, the 4-connected neighborhood around a pixel consists of the pixel and its north, south, east, and west neighbors. The 8-connected neighborhood around a pixel consists of all the pixels in a 3×3 window whose center is the given pixel.

Recall that recursive neighborhood operators are those for which a previously generated output may be one of the inputs to the neighborhood. In this manner the output memory is also part of the input. Nonrecursive neighborhood operators are those using independent image memory for input and output. Previous outputs cannot influence current outputs. Rosenfeld and Pfaltz (1966) call recursive operators sequential; nonrecursive operators, parallel.

6.2.1 Region-Growing Operator

The region-growing operator is nonrecursive and often has a symbolic data domain. It changes all pixels whose label is the background label to the non-background label of neighboring pixels. It is based on a two-argument primitive function h, which is a projection operator whose output is either its first argument or its second argument, depending on their values. If the first argument is the special symbol g for background, then the output of the function is its second argument. Otherwise the output is the first argument. Hence:

$$h(c,d) = \begin{cases} d & \text{if } c = g \\ c & \text{if } c \neq g \end{cases}$$

The region-growing operator uses the primitive function h in the following way. For the operator in the 4-connected mode, let $a_0 = x_0$. Define $a_n = h(a_{n-1}, x_n)$, $n = 1, \ldots, 4$. Then the output symbol y is defined by $y = a_4$. For the operator in the 8-connected mode, let $a_0 = x_0$. Define $a_n = h(a_{n-1}, x_n)$, $n = 1, \ldots, 8$. Then the output symbol y is defined by $y = a_8$. Figure 6.8 shows the operation of the region-growing operator in the 8-connected mode.

The region-growing operator is related to the binary dilation morphological operator with a structuring element that is a 4- or 8-connected neighborhood. However, instead of working on the binary images on which the binary dilation operator

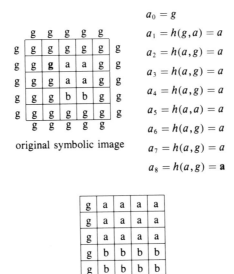

$$a_0 = g$$
$$a_1 = h(g,a) = a$$
$$a_2 = h(a,g) = a$$
$$a_3 = h(a,g) = a$$
$$a_4 = h(a,g) = a$$
$$a_5 = h(a,a) = a$$
$$a_6 = h(a,g) = a$$
$$a_7 = h(a,g) = a$$
$$a_8 = h(a,g) = \mathbf{a}$$

original symbolic image

filled image
(one iteration)

Figure 6.8 Operation of the region growing operator in the 8-connected mode.

works, the region-growing operator works on labeled regions. In this sense it is a generalization of dilation. A more sophisticated region-growing operator grows background border pixels to the region label that a majority of its neighbors have. In the 8-connected mode, such an operator sets $a_n = h(x_0, x_n)$, $n = 1, \ldots, 8$ and defines the output symbol y by $y = c$, where $\#\{n \mid a_n = c\} > \#\{n \mid a_n = c'\}$ for all c'.

6.2.2   Nearest Neighbor Sets and Influence Zones

Given a symbolic image with background pixels labeled g and each connected set of nonbackground pixels labeled with a unique label, we can label each background pixel with the label of its closest nonbackground neighboring pixel. Serra (1982) calls these nearest neighbor sets *influence zones*. To accomplish this labeling, simply iteratively grow the nonbackground labels into the background labels by using the 8-neighborhood if the max distance is desired, or the 4-neighborhood if the city-block distance is desired, employing the 4-neighborhood and 8-neighborhood alternately in the ratio of $\sqrt{2}$ for Euclidean distance.

6.2.3   Region-Shrinking Operator

The region-shrinking operator is nonrecursive and has a symbolic data domain. It changes the label on all border pixels to the background label. The region-shrinking operator defined here can change the connectivity of a region and can even entirely delete a region upon repeated application. It is based on a two-argument primitive function h that can recognize whether or not its arguments are identical. If the arguments are the same, h outputs the value of the argument. If the arguments differ, h outputs the special symbol g for background. Hence

$$h(c,d) = \begin{cases} c & \text{if } c = d \\ g & \text{if } c \neq d \end{cases}$$

The region-shrinking operator uses the primitive function h in the following way. For the operator in the 4-connected mode, let $a_0 = x_0$. Define $a_n = h(a_{n-1}, x_n)$, $n = 1, \ldots, 4$. Then the output symbol y is defined by $y = a_4$. For the operator in the 8-connected mode, let $a_0 = x_0$. Define $a_n = h(a_{n-1}, x_n)$, $n = 1, \ldots, 8$. Then the output symbol y is defined by $y = a_8$. Figure 6.9 illustrates this operation. Region shrinking is related to binary erosion, except that region-shrinking operates on labeled regions instead of binary-1s.

A more sophisticated region-shrinking operator shrinks border pixels only if they are connected to enough pixels of unlike regions. In the 8-connected mode it sets $a_n = h(x_0, x_n)$, $n = 1, \ldots, 8$ and defines the output symbol y by

$$y = \begin{cases} g & \text{if } \#\{n \mid a_n = g\} > k \\ x_0 & \text{otherwise} \end{cases}$$

As mentioned in the section on nearest neighbor sets, to obtain a region-shrinking (or region growing) that is close to a Euclidean-distance region-shrinking (or growing), the 4-neighborhood and the 8-neighborhood must be used alternately, approximating as closely as possible the ratio $\sqrt{2}/1$ (Rosenfeld and Pfaltz, 1968). A ratio of 4/3 can be obtained by the sequence $4 : 3 = < 4, 8, 4, 8, 4, 8, 4 >$, and a ratio of 3/2 can be obtained by the sequence $3 : 2 = < 4, 8, 4, 8, 4 >$. Alternating these two sequences will give a ratio of 7/5, which is just under $\sqrt{2}$. Using one 4:3 sequence followed by two 3:2 sequences gives a ratio of 10/7, just over $\sqrt{2}$. Alternating between $< 4 : 3, 3 : 2, 3 : 2 >$ and $< 4 : 3, 3 : 2 >$ gives a ratio of 17/12, which differs from $\sqrt{2}$ by less than 2.5×10^{-3}, an approximation that should be good enough for most purposes.

The choice of 4-neighborhood or 8-neighborhood for the current iteration that best approximates the Euclidean distance can be determined dynamically. Let $N4$ be the number of uses of the 4-neighborhood so far and $N8$ be the number of uses of the 8-neighborhood so far. If $| N4 - \sqrt{2}(N8 + 1) | < | N4 + 1 - \sqrt{2}N8 |$, then use the 8-neighborhood for the current iteration; otherwise use the 4-neighborhood.

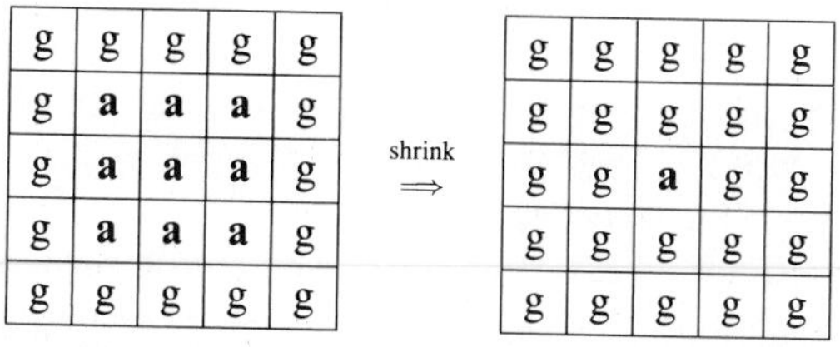

Figure 6.9 Operation of one iteration of the region-shrinking operator using an 8-connected neighborhood.

6.2.4 Mark-Interior/Border-Pixel Operator

The mark-interior/border-pixel operator is nonrecursive and has a symbolic data domain. It marks all interior pixels with the label i, and all border pixels with the label b. It is based on two primitive functions. One is a two-argument primitive function h very similar to that used in the region-shrinking operator. The other one is a one-argument primitive function f. The two-argument primitive function h can recognize whether or not its arguments are identical. For identical arguments it outputs the argument. For nonidentical arguments it outputs the special symbol b, for border. The one-argument primitive function f can recognize whether or not its argument is the special symbol b. If it is, it outputs b. If not, it outputs the special symbol i, for interior. Hence

$$h(c,d) = \begin{cases} c & \text{if } c = d \\ b & \text{if } c \neq d \end{cases}$$

$$f(c) = \begin{cases} b & \text{if } c = b \\ i & \text{if } c \neq b \end{cases}$$

The mark-interior/border-pixel operator uses the primitive function h in the following way. For the operator in the 4-connected mode, let $a_0 = x_0$. Define $a_n = h(a_{n-1}, x_n)$, $n = 1, \ldots, 4$. Then the output symbol y is defined by $y = f(a_4)$. For the operator in the 8-connected mode, let $a_0 = x_0$. Define $a_n = h(a_{n-1}, x_n)$, $n = 1, \ldots, 8$. Then the output symbol y is defined by $y = f(a_8)$.

6.2.5 Connectivity Number Operator

The connectivity number operator is nonrecursive and has a symbolic data domain. Its purpose is to classify the way a pixel is connected to its like neighbors. As shown in Fig. 6.10, there are six values of connectivity, five for border pixels and one for interior pixels. The border pixels consist of isolated pixels, edge pixels, connected pixels, branching pixels, and crossing pixels. The connectivity number operator associates with each pixel a symbol called the connectivity number of the pixel. The symbol, though a number, is really a label. It has no arithmetic number properties. The number designates which of the six kinds of connectivity a pixel has with its like neighbors.

Yokoi Connectivity Number

The definition we give here of connectivity number is based on a slight generalization of the definitions suggested by Yokoi, Toriwaki, and Fukumura (1975). The operator, as we define it, uses an 8-connected neighborhood and can be defined for either 4-connectivity or 8-connectivity.

For 4-connectivity, a pixel is an interior pixel if its value and that of each of its 4-connected neighbors are the same. In this case its 4-connectivity takes the index value 5. Otherwise the 4-connectivity of a pixel is given by the number of times a 4-connected neighbor has the same value but the corresponding three-pixel corner neighborhood does not. These corner neighbors are shown in Fig. 6.11.

```
*****  *              13221  0

  *                     2

  *                     2

********              12422222

  *      *              2     2

  *      *              2     1

****                   1211

****                   1551

**** *                 1551 0

****                   1111

Binary Image         Labeling of the
                       ' * '  Pixels


                     0  Isolated

                     1  Edge

                     2  Connecting

              Key:   3  Branching

                     4  Crossing

                     5  Interior
```

Figure 6.10 Connectivity number labeling of a binary image using 8-connectivity.

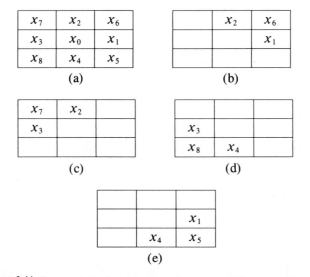

Figure 6.11 Corner neighborhood corresponding to each of the east, north, west, and south neighbors of the center pixel; (a) indexing pixels in a 3×3 neighborhood, (b) corner of x_1, (c) corner of x_2, (d) corner of x_3, and (e) corner of x_4.

For 8-connectivity, a pixel is an interior pixel if its value and that of each of its 8-connected neighbors are the same. Otherwise the 8-connectivity of a pixel is given by the number of times a 4-connected neighbor has a different value and at least one pixel in the corresponding three-pixel neighborhood corner has the same value.

The connectivity operator requires two primitive functions: a function h that can determine whether a three-pixel corner neighborhood is connected in a particular way and a function f that basically counts the number of arguments having a particular value.

For 4-connectivity, the function h of four arguments is defined by

$$h(b,c,d,e) = \begin{cases} q & \text{if } b = c \text{ and } (d \neq b \text{ or } e \neq b) \\ r & \text{if } b = c \text{ and } (d = b \text{ and } e = b) \\ s & \text{if } b \neq c \end{cases}$$

The function f of four arguments is defined by

$$f(a_1,a_2,a_3,a_4) = \begin{cases} 5 & \text{if } a_1 = a_2 = a_3 = a_4 = r \\ n & \text{where } n = \#\{a_k \mid a_k = q\}, \text{ otherwise} \end{cases}$$

The connectivity operator using 4-connectivity is then defined in the following way by letting

$$a_1 = h(x_0,x_1,x_6,x_2)$$

$$a_2 = h(x_0,x_2,x_7,x_3)$$

$$a_3 = h(x_0,x_3,x_8,x_4)$$

$$a_4 = h(x_0,x_4,x_5,x_1)$$

Define the connectivity number y by $y = f(a_1,a_2,a_3,a_4)$.

For 8-connectivity, the function h is slightly different. It is defined by

$$h(b,c,d,e) = \begin{cases} q & \text{if } b \neq c \text{ and } (d = b \text{ or } e = b) \\ r & \text{if } b = c \text{ and } (d = b \text{ and } e = b) \\ s & \text{otherwise} \end{cases}$$

Then, as before, the connectivity number y is defined by $y = f(a_1,a_2,a_3,a_4)$. Figure 6.12 illustrates the computation of the Yokoi connectivity number.

Rutovitz Connectivity Number

The Yokoi connectivity number is not the only definition of connectivity number. Another definition given by Rutovitz (1966) is based on the number of transitions from one symbol to another as one travels around the 8-neighborhood of a pixel. The definition we give here of the Rutovitz connectivity number, sometimes called a crossing number, is based on a slight generalization of the definitions suggested by Rutovitz (1966). The Rutovitz connectivity number simply counts the number of transitions from symbols that are different from that of the center pixel to symbols

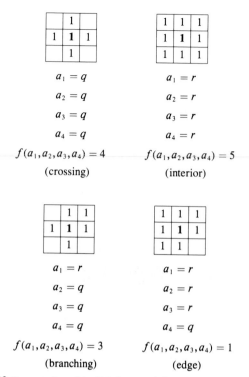

$a_1 = q$

$a_2 = q$

$a_3 = q$

$a_4 = q$

$f(a_1, a_2, a_3, a_4) = 4$

(crossing)

$a_1 = r$

$a_2 = r$

$a_3 = r$

$a_4 = r$

$f(a_1, a_2, a_3, a_4) = 5$

(interior)

$a_1 = r$

$a_2 = q$

$a_3 = q$

$a_4 = q$

$f(a_1, a_2, a_3, a_4) = 3$

(branching)

$a_1 = r$

$a_2 = r$

$a_3 = r$

$a_4 = q$

$f(a_1, a_2, a_3, a_4) = 1$

(edge)

Figure 6.12 Computation of the Yokoi connectivity number using 4-connectivity.

that are the same as that of the center pixel as one travels around the 8-neighborhood of a pixel.

The Rutovitz connectivity number requires a three-argument primitive function h defined by

$$h(a,b,c) = \begin{cases} 1 & \text{if } (a = b \text{ and } a \neq c) \text{ or } (a \neq b \text{ and } a = c) \\ 0 & \text{otherwise} \end{cases}$$

Then set

$$a_1 = h(x_0, x_1, x_6)$$

$$a_2 = h(x_0, x_6, x_2)$$

$$a_3 = h(x_0, x_2, x_7)$$

$$a_4 = h(x_0, x_7, x_3)$$

$$a_5 = h(x_0, x_3, x_8)$$

$$a_6 = h(x_0, x_8, x_4)$$

$$a_7 = h(x_0, x_4, x_5)$$

$$a_8 = h(x_0, x_5, x_1)$$

The output value y is then given by

$$y = \sum_{n=1}^{8} a_n$$

6.2.6   Connected Shrink Operator

The connected shrink operator is a recursive operator having a symbolic data domain. It is similar in certain respects to the connectivity number operator and the region-shrinking operator. Instead of labeling all border pixels with the background symbol g, the connected shrink operator labels only those border pixels that can be deleted from a connected region without disconnecting the region. Since it is applied recursively, pixels that are interior during one position of the scan may appear as border pixels at another position of the scan and eventually may be deleted by this operator. After one complete scan of the image, the set of pixels that get labeled as background is a strong function of the way in which the image is scanned with the operator. For example, as illustrated in Fig. 6.13, a top-down, left-right scan will delete all edge pixels that are not right-boundary edge pixels.

The theoretical basis of the connected shrink operator was explored by Rosenfeld and Pfaltz (1966), Rosenfeld (1970), and Stefanelli and Rosenfeld (1971). Basically a pixel's label is changed to g, for background, if upon deleting it from the region it belongs to, the region remains connected. The operator definition given here is based on Yokoi, Toriwaki, and Fukumura (1975). The operator uses an 8-connected neighborhood and can be defined for deleting either 4-deletable or 8-deletable pixels. It requires two primitive functions: a function h that can determine whether the three-pixel corner of a neighborhood is connected and a function g that basically counts the number of arguments having certain values.

In the 4-connectivity mode, the four-argument primitive function h is defined by using

$$h(b,c,d,e) = \begin{cases} 1 & \text{if } b = c \text{ and } (d \neq b \text{ or } e \neq b) \\ 0 & \text{otherwise} \end{cases}$$

In the 8-connectivity mode, the four-argument primitive function h is defined by

$$h(b,c,d,e) = \begin{cases} 1 & \text{if } c \neq b \text{ and } (d = b \text{ or } e = b) \\ 0 & \text{otherwise.} \end{cases}$$

```
        **
       ****
      ******              ***
      ** **              *   *
       *  **             *   *
       *  **             *   *
       *  **                 *
        (a)                 (b)
     input image      connected shrink
                        output image
```

Figure 6.13 Connected shrink operator applied in a top-down, left-right scan using 4-connectivity.

The five-argument primitive function f is defined by

$$f(a_1,a_2,a_3,a_4,x) = \begin{cases} g & \text{if exactly one of } a_1,a_2,a_3,a_4 = 1 \\ x & \text{otherwise} \end{cases}$$

Using the indexing convention of Fig. 6.11, we define the connected shrink operator by letting

$$a_1 = h(x_0,x_1,x_6,x_2)$$

$$a_2 = h(x_0,x_2,x_7,x_3)$$

$$a_3 = h(x_0,x_3,x_8,x_4)$$

$$a_4 = h(x_0,x_4,x_5,x_1)$$

The output symbol y is defined by $y = f(a_1,a_2,a_3,a_4,x_0)$. Figure 6.14 further illustrates the connected shrink operator.

The earliest discussion of connectivity in digital pictures can be found in Rosenfeld (1971). Rutovitz (1966) preceded Rosenfeld in the use of crossing numbers but did not use connectivity in his development. Related algorithms and discussion of connectivity can be found in Levialdi (1972), who introduced a parallel or nonrecursive shrinking algorithm for the purpose of counting the number of components in a binary image. This iterative algorithm does not employ the 1-deletability of the Yokoi, Toriwaki, and Fukumura method; it uses a 2×2 window rather than a 3×3 window in the shrinking process but requires the detection of an isolated element

Original Image

g	g	g	g	g	g	g	g	
g	1	1	g	g	g	1	1	g
g	1	1	1	g	g	1	1	g
g	1	1	1	1	1	1	1	g
g	1	1	1	g	g	1	1	g
g	1	1	g	g	g	1	1	g
g	g	g	g	g	g	g	g	

g	g	g
g	**1**	1
g	1	1

$a_1 = 1$ $\quad a_3 = 0$

$a_2 = 0$ $\quad a_4 = 0$

$f(1,0,0,0,1) = g$

Result

g	g	g	g	g	g	g	g
g	g	g	1	g	g	g	g
g	g	1	1	1	1	1	g
g	g	g	1	g	g	g	g
g	g	g	g	g	g	g	g

Figure 6.14 Application of the connected shrink operator to an image using 4-connectivity.

during the iterative process so that it may be counted before it is made to disappear by the process. A three-dimensional extension to this nonrecursive algorithm can be found in Arcelli and Levialdi (1972). Lobregt, Verbeck, and Groen (1980) discuss a recursive operator for three-dimensional shrinking.

6.2.7 Pair Relationship Operator

The pair relationship operator is nonrecursive and has a symbolic data domain. It is a general operator that labels a pixel on the basis of whether it stands in the specified relationship with a neighborhood pixel. An example of a pair relationship operator is one that relabels with a specified label all border pixels that are next to an interior pixel and either can relabel all other pixels with another specified label or can leave their labels alone. Formally, a pair relationship operator marks a pixel with the specified label p if the pixel has a specified label l and neighbors enough pixels having a specified label m. All other pixels it either marks with another specified label or leaves unmodified.

The pair relationship operator employs two primitive functions. The two-argument function h can recognize whether its first argument has the value of its second argument. It is defined by

$$h(a,m) = \begin{cases} 1 & \text{if } a = m \\ 0 & \text{otherwise} \end{cases}$$

For the 4-connected mode, the output value y is defined by

$$y = \begin{cases} q & \text{if } \sum_{n=1}^{4} h(x_n, m) < \theta \text{ or } x_0 \neq 1 \\ p & \text{if } \sum_{n=1}^{4} h(x_n, m) \geq \theta \text{ and } x_0 = 1 \end{cases}$$

where q can be either a specified output label or the label x_8.

For the 8-connected mode, the output y is defined by

$$y = \begin{cases} q & \text{if } \sum_{n=1}^{8} h(x_n, m) < \theta \text{ or } x_0 \neq 1 \\ p & \text{if } \sum_{n=1}^{8} h(x_n, m) \geq \theta \text{ and } x_0 = 1 \end{cases}$$

where q can be either a specified output or the label x_8.

6.2.8 Thinning Operator

The thinning operator discussed here is defined as a composition of three operators: the mark-interior/border-pixel operator, the pair relationship operator, and the marked-pixel connected shrink operator. It works by marking all border pixels that are next to interior pixels and then deleting (or shrinking) any marked pixel that is

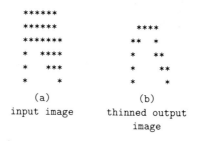

```
******
******              ****
*******           **   *
*  ****           *    **
*  ***            *    **
*     *           *     *
    (a)               (b)
input image      thinned output
                     image
```

Figure 6.15 Result of one application of the thinning operator using the 4-connectivity deletability condition.

deletable. The result of successively applying the thinning operator on a symbolic image is that all regions are symmetrically shrunk down until no interior pixels are left. What remains is their center lines, as shown in Fig. 6.15. This operator has the nice property that the center line is connected in exactly the same geometric and topologic way the original figure is connected. For other similar operators that thin without changing geometry or topology, see Rosenfeld and Davis (1976), Stefanelli and Rosenfeld (1971), or Arcelli and Sanniti di Baja (1978). To implement the operator as the composition of three operators, the mark-interior/border-pixel operator examines the original symbolic image to produce an interior/border image. The interior/border image is examined by the pair relationship operator, which produces an image whose pixels are marked if on the original image they were border pixels and were next to interior pixels. The marked-pixel image and the original symbolic image constitute the input to the marked-pixel connected shrink operator, which is exactly like the connected shrink operator except it shrinks only pixels that are deletable and marked.

The first discussions of thinning appeared in Hilditch (1969) and Deutsch (1969). These initial insights were later expanded by Fraser (1970), Stefenelli and Rosenfeld (1971), Deutsch (1972), Rosenfeld (1975), and Rosenfeld and Davis (1976). A brief comparison of thinning techniques can be found in Tamura (1978), who suggests that a smooth 8-connected thinning results if 8-deletable pixels are removed from thinning 4-connected curves. Tamura also notes that the thinning of Rosenfeld and Davis (1976) is very sensitive to contour noise when used in the 4-connected mode.

6.2.9 Distance Transformation Operator

The distance transformation operator can be implemented as either a recursive or a nonrecursive operator. It requires a binary image whose border pixels are labeled 0 and whose interior pixels are labeled i. The purpose of the distance transformation operator is to produce a numeric image whose pixels are labeled with the distance between each of them and their closest border pixel. The distance between two pixels can be defined by the length of the shortest 4-connected path (city-block distance) or 8-connected path (max or chessboard distance) between them.

As a nonrecursive operator, the distance transformation can be achieved by successive application of the pair relationship operator. In the first application the pair relationship labels with a 1 all pixels whose label is i and that are next to a pixel whose label is 0. All other pixels keep their labels. In the nth application, the pair relationship operator labels with an n all pixels whose label is i and that are next to a pixel whose label is $n - 1$. When no pixel has the label i, an application of the pair relationship operator changes no pixel value, and the resulting image is the distance transformation image. This implementation is related to the one given by Rosenfeld and Pfaltz (1968).

Another way of implementing this operator nonrecursively is by the iterative application of the primitive function defined by

$$h(a_0, \ldots, a_N) = \begin{cases} i & \text{if } a_n = i, \; n = 0, \ldots, N \\ \min \; \{b \mid \text{for some } n \leq N, a_n \neq i, \; b = a_n + 1\} \\ & \text{if } a_0 = i \text{ and there exists } n \text{ such that } a_n \neq i \\ a_0 & \text{if } a_0 \neq i \end{cases}$$

where i is the special interior pixel label.

In the 8-connected mode, the output y is defined by $y = h(x_0, x_1, \ldots, x_8)$, where $x_0, \ldots, x_8$ are pixel values coming from spatial positions defined in Fig. 6.7. In the 4-connected mode, the output symbol y is defined by $y = h(x_0, x_1, x_2, x_3, x_4)$. See Rosenfeld and Pfaltz (1966).

Another way (Rosenfeld and Pfaltz, 1966) of implementing the distance transformation involves the application of two recursive operators, the first operator being applied in a left-right, top-bottom scan and the second operator in a right-left, bottom-top scan. Both operators are based on similar primitive functions. For the first operator the primitive function h is defined by

$$h(a_1, \ldots, a_N; d) = \begin{cases} 0 & \text{if } a_N = 0 \\ \min\{a_1, \ldots, a_N\} + d & \text{otherwise} \end{cases}$$

In the 8-connected mode, the output symbol y of the first operator is defined by

$$y = h(x_2, x_6, x_7, x_3, x_0; 1)$$

In the 4-connected mode, the output symbol y is defined by

$$y = h(x_2, x_3, x_0; 1)$$

For the second operator, the primitive function is simply the minimum function. In the 8-connected mode, the output symbol y of the second operator is defined by

$$y = \min\{x_0, g(x_1, x_4, x_5, x_8; 1)\}$$

In the 4-connected mode, the output symbol y is defined by

$$y = \min\{x_0, g(x_1, x_4; 1)\}$$

where $g(a_1, \ldots, a_N; d) = \min\{a_1, \ldots, a_N\} + d$. Figure 6.16 illustrates the operation of the recursive distance operator (Rosenfeld and Pfaltz, 1968).

It is possible to compute a distance transformation that gives distances closely approximating Euclidean distance. For the first left-right, top-down pass, the output y is given by

$$y = \min\{h(x_2, x_3, x_0; d_1), h(x_6, x_7, x_0; d_2)\}$$

Original

0	0	0	0	0	0	0
0	0	1	1	1	1	0
0	0	1	1	1	1	0
0	1	1	1	1	1	0
0	0	1	1	1	1	0
0	0	1	1	1	1	0
0	0	0	0	0	0	0

Pass 1

0	0	0	0	0	0	0
0	0	1	1	1	1	0
0	0	1	2	2	1	0
0	1	2	2	2	1	0
0	0	1	2	2	1	0
0	0	1	1	1	1	0
0	0	0	0	0	0	0

Pass 2

0	0	0	0	0	0	0
0	0	1	1	1	1	0
0	0	1	2	2	1	0
0	1	1	2	2	1	0
0	0	1	2	2	1	0
0	0	1	1	1	1	0
0	0	0	0	0	0	0

Figure 6.16 Operation of the recursive Rosenfeld and Pfaltz distance operator, using 4-connectivity.

For the second right-left, bottom-up pass, the output y is given by

$$y = \min\{g(x_1, x_4; d_1), g(x_5, x_8; d_2), x_0\}$$

Montanari (1968) puts $d_1 = 1$ and $d_2 = \sqrt{2}$. This gives the correct Euclidean distance for all shortest paths that are vertical, horizontal, or diagonal. Barrow et al. (1977) and Nitzian and Agin (1979) use a scaled distance and put $d_1 = 2$ and $d_2 = 3$. Borgefors (1984) minimizes the maximum absolute value of the error between the correct Euclidean distance and the computed distance and determines that $d_1 = 1$ and $d_2 = \frac{1}{\sqrt{2}} + \sqrt{\sqrt{2} - 1} \approx 1.351$. For an integer approximation of scaled Euclidean distance, Borgefors recommends $d_1 = 3$ and $d_2 = 4$. Borgefors (1986) extends these ideas to using neighboring pixels whose Euclidean distance may be larger than $\sqrt{2}$ from the central pixel.

Vossepoel (1988) suggests $d_1 = .9413$ and $d_2 = 1.3513$, whereas Beckers and Smeulders (1989) argue that for isotropic distance transformations $d_1 = .9445$ and $d_2 = 1.3459$.

Verwer (1988) minimizes the maximum relative error and determines that $d_1 = .9604$ and $d_2 = 1.3583$. For an integer approximation of scaled Euclidean distance, Verwer recommends $d_1 = 5$ and $d_2 = 7$ or, for a better approximation, $d_1 = 12$ and $d_2 = 17$.

Danielsson (1980) propagates the pair of vertical and horizontal distances and is able thereby to compute a distance transformation that is almost exactly Euclidean, a small error occurring only in a few situations.

6.2.10   Radius of Fusion

Let I be a binary image. The radius of fusion for any connected component of I is the radius ρ of a disk satisfying the condition that if the binary image I is morphologically closed with a disk of radius ρ, then the given connected region will fuse with some other connected region.

To determine the radius of fusion for every binary-1 pixel, we begin by computing the connected components image for the given binary image I. In this way every binary-1 pixel can be labeled with a unique label corresponding to the connected region to which it belongs. The binary-0 labeled pixels are given the background label.

Exactly as we do to determine the nearest neighbor sets, we perform a region growing to label every binary-0 pixel with the label of its nearest labeled pixel. One iteration of a shrink operation on this image can label with a 0 all border pixels (pixels that have a neighbor with a different label). We use this image as the input to the distance transformation operator that labels nonzero every pixel with its distance to the nearest border. Then we mask this distance transformation image with the original image. Pixels having a nonbackground label on the original image get labeled with the distances associated with their spatial position on the distance transformation image. Then we give each pixel in a labeled region the minimum distance a pixel in the region has received. Pixels that are not labeled retain the background label.

The radius of fusion as defined here differs from the radius as defined by Rosenfeld and Pfaltz (1968). There the radius of fusion for a pixel is the smallest integer n such that after region-growing n iterations and region-shrinking $n + 1$ iterations, the pixel retains a nonbackground label. The difficulty with this definition for radius of fusion is that by using 4-neighborhoods, for example, it is possible for a pair or triangle of pixels never to fuse. The radius of fusion is therefore not defined. Defining it by some large number in such cases is artificial.

6.2.11   Number of Shortest Paths

Rosenfeld and Pfaltz (1968) describe the following neighborhood operator, which must be applied iteratively to count for each 0-pixel the number of shortest paths to the set that is represented as the binary-1 pixel on a binary image. Let the given

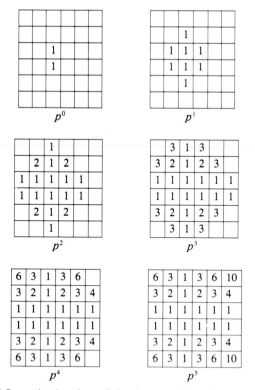

Figure 6.17 Successive iterations of the shortest-path-counting neighborhood operator.

binary image be denoted by $p^0(r,c)$. Define

$$
p^m(r,c) = \begin{cases} p^{m-1}(r,c) & \text{if } p^{m-1}(r,c) \neq 0 \\ \sum_{(r',c') \in N} p^{m-1}(r-r',c-c') & \text{if } p^{m-1}(r,c) = 0 \end{cases}
$$

where N can be the 4-neighborhood or the 8-neighborhood, as required. Since the application of this operator leaves nonzero pixels with their values and changes some of the 0-pixels to nonzero-labeled pixels, eventually successive applications of the operator make no more changes. If this happens after M iterations, then the value in pixel (r,c) of p^M will be the number of shortest paths from that pixel to the 1-pixels of image p^0, providing $p^0(r,c) = 0$. An example is given in Fig. 6.17.

6.3   Extremum-Related Neighborhood Operators

Finding pixels or regions that are relative minima and relative maxima can play an important role in the extraction of interesting points or region primitives for texture analysis or matching purposes. Operators for the determination of relative extrema and their reachability regions are more complex than simple 3×3 operators precisely because a relative extrema can be a region of pixels larger than 3×3.

In this section we discuss operators for the identification of nonminima and nonmaxima, for the identification of relative minima and maxima, and for the identification of the region of pixels reachable by ascending or descending pattern from relative extrema regions.

6.3.1 Non-Minima-Maxima Operator

The non-minima-maxima operator is a nonrecursive operator that takes a numeric input image and produces a symbolic output image in which each pixel is labeled with an index 0, 1, 2, or 3 indicating whether the pixel is nonmaximum, nonminimum, interior to a connected set of equal-valued pixels, or part of a transition region (a region having some neighboring pixels greater than and others less than its own value). A pixel whose value is the minimum of its neighborhood and that has one neighboring pixel with a value greater than its own may be a minimum or transition pixel, but it is certainly a nonmaximum pixel. Figure 6.18 illustrates how a pixel can be its neighborhood maximum yet not be part of any relative maximum.

The non-minima-maxima operator is based on the primitive function min and max. For the 4-connected case, let $a_0 = b_0 = x_0$ and define

$$a_n = \min\{a_{n-1}, x_0\} \quad n = 1, 2, 3, 4$$
$$b_n = \max\{b_{n-1}, x_0\} \quad n = 1, 2, 3, 4$$

The output index l is defined by

$$
l = \begin{cases}
0 \text{ (flat)} & \text{if } a_4 = x_0 = b_4 \\
1 \text{ (nonmaximum)} & \text{if } a_4 = x_0 < b_4 \\
2 \text{ (nonminimum)} & \text{if } a_4 < x_0 = b_4 \\
3 \text{ (transition)} & \text{if } a_4 < x_0 < b_4
\end{cases}
$$

1	1	1	1	4	1
1	1	1	1	4	1
1	1	3	3	3	1
1	1	3	3	3	1
1	1	3	3	3	1
1	1	1	1	1	1
1	1	1	1	1	1

Figure 6.18 Example of how a pixel can be its neighborhood maximum yet not be a part of any relative maximum. In its 8-neighborhood, the central 3 is a maximum, yet the flat of 3s it belongs to is a transition region.

For the 8-connected case, let $a_0 = b_0 = x_0$ and define

$$a_n = \min\{a_{n-1}, x_0\} \quad n = 1, 2, \ldots, 8$$
$$b_n = \min\{b_{n-1}, x_0\} \quad n = 1, 2, \ldots, 8$$

The output index l is defined by

$$l = \begin{cases} 0 \text{ (flat)} & \text{if } a_8 = x_0 = b_8 \\ 1 \text{ (nonmaximum)} & \text{if } a_8 = x_0 < b_8 \\ 2 \text{ (nonminimum)} & \text{if } a_8 < x_0 = b_8 \\ 3 \text{ (transition)} & \text{if } a_8 < x_0 < b_8 \end{cases}$$

6.3.2 Relative Extrema Operator

Relative extrema operators consist of the relative maximum operator and the relative minimum operator. They are recursive operators and have a numeric data domain. They require an input image that needs to be accessed but is not changed and an output image that is successively modified. Initially the output image is a copy of the input image. The operator must be successively applied in a top-down, left-right scan and then a bottom-up, right-left scan until no further changes are made. Each pixel on the output image contains the value of the highest extrema that can reach it by a monotonic path. Pixels on the output image that have the same value as those on the input image are the relative extrema pixels.

The relative maxima operator works as follows: Values are gathered from those pixels on the output image that corresponds to pixels on the input image that neighbor the given pixel and have input values greater than or equal to the input values of the given pixel. The maxima of these gathered values are propagated to the given output pixel. The relative minima operator works in an analogous fashion. Figure 6.19 illustrates the pixel designations for the normal and reverse scans.

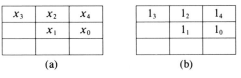

left-right top bottom scans

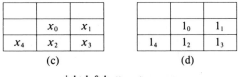

right-left bottom top scans

Figure 6.19 Pixel designations for the recursive operators that require forward and reverse scans and a numeric image and that recursively produce an output image. (a) and (c), input numeric images; (b) and (d), output images.

The relative maxima operator uses two primitive functions h and max. The four-argument function h selects the maximum of its last two arguments if its second argument is greater than or equal to its first argument. Otherwise it selects the third argument. Hence

$$h(b,c,d,e) = \begin{cases} \max \{d,e\} & \text{if } c \geq b \\ d & \text{if } c < b \end{cases}$$

The primitive function max selects the maximum of its arguments. In the 8-connected mode, the relative maxima operator lets

$$a_0 = l_0 \quad \text{and} \quad a_n = h(x_0, x_n, a_{n-1}, l_n), \qquad n = 1, 2, 3, \text{ and } 4$$

The output value l is defined by $l = a_4$. In the 4-connected mode, the operator is

$$a_0 = l_0 \quad \text{and} \quad a_n = h(x_0, x_n, a_{n-1}, l_n), \qquad n = 1 \text{ and } 2$$

The output value l is defined by $l = a_2$. Figure 6.20 illustrates the application of the relative maxima operator.

The relative minima operator is defined much like the relative maxima operator, with the max function replaced by the min function and all inequalities changed. Hence, for the relative minima operator, h is defined by

$$h(b,c,d,e) = \begin{cases} \min \{d,e\} & \text{if } c \leq b \\ d & \text{if } c > b \end{cases}$$

In the 8-connected mode, the relative minima operator lets $a_0 = l_0$ and

$$a_n = h(x_0, x_n, a_{n-1}, l_n), \qquad n = 1, 2, 3, \text{ and } 4$$

The output value l is defined by $l = a_4$. In the 4-connected mode, the operator lets $a_0 = l_0$ and

$$a_n = h(x_0, x_n, a_{n-1}l_n), \qquad n = 1 \text{ and } 2$$

The output value is defined by $l = a_2$.

An alternative kind of relative extrema operator can be defined by using the symbolic image created by the non-minima-maxima operator in combination with the original numeric image. Such an operator is a recursive operator and is based on the fact that by appropriate label propagation, all flat regions can be relabeled as transition, minima, or maxima regions and that the pixels originally labeled as nonminima or nonmaxima can be relabeled as transition regions or true relative minima or maxima.

The initial output image is taken to be the image created by the minima-maxima operator. Recursive propagation of the labels from one pixel to its neighbor on the output image is performed only if the two labels are not the same and the corresponding two gray levels on the original numeric image are equal.

Let any two neighboring pixels be x and y, labeled L_x and L_y, respectively, on the output image. As shown in Table 6.1, we have three cases to examine when $L_x \neq L_y$ and $x = y$:

1. Either L_x or L_y is a flat (0) and the other one is not (1,2,3). In this case we propagate the nonzero label into the zero label, thereby eliminating pixels marked as flats.

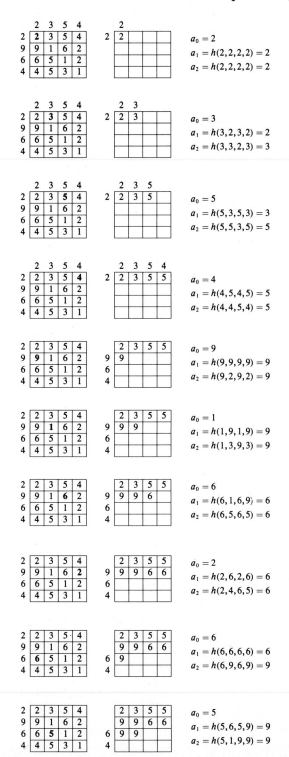

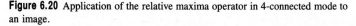

Figure 6.20 Application of the relative maxima operator in 4-connected mode to an image.

$a_0 = 1$
$a_1 = h(1,5,1,9) = 9$
$a_2 = h(1,6,9,6) = 9$

$a_0 = 2$
$a_1 = h(2,1,2,9) = 2$
$a_2 = h(2,2,2,6) = 6$

$\vdots$

Bottom-Up Pass

$a_0 = 9$
$a_1 = h(1,1,9,9) = 9$
$a_2 = h(1,1,9,9) = 9$

$a_0 = 6$
$a_1 = h(2,2,6,6) = 6$
$a_2 = h(2,1,6,9) = 6$

Result of Bottom-Up

Then it iterates down and up again until there are no more changes.

Final Result

Figure 6.20. *Continued.*

Table 6.1   Propagation table for the recursive relative extrema operator. The table gives the propagation label C for any pair a, b of neighboring pixels.

	a labels			
b labels	Nonmaxima	Nonminima	Flat	Transition
Nonmaxima	Nonmaxima	Transition	Nonmaxima	Transition
Nonminima	Transition	Nonminima	Nonminima	Transition
Flat	Nonmaxima	Nonminima	Flat	Transition
Transition	Transition	Transition	Transition	Transition

2. Either L_x is a minimum (1) and L_y is a maximum (2) or vice versa. In this case, since a region that is constant in value cannot simultaneously be a minimum and a maximum, we mark both pixels as transitions (3).

3. Either L_x or L_y is a transition (3). In this case, since a region that is constant in value and has one pixel marked as transition must be a transition region, we mark the nontransition-region pixel as a transition region, thereby propagating the transition label.

This propagation rule requires one four-argument primitive function h, defined by

$$
h(x,y,a,b) = \begin{cases}
a & \text{if } x \neq y \\[6pt]
3 \text{ (transition)} & \text{if } x = y \text{ and } (a = 3) \text{ or } (b = 3) \\
& (a = 1 \text{ and } b = 0) \text{ or} \\
& (a = 0 \text{ and } b = 1) \\[6pt]
2 \text{ (flat)} & \text{if } x = y \text{ and } (a = 2 \text{ and } b = 2) \\[6pt]
1 \text{ (nonminimum)} & \text{if } x = y \text{ and } (a = 1 \text{ and } b = 2) \text{ or} \\
& (a = 2 \text{ and } b = 1) \text{ or} \\
& (a = 1 \text{ and } b = 1) \\[6pt]
0 \text{ (nonmaximum)} & \text{if } x = y \text{ and } (a = 0 \text{ and } b = 0) \text{ or} \\
& (a = 0 \text{ and } b = 2) \text{ or} \\
& (a = 2 \text{ and } b = 0)
\end{cases}
$$

Values of pixels in the original numeric input image are denoted by x_n. Values of pixels in the non-minima-maxima-labeled image are denoted by l_n. For the operator using 4-connectedness and the standard 3×3 neighborhood designations, let $a_0 = l_0$ and define

$$a_n = h(x_0, x_n, a_{n-1}, l_n), \quad n = 1, 2, 3, \text{ and } 4$$

The output l is a_4. For the operator using 8-connectedness, let $a_0 = l_0$ and define

$$a_n = h(x_0, x_n, a_{n-1}, l_n), \quad n = 1, \ldots, 8$$

The output l is a_8.

Propagation can also be achieved by using the forward and reverse scan technique. In this case the left-right, top-bottom scan is alternated with the right-left, bottom-top scan. Employing the pixel designations in Fig. 6.11 for the operator using 4-connectedness, let $a_0 = l_0$ and define

$$a_n = h(x_0, x_n, a_{n-1}, l_n), \quad n = 1, 2, 3, \text{ and } 4$$

The output l is a_4.

6.3.3 Reachability Operator

Reachability operators consist of the descending reachability operator and the ascending reachability operator. The operators are recursive and require a numeric input and a symbolic image used for both input and output. Initially the symbolic image has all relative extrema pixels marked with unique labels (relative maxima for the descending reachability case and relative minima for the ascending reachability case). The unique labeling of extrema can be obtained by the connected component operator operating on the relative extrema image. Pixels that are not relative extrema must be labeled with the background symbol g. The reachability operator, like the connected component operator, must be iteratively and alternately applied in a top-down, left-right scan followed by a bottom-up, right-left scan until no further change is produced. The resulting output image has each pixel labeled with the unique label of the relative extrema region that can reach it by a monotonic path if it can only be reached by one extremum. If more than one extremum can reach it by a monotonic path, then the pixel is labeled c, for common region.

The operator works by successively propagating labels from all neighboring pixels that can reach the given pixel by monotonic paths. In case of conflicts the label c is propagated. Figure 6.19 illustrates the pixel designations for the reachability operator. To propagate the label, the descending reachability operator employs the four-argument primitive function h. Its first two arguments are labels from the output image, and its last two arguments are pixel values from the input image. It is defined by

$$h(a,b,x,y) = \begin{cases} a & \text{if } (b = g \text{ or } a = b) \text{ and } x < y \\ b & \text{if } a = g \text{ and } x < y \\ c & \text{if } a \neq g, \ b \neq g, \ a \neq b, \text{ and } x < y \\ a & \text{if } x > y \end{cases}$$

The operator uses the primitive function h in the 8-connected mode by letting $a_0 = l_0$ and defining $a_n = h(a_{n-1}, l_n, x_0, x_n)$, $n = 1, 2, 3$, and 4. The output label l is defined by $l = a_4$.

The 4-connected mode sets $a_0 = l_0$ and defines $a_n = h(a_{n-1}, l_n, x_0, x_n)$, $n = 1$ and 2. The output label l is defined by $l = a_2$.

The ascending reachability operator is defined just as the descending reachability operator is, except that the inequalities are changed. Hence, for the ascending reachability operator, the primitive function h is defined by

$$h(a,b,x,y) = \begin{cases} a & \text{if } (b = g \text{ or } a = b) \text{ and } x > y \\ b & \text{if } a = g \text{ and } x > y \\ c & \text{if } a \neq g, b \neq g, a \neq b, \text{ and } x > y \\ a & \text{if } x < y \end{cases}$$

6.4   Linear Shift-Invariant Neighborhood Operators

The linear shift-invariant neighborhood operator is the fundamental object of study in image and signal processing. Much has been written about the relationship between it, the discrete Fourier transform, and the frequency domain; for example, see Pratt (1978), Rosenfeld and Kak (1982), Gonzalez and Wintz (1987), Jain (1989), and Hall (1979). In this section we limit our discussion to the spatial domain. We begin by restating the definition for convolution. Then we prove that the convolution operator is commutative, associative, distributer over sums, and is homogeneous. We also prove that the reflection of a correlation is the convolution of the reflection.

6.4.1 Convolution and Correlation

The *convolution* of an image f with kernel w is defined by

$$(f * u)(r, c) = \sum_{\substack{(r', c') \in W \\ (r-r', c-c') \in F}} f(r - r', c - c') w(r', c')$$

Figure 6.21 illustrates a convolution in one dimension. Convolution has a number of mathematical properties, among which are:

1. $w * v = v * w$,
2. $(f * w) * v = f * (w * v)$,
3. $(f + g) * w = f * w + g * w$,
4. $(\alpha f) * w = \alpha(f * w)$ for any constant α,
5. $(w * v)\check{} = \check{w} * \check{v}$, where $\check{f}$ designates the reflection of f, $\check{f}(r, c) = f(-r, -c)$.

We now proceed to establish each of these properties.

x	-1	0	1
$k(x)$	1	2	3

x	4	5	6	7	8
$f(x)$	31	55	59	43	7

y	1	0	-1
$k(y)$	3	2	1
$f(3-y)$	—	—	31
$f(3-y)k(y)$	—	—	31
$(f*k)(3) = \sum\limits_{y=-1}^{1} f(3-y)k(y) = 31$			

y	1	0	-1
$k(y)$	3	2	1
$f(4-y)$	—	31	55
$f(4-y)k(y)$	—	62	55
$(f*k)(4) = \sum\limits_{y=-1}^{1} f(4-y)k(y) = 117$			

y	1	0	-1
$k(y)$	3	2	1
$f(5-y)$	31	55	59
$f(5-y)k(y)$	93	110	59
$(f*k)(5) = \sum\limits_{y=-1}^{1} f(5-y)k(y) = 262$			

y	1	0	-1
$k(y)$	3	2	1
$f(6-y)$	55	59	43
$f(6-y)k(y)$	165	118	43
$(f*k)(6) = \sum\limits_{y=-1}^{1} f(6-y)k(y) = 326$			

Figure 6.21 Example of how a one-dimensional convolution is peformed. The kernel k is defined as domain $\{-1,0,1\}$, and the function f to be convolved is defined as domain $\{4,5,6,7,8\}$. The convolution $f*k$ is defined on domain $\{3,4,5,6,7,8,9\}$. Notice that as f slips through the window of length 3, it meets k reflected to form the sum of products.

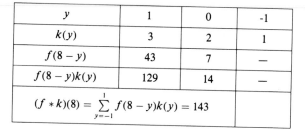

y	1	0	-1
$k(y)$	3	2	1
$f(7-y)$	59	43	7
$f(7-y)k(y)$	177	86	7
$(f*k)(7) = \sum_{y=-1}^{1} f(7-y)k(y) = 270$			

y	1	0	-1
$k(y)$	3	2	1
$f(8-y)$	43	7	—
$f(8-y)k(y)$	129	14	—
$(f*k)(8) = \sum_{y=-1}^{1} f(8-y)k(y) = 143$			

y	1	0	-1
$k(y)$	3	2	1
$f(9-y)$	7	—	—
$f(9-y)k(y)$	21	—	—
$(f*k)(9) = \sum_{y=-1}^{1} f(9-y)k(y) = 21$			

Figure 6.21. *Continued.*

Proposition 6.1: Let domain $(w) = W$ and domain $(v) = V$. Then

$$(w*v)(r,c) = (v*w)(r,c), \quad (r,c) \in W \oplus V$$

where $W \oplus V = \{(a,b)|$ for some $(c,d) \in W$ and $(e,f) \in V$, $a = c+e$, $b = d+f\}$.

Proof:

Let $(r,c) \in W \oplus V$. Then

$$(w*v)(r,c) = \sum_{\substack{(a,b) \in V \\ (r-a,c-b) \in W}} w(r-a,c-b)v(a,b)$$

Make a change of variables; let $\alpha = r-a, \beta = c-b$. Then

$$(w*v)(r,c) = \sum_{\substack{(r-\alpha,c-\beta) \in V \\ (\alpha,\beta) \in W}} w(\alpha,\beta)v(r-\alpha,c-\beta)$$

$$= \sum_{\substack{(\alpha,\beta) \in W \\ (r-\alpha,c-\beta) \in V}} v(r-\alpha,c-\beta)w(\alpha,\beta) = (v*w)(r,c)$$

Proposition 6.2: Let domain $(f) = F$, domain $(w) = W$, and domain $(v) = V$. Then
$$[(f * w) * v](r,c) = [f * (w * v)](r,c), \quad (r,c) \in F \oplus W \oplus V$$

Proof:

Let $(r,c) \in F \oplus W \oplus V$. By definition,

$$[(f * w) * v](r,c) = \sum_{(a,b) \in V} (f * w)(r-a, c-b)v(a,b)$$

$$= \sum_{(a,b) \in V} v(a,b) \sum_{\substack{(i,j) \in W \\ (r-a-i, c-b-j) \in F}} f(r-a-i, c-b-j)w(i,j)$$

Making a change of variables in the second summation, let $\alpha = a + i$ and $\beta = b + j$. Then

$$[(f * w) * v](r,c) = \sum_{(a,b) \in V} v(a,b)$$

$$\times \sum_{\substack{(\alpha - a, \beta - b) \in W \\ (r - \alpha, c - \beta) \in F}} w(\alpha - a, \beta - b)f(r - \alpha, c - \beta)$$

But $(a,b) \in V$ and $(\alpha - a, \beta - b) \in W$ imply $(\alpha, \beta) \in W \oplus V$. And $(\alpha, \beta) \in W \oplus V$ implies that for some $(a,b) \in V, (\alpha - a, \beta - b) \in W$. Hence the summations may be rearranged.

$$[(f * w) * v](r,c) = \sum_{\substack{(\alpha, \beta) \in W \oplus V \\ (r - \alpha, c - \beta) \in F}} f(r - \alpha, c - \beta)$$

$$\times \sum_{\substack{(a,b) \in V \\ (\alpha - a, \beta - b) \in W}} w(\alpha - a, \beta - b)v(a,b)$$

$$= \sum_{\substack{(\alpha, \beta) \in W \oplus V \\ (r - \alpha, c - \beta) \in F}} f(r - \alpha, c - \beta)(w * v)(\alpha, \beta)$$

$$= [f * (w * v)](r,c)$$

Proposition 6.3: Suppose $F = $ domain $(f) = $ domain $(g) = G$. Then

1. $[(f + g) * w](r,c) = (f * w)(r,c) + (g * w)(r,c)$,
2. $[(\alpha f) * w](r,c) = \alpha(f * w)(r,c)$ for any constant α.

Proof:

1. $\left[(f+g)*w\right](r,c) = \displaystyle\sum_{\substack{(a,b)\in W \\ (r-a,c-b)\in F}} (f+g)(r-a,c-b)w(a,b)$

    $\qquad\qquad = \displaystyle\sum_{\substack{(a,b)\in W \\ (r-a,c-b)\in F}} \left[f(r-a,c-b)+g(r-a,c-b)\right]w(a,b)$

    $\qquad\qquad = \displaystyle\sum_{\substack{(a,b)\in W \\ (r-a,c-b)\in F}} f(r-a,c-b)w(a,b)$

    $\qquad\qquad\quad + \displaystyle\sum_{\substack{(a,b)\in W \\ (r-a,c-b)\in G}} g(r-a,c-b)w(a,b)$

    $\qquad\qquad = (f*w)(r,c)+(g*w)(r,c)$

2. $\left[(\alpha f)*w\right](r,c) = \displaystyle\sum_{\substack{(a,b)\in W \\ (r-a,c-b)\in F}} (\alpha f)(r-a,c-b)w(a,b)$

    $\qquad\qquad = \displaystyle\sum_{\substack{(a,b)\in W \\ (r-a,c-b)\in F}} \alpha\, f(r-a,c-b)w(a,b)$

    $\qquad\qquad = \alpha \displaystyle\sum_{\substack{(a,b)\in W \\ (r-a,c-b)\in F}} f(r-a,c-b)w(a,b) = \alpha(f*w)(r,c)$

The last property $(w*v)\check{} = \check{w}*\check{v}$ can be also demonstrated by direct calculation.

Proposition 6.4: $(w*v)\check{} = \check{w}*\check{v}$.

Proof:

By definition,

$$(w*v)\check{}\,(r,c) = (w*v)(-r,-c)$$

$$\qquad = \sum_{\substack{(a,b)\in V \\ (-r-a,-c-b)\in W}} w(-r-a,-c-b)v(a,b)$$

Letting the reflection of a set A be denoted by $\check{A}$, we obtain $\check{A} = \{a\,|-a \in A\}$. Then we have

$$(w*v)\check{}(r,c) = \sum_{\substack{(-a,-b)\in\check{V} \\ (-r-a,-c-b)\in W}} w(-r-a,-c-b)v(a,b)$$

Making a change of variables, we let $a' = -a$ and $b' = -b$. Then

$$(w * v)(r, c) = \sum_{\substack{(a',b') \in \breve{V} \\ (-r+a', -c+b') \in W}} w(-r+a', -c+b')v(-a', -b')$$

$$= \sum_{\substack{(a',b') \in \breve{V} \\ (r-a', c-b') \; W}} \breve{w}(r-a', c-b')\breve{v}(a', b')$$

$$= (\breve{w} * \breve{v})(r, c)$$

The *cross-correlation* of f with w is defined by

$$(f \otimes w)(r, c) = \sum_{\substack{(a,b) \in W \\ (r+a, c+b) \in F}} f(r+a, c+b)w(a, b)$$

There is a direct relationship between convolution and cross-correlation:

$$f \otimes w = f * \breve{w}$$

The demonstration is direct. By definition,

$$(f \otimes w)(r, c) = \sum_{\substack{(a,b) \in W \\ (r+a, c+b) \in F}} f(r+a, c+b)w(a, b)$$

Making a change of variables, we let $a' = -a$ and $b' = -b$. Then

$$(f \otimes w)(r, c) = \sum_{\substack{(-a', -b') \in W \\ (r-a', c-b') \in F}} f(r-a', c-b')w(-a', -b')$$

$$= \sum_{\substack{(-a', -b') \in W \\ (r-a', c-b') \in \breve{F}}} f(r-a', c-b')\breve{w}(a', b')$$

$$= (f * \breve{w})(r, c)$$

Using the associative property for correlation and the relation $f \otimes w = f * \breve{w}$ between convolution and cross-correlation, we can determine whether cross-correlation is associative. It is not. However, it has a close analog. Consider

$$(f \otimes w) \otimes v = (f \otimes w) * \breve{v}$$

$$= (f * \breve{w}) * \breve{v}$$

$$= f * (\breve{w} * \breve{v})$$

$$= f \otimes (\breve{w} * \breve{v})^{\smile}$$

$$= f \otimes (w * v)$$

$$= f \otimes (w \otimes \breve{v})$$

Finally, the commutivity of convolution implies that the cross-correlation of w with v is the reflection of the cross-correlation of v with w.

$$w \otimes v = w * \breve{v} = \breve{v} * w = (v * \breve{w})^{\smile} = (v \otimes w)^{\smile}$$

Consider an image f defined on a domain F whose center is the origin $(0,0)$. When f has the special form of a discrete impulse,

$$f(r,c) = \begin{cases} 0 & (r,c) \neq (0,0) \\ 1 & (r,c) = (0,0) \end{cases}$$

the convolution of f with w gives

$$(f * w)(r,c) = \sum_{\substack{(r',c') \in W \\ (r-r',c-c') \in F}} f(r - r', c - c')w(r',c')$$

$$= \sum_{\substack{(r-a,c-b) \in W \\ (a,b) \in F}} f(a,b)w(r - a, c - b)$$

$$= \begin{cases} w(r,c) & (r,c) \in W \\ 0 & (r,c) \notin W \end{cases}$$

The result is just the kernel of the convolution, which suggests naming w as the *impulse response function* or the *point spread function*.

6.4.2 Separability

When the weight matrix w of a linear shift-invariant operator has a product decomposition, considerable savings can be obtained in the computation of the resultant image by performing the computation in a separable way. If the domain of w is a $(2M + 1) \times (2N + 1)$ neighborhood, then a straightforward computation would require $(2M + 1) \times (2N + 1)$ multiplications and additions for each output value generated. When w has a product decomposition, it may be written as

$$w(r',c') = u(r')v(c')$$

as illustrated in Fig. 6.22. In this case we can structure the computation by computing first along the columns for each row of the image and then along the rows

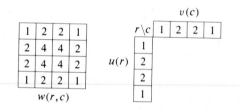

Figure 6.22 A separable mask w that can be decomposed into the two masks u and v as shown.

for each column of the image resulting from the first computation:

$$g(r,c) = \sum_{\substack{(r',c')\in W \\ (r+r',c+c')\in F}} f(r+r',c+c')w(r',c')$$

$$= \sum_{\substack{r'=-M \\ (r+r',c+c')\in F}}^{M} \sum_{c'=-N}^{N} f(r+r',c+c')u(r')v(c')$$

$$= \sum_{r'=-M}^{M} \left[\sum_{\substack{c'=-N \\ (r+r',c+c')\in F}}^{N} f(r+r',c+c')v(c') \right] u(r')$$

The bracketed term is a computation along the columns of row $r+r'$. Letting

$$h(r,c) = \sum_{\substack{c'=-N \\ (r,c+c')\in F}}^{N} f(r,c+c')v(c')$$

we clearly see that the computation of each $h(r,c)$ requires $2N+1$ multiplications and additions. Then $g(r,c)$ can be written as a computation along the rows:

$$g(r,c) = \sum_{r'=-M}^{M} h(r+r',c)u(r')$$

The computation of each $g(r,c)$ requires $2M+1$ multiplications and additions. Hence the total computation requires $(2M+1)+(2N+1)$ multiplications and additions.

When put in vector representation, weight matrices that are separable can be written as a Kronecker product of two vectors, one corresponding to the row function and one to the column function. More detailed discussion can be found in Chaper 7 on determining optimal weights from isotropic noise covariance matrices.

Next suppose that a kernel k has a representation as the sum of M separable kernels:

$$k(r,c) = \sum_{m=1}^{M} k_m(r,c)$$

Then the convolution of f with k has an implementation as the sum of M separable convolutions since convolution is linear:

$$(f * k)(r,c) = \left(f * \sum_{m=1}^{K} k_m \right)(r,c)$$

$$= \sum_{m=1}^{K} (f * k_m)(r,c)$$

Such a separable representation can be determined for any kernel defined on a rectangular neighborhood of support by the use of the singular-value decompositions

(Rao and Mitra, 1971), subroutines for which are available in most libraries of linear routines.

The *singular-value decomposition* of an $I \times J$ matrix K is given by

$$K = U\Lambda V$$

where U is an $I \times I$ orthonormal matrix, Λ is an $I \times J$ matrix all of whose nonzero entries are on the diagonal, and V is a $J \times J$ orthonormal matrix. The diagonal entries of Λ are nonnegative, and we assume that they are arranged in order of decreasing value.

Examining the case $I \leq J$ (the case $I \geq J$ can be examined in an exactly symmetric manner), we let the I columns of the matrix U be $u_1, \ldots, u_I$, each column u_i being an $I \times 1$ vector

$$U = (u_1, u_2, \ldots, u_I)$$

and we let the rows of the matrix V be $v_1, \ldots, v_J$, each row v_j being a $1 \times J$ vector

$$V = \begin{pmatrix} v_1 \\ v_2 \\ \vdots \\ v_J \end{pmatrix}$$

Then we can rewrite the matrix multiplication $U\Lambda V$ as

$$U\Lambda V = \sum_{i=1}^{I} \lambda_i u_i v_i$$

Letting the rth row of u_i be $u_i(r)$ and the cth column of v_j be $v_j(c)$, we can express any kernel k defined on a $I \times J$ neighborhood as

$$k(r,c) = \sum_{i=1}^{I} [\lambda_i u_i(r)] v_i(c)$$

In practice, in determining a separable implementation for a given kernel k, the diagonal entries of Λ often decrease rapidly, and only the first few highest entries need be retained. This provides for a relatively efficient implementation.

■ Exercises

6.1. Suppose $g(r,c) = \phi[f(r+r', c+c') : (r',c') \in W]$. Show that ϕ is a shift-invariant operator.

6.2. Suppose $g(r,c) = \phi[f(r-r', c-c') : (r',c') \in W]$. Show that ϕ is a shift-invariant operator.

6.3. Programming neighborhood operators to execute on images efficiently is important. Many neighborhood operators can be expressed in the iterative form, where

$t_1, \ldots, t_n$ represent two-dimensional spatial shifts. The output image is g_N and the input image is f.

$$g_1 = k_n(f_{t_1})$$
$$g_n = h[g_{n-1}, k_n(f_{t_n})], \qquad n = 2, \ldots, N$$

If $k_n(x) = \alpha_n x$ and $h(a,b) = a + b$, then g_N is the convolution of f with a kernel having a value of α_n at position t_n. If $k_n(x) = x + \alpha_n$ and $h(a,b) = \max\{a,b\}$, then g_N is the dilation of f with a structuring element having a height of α_n at position t_n. Assuming that $g_1, \ldots, g_N$ occupy the same memory buffer and that f and g_n can be held in memory all at once, determine the number of memory reads and writes, the number of times the outermost do loop is set up where the outermost loop runs through the N shifts $t_1, \ldots, t_N$, the number of times the middle do loop is set up (it runs through the input image rows), the number of times the innermost do loop is set up (it runs through the input image columns), and the number of innermost loop address calculations and operations to do computations of the form $h(a, k(b))$.

6.4. An alternative way to consider a neighborhood operator is to fix an output pixel position (r,c) and determine the value to be calculated at that position as a function of the values in the neighborhood of that pixel position on the input image. In this alternative, the outermost loop runs through the number of rows on the output image, the middle loop runs through the number of columns on the output image, and the innermost loop runs through the N different spatial shifts $t_1, \ldots, t_N$. Determine the number of memory reads and writes, the number of times each loop has to be set up, and the number of times address calculations and operations must be done in the innermost loop.

6.5. Program a neighborhood operator to do convolution or gray scale dilation using the strategy described in Exercise 6.3.

6.6. Design and carry out an experiment on a computer or workstation that uses your neighborhood operator implementation and that measures the CPU time by varying the number of rows and columns of the image being processed and the number of spatial shifts associated with the structuring element. Then do a linear regression analysis to determine the CPU time as a function of the variables identified in Exercise 6.3.

6.7. Program a neighborhood operator to do convolution or gray scale dilation using the strategy described in Exercise 6.4.

6.8. Repeat Exercise 6.6 using the neighborhood operator programmed in Exercise 6.7.

■ Bibliography

Arcelli, C., and S. Levialdi, "Parallel Shrinking by Three Dimensions," *Computer Graphics and Image Processing,* Vol. 1, 1972, pp. 21–30.

Arcelli, C., and G. Sanniti di Baja, "On the Sequential Approach to Medial Line Transformation," *IEEE Transactions on Systems, Man, and Cybernetics,* Vol. SMC-8, 1978, pp. 139–144.

Barrow, H. G., et al., "Parametric Correspondence and Chamfer Matching: Two New Techniques for Image Matching," *Proceedings of the Fifth International Conference on Artificial Intelligence,* Cambridge, MA, 1977, pp. 659–663.

Beckers, A. L. D., and A. W. M. Smeulders, "A Comment on 'A Note on Distance Transformations in Digital Images,'" *Computer Vision, Graphics, and Image Processing,* Vol. 47, 1989, pp. 89–91.

Borgefors, G., "Distance Transformations in Arbitrary Dimensions," *Computer Vision, Graphics, and Image Processing,* Vol. 27, 1984, pp. 321–345.

——, "Distance Transformations in Digital Images," *Computer Vision, Graphics, and Image Processing,* Vol. 34, 1986, pp. 344–371.

Chen, L.-H., and W.-H. Tsai, "Moment-Preserving Sharpening—A New Approach to Digital Picture Deblurring," *Computer Vision, Graphics, and Image Processing,* Vol. 41, 1987, pp. 1–13.

Danielsson, P.-E., "Euclidean Distance Mapping," *Computer Graphics and Image Processing,* Vol. 14, 1980, pp. 227–248.

Deutsch, E., "Comments on a Line Thinning Scheme," *Computer Journal,* Vol. 12, 1969, p. 412.

——, "Thinning Algorithms on Rectangular, Hexagonal, and Triangular Arrays," *Communications of the ACM,* Vol. 15, 1972, pp. 827–837.

Fraser, J., "Further Comments on a Line Thinning Scheme," *Computer Journal,* Vol. 13, 1970, pp. 221–222.

Gonzalez, R. C., and P. Wintz, *Digital Image Processing,* 2d ed., Addison-Wesley, Reading, MA, 1987.

Gray, S. B., "Local Properties of Binary Images in Two Dimensions," *IEEE Transactions on Computers,* Vol. C-20, 1971, pp. 551–561.

Hall, E., *Computer Image Processing and Recognition,* Academic Press, New York, 1979.

Haralick, R. M., "Some Neighborhood Operators," in *Real Time Parallel Computing Image Analysis,* K. Onoe, K. Preston, and A. Rosenfeld (eds), Plenum Press, New York, 1981, pp. 11–35.

Haralick, R. M., N. Griswold, and N. Kattiyakulwanich, "A Fast Two-Dimensional Karhunen-Loeve Transform," *SPIE Proceedings of the Conference on Efficient Transmission of Pictorial Information,* Palos Verdes, CA, Vol. SPIE-66, 1975, pp. 144–159.

Hilditch, C., "Linear Skeletons from Square Cupboards," in *Machine Intelligence,* Meltzer and Michie (eds.), Edinburgh University Press, Edinburgh, 1969, pp. 403–420.

Jain, A. K., *Fundamentals of Digital Image Processing,* Prentice-Hall, Englewood Cliffs, NJ, 1989.

Levialdi, S., "On Shrinking of Binary Picture Patterns," *Communications of the ACM,* Vol. 15, 1972, pp. 7–10.

Lobregt, S., P. W. Verbeck, and F. C. A. Goen, "Three-Dimensional Skeletonizations: Principle and Algorithm," *IEEE Transactions on Pattern Analysis and Machine Intelligence,* Vol. PAMI-2, 1980, pp. 75–77.

Montanari, U., "A Method for Obtaining Skeletons Using a Quasi-Euclidean Distance," *Journal of the ACM,* Vol. 15, 1968, pp. 600–624.

Newman, T. G., and H. Dirilten, "A Nonlinear Transformation for Digital Picture Processing," *IEEE Transactions on Computers,* Vol. C-22, 1973, pp. 869–873.

Nitzian, D., and G. J. Agin, "Fast Methods for Finding Object Outlines," *Computer Graphics and Image Processing,* Vol. 9, 1979, pp. 22–39.

Pratt, W. K., *Digital Image Processing,* Wiley, New York, 1978.

Rao, C. R., and S. K. Mitra, *Generalized Inverse of Matrices and Its Applications,* Wiley, New York, 1971.

Ritter, G. X., and J. N. Wilson, "Image Algebra in a Nutshell," *Proceedings of the First International Conference on Computer Vision,* London, 1987, pp. 1–5.

Ritter, G. X., M. A. Shrader-Frechette, and J. N. Wilson, "Image Algebra: A Rigorous and Translucent Way of Expressing All Image Processing Operations," *Proceedings of the Southeastern Technical Symposium on Optics, Electro-Optics, and Sensors,* Orlando, FL, 1987, pp. 1–6.

Rosenfeld, A., "Connectivity by Digital Pictures," *Journal of the ACM,* Vol. 17, 1970, pp. 146–160.

————, "A Characterization of Parallel Thinning Algorithms," *Information and Control,* Vol. 29, 1975, pp. 286–291.

Rosenfeld, A., and L. Davis, "A Note on Thinning," *IEEE Transactions on Systems, Man, and Cybernetics,* Vol. SMC-6, 1976, pp. 226–228.

Rosenfeld, A., and A. Kak, *Digital Picture Processing,* 2d ed., Vols. 1 and 2, Computer Science and Applied Mathematics, Academic Press, Orlando, FL, 1982.

Rosenfeld, A., and J. Pfaltz, "Sequential Operation in Digital Picture Processing," *Journal of the ACM,* Vol. 12, 1966, pp. 471–494.

————, "Distance Function on Digital Pictures," *Pattern Recognition,* Vol. 1, 1968, pp. 33–61.

Rutovitz, D., "Pattern Recognition," *Journal of the Royal Statistics Society,* Vol. 129A, 1966, pp. 504–530.

Serra, J., *Image Analysis and Mathematical Morphology,* Academic Press, New York, 1982.

Stefanelli, R., and A. Rosenfeld, "Some Parallel Thinning Algorithms for Digital Pictures," *Journal of the ACM,* Vol. 18, 1971, pp. 255–264.

Tamura, H., "A Comparison of Line Thinning Algorithms from Digital Geometry Viewpoint," *Proceedings of the Fourth International Japanese Conference on Computers and Pattern Recognition,* Tokyo, 1978.

Verwer, B. J. H., "Improved Metrics in Image Processing Applied to the Hilditch Skeleton," *Proceedings of the Ninth International Conference on Pattern Recognition,* Rome, 1988, pp. 137–142.

Vossepoel, A., "A Note on Distance Transformations in Digital Images," *Computer Vision, Graphics, and Image Processing,* Vol. 43, 1988, pp. 88–97.

Wilson, J. N., and G. X. Ritter, "Functional Specification of Neighborhoods in an Image Processing Language," *Proceedings of the SPIE International Conference on Image Processing,* The Hague, 1987, pp. 1–6.

Yokoi, S., J. Toriwaki, and T. Fukumura, "An Analysis of Topological Properties of Digitized Binary Pictures Using Local Features," *Computer Graphics and Image Processing,* Vol. 4, 1975, pp. 63–73.

7 CONDITIONING AND LABELING

7.1 Introduction

Conditioning and labeling are among the most common uses of neighborhood operators. Conditioning is based on a model that suggests the observed image is composed of an informative pattern modified by uninteresting variations that typically add to or multiply the informative pattern. Conditioning estimates the informative pattern on the basis of the observed image. Thus conditioning suppresses noise, which can be thought of as random, unpatterned variations affecting all measurements. Conditioning can also perform background normalization by suppressing uninteresting systematic or patterned variations. Conditioning is typically applied uniformly and is usually context independent.

Labeling is based on a model that suggests the informative pattern has structure as a spatial arrangement of events, each spatial event being a set of connected pixels. Labeling determines in what kinds of spatial events each pixel participates. For example, if the interesting spatial events of the informative pattern are only those of high-valued and low-valued pixels, then the thresholding operation can be considered a labeling operation. Other kinds of labeling operations include edge detection, corner finding, and identification of pixels that participate in various shape primitives.

This chapter is organized by application. We discuss neighborhood operators for the conditioning operations of noise cleaning and sharpening and for the labeling operations of edge and line detection.

7.2 Noise Cleaning

Noise cleaning is very often one of the first operators applied to an image in a computer vision task. Noise cleaning uses neighborhood spatial coherence and neighborhood pixel value homogeneity as its basis. Noise-cleaning techniques detect lack of coherence and either replace the incoherent pixel value by something more spatially coherent by using some or all of the pixels in a neighborhood containing the given pixel or they average or smooth the pixel value with others in an appropriate neighborhood. Mastin (1985) reviews a number of approaches. Typical masks for the 3×3 and 5×5 neighborhoods are shown in Figs. 6.2 and 6.3 of the preceding chapter.

The operator that computes the equally weighted average is called the *box filter operator*. The operator is important because of the ease with which it can be made to execute quickly. Not only is the operator separable, but by implementing it as a recursive operator, any sized neighborhood box filter can be implemented by using just a constant five operations per pixel, independent of neighborhood size. The operations are two additions, two subtractions, and one division (McDonnell, 1981).

The box filter operator with a $(2M + 1) \times (2N + 1)$ neighborhood-smoothing image f is defined by

$$k(r,c) = \frac{1}{(2M + 1)(2N + 1)} \sum_{r'=-M}^{M} \sum_{c'=-N}^{N} f(r + r', c + c') \qquad (7.1)$$

The recursive calculation then proceeds in the following way. Suppose row r has just been processed and we are beginning to process row $r + 1$. Then the partial row sum function $h(r + 1, c)$, defined by

$$h(r + 1, c) = \sum_{c'=-N}^{N} f(r + 1, c + c')$$

is computed for each c by the recursive relation

$$h(r + 1, c + 1) = h(r + 1, c) - f(r + 1, c - N) + f(r + 1, c + 1 + N)$$

This requires two operations per pixel. The partial row sums

$$h(r - M, c), \ h(r + 1 - M, c), \ldots, h(r + 1 + M, c)$$

for the previous $2M + 1$ rows as well as for the current row must be kept available. Then the partial column sum function $g(r + 1, c)$ defined by

$$g(r + 1, c) = \sum_{r'=-M}^{M} h(r + 1 + r', c)$$

for row $r + 1$ is recursively computed by

$$g(r + 1, c) = g(r, c) - h(r - M, c) + h(r + 1 + M, c)$$

Again this takes two more operations per pixel. Finally, the box filter output is calculated by

$$k(r,c) = \frac{1}{(2M + 1)(2N + 1)} g(r,c)$$

—a cost of one division per pixel.

A common linear smoother is the Gaussian filter. Here the weight matrix w is given by

$$w(r,c) = k \, e^{-\frac{1}{2}\left(\frac{r^2+c^2}{\sigma^2}\right)} \tag{7.2}$$

for all $(r,c) \in W$, where

$$k = \frac{1}{\sum\limits_{(r,c)\in W} e^{-\frac{1}{2}\left(\frac{r^2+c^2}{\sigma^2}\right)}}$$

The neighborhood W must be big enough to allow the pixels on the periphery of the neighborhood to be a distance of two or three σ from the center. The two-dimensional filter can be written as a product of two one-dimensional Gaussians, which makes it possible to implement the Gaussian filters efficiently and separably, first convolving a one-dimensional Gaussian in the row direction and then convolving a one-dimensional Gaussian in the column direction. That is, if

$$w(r,c) = \left(\sqrt{k}e^{-\frac{1}{2}\frac{r^2}{\sigma^2}}\right)\left(\sqrt{k}e^{-\frac{1}{2}\frac{c^2}{\sigma^2}}\right)$$
$$= w_1(r)w_2(c)$$

then $I * w = (I * w_1) * w_2$.

The application of linear noise-cleaning filters has the effect of defocusing the image. Edges become blurred. Narrow lines become attenuated. All other things being equal, the larger the neighborhood of the filter, the greater the defocusing action. The proper determination of neighborhood size and mask values depends on the correct balance between the better job of noise removal that large neighborhood operators can provide and the loss of detail that this entails. Determination of the correct balance depends on having a model that relates the observed neighborhood pixel values to the true underlying neighborhood pixel values and the effect the noise has on the latter. We discuss this relationship from a statistical point of view.

7.2.1 A Statistical Framework for Noise Removal

Suppose that we wish to apply an $M \times M$ shift-invariant linear neighborhood operator to an image in order to reduce noise. In this case the pixel values in each image neighborhood can be considered to constitute a vector of $N = M^2$ components. Suppose we adopt the idealization that if there were no noise, the pixel values in each image neighborhood would be the same constant. Obviously this idealization has stretched reality, because if, under the ideal situation, every pixel in each neighborhood takes the same value, then, since the neighborhoods overlap, every pixel value in the image would be the same. We can get around this trivialization, however, by being inconsistent and treating each neighborhood independently. Hence the constant value associated with any neighborhood is allowed to be different from the underlying constant value in any other neighborhood, including any neighborhood with which it overlaps.

Let us fix our attention on one neighborhood having N pixels. The pixels of the neighborhood are ordered in a left-to-right, top-to-bottom order. In this order this value of the pixels becomes the components of an N-dimensional vector x. Suppose that μ is the underlying unknown constant value that, if there were no noise, would be the value each pixel would take. Let $\mathbf{1}$ designate the N-dimensional vector all of whose components are 1s. The observed vector x can then be considered a random vector whose expected value is $\mu\mathbf{1} : E[x] = \mu\mathbf{1}$.

The neighborhood operator we wish to employ is a linear shift-invariant operator that uses all the pixels in the central $N = M \times M$ neighborhood to estimate the value of μ it will assign to the output pixel whose position is at the neighborhood's center. We seek, therefore, an N-dimensional vector c such that $\hat{\mu} = c'x$ is the estimated value of μ computed from the observed neighborhood pixel values in the components of the vector x. We desire the estimator $\hat{\mu}$ to be good in the sense both of being unbiased and of having minimum variance. For $\hat{\mu}$ to be unbiased, $E[\hat{\mu}] = \mu$. Now by the algebra of expectations

$$E[\hat{\mu}] = E[c'x] = c'E[x] = \mu c'\mathbf{1}$$

Since we desire $E[\hat{\mu}] = \mu$, the N-dimensional vector c must satisfy $c'\mathbf{1} = 1$.

Next we determine an expression for the variance of $\hat{\mu}$.

$$\begin{aligned} V[\hat{\mu}] &= E\left[(\hat{\mu} - E[\hat{\mu}])^2\right] \\ &= E[(c'x - \mu)^2] \\ &= E[(c'x - c'\mathbf{1}\mu)^2] \\ &= E[c'(x - \mathbf{1}\mu)(x - \mathbf{1}\mu)'c] \\ &= c'E[(x - \mathbf{1}\mu)(x - \mathbf{1}\mu)']c \end{aligned}$$

Recognizing $E[(x - \mathbf{1}\mu)(x - \mathbf{1}\mu)']$ as the covariance matrix Σ for x, we obtain

$$V[\hat{\mu}] = c'\Sigma c$$

To find the N-dimensional vector c that minimizes $V[\hat{\mu}] = c'\sum c$ subject to the constraint $c'\mathbf{1} = 1$, we can use the Lagrange multiplier technique. Let

$$f(c) = c'\Sigma c + \lambda(c'\mathbf{1} - 1)$$

Taking partial derivatives of f with respect to each component of c and using the fact that Σ is symmetric, we find that the vector of partial derivatives of f with respect to the components of c is given by

$$\frac{\partial f}{\partial c} = \begin{pmatrix} \frac{\partial f(c)}{\partial c_1} \\ \frac{\partial f(c)}{\partial c_2} \\ \vdots \\ \frac{\partial f(c)}{\partial c_N} \end{pmatrix} = 2\Sigma c + \lambda\mathbf{1}$$

We set this equal to 0 and solve for c in terms of the Lagrange multiplier λ. Hence

$$c = \left(\frac{-\lambda}{2}\right)\Sigma^{-1}\mathbf{1}$$

Substituting this value of c into the constraint $c'\mathbf{1} = 1$, we may solve for λ.

$$c'\mathbf{1} = \left(\frac{-\lambda}{2}\right)(\Sigma^{-1}\mathbf{1})'\,\mathbf{1} = \left(\frac{-\lambda}{2}\right)\mathbf{1}'(\Sigma^{-1})'\,\mathbf{1}$$

Since $\Sigma = \Sigma'$, we must also have $\Sigma^{-1} = (\Sigma')^{-1} = (\Sigma^{-1})'$. Hence $c'\mathbf{1} = \left(\frac{-\lambda}{2}\right)\mathbf{1}'\Sigma^{-1}\mathbf{1} = 1$, so that

$$\lambda = \frac{-2}{\mathbf{1}'\Sigma^{-1}\mathbf{1}}$$

Therefore

$$c = -\frac{1}{2}\frac{-2}{\mathbf{1}'\Sigma^{-1}\mathbf{1}}\Sigma^{-1}\mathbf{1}$$

$$= \frac{1}{(\mathbf{1}'\Sigma^{-1}\mathbf{1})}\Sigma^{-1}\mathbf{1}$$

(7.3)

The variance of the estimator $\hat{\mu}$ can now be easily calculated:

$$V(\hat{\mu}) = c'\Sigma c$$

$$= \frac{(\Sigma^{-1}\mathbf{1})'\,\Sigma(\Sigma^{-1}\mathbf{1})}{(\mathbf{1}'\Sigma^{-1}\mathbf{1})\,\mathbf{1}'\Sigma^{-1}\mathbf{1}}$$

(7.4)

$$= \frac{1}{\mathbf{1}'\Sigma^{-1}\mathbf{1}}$$

EXAMPLE 7.1

Consider the case when the neighborhood is 3×3 and the random noise is uncorrelated. To account for the reality that the greater the distance between a given pixel and the center pixel of the neighborhood, the greater its deviation from the expected value, we take the variance of the north, south, east, and west nearest neighbors of the center pixel to be α, $\alpha \geq 1$, times the variance of the center pixel, and the variance of the diagonal neighbors to be β, $\beta \geq \alpha$, times the variance of the center pixel. Figure 7.1(a) and (b) illustrates these conventions.

x_1	x_2	x_3
x_4	x_5	x_6
x_7	x_8	x_9

(a)

$\beta\sigma^2$	$a\sigma^2$	$\beta\sigma^2$
$\alpha\sigma^2$	σ^2	$\alpha\sigma^2$
$\beta\sigma^2$	$a\sigma^2$	$\beta\sigma^2$

(b)

β^{-1}	α^{-1}	β^{-1}
α^{-1}	1	α^{-1}
β^{-1}	α^{-1}	β^{-1}

(c)

Figure 7.1 (a) Correspondences between the components of the vector $x' = (x_1, x_2, \ldots, x_9)$ and their spatial position in a 3×3 neighborhood. (b) Variances associated with each spatial position; in a typical circumstance, $\alpha < \beta$. (c) Unnormalized minimum variance weight mark. The normalization constant divides each entry by $1 + 4\alpha^{-1} + 4\beta^{-1}$.

1	1	1
1	1	1
1	1	1

(a) $\frac{1}{9}$

1	1	1
1	2	1
1	1	1

(b) $\frac{1}{10}$

1	2	1
2	4	2
1	2	1

(c) $\frac{1}{16}$

Figure 7.2 Three common 3×3 masks for noise reduction. For (a) $\alpha = \beta = 1$; (b) $\alpha = \beta = 2$; and (c) $\alpha = 2, \beta = 4$.

The diagonal covariance matrix Σ is then given by

$$\Sigma = \begin{pmatrix} \beta &&&&&&&& \\ & \alpha &&&&&&& \\ && \beta &&&&&& \\ &&& \alpha &&&&& \\ &&&& 1 &&&& \\ &&&&& \alpha &&& \\ &&&&&& \beta && \\ &&&&&&& \alpha & \\ &&&&&&&& \beta \end{pmatrix} \sigma^2$$

Since the optimal c is determined by

$$c = \frac{\Sigma^{-1}\mathbf{1}}{\mathbf{1}'\Sigma^{-1}\mathbf{1}}$$

there results

$$c = \frac{1}{1 + 4\alpha^{-1} + 4\beta^{-1}} \begin{pmatrix} \beta^{-1} \\ \alpha^{-1} \\ \beta^{-1} \\ \alpha^{-1} \\ 1 \\ \alpha^{-1} \\ \beta^{-1} \\ \alpha^{-1} \\ \beta^{-1} \end{pmatrix}$$

This is shown in Fig. 7.1(c). Figure 7.2 shows particular 3×3 linear operators and their associated values of α and β.

EXAMPLE 7.2

We again consider a 3×3 neighborhood but assume that the noise is correlated in such a way that adjoint pixels have correlation ρ and with a distance n apart have correlations ρ^n, $n > 1$, and that all pixel values have the same variance.

In this case the covariance matrix has the following form.

$$\Sigma = \sigma^2 \begin{pmatrix}
1 & \rho & \rho^2 & \rho & \rho^2 & \rho^3 & \rho^2 & \rho^3 & \rho^4 \\
\rho & 1 & \rho & \rho^2 & \rho & \rho^2 & \rho^3 & \rho^2 & \rho^3 \\
\rho^2 & \rho & 1 & \rho^3 & \rho^2 & \rho & \rho^4 & \rho^3 & \rho^2 \\
\rho & \rho^2 & \rho^3 & 1 & \rho & \rho^2 & \rho & \rho^2 & \rho^3 \\
\rho^2 & \rho & \rho^2 & \rho & 1 & \rho & \rho^2 & \rho & \rho^2 \\
\rho^3 & \rho^2 & \rho & \rho^2 & \rho & 1 & \rho^3 & \rho^2 & \rho \\
\rho^2 & \rho^3 & \rho^4 & \rho & \rho^2 & \rho^3 & 1 & \rho & \rho^2 \\
\rho^3 & \rho^2 & \rho^3 & \rho^2 & \rho & \rho^2 & \rho & 1 & \rho \\
\rho^4 & \rho^3 & \rho^2 & \rho^3 & \rho^2 & \rho & \rho^2 & \rho & 1
\end{pmatrix}$$

The inverse covariance matrix is then given by

$$\Sigma^{-1} = \frac{1}{\sigma^2(1-\rho^2)^2}$$

$$\begin{pmatrix}
1 & -\rho & 0 & -\rho & \rho^2 & 0 & 0 & 0 & 0 \\
-\rho & 1+\rho^2 & -\rho & \rho^2 & -\rho(1+\rho^2) & \rho^2 & 0 & 0 & 0 \\
0 & -\rho & 1 & 0 & \rho^2 & -\rho & 0 & 0 & 0 \\
-\rho & \rho^2 & 0 & 1+\rho^2 & -\rho(1+\rho^2) & 0 & -\rho & \rho & 0 \\
\rho^2 & -\rho(1+\rho^2) & \rho^2 & -\rho(1+\rho^2) & (1+\rho^2)^2 & -\rho(1+\rho^2) & \rho^2 & -\rho(1+\rho^2) & \rho^2 \\
0 & \rho & -\rho & 0 & -\rho(1+\rho^2) & 1+\rho^2 & 0 & \rho^2 & -\rho \\
0 & 0 & 0 & -\rho & \rho^2 & 0 & 1 & -\rho & 0 \\
0 & 0 & 0 & \rho^2 & -\rho(1+\rho^2) & \rho^2 & -\rho & 1+\rho^2 & -\rho \\
0 & 0 & 0 & 0 & \rho^2 & -\rho & 0 & -\rho & 1
\end{pmatrix}$$

from which it follows that

$$c = \frac{1}{(3-\rho)^2} \begin{pmatrix}
1 \\
1-\rho \\
1 \\
1-\rho \\
(1-\rho)^2 \\
1-\rho \\
1 \\
1-\rho \\
1
\end{pmatrix}$$

Figure 7.3 shows this result as well as some particular 3×3 linear operators with their associated values of ρ.

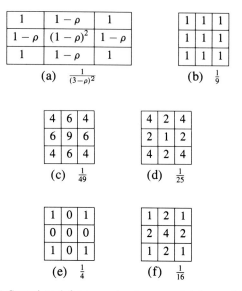

Figure 7.3 (a) General mask for an equal variance correlated case; (b) mask for $\rho = 0$; (c) mask for $\rho = -1/2$; (d) mask for $\rho = 1/2$; (e) mask for $\rho = 1$; and (f) mask for $\rho = -1$.

7.2.2 Determining Optimal Weight from Isotropic Covariance Matrices

Let μ denote the expected value of the neighborhood mean. Figure 7.4 illustrates the naming conventions for pixel values in an $M \times N$ neighborhood. Let

$$\sigma(i,j,m,n) = E[(x_{ij} - \mu)(x_{mn} - \mu)]$$

The second-order statistics of an image is said to be stationary when the covariances for a pair of pixels that stand in the same translational relationship are identical regardless of the absolute location of the pair on the image. That is, the second-order statistics are stationary when

$$\sigma(i+a,j+b,m+a,n+b) = \sigma(i,j,m,n)$$

for all a satisfying $1 \le i + a \le M$, $1 \le m + a \le M$, and for all b satisfying $1 \le j + b \le N$, $1 \le n + b \le N$. In this case the covariance can be written more simply as a function $\sigma(i - m, j - n)$.

(1,1)	(1,2)	(1,3)	(1,4)
(2,1)	(2,2)	(2,3)	(2,4)
(3,1)	(3,2)	(3,3)	(3,4)
(4,1)	(4,2)	(4,3)	(4,4)

Figure 7.4 Naming convention for pixels in an $M \times N$ neighborhood where M and $N = 4$.

	(1,1)	(1,2)	(1,3)	(1,4)	(2,1)	(2,2)	(2,3)	(2,4)	(3,1)	(3,2)	(3,3)	(3,4)	(4,1)	(4,2)	(4,3)	(4,4)
(1,1)	aa	ab	ac	ad	ae	af	ag	ah	ai	aj	ak	al	am	an	ao	ap
(1,2)		bb	bc	bd	be	bf	bg	bh	bi	bj	bk	bl	bm	bn	bo	bp
(1,3)			cc	cd	ce	cf	cg	ch	ci	cj	ck	cl	cm	cn	co	cp
(1,4)				dd	de	df	dg	dh	di	dj	dk	dl	dm	dn	do	dp
(2,1)					ee	ef	eg	eh	ei	ej	ek	el	em	en	eo	ep
(2,2)						ff	fg	fh	fi	fj	fk	fl	fm	fn	fo	fp
(2,3)							gg	gh	gi	gj	gk	gl	gm	gn	go	gp
(2,4)								hh	hi	hj	hk	hl	hm	hn	ho	hp
(3,1)									ii	ij	ik	il	im	in	io	ip
(3,2)										jj	jk	jl	jm	jn	jo	jp
(3,3)											kk	kl	km	kn	ko	kp
(3,4)												ll	lm	ln	lo	lp
(4,1)													mm	mn	mo	mp
(4,2)														nn	no	np
(4,3)															oo	op
(4,4)																pp

Figure 7.5 Covariance matrix associated with a 4 × 4 neighborhood for an image having nonstationary statistics. Each of the 136 distinct entries has a two-character label.

To illustrate this, consider Fig. 7.5, which shows the upper half of a covariance matrix associated with a 4 × 4 neighborhood. No two entries are identical. Table 7.1 lists all pairs of pixel locations that stand in the same translational relationship. When the image second-order statistics are stationary, then the covariance matrix takes the form shown in Fig. 7.6.

When the second-order statistics are stationary and isotropic, all pairs of pixels with the same distance between them have the same covariance. In this case the covariance can be written as a function

$$\sigma \left[(i - m)^2 + (j - n)^2 \right]$$

when the distance involved is the Euclidean distance. Table 7.2 lists all pairs of pixel locations in the 4 × 4 neighborhood standing in the same Euclidean distance relationship. The resulting isotropic covariance matrix is shown in Fig. 7.7.

Let

$$S_1 = \begin{pmatrix} y & r & k & d \\ r & y & r & k \\ k & r & y & r \\ d & k & r & y \end{pmatrix}$$

$$S_2 = \begin{pmatrix} r & q & j & c \\ q & r & q & j \\ j & q & r & q \\ c & j & q & r \end{pmatrix}$$

Table 7.1   Pairs of pixel locations situated in the same translational relationship. For example, all the pixel location pairs under column **c** are related by three rows down and one row across.

a	b	c	d	e	f	g
(3,3)	(3,2)	(3,1)	(3,0)	(3,-1)	(3,-2)	(3,-3)
(1,1)-(4,4)	(1,1)-(4,3)	(1,1)-(4,2)	(1,1)-(4,1)	(1,2)-(4,1)	(1,3)-(4,1)	(1,4)-(4,1)
	(1,2)-(4,4)	(1,2)-(4,3)	(1,2)-(4,2)	(1,3)-(4,2)	(1,4)-(4,2)	
		(1,3)-(4,4)	(1,3)-(4,3)	(1,4)-(4,3)		
			(1,4)-(4,4)			

h	i	j	k	l	m	n
(2,3)	(2,2)	(2,1)	(2,0)	(2,-1)	(2,-1)	(2,-3)
(1,1)-(3,4)	(1,1)-(3,3)	(1,1)-(3,2)	(1,1)-(3,1)	(1,2)-(3,1)	(1,3)-(3,1)	(1,4)-(4,1)
(2,1)-(4,4)	(1,2)-(3,4)	(1,2)-(3,3)	(1,2)-(3,2)	(1,3)-(3,2)	(1,4)-(3,2)	(2,4)-(4,1)
	(2,1)-(4,3)	(1,3)-(3,4)	(1,3)-(3,3)	(1,4)-(3,3)	(2,3)-(4,1)	
	(2,2)-(4,4)	(2,1)-(4,2)	(1,4)-(3,4)	(2,2)-(4,1)	(2,4)-(4,2)	
		(2,2)-(4,3)	(2,1)-(4,1)	(2,3)-(4,2)		
		(2,3)-(4,4)	(2,2)-(4,2)	(2,4)-(4,3)		
			(2,3)-(4,3)			
			(2,4)-(4,4)			

o	p	q	r	s	t	u
(1,3)	(1,2)	(1,1)	(1,0)	(1,-1)	(1,-2)	(1,-3)
(1,1)-(2,4)	(1,1)-(2,3)	(1,1)-(2,2)	(1,1)-(2,1)(3,1)-(4,1)	(1,2)-(2,1)	(1,3)-(2,1)	(1,4)-(2,1)
(2,1)-(3,4)	(1,2)-(2,4)	(1,2)-(2,3)	(1,2)-(2,2)(3,2)-(4,2)	(1,3)-(2,2)	(1,4)-(2,2)	(2,4)-(3,1)
(3,1)-(4,4)	(2,1)-(3,3)	(1,3)-(2,4)	(1,3)-(2,3)(3,3)-(4,3)	(1,4)-(2,3)	(2,3)-(3,1)	(3,4)-(4,1)
	(2,2)-(3,4)	(2,1)-(3,2)	(1,4)-(2,4)(3,4)-(4,4)	(2,2)-(3,1)	(2,4)-(3,2)	
	(3,1)-(4,3)	(2,2)-(3,3)	(2,1)-(3,1)	(2,3)-(3,2)	(2,3)-(4,1)	
	(3,2)-(4,4)	(2,3)-(3,4)	(2,2)-(3,2)	(2,4)-(3,3)	(3,4)-(4,2)	
		(3,1)-(4,2)	(2,3)-(3,3)	(3,2)-(4,1)		
		(3,2)-(4,3)	(2,4)-(3,4)	(3,3)-(4,2)		
		(3,3)-(4,4)		(3,4)-(4,3)		

v	w	x	y
(0,3)	(0,2)	(0,1)	(0,0)
(1,1)-(1,4)	(1,1)-(1,3)	(1,1)-(1,2)(3,3)-(3,4)	(1,1)-(1,1)(3,1)-(3,1)
(2,1)-(2,4)	(1,2)-(1,4)	(1,2)-(1,3)(4,1)-(4,2)	(1,2)-(1,2)(3,2)-(3,2)
(3,1)-(3,4)	(2,1)-(2,3)	(1,3)-(1,4)(4,2)-(4,3)	(1,3)-(1,3)(3,3)-(3,3)
(4,1)-(4,4)	(2,2)-(2,4)	(2,1)-(2,2)(4,3)-(4,4)	(1,4)-(1,4)(3,4)-(3,4)
	(3,1)-(3,3)	(2,2)-(2,3)	(2,1)-(2,1)(4,1)-(4,1)
	(3,2)-(3,4)	(2,3)-(2,4)	(2,2)-(2,2)(4,2)-(4,2)
	(4,1)-(4,3)	(3,1)-(3,2)	(2,3)-(2,3)(4,3)-(4,3)
	(4,2)-(4,4)	(3,2)-(3,3)	(2,4)-(2,4)(4,4)-(4,4)

$$S_3 = \begin{pmatrix} k & j & i & b \\ j & k & j & i \\ i & j & k & j \\ b & i & j & k \end{pmatrix}$$

$$S_4 = \begin{pmatrix} d & c & b & a \\ c & d & c & b \\ b & c & d & c \\ a & b & c & d \end{pmatrix}$$

Then the isotropic covariance matrix of Fig. 7.7 can be written as a partitioned

	(1,1)	(1,2)	(1,3)	(1,4)	(2,1)	(2,2)	(2,3)	(2,4)	(3,1)	(3,2)	(3,3)	(3,4)	(4,1)	(4,2)	(4,3)	(4,4)
(1,1)	y	x	w	v	r	q	p	o	k	j	i	h	d	c	b	a
(1,2)	x	y	x	w	s	r	q	p	l	k	j	i	e	d	c	b
(1,3)	w	x	y	x	t	s	r	q	m	l	k	j	f	e	d	c
(1,4)	v	w	x	y	u	t	s	r	n	m	l	k	g	f	e	d
(2,1)	r	s	t	u	y	x	w	v	r	q	p	o	k	j	i	h
(2,2)	q	r	s	t	x	y	x	w	s	r	q	p	l	k	j	i
(2,3)	p	q	r	s	w	x	y	x	t	s	r	q	m	l	k	j
(2,4)	o	p	q	r	v	w	x	y	u	t	s	r	n	m	l	k
(3,1)	k	l	m	n	r	s	t	u	y	x	w	v	r	q	p	o
(3,2)	j	k	l	m	q	r	s	t	x	y	x	w	s	r	q	p
(3,3)	i	j	k	l	p	q	r	s	w	x	y	x	t	s	r	q
(3,4)	h	i	j	k	o	p	q	r	v	w	x	y	u	t	s	r
(4,1)	d	e	f	g	k	l	m	n	r	s	t	u	y	x	w	v
(4,2)	c	d	e	f	j	k	l	m	q	r	s	t	x	y	x	w
(4,3)	b	c	d	e	i	j	k	l	p	q	r	s	w	x	y	x
(4,4)	a	b	c	d	h	i	j	k	o	p	q	r	v	w	x	y

Figure 7.6 Covariance matrix associated with a 4×4 neighborhood for an image whose statistics satisfy the stationary assumption.

matrix:

$$\Sigma = \begin{pmatrix} S_1 & S_2 & S_3 & S_4 \\ S_2 & S_1 & S_2 & S_3 \\ S_3 & S_2 & S_1 & S_2 \\ S_4 & S_3 & S_2 & S_1 \end{pmatrix}$$

When each submatrix S_1, S_2, S_3, and S_4 is some multiple of the same submatrix S, we can then write Σ as

$$\Sigma = \begin{pmatrix} v_1 S & v_2 S & v_3 S & v_4 S \\ v_2 S & v_1 S & v_2 S & v_3 S \\ v_3 S & v_2 S & v_1 S & v_2 S \\ v_4 S & v_3 S & v_2 S & v_1 S \end{pmatrix}$$

where v_1, v_2, v_3, and v_4 are scalars. The composite matrix Σ can then be expressed as a matrix Kronecker product.

$$\Sigma = V \times S$$

where

$$V = \begin{pmatrix} v_1 & v_2 & v_3 & v_4 \\ v_2 & v_1 & v_2 & v_3 \\ v_3 & v_2 & v_1 & v_2 \\ v_4 & v_3 & v_2 & v_1 \end{pmatrix}$$

Empirical experiments with image data indicate that actual covariance matrices do not often deviate too far from this form. The inverse of a matrix that can be represented as a Kronecker product is the Kronecker product of the inverses. Hence

$$\Sigma^{-1} = V^{-1} \times S^{-1}$$

Table 7.2	Pairs of pixel locations situated in the same distance relationship. For example, all the pixel location pairs under column **c** are related by distance $\sqrt{10}$.

a $d^2 = 18$	**b** $d^2 = 13$	**c** $d^2 = 10$	**d** $d^2 = 9$
(1,1)-(4,4)	(1,1)-(4,3)	(1,1)-(4,2)	(1,1)-(4,1)
(1,4)-(4,1)	(1,2)-(4,4)	(1,2)-(4,3)	(1,2)-(4,2)
	(1,3)-(4,1)	(1,3)-(4,4)	(1,3)-(4,3)
	(1,4)-(4,2)	(1,2)-(4,1)	(1,4)-(4,4)
	(1,4)-(3,1)	(1,3)-(4,2)	(1,1)-(1,4)
	(2,4)-(4,1)	(1,4)-(4,3)	(2,1)-(2,4)
	(1,1)-(3,4)	(1,4)-(2,1)	(3,1)-(3,4)
	(2,1)-(4,4)	(2,4)-(3,1)	(4,1)-(4,4)
		(3,4)-(4,1)	
		(1,1)-(2,4)	
		(2,1)-(3,4)	
		(3,1)-(4,4)	

i $d^2 = 8$	**j** $d^2 = 5$		**k** $d^2 = 4$	
(1,1)-(3,3)	(1,1)-(3,2)	(1,2)-(3,1)	(1,1)-(3,1)	(1,1)-(1,3)
(1,2)-(3,4)	(1,2)-(3,3)	(1,3)-(3,2)	(1,2)-(3,2)	(1,2)-(1,4)
(2,1)-(4,3)	(1,3)-(3,4)	(1,4)-(3,3)	(1,3)-(3,3)	(2,1)-(2,3)
(2,2)-(4,4)	(2,1)-(4,2)	(2,2)-(4,1)	(1,4)-(3,4)	(2,2)-(2,4)
(1,3)-(3,1)	(2,2)-(4,3)	(2,3)-(4,2)	(2,1)-(4,1)	(3,1)-(3,3)
(1,4)-(3,2)	(2,3)-(4,4)	(2,4)-(4,3)	(2,2)-(4,2)	(3,2)-(3,4)
(2,3)-(4,1)	(1,1)-(2,3)	(1,3)-(2,1)	(2,3)-(4,3)	(4,1)-(4,3)
(2,4)-(4,2)	(1,2)-(2,4)	(1,4)-(2,2)	(2,4)-(4,4)	(4,2)-(4,4)
	(2,1)-(3,3)	(2,3)-(3,1)		
	(2,2)-(3,4)	(2,4)-(3,2)		
	(3,1)-(4,3)	(3,3)-(4,1)		
	(3,2)-(4,4)	(3,4)-(4,2)		

q $d^2 = 2$		**r** $d^2 = 1$	
(1,1)-(2,2)	(1,2)-(2,1)	(1,1)-(2,1)	(1,1)-(1,2)
(1,2)-(2,3)	(1,3)-(2,2)	(1,2)-(2,2)	(1,2)-(1,3)
(1,3)-(2,4)	(1,4)-(2,3)	(1,3)-(2,3)	(1,3)-(1,4)
(2,1)-(3,2)	(2,2)-(3,1)	(1,4)-(2,4)	(2,1)-(2,2)
(2,2)-(3,3)	(2,3)-(3,2)	(2,1)-(3,1)	(2,2)-(2,3)
(2,3)-(3,4)	(2,4)-(3,3)	(2,2)-(3,2)	(2,3)-(2,4)
(3,1)-(4,2)	(3,2)-(4,1)	(2,3)-(3,3)	(3,1)-(3,2)
(3,2)-(4,3)	(3,3)-(4,2)	(2,4)-(3,4)	(3,2)-(3,3)
(3,3)-(4,4)	(3,4)-(4,3)	(3,1)-(4,1)	(3,3)-(3,4)
		(3,2)-(4,2)	(4,1)-(4,2)
		(3,3)-(4,3)	(4,2)-(4,3)
		(3,4)-(4,4)	(4,3)-(4,4)

y $d^2 = 0$	
(1,1)-(1,1)	(3,1)-(3,1)
(1,2)-(1,2)	(3,2)-(3,2)
(1,3)-(1,3)	(3,3)-(3,3)
(1,4)-(1,4)	(3,4)-(3,4)
(2,1)-(2,1)	(4,1)-(4,1)
(2,2)-(2,2)	(4,2)-(4,2)
(2,3)-(2,3)	(4,3)-(4,3)
(2,4)-(2,4)	(4,4)-(4,4)

	(1,1)	(1,2)	(1,3)	(1,4)	(2,1)	(2,2)	(2,3)	(2,4)	(3,1)	(3,2)	(3,3)	(3,4)	(4,1)	(4,2)	(4,3)	(4,4)
(1,1)	y	r	k	d	r	q	j	c	k	j	i	b	d	c	b	a
(1,2)	r	y	r	k	q	r	q	j	j	k	j	i	c	d	c	b
(1,3)	k	r	y	r	j	q	r	q	i	j	k	j	b	c	d	c
(1,4)	d	k	r	y	c	j	q	r	b	i	j	k	a	b	c	d
(2,1)	r	q	j	c	y	r	k	d	r	q	j	c	k	j	i	b
(2,2)	q	r	q	j	r	y	r	k	q	r	q	j	j	k	j	i
(2,3)	j	q	r	q	k	r	y	r	j	q	r	q	i	j	k	j
(2,4)	c	j	q	r	d	k	r	y	c	j	q	r	b	i	j	k
(3,1)	k	j	i	b	r	q	j	c	y	r	k	d	r	q	j	c
(3,2)	j	k	j	i	q	r	q	j	r	y	r	k	q	r	q	j
(3,3)	i	j	k	j	j	q	r	q	k	r	y	r	j	q	r	q
(3,4)	b	i	j	k	c	j	q	r	d	k	r	y	c	j	q	r
(4,1)	d	c	b	a	k	j	i	b	r	q	j	c	y	r	k	d
(4,2)	c	d	c	b	j	k	j	i	q	r	q	j	r	y	r	k
(4,3)	b	c	d	c	i	j	k	j	j	q	r	q	k	r	y	r
(4,4)	a	b	c	d	b	i	j	k	c	j	q	r	d	k	r	y

Figure 7.7 Isotropic covariance form.

The multiplication of a Kronecker product matrix with a Kronecker product vector is also a Kronecker product. The Kronecker product of a $J \times 1$ vector u with an $N \times 1$ vector v is a $JN \times 1$ vector. If

$$u = \begin{pmatrix} u_1 \\ u_2 \\ \vdots \\ u_J \end{pmatrix}$$

then the Kronecker product $u \times v$ is the $JN \times 1$ vector defined by

$$u \times v = \begin{pmatrix} u_1 v \\ u_2 v \\ \vdots \\ u_J v \end{pmatrix}$$

More precisely, if A is an $I \times J$ matrix, B is an $M \times N$ matrix, u is a $J \times 1$ vector, and v is an $N \times 1$ vector, then

$$(A \times B)(u \times v) = (Au) \times (Bv)$$

This makes the matrix Σ^{-1} easy to calculate:

$$\Sigma^{-1}\mathbf{1} = (V^{-1} \times S^{-1})(\mathbf{1} \times \mathbf{1})$$
$$= (V^{-1}\mathbf{1}) \times (S^{-1}\mathbf{1})$$

Hence the desired weight vector

$$w = \frac{\Sigma^{-1}\mathbf{1}}{\mathbf{1}'\Sigma'\mathbf{1}}$$

has a Kroneker product form, which means that it can be written as a product of a row function times a column function, thereby permitting fast implementation as a separable computation.

Afrait (1954), Andrews and Kane (1970), Andrews and Caspari (1971), and Haralick, Griswold, and Kattiyakulwanich (1975) give more details about the algebra associated with the separable implementation.

7.2.3   Outlier or Peak Noise

In outlier or peak noise, the value of a pixel is simply replaced by a random noise value typically having little to do with the underlying pixel's value. This can happen when there is a transmission error, when there is a bad spot on a vidicon or CCD array, when external noise affects the analog-to-digital-conversion process, or when something small and irrelevant occludes the object of interest. A neighborhood operator can be employed to detect and reduce such noise. The size of the neighborhood must be larger than the size of the noise structure and smaller than the size of the details to be preserved. The basis of the operator is to compare an estimate of the representative neighborhood value with the observed value of the neighborhood's center pixel. The center pixel value is an outlier if this difference is too large.

Let $x_1, \ldots, x_N$ denote all the pixel values in the neighborhood with the exception of the center pixel value. Such a neighborhood is called the *center-deleted neighborhood*. Let y denote the center pixel value. Let $\hat{\mu}$ be the estimate of the representative value of the center-deleted neighborhood. We take $\hat{\mu}$ to be the value that minimizes the sum of the squared differences between $\hat{\mu}$ and $x_1, \ldots, x_N$. That is, $\hat{\mu}$ minimizes $\sum_{n=1}^{N}(x_n - \hat{\mu})^2$. The minimizing $\hat{\mu}$ is quickly found to be the mean of the center-deleted neighborhood: $\hat{\mu} = \frac{1}{N}\sum_{n=1}^{N} x_n$. If y is reasonably close to $\hat{\mu}$, we can infer that y is not an outlier value.

The output value $z_{\text{outlier removal}}$ of the neighborhood operator is defined by

$$z_{\text{outlier removal}} = \begin{cases} y & \text{if } |y - \hat{\mu}| < \theta \\ \hat{\mu} & \text{otherwise} \end{cases} \tag{7.5}$$

Using $|y - \hat{\mu}|$ as the test statistic poses some problems. If θ is too small, the edges will be blurred. If θ is too large, the noise cleaning will not be good.

If y is statistically significantly different from $\hat{\mu}$, then we can infer that y is an outlier value. Statistically significant implies a comparison of $y - \hat{\mu}$ to the center-deleted neighborhood variance $\hat{\sigma}^2$, which is defined by $\hat{\sigma}^2 = \frac{1}{N-1}\sum_{n=1}^{N}(x_n - \hat{\mu})^2$ This suggests using the test statistic

$$t = \left| \frac{y - \hat{\mu}}{\hat{\sigma}} \right|$$

and rejecting the hypothesis of significant difference when t is small enough, small being smaller than threshold θ. The output value with a contrast-dependent-threshold neighborhood operator can be determined by

$$z_{\text{constrast--dependent outlier removal}} = \begin{cases} y & \text{if } \left| \frac{y-\hat{\mu}}{\hat{\sigma}} \right| < \theta \\ \hat{\mu} & \text{otherwise} \end{cases} \qquad (7.6)$$

This operator replaces a pixel value with the neighborhood mean if the pixel's value is sufficiently far from the neighborhood mean.

Instead of making the replacement occur completely or not at all, we can define a smooth replacement. The output value z is a convex combination of the input pixel value y and the neighborhood mean, where the weights of the convex combination depend on $\left| \frac{y-\hat{\mu}}{\hat{\sigma}} \right|$:

$$z = \frac{\left| \frac{y-\hat{\mu}}{\hat{\sigma}} \right|}{\left| \frac{y-\hat{\mu}}{\hat{\sigma}} \right| + K} \hat{\mu} + \frac{K}{\left| \frac{y-\hat{\mu}}{\hat{\sigma}} \right| + K} y \qquad (7.7)$$

7.2.4 k-Nearest Neighbor

Davis and Rosenfeld (1978) suggest a k-nearest neighbor averaging technique for noise cleaning. All the pixel values in the neighborhood are compared with the central pixel value. The k-closest pixel values are determined. The k-nearest neighbor average is then the equally weighted average of the k-nearest neighbors. For 3×3 neighborhoods Davis and Rosenfeld found $k = 6$ to perform better than other values of k. They also found that iterating the operator for three or four iterations produced better results than just one application.

7.2.5 Gradient Inverse Weighted

Wang, Vagnucci, and Li (1981) suggest a gradient inverse weighted noise-cleaning technique that they empirically show reduces the sum-of-squares error within homogeneous regions while keeping the sums of squares between homogeneous regions relatively constant. The neighborhood operator is a linear operator where the weights are a function of the spatial configuration of the pixel values. This makes the operator a shift-invariant operator, but not a linear shift-invariant operator.

The idea behind the operator is simple and is not unrelated to the k-nearest neighbor technique. In estimating the underlying value for a pixel, the neighboring pixel values should contribute in accordance with how close they are to the observed value of the given pixel. In the k-nearest neighbor technique, those k-neighboring pixels having values that are closest to the observed given pixel value are used in an equally weighted average. Wan, Vagnucci, and Li's idea is to use all neighboring pixel values, weighted according to how close they are. At each pixel position the weights are inversely proportional to the absolute value of the difference between the given pixel's value and the neighboring pixel's value. That is,

$$w(r',c',r,c) = \begin{cases} \frac{1}{2} & (r'c') = (r,c) \\ \frac{k}{\max\{\frac{1}{2}, |f(r',c')-f(r,c)|\}} & \text{otherwise} \end{cases} \qquad (7.8)$$

where

$$k = \frac{1}{2} \sum_{r'=r-1}^{r+1} \sum_{\substack{c'=c-1 \\ (r',c')\neq(r,c)}}^{c+1} \frac{1}{\max\{\frac{1}{2}, |f(r',c') - f(r,c)|\}}$$

and the noise-cleaned output g is given by a convex combination of the pixel neighborhood values

$$g(r,c) = \sum_{(r',c')\in W(r,c)} w(r',c',r,c)f(r',c') \tag{7.9}$$

The gradient inverse weighted noise-cleaning operator may be iterated to provide improved performance.

7.2.6 Order Statistic Neighborhood Operators

The order statistic approach (Bovik, Huang, and Munson, 1983) takes linear combinations of the sorted values of all the neighborhood pixel values $x_1, \ldots, x_N$. Conceptually we can visualize the operator as sorting the pixel values from smallest to largest and taking a linear combination of these sorted values. We denote the sorted neighborhood values by $x_{(1)}, \ldots, x_{(N)}$. Hence the order statistic operator produces an output value z for the position of the center of the neighborhood that is defined by using

$$z = \sum_{n=1}^{N} w_n x_{(n)} \tag{7.10}$$

Order statistic filtering commutes with any linear monotonically increasing transformation. To see this, note that for any positive constant a and any constant b, if $y_n = ax_n + b$, then $y_{(n)} = ax_{(n)} + b$. Hence

$$\sum_{n=1}^{N} w_n y_{(n)} = \sum_{n=1}^{N} w_n [ax_{(n)} + b]$$

$$= a \sum_{n=1}^{N} w_n x_{(n)} + b \sum_{n=1}^{N} w_n$$

$$= a \left[\sum_{n=1}^{N} w_n x_{(n)} \right] + b$$

Median Operator

The most common order statistic operator used to do noise cleaning is the median. For $K \times K$ neighborhoods where K is odd, $N = K \times K$ will also be odd, and the median is given by

$$z_{median} = x_{(\frac{N+1}{2})} \tag{7.11}$$

This operator was introduced by Tukey (1971).

Gallagher and Wise (1981) showed that repeatedly applying a median filtering operation to a one-dimensional signal must produce a result that is unchanged by further median filtering operations. The fixed-point result of a median filter is called the *median root*. Median roots consist only of constant-valued neighborhoods and sloped edges.

Narendra (1981) discusses an implementation of a separable median filter. For an $N \times N$ separable median filter, the image is first filtered with an $N \times 1$ median filter and then a $1 \times N$ median filter. This implementation reduces the computational complexity of the median filter. Narendra demonstrates that although the output of the separable median filter is not identical to the full two-dimensional median filter, the performance is sufficiently close.

Nodes and Gallagher (1983) show that it is almost always the case that repeated applications of the separable two-dimensional median filter results in a two-dimensional median root.

Fitch, Coyle, and Gallagher (1985) suggest that the neighborhood size and shape of a median filter be chosen so that the underlying noise-free image will be a median root for this filtering operation with the given neighborhood size and shape.

The running median does a good job of estimating the true pixel values in situations where the underlying neighborhood trend is flat or monotonic and the noise distribution has fat tails, such as double-sided exponential or Laplacian noise. Thus it does well in situations where the neighborhood is homogeneous or when the central feature in the neighborhood is a step edge.

The running median is effective for removing impulsive noise. However, when the neighborhood contains fine detail such as thin lines, they are distorted or lost. Corners can be clipped. Also it sometimes produces regions of constant or nearly constant values that are perceived as patches, streaks, or amorphous blotches. This can give the image a mottled appearance. Such artifacts may suggest boundaries that really do not exist. Bovik (1987) gives an analysis of this effect.

Brownrigg (1984) defines a weighted-median filter. The weights are given by a weight matrix w defined on domain $W = \{(i,j) | -N \leq i \leq N, -N \leq j \leq N\}$ for an odd-sized $2N+1 \times 2N+1$ neighborhood. The sum L of the weights is required to be odd:

$$L = \sum_{i=-N}^{N} \sum_{j=-N}^{N} w(i,j)$$

Let $x(i,j), (i,j) \in W$ denote the value of the (i,j)th pixel in a neighborhood. The weighted median first forms a list $y_1, \ldots, y_L$ of values. For each $(i,j) \in W$, $x(i,j)$ is put into the list $w(i,j)$ times. The weighted median is then given by the median of the values in the list:

$$z_{\text{weighted median}} = y_{\left(\frac{L+1}{2}\right)} \tag{7.12}$$

Brownrigg analyzes the 3×3 neighborhood case to determine a weight matrix w that satisfies the following two requirements:

1. One-pixel-wide streaks, straight or bent, should be removed.

2. Rectangular blotches of constant value should be preserved.

He finds that the weights with the smallest sum that satisfy the requirements is the weight matrix whose center weight has value 3 and whose other weights have value 1. The operator of the weighted median is illustrated in Fig. 7.8.

The running-median operator can be put into a context-dependent threshold form (Scollar, Weidner, and Huang, 1984). Define the interquartile distance Q by

$$Q = x_{\left(\frac{3N+2}{4}\right)} - x_{\left(\frac{N+2}{4}\right)}$$

where truncation is used for those cases that are not evenly divisible. The output value z of the median with contrast-dependent threshold is given by

$$z = \begin{cases} y & \text{if } \left|\frac{y - z_{\text{median}}}{Q}\right| < \theta \\ z_{\text{median}} & \text{otherwise} \end{cases} \tag{7.13}$$

Arce and McLaughlin (1987), Nieminen and Neuvo (1988), and Nieminen, Heinonen, and Neuvo (1987) discuss other variations of the running-median operator.

Trimmed-Mean Operator

Another common order statistic operator that works well when the noise distribution has a fat tail is the trimmed-mean operator (Bedner and Watt, 1984). Here the first k and last k order statistics are not used, and an equal weighted average of the central $N - 2k$ order statistics is used. When $\alpha = kN$, the result is called the α-*trimmed mean*.

$$z_{\text{trimmed mean}} = \frac{1}{N - 2k} \sum_{n=1+k}^{N-k} x_{(n)} \tag{7.14}$$

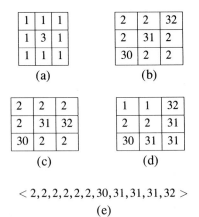

$$< 2, 2, 2, 2, 2, 2, 30, 31, 31, 31, 32 >$$
$$\text{(e)}$$

Figure 7.8 How the weighted-median operator works. (a) Weight matrix; (b) and (c) two configurations for which the one-pixel-wide, high-valued streak is to be eliminated; (d) configuration for which the block of 2s is to be preserved. Using the weight matrix (a), configuration (b), (c), and (d) produce the same list of sorted values (e) whose median value is 2.

Lee and Kassam (1985) indicate that when the noise has a double-exponential distribution, a value for α around .4 gives the minimum variance among all α-trimmed mean estimators. Peterson, Lee, and Kassam (1988) show that the trimmed-mean filter can perform better than the linear box filter as well as the median filter in white noise suppression, while at the same time having midrange edge-preserving characteristics comparable to those of the median.

Midrange

When the noise distribution has tails that are light and smooth, the midrange estimator can be more efficient than the mean (Rider, 1957; Arce and Fontana, 1988). It is defined by

$$z_{\text{midrange}} = \frac{1}{2}[x_{(1)} + x_{(N)}] \tag{7.15}$$

7.2.7 A Decision Theoretic Approach to Estimating Mean

Let $x_1, \ldots, x_N$ be observed noisy values from a neighborhood of pixels whose mean μ needs to be estimated by the neighborhood operator. Let $\hat{\mu}$ be the estimator for μ. Let $L(\hat{\mu}, \mu)$ be the loss incurred if $\hat{\mu}$ is the estimate of the mean when the true value for the mean is μ. The decision theoretic framework suggests defining $\hat{\mu}$ to be the estimator that minimizes the expected loss

$$\int_\mu L(\hat{\mu}, \mu) P(\mu \mid x_1, \ldots, x_N) d\mu$$

By definition of conditional probability,

$$P(\mu \mid x_1, \ldots, x_N) = \frac{P(x_1, \ldots, x_N, \mu)}{P(x_1, \ldots, x_N)}$$

Hence minimizing the expected loss is equivalent to minimizing

$$\int_\mu L(\hat{\mu}, \mu) P(x_1, \ldots, x_N \mid \mu) P(\mu) d\mu$$

As is often assumed, we assume the observations are independent so that

$$P(x_1, \ldots, x_N \mid \mu) = \prod_{n=1}^{N} P(x_n \mid \mu)$$

Typically the density $P(x_n \mid \mu)$ has a functional form that depends only on $(\mu - x_n)^2$. In this case we seek the estimator $\hat{\mu}$ that minimizes

$$\int_\mu L(\hat{\mu}, \mu) \prod_{n=1}^{N} P[(\mu - x_n)^2] P(\mu) d\mu$$

If we take the prior $P(\mu)$ to be uniform and the loss function to be the win-and-lose-all loss function—infinite gain when $\hat{\mu} = \mu$ (a negative infinite loss) and zero loss when $\hat{\mu} \neq \mu$—then the estimator $\hat{\mu}$ must maximize

$$\prod_{n=1}^{N} P\left[(\hat{\mu} - x_n)^2\right]$$

In this case $\hat{\mu}$ is the standard maximum-likelihood estimator. The $\hat{\mu}$ that maximizes

$$\log \prod_{n=1}^{N} P\left[(\hat{\mu} - x_n)^2\right]$$

is the same as that which maximizes

$$\sum_{n=1}^{N} \log P\left[(\hat{\mu} - x_n)^2\right]$$

Differentiating with respect to $\hat{\mu}$ gives the necessary condition

$$\sum_{n=1}^{N} \frac{P'\left[(\hat{\mu} - x_n)^2\right] 2(\hat{\mu} - x_n)}{P\left[(\hat{\mu} - x_n)^2\right]} = 0$$

which can be rewritten as

$$\hat{\mu} = \frac{\sum\limits_{n=1}^{N} x_n w_n}{\sum\limits_{n=1}^{N} w_n}$$

where

$$w_n = \frac{P'\left[(\hat{\mu} - x_n)^2\right]}{P\left[(\hat{\mu} - x_n)^2\right]}$$

In the Gaussian case

$$P(y) = \frac{e^{-\frac{1}{2}(y/\sigma^2)}}{\sqrt{2\pi}\sigma}$$

where $y = (\mu - x_n)^2$. Hence $P'(y)/P(y) = -\frac{1}{2\sigma^2}$, and $\hat{\mu}$ becomes the equally weighted neighborhood mean.

In the case of a mixture of a Gaussian with a uniform $U\left[-\frac{1}{\epsilon}, \frac{1}{\epsilon}\right]$,

$$P(y) = (1 - \epsilon) \frac{1}{\sqrt{2\pi}\sigma} e^{-\frac{y}{2\sigma^2}} + \epsilon\lambda$$

so that $\frac{P'(y)}{P(y)}$ is proportional to

$$\frac{(1 - \epsilon)e^{-\frac{y}{2\sigma^2}}}{(1 - \epsilon)e^{-\frac{y}{2\sigma^2}} + \epsilon\lambda\sqrt{2\pi}\sigma}$$

For small y this is just smaller than 1, and for large y it approaches 0. Values far from the estimate are weighted less and less. A two-term Taylor series expansion of

$\frac{P'(y)}{P(y)}$ around zero gives an approximation proportional to

$$1 - \frac{1}{2}\frac{\epsilon\lambda\sqrt{2\pi}\sigma}{1 - \epsilon + \lambda\epsilon\sqrt{2\pi}\sigma}y$$

where

$$y = \left(\frac{\mu - x}{\sigma}\right)^2$$

If we take the range of the contaminating uniform to be 6σ and the contaminating fraction ϵ to be $\frac{3}{3+4\sqrt{2\pi}}$, just short of .25, then $\frac{P'(y)}{P(y)}$ becomes related to Tukey's biweight, which is used in robust estimation

$$\begin{cases} \left[1 - \left(\frac{\hat{\mu}-x}{cS}\right)^2\right]^2 & \text{for } \left(\frac{\hat{\mu}-x}{cS}\right)^2 < 1 \\ 0 & \text{otherwise} \end{cases}$$

Tukey usually takes S to be the sample median absolute deviation and the constant c to be 6 or 9. Thus x_i that are more than four standard deviations away from the estimate $\hat{\mu}$ will get weight zero ($c = 9$).

There are other kinds of loss function than the win-and-lose-all kind. Another common one is the squared loss function $L(\hat{\mu}, \mu) = (\hat{\mu} - \mu)^2$. Assuming again a uniform prior, we seek to find a $\hat{\mu}$ that minimizes

$$\int_\mu (\hat{\mu} - \mu)^2 \prod_{n=1}^N P[(\mu - x_n)^2]\,d\mu$$

This corresponds to a minimum variance estimate. Carrying out the minimization yields

$$\hat{\mu} = \frac{\int \mu \prod_{n=1}^N P[(\mu - x_n)^2]\,d\mu}{\int \prod_{n=1}^N P[(\mu - x_n)^2]\,d\mu} \tag{7.16}$$

The product form makes this integration difficult to do analytically. A numerical approximation, however, is easily obtained. We use the neighborhood order statistics $x_{(1)}, x_{(2)}, \ldots, x_{(N)}$, where $x_{(1)} \le x_{(2)} \le \cdots \le x_{(N)}$, and assume that the integral is zero outside the interval (x_1, x_N).

Approximate the integral

$$\int_{x_{(n-1)}}^{x_{(n)}} \mu \prod_{m=1}^N P[(\mu - x_{(m)})^2]\,d\mu$$

by

$$\left(\frac{x_{(n)} + x_{(n-1)}}{2}\right)\left\{\prod_{m=1}^N P\left[\left(\frac{x_{(n)} + x_{(n-1)}}{2} - x_{(m)}\right)^2\right]\right\}(x_{(n)} - x_{(n-1)})$$

and the integral

$$\int_{x_{(n-1)}}^{x_{(n)}} \prod_{m=1}^N P[(\mu - x_{(m)})^2]\,d\mu$$

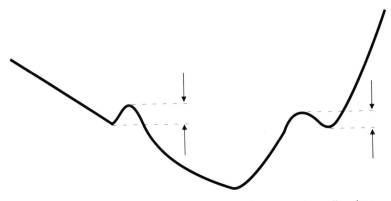

Figure 7.9 Definition for height of a relative maximum on a descending slope and height of a relative minimum on an ascending slope.

by

$$
w_n = \left\{ \prod_{m=1}^{N} P \left[\left(\frac{x_{(n)} + x_{(n-1)}}{2} - x_{(m)} \right)^2 \right] \right\} (x_{(n)} - x_{(n-1)})
$$

We then have

$$
\hat{\mu} = \frac{\displaystyle\sum_{n=2}^{N} \left(\frac{x_{(n)} + x_{(n-1)}}{2} \right) w_n}{\displaystyle\sum_{n=2}^{N} w_n} = \frac{\displaystyle\sum_{n=1}^{N} x_{(n)} \left(\frac{w_n + w_{(n+1)}}{2} \right)}{\displaystyle\sum_{n=1}^{N} w_n} \tag{7.17}
$$

where $w_1 = w_{(N+1)} = 0$.

Reflecting on the meaning of this equation, we see that as $x_{(n)}$ gets farther away from the center of the distribution, w_n will become smaller.

7.2.8 Hysteresis Smoothing

Hysteresis smoothing can remove minor fluctuations while preserving the structure of all major transients. Ehrich (1978) introduced a symmetric hysteresis noise-cleaning technique. A minor fluctuation is defined as a segment either having a relative maximum on a monotonically decreasing slope where the relative height of the maximum is smaller than h or having a relative minimum on a monotonically increasing slope where the relative depth of the minimum is smaller than h. Figure 7.9 illustrates these definitions.

The hysteresis algorithm is applied in a row-by-row fashion and then in a column-by-column fashion. It is most directly described in terms of a state machine. The machine has two states, UP and DOWN. At position $n + 1$, the output value $g(n + 1)$ is equal to the input value $f(n + 1)$, and the state remains the same so long as the state is UP and $f(n + 1) > f(n)$ or the state is DOWN and $f(n + 1) \leq f(n)$. If the state is UP and $f(n+1) \leq f(n)$, let k_0 be the smallest positive integer for which $f(n+k_0) < f(n+k_0+1)$ and $f(n+k_0) < f(n+k_0-1)$. This makes $n+k_0$ the location of the next relative minimum. If the state is DOWN and $f(n+1) > f(n)$, let j_0 be the smallest positive integer for which $f(n+j_0) > f(n+j_0+1)$ and $f(n+j_0) > f(n+j_0-1)$. This makes $n+j_0$ the location of the next relative maximum.

Now if the state is UP and if $f(n+1) \leq f(n)$ and $f(n)-f(n+k_0) < h$, indicating that the relative minimum is a minor fluctuation, then the output value remains the same: $g(n+1) = g(n)$, and the state remains UP. However, if $f(n+1) \leq f(n)$ and $f(n) - f(n+k_0) \geq h$, indicating that the relative minimum is significant, then the output value follows the input, $g(n+1) = f(n+1)$, and the state changes to DOWN. Finally, if the state is DOWN and if $f(n+1) > f(n)$ and $f(n+j_0) - f(n) < h$, indicating that the relative maximum is a minor fluctuation, then the output value remains the same: $g(n+1) = g(n)$, and the state remains DOWN. But, if $f(n+1) > f(n)$ and $f(n+j_0) - f(n) \geq h$, indicating that the relative maximum is significant, then the output value follows the input, $g(n+1) = f(n+1)$, and the state changes to UP. Tables 7.3 and 7.4 summarize the next state/output table for the state machine.

Ehrich suggests that the hysteresis smoothing be applied twice to the input image data: once in a left-to-right or forward order, and then in a right-to-left or reversed order. The output of the symmetric hysteresis smoother is the average of the two results.

7.2.9 Sigma Filter

The sigma filter (Lee, 1983b) is another way in which a pixel can be averaged with its neighbors that are close in value to it. Lee suggests looking to all the values in the neighborhood of the given pixel value y and averaging y only with those values that are within a two-sigma interval of y. If $x_1, \ldots, x_N$ are the neighboring values, then the estimate $\hat{y}$ is determined by

$$\hat{y} = \frac{1}{\#M} \sum_{n \in M} x_n \tag{7.18}$$

where $M = \{n \mid y - 2\sigma \leq x_n \leq y + 2\sigma\}$

When the number of neighboring pixels in the two-sigma ranges is too small, Lee recommends taking $\hat{y}$ as the average of all its eight immediate neighborhoods. For a 7×7 neighborhood, Lee suggests that too small is less than four.

Experiments done by Lee (1983b) indicate that the performance of the sigma filter is better than that of the gradient inverse weighted filter, the median, and the selected-neighborhood average filter.

7.2.10 Selected-Neighborhood Averaging

Selected-neighborhood averaging (Graham, 1962; Newman and Dirilten, 1973; Tomita and Tsuji, 1977; Nagao and Matsuyama, 1979; Haralick and Watson, 1981)

Table 7.3   Input to the state machine as a function of the input f and the previously computed output g.

Input	Condition
a	$f(n+1) > f(n),\ f(n+j_0) - f(n) \geq h$
b	$f(n+1) > f(n),\ f(n+j_0) - f(n) < h$
c	$f(n+1) \leq f(n),\ f(n) - f(n+k_0) < h$
d	$f(n+1) \leq f(n),\ f(n) - f(n+k_0) \geq h$

takes the point of view that the pixels that are averaged should be ones that form a tight spatial configuration as well as ones that are homogeneous and related to the given pixel. To understand selected-neighborhood averaging, we must make a change in point of view from the central neighborhood around a given pixel to a collection of all neighborhoods that contain a given pixel. For example, there are nine 3×3 neighborhoods that contain a given pixel. Neighborhoods in the collection, however, are not required to be square. Some may be square, some rectangular, and some diagonal. Nagao and Matsuyama use pentagonal and hexagonal neighborhoods. Graham uses a three-pixel vertical or horizontal neighborhood. Newman and Dirilten suggest a five-pixel strip neighborhood oriented orthogonally to the gradient direction.

Each neighborhood that contains the given pixel has a mean and variance. One of the neighborhoods that contains the given pixel will have the lowest variance. The noise-filtered value is computed as the mean value from the lowest variance neighborhood containing the given pixel.

Table 7.4   Specification of the next state/output for the state machine.

Current State	a	b	c	d
UP	UP $f(n+1)$	UP $f(n+1)$	UP $g(n)$	DOWN $f(n+1)$
DOWN	UP $f(n+1)$	DOWN $g(n)$	DOWN $f(n+1)$	DOWN $f(n+1)$

The model under which selected-neighborhood averaging appears to be a good noise-smoothing technique is one that assumes each pixel is a part of a homogeneous region, and in this region the pixel can be covered by one neighborhood that is entirely contained within the region. If this is the case, the neighborhood found to be the lowest-variance neighborhood is likely to be the neighborhood that is entirely contained in the region. Certainly it will not be a neighborhood that contains a step edge, for such a neighborhood would undoubtedly have a high variance. In this way the selected-neighborhood averaging operator will never average pixels across an edge boundary.

7.2.11 Minimum Mean Square Noise Smoothing

Lee (1980) introduced a minimum mean square noise-smoothing technique suitable for additive or multiplicative noise. Here the true image is regarded as constituting a set of random variables—one at each pixel. In our description we fix on a particular pixel and let Y denote its value. The mean of the random variable Y is denoted by μ_Y, and its variance is σ_Y^2. Both μ_Y and σ_Y^2 are considered known and to vary over the image. The random value that Y takes as it differs from the mean is not regarded as noise. It is simply regarded as the way in which an image pixel naturally varies from its mean.

The observed image is modeled as the true image perturbed by noise. We consider first the case of additive noise. Let ξ denote the noise random variable at the given pixel position. Its mean is assumed to be 0, and its variance σ^2 is assumed known. The noise random variable ξ and the image random variable Y are assumed uncorrelated. Letting Z denote the observed pixel value, we have

$$Z = Y + \xi$$

Having observed Z, Lee says that the problem is to determine an estimate $\hat{Y}$ of Y on the basis of Z. Constraining this estimate to be of the form

$$\hat{Y} = \alpha Z + \beta$$

we can use a least-square criterion to determine α and β. Let

$$\epsilon^2 = E\left[\left(\hat{Y} - Y\right)^2\right] = E\left\{[\alpha(Y + \xi) + \beta - Y]^2\right\}$$
$$= \alpha^2 \sigma^2 + \beta^2 - 2\beta(1 - \alpha)\mu_Y + (1 - \alpha)^2(\sigma_Y^2 + \mu_Y^2)$$

To determine the minimizing α and β, we take partial derivatives of ϵ^2 with respect to α and β, set them to zero, and solve the resulting system of equations.

$$\frac{\partial \epsilon^2}{\partial \alpha} = 0 = 2\alpha\sigma^2 + 2\beta\mu_Y - 2(1 - \alpha)(\sigma_Y^2 + \mu_Y^2)$$

$$\frac{\partial \epsilon^2}{\partial \beta} = 0 = 2\beta - 2(1 - \alpha)\mu_Y$$

This immediately results in

$$\alpha = \frac{\sigma_Y^2}{\sigma_Y^2 + \sigma^2}$$

$$\beta = (1 - \alpha)\mu_Y$$

making the estimate $\hat{Y}$ a convex combination of the observed pixel value Z and the mean μ_Y.

$$\hat{Y} = \frac{\sigma_Y^2}{\sigma_Y^2 + \sigma^2}Z + \frac{\sigma^2}{\sigma_Y^2 + \sigma^2}\mu_Y \qquad (7.19)$$

To use this estimate, σ_Y^2, μ_Y, and σ^2 all need to be known. In the case of stationary non-signal-dependent noise, the noise variance σ^2 can be regarded as constant over the whole image. It is reasonable to take it to be known. However, μ_Y and σ_Y^2 change over the image, and it is not reasonable to regard them as known. They may be estimated as the mean and variance of the central neighborhood around the given pixel. If $x_1, \ldots, x_N$ denote the values in the neighborhood, then

$$\hat{\mu}_Z = \frac{1}{N}\sum_{n=1}^{N} x_n$$

and

$$\hat{\sigma}_Z = \frac{1}{N-1}\sum_{n=1}^{N}(x_n - \hat{\mu}_Z)$$

are the estimated neighborhood mean and variance. We take these to be the true mean and variance:

$$\mu = \hat{\mu}_Z \quad \text{and} \quad \sigma_Y^2 = \hat{\sigma}_Z^2$$

Not all noise is additive. Under low light conditions, the noise has more of a Poisson character, which is better modeled by multiplicative noise. Here the observed Z can be represented as

$$Z = \xi Y$$

where the expected value of ξ is 1. We seek a least mean square estimate $\hat{Y}$ of Y from the observed Z.

$$\hat{Y} = \alpha Z + \beta$$

Let

$$\epsilon^2 = E[(\hat{Y} - Y)^2]$$

$$= E[(\alpha\xi Y + \beta - Y)^2]$$

$$= (\alpha - 1)^2(\mu_Y^2 + \sigma_Y^2) + \alpha^2\sigma^2(\mu_Y^2 + \sigma_Y^2) + 2(\alpha - 1)\beta\mu_Y + \beta^2$$

Taking the partial derivative of ϵ^2 with respect to α and β and setting them to zero results in

$$\frac{\partial \epsilon^2}{\partial \alpha} = 0 = 2(\alpha - 1)(\mu_Y^2 + \sigma_Y^2) + 2\alpha\sigma^2(\mu_Y^2 + \sigma_Y^2) + 2\beta\mu_Y$$

$$\frac{\partial \epsilon^2}{\partial \beta} = 0 = 2(\alpha - 1)\mu_Y + 2\beta$$

Solving this system of equations results in

$$\alpha = \frac{\sigma_Y^2}{\sigma_Y^2 + \sigma^2(\mu_Y^2 + \sigma_Y^2)}$$

$$\beta = (1 - \alpha)\mu_Y$$

The estimated $\hat{Y}$ is then given by

$$\hat{Y} = \frac{\sigma_Y^2}{\sigma_Y^2 + \sigma^2(\mu_Y^2 + \sigma_Y^2)}Z + \frac{\sigma^2(\mu_Y^2 + \sigma_Y^2)}{\sigma_Y^2 + \sigma^2(\mu_Y^2 + \sigma_Y^2)}\mu_Y \tag{7.20}$$

As in the additive noise case, the required values for μ_Y and σ_Y^2 are obtained as the neighborhood mean and variance. Lee (1980) makes a linearizing assumption, gets a result close to the one given here, and shows its application to radar imagery (Lee, 1981). Kuan et al. (1985) give the formulation expressed here.

7.2.12 Noise-Removal Techniques— Experiments

In this section we describe the performance of the noise-removal techniques outlined previously. For our experiments we used an image of blocks, to which we added the following types of noise:
    Uniform
    Gaussian
    Salt and pepper
    Varying noise (The noise energy varies across the image).
Figure 7.10 gives the image with no noise. Figure 7.11 shows the image generated by appending the images obtained after addition of each of the noise types listed above. The top left portion is corrupted with additive uniform noise. The top right portion is corrupted with additive Gaussian noise. The bottom left portion is corrupted with salt and pepper noise while the bottom right portion is corrupted with varying noise.

In order to study effectively the performance of each noise-removal technique relative to the noise type, the S/N ratio in each portion of the image was made the same. The S/N ratio was set at -1 dB. The signal-to-noise ratio is defined as $S = 10 * \log_{10}(VS/VN)$, where VS is the image gray level variance and VN is the noise variance. In our implementation the salt and pepper noise generation was done by specifying the minimum gray value ($i_{\min}$) and the maximum gray value ($i_{\max}$) for noise pixels and the fraction (p) of the image that is to be corrupted with noise. Assuming that u is a uniform random variable in the interval $[0, 1]$, we find that the

Figure 7.10 Image without noise.

gray value at a given pixel (r,c) in the output image with salt and pepper noise is given by

$$O(r,c) = \begin{cases} I(r,c) & \text{if } u < p \\ i_{\min} + (i_{\max} - i_{\min}) * u & \text{otherwise} \end{cases}$$

The results obtained by processing the four images of Fig. 7.11 with the different operators are given in Figs. 7.12 through 7.20. Figure 7.12 shows the result

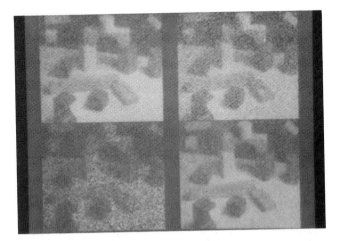

Figure 7.11 Image after the addition of four types of noise. The top left image is corrupted with additive uniform noise; the top right, with additive Gaussian noise; the bottom left, with salt and pepper noise; and the bottom right, with noise that varies across the image. The signal-to-noise ratio was set at -1 dB.

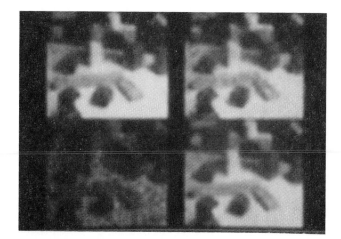

Figure 7.12 Result obtained by contrast-dependent noise removal with a 9 × 9 neighborhood and a threshold of 0.1.

obtained by performing contrast-dependent noise removal with a 9 × 9 neighborhood and a threshold of 0.1. Figure 7.13 shows the result obtained by performing contrast-dependent peak noise removal with smooth replacement with a 9 × 9 neighborhood, convex combination parameter value 0.2 and a threshold of 0.4. Figure 7.14 shows the result obtained by performing default peak noise removal (Eq. 7.5) with a 9 × 9 neighborhood and a threshold of 0.2. Figure 7.15 shows the result obtained by performing hysteresis smoothing. Figure 7.16 shows the result obtained by using the interquartile mean filter using a 7 × 7 neighborhood. Figure 7.17 shows the result obtained by using a 7 × 7 neighborhood midrange filter. Figure 7.18 shows

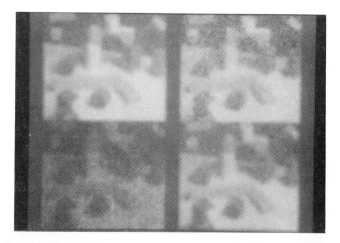

Figure 7.13 Result obtained by contrast-dependent peak noise removal with smooth replacement with a 9 × 9 neighborhood, a convex combination parameter value of 0.2, and a threshold of 0.4.

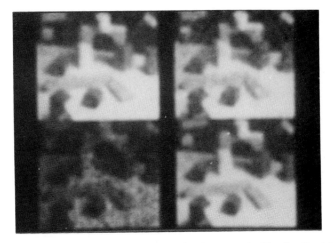

Figure 7.14 Result obtained by default peak noise removal with a 9 × 9 neighborhood and a threshold of 0.2.

the result obtained by using a 7 × 7 neighborhood running mean filter. Figure 7.19 shows the result obtained by using a sigma filter with 9 × 9 neighborhood and 0.2 sigma parameter. In Fig. 7.20 the result was obtained by using a 7 × 7 neighborhood weighted median filter with kernel as given below:

$$
\begin{matrix}
1 & 1 & 1 & 1 & 1 & 1 & 1 \\
1 & 2 & 2 & 2 & 2 & 2 & 1 \\
1 & 2 & 3 & 3 & 3 & 2 & 1 \\
1 & 2 & 3 & 4 & 3 & 2 & 1 \\
1 & 2 & 3 & 3 & 3 & 2 & 1 \\
1 & 2 & 2 & 2 & 2 & 2 & 1 \\
1 & 1 & 1 & 1 & 1 & 1 & 1
\end{matrix}
$$

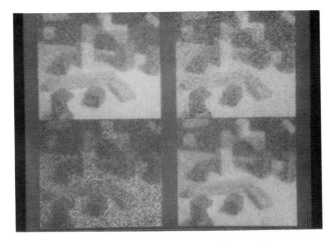

Figure 7.15 Result obtained by hysteresis smoothing.

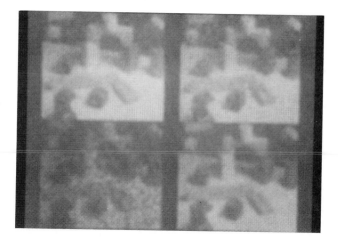

Figure 7.16 Result obtained by using the interquartile mean filter with a 7 × 7 neighborhood.

Table 7.5 gives the gain in S/N ratio (in decibels) for each noise-removal operator for different noise types.

It can be seen that the best operator for uniform noise was the midrange filter, followed by the contrast-dependent peak noise-removal filter. For an image with Gaussian noise, the best operator was the contrast-dependent peak noise-removal filter; for an image with salt and pepper noise, the interquartile mean filter; and for an image with varying noise, the contrast-dependent peak noise-removal filter.

Figure 7.17 Result obtained by using a 7 × 7 neighborhood midrange filter.

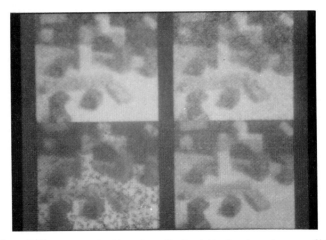

Figure 7.18 Result obtained by using a 7 × 7 neighborhood running-mean filter.

7.3   Sharpening

The simplest neighborhood operator method for sharpening or crispening an image is to subtract from each pixel some fraction of the neighborhood mean and then scale the result. If $x_1, \ldots, x_N$ are all the values in the neighborhood, including the value y of the center pixel, and $\hat{\mu} = \frac{1}{N} \sum_{n=1}^{N} x_n$ is the neighborhood mean, the output value is given by

$$z_{\text{sharpened}} = s[y - k\hat{\mu}]$$

where s is a scaling constant. Schreiber (1970) suggests that reasonable values for k are between $\frac{1}{5}$ and $\frac{2}{3}$, the larger values providing the greater amount of sharpening. Rosenfeld (1969) calls this technique *unsharp masking*.

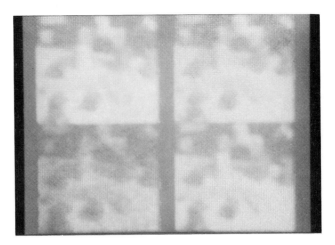

Figure 7.19 Result obtained by using a sigma filter with a 9 × 9 neighborhood and a 0.2 sigma parameter.

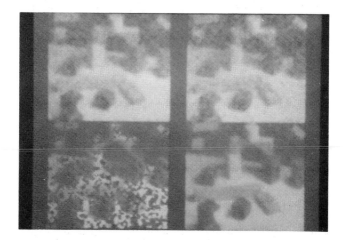

Figure 7.20 shows the result obtained by using a 7 by 7 neighborhood weighted median filter.

In areas of the image with high-contrast step edges, the technique of unsharp masking can result in overshooting, creating dark and light banding about the edge. Scollar, Weidner, and Huang (1984) suggest replacing the neighborhood mean with the neighborhood median.

$$z_{\text{median sharpened}} = s[y - kz_{\text{median}}]$$

They also suggest the possibility of combining noise cleaning and sharpening. If the value of the center pixel is statistically significantly different from the neighborhood median, then the pixel is likely to have been highly affected by noise. Since its value

Table 7.5   Gain in S/N ratio (in dB) obtained by noise filtering of an image corrupted with uniform, Gaussian, salt and pepper (S&P), and varying noise.

Uniform	Gaussian	S&P	Varying	Noise-Removal Operation
1.4973	1.5057	0.9380	1.5445	Contrast-dependent peak noise removal
1.3286	0.3144	−0.6314	1.1230	Contrast-dependent peak noise removal with smoothing
1.4973	1.5057	0.9380	1.5445	Default peak noise removal
−0.2526	−2.4267	−2.5693	−0.4262	Hysteresis smoothing
1.2831	1.2925	1.0814	1.3316	Interquartile mean filter
1.5692	0.8410	−1.2223	0.9851	Midrange filter
0.2456	−1.0347	1.0465	0.2308	Running-mean filter
1.3680	1.2477	0.6416	1.3897	Sigma filter
1.0557	1.1140	0.9214	1.1124	Weighted-median filter

is unreliable, replace it with the neighborhood median. On the other hand, if the value of the center pixel is close to the neighborhood median, then to bring out or sharpen the spatial detail of which it is part, replace its value with the median sharpened value. Thus we have a neighborhood operator defined by

$$z = \begin{cases} z_{\text{median}} & \text{if} \left|\frac{y - z_{\text{median}}}{Q}\right| > \theta \\ s[y - k z_{\text{median}}] & \text{otherwise} \end{cases}$$

Wallis (1976) suggested a form of unsharp masking that adjusts the neighborhood brightness and contrast toward given desired values. The Wallis neighborhood operator is defined by

$$z_{\text{Wallis}} = \frac{A\sigma_d}{A\hat{\sigma} + \sigma_d}[y - \hat{\mu}] + \alpha\mu_d + (1 - \alpha)\hat{\mu}$$

where μ_d is the desired neighborhood mean, σ_d^2 is the desired neighborhood variance, A is a gain or contrast expansion constant governing the degree to which the neighborhood variance is adjusted toward the desired variance, and α is a constant governing the degree to which the neighborhood mean is adjusted to the desired mean. Reasonable values for A range from 3 to 25 and for α from 0 to 0.4. For this operator to be effective, the neighborhood length N must be around $\frac{1}{20}$ of the image side length.

The Wallis operator can be put in the median mode as well by replacing $\hat{\mu}$ with z_{median}, $\hat{\sigma}$ with the observed interquartile range Q, and σ_d with the desired interquartile range Q_d.

7.3.1 Extremum Sharpening

The extremum-sharpening neighborhood operator (Kramer and Bruckner, 1975) is one that may be iteratively applied and is most appropriate for images that have large contrast regions. The output value $z_{\text{extremum sharpened}}$ is the closer of the neighborhood minimum or maximum to the value of the pixel at the neighborhood's center. More formally, let W be the neighborhood. Define z_{min} and z_{max} by

$$z_{\text{min}} = \min\{f(r + r', c + c')|(r',c') \in W\} \text{ and}$$

and

$$z_{\text{max}} = \max\{f(r + r', c + c')|(r',c') \in W\}$$

Then

$$z_{\text{extremum sharpened}} = \begin{cases} z_{\text{min}} & \text{if } f(r,c) - z_{\text{min}} < z_{\text{max}} - f(r,c) \\ z_{\text{max}} & \text{otherwise} \end{cases}$$

Kramer and Bruckner used the extremum-sharpening operator in a character recognition application. Lester, Brenner, and Selles (1980) report good results with the extremum-sharpening operator in biomedical image analysis applications. They also indicate that after one or two applications of the extremum sharpening operator, the application of the median neighborhood operator proved to be of considerable benefit prior to image segmentation.

7.4 **Edge Detection**

What is an edge in a digital image? The first intuitive notion is that a digital edge is the boundary between two pixels that appears when their brightness values are significantly different. Here "significantly different" may depend on the distribution of brightness values around each pixel.

On an image we often point to a region and say it is brighter than its surrounding area. We might then say that an edge exists between each pair of neighboring pixels where one pixel is inside the brighter region and the other is outside. Such edges are referred to as step edges. Hence we use the word *edge* to refer to a place in the image where brightness value appears to jump. Jumps in brightness value are associated with bright values of first derivative and are the kinds of edges that Roberts (1965) originally detected.

One clear way to interpret jumps in value when referring to a discrete array of values is to assume that the array comes about by sampling a real-valued function f defined on the domain of the image that is a bounded and connected subset of the real plane R^2. The finite difference typically used in the numerical approximation of first-order derivatives is usually based on the assumption that the function f is linear. From this point of view, the jumps in value really must refer to points of high first derivative of f. Edge detection must then involve fitting a function to the sample values. Prewitt (1970), Hueckel (1973), Brooks (1978), Haralick (1980), Haralick and Watson (1981), Morgenthaler and Rosenfeld (1981), Zucker and Hummel (1979), and Morgenthaler (1981b) all use the surface fit concept in determining edges. Roberts (1965) and Sobel (1970) explain edge detectors in terms of fitting as well. In this section we review other approaches to edge detection. We begin with some of the basic gradient edge operators, which measure a quantity related to edge contrast or gradient as well as edge or gradient direction. We also discuss zero-crossing edge operators, the performance characterization of edge operators, and some line detectors.

7.4.1 Gradient Edge Detectors

One of the early edge operators was employed by Roberts (1965). He used two 2×2 masks to calculate the gradient across the edge in two diagonal directions (Fig. 7.21). Letting r_1 be the value calculated from the first mask and r_2 the value calculated from the second mask, he obtained that the gradient magnitude is $\sqrt{r_1^2 + r_2^2}$.

Prewitt (1970) used two 3×3 masks oriented in the row and column direction (Fig. 7.22). Letting p_1 be the value calculated from the first mask and p_2 the value calculated from the second mask, she obtained that the gradient magnitude g is $\sqrt{p_1^2 + p_2^2}$ and the gradient direction θ taken in a clockwise angle with respect to the column axis is $\arctan(p_1/p_2)$.

Sobel (1970) used two 3×3 masks oriented in the row and column direction (Fig. 7.23). Letting s_1 be the value calculated from the first mask and s_2 the value calculated from the second mask, he obtained that the gradient magnitude g is

Figure 7.21 Masks used for the Roberts operators.

$\sqrt{s_1^2 + s_2^2}$ and the gradient direction θ taken in a counter-clockwise angle with respect to the column axis is $\arctan(s_1/s_2)$.

Frei and Chen (1977) used a complete set of nine orthogonal masks to detect edges and lines as well as to detect nonedgelike and nonlinelike neighborhoods. Two of the nine are appropriate for edge detection (Fig. 7.24). As before, letting f_1 be the value calculated from the first mask and f_2 the value calculated from the second mask, they obtained that the gradient magnitude g is $\sqrt{f_1^2 + f_2^2}$ and the gradient direction θ taken in a counterclockwise angle with respect to the column axis is $\arctan(f_1/f_2)$.

Kirsch (1971) describes a set of eight compass template edge masks (Fig. 7.25). The gradient magnitude g is

$$\max_{\substack{n \\ n=0,\dots,7}} k_n$$

and the gradient direction θ is $45°$ $\operatorname{argmax} k_n$.

To simplify computation, Robinson (1977) used a compass template mask set having values of only $0, \pm 1, \pm 2$ (Fig. 7.26). In actual practice, since the negation of each mask is also a mask, computation need only be done by using four masks. Gradient magnitude and direction are computed as for the Kirsch operator. Nevatia and Babu (1980) use a set of six 5×5 compass template masks (Fig. 7.27). The Robinson and Kirsch compass operators detect lineal edges (Fig. 7.28).

The edge contour direction is defined as the direction along the edge whose right side has higher gray level values and whose left side has lower gray level values. The edge contour direction is $90°$ more than the gradient direction.

From this discussion it might appear that one can simply design any kind of vertical and horizontal difference pattern and make an edge operator. However, each such operator has properties that differ from one another. So first we explore four important properties that an edge operator might have: (1) its accuracy in estimating gradient magnitude; (2) its accuracy in estimating gradient direction; (3) its accuracy in estimating step edge contrast; and (4) its accuracy in estimating step edge direction. For gradient direction and magnitude we suppose, without loss of generality, that the gray level values in a 3×3 neighborhood can be described by

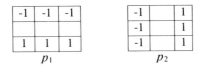

Figure 7.22 Prewitt edge detector masks.

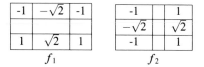

Figure 7.23 Sobel edge detector masks.

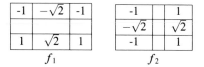

Figure 7.24 Frei and Chen gradient masks.

a simple linear relationship $I(r,c) = \alpha r + \beta c + \gamma$ (Fig. 7.29a) and that the masks used for the vertical and horizontal differences are those shown in Fig. 7.29(b). For such a linear gray level intensity surface, the gradient magnitude is $\sqrt{\alpha^2 + \beta^2}$, and the gradient direction θ satisfies $\tan \theta = \alpha/\beta$.

The row and column differences computed by this edge operator are

$$g_r = 2\alpha(2a + b)$$
$$g_c = 2\beta(2a + b)$$

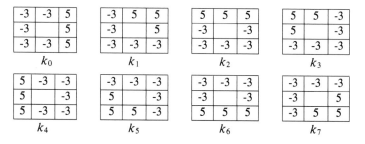

Figure 7.25 Kirsch compass masks.

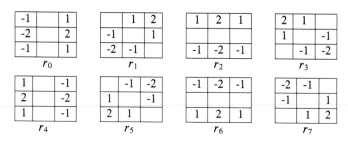

Figure 7.26 Robinson compass masks.

100	100	100	100	100
100	100	100	100	100
0	0	0	0	0
-100	-100	-100	-100	-100
-100	-100	-100	-100	-100

0°

100	100	100	100	100
100	100	100	78	-32
100	92	0	-92	-100
32	-78	-100	-1100	-100
-100	-100	-100	-100	-100

30°

100	100	100	32	-100
100	100	92	-78	-100
100	100	0	-100	-100
100	78	-92	-100	-100
100	32	-100	-100	-100

60°

-100	-100	0	100	100
-100	-100	0	100	100
-100	-100	0	100	100
-100	-100	0	100	100
-100	-100	0	100	100

90°

-100	32	100	100	100
-100	-78	92	100	100
-100	-100	0	100	100
-100	-100	-92	78	100
-100	-100	-100	-32	100

120°

100	100	100	100	100
-32	78	100	100	100
-100	-92	0	92	100
-100	-100	-100	-78	32
-100	-100	-100	-100	-100

150°

Figure 7.27 Nevatia-Babu 5 × 5 compass template masks.

The gradient magnitude computed by the operator is then

$$g = \sqrt{g_r^2 + g_c^2} = 2(2a + b)\sqrt{\alpha^2 + \beta^2}$$

Hence for this operator to compute gradient magnitude correctly, a and b must satisfy $2(2a + b) = 1$. The gradient direction θ computed by the operator satisfies

$$\tan \theta = \frac{g_r}{g_c} = \frac{\alpha}{\beta}$$

which is precisely the correct value.

The choice of the values for a and b under the constraint $2(2a + b) = 1$ has consequences relative to the effect the noise has on the value produced by the edge operator. For example, if

$$I(r,c) = \alpha r + \beta c + \gamma + \xi(r,c)$$

where $\xi(r,c)$ is independent noise having mean 0 and variance $\sigma^2(r,c)$, then

$$g_r = \alpha 2(2a+b) + a[\xi(-1,-1) + \xi(-1,1) + \xi(1,-1) + \xi(1,1)] + b[\xi(-1,0) + \xi(1,0)]$$

will have expected value $\alpha 2(2a + b) = \alpha$, since $2(2a + b) = 1$, and will have variance

$$a^2[\sigma^2(-1,-1) + \sigma^2(-1,1) + \sigma^2(1,-1) + \sigma^2(1,1)] + b^2[\sigma^2(-1,0) + \sigma^2(1,0)]$$

If $\sigma^2(-1,-1) = \sigma^2(-1,1) = \sigma^2(1,-1) = \sigma^2(1,1) = \sigma_a^2$, and $\sigma^2(-1,0) = \sigma^2(1,0) = \sigma_b^2$, then the variance $V[g_r] = 4a^2\sigma_a^2 + 2b^2\sigma_b^2$. Since $2(2a + b) = 1$,

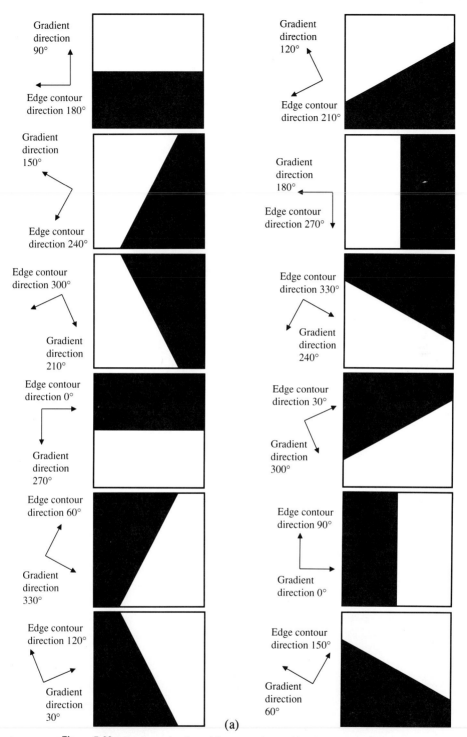

Figure 7.28 Lineal gray level spatial patterns detected by the compass edge operator. The white boxes show pixels with low values, and the gray boxes show pixels with high values. Both edge contour and gradient directions are indicated. Compass edge operator with maximal response for edges in the indicated direction. White boxes indicate pixels with high values; black boxes indicate pixels with low values.

341

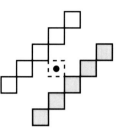
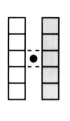
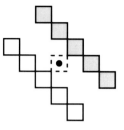
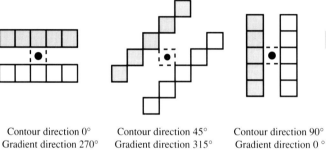

| Contour direction 180° | Contour direction 225° | Contour direction 270° | Contour direction 315° |
| Gradient direction 90° | Gradient direction 135° | Gradient direction 180° | Gradient direction 225° |

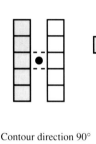
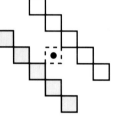

| Contour direction 0° | Contour direction 45° | Contour direction 90° | Contour direction 135° |
| Gradient direction 270° | Gradient direction 315° | Gradient direction 0 ° | Gradient direction 45° |

(b)

Figure 7.28. *Continued.*

$V[g_r] = 4a^2\sigma_a^2 + \frac{1}{2}(1 - 8a + 16a^2)\sigma_b^2$. The value of a that minimizes the variance $V[g_r]$ is then

$$a = \frac{\sigma_b^2}{2\sigma_a^2 + 4\sigma_b^2}$$

When $\sigma_a^2 = \sigma_b^2$, $a = \frac{1}{6}$, and since $2(2a + b) = 1$, then $b = \frac{1}{6}$. The result is a $\frac{1}{6}$ multiple of the Prewitt operator. When $\sigma_a^2 = 2\sigma_b^2$, $a = \frac{1}{8}$, and since $2(2a + b) = 1$, $b = \frac{1}{4}$. The result is a $\frac{1}{8}$ multiple of the Sobel operator. Hence we see that the choice of the Prewitt, Sobel, or Frei and Chen masks for edge detection should not be by a flip of the coin but should be based on a noise model. In other words, selection of a particular operator in effect commits us to a particular noise model.

To determine the properties of an edge operator for edge direction and contrast,

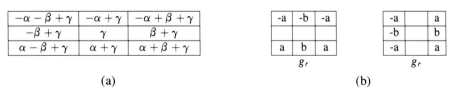

$-\alpha - \beta + \gamma$	$-\alpha + \gamma$	$-\alpha + \beta + \gamma$
$-\beta + \gamma$	γ	$\beta + \gamma$
$\alpha - \beta + \gamma$	$\alpha + \gamma$	$\alpha + \beta + \gamma$

(a)

-a	-b	-a
a	b	a

g_r

-a		a
-b		b
-a		a

g_r

(b)

Figure 7.29 (a) Gray level pattern for a linear gray level intensity surface; (b) 3×3 masks to compute differences in the row and column directions.

we must assume an appropriate edge model. The model we choose is the step edge. We assume that a straight step edge passes directly through the center point of the center pixel of the 3×3 neighborhood. All points on the bright side of the edge have the same value H, and all points on the dark side of the edge boundary have the same value L. Hence for pixels on or near the edge boundary, some of the pixel's area will have high values and some low values. We assume a model in which each pixel value is the convex combination of the high and low values, where the coefficients of the convex combination are just the areas of high and low values and where the areas of pixels are unit squares.

Using this edge model, we find from Fig. 7.30 that when edge direction θ satisfies $\frac{1}{3} \leq \tan\theta \leq 1$,

$$g_r = (H - L)[2aW + b(1 - 2V)]$$
$$g_c = (H - L)[2a(1 - W) + b]$$

From simple trigonometry the areas V and W are given by

$$V = \frac{\frac{1}{8}(1 - \tan\theta)^2}{\tan\theta}$$

$$W = \frac{1}{8}(9\tan\theta - 6 + 1/\tan\theta)$$

When $0 \leq \tan\theta \leq \frac{1}{3}$, the analysis is a little simpler and we have

$$g_r = 2b(H - L)\tan\theta$$
$$g_c = (2a + b)(H - L)$$

In either case the gradient magnitude $g = \sqrt{g_r^2 + g_c^2}$ now clearly depends on the gradient direction.

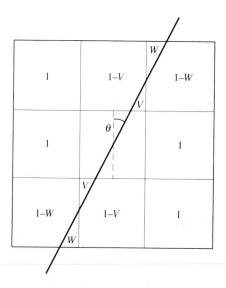

Figure 7.30 Edge boundary passing though the center of the 3×3 neighborhood and the areas of each pixel on each side of the edge boundary.

A straightforward computer calculation shows that when $2a + b = .958$, the computed edge contrast will be between $0.958(H - L)$ and $1.042(H - L)$. So the slight dependency on edge direction causes the constant to be off by no more than 4.2%. The true edge contrast is $H - L$. Kittler, Illingworth, and Paler (1983) show, using an analysis similar to ours, that the edge contrast is less than 1.6% different from what it would be for the Robinson compass operator.

The computed edge direction θ satisfies $\tan \theta = (g_r/g_c)$, and from computer simulations we find that when $a = 0.2278$ and $b = 0.5025$, the maximum difference between the computed edge direction and the true edge direction is less than $0.851°$, and this occurs at $\theta = 20.321°$. In contrast, the maximum difference between the computed edge direction and the true edge direction for the Sobel operator is $1.423°$, and this occurs at $34°$. For the Prewitt operator the maximum difference between the computed edge direction and the true edge direction is $7.429°$, and this occurs at $\theta = 20.734°$. Related analyses can be found in Deutsch and Fram (1978), Davies (1986), and Kitchen and Malin (1989).

To detect an edge with a gradient edge operator, one must examine the gradient magnitude output of the operator at each pixel. If it is high enough, then an edge is detected passing through the pixel, and the pixel will be labeled an edge pixel. If the gradient magnitude is smaller than a threshold, the pixel is labeled as having no edge.

Both a gradient magnitude and a gradient direction can be associated with each edge pixel. Although the magnitude is used for detection purposes, once detection has taken place, the direction can be used for edge organization, selection, and linking. Figure 7.31 illustrates a simple polyhedral object, its gradient magnitude image, and the binary edge image obtained by labeling a pixel an edge if the gradient magnitude is greater than 12. If only edge pixels with orientation directions of between $0°$ and $22°$ are selected, the reduced edge image of Fig. 7.31(d) results. Bowker (1974) describes an early use of edge orientation information. Robinson (1977) describes a constraint technique to eliminate detected edge pixels having directions that are not consistent with their neighboring edge pixel directions. Ikonomopoulos (1982) develops a local operator procedure that also uses orientation consistency to eliminate false edges from among the detected edges. Hancock and Kittler (1990) use a dictionary-based relaxation technique.

The basic idea of the edge detection technique with enforced orientation consistency is to examine every pixel labeled an edge pixel on the input image. Check each one of its eight neighbors to see if it has at least one edge-labeled neighbor whose direction orientation is consistent with its own orientation. If so, then the corresponding pixel on the output image is labeled an edge. If not, then the corresponding pixel on the output image is labeled a nonedge. The technique can be iterated by using the output edge-labeled image as the input edge-labeled image for the next iteration. The iterations can continue until there are no further changes. Each edge-labeled pixel in the resulting edge-labeled image is guaranteed to have some neighboring edge-labeled pixel whose directional orientation is consistent with its own. For the case of the compass edge operators, Table 7.6 lists an example set of consistent orientations for pairs of 8-neighboring pixels. It is always consistent for an edge-labeled pixel to be adjacent to a non-edge-labeled pixel.

The major problem with gradient edge operators is that they generally produce

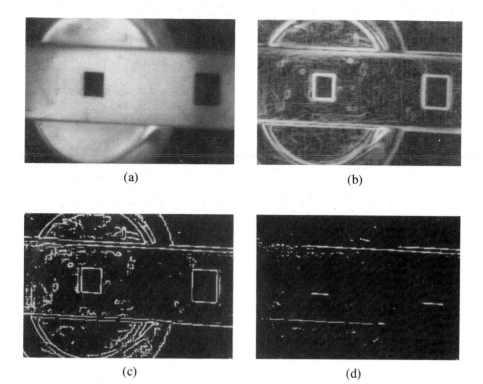

(a)   (b)

(c)   (d)

Figure 7.31 (a) Simple polyhedral object, (b) its gradient magnitude image, (c) the detected binary edge image, and (d) the detected binary edge image for pixels with gradient directions between $0°$ and $22°$.

noisy results. The noisy output can to some extent be reduced by applying one of the appropriate noise-cleaning conditioning operators described in Section 7.2 before applying the edge operator. Care, however, must be used if the domain of a noise-cleaning operator is too large. In this case edges that are close together will not be detected in the noise-cleaned image. Ideally noise-removal smoothing needs to be done only in a direction along the edge contour and not in the gradient direction, which is the direction across the edge. However, isotropic noise-removal conditioning with Gaussian and median filters is commonly used. Bovik, Huang, and Munson (1987) discuss the effectiveness of median filters for this application.

A second problem with gradient edge operators is that they may produce thick edges—edges much wider than one pixel. This happens when edges are not abrupt or when some kind of running-average noise-cleaning step is applied prior to the edge detector step. Therefore the edge-detector step often incorporates nonmaxima suppression. In nonmaxima suppression, not only must the gradient magnitude be high enough to detect an edge, but as one crosses the pixel in the direction of the gradient, the gradient magnitude of the pixel must be higher than the gradient magnitude of the preceding and succeeding neighboring pixels in order for the pixel to be detected on an edge pixel. Eberlein (1976) discusses an iterative technique based on this idea.

Table 7.6   Legal consistent orientation pairs for edge pixels detected by a compass edge operator.

a	b	a	b	a	b	a	b
0	0	0	0	45	45	0	0
45	45	90	90	90	90	45	45
135	135	135	135	135	135	90	90
180	180	180	180	225	225	180	180
225	225	270	270	270	270	225	225
315	315	315	315	315	315	270	270
0	45	135	180	90	135	45	0
45	0	180	135	135	90	0	45
0	315	135	90	90	45	45	90
315	0	90	135	45	90	90	45
180	225	0	315	270	315	225	180
225	180	315	0	315	270	180	225
180	135	315	270	270	225	135	180
135	180	270	315	225	270	180	135

7.4.2 Zero-Crossing Edge Detectors

The nonmaxima suppression can be incorporated into and made an integral part of the edge operator. Such operators are called zero-crossing edge operators. The way they work can be easily illustrated by the one-dimensional step edge example shown in Fig. 7.32. The place where the first derivative of the step is maximum is exactly the place where the second derivative of the step has a zero crossing. The isotropic generalization of the second derivative to two dimensions is the Laplacian.

The Laplacian of a function $I(r, c)$ is defined by

$$\nabla^2 I = \left(\frac{\partial^2}{\partial r^2} + \frac{\partial^2}{\partial c^2} \right) I = \frac{\partial^2 I}{\partial r^2} + \frac{\partial^2 I}{\partial c^2}$$

Two of the common 3×3 masks employed to calculate the digital Laplacian are shown in Fig. 7.33. It is easy to verify that if $I(r, c) = k_1 + k_2 r + k_3 c + k_4 r^2 + k_5 rc + k_6 c^2$, then the 3×3 values of I are as given in Fig. 7.34, and that each of the masks of Fig. 7.33 produces the correct value of the Laplacian of I, which is $2k_4 + 2k_6$.

The general pattern for the computation of an isotropic digital Laplacian is shown in Fig. 7.35. If we multiply the weights of Fig. 7.35 with the values of Fig. 7.34 and then add, the result must be $2k_4 + 2k_6$. This implies that $2a + b = 1$. It is easy to see from the equation relating the k_1 term that $e = -(4a + 4b)$.

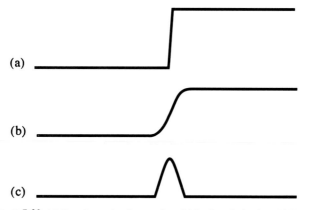

Figure 7.32 (a) One-dimensional step edge. (b) Its first derivative. (c) Its second derivative.

Figure 7.33 Two common 3×3 masks employed to calculate the Laplacian.

The various 3×3 masks that correctly compute the digital Laplacian have different performance characteristics under noise. Suppose that the values in a local 3×3 neighborhood can be modeled by

$$I(r,c) = k_1 + k_2 r + k_3 c + k_4 r^2 + k_5 rc + k_6 c^2 + \xi(r,c)$$

$k_1 - k_2 - k_3$ $+k_4 + k_5 + k_6$	$k_1 - k_2 + k_4$	$k_1 - k_2 + k_3$ $+k_4 - k_5 + k_6$
$k_1 - k_3 + k_6$	k_1	$k_1 + k_3 + k_6$
$k_1 + k_2 - k_3$ $+k_4 - k_5 + k_6$	$k_1 + k_2 + k_4$	$k_1 + k_2 + k_3$ $+k_4 + k_5 + k_6$

Figure 7.34 The 3×3 neighborhood values of an image function $I(r,c) = k_1 + k_2 r + k_3 c + k_4 r^2 + k_5 rc + k_6 c^2$.

a	b	a
b	e	b
a	b	a

Figure 7.35 General pattern for a 3×3 mask computing a digital Laplacian. The constraints are that $e = -(4a + 4b)$ and that $2a + b = 1$.

where $\xi(r,c)$ is independent noise having mean 0 and variance $\sigma^2(r,c)$. If the noise variance is constant, then the variance V of the digital Laplacian will be $V = \sigma^2[4a^2 + 4b^2 + (4a + 4b)^2]$. The values of a and b that minimize the variance of the Laplacian can then be determined easily. Minimize $\sigma^2[4a^2 + 4b^2 + (4a + 4b)^2]$ subject to $2a + b = 1$.

Using the Lagrangian multiplier solution technique, let $\epsilon^2 = \sigma^2[4a^2 + 4b^2 + (4a + 4b)^2] + \lambda(2a + b - 1)$. Then

$$\frac{\partial \epsilon^2}{\partial a} = \sigma^2[8a + 2(4a + 4b)4] + 2\lambda$$

$$\frac{\partial \epsilon^2}{\partial b} = \sigma^2[8b + 2(4a + 4b)4] + \lambda$$

$$\frac{\partial \epsilon^2}{\partial \lambda} = 2a + b - 1$$

Setting each of the partial derivatives to zero and solving for a and b yields $a = \frac{2}{3}$ and $b = \frac{-1}{3}$. Since $e = -(4a + 4b)$, $e = \frac{-4}{3}$. The resulting mask is shown in Fig. 7.36. Of course different noise models will necessitate different weights for the digital Laplacian mask.

As we have seen with the previous edge operators, the differencing entailed by taking first or second derivatives needs to be stabilized by some kind of smoothing or averaging. Marr and Hildreth (1980) suggest using a Gaussian smoother. The resulting operator is called the Laplacian of Gaussian zero-crossing edge detector.

Since convolution is an associative and commutative operation, smoothing an image by convolving it with a Gaussian kernel and then taking its Laplacian by convolving the result with a Laplacian kernel is exactly the same as taking the Laplacian of the Gaussian kernel (LOG) and convolving the image with it. The Laplacian of the Gaussian kernel is given by

$$LOG(r,c) = \left(\frac{\partial^2}{\partial r^2} + \frac{\partial^2}{\partial c^2}\right)\frac{1}{2\pi\sigma^2}e^{-\frac{1}{2}\left(\frac{r^2+c^2}{\sigma^2}\right)}$$

$$= \frac{-1}{2\pi\sigma^4}\left(2 - \frac{r^2 + c^2}{\sigma^2}\right)e^{-\frac{1}{2}\left(\frac{r^2+c^2}{\sigma^2}\right)}$$

The central negative area of the kernel is a disk of radius $\sqrt{2}\sigma$. The domain of the Laplacian of the Gaussian kernel must be at least as large as a disk of

$$\frac{1}{3}\quad\begin{array}{|c|c|c|}\hline 2 & -1 & 2 \\ \hline -1 & -4 & -1 \\ \hline 2 & -1 & 2 \\ \hline\end{array}$$

Figure 7.36 The 3×3 mask for computing a minimum-variance digital Laplacian when the noise is independent and has the same variance for every pixel position.

radius $3\sqrt{2}\sigma$. In actual practice, since only a zero crossing is being looked for, the Laplacian of the Gaussain kernel is multiplied by some constant, and the resulting values are quantized to integers, with some care being taken to do the quantization so that the sum of the positive entries equals the absolute values of the sum of the negative entries. One way of accomplishing this is to define

$$LOG(r,c) = \text{truncate}\left[A\left(1 - k\frac{r^2 + c^2}{\sigma^2}\right)e^{-\frac{1}{2}\frac{r^2+c^2}{\sigma^2}}\right]$$

where k is defined to be the value that makes

$$0 = \sum_{r=-N}^{N}\sum_{c=-N}^{N} LOG(r,c) \qquad \text{where} \qquad N = \lfloor 3\sqrt{2}\sigma \rfloor$$

and A is chosen to be just less than the largest value of A that would make $LOG(N,N) = 0$. Figure 7.37 shows a Laplacian of the Gaussian kernel suitable for an 11×11 mask ($\sigma = 1.4$).

From our discussion of variance of the 3×3 digital Laplacian, it is clear that the masks of Fig. 7.33 for computing the digital Laplacian are not necessarily optimal. To determine the optimal mask values, a noise model will have to be assumed. If this noise model is independent, identically distributed noise, then the Gaussian smoothing will introduce spatial correlation, which will then have to be appropriately taken into account. It appears that this kind of minimum-variance optimization for smoothed images has not been utilized, although it is not difficult to do.

Once the image is convolved with the Laplacian of the Gaussian kernel, the zero crossings can be detected in the following way: A pixel is declared to have a zero crossing if it is less than $-t$ and one of its eight neighbors is greater than t, or if it is greater than t and one of its eight neighbors is less than $-t$, for some fixed threshold t. Figure 7.38 shows the image of Fig. 7.31 processed with a Laplacian of Gaussian model $\sigma = 1.4$ and then with a zero-crossing detection having a threshold $t = 1$.

0	0	0	-1	-1	-2	-1	-1	0	0	0
0	0	-2	-4	-8	-9	-8	-4	-2	0	0
0	-2	-7	-15	-22	-23	-22	-15	-7	-2	0
-1	-4	-15	-24	-14	-1	-14	-24	-15	-4	-1
-1	-8	-22	-14	52	103	52	-14	-22	-8	-1
-2	-9	-23	-1	103	178	103	-1	-23	-9	-2
-1	-8	-22	-14	52	103	52	-14	-22	-8	-1
-1	-4	-15	-24	-14	-1	-14	-24	-15	-4	-1
0	-2	-7	-15	-22	-23	-22	-15	-7	-2	0
0	0	-2	-4	-8	-9	-8	-4	-2	0	0
0	0	0	-1	-1	-2	-1	-1	0	0	0

Figure 7.37 An 11×11 Laplacian of the Gaussian kernel for $\sigma = 1.4$.

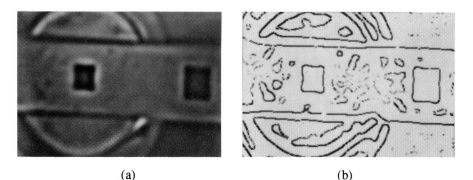

(a)   (b)

Figure 7.38 Laplacian of a Gaussian zero-crossing operator applied to the image of Fig. 7.31.

Berzins (1984) shows that the Marr and Hildreth analysis of the Laplacian of the Gaussian edge operator breaks down at corners, curves, and where the gray level intensity function varies in a nonlinear fashion along the edge. As a result of the breakdown, the displacement of the position of the zero crossing from its correct place at a corner can be as high as the standard deviation of the smoothing Gaussian.

Shah, Sood, and Jain (1986) analytically determine the response of the one-dimensional second derivative of the Gaussian edge operator on ideal infinite-width step edges, ramp edges, finite-width step edges, and staircase step edges. They show that for the ideal step and ramp edges, the location of the zero crossing is exactly where one would hope it to be. However, for the finite-width step and the staircase step edges, the zero-crossing location is shifted from where one would want the zero crossing to be. This shift is a function of the standard deviation of the Gaussian. As the standard deviation of the Gaussian increases, the zero crossings move away from one another for the finite-width step edge, whereas for the staircase edge they move toward one another.

Huertas and Medioni (1986) fit a local biquadratic to the response of the Laplacian of the Gaussian zero-crossing edge operator and from the fitted surface are able to determine the position of the zero crossing to subpixel accuracy. More-detailed discussions of this kind of technique can be found in Chapter 8.

A higher-performance edge operator can be obtained by differencing in a direction across an edge. Canny (1986) recommends conditioning the image by convolving it with a two-dimensional Gaussian. At each pixel position of the smoothed image, the gradient direction may be found by using, for example, the Prewitt operator. Then a line in the gradient direction can be passed through the given pixel, and the two pixels through which the line passes on either side of the given pixel are obtained. The resulting five-pixel values are then multiplied by a five-pixel weight mask, which is a sampling of the first derivative of a Gaussian having a σ of 1 or just less than 1. Canny also suggests that when the variance of the pixel values in the contour direction (a direction orthogonal to the gradient direction) is too high, then even when the value of the directional derivative is high, the edge detection should be suppressed. This edge operator has come to be known as the Canny operator. Its various implementations differ in the details of the establishment of the gradient direction, the suppression of nonedgelike neighborhoods, and the directional differencing.

7.4.3 Edge Operator Performance

Associated with any edge detector is its performance characteristics, which are defined by its misdetection rate and false-alarm rate. For an edge contrast of C in a direction θ on an image where the noise has standard deviation σ, there is a probability that an edge detector will in fact detect the edge. We denote this probability by Prob(edge is detected in direction $\hat{\theta}$, $|\hat{\theta} - \theta| < \delta|$, edge contrast is C, edge direction is θ, noise variance is δ^2), where δ is some fixed small-angle interval. Then each edge detector will be associated with this detection probability, which is a function of θ, C, and σ, in general. For an edge detector that is properly designed, the detection probability will be to a first approximation a function of C/σ and only to a slight degree a function of θ. The misdetection rate P_M is 1 minus the detection rate. Hence we see that $P_M = P_M(C/\sigma, \theta)$.

The false-alarm rate, P_F, is the probability that the detector declares an edge pixel given that there is no edge. It will be a function of noise variance σ^2.

The performance characteristics of an edge operator can easily be determined empirically by the following kind of experiment. To determine the false-alarm rate, generate images in which each pixel has a value from a pseudorandom variable having a normal distribution with fixed mean μ and variance σ^2. For colored noise this random image can be smoothed with a small-sized box or Gaussian smoothing filter. The edge detector can be run on these images, and for each σ the false-alarm rate can be estimated as the number of pixels declared to be an edge divided by the number of pixels processed.

To determine the misdetection rate, fix an edge contrast C, an edge orientation θ, and a noise variance σ^2. Generate an ideal image with a long step edge of contrast C and orientation θ. Then to generate a single pixel-wide edge, smooth the ideal image with a 2×2 box filter. Now add a noise image having variance σ^2. Run the edge detector on the noisy edge image and count the number of edge pixels not detected. This figure divided by the total number of edge pixels that would ideally be detected is the misdetection rate.

Several comparisons have been made between edge detectors and evaluations of edge detector performance. These include Deutsch and Fram (1978), Pratt and Abdou (1979), Bryant and Bouldin (1979), Kitchen and Rosenfeld (1981a and b), Peli and Malah (1982), Haralick (1984), Delp and Chu (1985), and Haralick and Lee (1990). All the evaluation metrics, however, leave something to be desired, for they are mainly not appropriate for describing edge random perturbations for an edge-grouping processing step, which is the most likely next step after edge detection.

-1	-1	-1
2	2	2
-1	-1	-1

0°

-1	-1	2
-1	2	-1
2	-1	-1

45°

-1	2	-1
-1	2	-1
-1	2	-1

90°

2	-1	-1
-1	2	-1
-1	-1	2

135°

Figure 7.39 Template masks for a compass line detector having four orientation directions.

7.5   Line Detection

A line segment on an image can be characterized as an elongated rectangular region having a homogeneous gray level bounded on both its longer sides by homogeneous regions of a different gray level. For a dark line the different gray levels of the side regions have higher values than the center elongated region containing the dark line. For a bright line the different gray levels of the side level have lower values than the center elongated region containing the bright line. Different line segments may differ in width. The width along the same line segment may also vary. A general line detector should be able to detect lines in a range of widths.

One-pixel-wide lines can be detected by compass line detectors, as shown in Fig. 7.39. Vanderburg suggests a semilinear line detector created by a step edge on

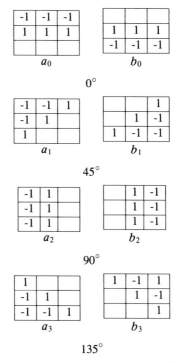

Figure 7.40 Template masks for a semilinear compass line detector having four orientations.

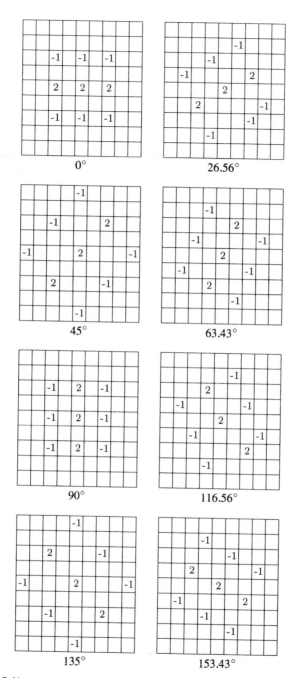

Figure 7.41 Template masks for a line detector capable of detecting lines of one to three pixels in width.

either side of the line. Using the template masks shown in Fig. 7.39, he calculated the line strength s at a pixel position as

$$s = \max\{a_i + b_i | a_i > t \text{ and } b_i > t\}$$

in a direction θ defined by

$$\theta = 45°i, \quad \text{where} \quad a_i + b_i = s$$

His qualitative experiments indicated that the semilinear line detector performs slightly better than the linear line detector of Fig. 7.40.

For lines that have a width greater than one pixel, the template masks of Figs. 7.39 and 7.40 are not satisfactory. For lines two pixels in width, the line detector of Fig. 7.39 produces half the response of what it would for one-pixel-wide lines. For lines three pixels or more in width, it produces no response. For lines two pixels in width, the semilinear detector of Fig. 7.40 fails when $t > 0$. And if $t = 0$, then it will produce many false detections. One possible way of handling a variety of line widths is to condition the image with a Gaussian smoothing, using a standard deviation equal to the largest-width line that the detector is required to detect. The smoothing has the effect of changing the gray level intensity profile across a wide line from constant to convex downward, which makes it possible for the simple line detectors of Figs. 7.39 and 7.40 to work.

Another way to handle wider lines is to use a greater sampling interval, as suggested by Paton (1979). The template masks compare gray level values from the center of the line to values at a distance of two to three pixels away from the center line. Template masks for eight directions are shown in Fig. 7.41. As long as the regions at the sides of the line are larger than two pixels in width, the technique will work for lines of one to three pixels in width. Larger-width lines can be accommodated by even longer interval spacings.

■ Exercises

7.1. Show that if $w_n = w_{N+1-n}$, then order-statistic filtering commutes with any linear transformation. That is, for any constants a and b, if $y_n = ax_n + b$, then

$$\sum_{n=1}^{N} w_n y_{(n)} = a \left[\sum_{n=1}^{N} w_n x_{(n)} \right] + b$$

7.2. Generate and examine the appearance of the following noisy images obtained by independently distorting each pixel of an image of a real scene by the following methods:
   a. Adding Gaussian noise with standard deviation from 1 to 21 by 4.
   b. Adding replacement noise with replacement fractions $p = 0.001, 0.002, 0.005, 0.01, 0.02, 0.05$. (Adding replacement noise means choosing a fraction p of pixels of the image at random and replacing their values with random values within the range of the image values.)
   c. Distorting the image with multiplicative noise by multiplying each pixel value with a uniform random variable in the range [0.8, 1.2].

7.3. Using the noise images generated in Example 7.2, apply a box filter of different neighborhood sizes, a Gaussian filter of different standard deviations, and a median filter to try to clean the noisy image. Measure the performance by computing the RMS error between the original image without noise and the noisy image, the original image and the cleaned image, and the noisy image and the cleaned image.

7.4. Show that the Sobel edge operator contains a built-in smoothing because it can be obtained by the following convolution:

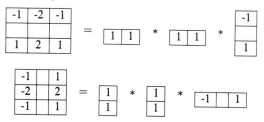

7.5. Show that the squared gradient magnitude of the Roberts operator is exactly one half the squared gradient magnitude $g^2 = \sqrt{d_1^2 + d_2^2}$ obtained from

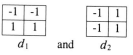

7.6. Determine the misdetection and false-alarm rates for an edge detector by using the Prewitt operator where the threshold or gradient magnitude is determined as the minimum edge contrast desired to be detected plus k times the noise standard deviation. As k varies, the misdetection and false-alarm rates will vary. Plot the misdetection rate against the false-alarm rate.

7.7. Repeat the experiment of Exercise 7.6, but this time presmooth the image with a Gaussian filter. Now the misdetection and false-alarm rates will depend on the parameter k and the standard deviation of the Gaussian filter. Plot the misdetection rate against the false-alarm rate.

7.8. Determine the misdetection and false alarm rates for a Laplacian of Gaussian edge detector where the detection of a new zero crossing is governed by the parameter t as described in Section 7.4.2. As t varies and as the standard deviation of the Gaussian varies, the misdetection and false-alarm rates will vary. Plot the misdetection rate against the false-alarm rate.

7.9. Suppose we desire to design the weights of the 3×3 mask shown below to produce the correct value of the Laplacian for any quadratic function $k_1 + k_2 r + k_3 c + k_4 r^2 + k_5 rc + k_6 c^2$.

a	b	c
d	e	f
g	h	i

If the mask is to satisfy corner symmetry—that is, if $a = c = g = i$—show that $b = d = f = h$ and that $2a + b = 1$.

7.10. The second derivative of the one-dimensional Gaussian kernel $e^{-z^2/2\sigma^2}$ is

$$\left(1 - \frac{z^2}{\sigma^2}\right) e^{-z^2/2\sigma^2}.$$

Determine in the continuous case the response of the one-dimensional second derivative of the Gaussian zero crossing operator for the ideal step edge

$$f(z) = \begin{cases} 0 & z < 0 \\ h & z \leq 0 \end{cases}$$

Determine the response of the one-dimensional second derivative zero-crossing operator for the ideal ramp edge

$$f(z) = \begin{cases} 0 & z < 0 \\ h_1 t & 0 \leq z \leq t \\ h_2 & z > 5 \end{cases}$$

Show that the locations of the zero crossings are independent of σ.

7.11. Consider the response of the one-dimensional second derivative of the Gaussian zero-crossing operator for an ideal step edge of finite width w, defined by

$$f(z) = \begin{cases} 0 & z < 0 \\ h & 0 \leq z \leq w \\ 0 & z > w \end{cases}$$

Show that the locations of the zero crossings are a function of σ. As σ increases, the zero crossings move away from one another.

7.12. Consider the response of the one-dimensional second derivative of the Gaussian zero-crossing operator for an ideal staircase edge defined by

$$f(z) = \begin{cases} 0 & z < 0 \\ h_1 & 0 \leq z \leq w \\ h_2 & z > 0 \end{cases}, \quad \text{where } h_2 > h_1$$

Show that the locations of the zero crossings are a function of σ and that as σ increases, the zero crossings move toward one another, eventually merging into one zero crossing.

7.13. The zero-crossing edge operator can be defined such that an edge position to subpixel precision can be computed. How would you make a zero-crossing edge operator produce a subpixel precision edge?

7.14. The locational accuracy of subpixel precision edge operators can be empirically determined by making up images having widely spaced straight step edges at random orientations. Pixels that have an edge boundary running through them are given values that are a convex combination of the values on either side of the edge, the convex combinations being simply the proportional areas. Additive independent Gaussian noise with different variances can be added to the synthetic image and the subpixel precision edge operator run. The subpixel edge boundary will have an orientation and distance to the pixel center. Positional accuracy can be measured by the difference between the true distance and the reported distance to the pixel center for all pixels that are correctly assigned edge pixels. For the definition of subpixel precision given in Exercise 7.13, plot the absolute value of the difference between the true distance and the computed distance to the center of the pixel as a function of the noise standard deviation.

7.15. An important characteristic of edge operators is their ability to distinguish between two closely spaced parallel edges. Design an experiment varying the distance between parallel edges of fixed edge contrast, the standard deviation of a Gaussian presmoother, and additive Gaussian noise to determine the best standard deviation for the Gaussian presmoother as a function of distance between parallel edges and the standard deviation of additive noise for any edge operator you like.

■ Bibliography

Abramatic, J. F., "Why the Simplest 'Huekel' Edge Detector Is a Roberts Operator," *Computer Graphics and Image Processing,* Vol. 17, 1981, pp. 79–83.

Afrait, S. N., " Composite Matrices," *Quarterly Journal of Mathematics,* Vol. 2, 1954, pp. 81–88.

Akagawa, Y., and A. Rosenfeld, "Edge/Border Coincidence as an Aid in Edge Extraction," *IEEE Transactions on Systems, Man, and Cybernetics,* Vol. SMC-8, 1978, pp. 899–901.

Andrews, H. C., and K. L. Caspari, "Degrees of Freedom and Modular Structure in Matrix Multiplication," *IEEE Transactions on Computers,* Vol. C-20, 1971, pp. 133–141.

Andrews, H. C., and J. Kane, "Kronecker Products, Computer Implementation and Generalized Spectra," *Journal of the ACM,* Vol. 17, April, 1970, pp. 260–268.

Arce, G. R., and S. A. Fontana, "On the Midrange Estimator," *IEEE Transactions on Acoustics, Speech, and Signal Processing,* Vol. ASSP-36, 1988, pp. 920–922.

Arce, G. R., and M. P. McLaughlin, "Theoretical Analysis of The Max/Median Filter," *IEEE Transactions on Acoustics, Speech, and Signal Processing,* Vol. ASSP-35, 1987, pp. 60–69.

Arce, G. R., and R. E. Foster, "Detail-Preserving Ranked-Order Based Filters for Image Processing," *IEEE Transactions on Acoustics, Speech, and Signal Processing,* Vol. 37, 1989, pp. 83–98.

Arnold, R. D., "Local Context in Matching Edges for Stereo Vision," *Proceedings of the ARPA in Workshop,* 1978, pp. 65–72.

Artzy, E., G. Frieder, and G. Herman, "The Theory, Design, Implementation and Evaluation of a Three-Dimensional Surface Detection Algorithm," *Computer Graphics and Image Processing,* Vol. 15, 1981, pp. 1–24.

Ashkar, G. P., and J. W. Modestino, "The Contour Extraction Problem with Biomedical Applications," *Computer Graphics and Image Processing,* Vol. 7, 1978, pp. 331–355.

Bailey, D. G., and R. M. Hodgson, "Range Filters: Local-Intensity Subrange Filters and Their Properties," *Image and Vision Computing,* Vol. 3, 1985, pp. 99–110.

Baker, H., and T. Binford, "Depth from Edge and Intensity Based Stereo," *Proceedings of the International Joint Conference on Artificial Intelligence,* 1981, pp. 631–636.

Barbaud, J., et al., "Uniqueness of the Gaussian Kernel for Scale-Space Filtering," *IEEE Transactions on Pattern Analysis and Machine Intelligence,* Vol. PAMI-8, 1986, pp. 26–33.

Basu, A., and C. M. Brown, "Algorithms and Hardware for Efficient Image Smoothing," *Computer Vision, Graphics, and Image Processing,* Vol. 40, 1987, pp. 131–146.

Bazakos, M., and N. Vu, "Methodologies for Understanding and Evaluation of Image Processing Algorithms," *Intelligent Robots and Computer Vision,* Vol. 521, 1984, pp. 119–132.

Beaudet, P., "Rotationally Invariant Image Operators," *Proceedings of the Fourth International Japanese Conference on Pattern Recognition,* Kyoto, Japan, 1978, pp. 579–583.

Bedner, J. B., and T. L. Watt, "Alpha-Trimmed Means and Their Relationships to Median Filters," *IEEE Transactions on Acoustics, Speech, and Signal Processing,* Vol. ASSP-32, 1984, pp. 145–153.

Bergholm, F., "Edge Focusing," *IEEE Transactions on Pattern Analysis and Machine Intelligence,* Vol. PAMI-9, 1987, pp. 726–741.

Berzins, V., "Accuracy of Laplacian Edge Detectors," *Computer Vision, Graphics, and Image Processing,* Vol. 27, 1984, pp. 195–210.

Birk, J., et al., "Image Feature Extraction Using Diameter-Limited Gradient Direction Histograms," *IEEE Transactions on Pattern Analysis and Machine Intelligence,* Vol. PAMI-1, 1979, pp. 228–235.

Bovik, A. C., "Streaking in Median Filtered Images," *IEEE Transactions on Acoustics, Speech, and Signal Processing,* Vol. ASSP-35, 1987, pp. 493–503.

———, "On Detecting Edges in Speckle Imagery," *IEEE Transactions on Acoustics, Speech, and Signal Processing,* Vol. 36, 1988, pp. 1618–27.

Bovik, A. C., T. S. Huang, and D. C. Munson, "A Generalization of Median Filtering Using Linear Combinations of Order Statistics," *IEEE Transactions on Acoustics, Speech, and Signal Processing,* Vol. ASSP-31, 1983, pp. 1342–50.

———, "The Effect of Median Filtering on Edge Estimation and Detection," *IEEE Transactions on Pattern Analysis and Machine Intelligence,* Vol. PAMI-9, 1987, pp. 181–194.

Bovik, A. C., and D. C. Munson, "Edge Detection Using Median Comparisons," *Computer Vision, Graphics, and Image Processing,* Vol. 33, 1986, pp. 377–389.

Bowker, J. K., "Edge Vector Image Analysis," *Proceedings of the Second International Conference on Pattern Recognition,* Copenhagen, 1974, pp. 1–5.

Brooks, M. J., "Rationalizing Edge Detectors," *Computer Graphics and Image Processing,* Vol. 8, 1978, pp. 277–285.

Brownrigg, D. R. K., "The Weighted Median Filter," *Communications of the ACM,* Vol. 27, 1984, pp. 807–818.

Bryant, D., and D. Bouldin, "Evaluation of Edge Operators Using Relative and Absolute Grading," *IEEE Conference on Pattern Recognition and Image Processing,* 1979, pp. 138–145.

Burns, J. B., A. Hanson, and E. Riseman, "Extracting Straight Lines," *Seventh International Conference on Pattern Recognition,* Montreal, 1984, pp. 482–485.

Canny, J., "A Computational Approach to Edge Detection," *IEEE Transactions on Pattern Analysis and Machine Intelligence,* Vol. PAMI-8, 1986, pp. 679–698.

Chen, J. S., and G. Medioni, "Detection, Localization, and Estimation of Edges," *IEEE Transactions on Pattern Analysis and Machine Intelligence,* Vol. 11, 1989, pp. 191–198.

Chen, P. C., and T. Pavlidis, "Image Segmentation as an Estimate Problem," *Computer Graphics and Image Processing,* Vol. 12, 1980, pp. 153–172.

Chien, R. T., and C. Jacobs, "Directional Derivatives in Computer Image Processing," *Proceedings of the Fourth International Japanese Conference on Pattern Recognition,* Tokyo, 1978, pp. 684–688.

Chien, Y. P., and K. S. Fu, "A Decision Function Method for Boundary Detection," *Computer Graphics and Image Processing,* Vol. 3, 1974, pp. 125–140.

Chin, R., and C. Yeh, "Quantitative Evaluation of Some Edge-Preserving Noise-Smoothing Techniques," *Computer Vision, Graphics, and Image Processing,* Vol. 23, 1983, pp. 67–91.

Chitteneni, C., "Edge and Line Detection in Multidimensional Noisy Imagery Data," *IEEE Transactions on Geoscience and Remote Sensing,* Vol. GE-21, 1983, pp. 163–174.

Clark, J., "Singularity Theory and Phantom Edges in Scale Space," *IEEE Transactions on Pattern Analysis and Machine Intelligence,* Vol. 10, 1988, pp. 720–727.

Clark, J., "Authenticating Edges Produced by Zero-Crossing Algorithms," *IEEE Transactions on Pattern Analysis and Machine Intelligence,* Vol. 11, 1989, pp. 43–57.

Cohen, M., and G. Toussaint, "On the Detection of Structures in Noisy Pictures," *Pattern Recognition,* Vol. 9, 1976, pp. 95–98.

Cooper, D., "Maximum Likelihood Estimation of Markov-Process Blob Boundaries in Noisy Images," *IEEE Transactions on Pattern Analysis and Machine Intelligence,* Vol. PAMI-1, 1979, pp. 372–384.

Cooper, D., et al., "Stochastic Boundary Estimation and Object Recognition," *Computer Graphics and Image Processing,* Vol. 12, 1980, pp. 326–356.

Cooper, D., and F. Sung, "Multiple-Window Parallel Adaptive Boundary Finding in Computer Vision," *IEEE Transactions on Pattern Analysis and Machine Intelligence,* Vol. PAMI-5, 1983, pp. 299–316.

Costabile, M., and G. Pieroni, "Boundary Detection Algorithms in Nuclear Medicine Imagery," *Computer Graphics and Image Processing,* Vol. 17, 1981, pp. 362–374.

Danielsson, P., "Rotation-Invariant Linear Operators with Directional Response," *Proceedings of the Fifth Annual Conference on Pattern Recognition,* Vol. 2 of 2, Miami Beach, FL, 1980.

——, "Getting the Median Faster," *Computer Graphics and Image Processing,* Vol. 17, 1981, pp. 71–78.

Davies, E., "Circularity—A New Principle Underlying the Design of Accurate Edge Orientation Operators," *Image and Vision Computing,* Vol. 2, 1984, pp. 134–142.

——, "Constraints on the Design of Template Masks for Edge Detection," *Pattern Recognition Letters,* Vol. 4, 1986, pp. 111–120.

Davis, L., "A Survey of Edge Detection Techniques," *Computer Graphics and Image Processing,* 1975, Vol. 4, pp. 248–270.

——, "On Models for Line Detection," *IEEE Transactions on Systems, Man, and Cybernetics,* Vol. SMC-6, 1976, pp. 127–133.

——, "Edge Detection in Textures—Maxima Selection," Department of Computer Sciences, University of Texas at Austin, 1980.

Davis, L., and A. Mitchie, "Edge Detection in Textures—Maxima Selection," *Computer Graphics and Image Processing,* Vol. 16, 1981, pp. 158–165.

——, "MITES (mit-es): A Model-Driven, Iterative Texture Segmentation Algorithm," *Computer Graphics and Image Processing,* Vol. 19, 1982, pp. 95–110.

Davis, L., and A. Rosenfeld, "Detection of Step Edges in Noisy One-Dimensional Data," *IEEE Transactions on Computers,* 1975, pp. 1006–10.

——, "Noise Cleaning by Iterated Local Averaging," *IEEE Transactions on Systems, Man, and Cybernetics,* Vol. SMC-8, 1978, pp. 705–710.

Delp, E., and C. H. Chu, "Detecting Edge Segments," *IEEE Transactions on Systems, Man, and Cybernetics,* Vol. SMC-15, 1985, pp. 144–152.

De Souza, P., "Edge Detection Using Sliding Statistical Tests," *Computer Vision, Graphics, and Image Processing,* Vol. 23, 1983, pp. 1–14.

Deutsch, E., and J. Fram, "A Quantitative Study of the Orientation Bias of Some Edge Detector Schemes," *IEEE Transactions on Computers,* Vol. C-27, 1978, pp. 205–213.

Di Zenso, S., "A Note on the Gradient of a Multi-Image," *Computer Vision, Graphics, and Image Processing,* Vol. 33, 1986, pp. 116–125.

Dunn, J., "Group Averaged Linear Transforms that Detect Corners and Edges," *IEEE Transactions on Computers,* Vol. C-24, 1975, pp. 1191–1201.

Eberlein, R., "An Iterative Gradient Edge Detection Algorithm," *Computer Graphics and Image Processing,* Vol. 5, 1976, pp. 245–253.

Eberlein, R., and J. Weszka, "Mixtures of Derivative Operators as Edge Detectors," *Computer Graphics and Image Processing,* Vol. 4, 1975, pp. 180–183.

Ehrich, R., "Detection of Global Edges in Textured Images," *IEEE Transactions on Computers,* Vol. C-26, 1977, pp. 589–603.

———, "A Symmetric Hysteresis Smoothing Algorithm that Preserves Principal Features," *Computer Graphics and Image Processing,* Vol. 8, 1978, pp. 121–126.

Ehrich, R., and F. Schroederm, "Contextual Boundary Formation by One-Dimensional Edge Detection and Scan Line Matching," *Computer Graphics and Image Processing,* Vol. 16, 1981, pp. 116–149.

Eichel, P., and E. Delp, "Quantitative Analysis of a Moment Based Edge Operator," *IEEE Transactions on Systems, Man, and Cybernetics,* Vol. 20, 1990, pp. 59–66.

Eklundh, J. O., T. Elfing, and S. Nyberg, "Edge Detection Using the Marr-Hildreth Operator with Different Sizes," *Proceedings of the Sixth International Conference on Pattern Recognition,* Munich, 1982, pp. 1109–12.

Eklundh, J. O., and A. Rosenfeld, "Image Smoothing Based on Neighbor Linking," *IEEE Transactions on Pattern Analysis and Machine Intelligence,* Vol. PAMI-3, 1981, pp. 679–683.

Elliott, H., D. B. Cooper, and P. Symosek, "Implementation, Interpretation, and Analysis of a Suboptimal Boundary Finding Algorithm," *Proceedings of the Pattern Recognition and Image Processing Conference,* Chicago, 1979, pp. 122–129.

Elliott, H., et al., "Implementation, Interpretation, and Analysis of a Suboptimal Boundary Finding Algorithm," *IEEE Transactions on Pattern Analysis and Machine Intelligence,* Vol. PAMI-4, 1982, pp. 167–181.

Elliott, H., and F. R. Hansen, "An Application of Adaptive Algorithms to Image Processing," *IEEE,* 1980, pp. 472–477.

Elliott, H., and L. Srinivasan, "An Application of Dynamic Programming to Sequential Boundary Detection," *Computer Graphics and Image Processing,* Vol. 17, 1981, pp. 291–314.

Englander, A. C., "Edge Detection Techniques for Industrial Machine Vision," *Conference Proceedings of VISION '86,* Detroit, 1986, pp. 5-85–5-105.

Feng, H. Y. F., and T. Pavlidis, "The Generation of Polygonal Outlines of Objects from Gray Level Pictures," *IEEE Transactions on Circuits and Systems,* Vol. CAS-22, 1975, pp. 427–439.

Fitch, J. P., E. J. Coyle, and N. C. Gallagher, Jr., "Root Properties and Convergence Rates of Medial Filters," *IEEE Transactions on Acoustics, Speech, and Signal Processing,* Vol. ASSP-33, 1985, pp. 230–240.

Fong, A., "Algorithms and Architectures for a Class of Non-Linear Hybrid Filters," *Computer Vision, Graphics, and Image Processing,* Vol. 50, 1990, pp. 101–111.

Forshaw, M. R. B., "Speeding up the Marr-Hildreth Edge Operator," *Computer Vision, Graphics, and Image Processing,* Vol. 41, 1988, pp. 172–185.

Fram, J. R., and E. S. Deutsch, "On the Quantitative Evaluation of Edge Detection Schemes and Their Comparison with Human Performance," *IEEE Transactions on Computers,* Vol. C-24, 1975, pp. 616–628.

Frei, W., and C. C. Chen, "Fast Boundary Detection: A Generalization and a New Algorithm," *IEEE Transactions on Computers,* Vol. C-26, 1977, pp. 556–566.

Frost, V. S., et al., "A Model for Radar Images and Its Application to Adaptive Digital Filtering of Multiplicative Noise," *IEEE Transactions on Pattern Analysis and Machine Intelligence,* Vol. PAMI-4, 1982, pp. 157–166.

Furst, M. A., and P. E. Caines, "Edge Detection for Digital Grey Level Images via Dynamic Programming," *Proceedings of the Seventh International Conference on Pattern Recognition,* Montreal, 1984, pp. 55–58.

——, "Edge Detection with Image Enhancement via Dynamic Programming," *Computer Vision, Graphics, and Image Processing,* Vol. 33, 1986, pp. 263–279.

Gallagher, N. C., Jr., and G. L. Wise, "A Theoretical Analysis of the Properties of Median Filters," *IEEE Transactions on Acoustics, Speech, and Signal Processing,* Vol. ASSP-29, 1981, pp. 1136–41.

Gath, I., and A. B. Geva, "Unsupervised Optimal Fuzzy Clustering," *IEEE Transactions on Pattern Analysis and Machine Intelligence,* Vol. PAMI-11, 1989, pp. 773–781.

Gonzalez, R. C., and P. Wintz, *Digital Image Processing,* Addison-Wesley, Reading, MA, 1987.

Graham, R. E., "Snow Removal—A Noise-Stripping Process for Picture Signals," *IEEE Transactions on Information Theory,* Vol. IT-8, 1962, pp. 129–144.

Grant, G., and A. F. Reid, "An Efficient Algorithm for Boundary Tracing and Feature Extraction," *Computer Graphics and Image Processing,* Vol. 17, 1981, pp. 225–237.

Grender, G. C., "TOPO II: A Fortran Program for Terrain Analysis," *Computers and Geosciences,* Vol. 2, 1976, pp. 195–209.

Griffith, A., "Mathematical Models for Automatic Line Detection," *Journal of the Association for Computing Machinery,* Vol. 22, 1973a, pp. 62–80.

——, "Edge Detection in Simple Scenes Using *A Priori* Information," *IEEE Transactions on Computers,* Vol. C-22, 1973b, pp. 371–381.

Gritton, C. W. K., and E. A. Parrish, Jr., "Boundary Location from an Initial Plan: The Bead Chain Algorithm," *IEEE Transactions on Pattern Analysis and Machine Intelligence,* Vol. PAMI-5, 1983, pp. 8–13.

Groch, W-D., "Extraction of Line Shaped Objects from Aerial Images Using a Special Operator to Analyze the Profiles of Functions," *Computer Graphics and Image Processing,* Vol. 18, 1982, pp. 347–358.

Haddon, J. F., "Generalized Threshold Selection for Edge Detection," *Pattern Recognition,* Vol. 21, 1988, pp. 195–203.

Hancock, E. R., and J. Kittler, "Edge-Labeling Using Dictionary-Based Relaxation," *IEEE Transactions on Pattern Analysis and Machine Intelligence,* Vol. 12, 1990, pp. 165–181.

Hanson, A. R., E. M. Riseman, and F. C. Glazer, "Edge Relaxation and Boundary Continuity," *COINS Technical Report 80-11,* Computer and Information Science, University of Massachusetts at Amherst, 1980.

Haralick, R. M., "Edge and Region Analysis for Digital Image Data," *Computer Vision, Graphics, and Image Processing,* Vol. 12, 1980, pp. 60–73.

——, "Digital Step Edges from Zero Crossing of Second Directional Derivatives," *IEEE Transactions on Pattern Analysis and Machine Intelligence,* Vol. PAMI-6, 1984, pp. 58–68.

Haralick, R. M., N. Griswold, and N. Kattiyakulwanich, "A Fast Two-Dimensional Karhunen-Loeve Transform," *SPIE Proceedings of the Conference on Efficient Transmission of Pictorial Information,* Palos Verdes, CA, Vol. SPIE-66, 1975, pp. 144–159.

Haralick, R. M., and J. Lee, "Context Dependent Edge Detection and Evaluation," *Pattern Recognition,* Vol. 23, 1990, pp. 1–19.

Haralick, R. M., and L. Watson, "A Facet Model for Image Data," *Computer Graphics and Image Processing,* Vol. 15, 1981, pp. 113–129.

Hartley, R., "A Gaussian-Weighted Multiresolution Edge Detector," *Computer Vision, Graphics, and Image Processing,* Vol. 30, 1985, pp. 70–83.

Hashimoto, M., P. V. Sankar, and J. Sklansky, "Detecting the Edges of Lung Tumors by Classification Techniques," *Proceedings of the Sixth International Conference on Pattern Recognition,* Munich, 1982, pp. 276–279.

Hashimoto, M., and J. Sklansky, "Edge Detection by Estimation of Multiple-Order Derivatives," *Transactions of the IEEE Computer Society Conference on Computer Vision and Pattern Recognition,* Irvine, CA, 1983, pp. 318–325.

Haynes, S. M., and R. Jain, "Detection of Moving Edges," *Computer Vision, Graphics, and Image Processing,* Vol. 21, 1983, pp. 345–367.

Herman, G. T., and H. K. Liu, "Dynamic Boundary Surface Detection," *Computer Graphics and Image Processing,* Vol. 7, 1978, pp. 130–138.

Heygster, G., "Rank Filters in Digital Processing," *Computer Vision, Graphics, and Image Processing,* Vol. 19, 1982, pp. 148–164.

Hildreth, E. C., "Edge Detection in Man and Machine," *Robotics Age,* Vol. 3, 1981, pp. 8–14.

———, "The Detection of Intensity Changes by Computer and Biological Vision Systems," *Computer Vision, Graphics, and Image Processing,* Vol. 22, 1983, pp. 1–27.

Holdermann, F., and H. Kazmierczak, "Preprocessing of Gray-Scale Pictures," *Computer Graphics and Image Processing,* Vol. 1, 1972, pp. 66–80.

Hong, T., et al., "Image Smoothing and Segmentation by Multiresolution Pixel Linking: Further Experiments and Extensions," *IEEE Transactions on Systems, Man, and Cybernetics,* Vol. SMC-12, 1982, pp. 611–622.

Hong, T., M. Shneier, and A. Rosenfeld, "Border Extraction Using Linked Edge Pyramids," *IEEE Transactions on Systems, Man, and Cybernetics,* Vol. SMC-12, 1982, pp. 660–668.

Horowitz, S. L., and T. Pavlidis, "Picture Segmentation by a Tree Traversal Algorithm," *Journal of the ACM,* Vol. 23, 1976, pp. 368–388.

Huang, J. S., and D. H. Tseng, "Statistical Theory of Edge Detection," *Computer Vision, Graphics, and Image Processing,* Vol. 43, 1988, pp. 337–346.

Hueckel, M., "A Local Visual Operator Which Recognizes Edges and Lines," *Journal of the ACM,* Vol. 20, 1973, pp. 634–647.

Huertas, A., and G. Medioni, "Detection of Intensity Changes with Subpixel Accuracy Using Laplacian-Gaussian Masks," *IEEE Transactions on Pattern Analysis and Machine Intelligence,* Vol. PAMI-8, 1986, pp. 651–664.

Hwang, J. J., C. C. Lee, and E. L. Hall, "Segmentation of Solid Objects Using Global and Local Edge Coincidence," *Proceedings of the Pattern Recognition and Image Processing Conference,* Chicago, 1979, pp. 114–121.

Iannino, A., "An Iterative Generalization of the Sobel Edge Detection Operator," *Proceedings of the Pattern Recognition and Image Processing Conference,* Chicago, 1979, pp. 130–137.

Ikonomopoulos, A., "An Approach to Edge Detection Based on the Direction of Edge Elements," *Computer Graphics and Image Processing,* Vol. 19, 1982, pp. 179–195.

Inokuchi, S., T. Nita, F. Matsuda and Y. Sakurai, "Feature Detection Using Basis Functions," *Computer Graphics and Image Processing,* Vol. 9, 1979, pp. 40–55.

Inokuchi, S., et al. "A Three-Dimensional Edge Region Operator for Range Pictures," *Proceedings of the Sixth International Conference on Pattern Recognition,* Munich, 1982, pp. 918–920.

Jacobus, C. J., and R. T. Chen, "Two New Edge Detectors," *IEEE Transactions on Pattern Analysis and Machine Intelligence,* Vol. PAMI-3, 1981, pp. 581–592.

Jain, R., and D. Rheaume, "A Two-Stage Method for Fast Edge Detection," *Computer Graphics and Image Processing,* Vol. 14, 1980, pp. 177–181.

Kadar, I., and L. Kurz, "A Class of Three-Dimensional Recursive Parallelepiped Masks," *Computer Graphics and Image Processing,* Vol. 11, 1979a, pp. 262–280.

——, "A Class of Robust Edge Detectors Based on Latin Squares," *Pattern Recognition,* Vol. 11, 1979b, pp. 329–339.

Kasvand, T., "Iterative Edge Detection," *Computer Graphics and Image Processing,* Vol. 4, 1975, pp. 279–286.

Kelly, M. D., "Edge Detection in Pictures by Computer Using Planning," *Machine Intelligence,* Vol. 6, 1971, pp. 397–409.

Kelly, P. A., H. Derin, and K. D. Harit, "Adaptive Segmentation of Speckled Images Using a Hierarchical Random Field Model," *IEEE Transactions on Acoustics, Speech, and Signal Processing,* Vol. 36, 1988, pp. 1628–41.

Kiroch, R., "Computer Determination of the Constituent Structure of Biologic Image," *Computer Biomedical Research,* Vol. 4, 1971, pp. 315–328.

Kitchen, L., "Relaxation Applied to Matching Quantitative Relational Structures," *IEEE Transactions on Systems, Man, and Cybernetics,* Vol. SMC-10, 1980, pp. 96–101.

Kitchen, L., and J. Malin, "The Effect of Spatial Discretization on the Magnitude and Direction Response of Simple Differential Edge Operators on a Step Edge," *Computer Vision, Graphics, and Image Processing,* Vol. 47, 1989, pp. 243–258.

Kitchen, L., and A. Rosenfeld, "Edge Evaluation Using Local Edge Coherence," *IEEE Transactions on Systems, Man, and Cybernetics,* Vol. SMC-11, 1981a, pp. 597–605.

——, "Edge Evaluation Using Local Edge Coherence," *SPIE Techniques and Applications of Image Understanding,* Vol. 281, 1981b, pp. 284–298.

Kittler, J., J. Illingworth, and K. Paler, "The Magnitude Accuracy of the Template Edge Detector," *Pattern Recognition,* Vol. 16, 1983, pp. 607–613.

Kramer, H. P., and J. B. Bruckner, "Iteration of Non–Linear Transformations for Enhancement of Digital Images," *Pattern Recognition,* Vol. 7, 1975, pp. 53–58.

Kuan, D. T., et al., "Adaptive Noise Smoothing Filter for Images with Signal-Dependent Noise," *IEEE Transactions on Pattern Analysis and Machine Intelligence,* Vol. PAMI-7, 1985, pp. 165–177.

Kundu, A., and S. K. Mitra, "A New Algorithm for Image Edge Extraction Using a Statistical Classifier Approach," *IEEE Transactions on Pattern Analysis and Machine Intelligence,* Vol. PAMI-9, 1987, pp. 569–577.

Lacroix, V., "A Three-Module Strategy for Edge Detection," *IEEE Transactions on Pattern Analysis and Machine Intelligence,* Vol. 10, 1988, pp. 803–810.

Leclerc, Y., and S. W. Zucker, "The Local Structure of Image Discontinuities in One Dimension," *IEEE Transactions on Pattern Analysis and Machine Intelligence,* Vol. PAMI-9, 1987, pp. 341–355.

——, "The Local Structure of Image Discontinuities in One Dimension," *Proceedings of the Seventh International Conference on Pattern Recognition,* Montreal, 1987, pp. 46–48.

Lee, D., "Coping with Discontinuities in Computer Vision: Their Detection, Classification, and Measurement," *Proceedings of the Second International Conference of IEEE,* Tampa, FL, 1988, pp. 546–557.

Lee, J-S., "Digital Image Enhancement and Noise Filtering," *IEEE Transactions on Pattern Analysis and Machine Intelligence,* Vol. PAMI-2, 1980, pp. 165–168.

——, "Refined Filtering of Image Noise Using Local Statistics," *Computer Graphics and Image Processing,* Vol. 15, 1981a, pp. 380–389.

——, "Speckle Analysis and Smoothing of Synthetic Aperture Radar Images," *Computer Graphics and Image Processing,* Vol. 17, 1981b, pp. 24–32.

——, "A Simple Speckle Smoothing Algorithm for Synthetic Aperture Radar Images," *IEEE Transactions on Systems, Man, and Cybernetics,* Vol. SMC-13, 1983a, pp. 85–89.

——, "Digital Image Smoothing and the Sigma Filter," *Computer Vision, Graphics, and Image Processing,* Vol. 24, 1983b, pp. 255–269.

Lee, Y. H., and S. A. Kassan, "Generalized Median Filtering and Related Nonlinear Filtering Techniques," *IEEE Transactions on Acoustics, Speech, and Signal Processing,* Vol. ASSP-33, 1985, pp. 672–683.

Lester, J. M., J. F. Brenner, and W. D. Selles, "Local Transforms for Biomedical Image Analysis," *Computer Graphics and Image Processing,* Vol. 13, 1980, pp. 17–30.

Lester, J. M., et al., "Two Graph Searching Techniques for Boundary Finding in White Blood Cell Images," *Computer Biology and Medicine,* Vol. 8, 1978, pp. 293–308.

Leung, E., and X. Li, "Parallel Processing Approaches to Edge Relaxation," *Pattern Recognition,* Vol. 21, 1988, pp. 547–558.

Lev, A., and S. W. Zucker, "Iterative Enhancement of Noisy Images," *IEEE Transactions on Systems, Man, and Cybernetics,* Vol. SMC-7, 1977, pp. 435–442.

Lev, A., S. W. Zucker, and A. Rosenfeld, "Iterative Enhancement of Noisy Images," *IEEE Transactions on Systems, Man, and Cybernetics,* Vol. SMC-7, 1977, pp. 435–442.

Lin, L., and S. Sahni, "Fair Edge Deletion Problems," *IEEE Transactions on Computers,* Vol. 38, 1989, pp. 756–761.

Liu, H. K., "Two- and Three-Dimensional Boundary Detection," *Computer Graphics and Image Processing,* Vol. 6, 1977, pp. 123–134.

Lunscher, W. H. H. J., "The Asymptotic Optimal Frequency Domain Filter for Edge Detection," *IEEE Transactions on Pattern Analysis and Machine Intelligence,* Vol. PAMI-5, 1983, pp. 678–680.

Lunscher, W. H. H. J., and M.P. Beddoes, "Optimal Edge Detector Design I: Parameter Selection and Noise Effects," *IEEE Transactions on Pattern Analysis and Machine Intelligence,* Vol. PAMI-8, 1986a, pp. 164–177.

——, "Optimal Edge Detector Design II: Coefficient Quantization," *IEEE Transactions on Pattern Analysis and Machine Intelligence,* Vol. PAMI-8, 1986b, pp. 178–187.

——, "Optimal Edge Detector Evaluation," *IEEE Transactions on Systems, Man, and Cybernetics,* Vol. SMC-16, 1986c, pp. 304–312.

Lyvers, E. P., and O. R. Mitchell, "Precision Edge Contrast and Orientation Estimation," *IEEE Transactions on Pattern Analysis and Machine Intelligence,* Vol. 10, 1988, pp. 927–937.

Machuca, R., and A. L. Gilbert, "Finding Edges in Noisy Scenes," *IEEE Transactions on Pattern Analysis and Machine Intelligence,* Vol. PAMI-3, 1981, pp. 103–111.

MacVicar-Whelan, P. J., and T. O. Binford, "Line Finding with Subpixel Precision," *Techniques and Applications of Image Understanding,* SPIE, Vol. 281, 1981, pp. 211–216.

Marr, D., and E. Hildreth, "Theory of Edge Detection," *Proceeding of the Royal Society of London,* Vol. B-207, 1980, pp. 186–217.

Martelli, A., "Edge Detection Using Heuristic Search Methods," *Computer Graphics and Image Processing,* Vol. 1, 1972, pp. 169–182.

Martelli, A., "An Application of Heuristic Search Methods to Edge and Contour Detection," *Communications of the ACM,* Vol. 19, 1976, pp. 73–83.

Mascarenhas, N. D. A., and L. O. C. Prado, "A Bayesian Approach to Edge Detection in Images," *IEEE Transactions on Automatic Control,* Vol. AC-25, 1980, pp. 36–43.

Mastin, G. A., "Adaptive Filters for Digital Image Noise Smoothing: An Evaluation," *Computer Vision, Graphics, and Image Processing,* Vol. 31, 1985, pp. 103–121.

Mayhew, J. E. W., and J. P. Frisby, "The Computation of Binocular Edges," *Perception,* Vol. 9, 1980, pp. 69–86.

McDonnell, M. J., "Box-Filtering Techniques," *Computer Graphics and Image Processing,* Vol. 17, 1981, pp. 65–70.

McLean, G. F., and M. E. Jernigan, "Hierarchical Edge Detection," *Computer Vision, Graphics, and Image Processing,* Vol. 44, 1988, pp. 350–366.

Mero, L., "An Optimal Line Following Algorithm," *IEEE Transactions on Pattern Analysis and Machine Intelligence,* Vol. PAMI-3, 1981, pp. 593–598.

Mero, L., and T. Vamos, "Real-Time Edge-Detection Using Local Operators," *Proceedings of the Third International Joint Conference on Pattern Recognition,* Coronado, CA, 1976, pp. 31–36.

Mero, L., and Z. Vassy, "A Simplified and Fast Version of the Hueckel Operator for Finding Optimal Edges in Pictures," *ISCAI,* 1975, pp. 650–655.

Mitchie, A., and J. K. Aggarwal, "Detection of Edges Using Range Information," *IEEE Transactions on Pattern Analysis Machine Intelligence,* Vol. PAMI-5, 1983, pp. 174–178.

Modestino, J. W., and R. W. Fries, "Edge Detection in Noisy Images Using Recursive Digital Filtering," *Computer Graphics and Image Processing,* Vol. 6, 1977, pp. 409–433.

Montanari, U., "On the Optimal Detection of Curves in Noisy Pictures," *Communications of the ACM,* Vol. 14, 1971, pp. 335–345.

Morgenthaler, D. G., "A New Hybrid Edge Detector," *Computer Graphics and Image Processing,* Vol. 16, 1981a, pp. 166–176.

Morgenthaler, D. G., and A. Rosenfeld, "Multidimensional Edge Detection by Hypersurface Fitting," *IEEE Transactions on Pattern Analysis and Machine Intelligence,* Vol. PAMI-3, 1981b, pp. 482–486.

Mori, S., Y. Monden, and T. Mori, "Edge Representation in Gradient Space," *Computer Graphics and Image Processing,* Vol. 2, 1973, pp. 321–325.

Nadler, M., "A Note on the Coefficients of Compass Mask Convolutions," *Computer Vision, Graphics, and Image Processing,* Vol. 51, 1990, pp. 96–101.

Nagao, M., and T. Matsuyama, "Edge Preserving Smoothing," *Proceedings of the Fourth International Conference on Pattern Recognition,* Tokyo, 1978, pp. 518–520.

——, "Edge Preserving Smoothing," *Computer Graphics and Image Processing,* Vol. 9, 1979, pp. 394–407.

Nagata, M., "Image Processing for Boundary Extraction of Remotely Sensed Data," *Pattern Recognition,* Vol. 14, 1981, pp. 275–282.

Nahi, N. E., and M. H. Jahanshahi, "Image Boundary Estimation," *IEEE Transactions on Computers,* Vol. C-26, 1977, pp. 772–781.

Nakagawa, Y., and A. Rosenfeld, "Edge/Border Coincidence as an Aid in Edge Extraction," *IEEE Transactions on Systems, Man, and Cybernetics,* Vol. SMC-8, 1978, pp. 899–901.

Nalwa, V. S., "Edge-Detector Resolution Improvement by Image Interpretation," *IEEE Transactions on Pattern Analysis and Machine Intelligence,* Vol. PAMI-9, 1987, pp. 446–465.

Nalwa, V. S., and T. O. Binford, "On Detecting Edges," *IEEE Transactions on Pattern Analysis and Machine Intelligence,* Vol. PAMI-8, 1986, pp. 699–714.

Narayanan, K. A., K. P. O'Leary, and A. Rosenfeld, "An Optimization Approach to Edge Reinforcement," *IEEE Transactions on Systems, Man, and Cybernetics,* Vol. SMC-12, 1982, pp. 551–553.

Narendra, P. M., "A Separable Median Filter for Image Noise Smoothing," *IEEE Transactions on Pattern Analysis and Machine Intelligence,* Vol. PAMI-3, 1981, pp. 20–29.

Narendra, P. M., and M. Goldberg, "Image Segmentation with Directed Trees," *IEEE Transactions on Pattern Analysis and Machine Intelligence,* Vol. PAMI-2, 1980, pp. 185–191.

Nevatia, R., "Locating Object Boundaries in Textured Environments," *IEEE Transactions on Computers,* Vol. C-25, 1976, pp. 1170–75.

——, "Evaluation of a Simplified Hueckel Edge-Line Detector," *Computer Graphics and Image Processing,* Vol. 6, 1977, pp. 582–588.

Nevatia, R., and K. R. Babu, "Linear Feature Extraction and Description," *Computer Graphics and Image Processing,* Vol. 13, 1980, pp. 257–269.

Newman, T. G., and H. Dirilten, "A Nonlinear Transformation for Digital Picture Processing," *IEEE Transactions on Computers,* Vol. C-22, 1973, pp. 869–873.

Nieminen, A., P. Heinonen, and Y. Neuvo, "A New Class of Detail-Preserving Filters for Image Processing," *IEEE Transactions on Pattern Analysis and Machine Intelligence,* Vol. PAMI-9, 1987, pp. 74–90.

Nieminen, A., and Y. Neuvo, "Comments on 'Theoretical Analysis of the Max Median Filter,' " *IEEE Transactions on Acoustics, Speech, and Signal Processing,* Vol. 36, 1988, pp. 826–827.

Nishihara, H. K., "Hidden Information in Early Visual Processing," *Robotics and Industrial Inspection,* SPIE, Vol. 360, pp. 76–87.

Nodes, T. A., and N. C. Gallagher, "Two-Dimensional Root Structures and Convergence Properties of the Separable Median Filter," *IEEE Transactions on Acoustic Speech and Signal Processing,* Vol. ASSP-31, 1983, pp. 1350–65.

O'Gorman, F., and M. B. Clowes, "Finding Picture Edges Through Collinearity of Feature Points," *IEEE Transactions on Computers,* Vol. C-25, 1976, pp. 449–456.

Pal, S. K., and R. A. King, "On Edge Detection of X-Ray Images Using Fuzzy Sets," *IEEE Transactions on Pattern Analysis and Machine Intelligence,* Vol. PAMI-5, 1983, pp. 69–77.

Panda, D. P., "Nonlinear Smoothing of Pictures," *Computer Graphics and Image Processing,* Vol. 8, 1978, pp. 259–270.

Panda, D. P., and T. Dubitzki, "Statistical Analysis of Some Edge Operators," *Computer Graphics and Image Processing,* Vol. 11, 1979, pp. 313–348.

Papadimitriou, C. H., "On the Complexity of Edge Traversing," *Journal of the ACM,* Vol. 23, 1976, pp. 544–554.

Park, R. H., and W. Y. Choi, "A New Interpretation of the Compass Gradient Edge Operators," *Computer Vision, Graphics, and Image Processing,* Vol. 47, 1989, pp. 259–265.

Park, S. Y., and Y. H. Lee, "Double Smoothing of Images Using Median and Wiener Filters," *IEEE Transactions on Acoustics, Speech, and Signal Processing,* Vol. 37, 1989, pp. 943–946.

Paton, K., "Picture Description Using Legendre Polynomials," *Computer Graphics and Image Processing,* Vol. 4, 1975, pp. 40–54.

Paton, K., "Line Detection by Local Methods," *Computer Graphics and Image Processing,* Vol. 9, 1979, pp. 316–332.

Patrenahalli, M. N, "A Separable Median Filter for Image Noise Smoothing," *IEEE Transactions on Pattern Analysis and Machine Intelligence,* Vol. PAMI-3, 1981, pp. 20–29.

Pavlidis, T., "A Minimum Storage Boundary Tracing Algorithm and Its Application to Automatic Inspection," *IEEE Transactions on Systems, Man, and Cybernetics,* Vol. SMC-8, 1978, pp. 66–69.

Peli, T., and D. Malah, "A Study of Edge Detection Algorithms," *Computer Graphics and Image Processing,* Vol. 20, 1982, pp. 1–21.

Persoon, E., "A New Edge Detection Algorithm and Its Applications in Picture Processing," *Computer Graphics and Image Processing,* Vol. 5, 1976, pp. 425–446.

Peterson, S. R., Y-H. Lee, and S. A. Kassam, "Some Statistical Properties of Alpha-Trimmed Mean and Standard Type *M* Filters," *IEEE Transactions on Acoustics, Speech, and Signal Processing,* Vol. ASSP-36, 1988, pp. 707–713.

Pingle, K. K., "Visual Perception by a Computer," in *Automatic Interpretation and Classification of Images,* A. Grasselli (ed.), Academic Press, New York, 1969, pp. 277–284.

Pitas, I., and A. N. Venetsanopoulos, "Edge Detectors Based on Nonlinear Filters," *IEEE Transactions on Pattern Analysis and Machine Intelligence,* Vol. PAMI-8, 1986, pp. 538–550.

Poppi, S. J., and G. Herrmann, "Boundary Detection in Scintigraphic Images," *Computer Graphics and Image Processing,* Vol. 19, 1982, pp. 281–290.

Prager, J. M., "Extracting and Labeling Boundary Segments in Natural Scenes," *IEEE Transactions on Pattern Analysis and Machine Intelligence,* Vol. PAMI-2, 1980, pp. 16–27.

Pratt, W., and I. Abdou, "Quantitative Design and Evaluation of Enhancement/Thresholding Edge Detectors," *Proceedings of the IEEE,* Vol. 67, 1979, pp. 753–763.

Prewitt, J., "Object Enhancement and Extraction," in *Picture Processing and Psychopictorics,* B. Lipkin and A. Rosenfeld (eds.), Academic Press, New York, 1970, pp. 75–149.

Ranade, S., "Use of Quadtrees for Edge Enhancement," *IEEE Transactions on Systems, Man, and Cybernetics,* Vol. SMC-11, 1981, pp. 370–373.

Rao, V. V. B., and K. S. Rao, "A New Algorithm for Real-Time Median Filtering," *IEEE Transactions on Acoustics, Speech, and Signal Processing,* Vol. ASSP-34, 1986, pp. 1674–75.

Reeves, A. P., M. L. Akey, and O. R. Mitchell, "A Moment Based Two-Dimensional Edge Operator," *IEEE Computer Society Conference on Computer Vision and Image Processing,* Washington, D.C., 1983, pp. 312–317.

Rider, P. R. " The Midrange of a Sample as Estimator of the Population Midrange" *Journal of the American Statistical Association,* Vol. 52, No. 280, 1957, pp. 537–542.

Ritter, G. X., M. A. Shrader-Frechette, and J. N. Wilson, "Image Algebra: A Rigorous and Translucent Way of Expressing All Image Processing Operations," *Proceedings of the Southeastern Technical Symposium on Optics, Electro-Optics, and Sensors,* Orlando, FL, 1987, pp. 1–6.

Ritter, G. X., and J. N. Wilson, "Image Algebra in a Nutshell," *Proceedings of the First International Conference on Computer Vision,* London, 1987, pp. 1–5.

Roberts, L. G., "Machine Perception of Three Dimensional Solids," in *Optical and Electro-optical Information Processing,* J.T. Tippet et al. (eds.), MIT Press, Cambridge, MA, 1965, pp. 159–197.

Robinson, G. S., "Color Edge Detection," *Proceedings of the SPIE Conference on Advances in Image Transmission Techniques,* San Diego, 1976, pp. 126–133.

———, "Edge Detection by Compass Gradient Masks," *Computer Graphics and Image Processing,* Vol. 6, 1977, pp. 492–501.

Robinson, G. S., and J. J. Reis, "A Real-Time Edge Processing Unit," *Proceedings of the Workshop on Picture Data Description and Management,* Chicago, 1977, pp. 155–164.

Rosenfeld, A., *Picture Processing by Computer,* Academic Press, New York, 1969.

———, "The Simplest 'Hueckel' Edge Detector is a Roberts Operator," *Technical Report TR-77,* Computer Science Center, University of Maryland, College Park, 1979.

———, "The Max Roberts Operator Is a Huekel-Type Edge Detector," *IEEE Transactions on Pattern Analysis and Machine Intelligence,* Vol. PAMI-3, No. 1, 1981, pp. 101–103.

Rosenfeld, A., and A. C. Kak, *Digital Picture Processing,* Vols. 1 and 2, Academic Press, Orlando, FL, 1982.

Rosenfeld, A., and M. Thurston, "Edge and Curve Detection for Visual Scene Analysis," *IEEE Transactions on Computers,* Vol. C-20, 1971, pp. 562–569.

Rosenfeld, A., M. Thurston, and Y-H. Lee, "Edge and Curve Detection: Further Experiments," *IEEE Transactions on Computers,* Vol. C-21, 1972, pp. 677–714.

Rowe, P. P.,"Some Nonlinear Operators for Picture Processing," *Pattern Recognition,* Vol. 11, 1979, pp. 341–342.

Rutovitz, D., "Pattern Recognition," *Journal of the Royal Statisics Society,* Vol. 129A, 1966, pp. 504–530.

Salahi, A., and T. S. Huang, "Edge Smoothing," *Proceedings of the Pattern Recognition and Image Processing Conference,* Chicago, 1979, pp. 154–161.

Sankar, P. V., and J. Sklansky, "A Gestalt-Guided Heuristic Boundary Follower for X-Ray Images of Lung Nodules," *IEEE Transactions on Pattern Analysis and Machine Intelligence,* Vol. PAMI-4, 1982, pp. 326–331.

Schachter, B. J., and A. Rosenfeld, "Some New Methods of Detecting Step Edges in Digital Pictures," *Communications of the ACM,* Vol. 21, 1978, pp. 172–176.

Scher, A, M. Shneier, and A. Rosenfeld, "A Method for Finding Pairs of Antiparallel Straight Lines," *IEEE Transactions on Pattern Analysis and Machine Intelligence,* Vol. PAMI-4, 1982a, pp. 316–323.

———, "Clustering of Collinear Line Segments," *Pattern Recognition,* Vol. 15, 1982b, pp. 85–91.

Scher, A., F. R. D. Velasco, and A. Rosenfeld, "Some New Image Smoothing Techniques," *IEEE Transactions on Systems, Man, and Cybernetics,* Vol. SMC-10, 1980, pp. 153–158.

Schreiber, W. F., "Wirephoto Quality Improvement by Unsharp Masking," *Pattern Recognition,* Vol. 2, 1970, pp. 117–121.

Scollar, I., B. Weidner, and T. S. Huang, "Image Enhancement Using the Median and the Interquartile Distance," *Computer Vision, Graphics, and Image Processing,* Vol. 25, 1984, pp. 236–251.

Sethi, I. K., "Edge Detection Using Charge Analogy," *Computer Graphics and Image Processing,* Vol. 20, 1982, pp. 185–195.

Shah, M, A. Sood, and R. Jain, "Pulse and Staircase Edge Models," *Computer Vision, Graphics, and Image Processing,* Vol. 34, 1986, pp. 321–343.

Shanmugam, K. S., F. M. Dickey, and J. A. Green, "An Optimal Frequency Domain Filter for Edge Detection in Digital Pictures," *IEEE Transactions on Pattern Analysis and Machine Intelligence,* Vol. PAMI-1, 1979, pp. 37–49.

Sherman, A. B., et al., "A Method of Boundary Determination in Digital Images of Urothelial Cells," *Pattern Recognition,* Vol. 13, 1981, pp. 285–291.

Shipman, A. L., R. R. Bitmead, and G. A. Allen, "Diffuse Edge Fitting and Following: A Location-Adaptive Approach," *IEEE Transactions on Pattern Analysis and Machine Intelligence,* Vol. PAMI-6, 1984, pp. 96–102.

Shneier, M., "Two Hierarchical Linear Feature Representations: Edge Pyramids and Edge Quadtrees," *Computer Graphics and Image Processing,* Vol. 17, 1981, pp. 211–224.

Sjoberg, F., and F. Bergholm, "Extraction of Diffuse Edges by Edge Focusing," *Proceedings of the Fifth Scandinavian Conference on Image Analysis,* Stockholm, 1987, pp. 23–33.

Smith, M. W., and W. A. Davis, "A New Algorithm for Edge Detection," *Computer Graphics and Image Processing,* Vol. 4, 1975, pp. 55–62.

Sobel, I. E., *Camera Models and Machine Perception,* Ph.D. Thesis, Electrical Engineering Department, Stanford University, Stanford, CA, 1970.

Stern, D., and L. Kurz, "Edge Detection in Correlated Noise Using Latin Square Masks," *Pattern Recogntion,* Vol. 21, 1988, pp. 119–129.

Stimets, R. W., W. L. Ying, and K. Rasjasekharan, "Rapid Recognition of Object Outlines in Reduced Resolution Images," *Pattern Recognition,* Vol. 19, 1986, pp. 21–33.

Suenaga, Y., "Range Filters for Processing of Continuous-tone Pictures and Their Applications," *Systems, Computers, Controls,* Vol. 5, 1974, pp. 16–24.

Suk, M., and O. Song, "Curvilinear Feature Extraction Using Minimum Spanning Trees," *Computer Vision, Graphics, and Image Processing,* Vol. 26, 1984, pp. 400–411.

Tabatabai, A. J., and O. R. Mitchell, "Edge Location to Subpixel Values in Digital Imagery," *IEEE Transactions on Pattern Analysis and Machine Intelligence,* Vol. PAMI-6, 1984, pp. 188–200.

Tamura, S., R. S. Ledley, and L. S. Rotolo, "Boundary Extraction from Coarsely or Irregularly Scanned Images," *Pattern Recognition,* Vol. 16, 1983, pp. 557–562.

Tomita, F., and S. Tsuji, "Extraction of Multiple Regions by Smoothing in Selected Neighborhoods," *IEEE Transactions on Systems, Man, and Cybernetics,* Vol. SMC-7, 1977, pp. 107–109.

Torre, V., and T. A. Poggio, "On Edge Detection," *Transactions on Pattern Analysis and Machine Intelligence,* Vol. PAMI-8, 1986, pp. 147–163.

Toriwaki, J-I., and T. Fukumura, "Extraction of Structural Information from Grey Pictures," *Computer Graphics and Image Processing,* Vol. 7, 1978, pp. 30–51.

Triendl, E. E., "How to Get the Edge into the Map," *Proceedings of the Fourth International Joint Conference on Pattern Recognition,* Tokyo, 1978, pp. 946–950.

Tukey, J. W. *Exploratory Data Analysis,* Addison-Wesley, Menlo Park, CA, 1971.

VanderBrug, G. J., "Semilinear Line Detectors," *Computer Graphics and Image Processing,* Vol. 4, 1975, pp. 287–293.

VanderBrug, G. J., "Line Detection in Satellite Imagery," *IEEE Transactions on Geoscience Electronics,* Vol. GE-14, 1976, pp. 37–43.

Verma, M. R., A. K. Majumdar, and B. Chatterjee, "Edge Detection in Fingerprints," *Pattern Recognition,* Vol. 20, 1987, pp. 513–523.

Van Vliet, L. J., I. T. Young, and G. L. Beckers, "A Nonlinear Laplace Operator as Edge Detector in Noisy Images," *Computer Vision, Graphics, and Image Processing,* Vol. 45, 1989, pp. 167–195.

Wallis, R. H., "An Approach for the Space Variant Restoration and Enhancement of Images," *Proceedings of the Symposium on Current Mathematical Problems in Image Scenes,* Monterey, CA, 1976, pp. 329–340.

Wang, D. C. C., A. H. Vagnucci, and C. C. Li, "Gradient Inverse Weighted Smoothing Scheme and the Evaluation of Its Performance," *Computer Graphics and Image Processing,* Vol. 15, 1981, pp. 167–181.

Wiejak, J. S., H. Buxton, and B. F. Buxton, "Convolution with Separable Masks for Early Image Processing," *Computer Vision, Graphics, and Image Processing,* Vol. 32, 1985, pp. 279–90.

Wilson, J. N. and G. X. Ritter, "Functional Specification of Neighborhoods in an Image Processing Language," *Proceedings of the SPIE International Conference on Image Processing,* The Hague, 1987, pp. 1–6.

Wilson, R., H. Knutson, and G. H. Granlund, "The Operational Definition of the Position of Line and Edge," *Proceedings of the Sixth International Conference on Pattern Recognition,* Munich, 1982, pp. 846–849.

Wojik, Z. M., "An Approach to the Recognition of Contours and Line-Shaped Objects," *Computer Vision, Graphics, and Image Processing,* Vol. 25, 1984, pp. 184–204.

Wong, R. Y., and E. L. Hall, "Edge Extraction of Radar and Optical Images," *Proceedings of the IEEE Conference on Pattern Recognition and Image Processing,* Chicago, 1979, pp. 150–153.

Xie, Z., and L. Wu, "The $\delta^2 G$ Performance in the Presence of Noise," *Proceedings of the Ninth International Conference on Pattern Recognition,* Rome, 1988, pp. 637–639.

Yachida, M., M. Ikeda, and S. Tsuji, "A Knowledge Directed Line Finder for Analysis of Complex Scenes," *Proceedings of the Fourth International Joint Conference on Artificial Intelligence,* Tokyo, 1979, pp. 984–991.

Yakimovsky, Y., "Boundary and Object Detection in Real World Images," *Journal of the ACM,* Vol. 23, 1976, pp. 599–618.

Yang, G. J., and T. S. Huang, "The Effect of Median Filtering on Edge Location Estimation," *Computer Graphics and Image Processing,* Vol. 15, 1981, pp. 224–245.

Yuille, A. L., and T. A. Poggio, "Scaling Theorems for Zero Crossings," *IEEE Transactions on Pattern Analysis and Machine Intelligence,* Vol. PAMI-8, 1986, pp. 15–25.

Zucker, S. W., and R. A. Hummel, "A Three-Dimensional Edge Operator," *IEEE Transactions on Pattern Analysis and Machine Intelligence,* Vol. PAMI-3, 1981, pp. 324–331.

Zucker, S. W., R. A. Hummel, and A. Rosenfeld, "An Application of Relaxation Labeling to Line and Curve Enhancement," *IEEE Transactions on Computers,* Vol. C-26, 1977, pp. 394–403.

Zucker, S. W., Y. G. Leclerc, and J. L. Mohammed, "Continuous Relaxation and Local Maxima Selection: Conditions for Equivalence," *IEEE Transactions on Pattern Analysis and Machine Intelligence,* Vol. PAMI-3, 1981, pp. 117–127.

8 THE FACET MODEL

8.1 Introduction

The facet model principle states that the image can be thought of as an underlying continuum or piecewise continuous gray level intensity surface. The observed digital image is a noisy, discretized sampling of a distorted version of this surface. Processing of the digital image for conditioning or labeling must first be defined in terms of what the conditioning or labeling means with respect to the underlying gray level intensity surface. To actually carry out the processing with the observed digital image requires both a model that describes what the general form of the surface would be in the neighborhood of any pixel if there were no noise and a model of what any noise and distortion, such as defocusing or monotonic gray level transformation, does to the assumed form. On the basis of the general form, processing proceeds by implicitly or explicitly estimating the free parameters of the general form for each neighborhood and then calculating the appropriate conditioning or labeling values on the basis of the definitions relative to the underlying gray level intensity surface. Graham (1962) and Prewitt (1970) were the first to adopt this point of view.

The commonly used general forms for the facet model include piecewise constant (flat facet model), piecewise linear (sloped facet model), piecewise quadratic, and piecewise cubic. In the flat model, each ideal region in the image is constant in gray level. In the sloped model, each ideal region has a gray level surface that is a sloped plane. Similarly, in the quadratic and cubic models, regions have gray level surfaces that are bivariate quadratic and cubic surfaces, respectively.

Given a noisy, defocused image and assuming one of these models, we must first estimate both the parameters of the underlying surface for a given neighborhood and the variance of the noise. We can then use these estimates in a variety of ways, including edge detection, line detection, corner detection, and noise filtering, to accomplish labeling and conditioning. In Section 8.2 we illustrate the use of the facet model principle in an application of determining relative maxima in a one-dimensional sense. In Section 8.3 we review the parameter estimation problem for the sloped facet model and in Section 8.4 we use the sloped facet model for peak noise removal. In Section 8.5, we illustrate how a facet model can be used to partition an image into regions each of whose gray level intensity surface is planar. In Section 8.6 we illustrate its use in the classic gradient edge detector application. Section 8.7 discusses the Bayesian approach to deciding whether or not an observed gradient magnitude is statistically significantly different from zero. Section 8.8 discusses the zero crossing of second derivational derivative edge detectors. Section 8.9 discusses the integrated directional derivative gradient operator. Section 8.10 discusses the facet approach to corner detection. Section 8.11 discusses using the facet approach to compute higher order isotropic derivative magnitudes. Section 8.12 discusses the determination of lines, which topographically are ridges and ravines, and Section 8.13 concludes with the labeling of every pixel into one of a variety of topographic categories, some of which are invariant under monotonic gray scale transformation.

8.2   Relative Maxima

To illustrate the facet model principle, we consider a simple labeling application, which is to detect and locate all relative maxima, to subpixel accuracy, from a one-dimensional observation sequence $f_1, f_2, \ldots, f_N$ taken on successive equally spaced points a unit distance apart. Relative maxima are defined to occur at points for which the first derivative is zero and the second derivative is negative.

To find the relative maxima, we can least-squares fit a quadratic function $\hat{c}m^2 + \hat{b}m + \hat{a}$, $-k \leq m \leq k$, to each group of $2k + 1$ successive observations, taking the origin of each fit to be the position of the middle observation in each group of $2k + 1$. Then we analytically determine if the fitted quadratic has a relative maximum close enough to the origin.

The squared fitting error ϵ_n^2 for the nth group of $2k + 1$ can be expressed by

$$\epsilon_n^2 = \sum_{m=-k}^{k} (\hat{c}m^2 + \hat{b}m + \hat{a} - f_{n+m})^2 \tag{8.1}$$

Taking partial derivatives of ϵ_n^2 with respect to the free parameters $\hat{a}, \hat{b}$, and $\hat{c}$ results in the following:

$$\begin{pmatrix} \frac{\partial \epsilon_n^2}{\partial \hat{a}} \\ \frac{\partial \epsilon_n^2}{\partial \hat{b}} \\ \frac{\partial \epsilon_n^2}{\partial \hat{c}} \end{pmatrix} = 2 \sum_{m=-k}^{k} \begin{pmatrix} \hat{c}m^2 + \hat{b}n + \hat{a} - f_{n+m} \\ (\hat{c}m^2 + \hat{b}m + \hat{a} - f_{n+m})m \\ (\hat{c}m^2 + \hat{b}m + \hat{a} - f_{n+m})m^2 \end{pmatrix} \tag{8.2}$$

Assuming $k = 1$, setting these partial derivatives to zero, and simplifying yields the matrix equation

$$\begin{pmatrix} 2 & 0 & 2 \\ 0 & 2 & 0 \\ 3 & 0 & 2 \end{pmatrix} \begin{pmatrix} \hat{a} \\ \hat{b} \\ \hat{c} \end{pmatrix} = \sum_{m=-1}^{1} \begin{pmatrix} m^2 f_{n+m} \\ m f_{n+m} \\ f_{n+m} \end{pmatrix}$$ (8.3)

from which

$$\hat{a} = f_n$$

$$\hat{b} = \frac{1}{2}(f_{n+1} - f_{n-1})$$ (8.4)

$$\hat{c} = \frac{1}{2}(f_{n-1} - 2f_n + f_{n+1})$$

The quadratic $y = \hat{c}x^2 + \hat{b}x + \hat{a}$ has relative extrema at $x_0 = -\hat{b}/2\hat{c}$, and the extremum is a relative maximum when $\hat{c} < 0$. The algorithm then amounts to the following:

1. Test whether $\hat{c} < 0$. If not, then there is no chance of maxima.
2. If $\hat{c} < 0$, compute $x_0 = -\hat{b}/2\hat{c}$.
3. If $|x_0| < \frac{1}{2}$, then mark the point $n + x_0$ as a relative maximum.

To see how well this algorithm will perform under conditions of additive independent Gaussian noise, suppose that the observed f_n can be modeled by

$$f_n = g_n + \xi_n$$ (8.5)

where g_n is the true underlying value of the nth point and satisfies $g_{n+m} = cm^2 + bm + a$ for $-k \le m \le k$; ξ_n is the noise; and f_n is the noisy observed value. We take ξ_n to be a normally distributed random variable with mean 0 and variance σ^2; ξ_n has $N(0, \sigma^2)$. In this case the computed variates $\hat{b}$ and $\hat{c}$ are normally distributed. We can compute the expected value and variance for $\hat{b}$ and $\hat{c}$.

$$E[b] = E\left[\frac{1}{2}(f_{n+1} - f_{n-1})\right]$$

$$= \frac{1}{2}E[g_{n+1} - g_{n-1} + \xi_{n+1} - \xi_{n-1}]$$

$$= \frac{1}{2}(g_{n+1} - g_{n-1}) = b$$ (8.6)

$$V[\hat{b}] = E\left[\left(\frac{1}{2}(f_{n+1} - f_{n-1}) - \frac{1}{2}(g_{n+1} - g_{n-1})\right)^2\right]$$

$$= E\left[\left(\frac{1}{2}(\xi_{n+1} - \xi_{n-1})\right)^2\right] = \frac{1}{4}E\left[\xi_{n+1}^2 - 2\xi_{n-1}\xi_{n+1} + \xi_{n-1}^2\right]$$

$$= \frac{1}{4}(\sigma^2 + 0 + \sigma^2) = \frac{\sigma^2}{2}$$ (8.7)

$$E[\hat{c}] = E\left[\frac{1}{2}(f_{n-1} - 2f_n + f_{n+1})\right]$$

$$= E\left[\frac{1}{2}(g_{n-1} - 2g_n + g_{n+1}) + \frac{1}{2}(\xi_{n-1} - 2\xi_n + \xi_{n+1})\right]$$

$$= \frac{1}{2}(g_{n-1} - 2g_n + g_{n+1}) = c \tag{8.8}$$

$$V[\hat{c}] = E\left[\left(\frac{1}{2}(f_{n-1} - 2f_n + f_{n+1}) - \frac{1}{2}(g_{n-1} - 2g_n + g_{n+1})\right)^2\right]$$

$$= E\left[\left(\frac{1}{2}(\xi_{n-1} - 2\xi_n + \xi_{n+1})\right)^2\right]$$

$$= \frac{1}{4}E\left[\xi_{n-1}^2 + 4\xi_n^2 + \xi_{n+1}^2 - 4\xi_{n-1}\xi_n + 2\xi_{n-1}\xi_{n+1} - 4\xi_n\xi_{n+1}\right]$$

$$= \frac{1}{4}(\sigma^2 + 4\sigma^2 + \sigma^2) = \frac{3}{2}\sigma^2 \tag{8.9}$$

Also, by examining the covariance we can determine the statistical dependence or independence of $\hat{b}$ and $\hat{c}$.

$$E\left\{\left[\hat{b} - \frac{1}{2}(g_{n+1} - g_{n+1})\right]\left[\hat{c} - \frac{1}{2}(g_{n-1} - 2g_n + g_{n+1})\right]\right\}$$

$$= E\left[\frac{1}{2}(\xi_{n+1} - \xi_{n-1})\frac{1}{2}(\xi_{n-1} - 2\xi_n + \xi_{n+1})\right] \tag{8.10}$$

$$= \frac{1}{4}E[\xi_{n+1}^2 - \xi_{n-1}^2] = \frac{1}{4}[E(\xi_{n+1}^2) - E(\xi_{n-1}^2)] = \frac{1}{4}(\sigma^2 - \sigma^2) = 0$$

Hence $\hat{b}$ and $\hat{c}$ are uncorrelated, and since each is a normally distributed variate, they are statistically independent.

Having determined that

$$\begin{pmatrix} \hat{b} \\ \hat{c} \end{pmatrix} \text{ has } N\left[\begin{pmatrix} b \\ c \end{pmatrix}, \frac{\sigma^2}{2}\begin{pmatrix} 1 & 0 \\ 0 & 3 \end{pmatrix}\right] \tag{8.11}$$

we can ask questions relating to the probability of missing a peak. One such question has the form: What is the probability that the estimated $\hat{c}$ is greater than zero, given the value of c?

$$\text{Prob }(\hat{c} > 0|c) = \int_{c=0}^{\infty} \frac{1}{\sqrt{2\pi}\sqrt{\frac{3}{2}}\sigma} e^{\frac{1}{2}\frac{(\hat{c}-c)^2}{\frac{3}{2}\sigma^2}} dc$$

$$= 1 - \phi\left(\frac{-c}{\sqrt{\frac{3}{2}}\sigma}\right) \tag{8.12}$$

Our answer indicates that when c is negative but close to zero $\left(\text{e.g.,}\ \frac{-\sqrt{3}}{2}\sigma < c < 0\right)$, the chance that the estimated $\hat{c}$ will be greater than zero is significant, and therefore a maximum could be missed.

In a similar manner, we can ask questions relating to the probability of declaring a false peak. One such question has the form: What is the probability that the estimated $\hat{c}$ is less than zero, given the value c?

$$\text{Prob}\ (\hat{c} < 0|c) = \phi\left(\frac{-c}{\sqrt{\frac{3}{2}}\sigma}\right)$$

(8.13)

Our answer indicates that when c is positive but close to zero

$$\left(\text{e.g.,}\ 0 < c < \sqrt{\frac{3}{2}}\sigma\right)$$

the chance that the estimated $\hat{c}$ will be less than zero is significant, and therefore a false maximum could occur. To limit the probability of false maxima, this answer suggests that instead of only requiring $\hat{c} < 0$, we can require that $\hat{c} < c_\alpha$ for a given negative c_α. By doing so, we can limit the probability that a false maximum can occur.

In general, for the relative maximum labeling procedure "label the a pixel as having a relative maximum if $\hat{c} < c_\alpha$ and $-\hat{b}/2\hat{c} < \frac{1}{2}$," the knowledge that

$$\begin{pmatrix} \hat{b} \\ \hat{c} \end{pmatrix}$$

has

$$N\left[\begin{pmatrix} b \\ c \end{pmatrix}, \frac{\sigma^2}{2}\begin{pmatrix} 1 & 0 \\ 0 & 3 \end{pmatrix}\right]$$

(8.14)

can be used to determine or bound the misdetection rate and the false-detection rate performance characteristics.

8.3   Sloped Facet Parameter and Error Estimation

In this discussion we employ a least-squares procedure both to estimate the parameters of the sloped facet model for a given two-dimensional rectangular neighborhood whose row index set is R and whose column index set is C and to estimate the noise variance. The facet parameter estimates are obtained independently for the central neighborhood of each pixel on the image. We assume that the coordinates of the given pixel are $(0,0)$ in its central neighborhood. We also assume that for each $(r,c)\ \epsilon\ R\times C$, the image function g is modeled by

$$g(r,c) = \alpha r + \beta c + \gamma + \eta(r,c)$$

(8.15)

where η is a random variable indexed on $R\times C$, which represents noise. We will assume that η is noise having mean 0 and variance σ^2 and that the noise for any two pixels is independent.

The least-squares procedure determines an $\hat{\alpha}$, $\hat{\beta}$, and $\hat{\gamma}$ that minimize the sum of the squared differences between the fitted surface and the observed one:

$$\epsilon^2 = \sum_{r \in R} \sum_{c \in C} [\hat{\alpha} r + \hat{\beta} c + \hat{\gamma} - g(r,c)]^2 \qquad (8.16)$$

Taking the partial derivatives of ϵ^2 and setting them to zero results in

$$\begin{pmatrix} \frac{\partial \epsilon^2}{\partial \hat{\alpha}} \\ \frac{\partial \epsilon^2}{\partial \hat{\beta}} \\ \frac{\partial \epsilon^2}{\partial \hat{\gamma}} \end{pmatrix} = 2 \sum_{r \in R} \sum_{c \in C} [\hat{\alpha} r + \hat{\beta} c + \hat{\gamma} - g(r,c)] \begin{pmatrix} r \\ c \\ 1 \end{pmatrix} = 0 \qquad (8.17)$$

Without loss of generality, we choose our coordinate system $R \times C$ so that the center of the neighborhood $R \times C$ has coordinates $(0,0)$. When the number of rows and columns is odd, the center pixel of the neighborhood has coordinates $(0,0)$. When the number of rows and columns is even, there is no pixel in the center, but the point where the corners of the four central pixels meet has coordinates $(0,0)$. In this case pixel centers will have coordinates of an integer plus a half.

The symmetry in the chosen coordinate system leads to

$$\sum_{r \in R} r = 0 \quad \text{and} \quad \sum_{c \in C} c = 0$$

Hence

$$\sum_r \sum_c \hat{\alpha} r^2 = \sum_r \sum_c rg(r,c)$$

$$\sum_r \sum_c \hat{\beta} c^2 = \sum_r \sum_c cg(r,c) \qquad (8.18)$$

$$\sum_r \sum_c \hat{\gamma} = \sum_r \sum_c g(r,c)$$

Solving for $\hat{\alpha}$, $\hat{\beta}$, and $\hat{\gamma}$, we obtain

$$\hat{\alpha} = \frac{\sum_r \sum_c rg(r,c)}{\sum_r \sum_c r^2}$$

$$\hat{\beta} = \frac{\sum_r \sum_c cg(r,c)}{\sum_r \sum_c c^2} \qquad (8.19)$$

$$\hat{\gamma} = \frac{\sum_r \sum_c g(r,c)}{\sum_r \sum_c 1}$$

Replacing $g(r,c)$ by $\alpha r + \beta c + \gamma + \eta(r,c)$ and simplifying the equations will allow us to see explicitly the dependence of $\hat{\alpha}$, $\hat{\beta}$, and $\hat{\gamma}$ on the noise. We obtain

$$\hat{\alpha} = \alpha + \frac{\sum_r \sum_c r\eta(r,c)}{\sum_r \sum_c r^2}$$

$$\hat{\beta} = \beta + \frac{\sum_r \sum_c c\eta(r,c)}{\sum_r \sum_c c^2}$$

$$\hat{\gamma} = \gamma + \frac{\sum_r \sum_c \eta(r,c)}{\sum_r \sum_c 1} \qquad (8.20)$$

From this it is apparent that $\hat{\alpha}, \hat{\beta}$, and $\hat{\eta}$ are unbiased estimators for α, β, and γ, respectively, and have variances

$$V[\hat{\alpha}] = \frac{\sigma^2}{\sum_r \sum_c r^2}$$

$$V[\hat{\beta}] = \frac{\sigma^2}{\sum_r \sum_c c^2}$$

$$V[\hat{\gamma}] = \frac{\sigma^2}{\sum_r \sum_c 1} \tag{8.21}$$

Normally distributed noise implies that $\hat{\alpha}$, $\hat{\beta}$, and $\hat{\gamma}$ are normally distributed. The independence of the noise implies that $\hat{\alpha}$, $\hat{\beta}$, and $\hat{\gamma}$ are independent because they are normal and that

$$E\left[(\hat{\alpha} - \alpha)(\hat{\beta} - \beta)\right] = E[(\hat{\alpha} - \alpha)(\hat{\gamma} - \gamma)] = E[\hat{\beta} - \beta)(\hat{\gamma} - \gamma)] = 0$$

as a straightforward calculation shows.

Examining the squared error residual ϵ^2, we find that

$$\epsilon^2 = \sum_r \sum_c \{(\hat{\alpha}r + \hat{\beta}c + \hat{\gamma}) - [\alpha r + \beta c + \gamma + \eta(r, c)]\}^2$$

$$= \sum_r \sum_c [(\hat{\alpha} - \alpha)^2 r^2 + (\hat{\beta} - \beta)^2 c^2 + (\hat{\gamma} - \gamma)^2 + \eta^2(r, c)$$

$$- 2(\hat{\alpha} - \alpha)r\eta(r, c) - 2(\hat{\beta} - \beta)c\eta(r, c) - 2(\hat{\gamma} - \gamma)\eta(r, c)] \tag{8.22}$$

Using the fact that

$$(\hat{\alpha} - \alpha) = \frac{\sum_r \sum_c r\eta(r, c)}{\sum_r \sum_c r^2}$$

$$(\hat{\beta} - \beta) = \frac{\sum_r \sum_c c\eta(r, c)}{\sum_r \sum_c c^2}$$

$$(\hat{\gamma} - \gamma) = \frac{\sum_r \sum_c \eta(r, c)}{\sum_r \sum_c 1} \tag{8.23}$$

we may substitute into the last three terms for ϵ^2 and obtain after simplification

$$\epsilon^2 = \sum_r \sum_c \eta^2(r, c) - (\hat{\alpha} - \alpha)^2 \sum_r \sum_c r^2 - (\hat{\beta} - \beta)^2 \sum_r \sum_c c^2 - (\hat{\gamma} - \gamma)^2 \sum_r \sum_c 1$$

Now notice that

$$\sum_r \sum_c \eta^2(r, c)$$

is the sum of the squares of

$$\sum_r \sum_c 1$$

independently distributed normal random variables with mean 0 and variance σ^2. Hence

$$\frac{\sum_r \sum_c \eta^2(r, c)}{\sigma^2}$$

is distributed as a chi-squared variate with

$$\sum_r \sum_c 1$$

degrees of freedom. Because $\hat{\alpha}$, $\hat{\beta}$, and $\hat{\gamma}$ are independent normals,

$$\frac{(\hat{\alpha} - \alpha)^2 \sum_r \sum_c r^2 + (\hat{\beta} - \beta)^2 \sum_r \sum_c c^2 + (\hat{\gamma} - \gamma)^2 \sum_r \sum_c 1}{\sigma^2} \quad (8.24)$$

is distributed as a chi-squared variate with three degrees of freedom. Therefore ϵ^2/σ^2 is distributed as a chi-squared variate with

$$\sum_r \sum_c 1 - 3$$

degrees of freedom. This means that

$$\epsilon^2 / (\sum_r \sum_c 1 - 3)$$

can be used as an unbiased estimator for σ^2.

The next section discusses the use of the estimated facet parameters for peak noise removal. Section 8.5 discusses the use of the estimated facet parameters in the labeling operation called gradient edge detection.

8.4   Facet-Based Peak Noise Removal

A peak noise pixel is defined as a pixel whose gray level intensity significantly differs from those of the neighborhood pixels. In order to measure the difference between a pixel and its neighbors, we need to estimate local gray level statistics in the neighborhood in terms of the sloped facet model and afterward compare those statistics with the current pixel gray level. We should note here that peak noise is judged not from the univariate marginal distribution of the gray level intensities in the neighborhood but from their spatial distribution. Figure 8.1 illustrates an example of the spatial distribution dependency of peak noise. In Fig. 8.1(a) and (b) the central pixel has the same gray level "5," and the neighborhood is composed of four values {1,2,3,4}. However, the peakedness of gray level intensity is different between them. It is difficult to judge that the center pixel in part (b) is peak noise, whereas it is easier in part (a). This indicates that the gray level spatial statistics are important.

Let N be a set of neighborhood pixels that does not contain the center pixel. Note that the use of the deleted neighborhood makes this facet approach different from that used earlier. Let n be the number of pixels in the neighborhood N. By choosing this neighborhood, we may estimate the difference between the observed value of the center pixel's (r_c, c_c) gray level intensity and the value estimated from the neighboring pixels according to the sloped facet model (Yasuka and Haralick, 1983).

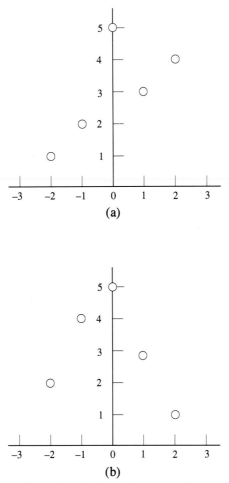

Figure 8.1 Spatial distribution dependency of peak noise.

Proceeding as before, we determine that the sloped facet model with the center-deleted neighborhood $N = R \times C - \{(0,0)\}$ is given by

$$g(r,c) = \alpha r + \beta c + \gamma + \eta(r,c) \text{ for } (r,c) \in N$$

where $\eta(r,c)$ is assumed to be independent additive Gaussian noise having mean 0 and variance σ^2. The least-squares procedure determines $\hat{\alpha}, \hat{\beta}$, and $\hat{\gamma}$, which minimize the sum of the squared differences between the fitted surface and the observed one:

$$\epsilon^2 = \sum_{(r,c) \in N} [\hat{\alpha} r + \hat{\beta} c + \hat{\gamma} - g(r,c)]^2$$

The minimizing $\hat{\alpha}, \hat{\beta}$, and $\hat{\gamma}$ are given by

$$\hat{\alpha} = \frac{\displaystyle\sum_{(r,c) \in N} r\, g(r,c)}{\displaystyle\sum_{(r,c) \in N} r^2}$$

$$\hat{\beta} = \frac{\displaystyle\sum_{(r,c)\in N} c\ g(r,c)}{\displaystyle\sum_{(r,c)\in N} c^2}$$

$$\hat{\gamma} = \frac{\displaystyle\sum_{(r,c)\in N} g(r,c)}{\#N}$$

At the center pixel of the neighborhood, the fitted value is $\hat{\gamma}$ and the observed value is $g(0,0)$. Under the hypothesis that $g(0,0)$ is not peak noise, $g(0,0) - \hat{\gamma}$ has a Gaussian distribution with mean 0 and variance $\sigma^2(1 + \frac{1}{\#N})$. Hence

$$\frac{g(0,0) - \hat{\gamma}}{\sigma\sqrt{1 + \frac{1}{\#N}}}$$

has mean 0 and variance 1. We have already obtained that ϵ^2/σ^2 has a chi-squared distribution with $\#N - 3$ degrees of freedom. Hence

$$t = \frac{g(0,0) - \hat{\gamma}}{\sqrt{(1 + \frac{1}{\#N})\epsilon^2}}$$

has a t-distribution with $\#N - 3$ degrees of freedom.

The center pixel is judged to be a peak noise pixel if a test of the hypothesis $g(0,0) = \hat{\gamma}$ rejects the hypothesis. Let $T_{N-3,p}$ be a number satisfying

$$P(t \le T_{\#N-3,p}) = 1 - p$$

Hence if $t > T_{\#N-3,p}$, the hypothesis of the equality of $g(0,0)$ and $\hat{\gamma}$ is rejected, and the output value for the center pixel is given by $\hat{\gamma}$. If $t \le T_{\#N-3,p}$, the hypothesis of the equality of $g(0,0)$ and γ is not rejected, and the output value for the center pixel is given by $g(0,0)$. A reasonable value for p is .05 to .01.

8.5   Iterated Facet Model

The iterated model for ideal image data assumes that the spatial domain of the image can be partitioned into connected regions called *facets*, each of which satisfies certain gray level and shape constraints. The gray levels in each facet must be a polynomial function of the row-column coordinates of the pixels in the facet. Hence if we consider the gray levels as composing a surface above the resolution cells of the facet, then for the ideal image having a degree-one polynomial function, the surface is a sloped plane. Thus the iterated sloped facet model would be an appropriate description of this specialized facet model.

The shape constraint is also simple: Each facet must be sufficiently smooth in shape. We assume that each region in the image can be exactly represented as the union of $K \times K$ blocks of pixels. The value of K associated with an image means that the narrowest part of each of its facets is at least as large as a $K \times K$ block of pixels. Hence images that can have large values of K have very smoothly shaped regions. Morphologically, we would say that the facet domains are open under a $K \times K$ structuring element.

To make these ideas precise, let R and C be the row and column index set for the spatial domain of an image. For any $(r,c) \in R \times C$, let $I(r,c)$ be the gray value of resolution cell (r,c) and let $B(r,c)$ be the $K \times K$ block of resolution cells centered around resolution cell (r,c). Let $\pi = \{\pi_1, \ldots, \pi_N\}$ be a partition of the spatial domain of $R \times C$ into its facets.

In the iterated sloped facet model, for every resolution cell $(r,c) \in \pi_n$, there exists a resolution cell $(i,j) \in R \times C$ such that

1. Shape region constraint: $(r,c) \in B(i,j) \subseteq \pi_n$;

2. Region gray level constraint: $I(r,c) = \alpha_n r + \beta_n c + \gamma_n$.

An observed image J differs from its corresponding ideal image I by the addition of random stationary noise having zero mean and covariance matrix proportional to a specified one.

$$J(r,c) = I(r,c) + \eta(r,c)$$

where

$$E[\eta(r,c)] = 0$$
$$E[\eta(r,c)\eta(r',c')] = k\sigma(r - r', c - c')$$

The flat facet model of Tomita and Tsuji (1977) and Nagao and Matsuyama (1979) differs from the sloped facet model only in that the coefficients α_n and β_n are assumed to be zero and Nagao and Matsuyama use a more generalized shape constraint, which is also suitable here.

The iterations generate images satisfying the facet form. The procedure has been proved to converge (Haralick and Watson, 1981) and has the following important properties: In a coordinated and parallel manner, the strong influence the weak in their neighborhoods, thereby causing the weak to become consistent with the strong.

The facet model suggests the following simple nonlinear iterative procedure to operate on the image until the image of ideal form is produced. Each resolution cell is contained in K^2 different $K \times K$ blocks. The gray level distribution in each of these blocks can be fit by a polynomial model. One of the K^2 blocks has the smallest error of fit. Set the output gray value to be that gray value fitted by the block having the smallest error of fit. For the flat facet model, this amounts to computing the variance for each $K \times K$ block in which a pixel participates. The output gray value is then the mean value of the block having the smallest variance (Tomita and Tsuji, 1977) and Nagao and Matsuyama (1979).

For the sloped facet model, the procedure amounts to fitting a sloped plane to each of the blocks in which a given resolution cell participates and outputting the fitted gray value of the given resolution cell from the block having the lowest fitting error.

The sloped facet model relaxation procedure examines each of the $K^2, K \times K$ blocks to which a pixel (r,c) belongs. For each block, a block error can be computed

8	5	2
5	2	-1
2	-1	-4

$\hat{J}(-1,-1)$

5	5	5
2	2	2
-1	-1	-1

$\hat{J}(-1,0)$

2	5	8
-1	2	5
-4	-1	2

$\hat{J}(-1,1)$

5	2	-1
5	2	-1
5	2	-1

$\hat{J}(0,-1)$

2	2	2
2	2	2
2	2	2

$\hat{J}(0,0)$

-1	2	5
-1	2	5
-1	2	5

$\hat{J}(0,1)$

2	-1	-4
5	2	-1
8	5	2

$\hat{J}(1,-1)$

-1	-1	-1
2	2	2
5	5	5

$\hat{J}(1,0)$

-4	-1	2
-1	2	5
2	5	8

$\hat{J}(1,1)$

Figure 8.2 The 3×3 linear estimators of a pixel's gray level for the nine different 3×3 neighborhoods in which the pixel participates. If the pixel's position is (i,j) in the neighborhood, the estimate is $\hat{J}(i,j)$. Each mask must be normalized by dividing by 18.

by using

$$\epsilon^2 = \sum_{r=-L}^{L} \sum_{c=-L}^{L} [\hat{J}(r,c) - J(r,c)]^2$$

where $\hat{J}(r,c) = \hat{\alpha}r + \hat{\beta}c + \hat{\gamma}$ is the least-squares fit to the block.

One of the $K \times K$ blocks will have the lowest error. Let the fit of the block having the smallest residual error in which the given pixel $l(r,c)$ participates have fitting function $\hat{J}$. Let (r^*, c^*) be the coordinates of the given pixel (r,c) in terms of the coordinate system of the block having the smallest residual error. The output gray value at pixel (r,c) is then given by $\hat{J}(r^*, c^*)$.

Figure 8.2 illustrates how replacing the pixel's value with the fitted value where the fitted value depends on the block having the smallest residual error is equivalent to replacing the pixel's value with a value that is a linear combination of pixel values coming from the best-fitting block.

8.6   Gradient-Based Facet Edge Detection

The facet edge finder regards the digital picture function as a sampling of the underlying function f, where some kind of random noise has been added to the true function values. To do this, the edge finder must assume some parametric form for the underlying function f, use the sampled brightness values of the digital picture function to estimate the parameters, and finally make decisions regarding the locations of discontinuities and the locations of relative extrema of partial derivatives based on the estimated values of the parameters.

Of course, it is impossible to determine the true locations of discontinuities in value directly from a sampling of the function values. The locations are estimated analytically after doing function approximation. Sharp discontinuities can reveal themselves in high values for estimates of first partial derivatives. This is the basis for gradient-based facet edge detection.

Suppose that our model of the ideal image is one in which each object part is imaged as a region that is homogeneous in gray level. In this case the boundary between object parts will manifest itself as jumps in gray level between successive pixels on the image. A small neighborhood on the image that can be divided into two parts by a line passing through the middle of the neighborhood and in which all the pixels on one side of the line have one gray level is a neighborhood in which the dividing line is indeed an edge line. When such a neighborhood is fitted with the sloped facet model, $\hat{\alpha} r + \hat{\beta} c + \hat{\gamma}$, a gradient magnitude of

$$\sqrt{\hat{\alpha}^2 + \hat{\beta}^2}$$

will result. The gradient magnitude will be proportional to the gray level jump. On the other hand, if the region is entirely contained within a homogeneous area, then the true surface $\alpha r + \beta c + \gamma$ will have $\alpha = \beta = 0$, and the fitted sloped facet model $\hat{\alpha} r + \hat{\beta} c + \hat{\gamma}$ will produce a value of

$$\sqrt{\hat{\alpha}^2 + \hat{\beta}^2}$$

which is near zero. Hence it is reasonable for edge detectors to use the estimated gradient magnitude

$$\sqrt{\hat{\alpha}^2 + \hat{\beta}^2}$$

as the basis for edge detection. Such edge detectors are called gradient-based edge detectors. There are other kinds of edge detectors, such as zero-crossing ones. A discussion of how the facet model can be used to determine zero crossings of second directional derivatives as edges can be found in Section 8.8.

The idea of fitting linear surfaces for edge detection is not new. Roberts (1965) employed an operator commonly called the Roberts gradient to determine edge strength in a 2×2 window in a blocks–world scene analysis problem. Prewitt (1970) used a quadratic fitting surface to estimate the parameters α and β in a 3×3 window for automatic leukocyte cell scan analysis. The resulting values for $\hat{\alpha}$ and $\hat{\beta}$ are the same for the quadratic or linear fit. O'Gorman and Clowes (1976) discussed the general fitting idea. Merò and Vamos (1976) used the fitting idea to find lines on a binary image. Hueckel (1973) used the fitting idea with low-frequency polar-form Fourier basis functions on a circular disk in order to detect step edges.

The fact that the Roberts gradient arises from a linear fit over the 2×2 neighborhood is easy to see. Let

$$
\begin{array}{cc}
a & b \\
c & d
\end{array}
$$

be the four gray level levels in the 2×2 window whose local spatial coordinates for pixel centers are

$$\left(-\frac{1}{2}, -\frac{1}{2}\right) \qquad \left(-\frac{1}{2}, \frac{1}{2}\right)$$
$$\left(\frac{1}{2}, -\frac{1}{2}\right) \qquad \left(\frac{1}{2}, \frac{1}{2}\right)$$

The Roberts gradient is defined by $\sqrt{(a - d)^2 + (b - c)^2}$. The least-squares fit for α and β is

$$\hat{\alpha} = \frac{1}{2}[(c + d) - (a + b)] \quad \text{and} \quad \hat{\beta} = \frac{1}{2}[(b + d) - (a + c)] \tag{8.25}$$

The gradient, which is the slope in the steepest direction, has magnitude $\sqrt{\hat{\alpha}^2 + \hat{\beta}^2}$.

$$\begin{aligned}
\sqrt{\hat{\alpha}^2 + \hat{\beta}^2} &= \frac{1}{2}\sqrt{[(c + d) - (a + b)]^2 + [(b + d)^2 - (a + c)]^2} \\
&= \frac{1}{2}\sqrt{2(a - d)^2 + 2(b - c)^2} \\
&= \sqrt{(a - d)^2 + (b - c)^2}/\sqrt{2} \tag{8.26}
\end{aligned}$$

which is exactly $1/\sqrt{2}$ times the Roberts gradient.

The quick Roberts gradient value is given by $|a - d| + |b - c|$. Now since $|x| + |y| = \max\{|x + y|, |x - y|\}$,

$$\begin{aligned}
|a - d| + |b - c| &= \max\ \{|a - d + b - c|, |a - d - b + c|\} \\
&= \max\ \{|-a + d - b + c|, |-a + d + b - c|\} \\
&= \max\ \{|2\hat{\alpha}|, |2\hat{\beta}|\} \tag{8.27}
\end{aligned}$$

There results

$$\max\{|\hat{\alpha}|, |\hat{\beta}|\} = \frac{1}{2}[|a - d| + |b - c|] \tag{8.28}$$

Hence the quick Roberts gradient is related to the parameters of the fitted sloped surface.

Finally, the max Roberts gradient is also related to the parameters of the fitted sloped surface. The max Roberts gradient value is defined by $\max\{|a - d|, |b - c|\}$. Since $\max\{|u|, |v|\} = \left|\frac{u+v}{2}\right| + \left|\frac{u-v}{2}\right|$,

$$\begin{aligned}
\max\{|a - d|, |b - c|\} &= \left|\frac{a - d + b - c}{2}\right| + \left|\frac{a - d - b + c}{2}\right| \\
&= \left|\frac{-a + d - b + c}{2}\right| + \left|\frac{-a + d + b - c}{2}\right| \\
&= |\hat{\alpha}| + |\hat{\beta}| \tag{8.29}
\end{aligned}$$

The most interesting question in the use of the estimated gradient $\sqrt{\hat{\alpha}^2 + \hat{\beta}^2}$ as an edge detector is, How large must the gradient be in order to be considered significantly different from zero? To answer this question, we begin by noting that $\hat{\alpha}$ is a normally distributed variate with mean α and variance

$$\sigma^2 / \sum_r \sum_c r^2$$

that $\hat{\beta}$ is a normally distributed variate with mean β and variance

$$\sigma^2 / \sum_r \sum_c c^2$$

and that $\hat{\alpha}$ and $\hat{\beta}$ are independent. Hence

$$\frac{(\hat{\alpha} - \alpha)^2 \sum_r \sum_c r^2 + (\hat{\beta} - \beta)^2 \sum_r \sum_c c^2}{\sigma^2}$$

is distributed as a chi-square variate with two degrees of freedom. From this it follows that to test the hypothesis of no edge under the assumption that $\alpha = \beta = 0$, we use the statistic G:

$$G = \frac{\hat{\alpha}^2 \sum_r \sum_c r^2 + \hat{\beta}^2 \sum_r \sum_c c^2}{\sigma^2}$$

which is distributed as a chi-squared variate with two degrees of freedom. If the statistic G has a high enough value, then we reject the hypothesis that there is no edge.

If the neighborhood used to estimate the facet is square, then

$$\sum_r \sum_c r^2 = \sum_r \sum_c c^2 \qquad (8.30)$$

so that the test statistic is a multiple of the estimated squared gradient magnitude $\hat{\alpha}^2 + \hat{\beta}^2$. For neighborhood sizes greater than 3×3, such an edge operator is a generalization of the Prewitt gradient edge operator. However, by knowing the conditional distribution given no edge, it becomes easier to choose a threshold. For example, suppose we want the edge detector to work with a controlled false-alarm rate. The false-alarm rate is the conditional probability that the edge detector classifies a pixel as an edge given that the pixel is not an edge. Suppose the false-alarm rate is to be held to 1%. Then since $P(\chi_2^2 > 9.21) = .01$, the threshold we must use must be at least 9.21.

Notice that, other things being equal, as the neighborhood size gets bigger, a fixed value of squared gradient becomes more statistically significant. Hence small gradient magnitudes estimated in small neighborhoods may not be statistically significant, but small gradient magnitudes may be statistically significant in large neighborhoods. Also notice that, other things being equal, the greater the noise variance, the greater the gradient magnitude must be in order to be statistically significant.

To use this technique, we must know the noise variance σ^2. Fortunately we can obtain a good estimate of σ^2. Each neighborhood's normalized squared residual error

$$\frac{\epsilon^2}{(\sum_r \sum_c 1 - 3)}$$

can constitute an estimator for σ^2. This estimator is available for each neighborhood of the image. Because there are usually thousands of pixels in the image, the average of $\epsilon^2 / (\sum_r \sum_c 1 - 3)$ taken over all the neighborhoods of the image is a very good and stable estimator of σ^2 if it can be assumed that the noise variance is the same in each neighborhood. If ϵ_n^2 represents the squared residual fitting error from the nth neighborhood and the image has N such neighborhoods, then we may use

$$\hat{\sigma}^2 = \frac{\frac{1}{N} \sum_{n=1}^{N} \epsilon_n^2}{(\sum_r \sum_c 1 - 3)} \qquad (8.31)$$

in place of σ^2. Hence our test statistic G becomes

$$G = \frac{\hat{\alpha}^2 \sum_r \sum_c r^2 + \hat{\beta}^2 \sum_r \sum_c c^2}{\hat{\sigma}^2} \qquad (8.32)$$

Under the hypothesis of no edge, G, being the ratio of two chi-squared statistics, would have an F distribution. But because the effective number of degrees of freedom of $\hat{\sigma}^2$ is so high, despite the dependencies among the ϵ_n, G has essentially a chi-squared distribution with two degrees of freedom. Thus if we wanted to detect edges and be assured that the false-alarm rate (the conditional probability of assigning a pixel as an edge given that it is not an edge) is less than p_o, we would use a threshold of θ_o, where $P(\chi_2^2 \geq \theta_o) = p_o$.

Figure 8.3 (upper left) shows a controlled 100×100 image having a disk of diameter 63. The interior of this disk has a gray level of 200. The background of the disk has a gray level of 0. Independent Gaussian noise having mean 0 and standard deviation 40, 50, and 75 is added to the controlled image. The noisy images are shown in the other parts of Fig. 8.3.

A sloped facet model is fitted to each 5×5 neighborhood of each image and its $\hat{\alpha}$, $\hat{\beta}$, and ϵ^2 are computed. For the ideal image of Fig. 8.3 (upper left), the average

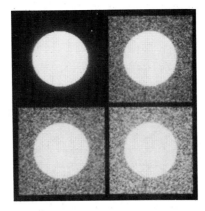

Figure 8.3 (Upper left), Controlled disk (background having value 0, disk having value 200) and noisy disks; (upper right), noise standard deviation of 40; (lower left), noise standard deviation of 50; (lower right), noise standard deviation of 75.

0	0	0	0	0
0	0	0	0	0
0	0	0	0	0
0	0	0	0	200
0	200	200	200	200

(a)

-64	-48	-32	-16	0
-28	-12	4	20	36
8	24 -	40	56	72
44	60	76	92	108
80	96	112	128	144

(b)

64	48	32	16	0
28	12	-4	-20	-36
-8	-24	-40	-56	-72
-44	-60	-76	-92	92
-80	104	88	72	56

(c)

Figure 8.4 (a) Neighborhood for which the slope fit is a relatively bad approximation. The fit produces an $\hat{\alpha} = 36$, $\hat{\beta} = 16$, and $\hat{\gamma} = 40$. (b) Slope-fitted neighborhood. (c) Residual fitting errors. The total squared error from (c) is 82,400. This divided by the degrees of freedom, $25 - 3 = 22$, yields an average squared error of 3746. The square root of 3746 is about 61.2, which represents the standard deviation of the residual fitting errors.

squared residual fitting error ϵ^2, the average being taken over all neighborhoods, is 302.33. This corresponds to a standard deviation of about 17.4, which is 8.7% of the dynamic range of the image.

Obviously in the noiseless image the fit will be perfect for all 5×5 neighborhoods that are entirely contained in the background or in the disk. The error must come from neighborhoods that contain some pixels from the background and some from the disk. In these neighborhoods the sloped fit is only an approximation. One neighborhood having the worst fit is shown in Fig. 8.4. The sloped fit there has an average squared residual error of 3746. The standard deviation of fitting error is then 61.2, which represents 30.6% of the dynamic range.

For the noisy image of Fig. 8.3 (upper right), the standard deviation of the fitting error is $\sigma = 77.3$. This is just a little higher than the standard deviation of the noise because it takes into account the extent to which the data do not fit the model. In fact, assuming that the imperfectedness of the model and the noise are independent, we would expect to find a standard deviation of $\sqrt{17.4^4 + 75^2} = 77$, which is close to the 77.3 measured.

Figure 8.5 (upper left) shows edges obtained when the statistic G computed on the ideal image of Fig. 8.3 is thresholded at the value 120. Since $\hat{\sigma}^2 = 302.33$ and for a 5×5 neighborhood $\sum_r \sum_c r^2 = \sum_r \sum_c c^2 = 50$, this corresponds to selecting all neighborhoods having slopes greater than 26.94. The other parts of Fig. 8.5 show the edges obtained when a 5×5 sloped facet model is employed and when the statistic G computed from each neighborhood of the noisy image of Fig. 8.3 (lower right) is thresholded at 4, 8, and 11. Since $\hat{\sigma}^2 = 5975.3$ for the

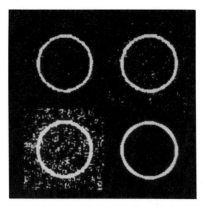

Figure 8.5 (Upper left), Edges obtained when the statistic G computed by using 5×5 neighborhoods on the ideal image of Fig. 8.3a is thresholded at the value 120; (upper right) edges obtained when the statistic G computed using 5×5 neighborhoods on the noisy image of Fig. 8.3 (lower right) is thresholded at the value 4; (lower left) and (lower right) thresholds of 8 and 11.

noisy image, a threshold of 8 corresponds to selecting all neighborhoods having slopes greater than 30.92. That is, $\frac{50(\hat{\alpha}^2 + \hat{\beta}^2)}{5975.3} > 8$ implies

$$\sqrt{\hat{\alpha}^2 + \hat{\beta}^2} > 30.92$$

These thresholds of 4, 8, and 11 guarantee (under the conditions of independent Gaussian noise) that the false-alarm rates must be less than .1353, .01832, and .0041, respectively. The observed false-alarm rates for these thresholds are .1231, .0164, and .0042, respectively. The corresponding misdetection rates are .0205, .0820, and .1598.

As just mentioned, corresponding to each possible threshold is a false-alarm rate and a misdetection rate. The misdetection rate is the conditional probability that a pixel is assigned "no edge" given that it is actually an "edge" pixel. One way to characterize the performance of an edge detector is to plot its false-alarm rate as a function of the misdetection rate in a controlled experiment. Such a plot is called an operating curve. Figure 8.6 shows two operating curves for the sloped facet edge detector. The higher one corresponds to a noisy disk with noise standard deviation 75. The lower one corresponds to a noisy disk with noise standard deviation 50. Notice that as the false-alarm rate decreases, the misdetection rate increases; as the false-alarm rate increases, the misdetection rate decreases. In a noisy world the false-alarm and misdetection rates cannot both be made arbitrarily small.

If we cannot assume that the noise variance is the same in each neighborhood, then the estimator using the average of the normalized squared residual errors for σ^2 is not proper. In this case we can use the local neighborhood residual squared error $\epsilon^2 / (\sum_r \sum_c 1 - 3)$ as an estimate of the variance in each neighborhood. However, this estimate is not as stable as the average squared residual error. It does have a higher variance than the estimate based on the average of the local variances, and it has a much lower number of degrees of freedom. Here, to test the hypothesis

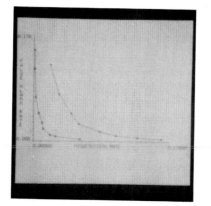

Figure 8.6 Two operating curves for the 5×5 sloped facet gradient edge detector. The higher one corresponds to a noisy disk with noise standard deviation of 75 and the upper one corresponds to a noisy disk with noise standard deviation of 50.

of no edge for the flat-world assumption, $\alpha = \beta = 0$, we use the ratio

$$F = \frac{\dfrac{\hat{\alpha}^2 \sum_r \sum_c r^2 + \hat{\beta}^2 \sum_r \sum_c c^2}{2}}{\dfrac{\epsilon^2}{\sum_r \sum_c 1 - 3}} \tag{8.33}$$

which has an F distribution with

$$\left(2, \sum_r \sum_c 1 - 3 \right)$$

degrees of freedom, and reject the hypothesis for large values of F.

Again notice that F may be regarded as a significance or reliability measure associated with the existence of a nonzero-sloped region in the domain $R \times C$. It is essentially proportional to the squared gradient of the region normalized by

$$\frac{\epsilon^2}{(\sum_r \sum_c 1 - 3)}$$

which is a random variable whose expected value is σ^2, the variance of the noise.

EXAMPLE 8.1

Consider the following 3×3 region:

3	5	9
4	7	7
0	3	7

Then $\hat{\alpha} = -1.17$, $\hat{\beta} = 2.67$, and $\hat{\gamma} = 5.00$. The estimated gray level surface is given by $\hat{\alpha}r + \hat{\beta}r + \hat{\gamma}$. Sampling it at the center of each pixel produces

3.50	6.16	8.83
2.33	5.00	7.67
1.17	3.83	6.50

The difference between the estimated and the observed surfaces is the error, and it is

0.50	1.17	−0.17
−1.67	−2.00	0.67
1.17	0.83	−0.50

From this we can compute the squared error $\epsilon^2 = 11.19$. The F statistic is then

$$\frac{[(-1.17)^2 \cdot 6 + (2.67)^2 \cdot 6]/2}{11.19/6} = 13.67 \qquad (8.34)$$

If we were compelled to make a hard decision about the significance of the observed slope in the given 3×3 region, we would probably call it a nonzero-sloped region, since the probability of a region with true zero slope giving an $F_{2,6}$ statistic of value less than 10.6 is 0.99. Because 13.67 is greater than 10.6, we are assured that the probability of calling the region nonzero sloped when it is in fact

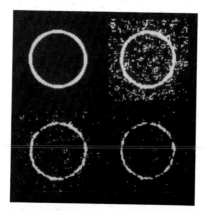

Figure 8.7 Edges obtained under a 5×5 sloped facet model using the F statistic. (Upper left) Thresholded F statistic from the noiseless disk; (upper right) F statistic image of the noisy disk of Fig. 8.3 (lower right) thresholded at 2.32; (lower left) and (lower right) thresholds of 5.04 and 7.06.

zero sloped is much less than 1%. The statistically oriented reader will recognize the test as a 1% significance level test.

Figure 8.7 shows the edges obtained when a 5×5 sloped facet model is employed and when the F statistic computed from each neighborhood of the noisy image of Fig. 8.3 (lower right) is thresholded at 2.32, 5.04, and 7.06. These thresholds should guarantee (under conditions of independent Gaussian noise) that the false-alarm rates are less than .1218, .0158, and .0042, respectively. These thresholds produce observed false alarm rates of .1236, .0165, and .0042, indicating these were small but negligible departures from the independent Gaussian assumptions. Since these observed false-alarm rates are almost identical to the observed false-alarm rates from the chi-square tests of Fig. 8.5, we may compare the corresponding misidentification rates. The observed misidentification rates for the F-test were .0792, .3224, and .5137, all of which are considerably higher than the observed misidentification rates of the corresponding chi-square tests. It is obvious from a comparison of these images that the edge noise is worse in the F-tests compared with the chi-square tests. All this is to be expected because the noise meets the assumption of the chi-square test, and the more one is able to make correct assumptions about reality, the better the results ought to be when the appropriate statistical test is used.

8.7   Bayesian Approach to Gradient Edge Detection

The Bayesian approach (Zuniga and Haralick, 1988a) to the decision of whether or not an observed gradient magnitude G is statistically significant and therefore participates in some edge is to decide there is an edge (statistically significant gradient) when,

$$P(\text{edge} \mid G) > P(\text{nonedge} \mid G)$$

By definition of conditional probability,

$$P(\text{edge } |G) = \frac{P(G| \text{ edge })P(\text{ edge })}{P(G)}$$

$$P(\text{ nonedge } |G) = \frac{P(G| \text{ nonedge })P(\text{ nonedge })}{P(G)} \qquad (8.35)$$

Hence a decision for edge is made whenever

$$P(G| \text{ edge })P(\text{ edge }) > P(G| \text{ nonedge })P(\text{ nonedge})$$

From the previous section, $P(G| \text{ nonedge})$ is known to be the density function of a χ_2^2 variate. But $P(G| \text{ edge })$ is not known.

It is possible to infer $P(G| \text{ edge })$ from the observed image data since $P(G)$, the density function of the histogram of observed gradient magnitude, is easily calculated.

Now

$$P(G) = P(G| \text{ edge })P(\text{ edge }) + P(G| \text{ nonedge })P(\text{ nonedge }) \qquad (8.36)$$

Hence

$$P(G| \text{ edge }) = \frac{P(G) - P(G| \text{ nonedge })P(\text{ nonedge })}{P(\text{ edge })}$$

$$= \frac{P(G) - P(G| \text{ nonedge })P(\text{ nonedge })}{1 - P(\text{ nonedge })} \qquad (8.37)$$

This means that once the prior probability for nonedge is specified, the density function for $P(G| \text{ edge })$ can be computed. Once $P(G| \text{ edge })$ is known, the appropriate threshold t for G is determined as that value t for which

$$P(t| \text{ edge })P(\text{ edge }) = P(t| \text{ nonedge })P(\text{ nonedge }) \qquad (8.38)$$

This relation, together with the relation for $P(G| \text{ edge })$, implies that the threshold t must satisfy

$$P(t) = 2P(t| \text{ nonedge })P(\text{ nonedge}) \qquad (8.39)$$

Here $P(t)$ is the observed density for the test statistic G evaluated at t, $P(t| \text{ nonedge})$ is the value of the density function of a χ_2^2 variate evaluated at t, and $P(\text{ nonedge})$ is a user-specified prior probability of nonedge. For many images values of .9 to .95 are reasonable.

8.8   Zero-Crossing Edge Detector

The gradient edge detector looks for high values of estimated first derivatives. The zero-crossing edge detector looks for relative maxima in the value of the first derivative taken across a possible edge. This permits the resulting edge to be thin and even localized to subpixel accuracy. In what follows we assume that in each neighborhood of the image, the underlying gray level intensity function f takes the form

$$f(r,c) = k_1 + k_2 r + k_3 c + k_4 r^2 + k_5 rc + k_6 c^2$$
$$+ k_7 r^3 + k_8 r^2 c + k_9 rc^2 + k_{10} c^3 \qquad (8.40)$$

As just mentioned, the zero-crossing edge detector places edges not at locations of high gradient but at locations of spatial gradient maxima. More precisely, a pixel is marked as an edge pixel if in its immediate area there is a zero crossing of the second directional derivative taken in the direction of the gradient (Haralick, 1982) and if the slope of the zero crossing is negative. Thus this kind of edge detector will respond to weak but spatially peaked gradients.

The underlying functions from which the directional derivatives are computed are easy to represent as linear combinations of the polynomials in any polynomial basis set. A polynomial basis set that permits the independent estimation of each coefficient would be the easiest to use. Such a basis is the discrete orthogonal polynomials.

8.8.1 Discrete Orthogonal Polynomials

The discrete orthogonal polynomial basis set of size N has polynomials from degree zero through degree $N - 1$. These unique polynomials are sometimes called the *discrete Chebyshev polynomials* (Beckmann, 1973). Here we show how to construct them for one or two variables.

Let the discrete integer index set R be symmetric in the sense that $r \in R$ implies $-r \in R$. Let $P_n(r)$ be the nth order polynomial. We define the construction technique for discrete orthogonal polynomials iteratively.

Define $P_0(r) = 1$. Suppose $P_0(r), \ldots, P_{n-1}(r)$ have been defined. In general, $P_n(r) = r^n + a_{n-1}r^{n-1} + \ldots + a_1 r + a_0$. $P_n(r)$ must be orthogonal to each polynomial $P_0(r), \ldots, P_{n-1}(r)$. Hence we must have the n equations

$$\sum_{r \in R} P_k(r)(r^n + a_{n-1}r^{n-1} + \ldots + a_1 r + a_0) = 0, \quad k = 0, \ldots, n - 1 \quad (8.41)$$

These equations are linear equations in the unknown $a_0, \ldots, a_{n-1}$ and are easily solved by standard techniques.

The first five polynomial function formulas are

$$P_0(r) = 1$$
$$P_1(r) = r$$
$$P_2(r) = r^2 - \frac{\mu_2}{\mu_0}$$
$$P_3(r) = r^3 - \frac{\mu_4}{\mu_2}r$$
$$P_4(r) = r^4 + \frac{(\mu_2\mu_4 - \mu_0\mu_6)r^2 + (\mu_2\mu_6 - \mu_4^2)}{\mu_0\mu_4 - \mu_2^2} \quad (8.42)$$

where

$$\mu_k = \sum_{s \in R} s^k \quad (8.43)$$

The discrete orthogonal polynomials defined on symmetric sets can be recursively generated (Forsythe, 1957) by the relation

$$P_{i+1}(r) = rP_i(r) - \beta_i P_{i-1}(r)$$

where

$$\beta_i = \frac{\sum_{r \in R} r P_i(r) P_{i-1}(r)}{\sum_{r \in R} P_{i-1}(r)^2}$$

$$P_0(r) = 1 \quad \text{and} \quad P_1(r) = r$$

8.8.2   Two-Dimensional Discrete Orthogonal Polynomials

Two-dimensional discrete orthogonal polynomials can be created from two sets of one-dimensional discrete orthogonal polynomials by taking tensor products. Let R and C be index sets satisfying the symmetry condition $r \in R$ implies $-r \in R$ and $c \in C$ implies $-c \in C$. Let $\{P_0(r), \ldots, P_N(r)\}$ be a set of discrete polynomials on R. Let $\{Q_0(c), \ldots, Q_M(c)\}$ be a set of discrete polynomials on C. Then the set $\{P_0(r)Q_0(c), \ldots, P_n(r)Q_m(c), \ldots, P_N(r)Q_M(c)\}$ is a set of discrete polynomials on $R \times C$.

The proof of this fact is easy. Consider whether $P_i(r)Q_j(c)$ is orthogonal to $P_n(r)Q_m(c)$ when $n \neq i$ or $m \neq j$. Then

$$\sum_{r \in R} \sum_{c \in C} P_i(r)Q_j(c)P_n(r)Q_m(c) = \sum_{r \in R} P_i(r)P_n(r) \sum_{c \in C} Q_j(c)Q_m(c) \qquad (8.44)$$

Since by assumption $n \neq i$ or $m \neq j$, the first or second sum must be zero, thereby proving the orthogonality.

Some one- and two-dimensional discrete orthogonal polynomials are as follows:

Index Set	Discrete Orthogonal Polynomial Set
$\{-\frac{1}{2}, \frac{1}{2}\}$	$\{1, r\}$
$\{-1, 0, 1\}$	$\{1, r, r^2 - \frac{2}{3}\}$
$\{-\frac{3}{2}, -\frac{1}{2}, \frac{1}{2}, \frac{3}{2}\}$	$\{1, r, r^2 - \frac{5}{4}, r^3 - \frac{41}{20}\}$
$\{-2, -1, 0, 1, 2\}$	$\{1, r, r^2 - 2, r^3 - \frac{17}{5}, r^4 + 3r^2 + \frac{72}{35}\}$
$\{-1, 0, 1\} \times \{-1, 0, 1\}$	$\{1, r, c, r^2 - \frac{2}{3}, rc, c^2 - \frac{2}{3}, r(c^2 - \frac{2}{3}),$ $c(r^2 - \frac{2}{3}), (r^2 - \frac{2}{3})(c^2 - \frac{2}{3})\}$

8.8.3   Equal-Weighted Least-Squares Fitting Problem

Let an index set R with the symmetry property $r \in R$ implies $-r \in R$ be given. Let the number of elements in R be N. Using the construction technique just described, we may construct the set $\{P_0(r), \ldots, P_{N-1}(r)\}$ of discrete orthogonal polynomials over R. Using the tensor product technique also described, we can construct discrete orthogonal polynomials over a two-dimensional neighborhood.

For each $r \in R$, let a data value $d(r)$ be observed. The exact fitting problem is to determine coefficients $a_0, \ldots, a_{N-1}$ such that

$$d(r) = \sum_{n=0}^{N-1} a_n P_n(r) \tag{8.45}$$

The approximate fitting problem is to determine coefficients $a_0, \ldots, a_K, K \le N - 1$ such that

$$e^2 = \sum_{r \in R} \left[d(r) - \sum_{n=0}^{K} a_n P_n(r) \right]^2 \tag{8.46}$$

is minimized. In either case the result is

$$a_m = \frac{\sum_{r \in R} P_m(r) d(r)}{\sum_{s \in R} P_m^2(s)} \tag{8.47}$$

The exact fitting coefficients and the least-squares coefficients are identical for $m = 0, \ldots, K$. Similar equations hold for the two-dimensional case. Readers who would like more technical details on the relationships between discrete least-square function fitting and orthogonal projection may consult Appendix B.

The equation for a_m means that each fitting coefficient can be computed as a linear combination of the data values. For each index r in the index set, the data value $d(r)$ is multiplied by the weight

$$\frac{P_m(r)}{\sum_{s \in R} P_m^2(s)}$$

which is just an appropriate normalization of an evaluation of the polynomial P_m at the index r. Figure 8.8 shows these weights for the 5×5 neighborhood.

Once the fitting coefficients $a_k, k = 0, \ldots, K$, have been computed, the estimated polynomial $Q(r)$ is given by

$$Q(r) = \sum_{n=0}^{K} a_n P_n(r) \tag{8.48}$$

This equation permits us to interpret $Q(r)$ as a well-behaved real-valued function defined on the real line. For example, to determine

$$\frac{dQ}{dr}(r_0)$$

we need only evaluate

$$\sum_{n=0}^{K} a_n \frac{dP_n}{dr}(r_0)$$

In this manner the estimate for any derivative at any point may be obtained. Similarly an estimate for any definite integral can be obtained.

The mathematics for weighted least squares is similar to the mathematics for equal-weighted least squares. The only difference is that the norm associated with the weighted least squares is a positive definite diagonal matrix instead of an identity matrix.

1	1	1	1	1
1	1	1	1	1
1	1	1	1	1
1	1	1	1	1
1	1	1	1	1

$[\frac{1}{25}]$ k_1 1

-2	-2	-2	-2	-2
-1	-1	-1	-1	-1
0	0	0	0	0
1	1	1	1	1
2	2	2	2	2

$[\frac{1}{50}]$ k_2 r

-2	-1	0	1	2
-2	-1	0	1	2
-2	-1	0	1	2
-2	-1	0	1	2
-2	-1	0	1	2

$[\frac{1}{50}]$ k_3 c

2	2	2	2	2
-1	-1	-1	-1	-1
-2	-2	-2	-2	-2
-1	-1	-1	-1	-1
2	2	2	2	2

$[\frac{1}{70}]$ k_4 $(r^2 - 2)$

4	2	0	-2	-4
2	1	0	-1	-2
0	0	0	0	0
-2	-1	0	1	2
-4	-2	0	2	4

$[\frac{1}{100}]$ k_5 rc

2	-1	-2	-1	2
2	-1	-2	-1	2
2	-1	-2	-1	2
2	-1	-2	-1	2
2	-1	-2	-1	2

$[\frac{1}{70}]$ k_6 $(c^2 - 2)$

-1	-1	-1	-1	-1
2	2	2	2	2
0	0	0	0	0
-2	-2	-2	-2	-2
1	1	1	1	1

$[\frac{1}{50}]$ k_7 $r^3 - 3.4r$

-4	-2	0	2	4
2	1	0	-1	-2
4	2	0	-2	-4
2	1	0	-1	-2
-4	-2	0	2	4

$[\frac{1}{140}]$ k_8 $(r^2 - 2)c$

-4	2	4	2	-4
-2	1	2	1	-2
0	0	0	0	0
2	-1	-2	-1	2
4	-2	-4	-2	4

$[\frac{1}{140}]$ k_9 $r(c^2 - 2)$

-1	2	0	-2	1
-1	2	0	-2	1
-1	2	0	-2	1
-1	2	0	-2	1
-1	2	0	-2	1

$[\frac{1}{50}]$ k_{10} $c^3 - 3.4c$

Figure 8.8 Kernels for estimating the coefficients $k_1, \ldots, k_{10}$ of the bivariate cubic $k_1 + k_2r + k_3c + k_4(r^2 - 2) + k_5rc + k_6(c^2 - 2) + k_7(r^3 - 3.4r) + k_8(r^2 - 2)c + k_9r(c^2 - 2) + k_{10}(c^3 - 3.4c)$.

8.8.4 Directional Derivative Edge Finder

We define the directional derivative edge finder as the operator that places an edge in all pixels having a negatively sloped zero crossing of the second directional derivative taken in the direction of the gradient.

Here we discuss the relationship between the directional derivatives and the coefficients from the polynomial fit. We denote the directional derivative of f at the point (r,c) in the direction α by $f'_\alpha(r,c)$. It is defined as

$$f'_\alpha(r,c) = \lim_{h \to 0} \frac{f(r + h\sin\alpha, c + h\cos\alpha) - f(r,c)}{h} \qquad (8.49)$$

The direction angle α is the clockwise angle from the column axis. It follows directly from this definition that

$$f'_\alpha(r,c) = \frac{\partial f}{\partial r}(r,c)\sin\alpha + \frac{\partial f}{\partial c}(r,c)\cos\alpha \qquad (8.50)$$

The simplest way to think about directional derivatives is to cut the surface $f(r,c)$ with a plane that is oriented in the desired direction and is orthogonal to the row-column plane. The intersection results in a curve. The derivative of the curve is the directional derivative. To cut the surface $f(r,c)$ with a plane in direction α, we simply require that $r = \rho\sin\alpha$ and $c = \rho\cos\alpha$, where ρ is the independent variable. This produces the curve $f_\alpha(\rho)$.

$$f_\alpha(\rho) = k_1 + (k_2\sin\alpha + k_3\cos\alpha)\rho + (k_4\sin^2\alpha + k_5\sin\alpha\cos\alpha + k_6\cos^2\alpha)\rho^2 +$$
$$(k_7\sin^3\alpha + k_8\sin^2\alpha\cos\alpha + k_9\sin\alpha\cos^2\alpha + k_{10}\cos^3\alpha)\rho^3$$

The first directional derivative of f in the direction α can be visualized as the first derivative of $f_\alpha(\rho)$ taken with respect to ρ.

$$f'_\alpha = \frac{\partial f}{\partial r}\sin\alpha + \frac{\partial f}{\partial c}\cos\alpha = k_2\sin\alpha + k_3\cos\alpha \qquad (8.51)$$

We denote the second directional derivative of f at the point (r,c) in the direction α by $f''_\alpha(r,c)$. It quickly follows by substituting f'_α for f that

$$f''_\alpha = \frac{\partial^2 f}{\partial r^2}\sin^2\alpha + 2\frac{\partial^2 f}{\partial r\partial c}\sin\alpha\cos\alpha + \frac{\partial^2 f}{\partial c^2}\cos^2\alpha \qquad (8.52)$$

Similarly,

$$f'''_\alpha = \frac{\partial^3 f}{\partial r^3}\sin^3\alpha + \frac{3\partial^3 f}{\partial r^2\partial c}\sin^2\alpha\cos\alpha + \frac{3\partial^3 f}{\partial r\partial c^2}\sin\alpha\cos^2\alpha + \frac{\partial^3 f}{\partial c^3}\cos^3\alpha \qquad (8.53)$$

Taking f to be a cubic polynomial in r and c that can be estimated by the discrete orthogonal polynomial fitting procedure, we can compute the gradient of f and the gradient direction angle α at the center of the neighborhood used to estimate f. In order for our notation to be invariant to the different discrete orthogonal polynomials that result from different neighborhood sizes, we rewrite this cubic in canonical form as

$$f(r,c) = k_1 + k_2 r + k_3 c$$
$$+ k_4 r^2 + k_5 rc + k_6 c^2$$
$$+ k_7 r^3 + k_8 r^2 c + k_9 rc^2 + k_{10} c^3 \qquad (8.54)$$

The kernels for directly estimating the coefficients $k_1, \ldots, k_{10}$ in the expression given above for a 5×5 window are shown in Fig. 8.9.

Notice that because linear combinations of linear combinations are linear combinations, the kernel associated with any monomial of Fig. 8.9 can be determined from the kernels associated with the orthogonal basis of Fig. 8.8 by taking on appropriate linear combinations. For example, for the monomial r, the kernel for k_2

in Fig. 8.8 involves r with a weight of 1, the kernel for k_7 involves r with a weight of -3.4, and the kernel for k_9 involves r with a weight of -2. Hence we can write a pictorial form for the kernel equation for r of Fig. 8.9 as

−2	−2	−2	−2	−2
−1	−1	−1	−1	−1
0	0	0	0	0
1	1	1	1	1
2	2	2	2	2

$$\frac{1}{50}$$

−1	−1	−1	−1	−1
2	2	2	2	2
0	0	0	0	0
−2	−2	−2	−2	−2
1	1	1	1	1

$$-\frac{3.4}{60}$$

−4	2	4	2	−4
−2	1	2	1	−2
0	0	0	0	0
2	−1	−2	−1	2
4	−2	−4	−2	4

$$-\frac{2}{140}$$

31	−5	−17	−5	31
−44	−62	−68	−62	−44
0	0	0	0	0
44	62	68	62	44
−31	5	17	5	−31

$$= \frac{1}{420}$$

We obtain the gradient angle α by

$$\sin \alpha = \frac{k_2}{\sqrt{(k_2^2 + k_3^2)}}$$

$$\cos \alpha = \frac{k_3}{\sqrt{(k_2^2 + k_3^2)}} \tag{8.55}$$

It is well defined whenever $k_2^2 + k_3^2 > 0$. At any point (r, c), the second directional derivative in the direction α is given by

$$
\begin{aligned}
f_\alpha''(r, c) = & (6k_7 \sin^2 \alpha + 4k_8 \sin \alpha \cos \alpha + 2k_9 \cos^2 \alpha)r \\
& + (6k_{10} \cos^2 \alpha + 4k_9 \sin \alpha \cos \alpha + 2k_8 \sin^2 \alpha)c \\
& + (2k_4 \sin^2 \alpha + 2k_5 \sin \alpha \cos \alpha + 2k_6 \cos^2 \alpha)
\end{aligned}
\tag{8.56}
$$

We wish to consider only points (r, c) on the line in direction α. Hence $r = \rho \sin \alpha$ and $c = \rho \cos \alpha$. Then

$$
\begin{aligned}
f_\alpha''(\rho) = & 6[k_7 \sin^3 \alpha + k_8 \sin^2 \alpha \cos \alpha \\
& + k_9 \sin \alpha \cos^2 \alpha + k_{10} \cos^3 \alpha]\rho \\
& + 2[k_4 \sin^2 \alpha + k_5 \sin \alpha \cos \alpha + k_6 \cos^2 \alpha] \\
= & A\rho + B
\end{aligned}
\tag{8.57}
$$

where

$$A = 6[k_7 \sin^3 \alpha + k_8 \sin^2 \alpha \cos \alpha + k_9 \sin \alpha \cos^2 \alpha + k_{10} \cos^3 \alpha] \tag{8.58}$$

-13	2	7	2	-13
2	17	22	17	2
7	22	27	22	7
2	17	22	17	2
-13	2	7	2	-13

$[\frac{1}{175}]$ k_1 1

31	-5	-17	-5	31
-44	-62	-68	-62	-44
0	0	0	0	0
44	62	68	62	44
-31	5	17	5	-31

$[\frac{1}{420}]$ k_2 r

31	-44	0	44	-31
-5	-62	0	62	5
-17	-68	0	68	17
-5	-62	0	62	5
31	-44	0	44	-31

$[\frac{1}{420}]$ k_3 c

2	2	2	2	2
-1	-1	-1	-1	-1
-2	-2	-2	-2	-2
-1	-1	-1	-1	-1
2	2	2	2	2

$[\frac{1}{70}]$ k_4 r^2

4	2	0	-2	-4
2	1	0	-1	-2
0	0	0	0	0
-2	-1	0	1	2
-4	-2	0	2	4

$[\frac{1}{100}]$ k_5 rc

2	-1	-2	-1	2
2	-1	-2	-1	2
2	-1	-2	-1	2
2	-1	-2	-1	2
2	-1	-2	-1	2

$[\frac{1}{70}]$ k_6 c^2

-1	-1	-1	-1	-1
2	2	2	2	2
0	0	0	0	0
-2	-2	-2	-2	-2
1	1	1	1	1

$[\frac{1}{60}]$ k_7 r^3

-4	-2	0	2	4
2	1	0	-1	-2
4	2	0	-2	-4
2	1	0	-1	-2
-4	-2	0	2	4

$[\frac{1}{140}]$ k_8 r^2c

-4	2	4	2	-4
-2	1	2	1	-2
0	0	0	0	0
2	-1	-2	-1	2
4	-2	-4	-2	4

$[\frac{1}{140}]$ k_9 rc^2

-1	2	0	-2	1
-1	2	0	-2	1
-1	2	0	-2	1
-1	2	0	-2	1
-1	2	0	-2	1

$[\frac{1}{60}]$ k_{10} c^3

Figure 8.9 Kernels for directly estimating the coefficients $k_1, \ldots, k_{10}$ of the bivariate cubic $k_1 + k_2r + k_3c + k_4r^2 + k_5rc + k_6c^2 + k_7r^3 + k_8r^2c + k_9rc^2 + k_{10}c^3$ for a 5×5 neighborhood.

and

$$B = 2\,[k_4 \sin^2\alpha + k_5 \sin\alpha \cos\alpha + k_6 \cos^2\alpha] \qquad (8.59)$$

If for some ρ, $|\rho| < \rho_0$, where ρ_0 is slightly smaller than the length of the side of a pixel, $f'''_\alpha(\rho) < 0, f''_\alpha(\rho) = 0$, and $f'_\alpha(\rho) \neq 0$, we have discovered a negatively sloped zero crossing of the estimated second directional derivative taken in the estimated direction of the gradient. We mark the center pixel of the neighborhood as an edge pixel, and if required we make a note of the subpixel location of the zero crossing.

If our ideal edge is the step edge, then we can refine these detection criteria by insisting that the cubic polynomial $f_\theta(\rho)$ have coefficients that make f_θ a suitable polynomial approximation of the step edge (Haralick, 1986). Now a step edge does not change in its essence if it is translated to the left or right or if it has a constant added to its height. Since the cubic polynomial is representing the step edge, we must determine what it is about the cubic polynomial that is its fundamental essence after an ordinate and abscissa translation.

To do this, we translate the cubic polynomial

$$f_\alpha(\rho) = c_0 + c_1\rho + c_2\rho^2 + c_3\rho^3 \qquad (8.60)$$

so that its inflection point is at the origin. Calling the new polynomial g, we have

$$g_\alpha(\rho) = f_\alpha\left(\rho - \frac{c_2}{3c_3}\right) - \left(c_0 + \frac{2c_2^3}{27c_3^2} - \frac{c_1c_2}{3c_3}\right)$$

$$= \left(\frac{3c_1c_3 - c_2^2}{3c_3}\right)\rho + c_3\rho^3 \qquad (8.61)$$

In our case since $c_1 = \sqrt{k_2^2 + k_3^2}$, we know $c_1 > 0$. If a pixel is to be an edge, the second directional derivative zero-crossing slope must be negative. Hence for edge pixel candidates, $c_3 < 0$. This makes $-3c_1c_3 + c_2^2 > 0$, which means that $g_\alpha(\rho)$ has relative extrema. The parameters of the cubic that are invariant under translation relate to these relative extrema. The parameters are the distance between the relative extrema in the abscissa direction and those in the ordinate direction. We develop these invariants directly from the polynomial equation $g_\alpha(\rho)$. First, we factor out the term

$$\frac{(c_2^2 - 3c_1c_3)^{1.5}}{3^{1.5}c_3^2}$$

This produces

$$g_\alpha(\rho) = \left[\frac{(c_2^2 - 3c_1c_3)^{1.5}}{3^{1.5}c_3^2}\right]\left[-c_3\sqrt{\frac{3}{c_2^2 - 3c_1c_3}}\,\rho + \frac{3^{1.5}c_3^3}{(c_2^2 - 3c_1c_3)^{1.5}}\rho^3\right]$$

For candidate edge pixels, $c_3 < 0$. This permits a rewrite to

$$g_\alpha(\rho) = \frac{(c_2^2 - 3c_1c_3)^{1.5}}{3^{1.5}c_3^2}\left[\sqrt{\frac{3c_3^2}{c_2^2 - 3c_1c_3}}\,\rho - \left(\frac{3c_3^2}{c_2^2 - 3c_1c_3}\right)^{1.5}\rho^3\right] \qquad (8.62)$$

Let the contrast be C and the scale S. They are defined by

$$C = \frac{(c_2^2 - 3c_1c_3)^{1.5}}{3^{1.5}c_3^2}$$

$$S = \sqrt{\frac{3c_3^2}{(c_2^2 - 3c_1c_3)}} \qquad (8.63)$$

Finally, we have

$$g_\alpha(\rho) = C\,(S\rho - S^3\rho^3) \tag{8.64}$$

In this form it is relatively easy to determine the character of the cubic. Differentiating, we have

$$g'_\alpha(\rho) = C\,(S - 3S^3\rho^2)$$
$$g''_\alpha(\rho) = -6CS^3\rho \tag{8.65}$$

The locations of the relative extrema depend only on S. They are located at $\pm 1/S\sqrt{3}$. The height difference between relative extrema depends only on the contrast. Their heights are $\pm 2C/3\sqrt{3}$. Other characteristics of the cubic depend on both C and S. For example, the magnitude of the curvature at the extreme is $2\sqrt{3}\ CS^2$, and the derivative at the inflection point is CS.

Of interest to us is the relationship between an ideal perfect step edge and the representation it has in the least-squares approximating cubic whose essential parameters are contrast C and scale S. We take an ideal step edge centered in an odd neighborhood size N to have $\frac{N-1}{2}$ pixels with value -1, a center pixel with value 0, and $\frac{N-1}{2}$ pixels with value $+1$. Using neighborhood sizes of 5 to 23, we find the values listed in Table 8.1 for contrast C and scale S of the least-squares approximating cubic.

The average contrast of the approximating cubic is 3.16257. The scale $S(N)$ appears to be inversely related to N; $S(N) = \frac{S_o}{N}$. The value of S_o minimizing the relative error

$$\frac{S(N) - \frac{S_o}{N}}{S(N)}$$

is 1.793157.

Table 8.1   Contrast C and scale S of the fitted cubic for an ideal step edge as a function of neighborhood size N.

Neighborhood Size N	Contrast C	Scale S
5	3.0867	0.37796
7	3.1357	0.26069
9	3.1566	0.20000
11	3.1673	0.16253
13	3.1734	0.13699
15	3.1773	0.11844
17	3.1799	0.10434
19	3.1817	0.09325
21	3.1830	0.08430
23	3.1841	0.07692

These two relationships

$$C = 3.16257$$
$$S_o = \frac{1.793157}{N}$$

$$(8.66)$$

for ideal step edges having a contrast of 2 can help provide additional criteria for edge selection. For example, the contrast across an arbitrary step edge can be estimated by

$$\text{Edge contrast} = \frac{2C}{3.16257}$$

$$(8.67)$$

If the edge contrast is too small, then the pixel is rejected as an edge pixel. In many kinds of images, too small means smaller than 5% of the image's true dynamic range. Interestingly enough, edge contrast C depends on the three coefficients c_1, c_2, and c_3 of the representing cubic. First-derivative magnitude at the origin, a value used by many edge gradient magnitude detection techniques, depends only on the coefficient c_1. First-derivative magnitude at the inflection point is precisely CS, a value that mixes together both scale and edge contrast.

The scale for the edge can be defined by

$$\text{Edge scale} = \frac{S_o N}{1.793157}$$

$$(8.68)$$

Ideal step edges, regardless of their contrast, will produce least-squares approximating cubic polynomials whose edge scale is very close to unity. Values of edge scale larger than 1 have the relative extrema of the representing cubic closer together than expected for an ideal step edge. Values of edge scale smaller than 1 have the relative extrema of the representing cubic farther away from each other than expected for an ideal step edge. Values of edge scale that are significantly different from unity may be indicative of a cubic representing a data value pattern very much different from a step edge. Candidate edge pixels with an edge scale very different from unity can be rejected as edge pixels.

The determination of how far from unity is different enough requires an understanding of what sorts of nonedge situations yield cubics with a high enough contrast and with an inflection point close enough to the neighborhood center. We have found that such nonedge situations occur when a steplike jump occurs at the last point in the neighborhood. For example, suppose all the observed values are the same except the value at an endpoint. If N is the neighborhood size, then the inflection point of the approximating cubic will occur at $\pm\frac{N+3}{14}$, the plus sign corresponding to a different left endpoint and the minus sign corresponding to a different right endpoint. Hence for neighborhood sizes of $N = 5, 7, 9$, or 11, the inflection point occurs within a distance of 1 from the center point of the neighborhood. So providing the contrast is high enough, the situation would be classified as an edge if scale were ignored. For neighborhood sizes of $N = 5, 7, 9, 11$, and 13, however, the scale of the approximating cubic is 1.98, 1.81, 1.74, 1.71, and 1.68, respectively. This suggests that scales larger than 1 are significantly more different from unity scale than corresponding scales smaller than 1. In many images restricting edge scale to between .4 and 1.1 works well.

If one is interested in only straight-line edges, a further refinement is possible. We can insist that the curvature of the contour at the zero-crossing point be sufficiently small. Let $(r_0, c_0) = (\rho_0 \sin \theta, \rho_0 \cos \theta)$ be the zero-crossing point. Let

$$f_r = k_2 + (2k_4 \sin \theta + k_5 \cos \theta)\rho_0 + (3k_7 \sin^2 \theta + 2k_8 \sin \theta \cos \theta + k_9 \cos^2 \theta)\rho_0^2$$
$$f_c = k_3 + (k_5 \sin \theta + 2k_6 \cos \theta)\rho_0 + (k_8 \sin^2 \theta + 2k_9 \sin \theta \cos \theta + 3k_{10} \cos^2 \theta)\rho_0^2$$
$$f_{rr} = 2k_4 + (6k_7 \sin \theta + 2k_8 \cos \theta)\rho_0$$
$$f_{rc} = k_5 + (2k_8 \sin \theta + 2k_9 \cos \theta)\rho_0$$
$$f_{cc} = 2k_6 + (2k_9 \sin \theta + 6k_{10} \cos \theta)\rho_0$$

Then the curvature K is defined by

$$K = \frac{(-f_c \quad f_r)\begin{pmatrix} f_{rr} & f_{rc} \\ f_{rc} & f_{cc} \end{pmatrix}\begin{pmatrix} -f_c \\ f_r \end{pmatrix}}{(f_r^2 + f_c^2)^{\frac{3}{2}}}$$

For straight lines, requiring K to be less than .05 is often reasonable.

8.9   Integrated Directional Derivative Gradient Operator

Accurate edge direction is important in techniques for grouping labeled pixels into arcs and segmenting arcs into line segments, as well as in Hough transformation techniques (Duda and Hart, 1972), which have been used extensively to detect lines (O'Gorman and Clowes, 1976), circles (Kimme, Ballard, and Sklansky, 1975), and arbitrary shapes (Ballard, 1981). Martelli (1972) and Ramer (1975) each use edge direction information to perform edge linking. Kitchen and Rosenfeld (1980) and Zuniga and Haralick (1983) use edge direction information in schemes to detect corners. The integrated directional derivative gradient operator (Zuniga and Haralick, 1987, 1988a), which we discuss here, permits a more accurate calculation of step edge direction than do techniques that use values of directional derivatives estimated at a point.

Local edge direction is defined as the direction that is orthogonal to the estimated gradient direction and in which, if one walked along the edge, the higher-valued area would be to the right. Knowledge of the directional derivatives D_1 and D_2 in any two orthogonal directions is sufficient to compute the directional derivative in any arbitrary direction. The gradient magnitude, which is defined as the maximum such directional derivative, is computed as $\sqrt{D_1^2 + D_2^2}$ and its direction as $\tan^{-1} D_2/D_1$. From this perspective, estimating gradient direction requires estimates of the directional derivatives D_1 and D_2.

In previous sections we discussed how different operators have been utilized to estimate these directional derivatives at a point. Examples are the Roberts operator (Roberts, 1965), the Prewitt operator (Prewitt, 1970), the Sobel operator (Duda and Hart, 1972), and the Hueckel operator (Hueckel, 1973). These gradient operators all face a problem: Their estimate of edge direction for a step edge is inherently biased as a function of true edge direction and displacement of the true edge from the pixel's center. The bias occurs because the step edge does not match the polynomial model.

Instead of computing directional derivatives at a point directly from the fitted surface, as in the case of the standard cubic facet gradient operator mentioned earlier, in this section we describe an operator that measures the integrated directional derivative strength as the integral of first directional derivative taken over a square area. The direction for the integrated derivative estimate that maximizes the integral defines the estimate of gradient direction.

Edge direction estimate bias of the integrated directional derivative gradient operator is sharply reduced as compared with the bias of the standard cubic facet, Sobel, and Prewitt gradient operators. Noise sensitivity is comparable to that of the Sobel and Prewitt operators and is much better than that of the standard cubic facet operator.

Also, unlike the standard cubic facet, Sobel, and Prewitt operators, increasing the neighborhood size decreases both estimate bias and noise sensitivity. For ramp edges the integrated operator is very nearly unbiased. The worst bias for the 7×7 operator is less than $0.09°$, for the 5×5 operator, less than $0.26°$.

Section 8.9.1 describes the mathematical analysis necessary to derive the new gradient estimate. Section 8.9.2 provides a comparison of the integrated directional derivative gradient operator against the standard cubic facet gradient, Prewitt, and Sobel operators for step and ramp edges contaminated by zero-mean Gaussian noise.

8.9.1 Integrated Directional Derivative

Let F_θ represent the integrated first directional derivative along lines orthogonal to the direction θ situated in a rectangle of length $2L$ and width $2W$ centered at the origin of the coordinate system and rotated by an angle of θ in the clockwise direction. Then

$$F_\theta = \frac{1}{4LW} \int_{-W}^{W} \int_{-L}^{L} f_\theta'(\rho \cos\theta + \omega \sin\theta, -\rho \sin\theta + \omega \cos\theta) d\rho d\omega \qquad (8.69)$$

for a given $N \times N$ neighborhood.

The integrated gradient estimate is

$$G = F_{\theta_{MAX}} u_{\theta_{MAX}} \qquad (8.70)$$

where $F_{\theta_{MAX}} = \max_\theta F_\theta$ and $u_{\theta_{MAX}}$ is a unit vector in the direction that maximizes F_θ.

Using the bivariate cubic fit, we obtain that $f_\theta'(\rho \cos\theta + \omega \sin\theta, -\rho \sin\theta + \omega \cos\theta)$ reduces to

$$
\begin{aligned}
& f_\theta'(\rho \cos\theta + \omega \sin\theta, -\rho \sin\theta + \omega \cos\theta) \\
&= [k_9 \sin^3\theta + k_8 \cos^3\theta + (3k_7 - 2k_9)\sin\theta \cos^2\theta + (3k_{10} - 2k_8)\sin^2\theta \cos\theta] \rho^2 \\
&\quad + 2[-k_8 \sin^3\theta + (3k_7 - 2k_9)\sin^2\theta \cos\theta + (2k_8 - 3k_{10})\sin\theta \cos^2\theta + k_9 \cos^3\theta] \rho\omega \\
&\quad + [3k_7 \sin^3\theta + 3k_{10} \cos^3\theta + 3k_9 \sin\theta \cos^2\theta + 3k_8 \sin^2\theta \cos\theta] \omega^2 \\
&\quad + [-k_5 \sin^2\theta + 2(k_4 - k_6)\sin\theta \cos\theta + k_5 \cos^2\theta] \rho \\
&\quad + 2[k_4 \sin^2\theta + k_5 \sin\theta \cos\theta + k_6 \cos^2\theta] \omega + k_2 \sin\theta + k_3 \cos\theta \qquad (8.71)
\end{aligned}
$$

Substituting Eq. (8.71) in Eq. (8.69) results in

$$F_\theta = \frac{1}{4LW} \int_{-W}^{W} \int_{-L}^{L} (A\rho^2 + B\rho\omega + C\omega^2 + D\rho + E\omega + F)d\rho d\omega$$

where $A, B, C, D, E,$ and F are the coefficients of the quadratic relation (8.71). Evaluating this integral results in

$$F_\theta = \frac{1}{3}AL^2 + \frac{1}{3}CW^2 + F$$

Finally,

$$F_\theta = \frac{1}{3}(k_9 L^2 + 3k_7 W^2)\sin^3\theta + \frac{1}{3}(k_8 L^2 + 3k_{10} W^2)\cos^3\theta$$

$$+ \frac{1}{3}\left[(3k_7 - 2k_9)L^2 + 3k_9 W^2\right]\cos^2\theta \sin\theta$$

$$+ \frac{1}{3}\left[(-2k_8 + 3k_{10})L^2 + 3k_8 W^2\right]\cos\theta \sin^2\theta + k_2 \sin\theta + k_3 \cos\theta \quad (8.72)$$

Thus F_θ reduces to a trigonometric expression in $\sin\theta$ and $\cos\theta$. Notice that if $L = W$, then

$$F_\theta = \frac{L^2}{3}\left[(k_9 + 3k_7)\sin^3\theta + (k_8 + 3k_{10})\cos^3\theta + (3k_7 + k_9)\cos^2\theta \sin\theta\right.$$

$$\left. + (3k_{10} + k_8)\cos\theta \sin^2\theta\right] + k_2 \sin\theta + k_3 \cos\theta$$

$$= \left[k_2 + \frac{L^2}{3}(k_9 + 3k_7)\right]\sin\theta + \left[k_3 + \frac{L^2}{3}(k_8 + 3k_{10})\right]\cos\theta \quad (8.73)$$

Hence F_θ is maximized when

$$\theta = \theta_{\text{MAX}} = \tan^{-1}\frac{L^2 k_7 + \frac{1}{3}L^2 k_9 + k_2}{L^2 k_{10} + \frac{1}{3}L^2 k_8 + k_3} \quad (8.74)$$

Then

$$F_{\theta_{\text{MAX}}} = \sqrt{D_1^2 + D_2^2} \quad (8.75)$$

where D_1 and D_2 are the numerator and denominator of the argument of the tangent function in Eq. (8.73). In the remainder of our discussion we take the area of integration to be square: $L = W$.

8.9.2 Experimental Results

Experiments that illustrate how the integrated directional derivative gradient operators perform use step and ramp edges contaminated by zero-mean Gaussian noise. The step edges are generated in a rectangular grid with orientations θ from $0°$ to $90°$ and with random displacement from the grid's center uniformly distributed within the range $(-D, D)$, with the maximum displacement D given by

$$\begin{cases} 0.5\cos\theta, & 0° \le \theta < 45° \\ 0.5\sin\theta, & 45° \le \theta \le 90° \end{cases}$$

if we assume a unit distance between two 4-neighbor pixels in the grid. A step edge passing through a pixel divides it into two parts having areas A_1 and A_2, with $A_1 + A_2 = 1$. If the corresponding gray level intensities on each side of the edge are I_1 and I_2, then the pixel is assigned a gray level intensity I according to the rule

$$I = I_1 A_1 + I_2 A_2$$

The experiments use values for I_1 and I_2 equal to 100 and 200, respectively, which implies that the edge contrast is 100.

Ramp edges are generated by defocusing step edges with a 3×3 equally weighted averaging filter. Finally, both step and ramp edges are contaminated by adding zero-mean Gaussian noise with a given standard deviation.

For comparison purposes we use two performance measurements, edge direction estimate bias and edge direction estimate standard deviation. The latter measures noise sensitivity. The estimate bias is defined as the difference between the estimate mean direction and the true edge direction. Combining the previous two measurements by the root-mean-square error formula produces a single performance measurement. The experiments show that the integrated directional derivative gradient operator achieves best performance in the root-mean-square error sense when $L = W = 1.8$ for a 5×5 neighborhood size and $L = W = 2.5$ for a 7×7 neighborhood size for both step and ramp edges and for a variety of noise levels.

We compare the following gradient operators: 5×5 extended Sobel (Iannino and Shapiro, 1979), 5×5 and 7×7 Prewitt, 5×5 and 7×7 standard cubic facet, and 5×5 and 7×7 integrated directional derivative. Figure 8.10 shows the 5×5 row derivative masks associated with each of the operators, and Fig. 8.11 shows the 7×7 row derivative mask for the integrated directional derivative gradient operator.

-116	-530	-668	-530	-116
-128	-335	-404	-335	-128
0	0	0	0	0
128	335	404	335	128
116	530	668	530	116

(a) $\frac{1}{10500}$

31	-5	-17	-5	31
-44	-62	-68	-62	-44
0	0	0	0	0
44	62	68	62	44
-31	5	17	5	-31

(b) $\frac{1}{420}$

-5	-8	-10	-8	-5
-4	-10	-20	-10	-4
0	0	0	0	0
4	10	20	10	4
5	8	10	8	5

(c) $\frac{1}{240}$

-2	-2	-2	-2	-2
-1	-1	-1	-1	-1
0	0	0	0	0
1	1	1	1	1
2	2	2	2	2

(d) $\frac{1}{50}$

Figure 8.10 Row derivative masks for gradient operators in 5×5 neighborhood size. (a) Integrated directional derivative; (b) standard cubic facet; (c) Prewitt; and (d) extended Sobel.

-3	-348	-555	-624	-555	-348	-3
-142	-372	-510	-556	-510	-372	-142
-113	-228	-297	-320	-297	-228	-113
0	0	0	0	0	0	0
113	228	297	320	297	228	113
142	372	510	556	510	372	142
3	348	555	624	555	348	3

$$\frac{1}{28224}$$

Figure 8.11 Row derivative mask for integrated directional derivative gradient operator for 7×7 neighborhood size.

The column derivative masks can be obtained from the row masks by rotation of 90°.

For a step or ramp edge of a given orientation and noise standard deviation, each operator is applied to the grid's center 10,000 times, each time with a different noisy sample and a different edge displacement from the grid's center. Edge orientations vary from 0° to 90° and noise standard deviation from 0 to 100. Edge contrast is 100. The results can be seen in Figs. 8.12 and 8.13.

Figures 8.12 and 8.13 show estimate bias against true edge direction for step and ramp edges under zero-noise conditions for the standard cubic facet gradient

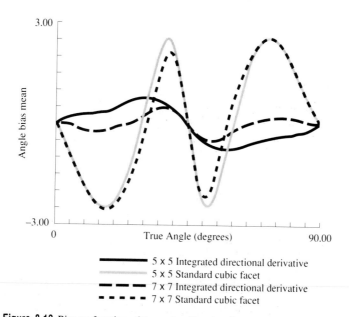

Figure 8.12 Bias as function of true edge direction for step edges under zero-noise conditions for four different edge operators.

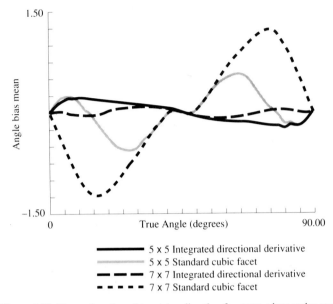

Figure 8.13 Bias as function of true edge direction for ramp edges under zero-noise conditions for four different edge operators.

operator and the integrated directional derivative gradient operator. Three observations can be made: (1) The integrated operator is clearly superior to the standard cubic facet gradient operator. (2) Under zero-noise conditions the 7×7 integrated directional derivative gradient operator has a worst bias of less than $0.09°$. And (3) the 5×5 integrated directional derivative gradient operator has a worst bias of less than $0.26°$ on ramp edges. For comparison purposes, the 7×7 standard cubic facet gradient operator has a worst bias of about $1.2°$, and the 5×5 standard cubic facet gradient operator has a worst bias of $0.5°$. This improvement in worst bias remains when the edges are contaminated by additive independent zero-mean Gaussian noise. The estimate bias decreases for the integrated operator as the neighborhood size increases, whereas the opposite happens with the standard cubic facet gradient operator. Both operators perform better with ramp edges than with step edges.

Figure 8.14 shows estimate standard deviation against noise standard deviation for a fixed step edge with orientation of $22.5°$ and additive independent Gaussian noise. Again, the integrated operator is uniformly superior to the standard cubic facet gradient operator for both step and ramp edges.

Under zero-noise conditions, Fig. 8.15 shows estimate bias of the Sobel and Prewitt operators as a function of true edge direction for step edges. The 7×7 integrated operator has the smallest bias, followed by the 5×5 extended Sobel and the 5×5 and 7×7 Prewitt operators. Notice that for ramp edges the response of the integrated operator is nearly flat about zero, that is, the operator is nearly unbiased. For the 7×7 integrated operator, the worst bias is less than $0.09°$, and for the 5×5

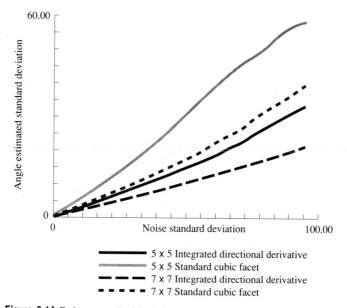

Figure 8.14 Estimate standard deviation as function of noise standard deviation for step edge. Edge orientation is 22.5°. Edge contrast is 100.

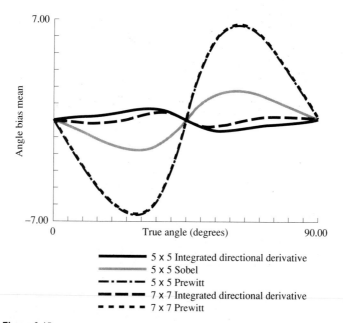

Figure 8.15 Estimate bias of the Sobel and Prewitt operators as function of true edge directionfor step edges under zero-noise conditions.

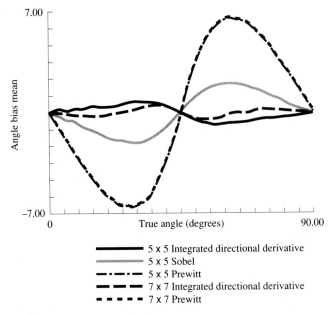

Figure 8.16 Estimate bias of the Sobel and Prewitt operators as function of true edge direction for step edge. Noise standard deviation is 25. Edge contrast is 100.

integrated operator, less than 0.26°. For comparison purposes the worst bias in the 7×7 Prewitt operator is about 5° and in the 5×5 Prewitt operator about 4°.

Figures 8.16 and 8.17 show estimate bias as a function of true edge direction for step and ramp edges when the noise standard deviation is equal to 25. The bias for all the operators shown is nearly identical to the bias under zero-noise conditions. It can be seen from the plots of estimate standard deviation that, as expected, the 7×7 operators are less sensitive to noise than the 5×5 operators.

8.10 Corner Detection

The detection of corners in images is extremely useful for computer vision tasks. For example, Huertas (1981) uses corners to detect buildings in aerial images. Nagel and Enkelmann (1982) use corner points to determine displacement vectors from a pair of consecutive images taken in time sequence. Some approaches to corner detection rely on prior segmentation of the image and subsequent analysis of region boundaries. Rutkowski and Rosenfeld (1978) provide a comparison of several corner detection techniques along those lines.

In this section we develop gray scale corner detectors, which detect corners by operating directly on the gray scale image. As Kitchen and Rosenfeld (1980) point out, the main advantage of such corner detectors is that their performance is not dependent on the success or failure of a prior segmentation step. Among

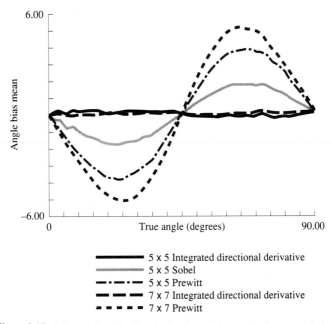

5 x 5 Integrated directional derivative

5 x 5 Sobel

5 x 5 Prewitt

7 x 7 Integrated directional derivative

7 x 7 Prewitt

Figure 8.17 Estimate bias of the Sobel, Prewitt, and integrated directional derivative operators as function of true edge direction for ramp edge. Noise standard deviation is 25. Edge contrast is 100.

the earliest gray scale corner detectors is Beaudet's (1978) DET operator, which responds significantly near corner and saddle points. Kitchen and Rosenfeld report results using several operators that measure cornerness by the product of gradient magnitude and rate of change of gradient direction. Dreschler and Nagel (1981) investigate points lying between extrema of Gaussian curvature as suitable candidates for corner points.

Corner detection is simply described by using the facet model. In general, what we are usually inclined to call a corner occurs where two edge boundaries meet at a certain angle or where the direction of an edge boundary is changing very rapidly. We associate corners therefore with two conditions: the occurrence of an edge and significant changes in edge direction. We discussed edge detection in Sections 8.6–8.9 Here we will concentrate on change in edge direction, which is equivalent to change in gradient direction since edge and gradient directions are orthogonal.

Corners occur at edge points where a significant change in gradient direction takes place. Now this change in gradient direction should ideally be measured as an incremental change along the edge boundary. We do not desire, however, to perform boundary following, since that would require a prior segmentation step. There are several ways to handle this situation based on the realization that according to our model the direction of an edge point—that is, the tangent to the edge boundary at that point—is orthogonal to the gradient vector at that same point. The simplest approach is to compute the incremental change in gradient direction along the tangent line to the edge at the point that is a corner candidate. The second approach is to evaluate the incremental change along the contour line that passes through the corner candidate. Finally, we can compute the instantaneous rate of change in gradient direction in the direction of the tangent line. We will discuss each of these approaches.

The properties of those neighborhood points away from the neighborhood center and possibly outside the pixel itself can be computed by two different methods: (a) using the surface fit from the central neighborhood and (b) using the surface fit from the neighborhood centered around the pixel closest to the given point.

Although the first method is computationally less expensive than the second one, the latter may be more accurate.

8.10.1 Incremental Change along the Tangent Line

Consider a row-column coordinate system centered at the corner candidate point. Let $\theta(r,c)$ be the gradient direction at coordinate (r,c), and let $\theta_0 = \theta(0,0)$. Then $(\sin\theta_0, \cos\theta_0)$ is a unit vector in the direction of the gradient at the origin. If the origin is an edge point, the direction of the line tangent to the edge boundary that passes through it is given by $(-\cos\theta, \sin\theta)$, and an arbitrary point lying on that line is $\rho(-\cos\theta, \sin\theta)$ for some ρ.

Consider two points $P_1 = (r_1, c_1), P_2 = (r_2, c_2)$ equidistant to the origin and lying on the tangent line (Fig. 8.18). P_1 and P_2 are given by $-R(-\cos\theta, \sin\theta)$ and $R(-\cos\theta, \sin\theta)$, respectively, where R is the distance from each point to the origin. If R is not too large, we can expect the true boundary to lie not too far away from either P_1 or P_2. In this case a suitable test to decide whether the origin $(0,0)$ is a corner point involves meeting the following two conditions:

1. $(0,0), (r_1, c_1)$, and (r_2, c_2) are edge points.
2. For a given threshold Ω, $|\theta(r_1, c_1) - \theta(r_2, c_2)| > \Omega$.

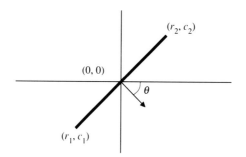

Figure 8.18 Two points equidistant to the origin and lying on the line tangent to the edge boundary passing through it.

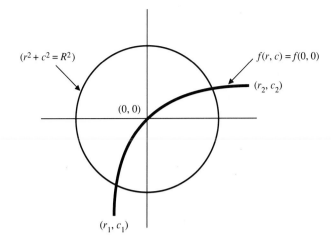

Figure 8.19 Two points equidistant to the origin and lying on the contour line passing through it.

8.10.2 Incremental Change along the Contour Line

It is reasonable to assume that points on the edge boundary to each side of the corner point and close to it are likely to have similar, but not necessarily the same, gray levels. This motivates us to approximate the edge boundary by the contour line $\{(r,c) \mid f(r,c) = f(0,0)\}$ that passes through the corner candidate point at the origin of the coordinate system.

We consider two points $P_1 = (r_1,c_1)$ and $P_2 = (r_2,c_2)$ equidistant to the origin and lying on the contour line (cf. Fig. 8.19). Let $\theta(r,c)$ be the gradient direction at coordinates (r,c). The test to decide whether the origin $(0,0)$ is a corner point is similar to the one used in the previous approach. That is, $(0,0)$ is declared to be a corner point if the following two conditions are satisfied:

1. $(0,0), (r_1,c_1)$, and (r_2,c_2) are edge points.
2. For a given threshold Ω, $|\theta(r_1,c_1) - \theta(r_2,c_2)| > \Omega$.

This approach is computationally more expensive than the previous one because of the need to intersect the cubic curve $f(r,c) = f(0,0)$ (the contour line) with the quadratic curve $r^2 + c^2 = R^2$ in order to determine the points P_1 and P_2 a distance R from the origin.

8.10.3 Instantaneous Rate of Change

Let $\theta(r,c)$ be the gradient direction at coordinates (r,c), and let $\theta_\alpha(r,c)$ be the first directional derivative of $\theta(r,c)$ in the direction α. We can compute $\theta'_\alpha(r,c)$ as follows:

Let $f(r,c)$ be the surface function underlying the neighborhood of pixel values centered at the corner candidate pixel. Let $f_r(r,c)$ and $f_c(r,c)$ denote the row and column partial derivatives of f. Consider the line passing through the origin in the direction α. An arbitrary point in this line is given by $\rho(\sin\alpha,\cos\alpha)$, and the gradient direction at that point is given by

$$\theta_\alpha(\rho\sin\alpha,\rho\cos\alpha) = \tan^{-1}\frac{f_r(\rho\sin\alpha,\rho\cos\alpha)}{f_c(\rho\sin\alpha,\rho\cos\alpha)} \qquad (8.76)$$

Since α can be considered fixed, we can write this as

$$\theta_\alpha(\rho) = \tan^{-1}\frac{f_r(\rho)}{f_c(\rho)} \qquad (8.77)$$

Differentiating with respect to the parameter ρ results in

$$\theta'_\alpha(\rho) = \frac{f_c(\rho)f'_r(\rho) - f_r(\rho)f'_c(\rho)}{[f_r(\rho)]^2 + [f_c(\rho)]^2} \qquad (8.78)$$

Using the bivariate cubic polynomial approximation for f, we have:

$$f_r(\rho) = k_2 + (2k_4\sin\alpha + k_5\cos\alpha)\rho + (3k_7\sin^2\alpha + 2k_8\sin\alpha\cos\alpha + k_9\cos^2\alpha)\rho^2$$

$$f_c(\rho) = k_3 + (k_5\sin\alpha + 2k_6\cos\alpha)\rho + (k_8\sin^2\alpha + 2k_9\sin\alpha\cos\alpha + 3k_{10}\cos^2\alpha)\rho^2$$

$$f'_r(\rho) = (2k_4\sin\alpha + k_5\cos\alpha) + 2(3k_7\sin^2\alpha + 2k_8\sin\alpha\cos\alpha + k_9\cos^2\alpha)\rho$$

$$f'_c(\rho) = (k_5\sin\alpha + 2k_6\cos\alpha) + 2(k_8\sin^2\alpha + 2k_9\sin\alpha\cos\alpha + 3k_{10}\cos^2\alpha)\rho$$

The rate of change of gradient direction in the direction α evaluated at the origin ($\rho = 0$) is then

$$\theta'_\alpha(0) = \frac{k_3(2k_4\sin\alpha + k_5\cos\alpha) - k_2(k_5\sin\alpha + 2k_6\cos\alpha)}{k_2^2 + k_3^2} \qquad (8.79)$$

We are interested in the value of $\theta'_\alpha(0)$ when the direction α is orthogonal to the gradient direction at the origin (the edge direction). Since (k_2, k_3) is the gradient vector at the origin, $(-k_3, k_2)$ is a vector orthogonal to it, and

$$\sin\alpha = \frac{-k_3}{\sqrt{k_2^2 + k_3^2}}, \qquad \cos\alpha = \frac{k_2}{\sqrt{k_2^2 + k_3^2}} \qquad (8.80)$$

Finally, using Eq. (8.80) in Eq. (8.79), we obtain

$$\theta'_\alpha(0,0) = \frac{-2(k_2^2 k_6 - k_2 k_3 k_5 + k_3^2 k_4)}{(k_2^2 + k_3^2)^{\frac{3}{2}}} \qquad (8.81)$$

The test to decide whether the origin $(0,0)$ is a corner point follows: We declare $(0,0)$ to be a corner point if these two conditions are satisfied:

1. $(0,0)$ is an edge point.
2. For a given threshold Ω, $|\theta_\alpha'(0)| > \Omega$.

If a zero-crossing edge detector is used to decide whether to label a pixel as edge, instead of employing the test at the origin, one can use it for $\rho = \rho_0$, where ρ_0 is the zero-crossing point.

8.10.4 Experimental Results

We illustrate the performance of the various facet model–based gray level corner detectors by applying them to two digital images. The first one represents a set of artificially generated rectangular shapes at different orientations. The second one is a real aerial image of an urban scene. The first image is 90×90 pixels and contains rectangular shapes of 20×20 pixels with orientations ranging from $0°$ to $90°$ in $10°$ increments. The rectangles have gray level intensity 175, and the background has gray level intensity 75. Independent Gaussian noise with mean 0 and standard deviation 10 has been added to this image. If we define the signal-to-noise ratio as 10 times the logarithm of the range of signal divided by the standard deviation of the noise, the artifically generated image has a 10DB signal-to-noise ratio. The perfect and noisy versions are shown in Fig. 8.20.

Facet Model–Based Corner Detectors

Each of the corner detection techniques discussed previously was applied to the artificially generated noisy image by using a neighborhood size of 7×7 pixels and a gradient strength threshold for edge detection equal to 20. If the gradient exceeds the threshold value and a negatively sloped zero crossing of the second directional derivative occurs in a direction of $\pm 14.9°$ of the gradient direction within a circle of radius one pixel length centered at the point of test, then this point is declared to be an edge point.

The thresholds for gradient direction change were selected to equalize as well as possible the conditional probability of assigning a corner within a given distance d from the true corner, given that there is a true corner, and the conditional probability of there being a true corner within a given distance d of an assigned corner when a corner is assigned.

A true corner is defined as the interior pixel in the rectangular shape where two adjacent sides meet. Table 8.2 shows the probability of correct corner assignment for each case for distances $d = 0$ and $d = 1$. This table shows that a very high percentage of the assigned corner points are guaranteed to lie within one pixel distance from the true corner point. The method that performs the best is the one that measures change in gradient direction as incremental change along a contour line and that computes properties of tested points away from the neighborhood center by using the surface fit from the neighborhood centered around the pixel closest to the

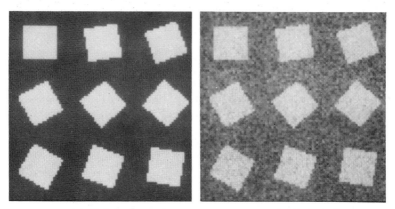

(a) Original   (b) Noisy

(c) Aerial scene

Figure 8.20 Perfect and noisy artificially generated images and the aerial scene.

tested point. Surprisingly, the next best is the simplest one, which uses incremental change along the tangent line and properties from the same corner candidate central neighborhood for all the tested points in the tangent line.

Comparison with Other Gray Tone Corner Detectors

Table 8.3 compares the performance of the best facet model–based corner detector according to Table 8.2 with the performance of two other gray level corner detectors: Kitchen-Rosenfeld (1980) and Dreschler-Nagel (1982).

Table 8.2   Performance of the facet model–based corner detectors.

Grad threshold −20	$d^a = 1$			$d = 0$		
	$P(AC/TC)^b$	$P(TC/AC)^c$	Angle Threshold	$P(AC/TC)$	$P(TC/AC)$	Angle Threshold
Incremental change along tangent line. Central neighborhood increment= 3.50 pixels.	0.97	0.99	47°	0.278	0.25	55°
Incremental change along tangent line. Nearest neighborhood increment= 3.50 pixels.	0.97	0.97	67°	0.111	0.108	80°
Incremental change along contour line. Central neighborhood increment= 3.50 pixels.	0.94	0.94	50°	0.278	0.294	63°
Incremental change along contour line. Nearest neighborhood increment= 4 pixels.	0.97	0.99	76°	0.361	0.361	94°
Instantaneous rate of change.	0.94	0.96	13°/pixel	0.083	0.075	16°/pixel

a. Parameter d is the maximum distance between assigned and true corners.

b. $P(AC/TC)$ is the conditional probability of assigning a corner given that there is a corner.

c. $P(TC/AC)$ is the conditional probability of there being a true corner when a corner is assigned.

Kitchen and Rosenfeld investigated several techniques for gray level corner detection. Each one computed for every pixel in the image a measure of cornerness, and then corners were obtained by thresholding. Their best results were achieved by measuring cornerness by the product of gradient magnitude and instantaneous rate of change in gradient direction evaluated from a quadratic polynomial gray level surface fit.

Dreschler and Nagel detected corners by the following procedure. First, they computed for each pixel in the image the Gaussian curvature. This entailed doing a local quadratic polynomial fit for each pixel and computing the Hessian matrix. The Gaussian curvature is the product of the main curvatures (eigenvalues of the

Table 8.3   Performance of the best facet model–based, Kitchen-Rosenfeld, and Dreschler-Nagel corner detectors.

	d = 1		d = 0	
	P(AC/TC)	P(TC/AC)	P(AC/TC)	P(TC/AC)
Best facet–model corner detector	0.97	0.97	0.361	0.361
Kitchen-Rosenfeld No gradient threshold	0.36	0.36	0.055	0.021
Kitchen-Rosenfeld Gradient threshold=20	0.83	0.84	0.055	0.05
Dreschler-Nagel Gradient threshold=20	0.33	0.35	0.055	0.059

Hessian matrix). Next, they found the locations of maximum and minimum Gaussian curvature. A pixel was declared to be a corner if the following conditions were satisfied.

1. The pixel's steepest slope was along the line that connected the location of maximum with the location of minimum Gaussian curvature. (This was done only for extrema lying within a given radius from the corner candidate pixel.)

2. The gray level intensity at the location of maximum Gaussian curvature was larger than the gray level intensity at the location of minimum Gaussian curvature.

3. The orientation of the main curvature that changed sign between the two extrema pointed into the direction of the associated extremum.

Figure 8.21 illustrates the results of applying the facet model–based, Kitchen-Rosenfeld, and Dreschler-Nagel gray level corner detectors to the artificially generated noisy image. In all cases we used a cubic polynomial fitting on a 7×7 pixel neighborhood. We slightly modified the Kitchen-Rosenfeld corner detector by considering only points whose gradient exceeded a given threshold. This resulted in substantial improvement of the original Kitchen-Rosenfeld method. The Dreschler-Nagel corner detector proved to be the most sensitive to noise, and a gradient threshold had to be used to improve its performance. Since all three methods use the same cubic polynomial surface fit and the same 7×7 pixel neighborhood size, the same gradient threshold of 20 was used in each to minimize the effects of the noise. The search for Gaussian curvature extrema was done in a 5×5 neighborhood. Table 8.3 shows the probability of correct corner assignment for each case. The best results according to this table are obtained by using the facet model–based corner

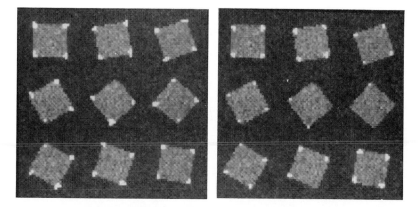

(a) Facet G-20   (b) Kit-Ross G-20

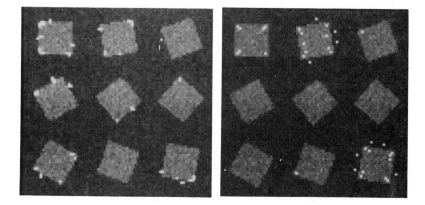

(c) Dre-Naq G-20   (d) Kit-Ross G-O

Figure 8.21 Comparison of the corner assignments for the facet model–based, the Kitchen-Rosenfeld (with and without gradient threshold), and the Dreschler-Nagel corner detectors (clockwise from top left). Parameters are shown in Table 8.3 for $d = 1$.

detector, followed by the Kitchen-Rosenfeld corner detector. The Dreschler-Nagel corner detector performs the worst.

Finally, Fig. 8.22 illustrates the results obtained by applying each of these corner detectors to the aerial image. In all cases we used a cubic polynomial fitting on a 7×7 pixel neighborhood. Gradient thresholds are equal to 16.

8.11   Isotropic Derivative Magnitudes

A gradient edge can be understood as arising from a first-order isotropic derivative magnitude. It should then come as no surprise that higher-order features can

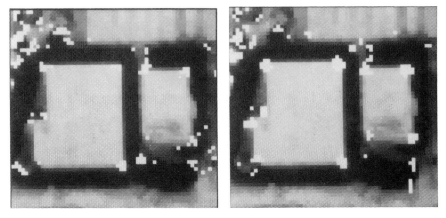

(a)   (b)

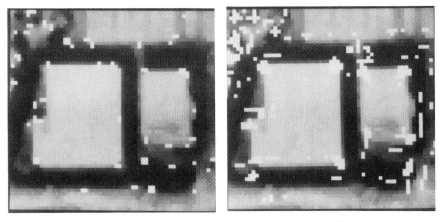

(c)   (d)

Figure 8.22 Comparison of the corner assignments in the aerial scene for the facet model–based, the Kitchen-Rosenfeld (with and without threshold), and the Dreschler-Nagel corner detectors (clockwise from top left).

arise from higher-order derivative magnitudes (Prewitt, 1970; Beaudet, 1978; and Haralick, 1981). In this section we determine those linear combinations of squared partial derivatives of two-dimensional functions that are invariant under rotation of the domain of the two-dimensional function. Let us first consider the simple linear function $f(r,c) = k_1 + k_2 r + k_3 c$. If we rotate the coordinate system by θ and call the resulting function g, we have in the new (r',c') coordinates

$$r = r \cos \theta - c' \sin \theta$$
$$c = r' \sin \theta + c' \cos \theta$$

and

$$g(r',c') = f(r,c)$$

so that

$$\left[\frac{\partial g}{\partial r}(r',c')\right]^2 + \left[\frac{\partial g}{\partial c}(r',c')\right]^2 = (k_2 \cos\theta - k_3 \sin\theta)^2 + (k_2 \sin\theta + k_3 \cos\theta)^2$$

$$= k_2^2 + k_3^2$$

$$= \left[\frac{\partial f}{\partial r}(r,c)\right]^2 + \left[\frac{\partial f}{\partial c}(r,c)\right]^2$$

Hence the sum of the squares of the first partials is the same constant $k_2^2 + k_3^2$, the squared gradient magnitude, for the original function or for the rotated function.

In the remainder of this section we explicitly develop the direction isotropic derivative magnitudes for the first and the second derivatives of an arbitrary function. Then we state the theorem giving the formula for the isotropic derivative magnitude of any order.

Proceeding as we did with the first-order case, upon writing the rotation equation with r' and c' as the independent variables, we have

$$r = r' \cos\theta - c' \sin\theta$$

$$c = r' \sin\theta + c' \cos\theta$$

Let the rotated function be g. Then $g(r',c') = f(r,c)$. Now expressing

$$\frac{\partial f}{\partial r'}(r,c) \quad \text{and} \quad \frac{\partial f}{\partial c'}(r,c)$$

in terms of

$$\frac{\partial f}{\partial r}(r,c) \quad \text{and} \quad \frac{\partial f}{\partial c}(r,c)$$

we have

$$\frac{\partial f}{\partial r'} = \frac{\partial f}{\partial r}\frac{\partial r}{\partial r'} + \frac{\partial f}{\partial c}\frac{\partial c}{\partial r'} = \frac{\partial f}{\partial r}\cos\theta + \frac{\partial f}{\partial c}\sin\theta$$

$$\frac{\partial f}{\partial c'} = \frac{\partial f}{\partial r}\frac{\partial r}{\partial c'} + \frac{\partial f}{\partial c}\frac{\partial c}{\partial c'} = \frac{-\partial f}{\partial r}\sin\theta + \frac{\partial f}{\partial c}\cos\theta$$

Then

$$\left[\frac{\partial g}{\partial r'}(r',c')\right]^2 + \left[\frac{\partial g}{\partial c'}(r',c')\right]^2$$

$$= \left[\frac{\partial f}{\partial r'}(r,c)\right]^2 + \left[\frac{\partial f}{\partial c'}(r,c)\right]^2$$

$$= \left[\frac{\partial f}{\partial r}(r,c)\cos\theta + \frac{\partial f}{\partial c}(r,c)\sin\theta\right]^2 + \left[\frac{-\partial f}{\partial r}(r,c)\sin\theta + \frac{\partial f}{\partial c}(r,c)\cos\theta\right]^2$$

$$= \left[\frac{\partial f}{\partial r}(r,c)\right]^2(\cos^2\theta + \sin^2\theta) + 2\left[\frac{\partial f}{\partial r}(r,c)\frac{\partial f}{\partial c}(r,c)(\cos\theta\sin\theta - \cos\theta\sin\theta)\right]$$

$$+ \left[\frac{\partial f}{\partial c}(r,c)\right]^2(\sin^2\theta + \cos^2\theta)$$

$$= \left[\frac{\partial f}{\partial r}(r,c)\right]^2 + \left[\frac{\partial f}{\partial c}(r,c)\right]^2$$

Thus for each point (r,c) in the unrotated coordinate system,

$$\left[\frac{\partial f}{\partial r}(r,c)\right]^2 + \left[\frac{\partial f}{\partial c}(r,c)\right]^2$$

produces the same value as

$$\left[\frac{\partial g}{\partial r}(r,c)\right]^2 + \left[\frac{\partial g}{\partial c}(r,c)\right]^2$$

in the rotated coordinate system, where $g(r',c') = f(r,c)$.

Proceeding in a similar manner for the second-order partials, we have

$$\frac{\partial^2 f}{\partial r'^2} = \frac{\partial^2 f}{\partial r^2}\cos^2\theta + 2\frac{\partial^2 f}{\partial r\partial c}\cos\theta\sin\theta + \frac{\partial^2 f}{\partial c^2}\sin^2\theta$$

$$\frac{\partial^2 f}{\partial r'\partial c'} = \frac{-\partial^2 f}{\partial r^2}\cos\theta\sin\theta + \frac{\partial^2 f}{\partial r\partial c}(\cos^2\theta - \sin^2\theta) + \frac{\partial^2 f}{\partial c^2}\cos\theta\sin\theta$$

$$\frac{\partial^2 f}{\partial c'^2} = \frac{\partial^2 f}{\partial r^2}\sin^2\theta - 2\frac{\partial^2 f}{\partial r\partial c}\cos\theta\sin\theta + \frac{\partial^2 f}{\partial c^2}\cos^2\theta$$

Looking for some constant λ that makes

$$\left(\frac{\partial^2 f}{\partial r'^2}\right)^2 + \lambda\left(\frac{\partial^2 f}{\partial r'\partial c'}\right)^2 + \left(\frac{\partial^2 f}{\partial c'^2}\right)^2 = \left(\frac{\partial^2 f}{\partial r^2}\right)^2 + \lambda\left(\frac{\partial^2 f}{\partial r\partial c}\right)^2 + \left(\frac{\partial^2 f}{\partial c^2}\right)^2$$

we discover that exactly one does exist, and its value is $\lambda = 2$. Thus for each point in the unrotated coordinate system,

$$\left[\frac{\partial^2 g}{\partial r'^2}(r',c')\right]^2 + 2\left[\frac{\partial^2 g}{\partial r'\partial c'}(r',c')\right]^2 + \left[\frac{\partial^2 g}{\partial c'^2}(r',c')\right]^2$$

produces the same value as

$$\left[\frac{\partial^2 f}{\partial r^2}(r,c)\right]^2 + 2\left[\frac{\partial^2 f}{\partial r \partial c}(r,c)\right]^2 + \left[\frac{\partial^2 f}{\partial c^2}(r,c)\right]^2$$

The direction isotropic second-derivative magnitude is therefore

$$\left(\frac{\partial^2 f}{\partial r^2}\right)^2 + 2\left(\frac{\partial^2 f}{\partial r \partial c}\right)^2 + \left(\frac{\partial^2 f}{\partial c^2}\right)^2$$

Higher-order direction isotropic derivative magnitudes can be constructed in a similar manner. The coefficients of the squared partials continue in a binomial coefficient pattern for the two-dimensional case we have been describing. To see this, consider the following theorem, which states that the sum of the squares of all the partials of a given total order is equal, regardless of which orthogonal coordinate system it is taken in. Specializing this to two dimensions and third-order partials, we obtain that the following is isotropic:

$$\left(\frac{\partial^3 f}{\partial r \partial r \partial r}\right)^2 + \left(\frac{\partial^3 f}{\partial r \partial r \partial c}\right)^2 + \left(\frac{\partial^3 f}{\partial r \partial c \partial r}\right)^2 + \left(\frac{\partial^3 f}{\partial r \partial c \partial c}\right)^2 +$$

$$\left(\frac{\partial^3 f}{\partial c \partial r \partial r}\right)^2 + \left(\frac{\partial^3 f}{\partial c \partial r \partial c}\right)^2 + \left(\frac{\partial^3 f}{\partial c \partial c \partial r}\right)^2 + \left(\frac{\partial^3 f}{\partial c \partial c \partial c}\right)^2$$

$$= \left(\frac{\partial^3 f}{\partial r^3}\right)^2 + 3\left(\frac{\partial^3 f}{\partial r^2 \partial c}\right)^2 + 3\left(\frac{\partial^3 f}{\partial r \partial c^2}\right)^2 + \left(\frac{\partial^3 f}{\partial c^3}\right)^2$$

It should be clear from this example that the binomial coefficients arise because of the commutivity of the partial differential operators.

Theorem 8.1: The sum of the squares of all partial derivatives of the same order is isotropic. Let $f : E^N \to E$ be C^∞, P be an $N \times N$ orthonormal matrix, and $y = Px$, where the (n,k)th entry of P is p_{nk}. Let M be any positive integer. Then

$$\sum_{(j_i,\ldots,j_M) \in \{1,\ldots,N\}^M} \left[\frac{\partial^M}{\partial x_{j_i}\ldots\partial x_{j_M}}f(y)\right]^2 = \sum_{(j_i,\ldots,j_M) \in \{1,\ldots,N\}^M} \left[\frac{\partial^M}{\partial y_{j_i}\ldots\partial y_{j_M}}f(y)\right]^2$$

Proof:

First notice that

$$\frac{\partial}{\partial x_k}f(y) = \sum_{n=1}^{N} \frac{\partial}{\partial y_n}f(y)\frac{\partial y_n}{\partial x_k}, \qquad k = 1,\ldots,N$$

Since $y = Px$, $\frac{\partial y_n}{\partial x_k} = p_{nk}$, so that

$$\frac{\partial}{\partial x_k}f(y) = \sum_{n=1}^{N} \frac{\partial}{\partial y_n}f(y)p_{nk}, \qquad k = 1,\ldots,N$$

To make our notation simpler, we denote $\partial/\partial y_n$ by $f_n(y)$ and can therefore write

$$\frac{\partial}{\partial x_k} f(y) = \sum_{n=1}^{N} f_n(y) p_{nk}, \quad k = 1, \ldots, N$$

Following the subscript notation for partial derivatives, we denote

$$\frac{\partial^M}{\partial y_{j_1} \ldots \partial y_{j_M}} f(y)$$

by $f_{j_1 \cdots j_M}(y)$. Now upon recursive application of these equations, we can write

$$\frac{\partial^M}{\partial x_{j_1} \ldots \partial x_{j_M}} f(y) = \sum_{(i_1,\ldots,i_M)\in\{1,\ldots,N\}^M} f_{i_1 \ldots i_M}(y) \prod_{m=1}^{M} p_{i_m j_m}$$

Then

$$A = \sum_{(j_1,\ldots,j_M)\in\{1,\ldots,N\}^M} \left[\frac{\partial^M}{\partial x_{j_1} \ldots \partial x_{j_M}} f(y) \right]^2$$

$$= \sum_{(j_1,\ldots,j_M)} \sum_{(i_1,\ldots,i_M)} f_{i_1 \ldots i_M}(y) \prod_{m=1}^{M} p_{i_m j_m} \sum_{(k_1,\ldots,k_M)} f_{k_1,\ldots,k_M}(y) \prod_{n=1}^{M} p_{k_n j_n}$$

$$= \sum_{(i_1,\ldots,i_M)(k_1,\ldots,k_M)} f_{i_1,\ldots,i_M}(y) f_{k_1,\ldots,k_M}(y) \sum_{(j_1,\ldots,j_M)} \prod_{m=1}^{M} p_{i_m j_m} \prod_{n=1}^{M} p_{k_n j_n}$$

$$= \sum_{(i_1,\ldots,i_M)} f_{i_1,\ldots,i_M}(y) \sum_{(k_1,\ldots,k_M)} f_{n_1,\ldots,n_M}(y) \prod_{m=1}^{M} \sum_{j_m=1}^{N} p_{i_m j_m} p_{k_m j_m}$$

But since p is orthonormal,

$$\sum_{j_m=1}^{N} = p_{i_m j_m} p_{k_m j_m} = \begin{cases} 1 & i_m = k_m \\ 0 & \text{otherwise} \end{cases}$$

Therefore

$$A = \sum_{(i_1,\ldots,i_m)\in\{1,\ldots,N\}^M} f_{i_1,\ldots,i_M}^2(y)$$

8.12   Ridges and Ravines on Digital Images

What is a ridge or a ravine in a digital image? The first intuitive notion is that a digital ridge (ravine) occurs on a digital image when there is a simply connected sequence of pixels with gray level intensity values that are significantly higher (lower) in the sequence than those neighboring the sequence. Significantly higher or lower may depend on the distribution of brightness values surrounding the sequence, as well as on the length of the sequence.

Ridges and ravines may arise from dark or bright lines or from an image that might be related to reflections, to variations, or to a three-dimensional surface structure. For elongated objects that have curved surfaces with a specular reflectance function, the locus of points on their surfaces having surface normals pointing in the direction of the camera generates pixels on a digital image that are ridges. Linearly narrow concavities on an object surface (such as cracks) are typically in shadow and generate pixels on a digital image that are ravines. Line and curve finding plays a universal role in object analysis. Therefore one important part of the computer vision algorithm lies in the detection of ridge and ravine pixels.

The facet model can be used to help accomplish ridge and ravine identification. To use the facet model, we must first translate our notion of ridge and ravine to the continuous-surface perspective. Here the concept of line translates in terms of directional derivatives. If we picture ourselves walking by the shortest distance across a ridge or ravine, we would walk in the direction having the greatest magnitude of second directional derivative. The ridge peak or the ravine bottom would occur when the first directional derivative has a zero crossing.

Thus to label pixels as ridges and ravines, we need to use the neighborhood of a pixel to estimate a continuous surface whose directional derivatives we can compute analytically. To do this, we can use a functional form consisting of a cubic polynomial in the two-variables row and column, just as we did for the facet edge operator.

8.12.1 Directional Derivatives

Recall that the first directional derivative of a function f in direction α at row-column position (r,c) is denoted by $f'_\alpha(r,c)$ and can be expressed as

$$f'_\alpha(r,c) = \frac{\partial f}{\partial r}(r,c)\sin\alpha + \frac{\partial f}{\partial c}(r,c)\cos\alpha \qquad (8.82)$$

From this it follows that the second directional derivative in direction α can be expressed by

$$f''_\alpha(r,c) = \frac{\partial^2 f}{\partial r^2}(r,c)\sin^2\alpha + 2\frac{\partial^2 f}{\partial r\partial c}(r,c)\sin\alpha\cos\alpha + \frac{\partial^2 f}{\partial c^2}(r,c)\cos^2\alpha \quad (8.83)$$

Rearranging the expression for f''_α, we find that the second directional derivative can be expressed as a linear combination of two terms, the first being the Laplacian of f and not depending on α and the second depending on α:

$$f''_\alpha = \frac{1}{2}\left(\frac{\partial^2 f}{\partial r^2} + \frac{\partial^2 f}{\partial c^2}\right) + \left[\frac{1}{2}\left(\frac{\partial^2 f}{\partial c^2} - \frac{\partial^2 f}{\partial r^2}\right)\cos 2\alpha + \frac{\partial^2 f}{\partial r\partial c}\sin 2\alpha\right] \qquad (8.84)$$

We can determine the direction α that extremizes f_α'' by differentiating f_α'' with respect to α, setting the derivative to zero, and solving for α:

$$\frac{\partial f_\alpha''}{\partial \alpha} = \left(\frac{\partial^2 f}{\partial r^2} - \frac{\partial^2 f}{\partial c^2} \right) \sin 2\alpha + 2 \frac{\partial^2 f}{\partial r \partial c} \cos 2\alpha \qquad (8.85)$$

Therefore

$$\sin 2\alpha = \pm \left(\frac{-2\partial^2 f}{\partial r \partial c} \right) / D \text{ and } \cos 2\alpha = \pm \left(\frac{\partial^2 f}{\partial r^2} - \frac{\partial^2 f}{\partial c^2} \right) / D \qquad (8.86)$$

where

$$D = \sqrt{4 \left(\frac{\partial^2 f}{\partial r \partial c} \right)^2 + \left(\frac{\partial^2 f}{\partial r^2} - \frac{\partial^2 f}{\partial c^2} \right)^2}$$

It is easy to see that when the plus signs are taken,

$$\frac{\partial^2 f_\alpha''}{\partial \alpha^2} > 0$$

indicating that the extremum is a relative minimum, and when the minus signs are taken,

$$\frac{\partial^2 f_\alpha''}{\partial \alpha^2} < 0$$

indicating that the extremum is a relative maximum. Also, the direction α that makes f_α'' a maximum differs from the α that makes f_α'' a minimum by $\pi/2$ radians.

8.12.2 Ridge-Ravine Labeling

To label a pixel as a ridge or a ravine, we set up a coordinate system whose origin runs through the center of the pixel. We select a neighborhood size to estimate the fitting coefficients of the polynomials. Using the fitted polynomials, we can compute all second partial derivatives at the origin, from which the two directions of the extremizing α can be computed by Eq. (8.86).

Having a direction α, we next need to see if by traveling along a line passing through the origin in the direction α, the first directional derivative has a zero crossing sufficiently near the center of the pixel. If so, we declare the pixel to be a ridge or a ravine. Of course, if in one direction we find a ridge and in the other a ravine, then the pixel is a saddle point.

To express this procedure precisely and without reference to a particular basis set of polynomials tied to a neighborhood size, we rewrite the fitted bicubic surface in a canonical form:

$$f(r,c) = k_1 + k_2 r + k_3 c + k_4 r^2 + k_5 rc$$

$$+ k_6 c^2 + k_7 r^3 + k_8 r^2 c$$

$$+ k_9 rc^2 + k_{10} c^2 \qquad (8.87)$$

Then the two directions for α are given by $\alpha = \pm \tan^{-1} k_5 / (k_6 - k_4)$.

To walk in the direction α, we constrain r and c by

$$r = \rho \sin \alpha \quad \text{and} \quad c = \rho \cos \alpha$$

Therefore in the direction α we have

$$f_\alpha(\rho) = A\rho^3 + B\rho^2 + C\rho + k_1 \tag{8.88}$$

where

$$A = (k_7 \sin^3 \alpha + k_8 \sin^2 \alpha \cos \alpha + k_9 \cos^2 \alpha \sin \alpha + k_{10} \cos^3 \alpha)$$

$$B = (k_4 \sin^2 \alpha + k_5 \sin \alpha \cos \alpha + k_6 \cos^2 \alpha)$$

$$C = k_2 \sin \alpha + k_3 \cos \alpha$$

The first directional derivative in direction α is given by

$$f'_\alpha(\rho) = 3A\rho^2 + 2B\rho + C \tag{8.89}$$

and the second directional derivative in the direction α at ρ away from the center of the pixel is given by

$$f''_\alpha(\rho) = 6A\rho + 2B \tag{8.90}$$

At those positions for ρ that make $f'_\alpha(\rho) = 0$, the value of $f''_\alpha(\rho)$ is proportional to the curvature of the surface. If $B^2 - 3AC > 0$, the largest-magnitude root ρ_L can be found by

$$\rho_L = \frac{-B - \text{sign}(B)\sqrt{B^2 - 3AC}}{3A} \tag{8.91}$$

The smallest-magnitude root ρ_S can be found by

$$\rho_S = \frac{C}{3A\rho_L} \tag{8.92}$$

If the smallest-magnitude root is sufficiently close to zero, the center point of the pixel, we label the pixel as a ridge or a ravine depending on the sign of the second directional derivative. Pixels that are both ridges and ravines can be labeled as saddles.

There are some practical complications to this basic procedure. The first complication is due to the fact that the fitted f_θ is, in general, a cubic. The cubics of interest have extrema. Such a fitted cubic arising from data that are as simple as piecewise constants with one jump have relative extrema, even though the data do not. This is an artifact that results from using a cubic fit. It may or may not be significant; that is, the relative extrema of the fit may or may not correspond to extrema in the data. We can analyze the significance in terms of the fitted cubic dynamic range, the relative depths of its extrema, and its inflection point.

The dynamic range of the cubic segment is defined by

$$\text{Range} = \max_\rho f_\theta(\rho) - \min_\rho f_\theta(\rho)$$

The relative depth is defined as follows: Suppose the extremum is a relative minimum. Let a represent the left endpoint of the interval, b the right endpoint of the interval, i the location of the inflection point, and v the location of the relative minimum. If the relative minimum occurs to the left of the relative maximum, the depth of the minimum is defined by

$$\text{Depth} \; = \; \min\{f_\theta(b), f_\theta(i)\} - f_\theta(v)$$

If the relative minimum occurs to the right of the inflection point, then the depth is defined by

$$\text{Depth} \; = \; \min\{f_\theta(a), f_\theta(i)\} - f_\theta(v)$$

The relative depth of the minimum is then defined by

$$\text{Relative depth} = \text{depth/range}$$

To illustrate, consider a one-dimensional data pattern that is a constant with a jump change at one end. Figure 8.23 shows an image and its first, second, and third isotropic derivative magnitude features. The derivative estimates were obtained by an equal-weight bivariate cubic fit over a 5×5 neighborhood.

In each of these cases the cubic fitted to the data "rings" around the large constant region where the data is zero. One extremum of this ringing is closer to the origin. This extremum is an artifact. Notice that in each of these cases the

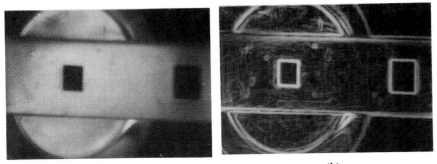

(a)   (b)

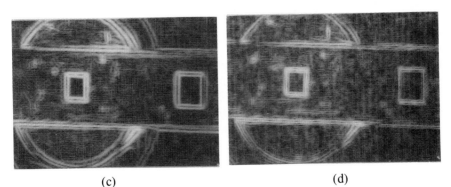

(c)   (d)

Figure 8.23 (a) Original image; (b) first isotropic derivative; (c) second isotropic derivative; and (d) third isotropic derivative.

Table 8.4   Relative depth data.

Neighborhood Size	Data	Position of Extremum Closest to Origin	Position of Inflection Point	Relative Depth
5	00009	.241	−.571	.0408
7	0000009	.533	−.714	.0610
9	000000009	.811	−.857	.0731
9	000000009	−.755	−2.14	.0205
11	0000000009	.0237	−1.75	.0338
13	00000000009	.519	−1.71	.0474
5	01300	−.527	1.00	.279
7	0013000	−.569	2.14	.419
9	000130000	−.589	3.67	.604
11	00001300000	−.600	5.57	.821
13	0000013000000	−.607	7.86	.849
5	01900	−.2235	2.71	.803
7	0019000	−.243	5.57	.874
9	000190000	−.246	9.38	.906
11	00001900000	−.247	14.14	.925
13	0000019000000	−.248	19.85	.937

inflection point is not too far from the origin, indicating a relatively high frequency ringing. Also for all these cases the relative depth, which measures the significance of the ringing, is close to zero.

Compare this situation to the case in which the data clearly have an extremum near the origin, as in the one-dimensional patterns of Table 8.4. Notice that in these cases the inflection points tend to be much farther away from the extremum indicating that the "ringing" behavior has a lower frequency. Also the relative depth tends to be much larger in the case of a true extremum.

What all this means is that in using f_θ to evaluate derivatives, we must understand and interpret the data through the "eyes" of a cubic polynomial. Not all extrema of the cubic are significant. A cubic extremum is significant in the sense that it reflects an extremum in the fitted data only if it passes the following tests:

1. | Position of extremum from origin | < radius threshold

2. | Position of inflection from origin | > distance

3. | Distance between roots | $> 1.756*$ size of interval

4. Relative depth $> .2$

5. $|f''_\theta(p*)| >$ curvature threshold

Test 1 guarantees that the extrema are close enough to the origin. Tests 2 and 3 guarantee that the "ringing" behavior has a long enough period, test 3 taking into account that for true extrema the period increases with the size of the fitting interval. Test 4 guarantees that the relative extrema have a significant enough height compared with the dynamic range of the fitted cubic segment. Test 5 guarantees that the curvature at the extrema is sufficiently high.

8.13   Topographic Primal Sketch

8.13.1   Introduction

The basis of the topographic primal sketch consists of the labeling and grouping of the underlying image-intensity surface patches according to the categories defined by monotonic, gray level, and invariant functions of directional derivatives. Examples of such categories are peak, pit, ridge, ravine, saddle, flat, and hillside. From this initial classification we can group categories to obtain a rich, hierarchical, and structurally complete representation of the fundamental image structure. We call this representation the *topographic primal sketch* (Haralick, Watson, and Laffey, 1983).

Invariance Requirement

A digital image can be obtained with a variety of sensing-camera gain settings. It can be visually enhanced by an appropriate adjustment of the camera's dynamic range. The gain-setting, or enhancing, point operator changes the image by some monotonically increasing function that is not necessarily linear. For example, non-linear, enhancing point operators of this type include histogram normalization and equal probability quantization.

In visual perception, exactly the same visual interpretation and understanding of a pictured scene occurs whether the camera's gain setting is low or high and whether the image is enhanced or unenhanced. The only diffference is that the enhanced image has more contrast, is nicer to look at, and can be understood more quickly by the eye.

The last fact is important because it suggests that many of the current low-level computer vision techniques, which are based on edges, cannot ever hope to have the robustness associated with human visual perception. They cannot have the robustness because they are inherently incapable of invariance under monotonic transformations. For example, edges based on zero crossings of second derivatives will change in position as the monotonic gray level transformation changes because convexity of a gray level intensity surface is not preserved under such transformations. However, the topographic categories of peak, pit, ridge, valley, saddle, flat, and hillside do have the required invariance.

Background

Marr (1976) argues that the first level of visual processing is the computation of a rich description of gray level changes present in an image, and that all subsequent computations are done in terms of this description, which he calls the *primal sketch*. Gray level changes are usually associated with edges, and Marr's primal sketch has, for each area of gray level change, a description that includes type, position, orientation, and fuzziness of edge. Marr (1980) illustrates that from this information it is sometimes possible to reconstruct the image to a reasonable degree.

The topographic primal sketch has richness and invariance and is very much in the spirit of Marr's primal sketch and the thinking behind Ehrich's relational trees (Ehrich and Foith 1978). Instead of concentrating on gray level changes as edges, as Marr does, or on one-dimensional extrema, as Ehrich and Foith do, we concentrate on all types of two-dimensional gray level variations. We consider each area on an image to be a spatial distribution of gray levels that constitutes a surface or facet of gray level intensities having a specific surface shape. It is likely that, if we could describe the shape of the gray level intensity surface for each pixel, then by assembling all the shape fragments we could reconstruct, in a relative way, the entire surface of the image's gray level intensity values. The shapes that have the invariance property are peak, pit, ridge, ravine, saddle, flat, and hillside, with hillside having noninvariant subcategories of slope, inflection, saddle hillside, convex hillside, and concave hillside.

Knowing that a pixel's surface has the shape of a peak does not tell us precisely where in the pixel the peak occurs; nor does it tell us the height of the peak or the magnitude of the slope around the peak. The topographic labeling, however, does satisfy Marr's (1976) primal sketch requirement in that it contains a symbolic description of the gray level intensity changes. Furthermore, upon computing and binding to each topographic label numerical descriptors such as gradient magnitude and direction, as well as directions of the extrema of the second directional derivative along with their values, we can obtain a reasonable absolute description of each surface shape.

8.13.2 Mathematical Classification of Topographic Structures

In this section we formulate the notion of topographic structures on continuous surfaces and show their invariance under monotonically increasing gray level transformations. We will use the following notation to describe the mathematical properties of our topographic categories for continuous surfaces.

$\nabla f =$ gradient vector of a function f

$\|\nabla f\| =$ gradient magnitude

$\omega^{(1)} =$ unit vector in the direction in which the second directional derivative
has the greatest magnitude

$\omega^{(2)} =$ unit vector orthogonal to $\omega^{(1)}$

$\lambda_1 =$ value of the second directional derivative in the direction of $\omega^{(1)}$

$\lambda_2 =$ value of the second directional derivative in the direction of $\omega^{(2)}$

$\nabla f \cdot \omega^{(1)} =$ value of the first directional derivative in the direction of $\omega^{(1)}$

$\nabla f \cdot \omega^{(2)} =$ value of the first directional derivative in the direction of $\omega^{(2)}$

Without loss of generality we assume $|\lambda_1| \geq |\lambda_2|$.

Each type of topographic structure in the classification scheme is defined in terms of the quantities listed above. In order to calculate these values, the first- and second-order partials with respect to r and c need to be approximated. These five partials are as follows:

$$\partial f/\partial r, \partial f/\partial c, \partial^2 f/\partial r^2, \partial^2 f/\partial c^2, \partial^2 f/\partial r\,\partial c$$

The gradient vector is simply $(\partial f/\partial r, \partial f/\partial c)$. The second directional derivatives may be calculated by forming the *Hessian*, where the Hessian is a 2×2 matrix defined as

$$H = \begin{pmatrix} \partial^2 f/\partial r^2 & \partial^2 f/\partial r\,\partial c \\ \partial^2 f/\partial c\,\partial r & \partial^2 f/\partial c^2 \end{pmatrix}$$

Hessian matrices are used extensively in nonlinear programming. Only three parameters are required to determine the Hessian matrix H, since the order of differentiation of the cross partials may be interchanged.

The eigenvalues of the Hessian are the values of the extrema of the second directional derivative, and their associated eigenvectors are the directions in which the second directional derivative is extremized. This can easily be seen by rewriting f_β'' as the quadratic form

$$f_\beta'' = (\sin \beta \; \cos \beta) H \begin{pmatrix} \sin \beta \\ \cos \beta \end{pmatrix}$$

Thus

$$H\omega^{(1)} = \lambda_1 \omega^{(1)} \quad \text{and} \quad H\omega^{(2)} = \lambda_2 \omega^{(2)}$$

Furthermore, the two directions represented by the eigenvectors are orthogonal to each other. Since H is a 2×2 symmetric matrix, calculation of the eigenvalues and eigenvectors can be done efficiently and accurately by using the method of Rutishauser (1971). We may obtain the values of the first directional derivative by simply taking the dot product of the gradient with the appropriate eigenvector:

$$\nabla f \cdot \omega^{(1)}$$

$$\nabla f \cdot \omega^{(2)}$$

A direct relationship exists between the eigenvalues λ_1 and λ_2 and curvature in the directions $\omega^{(1)}$ and $\omega^{(2)}$: When the first directional derivative $\nabla f \cdot \omega^{(i)} = 0$, then $\lambda_i / [1 + (\nabla f \cdot \nabla f)]^{1/2}$ is the curvature in the direction $\omega^{(i)}$, $i = 1$ or 2.

Having the gradient magnitude and direction and the eigenvalues and eigenvectors of the Hessian, we can describe the topographic classification scheme.

Peak

A peak (knob) occurs where there is a local maximum in all directions. In other words, we are on a peak if, no matter what direction we look in, we see no point that is as high as the one we are on (Fig. 8.24). The curvature is downward in all directions. At a peak the gradient is zero, and the second directional derivative is negative in all directions. To test whether the second directional derivative is negative in all directions, we simply examine the value of the second directional derivative in the directions that make it smallest and largest. A point is therefore classified as a peak if it satisfies the following conditions:

$$\|\nabla f\| = 0, \ \lambda_1 < 0, \ \lambda_2 < 0$$

Pit

A pit (sink, bowl) is identical to a peak except that it is a local minimum in all directions. At a pit the gradient is zero, and the

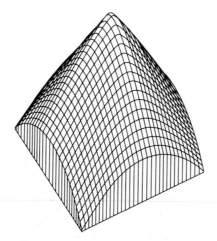

Figure 8.24 Right circular cone.

second directional derivative is positive in all directions. A point is classified as a pit if it satisfies the following conditions:

$$||\nabla f|| = 0, \; \lambda_1 > 0, \; \lambda_2 > 0$$

Ridge

A ridge occurs on a ridge line, a curve consisting of a series of ridge points. As we walk along the ridge line, the points to the right and left of us are lower than the ones we are on. Furthermore, the ridge line may be flat, sloped upward, sloped downward, curved upward, or curved downward. A ridge occurs where there is a local maximum in one direction, (Fig. 8.25). Therefore it must have a negative second directional derivative in the direction across the ridge and also a zero first directional derivative in the same direction. The direction in which the local maximum occurs may correspond to either of the directions in which the curvature is "extremized," since the ridge itself may be curved. For nonflat ridges, this leads to the first two cases listed below for ridge characterization. If the ridge is flat, then the ridge line is horizontal, and the gradient is zero along it. This corresponds to the third case. The defining characteristic is that the second directional derivative in the direction of the ridge line is zero and the second directional derivative across the ridge line is negative. A point is therefore classified as a ridge if it satisfies any one of the following three sets of conditions:

$$||\nabla f|| \neq 0, \lambda_1 < 0, \nabla f \cdot \omega^{(1)} = 0$$

or

$$||\nabla f|| \neq 0, \lambda_2 < 0, \nabla f \cdot \omega^{(2)} = 0$$

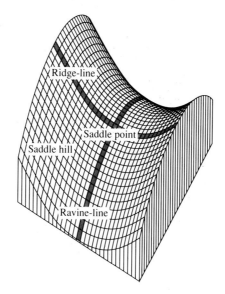

Figure 8.25 Saddle surface with ridge and ravine lines and saddle hillsides.

or

$$\|\nabla f\| = 0, \lambda_1 < 0, \lambda_2 = 0$$

A geometric way of thinking about the ridge definition is to realize that the condition $\nabla f \cdot \omega^{(1)} = 0$ means that the gradient direction (which is defined for nonzero gradients) is orthogonal to the direction $\omega^{(1)}$ of extremized curvature.

Ravine

A ravine (valley) is identical to a ridge except that it is a local minimum (rather than maximum) in one direction. As we walk along the ravine line, the points to the right and left of us are higher than the one we are on (see Fig. 8.25). A point is classified as a ravine if it satisfies any one of the following three sets of conditions:

$$\|\nabla f\| \neq 0, \lambda_1 > 0, \nabla f \cdot \omega^{(1)} = 0$$

or

$$\|\nabla f\| \neq 0, \lambda_2 > 0, \nabla f \cdot \omega^{(2)} = 0$$

or

$$\|\nabla f\| = 0, \lambda_1 > 0, \lambda_2 = 0$$

Saddle

A saddle occurs where there is a local maximum in one direction and a local minimum in a perpendicular direction (see Fig. 8.25). A saddle must therefore have a positive curvature in one direction and a negative curvature in a perpendicular direction. At a saddle the gradient magnitude must be zero, and the extrema of the second directional derivative must have opposite signs. A point is classified as a saddle if it satisfies the following conditions:

$$\|\nabla f\| = 0, \ \lambda_1 * \lambda_2 < 0$$

Flat

A flat (plain) is a simple, horizontal surface (Fig. 8.26). It therefore must have a zero gradient and no curvature. A point is classified as a flat if it satisfies the following conditions:

$$\|\nabla f\| = 0, \lambda_1 = 0, \lambda_2 = 0$$

Given that these conditions are true, we may further classify a flat as a *foot* or a *shoulder*. A foot occurs at the point where the flat just begins to turn up into a hill. At this point the third directional derivative in the direction toward the hill is nonzero, and the surface increases in this direction. The shoulder is an analogous case and occurs where the flat is ending and turning down into a hill. At this point the maximum magnitude of the third directional derivative is nonzero, and the surface decreases in the direction toward the hill. If the third directional derivative is zero

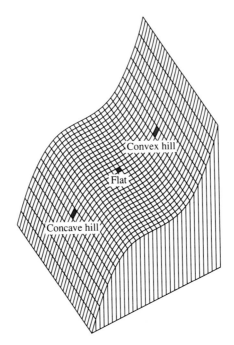

Figure 8.26 Hillside.

in all directions, then we are in a flat, not near a hill. Thus a flat may be further qualified as being a foot or a shoulder or not qualified at all.

Hillside

A hillside point is anything not covered by the previous categories. It has a nonzero gradient and no strict extrema in the directions of maximum and minimum second directional derivative. If the hill is simply a tilted flat (i.e., has a constant gradient), we call it a *slope*. If its curvature is positive (upward), we call it a *convex hill*. If its curvature is negative (downward), we call it a *concave hill*. If the curvature is up in one direction and down in a perpendicular direction, we call it a *saddle hill*. A saddle hill is illustrated in Fig. 8.25. If the curvature is 0 in all directions, the area is called a *flat*. The flat, the convex hill, and the concave hill are illustrated in Fig. 8.26.

A point on a hillside is an *inflection point* if it has a zero crossing of the second directional derivative taken in the direction of the gradient. When the slope of the second directional derivative is negative, the inflection point class is the same as the *step edge* defined in Section 8.8.

To determine whether a point is a hillside, we simply take the complement of the disjunction of the conditions given for all the previous classes. Thus if there is no curvature, then the gradient must be nonzero. If there is curvature, then the point must not be a relative extremum. Therefore a point is classified as a hillside if all three sets of the following conditions are true ($\rightarrow$ represents the operation of logical implication):

$$\lambda_1 = \lambda_2 = 0 \rightarrow ||\nabla f|| \neq 0$$

and

$$\lambda_1 \neq 0 \rightarrow \nabla f \cdot \omega^{(1)} \neq 0$$

and

$$\lambda_2 \neq 0 \rightarrow \nabla f \cdot \omega^{(2)} \neq 0$$

Rewritten as a disjunction rather than a conjunction of clauses, a point is classified as a hillside if any one of the following four sets of conditions is true:

$$\nabla f \cdot \omega^{(1)} \neq 0, \nabla f \cdot \omega^{(2)} \neq 0$$

or

$$\nabla f \cdot \omega^{(1)} \neq 0, \lambda_1 = 0$$

or

$$\nabla f \cdot \omega^{(2)} \neq 0, \lambda_2 = 0$$

or

$$||\nabla f|| \neq 0, \lambda_1 = 0, \lambda_2 = 0$$

We can differentiate between classes of hillsides by the values of the second directional derivative. The distinction can be made as follows:

Slope if $\lambda_1 = \lambda_2 = 0$

Convex if $\lambda_1 \geq \lambda_2 \geq 0$, $\lambda_1 \neq 0$

Concave if $\lambda_1 \leq \lambda_2 \leq 0$, $\lambda_1 \neq 0$

Saddle if $\lambda_1 * \lambda_2 < 0$

A slope, convex hill, concave hill, or saddle hill is classified as an inflection point if there is a zero crossing of the second directional derivative in the direction of the maximum first directional derivative (i.e., the gradient).

Summary of the Topographic Categories

Table 8.5 summarizes the mathematical properties of our topographic structures on continuous surfaces. The table exhaustively defines the topographic classes by their gradient magnitude, second directional derivative extrema values, and first directional derivatives taken in the directions that extremize second directional derivatives. Each entry in the table is either 0, +, −, or ∗. The 0 means not significantly different from zero; + means significantly different from zero on the positive side; − means significantly different from zero on the negative side; and ∗ means it does not matter. The label "Cannot occur" means that it is impossible for the gradient to be nonzero and for the first directional derivative to be zero in two orthogonal directions.

Table 8.5 Mathematical properties of topographic structures.

$\|\nabla f\|$	λ_1	λ_2	$\nabla f \cdot \omega^{(1)}$	$\nabla f \cdot \omega^{(2)}$	Label
0	−	−	0	0	Peak
0	−	0	0	0	Ridge
0	−	+	0	0	Saddle
0	0	0	0	0	Flat
0	+	−	0	0	Saddle
0	+	0	0	0	Ravine
0	+	+	0	0	Pit
+	−	−	−,+	−,+	Hillside (concave)
+	−	*	0	*	Ridge
+	*	−	*	0	Ridge
+	−	0	−,+	*	Hillside (concave)
+	−	+	−,+	−,+	Hillside (saddle)
+	0	0	*	*	Hillside (slope)
+	+	−	−,+	−,+	Hillside (saddle)
+	+	0	−,+	*	Hillside (convex)
+	+	*	0	*	Ravine
+	*	+	*	0	Ravine
+	+	+	−,+	−,+	Hillside (convex)
+	*	*	0	0	Cannot occur

From the table one can see that our classification scheme is complete. All possible combinations of first and second directional derivatives have a corresponding entry in the table. Each topographic category has a set of mathematical properties that uniquely determines it.

(*Note:* Special attention is required for the degenerate case $\lambda_1 = \lambda_2 \neq 0$, which implies that $\omega^{(1)}$ and $\omega^{(2)}$ can be *any* two orthogonal directions. In this case there *always* exists an extreme direction ω that is orthogonal to ∇f, and thus the first directional derivative $\nabla \cdot \omega$ is *always* zero in an extreme direction. To avoid spurious zero directional derivatives, we choose $\omega^{(1)}$ and $\omega^{(2)}$ such that $\nabla f \cdot \omega^{(1)} \neq 0$ and $\nabla f \cdot \omega^{(2)} \neq 0$, unless the gradient is zero.)

Invariance of the Topographic Categories

In this section we show that the topographic labels (peak, pit, ridge, ravine, saddle, flat, and hillside), the gradient direction, and the directions of second directional derivative extrema for peak, pit, ridge, ravine, and saddle are all invariant under monotonically increasing gray level transformations. We take *monotonically increasing* to mean positive derivative everywhere.

Let the original underlying gray level surface be $f(r,c)$. Let w be a monotonically increasing gray level transformation, and let $g(r,c)$ denote the transformed image: $g(r,c) = w[f(r,c)]$. It is directly derivable that

$$g'_\beta(r,c) = w'[f(r,c)] * f'_\beta(r,c)$$

from which we obtain that

$$g''_\beta(r,c) = w'[f(r,c)] * f''_\beta(r,c) + w''[f_\beta(r,c)] * f'_\beta(r,c)^2$$

Let us fix a position (r,c). Since w is a monotonically increasing function, w' is positive. In particular, w' is not zero. Hence the direction β that maximizes g'_β also maximizes f'_β, thereby showing that the gradient directions are the same. The categories peak, pit, ridge, ravine, saddle, and flat all have in common the essential property that the first directional derivative is zero when taken in a direction that extremizes the second directional derivative. To see the invariance, let β be an extremizing direction of f''_β. Then for points (r,c) having a label (peak, pit, ridge, ravine, saddle, or flat), $f'_\beta(r,c) = 0$ and $\partial f''_\beta(r,c)/\partial\beta = 0$. Notice that

$$\frac{\partial g''_\beta}{\partial\beta} = w' * \frac{\partial}{\partial\beta} f''_\beta + 2 * w'' * f'_\beta \frac{\partial f'_\beta}{\partial\beta} + (f'_\beta)^2 \frac{\partial w''}{\partial\beta}$$

Hence for these points, $g'_\beta(r,c) = 0$ and

$$\partial g''_\beta(r,c)/\partial\beta = 0$$

thereby showing that at these points the directions that extremize f''_β are precisely the directions that extremize g''_β, and that g''_β will always have the same sign as f''_β. A similar argument shows that if β extremizes g''_β and satisfies $g'_\beta = 0$, then β must also extremize f''_β and satisfy $f'_\beta = 0$. Therefore any points in the original image with the labels peak, pit, ridge, saddle, or flat retain the same label in the transformed image and, conversely, any points in the transformed image will have the same label in the original image.

Any pixel with a label not in the set (peak, pit, ridge, ravine, saddle, and flat) must have a hillside label. Thus a point labeled hillside must be transformed to a hillside-labeled point. However, the subcategories (inflection point, slope, convex hill, concave hill, and saddle hill) may change under the gray level transformation.

Ridge and Ravine Continua

Although the definitions given for ridge and ravine are intuitively pleasing, they may lead to the unexpected consequence of being entire areas of surface classified as all ridge or all ravine. To see how this can occur, observe that the eigenvalue $\lambda = \lambda(r,c)$ satisfies

$$\lambda(r,c) = \frac{1}{2} \left| \frac{\partial^2 f}{\partial r^2}(r,c) + \frac{\partial^2 f}{\partial c^2}(r,c) \right|$$

$$\pm \left[\left| \frac{\partial^2 f}{\partial r\, \partial c}(r,c) \right|^2 + \frac{1}{4} \left| \frac{\partial^2 f}{\partial r^2}(r,c) - \frac{\partial^2 f}{\partial c^2}(r,c) \right|^2 \right]^{1/2}$$

For a ridge or a ravine to exist at a point (r,c), the corresponding eigenvector $\omega(r,c)$ must be perpendicular to the gradient direction. Therefore $\nabla f \cdot \omega = 0$. If this equation holds for a point (r,c) and not for all points in a small neighborhood about (r,c), then a ridge or a ravine exists in the commonly understood sense. However, if this equation holds for all points in a neighborhood about (r,c), then a ridge or ravine continuum exists by our criteria.

Unfortunately, there are "nonpathologic" surfaces having ridge or ravine continua. Simple, radially symmetric examples include the inverted right circular cone defined by

$$f(r,c) = (r^2 + c^2)^{1/2}$$

the hemisphere defined by

$$f(r,c) = (K^2 - r^2 - c^2)^{1/2}$$

or in fact any function of the form $h(r^2 + c^2)$. In the case of the cone, the gradient is proportional to (r,c), and the unnormalized eigenvectors corresponding to eigenvalues

$$\lambda(r,c) = (r^2 + c^2)^{-1/2} \quad \text{and} \quad 0$$

are $(-c,r)$ and (r,c), respectively. The eigenvector corresponding to the nonzero eigenvalue is orthogonal to the gradient direction. The entire surface of the inverted cone, except for the apex, is a ravine. Other, nonradially symmetric examples exist as well.

The identification of points that are really ridge or ravine continua can be made as a postprocessing step. Points that are labeled ridge or ravine and have neighboring points in a direction orthogonal to the gradient that are also labeled ridge or ravine are ridge or ravine continua. These continua can be reclassified as hillsides if the label of ridge or ravine does not make sense in the application.

8.13.3   Topographic Classification Algorithm

The definitions of Section 8.13.2 cannot be used directly, because there is a problem of where in a pixel's area to apply the classification. If the classification were only applied to the point at the center of each pixel, then a pixel having a peak near one of its corners, for example, would be classified as a concave hill rather than as a peak. The problem is that the topographic classification we are interested in must be a sampling of the actual topographic surface classes. Most likely, the interesting categories of peak, pit, ridge, ravine, and saddle will never occur precisely at a pixel's center, and if they do occur in a pixel's area, then the pixel must carry that label rather than the class label of the pixel's center point. Thus one problem we must solve is how to determine the dominant label for a pixel, given the topographic class label of every point in the pixel. The next problem we must solve is how to determine, in effect, the set of all topographic classes occurring within a pixel's area without having to do the impossible brute-force computation.

To solve these problems, we divide the set of topographic labels into two subsets: (1) those that indicate that a strict, local, one-dimensional extremum has occurred (peak, pit, ridge, ravine, and saddle) and (2) those that do not indicate that a strict, local, one-dimensional extremum has occurred (flat and hillside). By *one-dimensional,* we mean along a line (in a particular direction). A strict, local, one-dimensional extremum can be located by finding those points within a pixel's area where a zero crossing of the first directional derivative occurs.

So that we do not search the pixel's entire area for the zero crossing, we search only in the directions of extreme second directional derivative, $\omega^{(1)}$ and $\omega^{(2)}$. Since these directions are well aligned with curvature properties, the chance of overlooking an important topographic structure is minimized, and more important, the computational cost is small.

When $\lambda_1 = \lambda_2 \neq 0$, the directions $\omega^{(1)}$ and $\omega^{(2)}$ are not uniquely defined. We handle this case by searching for a zero crossing in the direction given by $H^{-1} * \nabla f$. This is the *Newton direction,* and it points directly toward the extremum of a quadratic surface.

For inflection-point location (first derivative extremum), we search along the gradient direction for a zero crossing of the second directional derivative. For one-dimensional extrema, there are four cases to consider: (1) no zero crossing, (2) one zero crossing, (3) two zero crossings, and (4) more than two zero crossings of the first directional derivative. The next four sections discuss these cases.

Case One: No Zero Crossing

If no zero crossing is found along either of the two extreme directions within the pixel's area, then the pixel cannot be a local extremum and therefore must be assigned a label from the set (flat or hillside). If the gradient is zero, we have a flat. If it is nonzero, we have a hillside. If the pixel is a hillside, we classify it further into inflection point, slope, convex hill, concave hill, or saddle hill. If there is a zero crossing of the second directional derivative in the direction of the gradient within the pixel's area, the pixel is classified as an inflection point. If no such zero crossing occurs, the label assigned to the pixel is based on the gradient magnitude and Hessian eigenvalues calculated at the center of the pixel, local coordinates $(0,0)$, as in Table 8.6.

Case Two: One Zero Crossing

If a zero crossing of the first directional derivative is found within the pixel's area, then the pixel is a strict, local, one-dimensional extremum and must be assigned a label from the set (peak, pit, ridge, ravine, or saddle). At the location of the zero crossing, the Hessian and gradient are recomputed, and if the gradient magnitude at the zero crossing is zero, Table 8.7 is used.

If the gradient magnitude is nonzero, then the choice is either ridge or ravine. If the second directional derivative in the direction of the zero crossing is negative, we have a ridge. If it is positive, we have a ravine. If it is zero, we compare the function value at the center of the pixel, $f(0,0)$, with the function value at the zero crossing, $f(r,c)$. If $f(r,c)$ is greater than $f(0,0)$, we call it a ridge, otherwise we call it a ravine.

Table 8.6   Pixel label calculation for case 1: no zero crossing.

$\|\nabla f\|$	λ_1	λ_2	Label
0	0	0	Flat
+	−	−	Concave hill
+	−	0	Concave hill
+	−	+	Saddle hill
+	0	0	Slope
+	+	−	Saddle hill
+	+	0	Convex hill
+	+	+	Convex hill

Case Three: Two Zero Crossings

If we have two zero crossings of the first directional derivative, one in each direction of extreme curvature, then the Hessian and gradient must be recomputed at each zero crossing. Using the procedure just described, we assign a label to each zero crossing. We call these labels LABEL1 and LABEL2. The final classification given the pixel is based on these two labels and is shown in Table 8.8.

If both labels are identical, the pixel is given that label. In the case of both labels being ridge, the pixel may actually be a peak, but experiments have shown that this case is rare. An analogous argument can be made for both labels being ravine. If one label is ridge and the other ravine, this indicates we are at or very close to a saddle point, and thus the pixel is classified as a saddle. If one label is peak and the other ridge, we choose the category giving us the "most information," which in this case is peak. The peak is a local maximum in all directions, whereas the ridge

Table 8.7   Pixel label calculation for case 2: one zero crossing.

$\|\nabla f\|$	λ_1	λ_2	Label
0	−	−	Peak
0	−	0	Ridge
0	−	+	Saddle
0	+	−	Saddle
0	+	0	Ravine
0	+	+	Pit

Table 8.8   Final pixel classification, case 3: two zero crossings.

LABEL1	LABEL2	Resulting Label
Peak	Peak	Peak
Peak	Ridge	Peak
Pit	Pit	Pit
Pit	Ravine	Pit
Saddle	Saddle	Saddle
Ridge	Ridge	Ridge
Ridge	Ravine	Saddle
Ridge	Saddle	Saddle
Ravine	Ravine	Ravine
Ravine	Saddle	Saddle

is a local maximum in only one direction. Thus peak conveys more information about the image surface. An analogous argument can be made if the labels are pit and ravine. Similarly, a saddle gives us more information than a ridge or a ravine. Thus a pixel is assigned "saddle" if its zero crossings have been labeled ridge and saddle or ravine and saddle.

It is apparent from Table 8.8 that not all possible label combinations are accounted for. Some combinations, such as peak and pit, are omitted because of the assumption that the underlying surface is smooth and sampled frequently enough that a peak and a pit will not both occur within the same pixel's area. If such a case does occur, our convention is to choose arbitrarily either LABEL1 or LABEL2 as the resulting label for the pixel.

Case Four: More Than Two Zero Crossings

If more than two zero crossings occur within a pixel's area, then in at least one of the extrema directions there are two zero crossings. If this happens, we choose the zero crossing closest to the pixel's center and ignore the other. If we ignore the further zero crossings, then this case is identical to case 3. This situation has yet to occur in our experiments.

8.13.4 Summary of Topographic Classification Scheme

The scheme is a parallel process for topographic classification of every pixel, which can be done in one pass through the image. At each pixel of the image, the following four steps need to be performed.

1. Calculate the fitting coefficients, k_1 through k_{10}, of a two-dimensional cubic polynomial in an $n \times n$ neighborhood around the pixel. These coefficients are easily computed by convolving the appropriate masks over the image.

2. Use the coefficients calculated in step 1 to find the gradient, the gradient magnitude, and the eigenvalues and eigenvectors of the Hessian at the center of the pixel's neighborhood, (0,0).

3. Search in the direction of the eigenvectors calculated in step 2 for a zero crossing of the first directional derivative within the pixel's area. (If the eigenvalues of the Hessian are equal and nonzero, then search in the Newton direction.)

4. Recompute the gradient, the gradient magnitude, and the values of second directional derivative extrema at each zero crossing of the first directional derivative. Then apply the labeling scheme as described in Section 8.13.2.

Previous Work

Detection of topographic structures in a digital image is not a new idea. A wide variety of techniques for detecting pits, peaks, ridges, ravines, and the like have been described.

Peuker and Johnston (1972) characterize the surface shape by the sequence of positive and negative differences as successive surrounding points are compared with the central point. Peuker and Douglas (1975) describe several variations of this method for detecting one of the shapes from the set (pit, peak, pass, ridge, ravine, break, slope, flat). They start with the most frequent feature (slope) and proceed to the less frequent, thus making it an order-dependent algorithm.

Johnston and Rosenfeld (1975) attempt to find peaks by finding all points P such that no points in an $n \times n$ neighborhood surrounding P have greater elevation than P. Pits are found in an analogous manner. To find ridges, they identify points that are either east-west or north-south elevation maxima. This is done by using a "smoothed" array in which each point is given the highest elevation in a 2×2 square containing it. East-west and north-south maxima are also found on this array. Ravines are found in a similar manner.

Paton (1975) uses a six-term quadratic expansion in Legendre polynomials fitted to a small disk around each pixel. The most significant coefficients of the second-order polynomial yield a descriptive label chosen from the set (constant, ridge, valley, peak, bowl, saddle, ambiguous). He uses the continuous-fit formulation in setting up the surface fit equations as opposed to the discrete least-squares fit used in the facet model. The continuous fit is a more expensive computation than the discrete fit and results in a steplike approximation.

Grender's (1976) algorithm compares the gray level elevation of a central point with surrounding elevations at a given distance around the perimeter of a circular window. The radius of the window may be increased in successive passes through the image. This topographic-labeling set consists of slope, ridge, valley, knob, sink, and saddle.

Toriwaki and Fukumura (1978) take a totally different approach from all the others. They use two local features of gray level pictures, connectivity number and coefficient of curvature, for classification of the pixel into peak, pit, ridge, ravine, hillside, or pass. They then describe how to extract structural information from the image once the labelings have been made. This structural information consists of ridge lines, ravine lines, and the like.

Hsu, Mundy, and Beaudet (1978) use a quadratic surface approximation at every point on the image surface. The principal axes of the quadratic approximation are used as directions in which to segment the image. Lines emanating from the center pixel in these directions thus provide natural boundaries of patches approximating the surface. The authors then selectively generate the principal axes from some critical points distributed over an image and interconnect them into a network to get an approximation of the image data. In this network, which they call the *web representation,* the axes divide the image into regions and show important features, such as edges and peaks. They are then able to extract a set of primitive features from the nodes of the network by mask matching. Global features, such as ridge lines, are obtained by state transition rules.

Lee and Fu (1981) define a set of 3×3 templates that they convolve over the image to give each class except the class they call plain, a figure of merit. Their set of labels includes none, plain, slope, ridge, valley, foot, and shoulder. Thresholds are used to determine into which class the pixel will fall. In their scheme a pixel may satisfy the definition of zero, one, or more than one class. Ambiguity is resolved by choosing the class with the highest figure of merit.

■ Exercises

8.1. Suppose f is a function of two arguments (r, c). Let f_r denote $\frac{\partial}{\partial r} f$ and f_c denote $\frac{\partial}{\partial c} f$. Let $r = \rho \sin \theta$ and $c = \rho \cos \theta$. Show that

$$\frac{\partial}{\partial \rho} \frac{f_r}{\sqrt{f_r^2 + f_c^2}} = \frac{f_c (\sin \theta \cos \theta) \begin{pmatrix} f_{rr} f_{rc} \\ f_{rc} f_{cc} \end{pmatrix} \begin{pmatrix} f_c \\ -f_r \end{pmatrix}}{(f_r^2 + f_c^2)^{\frac{3}{2}}}$$

$$\frac{\partial}{\partial \rho} \frac{f_c}{\sqrt{f_r^2 + f_c^2}} = \frac{-f_r (\sin \theta \cos \theta) \begin{pmatrix} f_{rr} f_{rc} \\ f_{rc} f_{cc} \end{pmatrix} \begin{pmatrix} f_c \\ -f_r \end{pmatrix}}{(f_r^2 + f_c^2)^{\frac{3}{2}}}$$

8.2. Using the previous result, show that the change in a unit vector in the direction of the gradient taken in a direction of angle θ (θ being clockwise with respect to the column axis) is given by

$$\frac{(\sin \theta \cos \theta) \begin{pmatrix} f_{rr} f_{rc} \\ f_{rc} f_{cc} \end{pmatrix} \begin{pmatrix} f_c \\ -f_r \end{pmatrix}}{f_r^2 + f_c^2} \begin{pmatrix} f_x \\ -f_r \end{pmatrix} \frac{1}{\sqrt{f_r^2 + f_c^2}}$$

8.3. Show that the change in gradient direction taken in the direction of the gradient is given by

$$\frac{(f_r f_c) \begin{pmatrix} f_{rr} f_{rc} \\ f_{rc} f_{cc} \end{pmatrix} \begin{pmatrix} f_c \\ -f_r \end{pmatrix}}{(f_r^2 + f_c^2)^{\frac{3}{2}}} \left[\begin{pmatrix} f_c \\ -f_r \end{pmatrix} \frac{1}{\sqrt{f_r^2 + f_c^2}} \right]$$

8.4. Show that the change in gradient direction taken in the contour direction is given by

$$\frac{(f_r - f_c)\left(\frac{f_{rr}f_{rc}}{f_{rc}f_{cc}}\right)\left(\frac{f_c}{-f_r}\right)}{(f_r^2 + f_c^2)^{\frac{3}{2}}}\left[\left(\frac{f_c}{-f_r}\right)\frac{1}{\sqrt{f_r^2 + f_c^2}}\right]$$

8.5. Show that the change in gradient magnitude taken in the direction of the gradient is given by

$$\frac{(f_r f_c)\left(\frac{f_{rr}f_{rc}}{f_{rc}f_{cc}}\right)\left(\frac{f_c}{-f_r}\right)}{f_r^2 + f_c^2}$$

8.6. Suppose $f(r,c) = h(r^2 + c^2)$. Show that (a) the change in gradient direction taken in the direction of the gradient is zero; and (b) the change in gradient direction taken in the contour direction is given by $8h'(r^2 + c^2)^3(r^2 + c^2)$ times a unit vector in the contour direction.

8.7. Suppose $f(r,c) = h(\alpha r + \beta c + \gamma)$. Show that (a) the change in gradient direction taken in the direction of the gradient is zero; (b) the change in gradient direction taken in the direction of the contour is zero; and (c) the change in gradient magnitude taken in the direction of the gradient is $(\alpha^2 + \beta^2)h''(\alpha r + \beta c + \gamma)$.

8.8. Suppose the model is

$$g(x) = \sum_{n=1}^{n} \alpha_n f_n(x) + \eta(x)$$

where g is the observed surface at discretized values of x, the f_n are the orthonormal basis functions and η is an independent additive noise having mean 0 and variance σ^2 for each x. Show that the least-squares estimate $\hat{\alpha}_m$ for α_n is given by

$$\hat{\alpha}_m = \sum_{x} g(x) f_m(x)$$

8.9. Show that the expected value of $\hat{\alpha}_m$ is α_m; that is, $E[\hat{\alpha}_m] = \alpha_m$.

8.10. Show that $V[\hat{\alpha}_m] = E[(\hat{\alpha}_m - \alpha_m)^2] = \sigma^2$, so that if η has a normal distribution,

$$\hat{\alpha}_m \text{ has } N(\alpha_m, \sigma^2) \text{ and } \sum_{n=1}^{N}(\hat{\alpha}_n - \alpha_n)^2/\sigma^2$$

has χ_N^2 distribution.

8.11. If $e(x) = g(x) - \sum_{n=1}^{N} \hat{\alpha}_n(x)$ is the residual fitting error at x, show that

$$E[e^2(x)] = \sigma^2\left[1 - \sum_{n=1}^{N} fn^2(x)\right]$$

which implies that the residual variance is different at different positions.

8.12. Let the spatial domain of each f_n be the symmetric integer set $D = \{-M, \ldots, 0, \ldots, M\}$. Take the f_n to be the discretely orthonormal polynomials over the set D. For $N = 1, 2$, and 3 and $M = 1, 2$, and 3, plot $E[e^2(x)]$ as a function of x.

8.13. If η has a normal distribution, show that $\sum_{x} e^2(x)/\sigma^2$ has a χ_{M-N}^2 distribution.

8.14. The fitted function $\hat{g}(x) = \sum_{n=1}^{N} \hat{\alpha}_n f_n(x)$. Show that

$$E[\hat{g}(x)] = \sum_{n=1}^{N} \alpha_n f_n(x)$$

$$V[\hat{g}(x)] = \sigma^2 \sum_{n=1}^{N} f_n^2(x)$$

8.15. Show that $E[e^2(x)] + V[\hat{g}(x)] = \sigma^2$, which implies that at the x locations for which the fit is good, that is, x values for which $E[e^2(x)]$ is small, the variance of the fitted values will enlarge. And likewise, at the x locations for which the fit is bad, that is, x values for which $E[e^2(x)]$ is large, the variance of the fitted values will be small.

8.16. Suppose two surfaces $g_1(r,c) = \alpha_1 r + \beta_1 c + \gamma_1 rc + \delta_1$ and $g_2(r,c) = \alpha_2 r + \beta_2 c + \gamma_2 rc + \delta_2$ are given. If one surface is assumed to be a spatial and gray level translation of the other, that is

$$g_2(r,c) = g_1(r - r_o, c - c_o) + b_o$$

show that

$$r_o = \frac{\beta_1 - \beta_2}{\gamma_1}$$

$$c_o = \frac{\alpha_1 - \alpha_2}{\gamma_1}$$

$$b_o = \delta_2 - \delta_1 + \alpha_1 r_o + \beta_1 c_o - \gamma_1 r_o c_o$$

8.17. Suppose that the parameters $\alpha_1, \beta_1, \gamma_1, \delta_1$ and $\alpha_2, \beta_2, \gamma_2, \delta_2$ of the previous problem are unknown, but that unbiased, uncorrelated estimates $\hat{\alpha}_1, \hat{\beta}_1, \hat{\gamma}_1, \hat{\delta}_1, \hat{\alpha}_2, \hat{\beta}_2, \hat{\gamma}_2, \hat{\delta}_2$ are known and follow a Gaussian distribution. Show that the values of $\alpha_1, \beta_1, \gamma_1, \delta_1, \alpha_2, \beta_2, \gamma_2, \delta_2$ that maximize $\mathrm{prob}(\alpha_1, \beta_1, \gamma_1, \delta_1, \alpha_2, \beta_2, \gamma_2, \delta_2 | \hat{\alpha}_1, \hat{\beta}_1, \hat{\gamma}_1, \hat{\delta}_1, \hat{\alpha}_2, \hat{\beta}_2, \hat{\gamma}_2, \hat{\delta}_2)$ are given by

$$\alpha_1 = \hat{\alpha}_1, \qquad \alpha_2 = \hat{\alpha}_2$$
$$\beta_1 = \hat{\beta}_1, \qquad \beta_2 = \hat{\beta}_2$$
$$\delta_1 = \hat{\delta}_1, \qquad \delta_2 = \hat{\delta}_2$$

$$\gamma_1 = \gamma_2 = \frac{\hat{\gamma}_1 \sigma_{\gamma_2}^2 + \hat{\gamma}_2 \sigma_{\gamma_1}^2}{\sigma_{\gamma_1}^2 + \sigma_{\gamma_2}^2}$$

8.18. Show that the first four discretely orthogonal polynomials over the set $\{-2, -1, 0, 1, 2\}$ are given by

$$\frac{1}{\sqrt{5}} 1, \quad \frac{1}{\sqrt{10}} x, \quad \frac{1}{\sqrt{14}}(x^2 - 2), \quad \frac{1}{6\sqrt{10}}(5x^3 - 17x)$$

so that the discretized polynomials have the respective vector forms

$$\frac{1}{\sqrt{5}}\begin{pmatrix} 1 \\ 1 \\ 1 \\ 1 \\ 1 \end{pmatrix}, \quad \frac{1}{\sqrt{10}}\begin{pmatrix} -2 \\ -1 \\ 0 \\ 1 \\ 2 \end{pmatrix}, \quad \frac{1}{\sqrt{14}}\begin{pmatrix} 2 \\ -1 \\ -2 \\ -1 \\ 2 \end{pmatrix}, \quad \frac{1}{\sqrt{10}}\begin{pmatrix} -1 \\ 2 \\ 0 \\ -2 \\ 1 \end{pmatrix}$$

8.19. Do a least-squares fit for the observed values $a, a, a, a, a+b$ over the symmetric integer set $\{-2, -1, 0, 1, 2\}$. Graph the fitted function and determine the location of the zero of the second derivative of the fitted function. Show that the fitted values are given by vector form

$$
a \begin{pmatrix} 1 \\ 1 \\ 1 \\ 1 \\ 1 \end{pmatrix} + b \begin{pmatrix} -.0143 \\ .0571 \\ -.0857 \\ .0571 \\ .9857 \end{pmatrix}
$$

and in canonical form by

$$
\hat{g}(n) = b \left[\frac{n^3}{12} + \frac{n^2}{7} - \frac{n}{12} - \frac{3}{35} \right] + a, \quad n \in \{-2, -1, 0, 1, 2\}
$$

8.20. Show that the location n, which extremizes $\hat{g}(n)$ of Exercise 8.17, are the roots of the polynomial $21n^2 + 24n - 7$, which makes the zeros of $\hat{g}'(u)$ independent of the edge contrast b.

8.21. Show that the location n of the inflection point must satisfy $7n + 4 = 0$.

8.22. Let f be a function defined on the interval $[a, b]$ having an extremum at x_0 and an inflection point at x_i, both of which lie in the interval. Define the relative depth of the extremum x_0 by

$$
r(x_0) = \begin{cases} \min\{|f(a) - f(x_0)|, |f(x_i) - f(x_0)|\} & \text{if } x_0 < x \\ \min\{|f(b) - f(x_0)|, |f(x_i) - f(x_0)|\} & \text{otherwise} \end{cases}
$$

Define the dynamic range of f over the interval $[a, b]$ by

$$
R = \max_{a \le x \le b} f(x) - \min_{a \le x \le b} f(x)
$$

Define the relative depth of the extremum at x_0 by

$$
d = \frac{r(x_0)}{R}
$$

Determine the relative depth of the least-squares fitted function to the values

    a. $\alpha, \alpha, \alpha, \alpha, \beta$

    b. $\alpha, \alpha, \alpha, \beta, \beta$

where the observed values are those observed on the domain $\{-2, -1, 0, 1, 2\}$. Can the relative depth be used to distinguish between second derivative zero crossings arising from an edge near the middle of the domain and second derivative zero crossings arising from an edge near the end of the domain?

8.23. The line directional derivative $f_\theta'(r, c)$ of a function f, defined on the Euclidean plane, in the direction θ is defined by

$$
f_\theta'(r, c) = \lim_{d \to 0} \frac{f(r + d \sin \theta, c + d \cos \theta) - f(r - d \sin \theta, c - d \cos \theta)}{2d}
$$

Show

a. $\quad f_\theta''(r,c) = \dfrac{\partial f}{\partial r}(r,c)\sin\theta + \dfrac{\partial f}{\partial c}(r,c)\cos\theta$

b. $\quad f_\theta''(r,c) = \dfrac{\partial^2 f}{\partial r^2}(r,c)\sin^2\theta + 2\dfrac{\partial^2 f}{\partial r\partial c}(r,c)\sin\theta\cos\theta + \dfrac{\partial^2 f}{\partial c^2}(r,c)\cos^2\theta$

c. $\quad f_\theta''' = \left(\dfrac{\partial^3 f}{\partial r^3} - 3\dfrac{\partial^3 f}{\partial r\partial c^2}\right)\sin^3\theta + \left(\dfrac{\partial^3 f}{\partial c^3} - 3\dfrac{\partial^3 f}{\partial r^2\partial c}\right)\cos^3\theta$

$\qquad + 3\dfrac{\partial^3 f}{\partial r\partial c^2}\sin\theta + 3\dfrac{\partial^3 f}{\partial r^2\partial c}\cos\theta$

d. $\quad f_\theta'' = \dfrac{1}{2}\left(\dfrac{\partial^2 f}{\partial r^2} + \dfrac{\partial^2 f}{\partial c^2}\right) + \left(\dfrac{\partial^2 f}{\partial c^2} - \dfrac{\partial^2 f}{\partial r^2}\right)\dfrac{\cos 2\theta}{2} + \dfrac{\partial^2 f}{\partial r\partial c}\sin\theta$

8.24. Discuss the use of the form $w_1 f'\theta + w_2 f_\theta'''$ for a gradient-based edge detector, where θ is the gradient direction. How could reasonable choices for the values of w_1 and w_2 be made?

8.25. Define relative error e of an approximate value by

$$e = \frac{\text{approximate value} - \text{true value}}{\text{true value}}$$

(a) Over the worst possible values for a and b, what is the worst possible relative error of the approximation $|a| + |b|$ to $\sqrt{a^2 + b^2}$? (b) Over the worst possible values for a and b, what is the worst possible relative error of the approximation $|a| + |b| - \frac{1}{2}\min\{|a|, |b|\}$ to $\sqrt{a^2 + b^2}$? (c) Over the worst possible values for a and b, what is the worst possible relative error of the approximation $w_1(|a|+|b|) - w_2\min\{|a| = |b|\}$ to $\sqrt{a^2 + b^2}$?

8.26. Show that f_θ'' achieves a relative minimum over all θ when

$$\cos 2\theta = \frac{\frac{\partial^2 f}{\partial r^2} - \frac{\partial^2 f}{\partial c^2}}{\Delta} \quad \text{and} \quad \sin 2\theta = \frac{-2\frac{\partial^2 f}{\partial r\partial c}}{\Delta}$$

where

$$\Delta = \sqrt{\left(\frac{\partial^2 f}{\partial r^2}\right)^2 + 4\left(\frac{\partial^2 f}{\partial r\partial c}\right)^2}$$

Show that $f'' - \theta$ achieves a relative maximum over all θ when

$$\cos 2\theta = \frac{\left(\frac{\partial^2 f}{\partial r^2} - \frac{\partial^2 f}{\partial c^2}\right)}{\Delta} \quad \text{and} \quad \sin 2\theta = \frac{2\frac{\partial^2}{\partial r\partial c}}{\Delta}$$

■ Bibliography

Abdelmalek, N. N., "Noise Filtering in Digital Images and Approximation Theory," *Pattern Recognition,* Vol. 19, 1986, pp. 417–424.

Ballard, D. H., "Generalizing the Hough Transform to Detect Arbitrary Shapes," *Pattern Recognition,* Vol. 13, 1981, pp. 11–122.

Beaudet, P. R., "Rotationally Invariant Image Operators," *Proceedings of the Fourth International Joint Conference on Pattern Recognition,* Tokyo, 1978, pp. 579–583.

Beckman, P., *Orthogonal Polynomials for Engineers and Physicists,* Golem, Boulder, CO, 1973.

Dreschler, L., and H. Nagel, "Volumetric Model and 3D-Trajectory of a Moving Car Derived from Monocular TV-Frame Sequences of a Street Scene," *Proceedings of the International Joint Conference on Artificial Intelligence,* Vancouver, B.C., 1981, pp. 692–697.

Duda, R., *Pattern Classification and Scene Analysis,* Wiley, New York, 1973.

Duda, R., and P. Hart, "Use of Hough Transformation to Detect Lines and Curves in Pictures," *Communications of the ACM,* Vol. 15, 1972, pp. 11–15.

Ehrich, R. W., and J. P. Foith, "Topology and Semantics of Intensity Arrays," *Computer Vision Systems,* Academic Press, New York, 1978, pp. 111–128.

Forsythe, G. E., "Generation and Use of Orthogonal Polynomials for Data-Fitting with a Digital Computer," *Journal of the Society for Industrial Applied Mathematics,* Vol. 5, 1957, pp. 74–88.

Graham, R. F., "Snow Removal—A Noise Stripping Process for Picture Signals," *IRE Transaction on Information Theory,* Vol. II-8, 1962, pp. 129–144.

Grender, G. C., "TOPO: A Fortran Program for Terrain Analysis," *Computer Geoscience,* Vol. 2, 1976, pp. 195–209.

Haralick, R. M., "Edge and Region Analysis for Digital Image Data," *Computer Vision, Graphics, and Image Processing,* Vol. 12, 1980, pp. 60–73.

——, "The Digital Edge," *Proceedings of the IEEE Computer Society Conference on Pattern Recognition and Image Processing,* New York, 1981, pp. 285–294.

——, "Zero-Crossing of Second Directional Derivative Edge Operator," *SPIE Symposium on Robotic Vision,* Washington, DC, 1982, p. 23.

——, "Ridges and Valleys on Digital Images," *Computer Vision, Graphics, and Image Processing,* Vol. 22, 1983, pp. 28–38.

——, "Digital Step Edges from Zero Crossing of the Second Directional Derivatives," *IEEE Transactions on Pattern Analysis and Pattern Recognition,* Vol. PAMI-5, 1984, pp. 58–68.

——, "Cubic Facet Model Edge Detector and Ridge Valley Detector: Implementation Details," in *Pattern Recognition in Practice II,* E. S. Gelsema and L. Kanal (eds.), North Holland, Amsterdam, 1986.

Haralick, R. M., and L. T. Watson, "A Facet Model for Image Data," *Computer Graphics and Image Processing,* Vol. 15, 1981, pp. 113–129.

Haralick, R. M., L. T. Watson, and T. J. Laffey, "The Topographic Primal Sketch," *International Journal of Robotics Research,* Vol. 2, 1983, pp. 50–72.

Hsu, S., J. L. Mundy, and P. R. Beaudet, "Web Representation of Image Data," *Proceedings of the Fourth International Conference on Pattern Recognition,* New York, 1978, pp. 675–680.

Hueckel, M., "A Local Visual Operator Which Recognizes Edges and Lines," *Journal of the ACM,* Vol. 20, 1973, pp. 634–647.

Huertas, A., "Corner Detection for Finding Buildings in Aerial Images," *USCIPI Report 1050,* University of Southern California, 1981, pp. 61–68.

Iannino, A., and S. D. Shapiro, "An Iterative Generalization of the Sobel Edge Detection Operator," *Proceedings of the IEEE Conference on Pattern Recognition and Image Processing,* Chicago, 1979, pp. 130–137.

Johnston, E. G., and A. Rosenfeld, "Digital Detection of Pits, Peaks, Ridges, and Ravines," *IEEE Transactions on Systems, Man, and Cybernetics,* Vol. 5, 1975, pp. 472–480.

Kimme, C., D. Ballard, and J. Sklansky, "Finding Circles by an Array of Accumulators," *Communications of the ACM,* Vol. 18, 1975, pp. 120–122.

Kitchen, L., and A. Rosenfeld, "Gray Level Corner Detection," *Technical Report 887,* Computer Science Center, University of Maryland, College Park, 1980.

Laffey, T. J., R. M. Haralick, and L. T. Watson, "Topographic Classification of Digital Image Intensity," *Proceedings of the IEEE Workshop on Computer Vision,* New York, 1982, pp. 171–177.

Lee, H. C., and K. S. Fu, "The GLGS Image Representation and Its Application to Preliminary Segmentation," *Proceedings of the 1981 Conference on Pattern Recognition and Image Processing,* New York, 1981, pp. 256–261.

Marr, D., "Early Processing of Visual Information," *Philosophical Transactions of the Royal Society,* London, Vol. B-275, 1976, pp. 483–524.

——, "Visual Information Processing: The Structure and Creation of Visual Representations," *Philosophical Transactions of the Royal Society,* London, Vol. B-290, 1980, pp. 199–218.

Martelli, A., "Edge Detection Using Heuristic Search Methods," *Computer Graphics and Image Processing,* Vol. 1, 1972, pp. 169–182.

Merò, L., and T. Vamos, "Real-Time Edge-Detection Using Local Operators, *Proceedings of the Third International Joint Conference on Pattern Recognition,* Coronado, CA, 1976.

Nagar, M., and T. Matsuyama, "Edge Processing Smoothing," *Computer Graphics and Image Processing,* Vol. 9, 1979, pp. 394–407.

Nagel, H., and W. Enkelmann, "Investigation of Second Order Gray-Value Variations to Estimate Corner Point Displacements," *IEEE Conference on Pattern Recognition and Image Processing,* Munich, 1982.

O'Gorman, F., and M. B. Clowes, "Finding Picture Edges through Collinearity of Feature Points," *IEEE Transactions on Computers,* Vol. C-25, 1976, pp. 449–456.

Paton, K., "Picture Description Using Legendre Polynomials," *Computer Vision, Graphics, and Image Processing,* Vol. 4, 1975, pp. 40–54.

Peuker, T. K., and D. H. Douglas, "Detection of Surface-Specific Points by Local Parallel Processing of Discrete Terrain Elevation Data," *Computer Graphics and Image Processing,* Vol. 4, 1975, pp. 375–387.

Peuker, T. K., and E. G. Johnston, "Detection of Surface-Specific Points by Local Parallel Processing of Discrete Terrain Elevation Data," *Technical Report 206,* Computer Science Center, University of Maryland, College Park, 1972.

Prewitt, J., "Object Enhancement and Extraction," in *Picture Processing and Psychopictorics,* B. Lipkin and A. Rosenfeld (eds.), Academic Press, New York, 1970, pp. 75–149.

Ramer, E., "Transformation of Photographic Images into Stroke Arrays," *IEEE Transactions on Circuits and Systems,* Vol. CAS-22, 1975, pp. 363–373.

Roberts, L. G., "Machine Perception of Three-Dimensional Solids," in *Optical and Electro-optical Information Processing,* J. T. Tippet et al. (eds.), MIT Press, Cambridge, MA, 1965, pp. 159–197.

Rutishauser, H., "Jacobi Method for Real Symmetric Matrix," in *Handbook for Automatic Computation, Vol. 2: Linear Algebra,* J. H. Wilkinson and C. Reinsch (eds.), Springer-Verlag, New York, 1971.

Rutkowski, W. S., and A. Rosenfeld, "A Comparison of Corner Detection Techniques for Chain-Coded Curves," *Technical Report 623,* Computer Science Center, University of Maryland, College Park, 1978.

Sobel, I. E., *Camera Models and Machine Perception,* Ph.D. thesis, Stanford University, 1970.

Strang, G., *Linear Algebra and Its Applications,* 2d ed., Academic Press, New York, 1980, pp. 243–249.

Tomita F., and S. Tsuji, "Extraction of Multiple Regions by Smoothing in Selected Neighborhoods," *IEEE Transactions on Systems, Man, and Cybernetics,* Vol. SMC-7, 1977, pp. 107–109.

Toriwaki, J., and T. Fukumura, "Extraction of Structural Information from Grey Pictures," *Computer Graphics and Image Processing,* Vol. 7, 1978, pp. 30–51.

Yasuoka, Y., and R. M. Haralick, "Peak Noise Removal by a Facet Model," *Pattern Recognition,* Vol. 16, 1983, pp. 23–29.

Zuniga, O., and R. M. Haralick, "Corner Detection Using the Facet Model," *Proceedings of the IEEE Computer Vision and Pattern Recognition Conference,* Washington, D.C., 1983, pp. 30–37.

——, "Integrated Directional Derivative Gradient Operators," *IEEE Transactions on Systems, Man, and Cybernetics,* Vol. SMC-17, 1987, pp. 508–517.

——, "Gradient Threshold Selection Using the Facet Model," *Pattern Recognition,* Vol. 22, 1988a, pp. 493–503.

——, "Correction to Integrated Directional Derivative Gradient Operators," *IEEE Transactions on Systems, Man, and Cybernetics,* Vol. SMC-18, 1988b.

9 TEXTURE

9.1 Introduction

Texture is an important characteristic for the analysis of many types of images, from multispectral scanner images obtained from aircraft or satellite platforms, which the remote-sensing community analyzes, to microscopic images of cell cultures or tissue samples, which the biomedical community analyzes, to the outdoor scenes and object surfaces, which the machine vision community analyzes. Despite its importance and ubiquity in image data, a formal approach or precise definition of texture does not exist. The texture discrimination techniques are for the most part ad hoc. In this chapter we discuss some of the extraction techniques and models that have been used to measure textural properties and to compute three-dimensional shape from texture.

Ehrich and Foith (1978) summarize the following issues in texture analysis:

1. Given a textured region, determine to which of a finite number of classes the region belongs.

2. Given a textured region, determine a description or model for it.

3. Given an image having many textured areas, determine the boundaries between the differently textured regions.

Issue 1 has to do with the pattern recognition task of textural feature extraction. Issue 2 has to do with generative models of texture. Issue 3 has to do with using what we know about issues 1 and 2 to perform a texture segmentation of an image. In the remainder of this section we provide a brief historical elaboration of issues 1 and 2.

Early work in image texture analysis sought to discover useful features that had some relationship to the fineness and coarseness, contrast, directionality, roughness, and regularity of image texture. Tamura, Mori, and Yamawaki (1978) discuss the relationship of such descriptive measures to human visual perception. Typically, an image known to be texturally homogeneous was analyzed, and the problem was to measure textural features by which the image could be classified. For example, with microscopic imagery, analysts discriminated between eosinophils and large lymphocytes by using a textural feature for cytoplasm and a shape feature for cell nucleus (Bacus and Gose, 1972). With aerial imagery, they discriminated between areas having natural vegetation and trees and areas having manmade objects, buildings, and roads by using textural features (Haralick and Shanmugam, 1973). These statistical textural-feature approaches included use of the autocorrelation function, the spectral power density function, edgeness per unit area, spatial gray level co-occurrence probabilities, gray level run-length distributions, relative extrema distributions, and mathematical morphology.

Later approaches to image texture analysis sought a deeper understanding of what image texture is by the use of a generative image model. Given a generative model and the values of its parameters, one can synthesize homogeneous image texture samples associated with the model and the given value of its parameters. This association provides a theoretical and visual means of understanding the texture. Image texture analysis then amounts to verification and estimation. First one must verify that a given image texture sample is consistent with or fits the model. Then one must estimate the values of the model parameters on the basis of the observed sample. Autoregressive, moving-average, time-series models (extended to two dimensions), Markov random fields, and mosaic models are examples of model-based techniques.

The image texture we consider is nonfigurative and cellular. We think of this kind of texture as an organized-area phenomenon. When it is decomposable, it has two basic dimensions on which it may be described. The first dimension is concerned with the gray level primitives or local properties constituting the image texture, and the second dimension is concerned with the spatial organization of the gray level primitives. The basic textural unit of some textural primitives in their defining spatial relationships is sometimes called a *texel*, for texture element.

Gray level primitives are regions with gray level properties. The gray level primitive can be described in terms such as the average level or the maximum and minimum levels of its region. A region is a maximally connected set of pixels having a given gray level property. The gray level region can be evaluated in terms of its area and shape. The gray level primitive includes both its gray level and gray level region properties.

An image texture is described by the number and types of its primitives and their spatial organization or layout. The spatial organization may be random, may have a pairwise dependence of one primitive on a neighboring primitive, or may have a dependence of n primitives at a time. The dependence may be structural, probabilistic, or functional (like a linear dependence).

Image texture can be qualitatively evaluated as having one or more of the properties of fineness, coarseness, smoothness, granulation, randomness, lineation or as being mottled, irregular, or hummocky. Each of these qualities translates into some property of the gray level primitives and the spatial interaction between them. Unfortunately, few investigators have attempted experiments to map semantic meaning into precise properties of gray level primitives and their spatial distribution.

When the gray level primitives are small in size and the spatial interaction between gray level primitives is constrained to be very local, the resulting texture is a microtexture. The simplest example of a microtexture occurs when independent Gaussian noise is added to each pixel's value in a smooth gray level area (Fig. 9.1 a). As the Gaussian noise becomes more correlated, the texture becomes more of a microtexture. Finally, when the gray level primitives begin to have their own distinct shape and regular organization, the texture becomes a macrotexture. This illustrates an important point. Texture cannot be analyzed without a frame of reference in which a gray level primitive is stated or implied. For any textural surface there exists a scale at which, when the surface is examined, it appears smooth and textureless. Then as resolution increases, the surface appears as a fine texture and then a coarse one, and for multiple-scale textural surfaces the cycle of smooth, fine, and coarse may repeat.

Figure 9.1(a) shows a white-noise microtexture. Figure 9.1(b) is a box-filtered defocusing of the image in Part (a). It illustrates the beginning organization of some gray level primitives larger in size than the individual pixel. Parts (c) and (d) are examples of textures in which the gray level primitives have become regions. Parts (e) and (f) show textures in which the gray level primitives themselves have their own identifiable shape properties. These constitute macrotextures.

To use the gray level and textural pattern elements objectively, we must explicitly define the concepts of gray level and texture. Doing so, we discover that gray level and texture are not independent concepts. They bear an inextricable relationship to each other very much as do a particle and a wave. Whatever exists has both particle and wave properties, and depending on the situation, either particle or wave properties may predominate. Similarly, in the image context both gray level and texture are always there, although at times one property can dominate the other, and we tend to speak of only gray level or only texture. Hence, when we explicitly define gray level and texture, we are defining not two concepts but one gray level–texture concept.

The basic interrelationships in the gray level–texture concept are the following: When a small-area patch of an image has little variation of gray level primitives, the dominant property of that area is gray level. When a small-area patch has wide variation of gray level primitives, the dominant property is texture. Crucial in this distinction are the size of the small-area patch, the relative sizes and types of gray level primitives, and the number and placement or arrangement of the distinguishable primitives. As the number of distinguishable gray level primitives decreases, the gray level properties will predominate. In fact, when the small-area patch is only the size of a pixel, so that there is only one discrete feature, the only property present is simple gray level. As the number of distinguishable gray level primitives increases within the small-area patch, the texture property will predominate. When the spatial pattern in the gray level primitives is random and the gray level variation between primitives is wide, a fine texture results. As the spatial pattern becomes more definite and the gray level regions involve more and more pixels, a coarser texture results.

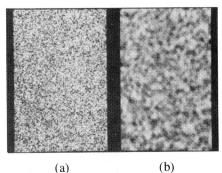

(a)   (b)

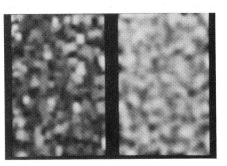

(c)   (d)

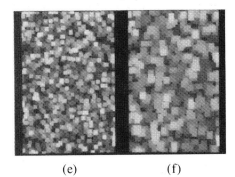

(e)   (f)

Figure 9.1 Four different kinds of texture: (a) White-noise texture, (b) colored-noise texture determined by box filtering the white-noise texture, (c) and (d) more macrotextures, (e) and (f) textures in which the primitives begin to have their own identifiable shape properties.

In summary, to characterize texture we must characterize the gray level primitive properties as well as the spatial relationships between them. This implies that texture-level is really a two-layered structure, the first layer having to do with specifying the local properties that manifest themselves in gray level primitives; the second layer, with specifying the organization among the gray level primitives. In images having texture gradients caused by nonfrontal views of a homogeneous texture, both primitives and their spatial relationships may change as a function of position within the image. We begin our discussion of texture with the gray level co-occurrence and the generalized co-occurrence approaches. From this perspective we describe a variety of other approaches. We conclude with a discussion on inferring three-dimensional shape from texture on a perspective projection image of a textured planar surface.

9.2   Gray Level Co-Occurrence

The gray level spatial dependence approach characterizes texture by the co-occurrence of its gray levels. Coarse textures are those for which the distribution changes only slightly with distance, and fine textures are those for which the distribution changes rapidly with distance.

The gray level co-occurrence can be specified in a matrix of relative frequencies P_{ij} with which two neighboring pixels separated by distance d occur on the image, one with gray level i and the other with gray level j. Such matrices of spatial gray level dependence frequencies are symmetric and a function of the angular relationship between the neighboring pixels as well as a function of the distance between them. For a $0°$ angular relationship, they explicitly average the probability of a left-right transition of gray level i to gray level j. Figure 9.2 illustrates the set of all horizontal neighboring pixels separated by distance 1. This set, along with the

(1,1)	(1,2)	(1,3)	(1,4)
(2,1)	(2,2)	(2,3)	(2,4)
(3,1)	(3,2)	(3,3)	(3,4)
(4,1)	(4,2)	(4,3)	(4,4)

$$L_y = \{1,2,3,4\}$$
$$L_x = \{1,2,3,4\}$$

$$R_H = \{((k,l),(m,n)) \in (L_y \times L_x) \times (L_y \times L_x) | k - m = 0, |l - n| = 1\}$$
$$= \{((1,1),(1,2)),((1,2),(1,1)),((1,2),(1,3)),((1,3),(1,2)),$$
$$((1,3),(1,4)),((1,4),(1,3)),((2,1),(2,2)),((2,2),(2,1)),$$
$$((2,2),(2,3)),((2,3),(2,2)),((2,3),(2,4)),((2,4),(2,3)),$$
$$((3,1),(3,2)),((3,2),(3,1)),((3,2),(3,3)),((3,3),(3,2)),$$
$$((3,3),(3,4)),((3,4),(3,3)),((4,1),(4,2)),((4,2),(4,1)),$$
$$((4,2),(4,3)),((4,3),(4,3)),((4,3),(4,4)),((4,4),(4,3))\}$$

Figure 9.2 The set of all distance-1 horizontal neighboring resolution cells on a 4×4 image.

image levels, would be used to calculate a distance-1 horizontal spatial gray level dependence matrix.

Formally, for angles quantized to 45° intervals, the unnormalized frequencies are defined by

$$P(i,j,d,0°) = \#\{[(k,\ell),(m,n)]|$$
$$k - m = 0, \; |\ell - n| = d$$
$$I(k,\ell) = i, \; I(m,n) = j\}$$

$$P(i,j,d,45°) = \#\{[(k,\ell),(m,n)]|$$
$$(k - m = d, \; \ell - n = -d)$$

or
$$(k - m = -d, \; \ell - n = d)$$
$$I(k,\ell) = i, \; I(m,n) = j\}$$

$$P(i,j,d,90°) = \#\{[(k,\ell),(m,n)]|$$
$$|k - m| = d, \; \ell - n = 0$$
$$I(k,\ell) = i, \; I(m,n) = j\}$$

$$P(i,j,d,135°) = \#\{[(k,\ell),(m,n)]$$
$$(k - m = d, \; \ell - n = d)$$

or
$$(k - m = -d, \; \ell - n = -d)$$
$$I(k,\ell) = i, \; I(m,n) = j\}$$

where $\#$ denotes the number of elements in the set.

Note that these matrices are symmetric; $P(i,j;d,a) = P(j,i;d,a)$. The distance metric ρ implicit in these equations can be explicitly defined by $\rho[(k,l),(m,n)] = \max\{|k - m|, |l - n|\}$. Other distances, such as Euclidean, could be used as well.

Consider Fig. 9.3(a), which represents a 4×4 image with four gray levels, ranging from 0 to 3. Figure 9.3(b) shows the general form of any gray level spatial dependence matrix. For example, the element in the (2,1)th position of the distance-1 horizontal P_H matrix is the total number of times two gray levels of value 2 and 1 occurred horizontally adjacent to each other. To determine this number, we count the number of pairs of resolution cells in R_H such that the first resolution cell of the pair has gray level 2 and the second resolution cell of the pair has gray level 1. In Fig. 9.3(c) through (f) we calculate all four distance-1 gray level spatial dependence matrices.

Using features calculated from the co-occurrence matrix (see Fig. 9.4), Haralick and Bosley (1973) performed a number of identification experiments. On a set of aerial imagery and eight terrain classes (old residential, new residential, lake, swamp, marsh, urban, railroad yard, scrub or wooded), an 82% correct identification was obtained. On a LANDSAT Monterey Bay, California, image, an 84% correct identification was obtained with the use of 64×64 subimages and both spectral and textural features on seven terrain classes: coastal forest, woodlands, annual grasslands, urban areas, large irrigated fields, small irrigated fields, and water. On a set of sandstone photo-micrographs, an 89% correct identification was obtained on five sandstone classes: Dexter-L, Dexter-H, St. Peter, Upper Muddy, and Gaskel.

Figure 9.3 Spatial co-occurrence calculations (Haralick, Shanmugam, and Dinstein, 1973).

The wide class of images in which they found that spatial gray level dependence carries much of the texture information is probably indicative of the power and generality of this approach.

The many possible co-occurrence features times the number of distance angle relationships for which the co-occurrence matrices can be computed lead to a potentially large number of dependent features. Zucker (1980) suggests using only the distance that maximizes a chi-square statistic of P. Tou and Chang (1977) discuss an eigenvector-based feature extraction approach to help reduce the dimension of feature space.

The power of the gray level co-occurrence approach is that it characterizes the spatial interrelationships of the gray levels in a textural pattern and can do so in a way that is invariant under monotonic gray level transformations. Its weakness is that it does not capture the shape aspects of the gray level primitives. Hence it is not likely to work well for textures composed of large-area primitives. Also, it cannot capture the spatial relationships between primitives that are regions larger than a pixel.

Julesz (1961) is the first to use co-occurrence statistics in visual human texture discrimination experiments. Darling and Joseph (1968) use statistics obtained from nearest neighbor gray level transition probability matrices to measure textures using spatial intensity dependence in satellite images taken of clouds. Deutsch and Belknap (1972) use a variant of co-occurrence matrices to describe image texture. Zobrist and Thompson (1985) use co-occurrence statistics in a Gestalt grouping experiment. Bartles and Wied (1975), and Bartles, Bahr, and Wied (1969) use one-dimensional co-occurrence statistics for the analysis of cervical cells. Rosenfeld and Troy (1970), Haralick (1971), and Haralick, Shanmugam, and Dinstein (1973) suggest the use of spatial co-occurrence for arbitrary distances and directions. Galloway (1975) uses gray level run-length statistics to measure texture. These statistics are computable from co-occurrence if one assumes that the image is generated by a

Uniformity of energy	$\sum_{i,j} P_{ij}^2$
(Related to the variance of $\{P_{i1}, \ldots, P_{ij}, \ldots, P_{NN}\}$)	
Entropy	$-\sum_{i,j} P_{ij} \log P_{ij}$
Maximum Probability	$\max_{i,j} P_{ij}$
Contrast	$\sum_{i,j} |i - j|^k (P_{ij})^\ell$
Inverse difference moment	$\sum_{\substack{i,j \\ i \neq j}} \frac{(P_{ij})^\ell}{|i - j|^k}$
Correlation	$\sum_{i,j} \frac{(i - \mu)(j - \mu)P_{ij}}{\sigma^2}$ where $\mu = \sum_{i,j} iP_{ij}$
Probability of a run of length n for gray level i (Assuming the image is Markov)	$\sum_i \frac{(P_i - P_{ii})^2 (P_{ii})^{n-1}}{P_i^n}$ where $P_i = \sum_j P_{ij}$
Homogeneity	$\sum_{i,j} \frac{P(i,j)}{1 + |i - j|}$
Cluster Tendency	$\sum_{i,j} (i + j - 2\mu)^k P_{ij}$

Figure 9.4 Eight of the common features computed from the co-occurrence probabilities.

Markov process. Chen and Pavlidis (1979) use the co-occurrence matrix in conjunction with a split-and-merge algorithm to segment an image at textural boundaries. Tou and Chang (1977) use statistics from the co-occurrence matrix, followed by a principal-components eigenvector-dimensionality-reduction scheme to reduce the dimensionality of the classification problem.

Statistics that Haralick, Shanmugam, and Dinstein (1973) compute from such co-occurrence matrices of equal probability quantized images (see also Conners and Harlow, 1978) are used to analyze textures in satellite images (Haralick and Shanmugam, 1974). An 89% classification accuracy is obtained. Additional applications of this technique include the analysis of microscopic images (Haralick and Shanmugam, 1973), pulmonary radiographs (Chien and Fu, 1974), and cervical cell, leukocyte, and lymph node tissue section images (Pressman, 1976).

Vickers and Modestino (1982) argue that using features of the co-occurrence matrix in a classification situation is surely suboptimal and that better results are obtained by using the co-occurrence matrix directly in a maximum-likelihood classifier. They report better than a 95% correct identification accuracy in distinguishing between tree bark, calf leather, wool, beach sand, pigskin, plastic bubbles, herring-bone weave, raffia, and wood grain textures.

Bacus and Gose (1972) use a gray level difference variant of the co-occurrence matrix to help distinguish between eosinophils and lymphocytes. They use the probability of a given contrast occurring in a given spatial relationship as a textural feature. This gray level difference probability can be defined in terms of the co-occurrence probabilities by

$$P(d) = \sum_i \sum_j P(i,j)$$

$$|i - j| = d$$

The probability of a small contrast d for a coarse texture will be much higher than for a fine texture. Bacus and Gose use statistics of the differences between a pixel on a red image and a displaced pixel on a blue image. Rosenfeld, Wang, and Wu (1982) also suggest using multispectral difference probabilities. Haralick and Shanmugam (1973) use multispectral co-occurrence probabilities.

Weszka, Dyer, and Rosenfeld (1976) use contrast, energy, entropy, and mean of $P(d)$ as texture measures and report that they did about as well as the co-occurrence probabilities. Sun and Wee (1983) suggest a variant of the gray level difference distribution. They fix a distance d and a contrast c and determine the number of pixels each having gray level g and each having n neighbors that are within distance d and within contrast c. That is,

$$P(g,n) = \#\{(i,j)|I(i,j) = g \quad \text{and}$$

$$\#\{(k,l)|\rho[(i,j),(k,l)] \le d \text{ and } |I(i,j) - I(k,l)| \le c\} = n\}$$

From $P(g,n)$ they compute a variety of features, such as entropy and energy. They report an 85% classification accuracy in distinguishing between textures of three different geological terrain types on LANDSAT imagery. Wechsler and Kidode (1979) and Wechsler (1980) use the gray level difference probabilities to define a random-walk model for texture. See de Souza (1983) and Percus (1983) for some comments on the random-walk model.

Haralick (1975) illustrates a way to use co-occurrence matrices to generate an image in which the value at each resolution cell is a measure of the texture in the resolution cell's neighborhood. All these studies produce reasonable results on different textures. Conners and Harlow (1976, 1980) conclude that this spatial gray level dependence technique is more powerful than spatial frequency (power spectra), gray level difference (gradient), and gray level run-length methods (Galloway, 1975) of texture quantification.

Dyer, Hong, and Rosenfeld (1980) and Davis, Clearman, and Aggarwal (1981) compute co-occurrence features for local properties, such as edge strength maxima and edge direction relationships. They suggest computing gray level co-occurrence involving only those pixels near edges. Zucker and Kant (1981) also suggest using generalized co-occurrence statistics. Terzopoulos and Zucker (1982) report a 13% increase in accuracy when combining gray level co-occurrence features with edge co-occurrence features in the diagnosis of osteogenesis imperfecta from images of fibroblast cultures.

Davis (1981) computes co-occurrence probabilities for spatial relationships parametrized by angular orientation. He defines the polarogram to be a statistic of these co-occurrence probabilities as a function of the angular orientation. See also Chetverikov (1981). Chetverikov (1984) uses co-occurrence statistics as a function of displacement to determine textural regularity.

9.2.1 Generalized Gray Level Spatial Dependence Models for Texture

A simple generalization of the primitive gray level co-occurrence approach is to consider more than two pixels at a time.

Given a specific kind of spatial neighborhood (such as a 3×2 or 5×5 neighborhood) and a subimage, one can parametrically estimate the joint probability distribution of the gray levels over the neighborhoods in the subimage. In the case of a 5×5 neighborhood, the joint distribution would be 25-dimensional. The generalized gray level spatial dependence model for texture is based on this joint distribution. Here the neighborhood is the primitive, the arrangement of its gray levels is the property, and the texture is characterized by the joint distribution of the gray levels in the neighborhood.

The prime candidate distribution for parametric estimation is the multivariate normal. If $x_1, \ldots, x_N$ represent the N K-normal vectors coming from neighborhoods in a subimage, then the mean vector μ and covariance matrix Σ can be estimated by

$$\mu = \mu_o \mathbf{1}, \text{ where } \mu_o = \frac{1}{N} \sum_{n=1}^{N} \mathbf{1} x_n$$

$$\text{and } \Sigma = \frac{1}{N} \sum_{n=1}^{N} (x_n - \mu)(x_m - \mu)'$$

where $\mathbf{1}$ is a column vector all of whose components have the volume 1.

9.3   Strong Texture Measures and Generalized Co-Occurrence

Strong texture measures take into account the co-occurrence between texture primitives. We call this generalized co-occurrence. On the basis of Julesz (1975) the most important interaction between texture primitives probably occurs as a two-way interaction. Textures with identical second- and lower-order interactions but with different higher-order interactions tend to be visually similar, although this is not universally true.

To describe generalized co-occurrence, we next focus on the primitive and then the spatial relationships between primitives. A primitive is a connected set of pixels characterized by a list of attributes. The simplest primitive is the pixel with its gray level attribute. The next more complicated primitive is a connected set of pixels homogeneous in level (Tsuji and Tomita, 1973). Such a primitive can be characterized by size, elongation, orientation, and average gray level. Useful texture measures include co-occurrence of primitives based on relationships of distance or adjacency. Maleson, Brown, and Feldman (1977) suggest using region-growing techniques and ellipsoidal approximations to define the homogeneous regions and degree of collinearity as one basis of co-occurrence. For example, for all primitives of elongation greater than a specified threshold, we can use the angular orientation of each primitive with respect to its closest neighboring primitive as a strong measure of texture.

Relative extrema primitives were proposed by Rosenfeld and Troy (1970), Mitchell, Myers, and Boyne (1977), Ehrich and Foith (1976), Mitchell and Carlton (1977), and Ehrich and Foith (1978a, 1978b). Co-occurrence between two relative extrema was suggested by Davis, Johns, and Aggarwal (1979). Because of their invariance under any monotonic gray scale transformation, relative extrema primitives are likely to be very important.

It is possible to segment an image on the basis of relative extrema (for example, relative maxima) in the following way. Label all pixels in each maximally connected relative maximum plateau with an unique label. Then label each pixel with the label of the relative maximum that can reach it by a monotonically decreasing path. If more than one relative maximum can reach it by a monotonically decreasing path, then label the pixel with a special label c, for common. We call the regions so formed the descending components of the image.

Sometimes it is useful to work with primitives that are maximally connected sets of pixels having a particular property, such as the same gray level or the same edge direction. Gray levels and local properties are not the only attributes that primitives may have. Other attributes include measures of shape and homogeneity of local property. For example, a connected set of pixels can be associated with its length, with the elongation of its shape, or with the variance of its local property.

Many kinds of primitives can be generated or constructed from image data by one or more applications of neighborhood operators. Included in this class of primitives are (1) connected components, (2) ascending or descending components, (3) saddle components, (4) relative maxima or minima components, and (5) central axis components. Neighborhood operators that compute these kinds of primitives can be found in various papers and will not be discussed here; see Arcelli and Sanniti di Baja (1978), Haralick (1978), Rosenfeld (1970), Rosenfeld and Davis (1976), Rosenfeld and Pfaltz (1966, 1968), Rosenfeld and Thurston (1971), and Yokoi, Toriwaki, and Fukumura (1975).

9.3.1 Spatial Relationships

Once the primitives have been constructed, we have available a list of primitives, their center coordinates, and their attributes. We might also have available some topological information, such as which primitives are adjacent to which. From these data we can select a simple spatial relationship, such as *adjacency* of primitives or *nearness* of primitives, and count how many primitives of each kind occur in the specified spatial relationship.

More complex spatial relationships include closest distance or closest distance within an angular window. In this case, for each kind of primitive situated in the texture, we could lay expanding circles around it and locate the shortest distance between it and every other kind of primitive. Our co-occurrence frequency would be three-dimensional, two dimensions for primitive kind and one dimension for shortest distance. This can be dimensionally reduced to two dimensions by considering only the shortest distance between each pair of like primitives.

To define the concept of generalized co-occurrence, it is necessary first to decompose an image into its primitives. Let Q be the set of all primitives on the image. Then we measure primitive properties, such as mean gray level, variance of gray levels, region size and region shape. Let T be the set of primitive properties and f be a function assigning to each primitive in Q a property of T. Finally, we need to specify a spatial relation between primitives, such as distance or adjacency. Let $S \subseteq Q \times Q$ be the binary relation pairing all primitives that satisfy the spatial relation. The generalized co-occurrence matrix P is defined by

$$P(t_1, t_2) = \frac{\#\{(q_1, q_2) \in S | f(q_1) = t_1 \text{ and } f(q_2) = t_2\}}{\#S}$$

$P(t_1, t_2)$ is just the relative frequency with which two primitives occur with specified spatial relationships in the image, one primitive having property t_1 and the other having property t_2.

Zucker (1974) suggests that some textures may be characterized by the frequency distribution of the number of primitives related to any given primitive. This probability $p(k)$ is defined by

$$p(k) = \frac{\#\{q \in Q | \#S(q) = k\}}{\#Q}.$$

Although this distribution is simpler than co-occurrence, no investigator appears to have used it in texture discrimination experiments.

9.4   Autocorrelation Function and Texture

From one point of view, texture relates to the spatial size of the gray level primitives on an image. Gray level primitives of larger size are indicative of coarser textures; gray level primitives of smaller size are indicative of finer textures. The autocorrelation function is a feature that describes the size of the gray level primitives.

We explore the autocorrelation function with the help of a thought experiment. Consider two image transparencies that are exact copies of each other. Overlay one transparency on top of the other, and with a uniform source of light measure the average light transmitted through the double transparency. Now translate one transparency relative to the other and measure only the average light transmitted through the portion of the image where one transparency overlaps the (x, y) translated positions. The two-dimensional autocorrelation function of the image transparency is their average normalized with respect to the $(0, 0)$ translation.

Let $I(u, v)$ denote the transmission of an image transparency at position (u, v). We assume that outside some bounded rectangular region $0 \leq u \leq L_x$ and $0 \leq$

$v \leq L_y$, the image transmission is zero. Let (x, y) denote the x-translation and y-translation, respectively. The autocorrelation function for the image transparency d is formally defined by

$$p(x,y) = \frac{\frac{1}{(L_x - |x|)(L_y - |y|)} \int_{-\infty}^{\infty} \int I(u,v)I(u+x, v+y)du \; dv}{\frac{1}{L_x L_y} \int_{-\infty}^{\infty} \int I^2(u,v)du \; dv} \qquad |x| < L_x \text{ and } |y| < L_y$$

If the gray level primitives on the image are relatively large, then the autocorrelation will drop off slowly with distance. If the gray level primitives are small, then the autocorrelation will drop off quickly with distance. To the extent that the gray level primitives are spatially periodic, the autocorrelation function will drop off and rise again in a periodic manner. The relationship between the autocorrelation function and the power spectral density function is well known: They are Fourier transforms of each other.

The gray level primitive in the autocorrelation model is the gray level. The spatial organization is characterized by the correlation coefficient that is a measure of the linear dependence one pixel has on another.

9.5   Digital Transform Methods and Texture

In the digital transform method of texture analysis, the digital image is typically divided into a set of nonoverlapping small square subimages. Suppose the size of the subimage is $n \times n$ resolution cells; then the n^2 gray levels in the subimage can be thought of as the n^2 components of an n^2-dimensional vector. The set of subimages then constitutes a set of n^2-dimensional vectors. In the transform technique each of these vectors is reexpressed in a new coordinate system. The Fourier transform uses the complex sinusoid basic set; the Hadamard transfer uses the Walsh function basis set, and the like. The point to the transformation is that the basis vectors of the new coordinate system have an interpretation that relates to spatial frequency or sequency, and since frequency is a close relative of texture, such transformations can be useful.

The gray level primitive in spatial frequency (sequency) models is the gray level. The spatial organization is characterized by the kind of linear dependence that measures projection lengths.

Gramenopoulos (1973) uses a transform technique employing the sine-cosine basis vectors (and implements it with the FFT algorithm) on LANDSAT imagery. He is interested in the power of texture and spatial patterns to do terrain type recognition. He uses subimages of 32×32 resolution cells and finds that on a Phoenix, AZ, LANDSAT image, spatial frequencies larger than 3.5 cycles/km and smaller than 5.9 cycles/km contain most of the information needed to discriminate between terrain types. His terrain classes are clouds, water, desert, farms, mountains, urban, riverbed, and cloud shadows. He achieves an overall identification accuracy of 87%.

Horning and Smith (1973) does work similar to Gramenopoulos, but with aerial multispectral scanner imagery instead of LANDSAT imagery.

Kirvida and Johnson (1973) compare the fast Fourier, Hadamard, and Slant transforms for textural features on LANDSAT imagery over Minnesota. They use 8×8 subimages and five categories: hardwoods, conifers, open, city, and water. Using only spectral information, they obtain 74% accuracy. When they add textural information, they increase their identification accuracy to 99%.

Maurer (1974a, 1974b) obtains encouraging results by classifying crops from low-altitude color photography on the basis of a one-dimensional Fourier series taken in a direction orthogonal to the rows.

Bajcsy (1973a, 1973b) and Bajcsy and Lieberman (1974, 1976) divide the image into square windows and use the two-dimensional power spectrum of each window. They express the power spectrum in a polar coordinate system of radius r versus angle ϕ, treating the power spectrum as two independent one-dimensional functions of r and ϕ. Directional textures tend to have peaks in the power spectrum as a function of ϕ. Bloblike textures tend to have peaks in the power spectrum as a function of r. The investigators show that texture gradients can be measured by locating the trends of relative maxima of r or ϕ as a function of the position of the window whose power spectrum is being taken. As the relative maxima along the radial direction tend to shift toward larger values, the image surface becomes more finely textured.

In general, features based on Fourier power spectra have been shown to perform more poorly than features based on second-order gray level co-occurrence statistics (Haralick, Shanmugam, and Dinstein, 1973) or those based on first-order statistics of spatial gray level differences (Weszka, Dyer, and Rosenfeld, 1976; Conners and Harlow, 1980). Presence of aperture effects has been hypothesized to account for part of the unfavorable performance by Fourier features compared with spatial-domain gray level statistics (Dyer and Rosenfeld, 1976), although experimental results indicate that this effect, if present, is minimal. However, D'Astous and Jernigan (1984) claim that the reason for the poorer performance is that earlier studies employing the Fourier transform features used summed spectral energies within band- or wedge-shaped regions in the power spectrum. They argue that additional discriminating information can be obtained from the power spectrum in terms of characteristics such as regularity, directionality, linearity, and coarseness. The degree of regularity can be measured by the relative strength of the highest non-DC peak in the power spectrum. Other peak features include the Laplacian at the peak, the number of adjacent neighbors of the peak containing at least 50% of the energy in the peak, the distance between the peak and the origin, and the polar angle of the peak. In the comparative experiment reported by D'Astous and Jernigan, the peak features yielded uniformly greater interclass differences than the co-occurrence features, and the co-occurrence features yielded uniformly greater interclass distances than the summed Fourier energy features.

Pentland (1984) computes the discrete Fourier transform for each block of 8×8 pixels of an image and determines the power spectrum. He then uses a linear regression technique on the log of the power spectrum as a function of frequency to estimate the fractal dimension D. For gray level intensity surfaces of textured scenes that satisfy the fractal model (Mandelbrot, 1983), the power spectrum satisfies

$$P(f) = Cf^{-(2D+1)}$$

Pentland reports a classification accuracy of 84.4% on a texture mosaic using fractal dimensions computed in two orthogonal directions.

Transforms other than the Fourier can be used for texture analysis. Kirvida (1976) compared the fast Fourier, Hadamard, and Slant Transforms for textural features on aerial images of Minnesota. Five classes (i.e., hardwood trees, conifers, open space, city, and water) were studied with the use of 8×8 subimages; a 74% correct classification rate was obtained by using only spectral information. This rate increased to 98.5% when textural information was also included in the analysis. These researchers reported no significant difference in the classification accuracy as a function of which transform was employed.

The simplest orthogonal transform that can be locally applied is the identity transformation. Lowitz (1983, 1984) and Carlotto (1984) suggest using the local histogram for textural feature extraction. Lowitz uses window sizes as large as 16×16; Carlotto, as large as 33×33.

The power of the spatial frequency approach to texture is the familiarity we have with these concepts. One of the inherent problems, however, is in regard to gray level calibration of the image. The procedures are not invariant under even a monotonic transformation of gray level. To compensate for this, probability quantizing can be employed. But the price paid for the invariance of the quantized images under monotonic gray level transformations is the resulting loss of gray level precision in the quantized image. Weszka, Dyer, and Rosenfeld (1976) compare the effectiveness of some of these techniques for terrain classification. They conclude that spatial frequency approaches perform significantly poorer than the other approaches.

9.6   Textural Energy

In the textural energy approach (Laws, 1980, 1985), the image is first convolved with a variety of kernels. If I is the input image and $g_1, \ldots, g_N$ are the kernels, the images $J_n = I * g_n$, $n = 1, \ldots, N$ are computed. Then each convolved image is processed with a nonlinear operator to determine the total textural energy in each pixel's 7×7 neighborhood. The energy image corresponding to the nth kernel is defined by

$$S_n(r,c) = \frac{1}{49} \sum_{i=-3}^{3} \sum_{j=-3}^{3} |J_n(r+1, c+j)|$$

Associated with each pixel position (r,c), therefore, is a textural feature vector $[S_1(r,c), \ldots, S_N(r,c)]$.

The textural energy approach is very much in the spirit of the transform approach, but it uses smaller windows or neighborhood supports. The kernels Laws uses have supports for 3×5, 5×5, and 7×7 neighborhoods. The one-dimensional forms are illustrated in Fig. 9.5. The two-dimensional forms are generated from the one-dimensional form by outer products. That is, if k_1 and k_2 are two one-

$$L3 = [\; 1 \quad 2 \quad 1\;]$$
$$E3 = [\; \text{-}1 \quad 0 \quad 1\;]$$
$$S3 = [\; \text{-}1 \quad 2 \quad \text{-}1\;]$$

$$L5 = [\; 1 \quad 4 \quad 6 \quad 4 \quad 1\;]$$
$$E5 = [\; \text{-}1 \quad \text{-}2 \quad 0 \quad 2 \quad 1\;]$$
$$S5 = [\; \text{-}1 \quad 0 \quad 2 \quad 0 \quad \text{-}1\;]$$
$$W5 = [\; \text{-}1 \quad 2 \quad 0 \quad \text{-}2 \quad 1\;]$$
$$R5 = [\; 1 \quad \text{-}4 \quad 6 \quad \text{-}4 \quad 1\;]$$

$$L7 = [\; 1 \quad 6 \quad 15 \quad 20 \quad 15 \quad 6 \quad 1\;]$$
$$E7 = [\; \text{-}1 \quad \text{-}4 \quad \text{-}5 \quad 0 \quad 5 \quad 4 \quad 1\;]$$
$$S7 = [\; \text{-}1 \quad \text{-}2 \quad 1 \quad 4 \quad 1 \quad \text{-}2 \quad \text{-}1\;]$$
$$W7 = [\; \text{-}1 \quad 0 \quad 3 \quad 0 \quad \text{-}3 \quad 0 \quad 1\;]$$
$$R7 = [\; 1 \quad \text{-}2 \quad \text{-}1 \quad 4 \quad \text{-}1 \quad \text{-}2 \quad 1\;]$$
$$O7 = [\; \text{-}1 \quad 6 \quad \text{-}15 \quad 20 \quad \text{-}15 \quad 6 \quad \text{-}1\;]$$

Figure 9.5 One-dimensional textural energy kernels. L stands for level, E for edge, S for shape, W for wave, R for ripple, and O for oscillation.

dimensional forms, each a row vector of K columns, then $k'_1 \, k_2$ constitutes a $K \times K$ kernel.

Laws shows that on a set of experiments with some sample textures, the textural energy approach is able to distinguish among eight textures with an identification accuracy of 94%, whereas the spatial gray level co-occurrence has an accuracy of only 72%.

The biggest difficulty with the textural energy approach as with the textural transfer approach is the possibility of introducing significant errors along boundaries between different textures, because it is exactly for positions by the boundary that the neighborhood support includes a mixture of textures. It is possible for the textural energy vector for a neighborhood of such mixed textures to be close to a vector prototype for a third texture having nothing to do with the textures of the mixture.

To handle this problem, Hsaio and Sawchuk (1989) do one more level of processing on each textural energy image. For each pixel position (r,c) of textural energy image J_n, they compute the mean and variance of the four 15×15 neighborhoods for which (r,c) is the southeast, the southwest, the northeast, and the northwest pixel, respectively. Then they create a smoothed textural energy image $\bar{J}_n$ in which $\bar{J}_n(r,c)$ is given the value of the mean of the 15×15 neighborhood that has the smallest variance.

Unser and Eden (1989) discuss multiscale modification of the textural energy approach. They take the textural energy image and iteratively smooth it with Gaussian kernels having a half-octave scale progression. They reduce feature dimensionality by simultaneously diagonalizing the scatter matrices at two successive levels of spatial resolution.

Unser (1984) notes that one could use a discrete orthogonal transform, such as the discrete sine or discrete cosine transform, applied locally to each pixel's neighborhood instead of using the ad hoc linear operators of Laws. He indicates a classification accuracy above 96% with the discrete sine transform in distinguishing between textures of paper, grass, sand, and raffia. Ikonomopoulos and Unser (1984) suggest local directional filters. Jernigan and D'Astous (1984) compute an FFT on windows and then use the entropy in different-sized regions for the normalized power spectrum for textural features.

9.7   Textural Edgeness

The autocorrelation function and digital transforms basically both reference texture to spatial frequency. Rosenfeld and Troy (1970) and Rosenfeld and Thurston (1971) conceive of texture not in terms of spatial frequency but in terms of edgeness per unit area. An edge passing through a pixel can be detected by comparing the values for local properties obtained in pairs of nonoverlapping neighborhoods bordering the pixel. To detect microedges, small neighborhoods can be used; to detect macroedges, large neighborhoods can be used (Fig. 9.6).

The local property that Rosenfeld and Thurston suggest is the quick Roberts gradient (the sum of the absolute value of the differences between diagonally opposite neighboring pixels). The Roberts gradient is an estimate of the image gradient. Thus a measure of texture for any subimage can be obtained by computing the Roberts gradient image for the subimage and from it determining the average value of the gradient in the subimage.

Sutton and Hall (1972) extend Rosenfeld and Thurston's idea by making the gradient a function of the distance between the pixels. Thus for every distance d and subimage I defined over neighborhood N, they compute

$$g(d) = \sum_{(i,j) \in N} \{ |I(i,j) - I(I+d,j)| + |I(i,j) - I(i-d,j)|$$
$$+ |I(i,j) - I(i,j+d)| + |I(i,j) - I(i,j-d)| \}$$

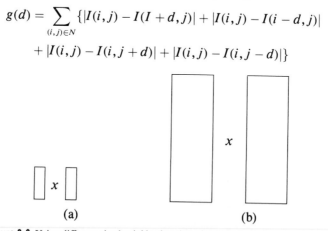

(a)   (b)

Figure 9.6 Using different-sized neighborhoods to determine micro- and macroedges. The difference between two average values in the left and right bordering neighborhoods to pixel x can be used to determine the vertical edge contrast. (a) Microedge. (b) Macroedge.

The curve of $g(d)$ is like the graph of the minus autocorrelation function translated vertically.

Sutton and Hall apply this textural measure in a pulmonary disease identification experiment and obtain an identification accuracy in the 80 percentile range for discriminating between normal and abnormal lungs when using a 128×128 subimage.

Triendl (1972) measures degree of edgeness by filtering the image with a 3×3 averaging filter and a 3×3 Laplacian filter. The two resulting filtered images are then smoothed with an 11×11 smoothing filter. The two values of average level and roughness obtained from the low- and high-frequency filtered image can be used as textural features.

Hsu (1977) determines textural edgeness by computing gradientlike measures for the gray levels in a neighborhood. If N denotes the set of resolution cells in a neighborhood about a pixel and g_c is the gray level of the center pixel, μ is the mean gray level in the neighborhood, and ρ is a metric, then Hsu suggests

$$\sum_{(i,j)\in N} \rho(I(i,j),\mu), \quad \sum_{(i,j)\in N} \rho(I(i,j),g_c), \quad \text{and} \quad \rho(\mu,g_c)$$

are all appropriate measures for textural edgeness of a pixel.

9.8   Vector Dispersion

The vector dispersion estimate for texture was first applied by Harris and Barrett (1978) in a cloud texture assessment study and is based on a theory developed by Fisher (1953). In the vector dispersion technique, the image texture is divided into mutually exclusive neighborhoods, and a sloped plane fit (see Chapter 8) to the gray levels is performed for each neighborhood. That is, using a relative coordinate system whose origin is the center of the neighborhood, one can model the gray levels in the neighborhood with

$$I(r,c) = \alpha r + \beta c + \gamma$$

A graphical representation of these fits is shown in Fig. 9.7.

The unit normal vector to the plane fit for the ith neighborhood is given by

$$\begin{pmatrix} l_i \\ m_i \\ n_i \end{pmatrix} = \frac{1}{\sqrt{\alpha_i^2 + \beta_i^2 + 1}} \begin{pmatrix} \alpha_i \\ \beta_i \\ -1 \end{pmatrix}$$

Then the maximum likelihood estimator of the unit vector $\begin{pmatrix} l \\ m \\ n \end{pmatrix}$ around which the

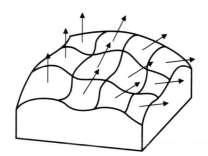

Figure 9.7 Graphical representation of the dispersion of a group of unit surface normal vectors for a patch of gray level intensity surface.

unit normal vectors are distributed is given by

$$\begin{pmatrix} l \\ m \\ n \end{pmatrix} = \frac{1}{R} \sum_{i=1}^{N} \begin{pmatrix} l_i \\ m_i \\ n_i \end{pmatrix}$$

where

$$R^2 = \left(\sum_{i=1}^{N} l_i \right)^2 + \left(\sum_{i=1}^{N} m_i \right)^2 + \left(\sum_{i=1}^{N} n_i \right)^2$$

According to Fisher (1953), the distribution of errors over the unit sphere is proportional to

$$e^{\kappa \cos \theta_i}$$

where $\cos \theta_i = ll_i + mm_i + nn_i$. The maximum likelihood estimate for κ satisfies

$$\coth \kappa - \frac{1}{\kappa} = \frac{R}{N}$$

and has the approximate solution

$$\kappa = \frac{N - 1}{N - R}$$

For smooth textures κ takes the value 1. For uneven or rough textures, κ takes a value near 0.

9.9   Relative Extrema Density

Rosenfeld and Troy (1970) suggest the number of extrema per unit area for a texture measure. They suggest defining extrema in one dimension only along a horizontal scan in the following way. In any row of pixels, a pixel i is a relative minimum if its gray level $g(i)$ satisfies

$$g(i) \leq g(i + 1) \quad \text{and} \quad g(i) \leq g(i - 1) \tag{9.1}$$

A pixel i is a relative maximum if

$$g(i) \geq g(i + 1) \quad \text{and} \quad g(i) \geq g(i - 1) \tag{9.2}$$

Note that with this definition each pixel in the interior of any constant gray level run of pixels is considered simultaneously a relative minimum and a relative maximum. This is so even if the constant run is just a plateau on the way down to or on the way up from a relative extremum.

The algorithm employed by Rosenfeld and Troy marks every pixel in each row that satisfies Eq. (9.1) or (9.2). Then it centers a square window around each pixel and counts the number of marked pixels. The texture image created this way corresponds to a defocused marked image.

Mitchell, Myers, and Boyne (1977) suggest the extrema idea of Rosenfeld and Troy except they use true extrema and operate on a smoothed image to eliminate extrema due to noise (Carlton and Mitchell, 1977; Ehrich and Foith, 1976, 1978a, 1978b).

One problem with simply counting all extrema in the same extrema plateau as extrema is that extrema per unit area as a measure is not sensitive to the difference between a region having a few large plateaus of extrema and many single-pixel extrema. The solution to this problem is to count an extrema plateau only once. This can be achieved by locating some central pixel in the extrema plateau and marking it as the extremum associated with the plateau. Another way of achieving this is to associate a value of $1/N$ for every extremum in an N-pixel extrema plateau.

In the one-dimensional case, two properties can be associated with every extremum: its height and its width. The height of a maximum can be defined as the difference between the value of the maximum and the highest adjacent minimum. The height (depth) of a minimum can be defined as the difference between the value of the minimum and the lowest adjacent maximum. The width of a maximum is the distance between its two adjacent minima. The width of a minimum is the distance between its two adjacent maxima.

Two-dimensional extrema are more complicated than one-dimensional extrema. One way of finding extrema in the full two-dimensional sense is by the iterated use of some recursive neighborhood operators propagating extrema values in an appropriate way. Maximally connected areas of relative extrema may be areas of single pixels or may be plateaus of many pixels. We can mark each pixel in a relative extrema region of size N with the value h, indicating that it is part of a relative extremum having height h, or mark it with the value h/N, indicating that it is part of a relative extrema region with the value h. Alternatively, we can mark the most centrally located pixel in the relative extrema region with the value h. Pixels not marked can be given the value 0. Then for any specified window centered on a given pixel, we can add up the values of all the pixels in the window. This sum divided by the window size is the average height of extrema in the area. Alternatively we could set h to 1, and the sum would be the number of relative extrema per unit area to be associated with the given pixel.

Going beyond the simple counting of relative extrema, we can associate properties with each relative extremum. For example, given a relative maximum, we can determine the set of all pixels reachable only by the given relative maximum, not by any other, by monotonically decreasing paths. This set of reachable pixels is a connected region and forms a mountain. Its border pixels may be relative minima or saddle pixels.

The relative height of the mountain is the difference between its relative maximum and the highest of its exterior border pixels. Its size is the number of pixels that constitute it. Its shape can be characterized by features such as elongation, circularity, and symmetric axis. Elongation can be defined as the ratio of the larger to the smaller eigenvalue of the 2×2 second-moment matrix obtained from the $\binom{x}{y}$ coordinates of the border pixels (Bachi, 1973; Frolov, 1975). Circularity can be defined as the ratio of the standard deviation to the mean of the radii from the region's center to its border (Haralick, 1975). The symmetric axis feature can be determined by thinning the region down to its skeleton and counting the number of pixels in the skeleton. For regions that are elongated, it may be important to measure the direction of the elongation or the direction of the symmetric axis.

Osman and Saukar (1975) use the mean and variance of the height of mountain or the depth of valley as properties of primitives. Tsuji and Tomita (1973) use size. Histograms and statistics of histograms of these primitive properties are all suitable measures for textural primitive properties.

9.10   Mathematical Morphology

The morphological approach to the texture analysis of binary images was proposed by Matheron (1975) and Serra and Verchery (1973). Mathematical morphology was discussed in Chapter 5. Here we review the basic definitions to make this discussion readable by itself. The approach requires the definition of a structuring element (i.e., a set of pixels constituting a specific shape, such as a line, a disk, or a square) and the generation of binary images that result from the translation of the structuring element through the image and the erosion of the image by the structuring element. The textural features can be obtained from the new binary images by counting the number of pixels having the value 1. This mathematical morphology approach of Serra and Matheron is the basis of the Leitz texture analyser (TAS) (Mueller and Herman, 1974; Mueller, 1974; Serra, 1974) and the Cyto computer (Sternberg, 1979). A broad spectrum of applications has been found for this quantitative analysis of microstructures method in materials science and biology.

We begin by examining the texture of binary images. Let H, a subset of pixels, be the structuring element. We define the translate of H by row-column coordinates (r,c) as $H(r,c)$, where

$$H(r,c) = \{(i,j)| \text{ for some } (r',c') \in H, i = r + r', j = c + c'\}$$

The erosion of F by the structuring element H, written as $F \ominus H$, is defined as

$$F \ominus H = \{(m,n)|H(m,n) \subseteq F\}$$

The eroded image J obtained by eroding F with structuring element H is a binary image where pixels take the value 1 for all pixels in $F \ominus H$. Textural properties can be obtained from the erosion process by appropriately parameterizing the structuring element (H) and determining the number of elements of the erosion as a function of the parameter's value.

For example, a two-pixel structuring element can be parameterized by fixing a row distance and a column distance between two pixels. The normalized area of the erosion as a function of row and column distance is the autocorrelation function of the binary image. A disk and a one-pixel wide annulus are two more examples of one-parameter structuring elements. The parameter in both cases is the radius. The area of the eroded image as a function of the parameter provides a statistical descriptor of the shape description of the image's shape distribution.

The dual operation of erosion is dilation. The dilation of F by structuring element H, written $F \oplus H$, is defined by

$$F \oplus H = \{(m,n)| \text{ for some } (i,j) \in F \text{ and } (r,s) \in H, m = i + r \text{ and } n = j + s\}$$

Composition of erosions and dilations determines two other important morphological operations that are idempotent and are duals of one another: openings and closings. The opening of F by H is defined by $F \circ H = (F \ominus H) \oplus H$. The closing of F by H is defined by $F \circ H = (F \oplus H) \ominus H$.

The number of binary-1 pixels of the opening as a function of the size parameter of the structuring element can determine the size distribution of the grains in an image. We simply take H_d to be a line structuring element of length d or a disk structuring element of diameter d. Then we can define the granularity of the image F by

$$G(d) = 1 - \frac{\#F \circ H_d}{\#F}$$

where $\#F$ means the number of elements in F. $G(d)$ measures the properties of grain pixels that cannot be contained in some translated structuring element of size d that is entirely contained in the grain and contains the given pixel. Thus it measures the proportion of pixels participating in grains of a size smaller than d.

Sternberg (1983) has extended the morphological definition of erosion to gray level images. The erosion of gray level image I by gray level structuring element H produces a gray level image J defined by

$$J(r,c) = \min_{(i,j)}\{I(r+i, c+j) - H(i,j)\} = (I \ominus H)(r,c)$$

The dilation of gray level image I by gray level structuring element H produces a gray level image J defined by

$$J(r,c) = \max_{(i,j)}\{I(r-i, c-j) + H(i,j)\} = (I \oplus H)(r,c)$$

The gray level opening is defined as a gray level erosion followed by a gray level dilation. The gray level closing is defined as a gray level dilation followed by a gray level erosion. Commonly used gray level structuring elements include rods, disks, cones, paraboloids, and hemispheres.

Peleg et al. (1984) use gray level erosion and dilation to determine the fractal surface of the gray level intensity surface of a textural scene. They define the scale-k volume of the blanket around a gray level intensity surface I by

$$V(k) = \sum_{(r,c)} (I \oplus H)(r,c) - (I \ominus H)(r,c)$$

where $\oplus$ means a k-fold dilation with the structuring element, and $\ominus$ means a k-fold erosion with the structuring element. Peleg et al. defined the structuring element H over the five-pixel cross neighborhood taking the value of 1 for the center pixel and 0 elsewhere. The fractal surface area A at scale k is then defined by

$$A(k) = \frac{V(k) - V(k-1)}{2}$$

and the fractal signature S at scale k is defined by

$$S(k) = \frac{d}{d \log k} \log A(k) = \frac{kA'(k)}{A(k)}$$

Peleg et al. compare the similarity between textures by the weighted distance D between their fractal signatures

$$D = \sum_k [S_1(k) - S_2(k)]^2 \log \left(\frac{k + \frac{1}{2}}{k - \frac{1}{2}} \right)$$

Werman and Peleg (1984) give a fuzzy set generalization to the morphological operators. Meyer (1979) and Lipkin and Lipkin (1974) demonstrate the capability of morphological textural parameters in biomedical image analysis. Theoretical properties of the erosion operator as well as those of other operators are presented by Matheron (1963), Serra (1978), and Lantuejoul (1978). The importance of this approach to texture analysis is that properties obtained by the application of operators in mathematical morphology can be related to physical three-dimensional shape properties of the materials imaged.

9.11 Autoregression Models

The autoregression model provides a way to use linear estimates of a pixel's gray level, given the gray levels in a neighborhood containing it, in order to characterize texture. For coarse textures, the coefficients will all be similar. For fine textures, the coefficients will vary widely.

The linear dependence that one pixel of an image has on another is well known and can be illustrated by the autocorrelation function. This linear dependence is exploited by the autoregression model for texture, which was first used by McCormick and Jayaramamurthy (1974). These researchers employ the Box and Jenkins (1970) time-series seasonal-analysis method to estimate the parameters of a given texture. They then use the estimated parameters and a given set of starting values to illustrate that the synthesized texture is close in appearance to the given texture. Deguchi and Morishita (1976), Tou, Kao, and Chang (1976), and Tou and Chang (1976) also use a similar technique.

Figure 9.8 shows this texture synthesis model. Given a randomly generated noise image and any sequence of K-synthesized gray level values in a scan, the next gray level value can be synthesized as a linear combination of the previously

b_1	b_2	b_3	b_4	..	..
..	..	..	..	..	..
..	..	..	..	..	..
..	..	b_n			

a_1	a_2	a_3	a_4	..	..
..	..	..	..	..	..
..	..	..	..	..	..
..	..	..	a_n		

$$a_{N+1} = \underbrace{\sum_{k=0}^{K-1} \alpha_k a_{N-k}}_{\text{Auto-regressive Terms}} + \underbrace{\sum_{\ell=0}^{L-1} \beta_\ell b_{N-\ell}}_{\text{Moving Average Terms}}$$

Figure 9.8 How, from a randomly generated noise image and a given starting sequence $a_1, \ldots, a_K$ representing the initial boundary conditions, all values in a texture image can be synthesized by a one-dimensional autoregressive model.

synthesized values plus a linear combination of previous L random-noise values. The coefficients of these linear combinations are the parameters of the model.

Although the one-dimensional model employed by Read and Jayaramamurthy (1972) worked reasonably well for the two vertical streaky textures on which they illustrated their method, their performance would be poorer on diagonal wiggly streaky textures. Better performance on general textures would be achieved by a full two-dimensional model, as illustrated in Fig. 9.9. Here a pixel (i, j) depends on a two-dimensional neighborhood $N(i, j)$ consisting of pixels above or to the left of it as opposed to the simple sequence of the previous pixels a raster scan could define. For each pixel (k, l) in an order-D neighborhood for pixel (i, j), (k, l) must be previous to pixel (i, j) in a standard raster sequence, and (k, l) must not have any coordinates more than D units away from (i, j). Formally the order-D neighborhood is defined by

$$N(i, j) = \{(k, l) \quad | \quad (i - D \leq k < i$$
$$\text{and} \quad j - D \leq l \leq j + D)$$
$$\text{or} \quad (k = i \text{ and } j - D \leq l < j)\}$$

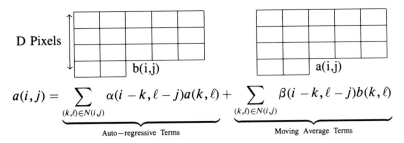

$$a(i, j) = \underbrace{\sum_{(k, \ell) \in N(i, j)} \alpha(i - k, \ell - j) a(k, \ell)}_{\text{Auto-regressive Terms}} + \underbrace{\sum_{(k, \ell) \in N(i, j)} \beta(i - k, \ell - j) b(k, \ell)}_{\text{Moving Average Terms}}$$

Figure 9.9 How, from a randomly generated noise image and a given starting sequence for the first-order D neighborhood in the image, all values in a texture image can be synthesized by a two-dimensional autoregressive model.

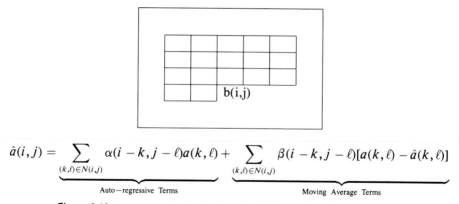

$$\hat{a}(i,j) = \underbrace{\sum_{(k,\ell)\in N(i,j)} \alpha(i-k,j-\ell)a(k,\ell)}_{\text{Auto-regressive Terms}} + \underbrace{\sum_{(k,\ell)\in N(i,j)} \beta(i-k,j-\ell)[a(k,\ell)-\hat{a}(k,\ell)]}_{\text{Moving Average Terms}}$$

Figure 9.10 How a gray level value for pixel (i,j) can be estimated by using the gray level values in the neighborhood $N(i,j)$ and the differences between the actual values and the estimated values in the neighborhood.

The autoregressive model can be employed in texture segmentation applications as well as texture synthesis applications. Let $\{\alpha_c(m,n), \beta_c(m,n)\}$ be the coefficients for texture category c, and let θ be a threshold value. Define the estimated value of the gray level at resolution cell (i,j) by

$$\hat{a}_c(i,j) = \sum_{(k,l)\in N(i,j)} \alpha_c(i-k,j-l)a_c(k,l)$$

$$+ \sum_{(k,l)\in N(i,j)} \beta_c(i-k,j-l)[a_c(k,l)-\hat{a}_c(k,l)]$$

See Fig. 9.10.

Assuming a uniform prior distribution, we can decide that pixel (i,j) has texture category k if

$$|a(i,j) - \hat{a}_k(i,j)| \le |a(i,j) - \hat{a}_l(i,j)| \text{ for every } l \text{ and } |a(i,j) - \hat{a}_k(i,j)| \le \theta$$

If $|a(i,j) - a_k(i,j)| > \theta$, then we can decide that pixel (i,j) is a boundary pixel.

The power of the autoregression linear estimator approach is that it is easy to use the estimator in a mode that synthesizes textures from any initially given linear estimator. In this sense the autoregressive approach is sufficient to capture everything about a texture. Its weakness is that the textures it can characterize are likely to consist mostly of microtextures.

9.12   Discrete Markov Random Fields

The Markov random field model for texture assumes that the texture field is stochastic and stationary and satisfies a conditional independence assumption. Let $R \times C$ be the spatial domain of an image, and for any $(r,c) \in R \times C$ let $N(r,c)$ denote the neighbors of (r,c). $N(r,c)$ does not include (r,c). Because the field is stationary, $(a,b) \in N(r,c)$ if and only if $(a+i,c+j) \in N(r+i,c+j)$ for any (i,j). Hence the spatial neighborhood configuration is the same all over the image. There is an obvious difficulty with this condition holding at pixels near the image boundary. The usual way of handling the problem theoretically is to assume the image is wrapped around a torus. In this case the canonical spatial neighborhood can be given as $N(0,0)$. For any (r,c), $N(r,c)$ is then a translation of $N(0,0)$.

The conditional independence assumption is that the conditional probability of the pixel given all the remaining pixels in the image is equal to the conditional probability of the pixel given just the pixels in its neighborhood. That is,

$$P[I(r,c)|I(i,j) : (i,j) \in R \times C, (i,j) \neq (r,c)] = P[I(r,c)|I(i,j) : (i,j) \in N(r,c)]$$

Markov mesh models were first introduced into the pattern recognition community by Chow (1962) and then by Abend, Harley, and Kanal (1965). One important issue is how to compute the joint probability function $P[I(r,c) : (r,c) \in R \times C]$. Hassner and Sklansky (1980) note that this can be done by identifying the conditional probability assumption with Gibbs ensembles, which are studied in statistical mechanics. Woods (1972) shows that when the distributions are Gaussian, the discrete Gauss-Markov field can be written as an equation in which each pixel's value is a linear combination of the values in its neighborhood plus a correlated noise term. That is,

$$I(r,c) = \sum_{(i,j) \in N(0,0)} I(r-i, c-j)h(i,j) + u(r,c) \qquad (9.3)$$

where the coefficients of the linear combination are given by the function h, and the set $\{u(r,c)|(r,c) \in R \times C\}$ represents a joint set of possible correlated Gaussian random variables. This equation has a lot of similarity to the autoregressive moving-average time-series models of Box and Jenkins (1970). There the relationship would be expressed by

$$I(r,c) = \sum_{(i,j) \in K(0,0)} I(r-i, c-j)h(i,j) + \sum_{(i,j) \in K(0,0)} u(r-i, c-j)k(i,j)$$

where $K(0,0)$ represents a domain that contains only pixels occurring after $(0,0)$ in the usual top-down raster scan order of an image. Hence each term in the summation $I(r-i, c-j)$ contains only pixels occurring before pixel (i,j) in the raster scan order. The first summation is called the autoregressive term, and the second term is called the moving-average term. When $K(0,0)$ contains pixels occurring before and after $(0,0)$ in the raster scan order, the model is called a simultaneous autoregressive model.

To determine the coefficients $h(i,j)$ for $(i,j) \in N(0,0)$, we can proceed by least squares. Define

$$\epsilon^2 = \sum_{r,c} \left[I(r,c) - \sum_{(i,j) \in N(0,0)} I(r-i, c-j)h(i,j) \right]^2$$

Now take the partial derivatives of ϵ^2 with respect to $h(m,n)$ and set these partial derivatives to zero. There results the system of equations

$$\sigma(m,n) = \sum_{i,j} h(i,j)\sigma(m-i,n-j) \tag{9.4}$$

where $\sigma(m,n) = \sum_{(r,c)} I(r,c)I(r-m,c-n)$, and because of an assumed stationarity,

$$\sigma(m,n) = \sum_{(r,c)} I(r+a,c+b)I(r+a-m,c+b-n)$$

for every (a,b).

The linear system of Eq. (9.4) can be solved for the coefficients $h(i,j)$. Texture classification can then be done by comparing a computed set of coefficients from an observed image with the prototypical set of coefficients from the different texture classes.

Besag (1974) and Cross and Jain (1983) discuss the autobinomial form for a discrete random Markov field. Here the probability that a pixel takes a particular gray level has a binomial form, with the binomial parameter depending on the values of the neighboring gray level. That is,

$$P[I(r,c) = k | I(i,j) : (i,j) \in N(r,c)] = \binom{K}{k} \theta^k (1-\theta)^{K-k}$$

where

$$\theta = \frac{e^{T-a}}{1 + e^{T-a}}$$

and

$$T = \sum_{(i,j) \in N(0,0)} I(r-i,c-j)b(i,j)$$

The texture parameters here are a and $b(i,j)$ for $(i,j) \in N(0,0)$.

It is apparent that the discrete Markov random field model is a generalization of time-series autoregressive moving-average models that were initially explored for image texture analysis by McCormick and Jayaramamurthy (1974), Tou and Chang (1976), Tou, Kao, and Chang (1976), and Deguchi and Morishita (1978). Related papers include Delp, Kashyap, and Mitchell (1979), Tou (1980), Chen (1980), Faugeras (1980), Therrien (1980), and Jau, Chin, and Weinman (1984). Issues concerning the estimation of h from texture samples can be found in Kashyap and Chellappa (1981). De Souza (1982) develops a chi-square test to discriminate microtextures described by autoregressive models.

Pratt, Faugeras, and Gagalowicz (1978) and Faugeras and Pratt (1980) consider only the autoregressive term with independent noise and rewrite the autoregressive equation as

$$I(r,c) - \sum_{(k,j) \in N(0,0)} I(r-i,c-j)h(i,j) = u(r,c)$$

Here $\{u(r,c) | (r,c) \in R \times C\}$ represents independent random variables, not necessarily Gaussian. The left-hand side represents a convolution that decorrelates the image. Faugeras and Pratt characterize the texture by the mean, variance, skewness, and kurtosis of the decorrelated image that is obtained by either estimating h or by using a given gradient of a Laplacianlike operator to perform the decorrelation.

9.13 Random Mosaic Models

The random mosaic models are constructed in two steps. The first step provides a means of tessellating a plane into cells, and the second step assigns a property value to each cell. In the Poisson line model (Miles, 1969), a Poisson process of intensity λ/π determines an ordered pair $(\theta, p) \in [0, \pi] \times (-\infty, \infty)$. Each ordered pair (θ, p) is associated with a line $x \cos \theta + y \sin \theta = p$. The lines generated tessellate a finite plane region into convex cells whose boundary consists of line segments from the lines in the random set. In the occupancy model (Miles, 1970), a tessellation is produced by a Poisson process of intensity λ, which plants points in the plane. Each point determines a cell that consists of all points in the plane closest to the given planted point. In the Delauney model, a line segment is drawn between each pair of planted points whose corresponding cells in the occupancy model share a common border segment. Table 9.1 shows the expected value of the area, the perimeter length, and the number of sides to a convex cell for each of the processes.

Schacter, Rosenfeld, and Davis (1978) and Schacter and Ahuja (1979) derive the statistical properties for these random mosaic models. Ahuja, Dubitzki, and Rosenfeld (1980) compare properties of synthetically generated textures with their theoretical values. Schacter (1980b) summarizes how texture characteristics are related to the texture's variogram and correlation function. Modestino, Fries, and Vickers (1980, 1981) compute the power spectral density function for a plane tessellated by a random line process and in which the gray levels of one cell have a Markov dependence on the gray levels of the cells around them. They give a maximum likelihood texture discriminant for this mosaic model and illustrate its use on some sample images. Therrien (1983) uses an autoregressive model for each cell and, like Modestino, Fries, and Vickers (1980, 1981), superimposes a Markov random field to describe transitions between cells. Other models include the Johnson-Mehl model (Gilbert, 1962) and the bombing model (Switzer, 1967).

Table 9.1 Expected value for area A, perimeter length S, and number of sides N for the line model, the occupancy model, and the Delauney model.

Expected Value	Line Model	Occupancy Model	Delauney Model
E[A]	$\frac{\pi}{\lambda^2}$	$\frac{1}{\lambda}$	$\frac{1}{2\lambda}$
E[S]	$\frac{2}{\lambda}$	$\frac{4}{\sqrt{\lambda}}$	$\frac{32}{3\pi\sqrt{\lambda}}$
E[N]	4	6	3

9.14 Structural Approaches to Texture Models

Pure structural models of texture are based on the view that textures are made up of primitives that appear in nearly regular repetitive spatial arrangements. To describe the texture, we must describe the primitives and the placement rules (Rosenfeld and Lipkin, 1970). The choice of primitive from a set of primitives and the probability of the chosen primitive being placed at a particular location can be a strong or weak function of location or of the primitives near the location.

Carlucci (1972) suggests a texture model using primitives of line segments, open polygons, and closed polygons in which the placement rules are given syntactically in a graphlike language. Zucker (1976a, 1976b) conceives of real texture as being a distortion of an ideal texture. The underlying ideal texture has a nice representation as a regular graph in which each node is connected to its neighbors in an identical fashion. Each node corresponds to a cell in a tessellation of the plane. The underlying ideal texture is transformed by distorting the primitive at each node to make a realistic texture. Zucker's model is more a competence-based model than a performance-based model.

Lu and Fu (1978) give a tree-grammar syntactic approach for texture. They divide a texture up into small square windows (9×9). The spatial structure of the resolution cells in the window is expressed as a tree. The assignment of gray levels to the resolution is given by the rules of a stochastic tree grammar. Finally, special care is given to the placement of windows with respect to one another in order to preserve the coherence among windows. Lu and Fu illustrate the power of their technique with both texture synthesis and texture experiments. Other work with structural approaches to texture includes Leu and Wee (1985).

9.15 Texture Segmentation

Most work in image texture analysis has been devoted to textural feature analysis of an entire image. It is apparent, however, that an image is not necessarily homogeneously textured. An important image-processing operation, therefore, is the segmentation of an image into regions, each of which is differently textured. The constraint is that each region has a homogeneous texture, such as that arising from a frontal view, and that each pair of adjacent regions is differently textured. Bajcsy (1973a, 1973b) is one of the first researchers to do texture segmentations for outdoor scenes. Her algorithm merges small, nearly connected regions having similar local texture or color descriptors. For texture descriptors she uses Fourier transform features. The descriptors for each region include an indication of whether the texture is isotropic or directional, the size of the texture element, and the separation between texture elements. If the texture is considered directional, then the description includes the orientation.

Chen and Pavlidis (1979) use the split-and-merge algorithm on the co-occurrence matrix of the regions as the basis for merging. Let the four $2^{N-1} \times 2^{N-1}$ windows in a $2^N \times 2^N$ window have C^{NE}, C^{NW}, C^{SE}, and C^{SW} for their respective co-occurrence matrices. Then with only little error, the co-occurrence matrix C of the $2^N \times 2^N$

window can be computed by

$$C(i,j) = \frac{1}{4}[C^{NE}(i,j) + C^{NW}(i,j) + C^{SE}(i,j) + C^{SW}(i,j)]$$

Experiments by Hong, Wu, and Rosenfeld (1980) indicate that the error of this computation is minimal. The $2^N \times 2^N$ window is declared to be uniformly textured if for the user-specified threshold T,

$$\sum_{(i,j)}[\max\{C^{NE}(i,j), C^{NW}(i,j), C^{SE}(i,j), C^{SW}(i,j)\} -$$

$$\min\{C^{NE}(i,j), C^{NW}(i,j), C^{SE}(i,j), C^{SW}(i,j)\}] < T$$

Using this criteria, Chen and Pavlidis begin the merging process using 16×16 windows. Any 16×16 window not merged is split into four 8×8 windows. The splitting continues until the window size is 4×4. The gray levels of the images are quantized to eight levels. Chen and Pavlidis (1983) use a similar split-and-merge algorithm, with the correlation coefficients between vertically adjacent and horizontally adjacent pixels as the feature vectors. Modestino, Fries, and Vickers (1981) use a Poisson line process to partition the plane and assign gray levels to each region by a Gauss-Markov model using adjacent regions. They develop a maximum-likelihood estimator for the parameters of the process and show segmentation results on artificially generated images having three different texture types.

Conners, Trivedi, and Harlow (1984) use six features from the co-occurrence matrix to segment an aerial urban scene into nine classes: residential, commercial/industrial, mobile home, water, dry land, runway/taxiway, aircraft parking, multi-lane highway, and vehicle parking. Their work is important because it integrates the splitting idea of Chen and Pavlidis into a classification setting. They initially segmented the image into regions. Any region whose likelihood ratio for its highest-likelihood class against any other class was too low was considered a boundary region and split. Any region whose likelihood ratio for its highest-likelihood class against each other class was high enough was considered to be uniformly textured and assigned to the highest-likelihood class.

Kashyap and Khotanzad (1984) use a simultaneous autoregressive and circular autoregressive model for each 3×3 neighborhood of an image. Here each neighborhood produces a feature vector associated with the model. The set of feature vectors generated from the image is clustered, and each pixel is labeled with the cluster label of the feature vector associated with its 3×3 neighborhood. Pixels associated with outlier feature vectors are given the cluster label of the majority of their labeled neighbors. Therrien (1983) uses an autoregressive model for each textured region and superimposes a Markov random field to describe the transitions of one region to another. He uses maximum likelihood and maximum a posteriori estimation techniques to achieve a high-quality segmentation of aerial imagery.

9.16   Synthetic Texture Image Generation

A variety of approaches have been developed for the generation of synthetic texture images. Rather than giving a detailed description of each, we will provide a brief guide to some of the representative papers in the literature. McCormick and Jayaramamurthy (1974) use a time-series model for texture synthesis, as do Tou, Kao, and Chang (1976). Yokoyama and Haralick (1978) use a structured-growth model to synthesize a more complex image texture. Pratt, Faugeras, and Gagalowicz (1978) develop a set of techniques for generating textures with identical means, variances, and autocorrelation functions but different higher-order moments. Gagalowicz (1981) gives a technique for generating binary texture fields with prescribed second-order statistics. Chellappa and Kashyap (1981) describe a technique for the generation of images having a given Gauss-Markov random field.

Yokoyama and Haralick (1979) describe a technique that uses a Markov chain method. Schacter (1980a) uses a long-crested wave model. Monne, Schmitt, and Massaloux (1981) use an interlaced vertical and horizontal Markov chain method to generate a texture image. Garber and Sawchuk (1981) use a best-fit model instead of the Nth-order transition probabilities to make a good simulation of texture without exceeding computer memory limits on storing Nth-order probability functions. Schmitt et al. (1984) add vector quantization to the bidimensional Markov technique of Monne, Schmitt, and Massaloux (1981) to improve the appearance of the texture image. Gagalowicz (1984) describes a texture synthesis technique that produces textures as they would appear on perspective projection images of three-dimensional surfaces. Ma and Gagalowicz (1984) describe a technique to synthesize artificial textures in parallel from a compressed-data set and retain good visual similarity to natural textures.

9.17   Shape from Texture

Image texture gradients on oblique photography can be used to estimate surface orientation of the observed three-dimensional object. The techniques developed so far assume that the observed texture area has no depth changes and no texture changes within the observed area. They also do not take into account the possibility of subtextures. The first work of this kind was done by Carel, Purdy, and Lulow (1961) and Charton and Ferris (1965). They produced a conceptual design of a system called VISILOG, which could direct a freely moving vehicle through an undetermined environment. One important kind of guidance information needed by such a vehicle is the surface orientation of the surface over which the vehicle is moving. The basis of the design was an analysis that related surface slant to the texture gradient in the perspective projection image. Assumptions were that a stochastically regular surface was observed through a perspective projection, and the number of texture elements could be measured along two parallel line segments perpendicular to the view direction and two parallel line segments parallel to the view direction. They measured the number of texture elements in a line by measuring the number of changes in brightness along the line. The number of changes in brightness was the number of relative extrema.

Bajcsy and Lieberman (1976) used a Fourier transform to extract texture gradients, which were then related to three-dimensional distance. Witkin (1981) derived equations for the slant and tilt angles of a planar surface under orthographic projection by measuring the distribution of tangent directions of zero-crossing contours, assuming isotropic distribution of edge directions for frontally viewed textures. Witkin divided the tangent angle interval $[0, \pi]$ into n equal intervals, the ith interval being $[(i - 1)\pi/n, i\pi/n]$, $i = 1, \ldots, n$, and measured the number $k(i)$ of tangent directions that fell in the ith interval. The slant angle s and the tilt angle t of the observed surface were estimated to be that pair of values maximizing the a posteriori probability of (s, t), given the observed $k(i)$, $i = 1, \ldots, n$. Davis, Janos, and Dunn (1983) indicated some mistakes in the Witkin paper and gave the joint a posteriori probability of (s, t) as proportional to

$$\frac{\sin(s)\cos^n(s)}{\prod_{i=1}^{n}[1 - \sin^2(s)\sin^2\left(\frac{(2i-1)\pi}{2n}\right) - t)]}$$

They also gave a modified version of the two-dimensional Newton method for determining the (s, t) achieving the maximization.

Other work that relates to surface orientation recovery from texture includes that of Kender (1979), who described an aggregation Hough-related transform that groups together edge directions associated with the same vanishing point, assuming parallel edges in frontally viewed textures. The edge direction is the gradient direction. It is perpendicular to the direction along an edge boundary. In the case of a line segment, it is perpendicular to the direction along the line segment. A unit length edge direction $E' = (E_x, E_y)$ at position $P' = (P_x, P_y)$ has coordinates $T' = (T_x, T_y)$ in the transformed space where

$$T = (E'P)E$$

All lines that go through the point P map to a circle whose center is $P/2$ and whose radius is $\|P\|/2$. Kender gives a second transform defined by

$$T = \frac{f}{E'P}E$$

Here all lines that go through the point P are mapped to a line that goes through the point $fP/\|P\|^2$ in the orthogonal direction to P.

The way Kender makes use of this transform for the estimation of the normal to a plane in three-dimensional space is as follows: Consider that the plane is densely populated with texels that are just edge segments (edgels). Each has a position and orientation. Each such edgel on the plane in three-dimensional space can be represented as a set of points satisfying

$$\begin{pmatrix} x \\ y \\ z \end{pmatrix} + k \begin{pmatrix} \alpha \\ \beta \\ \gamma \end{pmatrix} \quad \text{for some small range of } k, |k| \leq T_o.$$

The point (x, y, z) can be thought of as the center position of the edgel on the three-dimensional plane, and (α, β, γ) are its direction cosines. From the perspective geometry (see Chapter 13), the perspective projection (u, v) of any point (x, y, z) satisfies

$$u = f\frac{x}{z} \qquad v = f\frac{y}{z}$$

where f is the distance the image projection plane is in front of the center of perspectivity. The perspective projection of the set of points on the edgel in the plane in three-dimensional space therefore satisfies

$$\begin{pmatrix} u(k) \\ v(k) \end{pmatrix} = \frac{f}{z + k\gamma} \begin{pmatrix} x + k\alpha \\ y + k\beta \end{pmatrix}$$

This set of perspective projection points constitutes a short-line segment or an edgel on the perspective projection image. The direction cosines for the edgel are proportional to

$$\begin{pmatrix} \gamma y - \beta z \\ -\gamma x + \alpha z \end{pmatrix}$$

The transform $T = \frac{f}{E'P} E$ of any point in position P,

$$P = \frac{f}{z + k\gamma} \begin{pmatrix} x + k\alpha \\ y + k\beta \end{pmatrix}$$

with unit direction

$$E = \frac{1}{\left\| \begin{matrix} \gamma y - \beta z \\ -\gamma x + \alpha z \end{matrix} \right\|} \begin{pmatrix} \gamma y - \beta z \\ -\gamma x + \alpha z \end{pmatrix}$$

is

$$\begin{pmatrix} p \\ q \end{pmatrix} = \frac{1}{(\alpha y - \beta x)} \begin{pmatrix} \gamma y - \beta z \\ -\gamma x + \alpha z \end{pmatrix}$$

It is directly verifiable that this point (p, q) satisfies

$$\alpha p + \beta q - \gamma = 0$$

So the transform of each edgel on the three-dimensional plane will be a point (p, q) that lies along an unknown line whose coefficients are directly related to the direction cosines of the three-dimensional line. And if the texel edgels are densely spaced on the plane in three-dimensional space, then those which have direction cosines (α, β, γ), regardless of their three-dimensional position, will densely populate the line

$$L = \left\{ \begin{pmatrix} p \\ q \end{pmatrix} \middle| \alpha p + \beta q - \gamma \right\}$$

And if the edgels on the three-dimensional plane have a variety of different directions, then the transform of all the pixels having the ith direction cosines $(\alpha_i, \beta_i, \gamma_i)$ will densely populate the line

$$L_i = \left\{ \begin{pmatrix} p \\ q \end{pmatrix} \middle| \alpha_i p + \beta_i q - \gamma_i = 0 \right\}$$

Notice now, that these lines L_i must intersect if there is more than one variety of directions to the three-dimensional edgels. Hence, around the intersection point there must be a higher concentration or density of transformed points. If, by this higher concentration, the intersection point (p_0, q_0) can be identified, then because the normal to the plane must be perpendicular to the direction cosines for all lines the plane contains, $(p_0, q_0, -1)$ must be in the direction of the normal to the three-dimensional plane, since $(p_0, q_0, -1)$ satisfies

$$\begin{pmatrix} \alpha_i \\ \beta_i \\ \gamma_i \end{pmatrix} \cdot \begin{pmatrix} p_0 \\ q_0 \\ -1 \end{pmatrix} = 0,$$

for all i's as can be seen from the definition of L_i.

Kanatani and Chou (1986) assume that textural density can be measured and discuss a differential geometry approach to relate the measured density of texture primitives on a perspective projection image to the surface normal of the planar or curved surface. Their argument leads to a nonlinear set of equations. Motivated by their idea, we give a simple geometric derivation of a procedure to recover a planar surface normal from the density of texture primitives.

We assume that the density of texture primitives—that is, the number of texture primitives per unit area—on the planar surface is constant and does not vary with position on the surface. We select a neighborhood on the perspective projection image of the textural surface and count the number of texture primitives in the neighborhood. The neighborhood size might be, for example, 25×25. A relationship exists between the measured density of texture primitives in a neighborhood at a given position and the surface normal.

To develop this relationship, we use the concept of solid angle, a complete discussion of which can be found in Chapter 12. Let Ω be the solid angle formed by the neighborhood and the center of perspectivity. Let the position of the center of the neighborhood be given by (u, v). Let the unknown plane where the textural surface is observed satisfy

$$Ax + By + Cz + D = 0 \tag{9.5}$$

where $A^2 + B^2 + C^2 = 1$.

From the perspective geometry (see Chapter 13) for any three-dimensional point (x, y, z), its perspective projection (u, v) satisfies

$$u = f\frac{x}{z}, \qquad v = f\frac{y}{z}$$

where f is the distance from the image projection plane to the front of the center of perspectivity. Hence

$$x = \frac{uz}{f} \quad \text{and} \quad y = \frac{vz}{f} \tag{9.6}$$

Substituting the expression of Eq. (9.6) into Eq. (9.5) and solving for z results in

$$z = \frac{-Df}{Au + Bv + Cf} \tag{9.7}$$

Let d be the distance between the center of perspectivity and the point determined by the intersection of the plane $Ax + By + Cf + D = 0$ with the ray $\lambda(u, v, f)$. This point is the three-dimensional point whose perspective projection is (u, v). Then $d^2 = x^2 + y^2 + z^2$. After substituting Eq. (9.6), there results

$$d^2 = \left(\frac{uz}{f}\right)^2 + \left(\frac{vz}{f}\right)^2 + z^2$$

After substituting Eq. (9.7), there results

$$d^2 = \frac{u^2 + v^2 + f^2}{f^2} \frac{D^2 f^2}{(Au + Bv + Cf)^2}$$

$$= \frac{D^2}{(n'\xi)^2}$$

where

$$n = \begin{pmatrix} A \\ B \\ C \end{pmatrix} \quad \text{and} \quad \xi = \frac{1}{\sqrt{u^2 + v^2 + f^2}} \begin{pmatrix} u \\ v \\ f \end{pmatrix}$$

are both unit length vectors.

Now the area orthogonal to the ray $\lambda(u,v,f)$ formed by the solid angle Ω at a distance d is Ωd^2. The area on the plane $Ax + By + Cz + D = 0$ that the solid angle makes is then $\Omega d^2/n'\xi = \Omega D^2/(n'\xi)^3$.

Let the density of texture primitives on the plane $Ax + By + Cz + D = 0$ be k primitives per unit area. The total number of primitives in the area $\Omega D^2/(n'\xi)^3$ is then $k\Omega D^2/(n'\xi)^3$.

Arguing in a similar manner, we obtain that the area on the image formed by the solid angle Ω is

$$\frac{\Omega f^2}{\begin{pmatrix} 0 \\ 0 \\ 1 \end{pmatrix}' \xi} = \frac{\Omega f^2}{f/\sqrt{u^2 + v^2 + f^2}}$$

$$= \Omega f \sqrt{u^2 + v^2 + f^2}$$

The density γ of texture primitives in this area is then

$$\gamma = \frac{k\Omega D^2}{(n'\xi)^3} \Big/ \left(\Omega f \sqrt{u^2 + v^2 + f^2} \right)$$

$$= \frac{kD^2}{f} \frac{1}{(n'\xi)^3 \sqrt{u^2 + v^2 + f^2}} \tag{9.8}$$

We have, without loss of generality, the freedom to choose the sign of n so that $n'\xi$ is positive. Hence, after taking cube roots, we can rewrite Eq. (9.8) in the form

$$\xi'n = \lambda_o \left[\frac{1}{\gamma \sqrt{u^2 + v^2 + f^2}} \right]^{\frac{1}{3}} \tag{9.9}$$

where

$$\lambda_o = \left[\frac{kD^2}{f} \right]^{\frac{1}{3}}$$

This is the desired relationship between primitive density γ at position (u,v) and the surface normal n of the unknown plane.

Suppose that the measurement of density of texture primitives is made at N different neighborhoods. Then there result the N equations

$$\xi_i' n = \lambda_o b_i \qquad (9.10)$$

where

$$\xi_i = \frac{1}{\sqrt{u_i^2 + v_i^2 + f^2}} \begin{pmatrix} u_i \\ v_i \\ f \end{pmatrix}$$

$$b_i = \left[\frac{1}{\gamma_i \sqrt{u_i^2 + v_i^2 + f^2}} \right]^{\frac{1}{3}}$$

γ_i is the measured density of the ith neighborhood, and (u_i, v_i) is the center position of the ith neighborhood.

Putting Eq. (9.10) in matrix form results in

$$\Psi n = \lambda_o b \qquad (9.11)$$

where

$$\Psi = \begin{pmatrix} \xi_1' \\ \vdots \\ \xi_N' \end{pmatrix} \quad \text{and} \quad b = \begin{pmatrix} b_1 \\ \vdots \\ b_N \end{pmatrix}$$

The system of Eq. (9.11) is overconstrained. The normal n is not known and must satisfy $n'n = 1$. The parameter λ_o is not known. We will find the n that maximizes the cosine of the angle between Ψn and $\lambda_o b$ subject to the constraint $n'n = 1$. An n maximizes the cosine of the angle between Ψn and $\lambda_o b$ if and only if the n maximizes $(\Psi n)'b$. Determining the n that maximizes $(\Psi n)'b$ is easy. Let

$$\epsilon = (\Psi n)'b + \eta(n'n - 1)$$

Taking partial derivatives of ϵ with respect to n and η results in

$$\frac{\partial \epsilon}{\partial n} = \Psi'b + 2\eta n$$

$$\frac{\partial \epsilon}{\partial \eta} = n'n - 1$$

Setting these partial derivatives to zero and solving yields

$$n = \frac{\Psi'b}{\|\Psi'b\|}$$

Ohta, Maenobu, and Sakai (1981) assume that there are effective procedures for finding texture primitives, that the texture primitives can be divided into types distinguishable from one another on the perspective projection image, and that the area of each instance of a textural primitive on the observed surface is the same. They do not require that the density of texture primitives be constant on the observed surface. They proceed by approximating the perspective projection with an affine transformation and developing the required relationships from the affine transformation. We will develop the analogous relationships in a more exact form using the reasoning we have already given with solid angles.

Let A_p be the area of each of the primitives on the textural plane surface. It is a constant. Let Ω be the solid angle formed by this area with respect to the center of perspectivity. Then

$$A_p = \frac{\Omega D^2}{(n'\xi)^3} \tag{9.12}$$

Both Ω and ξ are functions of the position of the primitive on the perspective projection image. Let A_I be the area of the perspective projection of the primitive. Then as we have already seen,

$$A_I = \Omega f \sqrt{u^2 + v^2 + f^2} \tag{9.13}$$

Of course the area A_I depends on (u, v).

From Eqs. (9.12) and (9.13) there follows

$$A_I = A_p \frac{(n'\xi)^3}{D^2} f \sqrt{u^2 + v^2 + f^2} \tag{9.14}$$

Proceeding as we have done before,

$$\xi'n = \left(\frac{D^2}{A_p f}\right)^{\frac{1}{3}} \left[\frac{A_I(u, v)}{\sqrt{u^2 + v^2 + f^2}}\right]^{\frac{1}{3}} \tag{9.15}$$

Consider the situation for two texture primitives having identical areas on the textured plane $Ax + By + Cz + D = 0$. Let the perspective projection image be A_{I1} and A_{I2}, respectively. Let

$$\xi_1 = \frac{1}{\sqrt{u_1^2 + v_1^2 + f^2}} \begin{pmatrix} u_1 \\ v_1 \\ f \end{pmatrix} \quad \text{and} \quad \xi_2 = \frac{1}{\sqrt{u_2^2 + v_2^2 + f^2}} \begin{pmatrix} u_2 \\ v_2 \\ f \end{pmatrix}$$

Then from Eq. (9.14)

$$\frac{A_{I1}}{A_{I2}} = \frac{(n'\xi_1)^3 \sqrt{u_1^2 + v_1^2 + f^2}}{(n'\xi_2)^3 \sqrt{u_2^2 + v_2^2 + f^2}} \tag{9.16}$$

Next consider the geometry illustrated in Fig. 9.11 of the distances h_1 and h_2 from the points (u_1, v_1) and (u_2, v_2) to the line $Au + Bv + Cf = 0$ on the image plane.

$$h_1 = \frac{|Au_1 + Bv_1 + Cf|}{\sqrt{A^2 + B^2}} = \frac{n'\xi_1 \sqrt{u_1^2 + v_1^2 + f^2}}{\sqrt{A^2 + B^2}}$$

$$h_2 = \frac{|Au_2 + Bv_2 + Cf|}{\sqrt{A^2 + B^2}} = \frac{n'\xi_2 \sqrt{u_2^2 + v_2^2 + f^2}}{\sqrt{A^2 + B^2}}$$

Hence

$$\frac{h_1}{h_2} = \frac{n'\xi_1}{n'\xi_2} \frac{\sqrt{u_1^2 + v_1^2 + f^2}}{\sqrt{u_2^2 + v_2^2 + f^2}} \tag{9.17}$$

Draw the line between (u_1, v_1) and (u_2, v_2) and extend it until it intersects the line $Au + Bv + Cf = 0$. Let f_1 be the distance from (u_1, v_1) along the extended line to the line $Au + Bv + Cf = 0$, and let f_2 be the distance from (u_2, v_2) along the

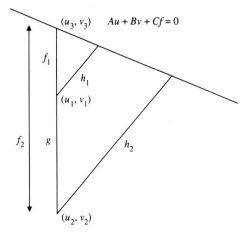

Figure 9.11 The similar triangle geometry generated between two perspective projection points (u_1, v_1) and (u_2, v_2) with their distance to a line $Ax + By + Cf = 0$.

extended line to the line $Au + Bv + Cf = 0$. Let (u_3, v_3) be the point of intersection between the extended line and the line $Au + Bv + Cf = 0$. From similar triangles

$$\frac{h_1}{h_2} = \frac{f_1}{f_2} \tag{9.18}$$

Let g be the distance between (u_1, v_1) and (u_2, v_2). Then $f_2 = g + f_1$. Substituting this into Eqs. (9.17) and (9.18) results in

$$\frac{f_1}{g + f_1} = \left[\frac{A_{I1}(u_1^2 + v_1^2 + f^2)}{A_{I2}(u_2^2 + v_2^2 + f^2)}\right]^{\frac{1}{3}}$$

and solving for f_1 results in

$$f_1 = \frac{g}{1 - \left[\frac{A_{I1}(u_1^2 + v_1^2 + f^2)}{A_{I2}(u_2^2 + v_2^2 + f^2)}\right]^{\frac{1}{3}}}$$

Notice that the right-hand side of Eq. (9.19) contains all measurable quantities, so that the distance f_1 can be determined. With f_1 determined, the intersection point (u_3, v_3) is given by

$$\begin{pmatrix} u_3 \\ v_3 \end{pmatrix} = \begin{pmatrix} u_1 \\ v_1 \end{pmatrix} + \frac{f_1}{\sqrt{(u_1 - u_2)^2 + (v_1 - v_2)^2}} \begin{pmatrix} u_1 - u_2 \\ v_1 - v_2 \end{pmatrix} \tag{9.19}$$

Then from the measured position and area of each pair of texture primitives on the perspective projection image, it is possible to determine one point on the line $Au + Bv + Cf = 0$. The only assumption is that the area of the texture primitives on the textured plane $Ax + By + Cz + D = 0$ is identical. From N pairs of such texture primitives, N points on the line $Au + Bv + Cf = 0$ can be determined. Since f is given, a fit of the N points to a line will produce the unknown coefficients $n' = (A, B, C)$, which is the unit normal to the textured plane.

Aloimonos and Swain (1988) use the same affine transformation approximation to the perspective projection that Ohta et al. (1981) do. In terms of the geometry we have been doing with solid angles, they derive the relationship between the area A_I on the image of a texture primitive located at (u,v) and the area A_p on the textured plane as

$$A_I = A_P \left[\frac{f \sqrt{u^2 + v^2 + f^2}}{d^2} \right] n'\xi \tag{9.20}$$

where d, the distance from the center of perspective to the texture primitive on the plane $Ax + By + Cz + D = 0$, must be considered a function of (u,v). From our perspective, however, Aloimonos and Swain make the approximation that $f \sqrt{u^2 + v^2 + f^2}/d^2$ is a constant, which is reasonable when the depth of field of the observed textured plane is narrow and $u^2 + v^2 << f^2$. In this case Eq. (9.20) becomes

$$A_I = \lambda n \xi \tag{9.21}$$

where they call λ the "textural albedo," noticing the similarity between Eq. (9.21) and the Lambertian reflectance equation (see Chapter 12).

Suppose the textural primitives are observed as all having identical area and lying on the textured plane $Ax + By + Cz + D = 0$. Then by Eq. (9.21), we have

$$\begin{pmatrix} \xi_1' \\ \xi_2' \\ \xi_3' \end{pmatrix} n = \frac{1}{\lambda} \begin{pmatrix} A_{I1} \\ A_{I2} \\ A_{I3} \end{pmatrix}$$

Hence

$$n = \frac{1}{\lambda} \begin{pmatrix} \xi_1' \\ \xi_2' \\ \xi_3' \end{pmatrix}^{-1} \begin{pmatrix} A_{I1} \\ A_{I2} \\ A_{I3} \end{pmatrix}$$

where λ is chosen so that $n'n = 1$.

Aloimonos and Swain suggest solving for λ and n for each triplet of neighboring textural primitives and determining a more accurate estimate of λ by taking the average of the individual λ's. Then they consider the individual unit normals as the initial approximations to the unit normal in an algorithm that constructs a set of unit surface normals satisfying a smoothness constraint.

Blostein and Ahuja (1987, 1989a, 1989b) also make the assumption that the area of the textural primitives is constant and do not require that the density of the texture primitives be constant. They develop a relationship between the area of a primitive on the perspective projection image and the tilt and slant of the textured planar surface. From the work we have already done, it is easy to derive such a relationship by using the surface normal of the textured planar surface rather than its slant and tilt angles.

If areas of texture primitives are measured at locations (u_i, v_i), $i = 1, \ldots, N$, then we have from Eq. (9.21) the overconstrained equation

$$\Psi n = \lambda_o b \tag{9.22}$$

where

$$\Psi = \begin{pmatrix} \xi_1' \\ \vdots \\ \xi_N' \end{pmatrix}$$

$$b = \begin{pmatrix} b_1 \\ \vdots \\ b_N \end{pmatrix}$$

$$\xi_i = \frac{1}{\sqrt{u_i^2 + v_i^2 + f^2}} \begin{pmatrix} u_i \\ v_i \\ f \end{pmatrix}$$

$$b_i = \left[\frac{A_i(u_i, v_i)}{\sqrt{u_i^2 + v_i^2 + f^2}} \right]^{\frac{1}{3}} \quad \text{and}$$

$$\lambda_o = \left(\frac{D^2}{A_p f} \right)^{\frac{1}{3}}$$

Blostein and Ahuja do not analytically solve for the (slant, tilt) angle. They do a brute-force search over a set of fixed slant-tilt angles to find the (slant, tilt) angle that best fits the observed areas. The motivation for the brute-force search is that they accept the reality that it is difficult to determine which regions have the texture of interest and which ones do not. By doing a global fit, they are able to identify simultaneously the true texels from among the candidate regions and the slant and tilt.

Blostein and Ahuja found the texel identification problem to be difficult and gave the detailed procedure they found most satisfactory among the ones they tried. They extracted texture disklike primitives by convolving the image with a Laplacian of Gaussian kernel

$$\nabla^2 G(u,v) = \frac{2\sigma^2 - (u^2 + v^2)}{\sigma^4} e^{-\frac{(u^2 + v^2)}{2\sigma^2}}$$

and a kernel that was the partial derivative of $\nabla^2 G$ with respect to G :

$$\frac{\partial}{\partial \sigma} \nabla^2 G(u,v) = \left[\frac{6(u^2 + v^2)}{\sigma^5} - \frac{(u^2 + v^2)^2}{\sigma^7} - \frac{4}{\sigma^3} \right] e^{-\frac{(u^2 + v^2)}{2\sigma^2}}$$

For an image having a disk of diameter D and contrast C centered at $(0,0)$, that is,

$$I(x,y) = \begin{cases} c \text{ if } x^2 + y^2 \leq D^2/4 \\ 0 \text{ elsewhere} \end{cases}$$

the response of the filters $\nabla^2 G$ and $\frac{\partial}{\partial \sigma} \nabla^2 G$ at the center of the disk was $(\pi C D^2/2\sigma^2) \times e^{-D^2/8\sigma^2}$ and $(\pi C D^2/2)[D^2/4\sigma^3 - 2/\sigma^3]e^{-D^2/8\sigma^2}$, respectively.

From these expressions, it is apparent that by dividing one expression by the other, it is possible to solve for both the diameter D and the contrast C of the disk.

This results in

$$D = 2\sigma\sqrt{\frac{\partial}{\partial\sigma}\nabla^2 G * I / (\nabla^2 G * I) + 2}$$

$$C = \frac{2\sigma^2}{\pi D^2} e^{D^2/8\sigma^2} (\nabla^2 G * I)$$

What Blostein and Ahuja did was to compute the convolutions $\nabla^2 G * I$ and $\frac{\partial}{\partial\sigma}\nabla^2 G * I$ at six σ values: $\sqrt{2}$, $2\sqrt{2}$, $3\sqrt{2}$, $4\sqrt{2}$, $5\sqrt{2}$, and $6\sqrt{2}$. They identified the position of the local extrema in the $\nabla^2 G * I$ image. At each local extremum, they used the value of $\frac{\partial}{\partial\sigma}\nabla^2 G * I$ and $\nabla^2 * I$ to compute disk diameter D and constant C. If $2\sqrt{2} - 2 \le D \le 2\sqrt{2}\sigma + 2$, a disk of diameter D was accepted to be centered at the position of the extremum. Finally, they identified texture primitives as either single disks that did not touch any other disk or the union of overlapping disks, providing the union did not have concavities that were too sharp.

9.18   Summary

We have discussed the conceptual basis of texture in terms of its primitives and their spatial relationships, and described several kinds of primitives and spatial relationships by which a texture can be characterized. We reviewed a number of different textural feature extraction techniques, including co-occurrence, autocorrelation, digital transform, edgeness, relative extrema density, mathematical morphology, autoregressive Markov random fields, random mosaic models, and structural approaches. Then we discussed texture segmentation and synthetic texture generation. Finally, we reviewed a variety of approaches to determine shape from texture. These approaches assume that either the density or the size of the texture primitives is constant, and they permit the calculation of a local surface normal on the basis of the texture density or size of texture primitives at multiple locations on the perspective projection image. Qualitatively, shape from texture can work; quantitatively, the techniques are generally not dependable. The degree of dependability could actually be determined by an analytic calculation of the variance of the computed quantities as a function of the Poisson density parameter for the primitive generating process. However, this has not yet been done.

■ Exercises

9.1.   Generate some synthetic 512×512 texture images by low-pass filtering a white-noise image with the Gaussian kernel

$$G(u,v) = \frac{1}{\sqrt{2\pi}\sigma} e^{-\frac{1}{2}u^2 + v^2\sigma^2}$$

for $\sigma = 1, 2, 3, 4, 5$.

9.2.   For each of the five images generated by Exercise 9.1, determine the entropy, energy, and homogeneity features of the co-occurrence matrix for distance $d = 1, 2, 3, 4, 5$.

What can you say about the relationship between the feature value as a function of σ and d?

9.3.   For each of the five images generated in Exercise 9.1, determine the relationship between the texture energy features of Laws and σ.

9.4.   For each of the five images generated in Exercise 9.1, determine the relationship between the textural edgeness features and σ.

9.5.   For each of the five images generated in Exercise 9.1, determine the relationship between the vector dispersion feature and σ.

9.6.   For each of the five images generated by Exercise 9.1, use the Markov random field model to estimate the coefficients of linear combinations $h(i,j)$ from Eq. (9.4). What can you infer about the relationship between σ and the $h(i,j)$ coefficients?

9.7.   Use the textured image of $\sigma = 5$ to texture a plane $Ax + By + Cz + D = 0$ in three-dimensional space. Then compute the perspective projection of this textured plane. Write a program to identify the position and size of the textural primitives on the perspective projection image.

9.8.   Use a method that assumes a constant density of texture primitives to estimate the surface normal (A,B,C) of the textured plane from the image produced in Exercise 9.7.

9.9.   Use a method that assumes a constant size of texture primitives to estimate the surface normal (A,B,C) of the textured plane.

9.10. Repeat Exercise 9.8 for a number of trials with different texture images generated in Exercises 9.1 and 9.7 with $\sigma = 5$. What is an appropriate way to estimate the variance of the estimated unit normal vector? What is this variance as a function of image size? Try images that are 64×64, 128×128, 256×256, and 512×512.

9.11. Repeat Exercise 9.9 for a number of trials with different texture images generated as in Exercises 9.1 and 9.7 with $\sigma = 5$. What is an appropriate way to estimate the variance of the estimated unit normal vectors? What is this variance as a function of image size? Try images that are 64×64, 128×128, 256×256, and 512×512.

9.12. Devise an approach that uses both the constant density and the constant size of texture primitives to estimate the surface normal (A,B,C) of the textured plane.

9.13. Write a program that uses the method of Exercise 9.12 to estimate the normal (A,B,C) of a textured plane from the image produced in Exercise 9.7.

9.14. Repeat Exercise 9.13 for a number of trials with different texture images generated as in Exercises 9.1 and 9.7 with $\sigma = 5$. What is the value for a suitable measure of the variance of the estimated unit normal vector as a function of image size? Try images that are 64×64, 128×128, 256×256, and 512×512.

■ Bibliography

Abend, K., T. J. Harley, and L. N. Kanal, "Classification of Binary Random Patterns," *IEEE Transactions on Information Theory,* Vol. IT-11, 1965, pp. 538–544.

Ahuja, N., T. Dubitzki, and A. Rosenfeld, "Some Experiments with Mosaic Models for Images," *IEEE Transactions on Systems, Man, and Cybernetics,* Vol. SMC-10, 1980, pp. 744–749.

Ahuja, N., and A. Rosenfeld, "Mosaic Models for Textures," *IEEE Transactions on Pattern Analysis and Machine Intelligence,* Vol. PAMI-3, 1981, pp. 1–11.

Alapati, N. K., and A. C. Sanderson, "Texture Classification Using Multi-Resolution Rotation-Invariant Operators," *Intelligent Robots and Computer Vision,* SPIE Vol. 579, 1985, pp. 27–38.

Albregtsen, F., "Fractal Texture Signature Estimated by Multiscale LIT-SNN and MAX-MIN Operators on LANDSAT-5 MSS Images of the Antarctic," *Sixth Scandinavian Conference on Image Analysis,* Oulu, Finland, 1989, pp. 995–1002.

Aloimonos, J., and M. J. Swain, "Shape from Texture," *Proceedings of the Ninth International Joint Conference on Artificial Intelligence,* Los Angeles, 1988, pp. 926–931.

Arcelli, C., and G. Sanniti di Baja, "On the Sequential Approach to Medial Line Transformation," *IEEE Transactions on Systems, Man, and Cybernetics,* Vol. SMC-8, 1978, pp. 139–144.

Bachi, R., "Geostatistical Analysis of Territories," *Proceedings of the Thirty-ninth Session— Bulletin of the International Statistical Institute,* Vienna, 1973.

Bacus, J. W., and E. E. Gose, "Leukocyte Pattern Recognition," *IEEE Transactions on Systems, Man, and Cybernetics,* Vol. SMC-2, 1972, pp. 513–526.

Bajcsy, R., "Computer Description of Textured Surfaces," *Third Joint International Conference on Artificial Intelligence,* Stanford, CA, 1973a, pp. 572–578.

——, "Computer Identification of Visual Surfaces," *Computer Graphics and Image Processing,* Vol. 2, 1973b, pp. 118–130.

Bajcsy, R., and L. Lieberman, "Computer Description of Real Outdoor Scenes," *Proceedings of the Second International Joint Conference on Pattern Recognition,* Copenhagen, 1974, pp. 174–179.

——, "Texture Gradient as a Depth Cue," *Computer Graphics and Image Processing,* Vol. 5, 1976, pp. 52–67.

Bartels, P. H., G. Bahr, and G. Weid, "Cell Recognition from Line Scan Transition Probability Profiles," *Acta Cytologica,* Vol. 13, 1969, pp. 210–217.

Bartels, P. H., and G. L. Wied, "Extraction and Evaluation of Information from Digitized Cell Images," *Mammalian Cells: Probes and Problems,* U.S. NTIS Technical Information Center, Springfield, VA, 1975, pp. 15–28.

Besag, J., "Spatial Interaction and the Statistical Analysis of Lattice Systems (with Discussion)," *Journal of the Royal Statistical Society,* Series B, Vol. 36, 1974, pp. 192–326.

Blostein, D., and N. Ahuja, "Representation and Three-Dimensional Interpretation of Image Texture: An Integrated Approach," *Proceedings of the First International Conference on Computer Vision,* London, 1987, pp. 444–449.

——, "A Multiscale Region Detector," *Computer Vision, Graphics, and Image Processing,* Vol. 45, 1989a, pp. 22–41.

——, "Shape from Texture: Integrating Texture-Element Extraction and Surface Estimation," *IEEE Transactions on Pattern Analysis and Machine Intelligence,* Vol. 11, 1989b, pp. 1233–50.

Box, J. E., and G. M. Jenkins, *Time Series Analysis,* Holden-Day, San Francisco, 1970.

Carel, W., W. Purdy, and R. Lulow, "The VISILOG: A Bionic Approach to Visual Space Perception and Orientation," *Proceedings of the 1961 National Aerospace Electronics Conference (NAECON),* Dayton, OH, 1961, pp. 295–300.

Carlotto, M. J., "Texture Classification Based on Hypothesis Testing Approach," *International Japanese Conference on Pattern Recognition,* Montreal, 1984, pp. 93–96.

Carlton, S. G., and O. R. Mitchell, "Image Segmentation Using Texture and Gray Level," *IEEE Computer Society Conference on Pattern Recognition and Image Processing,* Troy, NY, 1977, pp. 387–391.

Carlucci, L., "A Formal System for Texture Languages," *Pattern Recognition,* Vol. 4, 1972, pp. 53–72.

Charton, P. W., and E. E. Ferris, "The VISILOG: A Synthetic Eye," General Electric Co., Technical Report AL-TDR-64-185, DDC No. AD611539, 1965.

Chellappa, R., and R. L. Kashyap, "On the Correlation Structure of Random Field Models of Images and Textures," *IEEE Conference on Pattern Recognition and Image Processing,* Dallas, 1981, pp. 574–576.

Chellappa, R., and R. L. Kashyap, "Synthetic Generation and Estimation in Random Field Models of Images," *Proceedings of the 1981 Pattern Recognition Conference and Image Processing Conference,* Dallas, 1981, pp. 577–582.

Chen, C. H., "On Two-Dimensional ARMA Models for Image Analysis," *Fifth International Conference on Pattern Recognition,* Miami, 1980, pp. 1129–31.

Chen, P. C., and T. Pavlidis, "Segmentation by Texture Using a Co-occurrence Matrix and a Split-and-Merge Algorithm," *Computer Graphics and Image Processing,* Vol. 10, 1979, pp. 172–182.

——, "Segmentation by Texture Using Correlation," *IEEE Transactions on Pattern Analysis and Machine Intelligence,* Vol. PAMI-5, 1983, pp. 64–69.

Chetverikov, D., "Textural Anisotropy Features for Texture Analysis," *IEEE Conference on Pattern Recognition and Image Processing,* Dallas, 1981, pp. 583–588.

——, "Measuring the Degree of Texture Regularity," *International Conference on Pattern Recognition,* Montreal, 1984, pp. 80–82.

Chien, Y. P., and K-S. Fu, "Recognition of X-Ray Picture Patterns," *IEEE Transactions on Systems, Man, and Cybernetics,* Vol. SMC-4, 1974, pp. 145–156.

Chow, C. K., "A Recognition Method Using Neighbor Dependence," *IRE Transactions on Electronic Computers,* Vol. 11, 1962, pp. 683–690.

Clark, M., and A. C. Bovik, "Experiments in Segmenting Texton Patterns Using Localized Spatial Filters," *Pattern Recognition,* Vol. 22, 1989, pp. 707–717.

Cohen, F. S., and D. B. Cooper, "Real Time Textured-Image Segmentation Based on Noncausal Markovian Random Field Models," *Proceedings of SPIE, Intelligent Robots: Third International Conference on Robot Vision and Sensory Controls,* Cambridge, MA, 1983, pp. 17–28.

Cohen, P., C. T. LeDinh, and V. Lacasse, "Classification of Natural Textures by Means of Two-Dimensional Orthogonal Masks," *IEEE Transactions on Acoustics, Speech, and Signal Processing,* Vol. 37, 1989, pp. 125–128.

Cohen, P., and H. H. Nguyen, "Unsupervised Bayesian Estimation for Segmenting Textured Images," *Second International Conference on Computer Vision,* Tampa, FL, 1988, pp. 303–309.

Conners, R. W., and C. A. Harlow, "Some Theoretical Considerations Concerning Texture Analysis of Radiographic Images," *Proceedings of the 1976 IEEE Conference on Decision and Control,* Clearwater, FL, 1976.

——, "Equal Probability Quantizing and Texture Analysis of Radiographic Images," *Computer Graphics and Image Processing,* Vol. 8, 1978, pp. 447–463.

——, "A Theoretical Comparison of Texture Algorithms," *IEEE Transactions on Pattern Analysis and Machine Intelligence,* Vol. PAMI-2, 1980, pp. 204–222.

Conners, R. W., M. A. Trivedi, and C. A. Harlow, "Segmentation of a High Resolution Urban Scene Using Texture Operators," *Computer Vision, Graphics, and Image Processing,* Vol. 25, 1984, pp. 273–310.

Cross, G. R., and A. K. Jain, "Markov Random Field Texture Models," *IEEE Transactions on Pattern Analysis and Machine Intelligence,* Vol. PAMI-5, 1983, pp. 25–39.

Darling, E. M., and R. D. Joseph, "Pattern Recognition from Satellite Altitudes," *IEEE Transactions on Systems, Man, and Cybernetics,* Vol. SMC-4, 1968, pp. 38–47.

D'Astous, F., and M. E. Jernigan, "Texture Discrimination Based on Detailed Measures of the Power Spectrum," *IEEE International Conference on Pattern Recognition,* Montreal, 1984, pp. 83–86.

Davis, L. S., "Computing the Spatial Structure of Cellular Textures," *Computer Graphics and Image Processing,* Vol. 11, 1979, pp. 111–122.

———, "Polarograms: A New Tool for Image Texture Analysis," *Pattern Recognition,* Vol. 13, 1981, pp. 219–223.

Davis, L. S., M. Clearman, and J. K. Aggarwal, "An Empirical Evaluation of Generalized Co-occurrence Matrices," *IEEE Transactions on Pattern Analysis and Machine Intelligence,* Vol. PAMI-3, 1981, pp. 214–221.

Davis, L. S., S. M. Dunn, and L. Janos, "Recovery of the Orientation of Textured Surfaces," *Proceedings of SPIE, Intelligent Robots: Third International Conference on Robot Vision and Sensory Controls,* Cambridge, MA, 1983, pp. 409–418.

Davis, L. S., L. Janos, and S. M. Dunn, "Efficient Recovery of Shape from Texture," *IEEE Transactions on Pattern Analysis and Machine Intelligence,* Vol. PAMI-5, 1983, pp. 485–492.

Davis, L. S., S. A. Johns, and J. K. Aggarwal, "Texture Analysis Using Generalized Co-Occurrence Matrices," *IEEE Transactions on Pattern Recognition and Machine Intelligence,* Vol. PAMI-1, 1979, pp. 251–259.

Davis, L. S., and A. Mitiche, "Edge Detection in Textures," *Computer Graphics and Image Processing,* Vol. 12, 1980, pp. 25–39.

Deguchi, K., and I. Morishita, "Texture Characterization and Texture-Based Image Partitioning Using Two-Dimensional Linear Estimation Techniques," *IEEE Transactions on Computers,* Vol. C-27, 1976, pp. 739–745.

Delp, E. J., R. L. Kashyap, and O. R. Mitchell, "Image Data Compression Using Autoregressive Time Series Models," *Pattern Recognition,* Vol. 11, 1979, pp. 313–323.

de Ma, S., and A. Gagalowicz, "Natural Textures Synthesis with the Control of the Autocorrelation and Histogram Parameters," *Third Scandinavian Conference on Image Analysis,* Copenhagen, 1983, pp. 79–84.

Derin, H., and W. S. Cole, "Segmentation of Textured Images Using Gibbs Random Fields," *Computer Vision, Graphics, and Image Processing,* Vol. 35, 1986, pp. 72–98.

de Souza, P., "Texture Recognition via Autoregression," *Pattern Recognition,* Vol. 15, 1982, pp. 471–475.

———, "A Note on a Random Walk Model for Texture Analysis," *Pattern Recognition,* Vol. 16, 1983, pp. 219–222.

Deutsch, E. S., and N. J. Belknap, "Texture Descriptors Using Neighborhood Information," *Computer Graphics and Image Processing,* Vol. 1, 1972, pp. 145–168.

Dipanda, A., et al., "Segmentation of Echocardiographic Images," *Ninth International Conference on Pattern Recognition,* Rome, 1988, pp. 1255–59.

Doner, J., A. Adams, and M. Merickel, "An Organizational Approach to Texture Analysis," *Proceedings of the Computer Vision and Pattern Recognition Conference,* Miami Beach, 1986, pp. 431–434.

Dyer, C. R., T-H. Hong, and A. Rosenfeld, "Texture Classification Using Gray Level Cooccurrence Based on Edge Maxima," *IEEE Transactions on Systems, Man, and Cybernetics,* Vol. SMC-10, 1980, pp. 158–163.

Dyer, C. R., and A. Rosenfeld, "Fourier Texture Features: Suppression of Aperture Effects," *IEEE Transactions on Systems, Man, and Cybernetics,* Vol. SMC-6, 1976, pp. 703–705.

Ehrich, R. W., and J. P. Foith, "Representation of Random Waveforms by Relational Trees," *IEEE Transactions on Computers,* Vol. C-25, 1976, pp. 725–735.

——, "A View of Texture Topology and Texture Description," *Computer Graphics and Image Processing,* Vol. 8, 1978a, pp. 174–202.

——, "Topology and Semantics of Intensity Arrays," in *Computer Vision,* A. Hanson and E. Riseman (eds.), Academic Press, New York, 1978b.

Faugeras, O. D., "Autoregressive Modeling with Conditional Expectation or Texture Synthesis," *Fifth International Conference on Pattern Recognition,* Miami, 1980, pp. 792–794.

Faugeras, O. D., and W. K. Pratt, "Decorrelation Methods of Texture Feature Extraction." *IEEE Transactions on Pattern Analysis and Machine Intelligence,* Vol. PAMI-2, 1980, pp. 323–332.

Fisher, R., "Dispersion of a Sphere," *Proceedings of the Royal Society of London,* Vol. A217, 1953, pp. 295–305.

Francos, J. M., and A. Z. Meiri, "A Unified Structural-Stochastic Model for Texture Analysis and Synthesis," *Ninth International Conference on Pattern Recognition,* Rome, 1988, pp. 41–50.

Frolov, Y. S., "Measuring the Shape of Geographical Phenomena: A History of the Issue," *Soviet Geography,* Vol. 16, 1975, pp. 676–687.

Gagalowicz, A., "A New Method for Texture Fields Synthesis: Some Applications to the Study of Human Vision," *IEEE Transactions on Pattern Analysis and Machine Intelligence,* Vol. PAMI-3, 1981, pp. 520–533.

——, "Synthesis of Natural Textures on 3-D Surfaces," *Seventh International Conference on Pattern Recognition,* Montreal, 1984, pp. 1209–12.

Gagalowicz, A., and S. de Ma, "Sequential Synthesis of Natural Textures," *Computer Vision, Graphics, and Image Processing,* Vol. 30, 1985, pp. 289–315.

Gagalowicz, A., S. de Ma, and C. Tournier-Lasserve, "New Model for Homogeneous Textures," *Proceedings of the Fourth Scandinavian Conference on Image Analysis,* Trondheim, Norway, 1985, pp. 411–419.

Galloway, M. M., "Texture Analysis Using Gray Level Run Lengths," *Computer Graphics and Image Processing,* Vol. 4, 1975, pp. 172–179.

Garber, D., and A. A. Sawchuk, "Texture Simulation Using a Best Fit Model," *Pattern Recognition and Image Processing Conference,* Dallas, 1981, pp. 603–608.

Gilbert, E., "Random Subdivisions of Space into Crystals," *Annals of Mathematical Statistics,* Vol. 33, 1962, pp. 958–972.

Gong, X., and N. K. Huang, "Texture Segmentation Using Iterative Estimate of Energy States," *Ninth International Conference on Pattern Recognition,* Rome, 1988, pp. 51–63.

Gramenopoulos, N., "Terrain Type Recognition Using ERTS-1 MSS Images," *Record of the Symposium on Significant Results Obtained from the Earth Resources Technology Satellite,* NASA SP-327, 1973, pp. 1229–41.

Haralick, R. M., "A Texture-Context Feature Extraction Algorithm for Remotely Sensed Imagery," *Proceedings of the 1971 IEEE Decision and Control Conference,* Gainesville, FL, 1971, pp. 650–657.

——, "A Textural Transform for Images," *Proceedings of the IEEE Conference on Computer Graphics, Pattern Recognition, and Data Structure,* Beverly Hills, CA, 1975.

——, "Statistical and Structural Approaches to Texture Analysis," *Proceedings of Fourth International Joint Conference on Pattern Recognition,* Kyoto, 1978.

Haralick, R. M., and R. Bosley, "Texture Features for Image Classification," *Third ERTS Symposium,* NASA SP-351, 1973, pp. 1219–28.

Haralick, R. M., and K. Shanmugam, "Computer Classification of Reservoir Sandstones," *IEEE Transactions on Geoscience Electronics,* Vol. GE-11, 1973, pp. 171–177.

——, "Combined Spectral and Spatial Processing of ERTS Imagery Data," *Journal of Remote Sensing of the Environment,* Vol. 3, 1974, pp. 3–13.

Haralick, R. M., K. Shanmugam, and I. Dinstein, "On Some Quickly Computable Features for Texture," *Proceedings of the 1972 Symposium on Computer Image Processing and Recognition,* University of Missouri, Columbia, Vol. 2, 1972, pp. 12-2-1 to 12-2-10.

——, "Textural Features for Image Classification," *IEEE Transactions on Systems, Man, and Cybernetics,* Vol. SMC-3, 1973, pp. 610–621.

Harlow, C. A., M. M. Trivedi, and R. W. Conners, "Use of Texture Operators in Segmentation," *Applications of Artificial Intelligence II,* SPIE Vol. 548, 1985, pp. 10–15.

Harris, R., and R. C. Barrett, "Toward an Objective Nephanalysis," *Journal of Applied Meteorology,* Vol. 17, 1978, pp. 1258–66.

Harwood, D., M. Subbarao, and L. S. Davis, "Texture Classification by Local Rank Correlation," *Computer Vision, Graphics, and Image Processing,* Vol. 32, 1985, pp. 404–411.

Hassner, M., and J. Sklansky, "The Use of Markov Random Fields as Models of Texture," *Computer Graphics and Image Processing,* Vol. 12, 1980, pp. 357–370.

Hawkins, J. K., "Textural Properties for Pattern Recognition," in *Picture Processing and Psychopictorics,* B. S. Lipkin and A. Rosenfeld (eds.), Academic Press, New York, 1969.

He, D-C., L. Wang, and J. Guibert, "Texture Discrimination Based on an Optimal Utilization of Texture Features," *Pattern Recognition,* Vol. 21, 1988, pp. 141–146.

Heitz, F., H. Maitre, and C. de Couessin, "Application of Autoregressive Models to Fine Arts Painting Analysis," *Signal Processing,* Vol. 13, 1987, pp. 1–14.

Hong, T. H., C. R. Dyer, and A. Rosenfeld, "Texture Primitive Extraction Using an Edge-Based Approach," *IEEE Transactions on Systems, Man, and Cybernetics,* Vol. SMC-10, 1980, pp. 659–675.

Hong, T. H., A. Y. Wie, and A. Rosenfeld, "Feature Value Smoothing as an Aid in Texture Analysis," *IEEE Transactions on Systems, Man, and Cybernetics,* Vol. SMC-10, 1980, pp. 519–524.

Horning, R. J., and A. J. Smith, " Application of Fourier Analysis in Multispectral/Spatial Recognition," paper presented at the *Management and Utilization of Remote Sensing Data ASP Symposium,* Sioux Falls, SD, 1973.

Hsiao, J. Y., and A. A. Sawchuk, "Unsupervised Image Segmentation Using Feature Smoothing and Probabilistic Relaxation Techniques," *Computer Vision, Graphics, and Image Processing,* Vol. 48, 1989, pp. 1–21.

Hsu, S-Y., "A Texture-Tone Analysis for Automated Landuse Mapping with Panchromatic Images," *Proceedings of the American Society for Photogrammetry,* 1977, pp. 203–215.

Iizuka, M., "Quantitative Evaluation of Similar Images with Quasi-Gray Levels," *Computer Vision, Graphics, and Image Processing,* Vol. 38, 1987, pp. 342–360.

Ikonomopoulos, A., and M. Unser, "A Directional Filtering Approach to Texture Discrimination," *International Conference on Pattern Recognition,* Montreal, 1984, pp. 87–89.

Jau, Y-C., R. T. Chin, and J. A. Weinman, "Time Series Modeling for Texture Analysis and Synthesis with Applications to Cloud Field Morphology Study," *International Conference on Pattern Recognition,* Montreal, 1984, pp. 1219–21.

Jernigan, M. E., and F. D'Astous, "Entropy-Based Texture Analysis in the Spatial Frequency Domain," *IEEE Transactions on Pattern Analysis and Machine Intelligence,* Vol. PAMI-6, 1984, pp. 237–243.

Julesz, B., "Visual Pattern Discrimination," *IRE Transactions on Information Theory,* February 1961, pp. 84–92.

——, "Texture and Visual Perception," *Scientific American,* February 1965, pp. 38–48.

——, "Experiments in the Visual Perception of Texture," *Scientific American,* 1975, pp. 34–43.

Kanal, L. N., "Markov Mesh Models," *Computer Graphics and Image Processing,* Vol. 12, 1980, pp. 371–375.

Kanatani, K-I., and T-C. Chou, "Shape from Texture: General Principle," *Proceedings of the IEEE Computer Society Conference on Computer Vision and Pattern Recognition,* Miami, 1986, pp. 578–583.

Kashyap, R. L., and R. Chellappa, "Decision Rules for Choice of Neighbors in Random Field Models of Images," *Computer Graphics and Image Processing,* Vol. 15, 1981, pp. 301–318.

Kashyap, R. L., and K-B. Eom, "Texture Boundary Detection Based on the Long Correlation Model," *IEEE Transactions on Pattern Analysis and Machine Intelligence,* Vol. PAMI-11, 1989, pp. 58–67.

Kashyap, R. L., and A. Khotanzad, "A Stochastic Model Based Technique for Texture Segmentation," *Seventh International Conference on Pattern Recognition,* Montreal, 1984, pp. 1202–05.

——, "A Model-Based Method for Rotation Invariant Texture Classification," *IEEE Transactions on Pattern Analysis and Machine Intelligence,* Vol. PAMI-8, 1986, pp. 472–482.

Keller, J. M., S. Chen, and R. M. Crownover, "Texture Description through Fractal Geometry," *Computer Vision, Graphics, and Image Processing,* Vol. 45, 1989, pp. 150–166.

Keller, J. M., R. M. Crownover, and R. Y. Chen, "Characteristics of Natural Scenes Related to the Fractal Dimension," *IEEE Transactions on Pattern Analysis and Machine Intelligence,* Vol. PAMI-9, pp. 621–627.

Kender, J. R., "Shape from Texture: An Aggregation Transform That Maps a Class of Textures into Surface Orientation," *Proceedings of the International Japanese Conference on Artificial Intelligence,* Tokyo, 1979, pp. 475–480.

Khotanzad, A., and J-Y. Chen, "Unsupervised Segmentation of Textured Images by Edge Detection in Multidimensional Features," *IEEE Transactions on Pattern Analysis and Machine Intelligence,* Vol. PAMI-11, 1989, pp. 414–421.

Khotanzad, A., and R. Kashyap, "Feature Selection for Texture Recognition Based on Image Symbols," *IEEE Transactions on Systems, Man, and Cybernetics,* Vol. SMC-17, 1987, pp. 1087–95.

Kirvida, L., "Texture Measurements for the Automatic Classification of Imagery," *IEEE Transactions on Electromagnetic Compatibility,* Vol. 18, 1976, pp. 38–42.

Kirvida, L., and G. Johnson, "Automatic Interpretation of ERTS Data for Forest Management," *Symposium on Significant Results Obtained from the Earth Resources Technology Satellite,* NASA SP-327, 1973.

Kube, P., and A. Pentland, "On the Imaging of Fractal Surfaces," *IEEE Transactions on Pattern Analysis and Machine Intelligence,* Vol. PAMI-10, 1988, pp. 704–707.

Kuni, T. L., and H. Arisawa, "A Texture Embedding Method in Computer Graphics," *Proceedings of the Conference on Computer Graphics, Pattern Recognition, and Data Structure,* Beverly Hills, CA, 1978, pp. 155–156.

Landeweerd, G. H., and E. S. Gelsema, "The Use of Nuclear Texture Parameters in the Automatic Analysis of Leukocytes," *Pattern Recognition,* Vol. 10, 1978, pp. 57–61.

Lantuejoul, C., "Grain Dependence Test in a Polycrystalline Ceramic," in *Quantitative Analysis of Microstructures in Materials Science, Biology, and Medicine,* J. L. Chernant (ed.), Riederer-Verlag, GmbH, Stuttgart, Germany, 1978, pp. 40–50.

Laws, K. I., "Rapid Texture Identification," *Proceedings of the SPIE Conference on Image Processing for Missile Guidance,* San Diego, 1980, pp. 376–380.

——, "Goal-Directed Textured-Image Segmentation," *Applications of Artificial Intelligence II,* SPIE Vol. 548, 1985, pp. 19–26.

Ledley, R. S., "Texture Problems in Biomedical Pattern Recognition," *Proceedings of the 1972 IEEE Conference on Decision and Control and the Eleventh Symposium on Adaptive Processes,* New Orleans, 1972.

Leu, J-G., and W. G. Wee, "Detecting the Spatial Structure of Natural Textures Based on Shape Analysis," *Computer Vision, Graphics, and Image Processing,* Vol. 31, 1985, pp. 67–88.

Lin, Z., and Y. Attikiouzel, "Two-Dimensional Linear Prediction Model-Based Decorrelation Method," *IEEE Transactions on Pattern Analysis and Machine Intelligence,* Vol. PAMI-11, 1989, pp. 661–664.

Lipkin, B. S., and L. E. Lipkin, "Textural Parameters Related to Nuclear Maturation in the Granulocytic Leukocytic Series," *Journal of Histochemistry and Cytochemistry,* Vol. 22, 1974, pp. 583–593.

Liu, S. S., and M. E. Jernigan, "Texture Analysis and Discrimination in Additive Noise," *Computer Vision, Graphics, and Image Processing,* Vol. 49, 1990, pp. 52–67.

Lowitz, G. E., "Can a Local Histogram Really Map Texture Information?" *Pattern Recognition,* Vol. 16, 1983, pp. 141–147.

——, "Mapping the Local Information Content of a Spatial Image," *Pattern Recognition,* Vol. 17, 1984, pp. 545–550.

Lu, D., J. T. Tou, and T. Gu, "A Simplified Procedure for Statistical Feature Extraction in Texture Processing," *Pattern Recognition and Image Processing Conference,* Dallas, 1981, pp. 589–592.

Lu, S. Y., and K. S. Fu, "A Syntactic Approach to Texture Analysis," *Computer Graphics and Image Processing,* Vol. 7, 1978, pp. 303–330.

——, "Stochastic Tree Grammar Inference for Texture Synthesis and Discrimination," *Computer Graphics and Image Processing,* Vol. 9, 1979, pp. 234–245.

Lumia, R., et al., "Texture Analysis of Aerial Photographs," *Pattern Recognition,* Vol. 16, 1983, pp. 39–46.

Ma, S., and A. Gagalowicz, "A Parallel Method for Natural Texture Synthesis," *Seventh International Conference on Pattern Recognition,* Montreal, 1984, pp. 90–92.

Maleson, J., C. Brown, and J. Feldman, "Understanding Natural Texture," Computer Science Department, University of Rochester, Rochester, NY, 1977.

Mandelbrot, B., *The Fractral Geometry of Nature,* W. H. Freeman, San Francisco, 1983.

Matheron, G., *Random Sets and Integral Geometry,* Wiley, New York, 1975.

Matheron, G., "Principles of Geostatistics," *Economic Geology,* Vol. 58, 1963, pp. 1246–66.

Matsuyama, T., S. I. Miura, and M. Nagao, "A Structural Analyzer for Regularly Arranged Textures," *Computer Graphics and Image Processing,* Vol. 18, 1982, pp. 259–279.

——, "Structural Analysis of Natural Textures by Fourier Transformation," *Computer Vision, Graphics, and Image Processing,* Vol. 24, 1983, pp. 347–362.

Maurer, H., "Measurement of Textures of Crop Fields with the Zeiss-Scanning-Microscope-Photometer 05," *Proceedings of the Seventh International Symposium on Remote Sensing of Environment,* Ann Arbor, MI, 1971, pp. 2329–42.

——, "Quantification of Textures—Textural Parameters and Their Significance for Classifying Agricultural Crop Types from Colour Aerial Photographs," *Photogrammetria,* Vol. 30, 1974a, pp. 21–40.

——, "Texture Analysis with Fourier Series," *Proceedings of the Ninth International Symposium on Remote Sensing of Environment,* Ann Arbor, MI, 1974b, pp. 1411–20.

McCormick, B. H., and S. N. Jayaramamurthy, "Time Series Model for Texture Synthesis," *International Journal of Computer and Information Sciences,* Vol. 3, 1974, pp. 329–343.

——, "A Decision Theory Method for the Analysis of Texture," *International Journal of Computer and Information Sciences,* Vol. 4, 1975, pp. 1–38.

Meyer, F., "Iterative Image Transformations for an Automatic Screening of Cervical Smears," *Journal of Histochemistry and Cytochemistry,* Vol. 27, 1979, pp. 128–135.

Mezei, L., M. Puzin, and P. Conroy, "Simulation of Patterns of Nature by Computer Graphics," *Information Processing,* Vol. 74, 1974, pp. 861–865.

Miles, R., "Random Polygons Determined by Random Lines in the Plane," *Proceedings of the National Academy of Sciences,* Vol. 52, 1969, pp. 901–907, 1157–60.

——, "On the Homogeneous Planar Poisson Point-Process," *Math Bioscience,* Vol. 6, 1970, pp. 85–127.

——, "A Survey of Geometrical Probability in the Plane, with Emphasis on Stochastic Image Modeling," *Computer Graphics and Image Processing,* Vol. 21, 1980, pp. 1–24.

Mitchell, O. R., and S. G. Carlton, "Image Segmentation Using a Local Extrema Texture Measure," *Pattern Recognition,* Vol. 10, 1978, pp. 205–210.

Mitchell, O. R., C. R. Myers, and W. Boyne, "A Max-Min Measure for Image Texture Analysis," *IEEE Transactions on Computers,* C-26, 1977, pp. 408–414.

Modestino, J. W., R. W. Fries, and A. L. Vickers, "Stochastic Image Models Generated by Random Tessellations of the Plane," *Computer Graphics and Image Processing,* Vol. 12, 1980, pp. 74–98.

——, "Texture Discrimination Based upon an Assumed Stochastic Texture Model," *IEEE Transactions on Pattern Analysis and Machine Intelligence,* Vol. PAMI-3, 1981, pp. 557–580.

Moerdler, M. L., "Multiple Shape-from-Texture into Texture Analysis and Surface Segmentation," *Proceedings of the Second International Conference on Computer Vision,* Tarpou Springs, MD, 1988, pp. 316–320.

Monne, J., F. Schmitt, and C. Massaloux, "Bidimensional Texture Synthesis by Markov Chains," *Computer Graphics and Image Processing,* Vol. 17, 1981, pp. 1–23.

Mueller, W., "The Leitz Texture Analyzes Systems," *Leitz Scientific and Technical Information,* Supplement 1, 4, 1974, pp. 101–116.

Mueller, W., and W. Herman, "Texture Analyzes Systems," *Industrial Research,* November 1974.

Ohta, Y., K. Maenobu, and T. Sakai, "Obtaining Surface Orientation from Texture under Perspective Projection," *Proceedings of the International Joint Conference on Artificial Intelligence,* Vancouver, BC, 1981, pp. 746–751.

Osman, M. O. M., and T. S. Saukar, "The Measurement of Surface Texture by Means of Random Function Excursion Techniques," *Advances in Test Measurement,* Vol. 12, *Proceedings of the Twenty-first International Instrumentation Symposium,* Pittsburgh, 1975.

Peet, F. G., and T. S. Sahota, "Surface Curvature as a Measure of Image Texture," *IEEE Transactions on Pattern Analysis and Machine Intelligence,* Vol. PAMI-7, 1985, pp. 734–738.

Peleg, S., et al., "Multiple Resolution Texture Analysis and Classification." *IEEE Transactions on Pattern Analysis and Machine Intelligence,* Vol. PAMI-6, 1984, pp. 518–523.

Pentland, A. P., "Fractal-based Description of Natural Scenes," *IEEE Transactions on Pattern Analysis and Machine Intelligence,* Vol. PAMI-6, 1984, pp. 661–674.

Percus, J. K., "On the Wechsler–De Souza Discussion," *Pattern Recognition,* Vol. 16, 1983, pp. 269–270.

Pickett, R. M., "Visual Analyses of Texture in the Detection and Recognition of Objects," in *Picture Processing and Psychopictorics,* B. S. Lipkin and A. Rosenfeld (eds.), Academic Press, New York, 1970, pp. 289–308.

Pietikäinen, M., and A. Rosenfeld, "Gray Level Pyramid Linking as an Aid in Texture Analysis," *IEEE Transactions on Systems, Man, and Cybernetics,* Vol. SMC-12, 1982a, pp. 422–430.

——, "Edge-Based Texture Measures," *IEEE Transactions on Systems, Man, and Cybernetics,* Vol. SMC-12, 1982b, pp. 585–594.

Pratt, W. K., *Digital Image Processing,* Wiley-Interscience, New York, 1978.

Pratt, W. K., O. D. Faugeras, and A. Gagalowicz, "Visual Discrimination of Stochastic Texture Fields," *IEEE Transactions on Systems, Man, and Cybernetics,* Vol. SMC-8, 1978, pp. 796–804.

——, "Applications of Stochastic Texture Field Models to Image Processing," *Proceedings of the IEEE,* Vol. 69, 1981, pp. 542–551.

Pressman, N. J., "Markovian Analysis of Cervical Cell Images," *Journal of Histochemistry and Cytochemistry,* Vol. 24, 1976, pp. 138–144.

Raafat, H. M., and A. K. C. Wong, "A Texture Information-Directed Region Growing Algorithm for Image Segmentation and Region Classification," *Computer Vision, Graphics, and Image Processing,* Vol. 43, 1988, pp. 1–21.

Read, J. S., and S. N. Jayaramamurthy, "Automatic Generation of Texture Feature Detectors," *IEEE Transactions on Computers,* C-21, 1972, pp. 803–812.

Reed, T. R., and H. Wechsler, "Segmentation of Textured Images and Gestalt Organization Using Spatial/Spatial-Frequency Representations," *IEEE Transactions on Pattern Analysis and Machine Intelligence,* Vol. PAMI-12, 1990, pp. 1–12.

Roan, S. J., J. K. Aggarwal, and W. N. Martin, "Multiple Resolution Imagery and Texture Analysis," *Pattern Recognition,* Vol. 20, 1987, pp. 17–31.

Rosenfeld, A., "Connectivity in Digital Pictures," *Journal of the ACM,* Vol. 17, 1970, pp. 146–160.

——, "A Note on Automatic Detection of Texture Gradients," *IEEE Transactions on Computers,* C-24, 1975, pp. 988–991.

Rosenfeld, A., and L. Davis, "A Note on Thinning," *IEEE Transactions on Systems, Man, and Cybernetics,* Vol. SMC-6, 1976, pp. 226–228.

Rosenfeld, A., and B. S. Lipkin, "Texture Synthesis," in *Picture Processing and Psychopictorics,* Lipkin and Rosenfeld, (eds.), Academic Press, New York, 1970.

Rosenfeld, A., and J. Pfaltz, "Sequential Operations in Digital Picture Processing," *Journal of the ACM,* Vol. 13, 1966, pp. 471–494.

——, "Distance Functions on Digital Images," *Pattern Recognition,* Vol. 1, 1968, pp. 33–61.

Rosenfeld, A., and M. Thurston, "Edge and Curve Detection for Visual Scene Analysis," *IEEE Transactions on Computers,* Vol. C-20, 1971, pp. 562–569.

Rosenfeld, A., and E. Troy, "Visual Texture Analysis," Technical Report 70-116, University of Maryland, College Park, 1970.

Rosenfeld, A., C-Y. Wang, and A.Y. Wu, "Multispectral Texture," *IEEE Transactions on Systems, Man, and Cybernetics,* Vol. SMC-12, 1982, pp. 79–84.

Rotolo, L. S., "Automatic Texture Analysis for the Diagnosis of Pneumoconiosis," *Proceedings of the Twenty-sixth ACEMB,* Minneapolis, 1973, p. 32.

Sato, M., and M. Ogata, "Texture Analysis by the Self-Organization Method," *Proceedings of the International Conference on Pattern Recognition,* Tokyo, 1984, pp. 1213–15.

Schachter, B., "Long Crested Wave Models," *Computer Graphics and Image Processing,* Vol. 12, 1980a, pp. 187–201.

——, "Model-Based Texture Methods," *IEEE Transactions on Pattern Analysis and Machine Intelligence,* Vol. PAMI-2, 1980b, pp. 169–171.

Schachter, B., and N. Ahuja, "Random Pattern Generation Processes," *Computer Graphics and Image Processing,* Vol. 10, 1979, pp. 95–114.

Schachter, B., A. Rosenfeld, and L.S. Davis, "Random Mosaic Models for Textures," *IEEE Transactions on Systems, Man, and Cybernetics,* Vol. SMC-8, 1978, pp. 694–702.

Schmitt, F., et al., "Texture Representation and Synthesis," *Seventh International Conference on Pattern Recognition,* Montreal, 1984, pp. 1222–25.

Serra, J., "Theoretical Bases of the Leitz Texture Analyses System," *Leitz Scientific and Technical Information,* Supplement 1, 4, 1974, pp. 125–136.

——, "One, Two, Three, . . . ,Infinity," *Quantitative Analysis of Microstructures in Material Science, Biology, and Medicine,* Stuttgart, Riederer-Verlag, 1978, pp. 9–24.

Serra, J., and G. Verchery, "Mathematical Morphology Applied to Fibre Composite Materials," *Film Science and Technology,* Vol. 6, 1973, pp. 141–158.

Shen, H. C., and A. K. C. Wong, "Generalized Texture Representation and Metric," *Computer Vision, Graphics, and Image Processing,* Vol. 23, 1983, pp. 187–206.

Siew, L. H., R. M. Hodgson, and E. J. Wood, "Texture Measures for Carpet Wear Assessment," *IEEE Transactions on Pattern Analysis and Machine Intelligence,* Vol. PAMI-10, 1988, pp. 92–125.

Silverman, J. F., and D. B. Cooper, "Bayesian Clustering for Unsupervised Estimation of Surface and Texture Models," *IEEE Transactions on Pattern Analysis and Machine Intelligence,* Vol. PAMI-10, 1988, pp. 482–495.

Sternberg, S. R., "Parallel Architectures for Image Processing," *Proceedings of IEEE International Computer Software and Applications Conference,* Chicago, 1979, pp. 712–7.

Sternberg, S. R., and E. S. Sternberg, "Industrial Inspection by Morphological Virtual Gauging," *IEEE Workshop on Computer Architecture, Pattern Analysis, and Image Database Management,* Pasadena, CA, 1983.

Sun, C., and W. G. Wee, "Neighboring Gray Level Dependence Matrix for Texture Classification," *Computer Vision, Graphics, and Image Processing,* Vol. 23, 1983, pp. 341–352.

Sutton, R. N., and E. L. Hall, "Texture Measures for Automatic Classification of Pulmonary Disease," *IEEE Transactions on Computers,* Vol. C-21, 1972, pp. 667–676.

Swerling, P., "Statistical Properties of the Contours of Random Surfaces," *IRE Transactions on Information Theory,* November 1962, p. 315–321.

Switzer, P., "Reconstructing Patterns from Sample Data," *Annals of Mathematical Statistics,* Vol. 38, 1967, pp. 138–154.

Tamura, H., S. Mori, and T. Yamawaki, "Textural Features Corresponding to Visual Perception," *IEEE Transactions on Systems, Man, and Cybernetics,* Vol. SMC-8, 1978, pp. 460–473.

Terzopoulos, D., and S. W. Zucker, "Detection of Osteogenesis Imperfecta by Automated Texture Analysis," *Computer Graphics and Image Processing,* Vol. 20, 1982, pp. 229–243.

Therrien, C. W., "Linear Filtering Models for Texture Classification and Segmentation," *Proceedings of the Fifth International Conference on Pattern Recognition,* Vol. 2 of 2, 1980, pp. 1132–35.

——, "An Estimation-Theoretic Approach to Terrain Image Segmentation," *Computer Vision, Graphics, and Image Processing,* Vol. 22, 1983, pp. 313–326.

Thomas, J. O., and P. G. Davey, *Proceedings of the British Pattern Recognition Association and Remote Sensing Society Joint Meeting on Texture Analysis,* Oxford, 1977.

Tomita, F., Y. Shirai, and S. Tsuji, "Description of Textures by a Structural Analysis," *IEEE Transactions on Pattern Analysis and Machine Intelligence,* Vol. PAMI-4, 1982, pp. 183–191.

Tomita, F., M. Yachida, and S. Tsuji, "Detection of Homogeneous Regions by Structural Analysis," *Third International Joint Conference on Artificial Intelligence,* Stanford, 1973, pp. 564–571.

Toriwaki, J., and T. Fukumura, "Extraction of Structural Information from Grey Pictures," *Computer Graphics and Image Processing,* Vol. 7, 1978, pp. 30–51.

Toriwaki, J., Y. Yashima, and S. Yokoi, "Adjacency Graphs on a Digitized Figure Set and Their Applications Texture Analysis," *Seventh International Conference on Pattern Recognition,* Montreal, 1984, pp. 1216–18.

Tou, J. T., "Pictorial Feature Extraction and Recognition via Image Modeling," *Computer Graphics and Image Processing,* Vol. 12, 1980, pp. 376–406.

Tou, J. T., and Y. S. Chang, "Picture Understanding by Machine via Textural Feature Extraction," *Proceedings of the IEEE Conference on Pattern Recognition and Image Processing,* Troy, NY, 1977, pp. 1–8.

——, "An Approach to Texture Pattern Analysis and Recognition," *Proceedings of the IEEE Conference on Decision and Control,* Clearwater, FL, 1976, pp. 1–7.

Tou, J. T., D. B. Kao, and Y. S. Chang, "Pictorial Texture Analysis and Synthesis," *Proceedings of the Third International Joint Conference on Pattern Recognition,* Coronado, CA, 1976, p. 590.

Triendl, E. E., "Automatic Terrain Mapping by Texture Recognition," *Proceedings of the Eighth International Symposium on Remote Sensing of Environment,* Environmental Research Institute of Michigan, Ann Arbor, 1972, pp. 771–776.

Trivedi, M. M., et al., "Object Detection Based on Gray Level Cooccurrence," *Computer Vision, Graphics, and Image Processing,* Vol. 28, 1984, pp. 199–219.

Troy, E. B., E. S. Deutsch, and A. Rosenfeld, "Gray-Level Manipulation Experiments for Texture Analysis," *IEEE Transactions on Systems, Man, and Cybernetics,* Vol. SMC-3, 1973, pp. 91–98.

Tsai, W. H., and K. S. Fu, "Image Segmentation and Recognition by Texture Discrimination: A Syntactic Approach," *Fourth International Joint Conference on Pattern Recognition,* Tokyo, 1978, pp. 560–564.

Tsuji, S., and F. Tomita, "A Structural Analyzer for a Class of Textures," *Computer Graphics and Image Processing,* Vol. 2, 1973, pp. 216–231.

Unser, M., "Local Linear Transforms for Texture Analysis," *Proceedings of the Seventh International Conference on Pattern Recognition,* Montreal, 1984, pp. 1206–08.

——, "Sum and Difference Histograms for Texture Classification," *IEEE Transactions on Pattern Analysis and Machine Intelligence,* Vol. PAMI-8, 1986, pp. 118–125.

Unser, M., and M. Eden, "Multiresolution Feature Extraction and Selection for Texture Segmentation," *IEEE Transactions on Pattern Analysis and Machine Intelligence,* Vol. PAMI-11, 1989, pp. 717–728.

Van Gool, L., P. Dewaele, and A. Oosterlinck, "Texture Analysis Anno 1983," *Computer Vision, Graphics, and Image Processing,* Vol. 29, 1985, pp. 336–357.

Vetter, H. G., and S. M. Pizer, "Perception of Quantum-Limited Images," *Photogrammetric Engineering,* Vol. 36, 1970, pp. 1179–88.

Vickers, A. L., and J. W. Modestino, "A Maximum Likelihood Approach to Texture Classification," *IEEE Transactions on Pattern Analysis and Machine Intelligence,* Vol. PAMI-4, 1982, pp. 61–68.

Vilnrotter, F., R. Nevatia, and K. Price, "Structural Analysis of Natural Textures," *IEEE Transactions on Pattern Analysis and Machine Intelligence,* Vol. PAMI-8, 1986, pp. 76–89.

Voorhees, H., and T. Poggio, "Detecting Textons and Texture Boundaries in Natural Images," *Proceedings of the First International Conference on Computer Vision,* London, 1987, pp. 250–258.

Wang, D., and S. N. Srihair, "Classification of Newspaper Image Blocks Using Texture Analysis," *Computer Vision, Graphics, and Image Processing,* Vol. 47, 1989, pp. 327–352.

Wang, S., et al., "Relative Effectiveness of Selected Texture Primitive Statistics for Texture Discrimination," *IEEE Transactions on Systems, Man, and Cybernetics,* Vol. SMC-11, 1981, pp. 360–370.

Wechsler, H., "Feature Extraction for Texture Classification," *Pattern Recognition,* Vol. 12, 1980, pp. 301–311.

Wechsler, H., and M. Kidode, "A Random Walk Procedure for Texture Discrimination," *IEEE Transactions on Pattern Analysis and Machine Intelligence,* Vol. PAMI-1, 1979, pp. 272–280.

Weid, G., G. Bahr, and P. Bartels, "Automatic Analysis of Cell Images," in *Automated Cell Identification and Cell Sorting,* Wied and Bahr (eds.), Academic Press, New York, 1970, pp. 195–360.

Werman, M., and S. Peleg, "Multiresolution Texture Signatures Using Min-Max Operators," *Proceedings of the Seventh International Conference on Pattern Recognition,* Montreal, 1984, pp. 97–99.

——, "Min-Max Operators in Texture Analysis," *IEEE Transactions on Pattern Analysis and Machine Intelligence,* Vol. PAMI-7, 1985, pp. 730–733.

Wermser, D., and C-E. Liedtke, "Texture Gradient: A New Tool for the Unsupervised Segmentation," *Proceedings of the Third International Conference on Image Analysis,* Copenhagen, 1983, pp. 85–89.

Weszka, J. S., C. R. Dyer, and A. Rosenfeld, "A Comparative Study of Texture Measures for Terrain Classification," *IEEE Transactions on Systems, Man, and Cybernetics,* Vol. SMC-6, 1976, pp. 269–285.

Witkin, A. P., "Recovering Surface Shape and Orientation from Texture," *Artificial Intelligence,* Vol. 17, 1981, pp. 17–45.

Woods, J.W., "Two-Dimensional Discrete Markovian Fields," *IEEE Transactions on Information Theory,* Vol. IT-18, 1972, pp. 232–240.

Yang, M. C., and C-C. Yang, "Image Enhancement for Segmentation by Self-Induced Autoregressive Filtering," *IEEE Transactions on Pattern Analysis and Machine Intelligence,* Vol. PAMI-11, 1989, pp. 655–661.

Yokoi, S., J. Toriwaki, and T. Fukumura, "An Analysis of Topological Properties of Digitized Binary Pictures Using Local Features," *Computer Graphics and Image Processing,* Vol. 4, 1975, pp. 63–73.

Yokoyama, R., and R. M. Haralick, "Texture Synthesis Using a Growth Model," *Computer Graphics and Image Processing,* Vol. 8, 1978, pp. 369–381.

———, "Texture Pattern Image Generation by Regular Markov Chains," *Pattern Recognition,* Vol. 11, 1979, pp. 225–234.

Zobrist, A. I., and W. B. Thompson, "Building a Distance Function for Gestalt Grouping," *IEEE Transactions on Computers,* Vol. C-4, 1985, pp. 718–728.

Zucker, S. W., "On the Foundations of Texture: A Transformational Approach," Technical Report TR-311, University of Maryland, College Park, 1974.

———, "On the Structure of Texture," *Perception,* Vol. 5, 1976a, pp. 419–436.

———, "Toward a Model of Texture," *Computer Graphics and Image Processing,* Vol. 5, 1976b, pp. 190–202.

———, "Finding Structure in Co-occurrence Matrices for Texture Analysis," *Computer Graphics and Image Processing,* Vol. 12, 1980, pp. 286–308.

Zucker, S. W., and K. Kant, "Multiple-level Representations for Texture Discrimination," *Pattern Recognition and Image Processing Conference,* Dallas, 1981, pp. 609–614.

Zucker, S. W., A. Rosenfeld, and L. S. Davis, "Picture Segmentation by Texture Discrimination," *IEEE Transactions on Computers,* C-24, 1975, pp. 1228–33.

10 IMAGE SEGMENTATION

10.1 Introduction

An *image segmentation* is the partition of an image into a set of nonoverlapping regions whose union is the entire image. The purpose of image segmentation is to decompose the image into parts that are meaningful with respect to a particular application. For example, in two-dimensional part recognition, a segmentation might be performed to separate the two-dimensional object from the background. Figure 10.1(a) shows a gray level image of an industrial part, and Figure 10.1(b) shows its segmentation into object and background. In this figure the object is shown in white and the background in black. In simple segmentations we will use gray levels to illustrate the separate regions. In more complex segmentation examples where there are many regions, we will use white lines on a black background to show the separation of the image into its parts.

It is very difficult to tell a computer program what constitutes a "meaningful" segmentation. Instead, general segmentation procedures tend to obey the following rules.

1. Regions of an image segmentation should be uniform and homogeneous with respect to some characteristic, such as gray level or texture.

2. Region interiors should be simple and without many small holes.

3. Adjacent regions of a segmentation should have significantly different values with respect to the characteristic on which they are uniform.

4. Boundaries of each segment should be simple, not ragged, and must be spatially accurate.

Achieving all these desired properties is difficult because strictly uniform and homogeneous regions are typically full of small holes and have ragged boundaries. Insisting that adjacent regions have large differences in values can cause regions to merge and boundaries to be lost.

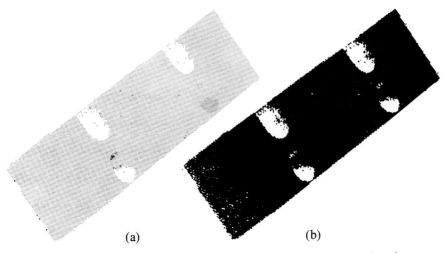

(a)   (b)

Figure 10.1 (a) Gray level image of an industrial part, and (b) segmentation of the image into object (white) and background (black).

Clustering in pattern recognition is the process of partitioning a set of pattern vectors into subsets called clusters (Young and Calvert, 1974). For example, if the pattern vectors are pairs of real numbers illustrated by the point plot of Figure 10.2, clustering consists of finding subsets of points that are "close" to one another in Euclidean 2-space. As there is no full theory of clustering, there is no full theory of image segmentation. Image segmentation techniques are basically ad hoc and differ precisely in the way they emphasize one or more of the desired properties and in the way they balance and compromise one desired property against another. The difference between image segmentation and clustering is that in clustering, the grouping is done in measurement space: In image segmentation, the grouping is done on the spatial domain of the image, and there is an interplay in the clustering between the (possibly overlapping) groups in measurement space and the mutually exclusive groups of the image segmentation.

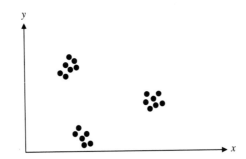

Figure 10.2 Set of points in a Euclidean measurement space that can be separated into three clusters of points. Each cluster consists of points that are in some sense close to one another.

This chapter describes the main ideas behind the major image segmentation techniques and gives example results for a number of them. Additional image segmentation surveys can be found in Zucker (1976), Riseman and Arbib (1977), Kanade (1980), and Fu and Mui (1981). Our point of view will be segmentation with respect to the gray level characteristic. Segmentation on the basis of some other characteristic, such as texture, can be achieved by first applying an operator that transforms local texture to a texture feature value. Texture segmentation can then be accomplished by applying segmentation with respect to the texture pattern value characteristic exactly as if it were a gray level characteristic.

10.2   Measurement-Space-Guided Spatial Clustering

The technique of measurement-space-guided spatial clustering for image segmentation uses the measurement-space-clustering process to define a partition in measurement space. Then each pixel is assigned the label of the cell in the measurement-space partition to which it belongs. The image segments are defined as the connected components of the pixels having the same label.

The segmentation process is, in general, an unsupervised clustering, since no a priori knowledge about the number and type of regions present in the image is available. The accuracy of the measurement-space-clustering image segmentation process depends directly on how well the objects of interest on the image separate into distinct measurement-space clusters. Typically the process works well in situations where there are a few kinds of distinct objects having widely different gray level intensities (or gray level intensity vectors, for multiband images) and where these objects appear on a nearly uniform background.

Clustering procedures that use the pixel as a unit and compare each pixel value with every other pixel value can require excessively long computation times because of the large number of pixels in an image. Iterative partition rearrangement schemes have to go through the image data set many times and, if done without sampling, can also take excessive computation time. Histogram mode seeking, because it requires only one pass through the data, probably involves the least computation time of the measurement-space-clustering technique, and it is the one we discuss here.

Histogram mode seeking is a measurement-space-clustering process in which it is assumed that homogeneous objects on the image manifest themselves as the clusters in measurement space. Image segmentation is accomplished by mapping the clusters back to the image domain where the maximal connected components of the mapped back clusters constitute the image segments. For images that are single-band images, calculation of this histogram in an array is direct. The measurement-space clustering can be accomplished by determining the valleys in this histogram and declaring the clusters to be the intervals of values between valleys. A pixel whose value is in the ith interval is labeled with index i, and the segment it belongs to is one of the connected components of all pixels whose label is i. The thresholding techniques discussed in Chapter 2 are examples of histogram mode seeking with bimodal histograms.

Figure 10.3 Enlarged polished mineral ore section. The bright areas are grains of pyrite; the gray areas constitute a matrix of pyrorhotite; the black areas are holes.

Figure 10.3 illustrates an example image that is the right kind of image for the measurement-space-clustering image segmentation process. It is an enlarged image of a polished mineral ore section. The width of the field is about 1mm. The ore is from Ducktown, Tennessee, and shows subhedral-to-enhedral pyrite porophyroblests (white) in a matrix of pyrorhotite (gray). The black areas are holes. Figure 10.4

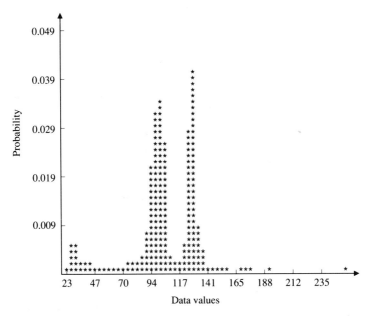

Figure 10.4 Histogram of the image in Fig. 10.3. The three nonoverlapping modes correspond to the black holes, the pyrorhotite, and the pyrite.

Figure 10.5 Segmentation of the image of Fig. 10.3 produced by clustering the histogram of Fig. 10.4.

shows the histogram of this image. The valleys are no trouble to find. The first cluster is from the left end to the first valley. The second cluster is from the first valley to the second valley. The third cluster is from the second valley to the right end. Assigning to each pixel the cluster index of the cluster to which it belongs and then assigning a unique gray level to each cluster label yields the segmentation shown in Fig. 10.5. This is a virtually perfect (meaningful) segmentation.

Figure 10.6 shows an example image that is not ideal for measurement-space-clustering image segmentation. Figure 10.7 shows its histogram, which has three modes and two valleys, and Fig. 10.8 shows the corresponding segmentation. Notice the multiple-boundary area. It is apparent that the boundary between the grain and

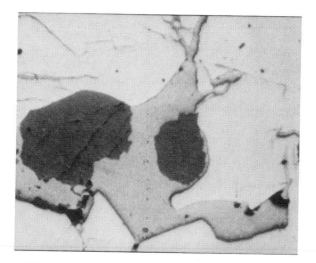

Figure 10.6 Image similar in some respects to the image of Fig. 10.3. Because some of the boundaries between regions are shadowed, homogeneous region segmentation may not produce the desired segmentation.

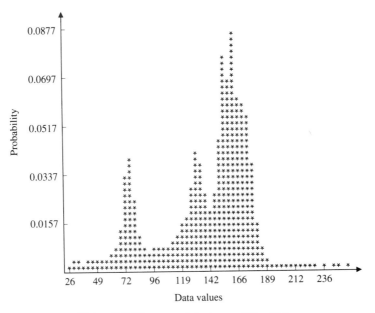

Figure 10.7 Histogram of the image of Fig. 10.6.

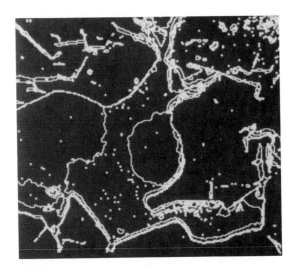

Figure 10.8 Segmentation of the image of Fig. 10.6 produced by clustering the histogram of Fig. 10.7.

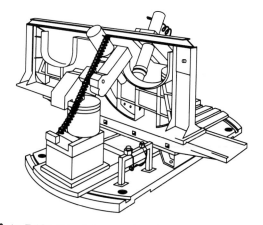

Figure 10.9 An F-15 bulkhead. Images of portions of the bulkhead are used as examples throughout this chapter.

the background is in fact shaded dark, and there are many such border regions that show up as dark segments. In this case we do not desire the edge borders to be separate regions, and although the segmentation procedure did exactly as it should have done, the results are not what we desired. This illustrates that segmentation into homogeneous regions is not necessarily a good solution to a segmentation problem.

The next example further illustrates the fallacies of measurement-space clustering. Figure 10.9 is a diagram of an F-15 bulkhead. Images of portions of the bulkhead, which were used as test data for an experimental robot guidance/inspection system, will be used as examples throughout the rest of this chapter. Figure 10.10

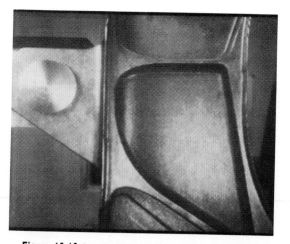

Figure 10.10 Image of a section of the F-15 bulkhead.

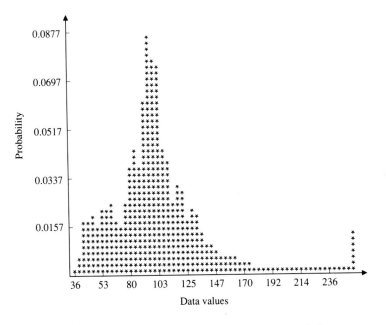

Figure 10.11 Histogram of the bulkhead image of Fig. 10.10.

illustrates an image of a section of the F-15 bulkhead. It is clear that the image has distinct parts, such as webs and ribs. Figure 10.11 shows the histogram of this image. It has two well-separated modes. The narrow one on the right with a long left tail corresponds to specular reflection points. The main mode has three valleys on its left side and two valleys on its right side. Defining the depth of a valley to be the probability difference between the valley bottom and the lowest valley side and eliminating the two shallowest valleys produces the segmentation shown in Fig. 10.12. The problem in the segmentation is apparent. Since the clustering was done in measurement space, there was no requirement for good spatial continuation, and the resulting boundaries are very noisy and busy. Separating the main mode into its two most dominant submodes produces the segmentation of Fig. 10.13. Here the boundary noise is less and the resulting regions are more satisfactory, but the detail provided is much less.

Ohlander, Price, and Reddy (1978) refine the clustering idea in a recursive way. They begin by defining a mask selecting all pixels on the image. Given any mask, a histogram of the masked image is computed. Measurement-space clustering enables the separation of one mode of the histogram set from another mode. Pixels on the image are then identified with the cluster to which they belong. If there is only one measurement-space cluster, then the mask is terminated. If there is more than one cluster, then each connected component of all pixels with the same cluster is, in turn, used to generate a mask that is placed on a mask stack. During successive iterations the next mask in the stack selects pixels in the histo-

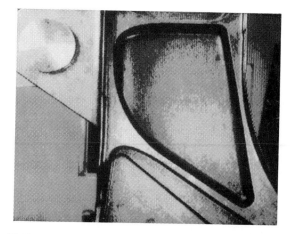

Figure 10.12 Segmentation of the bulkhead induced by a measurement-space clustering into five clusters.

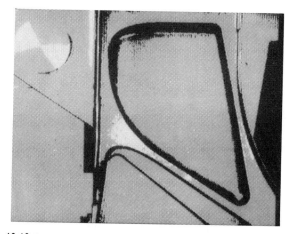

Figure 10.13 Segmentation of the bulkhead induced by a measurement-space clustering into three clusters.

gram computation process. Clustering is repeated for each new mask until the stack is empty.

Figure 10.14 illustrates this process, which we call a recursive histogram-directed spatial clustering. Figure 10.15 illustrates a recursive histogram-directed spatial-clustering technique applied to the bulkhead image of Fig. 10.10. It produces a result with boundaries being somewhat busy and with many small regions in areas of specular reflectance. Figure 10.16 illustrates the results of performing a morphological opening with a 3×3 square structuring element on each region in the segmentation of Fig. 10.15. Pixels, which are removed by the opening, are then given values by a single region growing process. The tiny regions are removed in this manner, but several important long, thin regions are also lost.

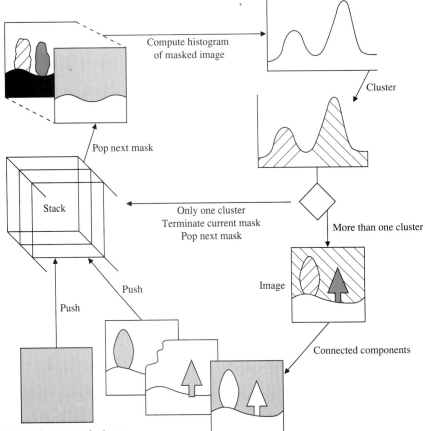

Compute histogram
of masked image

Cluster

Pop next mask

Stack

Only one cluster
Terminate current mask
Pop next mask

More than one cluster

Image

Push

Connected components

Push

Original mask covers entire image

Figure 10.14 Recursive histogram-directed spatial-clustering scheme of Ohlander.

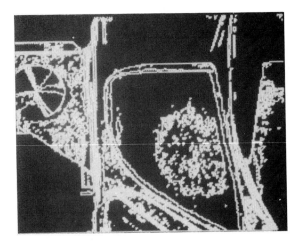

Figure 10.15 Results of the histogram-directed spatial clustering when applied to the bulkhead image.

518

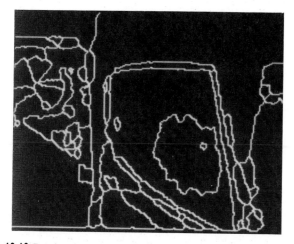

Figure 10.16 Results of performing a morphological opening with a 3×3 square structuring element on the segmentation of Fig. 10.15 and then filling in the removed pixels by a single region growing process.

Figure 10.17 A color image.

For ordinary color images Ohta, Kanade, and Sakai (1980) suggest that histograms not be computed individually on the red, green, and blue (RGB) color variables, but on a set of variables closer to what the Karhunen-Loeve (principal components) transform would suggest. They suggest $(R + G + B)/3$, $(R - B)/2$, and $(2G - R - B)/4$. Figure 10.17 illustrates a color image. Figure 10.18 shows two segmentations of the color image: one by recursive histogram-directed spatial clustering using the R, G, and B bands, and the second by the same method, but using the transformed bands suggested by Ohta, Kanade, and Sakai.

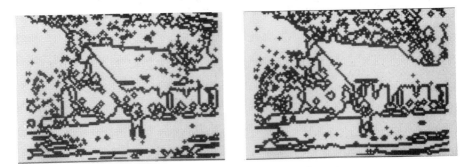

Figure 10.18 Two segmentations of the color image of Fig. 10.17. The left segmentation was achieved by recursive histogram-directed spatial clustering using the R, G, and B bands. The right segmentation was achieved by the same method but using the transformed bands $(R+G+B)/3$, $(R-B)/2$, and $(2G-R-B)/4$ suggested by Ohta, Kanade, and Sakai (1980).

10.2.1 Thresholding

If the image contains a bright object against a dark background and the measurement space is one-dimensional, measurement-space clustering amounts to determining a threshold such that all pixels whose values are less than or equal to the threshold are assigned to one cluster and the remaining pixels are assigned to the second cluster. In the easiest cases a procedure to determine the threshold need only examine the histogram and place the threshold in the valley between the two modes. Procedures of this kind were discussed in Chapter 2. Unfortunately, it is not always the case that the two modes are nicely separated by a valley. To handle this kind of situation, a variety of techniques can be used to combine the spatial information on the image with the gray level intensity information to help in threshold determination.

Chow and Kaneko (1972) suggest using a threshold that depends on the histogram determined from the spatially local area around the pixel to which the threshold applies. Thus, for example, a neighborhood size of 33×33 or 65×65 can be used to compute the local histogram. Chow and Kaneko avoided the local histogram computation for each pixel's neighborhood by dividing the image into mutually exclusive blocks, computing the histogram for each block, and determining an appropriate threshold for each histogram. This threshold value can be considered to apply to the center pixel of each block. To obtain thresholds for the remaining pixels, they spatially interpolated the block center-pixel thresholds to obtain a spatially adaptive threshold for each pixel.

Weszka, Nagel, and Rosenfeld (1974) suggest determining a histogram for only those pixels having a high Laplacian magnitude (see Chapter 6). They reason that there will be a shoulder of the gray level intensity function at each side of the boundary. The shoulder has high Laplacian magnitude. A histogram of all shoulder pixels will be a histogram of all interior pixels just next to the interior border of the region. It will not involve those pixels between regions that help make the histogram valley shallow. It will also have a tendency to involve equal numbers of pixels from the object and from the background. This makes the two histogram modes about the same size. Thus the valley-seeking method for threshold selection has a chance of working on the new histogram.

Weszka and Rosenfeld (1978) describe one method for segmenting white blobs against a dark background by a threshold selection based on busyness. For any threshold, busyness is the percentage of pixels having a neighbor whose thresholded value is different from their own thresholded value. A good threshold is the point near the histogram valley between the two peaks that minimizes the busyness.

Watanabe (1974) suggests choosing a threshold value that maximizes the sum of gradients taken over all pixels whose gray level intensity equals the threshold value. Kohler (1981) suggests a modification of the Watanabe idea. Instead of choosing a threshold that maximizes the sum of gradient magnitudes taken over all pixels whose gray level intensity equals the threshold value, Kohler suggests choosing the threshold that detects more high-contrast edges and fewer low-contrast edges than any other threshold.

Kohler defines the set $E(T)$ of edges detected by a threshold T to be the set of all pairs of neighboring pixels one of whose gray level intensities is less than or equal to T and one of whose gray level intensities is greater than T;

$$E(T) = \{[(i,j),(k,l)]| \tag{10.1}$$

1. pixels (i,j) and (k,l) are neighbors
2. $\min \{I(i,j),I(k,l)\} \leq T < \max\{I(i,j),I(k,l)\}$.

The total contrast $C(T)$ of edges detected by threshold T is given by

$$C(T) = \sum_{[(i,j),(k,l)]\in E(T)} \min\{|I(i,j) - T|, |I(k,l) - T|\} \tag{10.2}$$

The average contrast of all edges detected by threshold T is then given by $C(T)/\#E(T)$. The best threshold T_b is determined by the value that maximizes $C(T_b)/\#E(T_b)$.

Milgram and Herman (1979) reason that pixels that are between regions probably have in-between gray level intensities. If it is these pixels that are the cause of the shallow valleys, then it should be possible to eliminate their effect by considering only pixels having small gradients. They take this idea further and suggest that by examining clusters in the two-dimensional measurement space consisting of gray level intensity and gradient magnitude, it is even possible to determine multiple thresholds when more than one kind of object is present.

Panda and Rosenfeld (1978) suggest a related approach for segmenting a white blob against a dark background. Consider the histogram of gray levels for all pixels that have small gradients. If a pixel has a small gradient, then it is not likely to be an edge. If it is not an edge, then it is either a dark background pixel or a bright blob pixel. Hence the histogram of all pixels having small gradients will be bimodal, and for pixels with small gradients, the valley between the two modes of the histogram is an appropriate threshold point. Next, consider the histogram of gray levels for all pixels that have high gradients. If a pixel has a high gradient, then it is likely to be an edge. If it is an edge separating a bright blob against a dark background, and if the separating boundary is not sharp but somewhat diffuse, then the histogram will be unimodal, the mean being a good threshold separating the dark background pixels from the bright blob pixels. Thus Panda and Rosenfeld suggest determining two thresholds: one for low-gradient pixels and one for high-gradient pixels. By this means they perform the clustering in the two-dimensional measurement space consisting of gray level intensity and gradient. The form of the decision boundary in the two-dimensional measurement space is shown in Fig. 10.19.

Figure 10.20 illustrates a FLIR image from the NATO data base, which one might think has the right characteristics for this type of segmentation algorithm. Figure 10.21 illustrates the FLIR image thresholded at 159 and 190. Figure 10.22 shows the pixels having a large gradient magnitude, where the gradient is computed as the square root of the sum of the squares of the linear coefficients arising from a gray level intensity cubic fit (see Chapter 8) in a 7×7 window. Figure 10.23 shows the horseshoe-shaped cluster in the two-dimensional gray level intensity–gradient space where the gray level intensities and the gradient values have been equal-interval quantized.

Figure 10.24 illustrates the resulting segmentation. Notice that because there is a bright object with a slightly darker appendage on top, the assumption of a homogeneous object on a dark background is not met. The result is that only the boundary of the appendage is picked up. A survey of threshold techniques can be found in Weszka (1978).

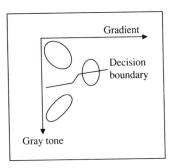

Figure 10.19 Diagram showing how the threshold of the Panda and Rosenfeld technique depends on the gradient magnitude.

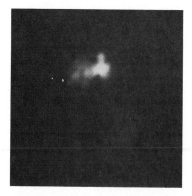

Figure 10.20 FLIR image from the NATO data base. To reduce noise, it was filtered with a Gaussian filter (see Chapter 6) with a sigma of 1.5 and a neighborhood size of 15.

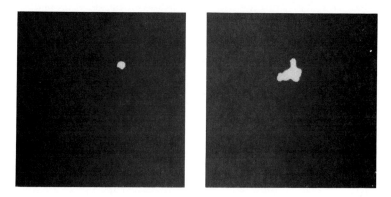

Figure 10.21 FLIR image of Fig. 10.20 thresholded at gray level intensity 159 (left) and 190 (right).

Figure 10.22 Pixels of the FLIR image having large gradient magnitude.

524

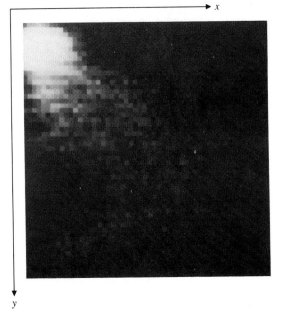

Figure 10.23 Scattergram of the gray level intensity–gradient measurement space for the image of Fig. 10.20. The gray level intensity is along the y-axis and the gradient is along the x-axis. Notice the nicely bimodal gray level intensity distribution for small gradient magnitudes.

10.2.2 Multidimensional Measurement–Space Clustering

A LANDSAT image comes from a satellite and consists of seven separate images called *bands*. The bands are registered so that pixel (i,j) in one band corresponds to pixel (i,j) in each of the other bands. Each band represents a particular range of wavelengths. For multiband images such as LANDSAT or Thematic Mapper, determining the histogram in a multidimensional array is not feasible. For example, in a six-band image where each band has intensities between 0 and 99, the array

Figure 10.24 Segmentation of the image in Fig. 10.20 using the Panda and Rosenfeld scheme.

would have to have $100^6 = 10^{12}$ locations. A large image might be 10,000 pixels per row by 10,000 rows. This constitutes only 10^8 pixels, a sample too small to estimate probabilities in a space of 10^{12} values were it not for some constraints of reality: (1) there is typically a high correlation between the band-to-band pixel values, and (2) there is a large amount of spatial redundancy in image data. Both these factors create a situation in which the 10^8 pixels can be expected to contain only between 10^4 and 10^5 distinct 6-tuples. Based on this fact, the counting required for the histogram is easily done by mapping the 6-tuples into array indexes. The programming technique known as *hashing*, which is described in most data structures texts, can be used for this purpose.

Clustering using the multidimensional histogram is more difficult than univariate histogram clustering, since peaks fall in different places in the different histograms. Goldberg and Shlien (1977, 1978) threshold the multidimensional histogram to select all N-tuples situated on the most prominent modes. Then they perform a measurement-space connected components on these N-tuples to collect all the N-tuples in the top of the most prominent modes. These measurement-space connected sets form the cluster cores. The clusters are defined as the set of all N-tuples closest to each cluster core.

An alternative possibility (Narendra and Goldberg, 1977) is to locate peaks in the multidimensional measurement space and region-grow around them, constantly descending from each peak. The region growing includes all successive neighboring N-tuples whose probability is no higher than the N-tuple from which it is growing. Adjacent mountains meet in their common valleys.

Rather than accomplish the clustering in the full measurement space, it is possible to work in multiple lower-order projection spaces and then reflect these clusters back to the full measurement space. Suppose, for example, that the clustering is done on a four-band image. If the clustering done in bands 1 and 2 yields clusters c_1, c_2, c_3 and the clustering done in bands 3 and 4 yields clusters c_4 and c_5, then each possible 4-tuple from a pixel can be given a cluster label from the set $\{(c_1, c_4), (c_1, c_5), (c_2, c_4), (c_2, c_5), (c_3, c_4), (c_3, c_5)\}$. A 4-tuple (x_1, x_2, x_3, x_4) gets the cluster label (c_2, c_4) if (x_1, x_2) is in cluster c_2 and (x_3, x_4) is in cluster c_4.

10.3   Region Growing

10.3.1 Single-Linkage Region Growing

Single-linkage region-growing schemes regard each pixel as a node in a graph. Neighboring pixels whose properties are similar enough are joined by an arc. The image segments are maximal sets of pixels all belonging to the same connected component. Figure 10.25 illustrates this idea with a simple image and the corresponding graph, with the connected components circled. In this example two pixels are connected by an edge if their values differ by less than 5 and they are 4–neighbors. Single-linkage image segmentation schemes are attractive for their simplicity. They

50	51	50	102
51	49	50	102
240	240	102	102
241	240	103	103

Figure 10.25 Simple gray level image and graph resulting from defining "similar enough" to be differing in gray level by less than 5 and using the 4-neighborhood to determine connected components (see Chapter 2).

do, however, have a problem with chaining, because it takes only one arc leaking from one region to a neighboring one to cause the regions to merge.

As illustrated in Fig. 10.25, the simplest single-linkage scheme defines "similar enough" by pixel difference. Two neighboring pixels are similar enough if the absolute value of the difference between their gray level intensity values is small enough. Bryant (1979) defines "similar enough" by normalizing the difference by the quantity $\sqrt{2}$ times the root-mean-square value of neighboring pixel differences taken over the entire image. For the image of Fig. 10.25, the normalization factor is 99.22. The random variable that is the difference of two neighboring pixels normalized by the factor 1/99.22 has a normal distribution with mean 0 and standard deviation 99.22. A threshold can now be chosen in terms of the standard deviation instead of as an absolute value. For pixels having vector values, the obvious generalization is to use a vector norm of the pixel difference vector.

10.3.2 Hybrid-Linkage Region Growing

Hybrid single-linkage techniques are more powerful than the simple single-linkage technique. The hybrid techniques seek to assign a property vector to each pixel where the property vector depends on the $K \times K$ neighborhood of the pixel. Pixels that are similar are so because their neighborhoods in some special sense are similar. Similarity is thus established as a function of neighboring pixel values, and this makes the technique better behaved on noisy data.

One hybrid single-linkage scheme relies on an edge operator to establish whether two pixels are joined with an arc. Here an edge operator is applied to the image, labeling each pixel as edge or nonedge. Neighboring pixels, neither of which is an edge, are joined by an arc. The initial segments are the connected components of the nonedge-labeled pixels. The edge pixels can either be left assigned as edges and considered as background or they can be assigned to the spatially nearest region having a label.

The quality of this technique is highly dependent on the edge operator used. Simple operators, such as the Roberts and Sobel operators, may provide too much region linkage, for a region cannot be declared a segment unless it is completely surrounded by edge pixels. Figure 10.26 shows an example of this phenomenon.

Figure 10.26 Edge image with gaps in the edges that can cause problems in a segmentation performed by taking connected components of nonedge pixels.

Haralick and Dinstein (1975), however, do report some success using this technique on LANDSAT data. They perform a dilation of the edge pixels in order to close gaps before performing the connected components operator. Perkins (1980) uses a similar technique.

Haralick (1982, 1984) discusses a very sensitive zero crossing of the second directional derivative edge operator. In this technique, each neighborhood is least-squares fitted with a cubic polynomial in two variables. The first and second partial derivatives are easily determined from the polynomial. The first partial derivatives at the center pixel determine the gradient direction. With the direction fixed to be the gradient direction, the second partials determine the second directional derivative. If the gradient is high enough and if, in the gradient direction, the second directional derivative has a negatively sloped zero crossing inside the pixel's area, then an edge is declared in the neighborhood's center pixel. (This edge operator is described in more detail in Chapter 8.)

Figure 10.27 shows the edges resulting from the second directional derivative

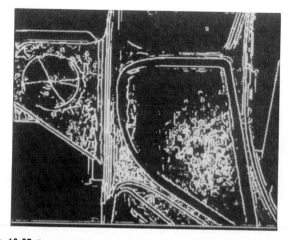

Figure 10.27 Second directional derivative zero-crossing operator using a gradient threshold of 4, a 9 × 9 neighborhood, and a zero-crossing radius of 0.85 applied to the bulkhead image of Fig. 10.10.

zero-crossing operator using a gradient threshold of 4, a 9×9 neighborhood, and a zero-crossing radius of 0.85. The edges are well placed, and a careful examination of pixels on perceived boundaries that are not classified as edge pixels will indicate the step edge pattern to be either nonexistent or weak. A connected components on the nonedge pixels accomplishes the initial segmentation. After the connected components operation, the edge pixels are assigned to their spatially closest component by a region-filling operation. Figure 10.28 shows the boundaries from the region-filled image. Obviously some regions have been merged. However, those boundaries that are present are placed correctly and they are reasonably smooth. Lowering the gradient threshold of the edge operator could produce an image with more edges and thereby reduce the edge gap problem. But this solution does not really solve the gap problem in general.

Yakimovsky (1976) assumes regions are normally distributed and uses a maximum-likelihood test to determine edges. Edges are declared to exist between pairs of contiguous and exclusive neighborhoods if the hypothesis that their means are equal and their variances are equal has to be rejected. For any pair of adjacent pixels with mutually exclusive neighborhoods R_1 and R_2 having N_1 and N_2 pixels, respectively, the maximum-likelihood technique computes the mean

$$\overline{X}_i = \frac{1}{N_i} \sum_{X \in R_i} X \tag{10.3}$$

and the scatter

$$S_i = \sum_{X \in R_i} (X - \overline{X}_i)^2 \tag{10.4}$$

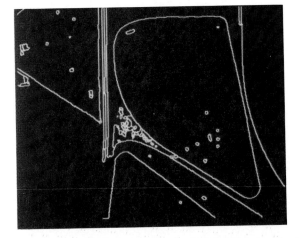

Figure 10.28 Hybrid-linkage region-growing scheme in which any pair of neighboring pixels, neither of which is an edge pixel, can link together. The resulting segmentation consists of the connected components of the nonedge pixels augmented by assigning edge pixels to their nearest connected component. This result was obtained from the edge image of Fig. 10.27.

as well as the grand mean

$$\overline{X} = \frac{1}{N_1 + N_2} \sum_{X \in R_1 \cup R_2} X \tag{10.5}$$

and the grand scatter

$$S = \sum_{X \in R_1 \cup R_2} (X - \overline{X})^2 \tag{10.6}$$

The likelihood ratio test statistic t is given by

$$t = \frac{[S^2/(N_1 + N_2)]^{N_1 + N_2}}{[S_1^2/N_1]^{N_1}[S_2^2/N_2]^{N_2}} \tag{10.7}$$

Edges are declared between any pair of adjacent pixels when the t-statistic from their neighborhoods is high enough. As N_1 and N_2 get large, $2 \log t$ is asymptotically distributed as a chi-squared variate with two degrees of freedom.

If it can be assumed that the variances of the two regions are identical, then the statistic

$$F = \frac{(N_1 + N_2 - 2)N_1 N_2}{N_1 + N_2} \frac{(\overline{X}_1 - \overline{X}_2)^2}{S_1^2 + S_2^2} \tag{10.8}$$

has an F-distribution with 1 and $N_1 + N_2 - 2$ degrees of freedom under the hypothesis that the means of the regions are equal. For an F-value that is sufficiently large, the hypothesis can be rejected and an edge declared to exist between the regions.

Haralick (1980) suggests fitting a plane to the neighborhood around the pixel and testing the hypothesis that the slope of the plane is zero. Edge pixels correspond to pixels between neighborhoods in which the zero-slope hypothesis has to be rejected. To determine a roof or V-shaped edge, Haralick suggests fitting a plane to the neighborhoods on either side of the pixel and testing the hypothesis that the coefficients of fit, referenced to a common framework, are identical.

Another hybrid technique first used by Levine and Leemet (1976) is based on the Jarvis and Patrick (1973) shared-nearest-neighbor idea. Using any kind of reasonable notion for similarity, each pixel examines its $K \times K$ neighborhood and makes a list of the N pixels in the neighborhood most similar to it. Call this list the similar-neighbor list, where we understand neighbor to be any pixel in the $K \times K$ neighborhood. An arc joins any pair of immediately neighboring pixels if each pixel is in the other's shared-neighbor list and if there are enough pixels common to their shared-neighbor lists, that is, if the number of shared neighbors is high enough.

To make the shared-neighbor technique work well, each pixel can be associated with a property vector consisting of its own gray level intensity and a suitable average of the gray level intensities of pixels in its $K \times K$ neighborhood. For example, we can have (x, a) and (y, b) denote the property vectors for two pixels if x is the gray level intensity value and a is the average gray level intensity value in the neighborhood of the first pixel, y is the gray level intensity value and b is the average gray level intensity value in the neighborhood of the second pixel. Similarity can be established by computing

$$S = w_1(x - y)^2 + w_2(x - b)^2 + w_3(y - a)^2 \tag{10.9}$$

where w_1, w_2, and w_3 are nonnegative weights. Thus the quantity S takes into account the difference between the gray levels of the two pixels in question and the difference between the gray level of each pixel and the average gray level of the neighborhood of the other pixel. The weights w_1, w_2, and w_3 can be learned from training data for a particular class of images. The pixels are called similar enough for small enough values of S.

Pong et al. (1984) suggest an approach to segmentation based on the facet model of images. The procedure starts with an initial segmentation of the image into small regions. The initial segmentations used by Pong group together pixels that have similar facet-fitting parameters (see Chapter 8), but any initial segmentation can be used. For each region of the initial segmentation, a property vector, which is a list of values of a set of predefined attributes, is computed. The attributes consist of such properties of a region as its area, its mean gray level, and its elongation. Each region with an associated property vector is considered a unit. In a series of iterations the property vector of a region is replaced by a property vector that is a function of its neighboring regions. (The function that worked best in Pong's experiments replaced the property vector of a region with the property vector of the best-fitting neighborhood of that region.) Then adjacent regions having similar final property vectors are merged. This gives a new segmentation, which can then be used as input to the algorithm. Thus a sequence of coarser and coarser segmentations is produced. Useful variations are to prohibit merging across strong edge boundaries or when the variance of the combined region becomes too large. Figures 10.29, 10.30, and 10.31 illustrate the results of the Pong approach on the image of Fig. 10.10 for one, two, and three iterations, respectively. Figure 10.32 illustrates the result of removing regions of size 25 or fewer pixels from the segmentation of Fig. 10.31.

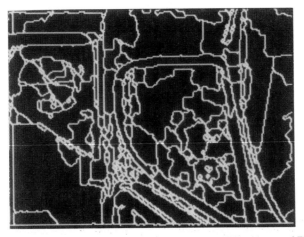

Figure 10.29 One iteration of the Pong algorithm on the bulkhead image of Fig. 10.10.

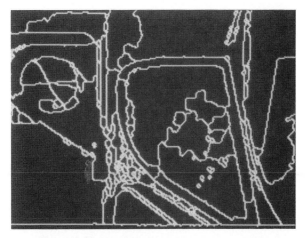

Figure 10.30 Second iteration of the Pong algorithm.

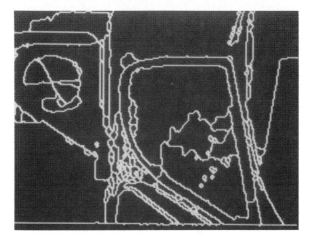

Figure 10.31 Third iteration of the Pong algorithm.

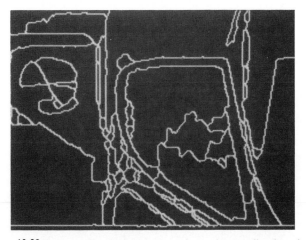

Figure 10.32 Segmentation obtained by removing regions smaller than size 25 from the segmentation of Fig. 10.31.

10.3.3 Centroid-Linkage Region Growing

In centroid-linkage region growing, in contrast to single-linkage region growing, pairs of neighboring pixels are not compared for similarity. Rather, the image is scanned in some predetermined manner, such as left-right, top-bottom. A pixel's value is compared with the mean of an already existing but not necessarily completed neighboring segment. If its value and the segment's mean value are close enough, then the pixel is added to the segment and the segment's mean is updated. If more than one region is close enough, then it is added to the closest region. However, if the means of the two competing regions are close enough, the two regions are merged and the pixel is added to the merged region. If no neighboring region has a close-enough mean, then a new segment is established having the given pixel's value as its first member. Figure 10.33 illustrates the geometry of this scheme.

Keeping track of the means and scatters for all regions as they are being determined does not require large amounts of memory space. There cannot be more regions active at one time than the number of pixels in a row of the image. Hence a hash table mechanism with the space of a small multiple of the number of pixels in a row can work well.

Another possibility is a single-band region-growing technique using the T-test. Let R be a segment of N pixels neighboring a pixel with gray level intensity y. Define the mean $\overline{X}$ and scatter S^2 by

$$\overline{X} = \frac{1}{N} \sum_{(r,c) \in R} I(r,c) \tag{10.10}$$

and

$$S^2 = \sum_{(r,c) \in R} [I(r,c) - \overline{X}]^2 \tag{10.11}$$

Under the assumption that all the pixels in R and the test pixel y are independent

2	3	4
1	y	

Figure 10.33 Region-growing geometry for one-pass scan, left-right, top-bottom region growing. Pixel i belongs to region R_i, whose mean is $X_i, i = 1, 2, 3,$ and 4. Pixel y is added to a region R_j if by a T-test the difference betwen y and $\overline{X}_j$ is small enough. If for two regions R_i and R_j, the difference is small enough, and if the difference between $\overline{X}_i$ and $\overline{X}_j$ is small enough, regions R_i and R_j are merged together, and y is added to the merged region. If the difference between $\overline{X}_i$ and $\overline{X}_j$ is significantly different, then y is added to the closest region.

and have identically distributed normals, the statistic

$$t = \left[\frac{(N-1)N}{(N+1)} (y - \overline{X})^2 / S^2 \right]^{\frac{1}{2}} \tag{10.12}$$

has a T_{N-1} distribution. If t is small enough, y is added to region R and the mean and scatter are updated by using y. The new mean and scatter are given by

$$\overline{X}_{new} \leftarrow (N\overline{X}_{old} + y)/(N+1) \tag{10.13}$$

and

$$S^2_{new} \leftarrow S^2_{old} + (y - \overline{X}_{new})^2 + N(\overline{X}_{new} - \overline{X}_{old})^2 \tag{10.14}$$

If t is too high, the value y is not likely to have arisen from the population of pixels in R. If y is different from all its neighboring regions, then it begins its own region. A slightly stricter linking criterion can require that not only must y be close enough to the mean of the neighboring regions, but a neighboring pixel in that region must have a close-enough value to y. This combines a centroid-linkage and a single-linkage criterion. The next section discusses a more powerful combination technique, but first we want to develop the concept of "significantly high."

To give a precise meaning to the notion of too high a difference, we use an α-level statistical significance test. The fraction α represents the probability that a T-statistic with $N - 1$ degrees of freedom will exceed the value $T_{N-1}(\alpha)$. If the observed T is larger than $T_{N-1}(\alpha)$, then we declare the difference to be significant. If the pixel and the segment really come from the same population, the probability that the test provides an incorrect answer is α.

The significance level α is a user-provided parameter. The value of $T_{N-1}(\alpha)$ is higher for small degrees of freedom and lower for larger degrees of freedom. Thus, region scatters considered to be equal, the larger a region is, the closer a pixel's value has to be to the region's mean in order to merge into the region. This behavior tends to prevent an already large region from attracting to it many other additional pixels and tends to prevent the drift of the region mean as the region gets larger.

Note that all regions initially begin as one pixel in size. To avoid the problem of division by 0 (for S^2 is necessarily 0 for one-pixel regions as well as for regions having identically valued pixels), a small positive constant can be added to S^2. One convenient way of determining the constant is to decide on a prior variance $V > 0$ and an initial segment size N. The initial scatter for a new one-pixel region is then given by NV, and the new initial region size is given by N. This mechanism keeps the degrees of freedom of the T-statistic high enough so that a significant difference is not the huge difference required for a T-statistic with a small number of degrees of freedom. To illustrate this method, consider the second image of the F-15 bulkhead shown in Fig. 10.34. Figure 10.35 illustrates the resulting segmentation of this bulkhead image for a 0.2% significance level test after all regions smaller than 25 pixels have been removed.

Pavlidis (1972) suggests a more general version of this idea. Given an initial segmentation where the regions are approximated by some functional fit guaranteed to have a small enough error, pairs of neighboring regions can be merged if for each region the sum of the squares of the differences between the

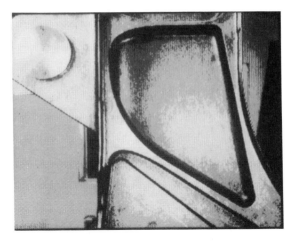

Figure 10.34 Second image of the F-15 bulkhead.

fitted coefficients for this region and the corresponding averaged coefficients, averaged over both regions, is small enough. Pavlidis gets his initial segmentation by finding the best way to divide each row of the image into segments with a sufficiently good fit. He also describes a combinatorial tree search algorithm to accomplish the merging that guarantees the best result. Kettig and Landgrebe (1975) successively merge small image blocks using a statistical test. They avoid much of the problem of zero scatter by considering only cells containing a 2×2 block of pixels.

Gupta et al. (1973) suggest using a T-test based on the absolute value of the difference between the pixel and the nearest region as the measure of dissimilarity.

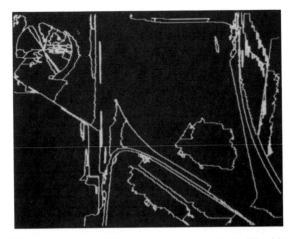

Figure 10.35 One-pass centroid-linkage segmentation of the bulkhead image of Fig. 10.34. A significance level of 0.2% was used.

Kettig and Landgrebe (1975) discuss the multiband situation leading to the F-test and report good success with LANDSAT data.

Nagy and Tolaba (1972) simply examine the absolute value between the pixel's value and the mean of a neighboring region formed already. If this distance is small enough, the pixel is added to the region. If there is more than one region, then the pixel is added to the region with the smallest distance.

The Levine and Shaheen (1981) scheme is similar. The difference is that Levine and Shaheen attempt to keep regions more homogeneous and try to keep the region scatter from becoming too high. They do this by requiring the differences to be more significant before a merge takes place if the region scatter is high. For a user-specified value θ, they define a test statistic t where

$$t = |y - \overline{X}_{\text{new}}| - (1 - S/\overline{X}_{\text{new}})\theta \qquad (10.15)$$

If $t < 0$ for the neighboring region R in which $|y - \overline{X}|$ is the smallest, then y is added to R. If $t > 0$ for the neighboring region in which $|y - \overline{X}|$ is the smallest, then y begins a new region. (Readers of the Levine and Shaheen paper should note that there are misprints in the formulas given there for region scatter and region scatter updating.)

Brice and Fennema (1970) accomplish the region growing by partitioning the image into initial segments of pixels having identical intensity. They then sequentially merge all pairs of adjacent regions if a significant fraction of their common border has a small enough intensity difference across it.

Simple single-pass approaches that scan the image in a left-right, top-down manner are, of course, unable to make the left and right sides of a V-shaped region belong to the same segment. To be more effective, the single pass must be followed by some kind of connected components merging algorithm in which pairs of neighboring regions having means that are close enough are combined into the same segment. This is easily accomplished by using the two-pass label propagation logic of the Lumia, Shapiro, and Zuniga (1983) connected components algorithm.

After the top-bottom, left-right scan, each pixel has already been assigned a region label. In the bottom-up, right-left scan, the means and scatters of each region can be recomputed and kept in a hash table. Whenever a pair of pixels from different regions neighbor each other, a T-test can check for the significance of the difference between the region means. If the means are not significant, then they can be merged. A slightly stricter criterion would insist not only that the region means be similar, but also that the neighboring pixels from the different regions be similar enough. Figure 10.36 shows the resulting segmentation of the bulkhead image for a 0.2% significance level after one bottom-up, right-left merging pass and after all regions smaller than 25 pixels have been removed.

One potential problem with region-growing schemes is their inherent dependence on the order in which pixels and regions are examined. A left-right, top-down scan does not yield the same initial regions as a right-left, bottom-up scan or for that matter a column major scan. Usually, however, differences caused by scan order are minor.

536

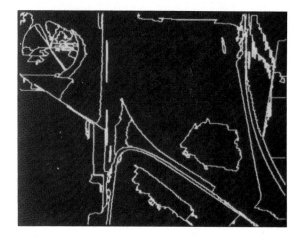

Figure 10.36 Two-pass centroid segmentation of the bulkhead image of Fig. 10.34. A significance level of 0.2% was used on both passes.

10.4 Hybrid-Linkage Combinations

The previous section mentioned the simple combination of centroid-linkage and single-linkage region growing. In this section we discuss the more powerful hybrid-linkage combination techniques.

The centroid linkage and the hybrid linkage can be combined in a way that takes advantage of their relative strengths. The strength of the single linkage is that boundaries are placed in a spatially accurate way. Its weakness is that edge gaps result in excessive merging. The strength of centroid linkage is its ability to place boundaries in weak gradient areas. It can do this because it does not depend on a large difference between the pixel and its neighbor to declare a boundary. It depends on a large difference between the pixel and the mean of the neighboring region to declare a boundary.

The combined centroid-hybrid linkage technique does the obvious thing. Centroid linkage is done only for nonedge pixels, that is, region growing is not permitted across edge pixels. Thus if the parameters of centroid linkage were set so that any difference, however large, between pixel value and region mean was considered small enough to permit merging, the two-pass hybrid combination technique would produce the connected components of the nonedge pixels. As the difference criterion is made more strict, the centroid linkage will produce boundaries in addition to those produced by the edges.

Figure 10.37 illustrates a one-pass scan combined centroid- and hybrid-linkage segmentation scheme using a significance level test of 0.2%. Edge pixels are assigned to their closest labeled neighbor, and regions having fewer than 25 pixels are eliminated. Notice that the resulting segmentation is much finer than that shown in Figs. 10.35 and 10.36. Also the dominant boundaries are nicely curved and smooth. Figure 10.38 illustrates the two-pass scan combined centroid- and hybrid-linkage region-growing scheme using a significance level test of 0.2%. The regions are somewhat simpler because of the merging done in the second pass.

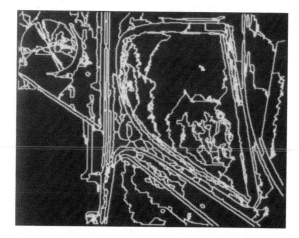

Figure 10.37 One-pass combined centroid- and hybrid-linkage segmentation of the bulkhead image of Fig. 10.34. A significance level of 0.2% was used.

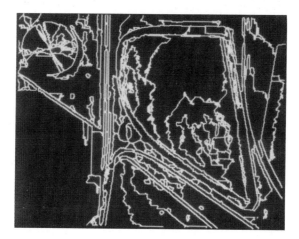

Figure 10.38 Two-pass combined centroid- and hybrid-linkage segmentation of the bulkhead image of Fig. 10.34. A significance level of 0.2% was used on both passes.

10.5   Spatial Clustering

It is possible to determine the image segments by simultaneously combining clustering in measurement space with a spatial region growing. We call such a technique spatial-clustering. In essence, spatial-clustering schemes combine the histogram-mode-seeking technique with a region-growing or a spatial-linkage technique.

Haralick and Kelly (1969) suggest that segmentation be done by first locating, in turn, all the peaks in the measurement-space histogram, and then determining all pixel locations having a measurement on the peak. Next, beginning with a pixel corresponding to the highest peak not yet processed, both spatial and measurement-space region growing are simultaneously performed in the following manner. Initially each segment is the pixel whose value is on the current peak. Consider for possible inclusion into this segment a neighbor of this pixel (in general, the neighbors of the pixel we are growing from) if the neighbor's value (an N-tuple for an N band image) is close enough in measurement space to the pixel's value and if its probability is not larger than the probability of the value of the pixel we are growing from. Matsumoto, Naka, and Yanamoto (1981) discuss a variation of this idea. Milgram (1979) defines a segment for a single-band image to be any connected component of pixels all of whose values lie in some interval I and whose border has a higher coincidence with the border created by an edge operator than for any other interval I. The technique has the advantage over the Haralick and Kelly technique in that it does not require the difficult measurement-space exploring done in climbing down a mountain. But, it does have to try many different intervals for each segment. Extending it to efficient computation in multiband images appears difficult. However, Milgram does report good results from segmenting white blobs against a black background. Milgram and Kahl (1979) discuss embedding this technique into the Ohlander (1978) recursive control structure.

Minor and Sklansky (1981) make more active use of the gradient edge image than Milgram but restrict themselves to the more constrained situation of small convexlike segments. They begin with an edge image in which each edge pixel contains the direction of the edge. The orientation is such that the higher-valued gray level is to the right of the edge. Then each edge sends out for a limited distance a message to nearby pixels and in a direction orthogonal to the edge direction. The message indicates the sender's edge direction. Pixels that pick up these messages from enough different directions must be interior to a segment.

The spoke filter of Minor and Sklansky counts the number of distinct directions appearing in each 3×3 neighborhood. If the count is high enough, Minor and Sklansky mark the center pixel as belonging to an interior of a region. Then the connected component of all marked pixels is obtained. The gradient-guided segmentation is completed by performing a region growing of the components. The region growing must stop at the high-gradient pixels, thereby assuring that no undesired boundary placements are made.

Burt, Hong, and Rosenfeld (1981) describe a spatial-clustering scheme that is a spatial pyramid constrained ISODATA kind of clustering. The bottom layer of the pyramid is the original image. Each successive higher layer of the pyramid is an image having half the number of pixels per row and half the number of rows of the image below it. Figure 10.39 illustrates the pyramid structure. Initial links between layers are established by linking each parent pixel to the spatially corresponding 4×4 block of child pixels. Each pair of adjacent parent pixels has eight child pixels in common. Each child pixel is linked to a 2×2 block of parent pixels. The iterations proceed by assigning to each parent pixel the average of its child pixels. Then each child pixel compares its value with each of its parent's values and links itself to its closest parent. Each parent's new value is the average of the children to which it is linked, and so on. The iterations converge reasonably quickly for the same reason the ISODATA iterations converge. If the top layer of the pyramid is

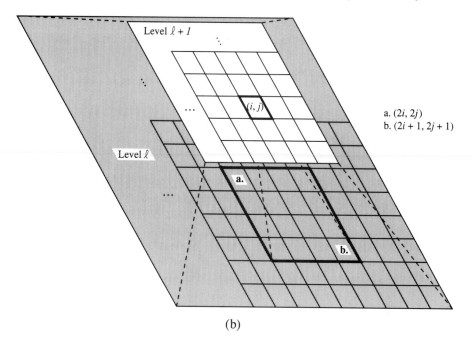

(b)

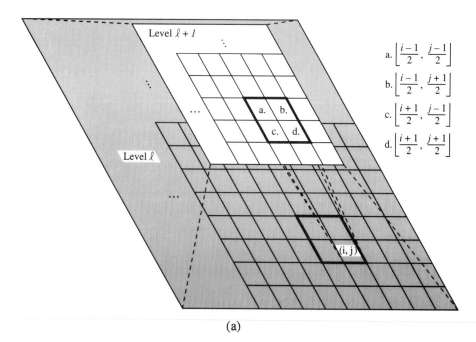

(a)

Figure 10.39 Pyramid structure used in the Burt, Hong, and Rosenfeld scheme.

a 2×2 block of great-grandparents, then there are at most four segments that are the respective great-grandchildren of these four great-grandparents. Pietikäinen and Rosenfeld (1981) extend this technique to segment an image using textural features.

10.6   Split and Merge

A splitting method for segmentation begins with the entire image as the initial segment. Then the method successively splits each of its current segments into quarters if the segment is not homogeneous enough; that is, if the difference between the largest and the smallest gray level intensities is large. A merging method starts with an initial segmentation and successively merges regions that are similar enough.

Splitting algorithms were first suggested by Robertson (1973) and Klinger (1973). Kettig and Landgrebe (1975) try to split all nonuniform 2×2 neighborhoods before beginning the region merging. Fukada (1980) suggests successively splitting a region into quarters until the sample variance is small enough. Efficiency of the split-and-merge method can be increased by arbitrarily partitioning the image into square regions of a user-selected size and then splitting these further if they are not homogeneous.

Because segments are successively divided into quarters, the boundaries produced by the split technique tend to be squarish and slightly artificial. Sometimes adjacent quarters coming from adjacent split segments need to be joined rather than remain separate. Horowitz and Pavlidis (1976) suggest the split-and-merge strategy to take care of this problem. They begin with an initial segmentation achieved by splitting into rectangular blocks of a prespecified size. The image is represented by a *segmentation tree,* which is a quadtree data structure (a tree whose nonleaf nodes each have four children). The entire image is represented by the root node. The children of the root are the regions obtained by splitting the root into four equal pieces, and so on. A segmentation is represented by a *cutset*, a minimal set of nodes separating the root from all of the leaves. In the tree structure the merging process consists of removing four nodes from the cutset and replacing them with their parent. Splitting consists of removing a node from the cutset and replacing it with its four children. The two processes are mutually exclusive; all the merging operations are followed by all the splitting operations. The splitting and merging in the tree structure is followed by a final grouping procedure that can merge adjacent unrelated blocks found in the final cutset. Figure 10.40 illustrates the result of a Horowitz and Pavlidis type split-and-merge segmentation of the bulkhead image. Muerle and Allen (1968) suggest merging a pair of adjacent regions if a statistical test determines that their gray level intensity distributions are similar enough. They recommend the Kolmogorov-Smirnov test.

Chen and Pavlidis (1980) suggest using statistical tests for uniformity rather than a simple examination of the difference between the largest and the smallest gray level intensities in the region under consideration for splitting. The uniformity test requires that there be no significant difference between the mean of the region

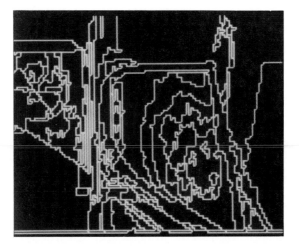

Figure 10.40 Split-and-merge segmentation of the bulkhead image of Fig. 10.10.

and the mean of each of its quarters. The Chen and Pavlidis tests assume that the variances are equal and known.

Let each quarter have K pixels with X_{ij} being the jth pixel in the ith region; let $X_i.$ be the mean of the ith quarter; and let $X..$ be the grand mean of all the pixels in the four quarters. Then in order for a region to be considered homogeneous, Chen and Pavlidis require that

$$|X_i. - X..| \leq \epsilon, \qquad i = 1,2,3,4 \tag{10.16}$$

where ϵ is a given threshold parameter.

We give here the F-test for testing the hypothesis that the means and variances of the quarters are identical. This is the optimal test when the randomness can be modeled as arising from additive Gaussian-distributed variates. The value of variance is not assumed known. Under the assumption that the regions are independent and have identically distributed normals, the optimal test is given by the statistic F, which is defined by

$$f = \frac{K \sum_{i=1}^{4} (X_i. - X..)^2 / 3}{\sum_{i=1}^{4} \sum_{k=1}^{K} (X_{ik} - X_i.)^2 / 4(K-1)} \tag{10.17}$$

It has an $F_{3,4(K-1)}$ distribution. If f is too high, the region is declared not uniform.

The data structures required to do a split and merge on images larger than 512×512 are extremely large. Execution of the algorithm on virtual-memory computers results in so much paging that the dominant activity may be paging rather than segmentation. Browning and Tanimoto (1982) give a description of a space-efficient version of the split-and-merge scheme that can handle large images, using only a small amount of main memory.

Rule-Based Segmentation

The rules behind each of the methods discussed so far are encoded in the procedures of the method. Thus it is not easy to try different concepts without complete reprogramming. Nazif and Levine (1984) solve this problem with a rule-based expert system for segmentation. The knowledge in the system is not application domain specific, but includes general-purpose, scene-independent knowledge about images and grouping criteria. Rule-based systems including higher-level knowledge are discussed in Chapter 19.

The Nazif and Levine system contains a set of processes—the initializer, the line analyzer, the region analyzer, the area analyzer, the focus of attention, and the scheduler—plus two associate memories, the short-term memory (STM) and the long-term memory (LTM). The short-term memory holds the input image, the segmentation data, and the output. The long-term memory contains the model representing the system knowledge about low-level segmentation and control strategies. As described in detail in Chapter 19, a system process matches rules in the LTM against the data stored in the STM. When a match occurs, the rule fires, and an action, usually involving data modification, is performed.

The model stored in the LTM has three levels of rules. At level 1 are knowledge rules that encode information about the properties of regions, lines, and areas in the form of situation-action pairs. The specific actions include splitting a region; merging two regions; adding, deleting, or extending a line; merging two lines; and creating or modifying a focus-of-attention area. Knowledge rules are classified by their actions. At level 2 are the control rules, which are divided into two categories: focus-of-attention rules and inference rules. Focus-of-attention rules find the next data entry to be considered: a region, a line, or an entire area. These rules control the focus-of-attention strategy. The inference rules are metarules in that their actions do not modify the data in the STM. Instead, they alter the matching order of different knowledge rule sets. Thus they control which process will be activated next. At level 3, the highest rule level, are strategy rules that select the set of control rules that executes the most appropriate control strategy for a given set of data.

The conditions of the rules in the rule base are made up of (1) a symbolic qualifier depicting a logical operation to be performed on the data, (2) a symbol denoting the data entry on which the condition is to be matched, (3) a feature of this data entry, (4) an optional NOT qualifier, and (5) an optional DIFFERENCE qualifier that applies the operation to differences in feature values. Table 10.1 shows the different types of data entries allowed. Tables 10.2 to 10.4 show the different kinds of features, and Tables 10.5 and 10.6 show the possible actions that can be associated with a rule. Table 10.7 illustrates several rules from the system.

The Nazif and Levine approach to segmentation is useful because it is general but allows more specific strategies to be incorporated without changing the code. Other rule-based segmentation systems tend to use high-level-knowledge models of the expected scene instead of general rules. The paper by McKeown discussed in Chapter 19 takes this approach for aerial images of airport scenes.

Table 10.1   Allowable data entry types in the Nazif and Levine rule–based segmentation system.

Data Entry	Symbol
Current region	REG
Current line	LINE
Current area	AREA
Region ADJACENT to current region	REGA
Region to the LEFT of current line	REGL
Region to the RIGHT of current line	REGR
Line NEAR current line	LINEN
Line in FRONT of current line	LINEF
Line BEHIND current line	LINEB
Line PARALLEL TO current line	LINEP
Line INTERSECTING current region	LINEI

Table 10.2   Numerical descriptive features that can be associated with the condition part of a rule.

Numerical Descriptive Features		
Feature 1	Feature 2	Feature 3
Variance 1	Variance 2	Variance 3
Intensity	Intensity variance	Gradient
Gradient variance	X-centroid	Y-centroid
Minimum X	Minimum Y	Maximum X
Maximum Y	Starting X	Starting Y
Ending X	Ending Y	Starting direction
Ending direction	Average direction	Length
Start-end distance	Size	Perimeter
Histogram bimodality	Circularity	Aspect ratio
Uniformity 1	Uniformity 2	Uniformity 3
Region contrast 1	Region contrast 2	Region contrast 3
Line contrast 1	Line contrast 2	Line contrast 3
Line connectivity	Number of regions	Number of lines
Number of areas		

Table 10.3   Numerical spatial features that can be associated with the condition part of a rule.

Numerical Spatial Features

Number of ADJACENT regions
Number of INTERSECTING regions
Distance to line in FRONT
Distance to line BEHIND
Distance to PARALLEL line
Adjacency of LEFT region
Number of lines in FRONT
Number of PARALLEL lines
Number of regions to the RIGHT

Adjacency values
Line content between regions
Nearest point on line in FRONT
Nearest point of line BEHIND
Number of PARALLEL points
Adjacency of RIGHT region
Number of lines BEHIND
Number of regions to the LEFT

Table 10.4   Logical features that can be associated with the condition part of a rule.

Logical Features

Histogram is bimodal
Line is open
Line is loop
Line start is open
Area is smooth
Area is bounded
One region to the LEFT

Region is bisected by line
Line is closed
Line end is open
Line is clockwise
Area is textured
Area is new
One region to the RIGHT

Same region LEFT and RIGHT of line
Same region LEFT of line 1 and line 2
Same region RIGHT of line 1 and line 2
Same region LEFT of line 1 and RIGHT of line 2
Same region RIGHT of line 1 and LEFT of line 2
Two lines are touching (8-connected)

Areas are absent
Lines are absent
Process was regions
Process was areas
Process was generate areas

Regions are absent
System is starting
Process was lines
Process was focus
Process was active

Table 10.5   Area, region, and line analyzer actions that can be associated with a rule.

Area Analyzer Actions

Create smooth area	Add to smooth area	Save smooth area
Create texture area	Add to texture area	Save texture area
Create bounded area	Add to bounded area	Save bounded area
Relabel area to smooth	Relabel area to texture	
Relabel area to bounded	Delete area	

Region Analyzer Actions

Split a region by histogram	Merge two regions
Split region at lines	

Line Analyzer Actions

Extend line forward	Extend line backward
Join lines forward	Join lines backward
Insert line forward	Insert line backward
Merge lines forward	Merge lines backward
Delete line	

10.8   Motion-Based Segmentation

In time-varying image analysis (Chapter 15) the data are a sequence of images instead of a single image. One paradigm under which such a sequence can arise is with a stationary camera viewing a scene containing moving objects. In each frame of the sequence after the first frame, the moving objects appear in different positions of the image from those in the previous frame. Thus the motion of the objects creates a change in the images that can be used to help locate the moving objects.

Jain, Martin, and Aggarwal (1979) used differencing operations to identify areas containing moving objects. The images of the moving objects were obtained by focusing the segmentation processes on these restricted areas. In this way motion was used as a cue to the segmentation process. Thompson (1980) developed a method for partitioning a scene into regions corresponding to surfaces with distinct velocities. He first computed velocity estimates for each point of the scene (see Chapter 15) and then performed the segmentation by a region-merging procedure that combined regions based on similarities in both intensity and motion.

Table 10.6   Focus-of-attention and supervisor actions that can be associated with a rule.

Focus-of-Attention Actions

Region with highest adjacency	Largest ADJACENT region
Region with lowest adjacency	Smallest ADJACENT region
Region with higher label	Next scanned region
Region to the LEFT of line	Region to the RIGHT of line
Closest line in front	Closest line BEHIND
Closest PARALLEL line	Shortest line that is near
Longest line that is near	Strongest line that is near
Weakest line that is near	Line with higher label
Next scanned line	Line INTERSECTING region
Defocus (focus on whole image)	Focus on areas
Clear region list	Clear line list
Freeze area	Next area (any)
Next smooth area	Next texture area
Next bounded area	

Supervisor Actions

Initialize regions	Initialize lines	Generate areas
Match region rules	Match line rules	Match area rules
Match focus rules	Start	Stop

Jain (1984) handled the more complex problem of segmenting dynamic scenes using a moving camera. He used the known location of the focus of expansion (see Chapter 15) to transform the original frame sequence into another camera-centered sequence. The ego-motion polar transform (EMP) works as follows:

Suppose that A is a point in 3-space having coordinates (x, y, z), and the camera at time 0 is located at (x_0, y_0, z_0). During the time interval between frames, the camera undergoes displacement (dx_0, dy_0, dz_0), and the point A undergoes displacement (dx, dy, dz). When the projection plane is at $z = 1$, the focus of expansion is at $(dx_0/dz_0, dy_0/dz_0)$. The projection A' of point A after the displacements is at (X, Y) in the image plane, where

$$X = \frac{(x + dx - x_0 - dx_0)}{(z + dz - z_0 - dz_0)}$$

and

$$Y = \frac{(y + dy - y_0 - dy_0)}{(z + dz - z_0 - dz_0)}$$

Table 10.7	Examples of rules from the Nazif and Levine system.

Region-Merging Rule:

IF: 1. The REGION SIZE is VERY LOW
2. The ADJACENCY with another REGION is HIGH
3. The DIFFERENCE in REGION FEATURE 1 is NOT HIGH
4. The DIFFERENCE in REGION FEATURE 2 is NOT HIGH
5. The DIFFERENCE in REGION FEATURE 3 is NOT HIGH

THEN: MERGE the two REGIONS

Region-Splitting Rule:

IF: 1. The REGION SIZE is NOT LOW
2. The REGION AVERAGE GRADIENT is HIGH
3. The REGION HISTOGRAM is BIMODAL

THEN: SPLIT the REGION according to the HISTOGRAM

Line-Merging Rule:

IF: 1. The LINE END point is OPEN
2. The LINE GRADIENT is NOT VERY LOW
3. The DISTANCE to the LINE IN FRONT is NOT VERY HIGH
4. The two LINES have the SAME REGION to the LEFT
5. The two LINES have the SAME REGION to the RIGHT

THEN: JOIN the LINES by FORWARD expansion

A Control Rule:

IF: 1. The LINE GRADIENT is HIGH
2. The LINE LENGTH is HIGH
3. SAME REGION LEFT and RIGHT of the LINE

THEN: GET the REGION to the LEFT of the LINE

The point A' is converted into its polar coordinates (r, θ), with the focus of expansion being the origin in the image plane. The polar coordinates are given by

$$\theta = tan^{-1}\left[\frac{dz_0(y + dy - y_0) - dy_0(z + dz - z_0)}{dz_0(x + dx - x_0) - dx_0(z + dz - z_0)}\right]$$

and

$$r = [(X - dx_0)^2 + (Y - dy_0)^2]^{\frac{1}{2}}$$

In (r, θ) space the segmentation is simplified. Assume that the transformed picture is represented as a two-dimensional image having θ along the vertical axis and r along the horizontal axis. If the camera continues its motion in the same direction, then the focus of expansion remains the same, and θ remains constant. Thus the radial motion of the stationary point A' in the image plane due to the motion of the camera is converted to horizontal motion in (r, θ) space. If the camera has only a translational component to its motion, then all the regions that show only horizontal velocity in the (r, θ) space can be classified as due to stationary surfaces. The regions having a vertical velocity component are due to nonstationary surfaces. The segmentation algorithm first separates the stationary and nonstationary components on the basis of their velocity components in (r, θ) space. The stationary components are then further segmented into distinct surfaces by using the motion to assign relative depths to the surfaces.

10.9   Summary

We have briefly surveyed the place of segmentation in vision algorithms as well as common techniques of measurement-space clustering, single linkage, hybrid linkage, region growing, spatial clustering, and split and merge used in image segmentation. The single-linkage region-growing schemes are the simplest and most prone to the unwanted region merge errors. The hybrid and centroid region-growing schemes are better in this regard. The split-and-merge technique is not as subject to the unwanted region merge error. However, it suffers from large memory usage and excessively blocky region boundaries. The measurement-space-guided spatial clustering tends to avoid both the region merge errors and the blocky boundary problems because of its primary reliance on measurement space. But the regions produced are not smoothly bounded, and they often have holes, giving the effect of salt and pepper noise. The spatial-clustering schemes may be better in this regard, but they have not been well-enough tested. The hybrid-linkage schemes appear to offer the best compromise between having smooth boundaries and few unwanted region merges. When the data form a time sequence of images instead of a single image, motion-based segmentation techniques can be used. All the techniques can be made to be more powerful if they are based on some kind of statistical test for equality of means assuming that each region may have some small fraction of outliers and more flexible if part of a rule-based system.

Not discussed as part of image segmentation is the fact that it might be appropriate for some segments to remain apart or to be merged not on the basis of the gray level distributions but on the basis of the object sections they represent. The use of this kind of semantic information in the image segmentation process is essential for the higher-level image understanding work. The work of McKeown, which is discussed under knowledge-based systems in Chapter 19, describes a system that uses domain-specific knowledge in this manner.

■ Exercises

10.1. Write a program to generate controlled images for the purpose of segmentation. One model for the generation of a controlled image is to establish a background gray-level value and then place nonconnecting or noninterfering shapes, such as disks and polygons, on the image, each having a given gray level. Next additive Gaussian noise can be included with a given standard deviation. This noise can be correlated by preaveraging it with a Gaussian filter with a given standard deviation. Finally, outlier noise can be added by choosing a number of pixels to be affected by the outlier noise from a Poisson distribution, then choosing the location of the pixels to be affected by a uniform distribution over the spatial domain of the image, and then choosing the value of the affected pixels from a uniform distribution over the range of gray levels. Control parameters include contrast between shape and background, area of shape, kind of shape, standard deviation of noise (after any presmoothing), autocorrelation function of noise due to presmoothing, and Poisson density parameter.

10.2. Think about how a figure of merit for a segmentation process can be defined. For example, for the image generated in Exercise 10.1, a 100% correct segmentation can be defined as an image I_c in which each background pixel is labeled 0 and each different disk or polygon created on the synthetic image has all of its pixels labeled with the same label. Any algorithm-produced segmentation I_s can be represented as an image in which each pixel is given a label designating the segment to which it belongs. A figure of merit for the segmentation of I_s with respect to the correct segmentation I_c can be created from the contingency table T defined by

$$T(i,j) = \#\{(r,c)|I_c(r,c) = i \text{ and } I_s(r,c) = j\}$$

The degree to which I_s is a refinement of I_c can be defined by

$$f_r = \frac{\sum_j \max_i T(i,j)}{\sum_i \sum_j T(i,j)}$$

The degree to which I_s is a coarsening of I_c can be defined by

$$f_c = \frac{\sum_i \max_j T(i,j)}{\sum_i \sum_j T(i,j)}$$

Possible figures of merit include $\frac{1}{2}(f_r + f_c)$, $\min\{f_r, f_c\}$, and $\sqrt{f_r f_c}$. What aspects of segmentation errors are not included in these figures of merit? What other definitions of figures of merit can you think of?

10.3. Write a program to perform a segmentation by histogram-mode seeking.

10.4. Design and carry out an empirical experiment that characterizes the performance of any histogram-mode-seeking segmentation procedure in terms of the control parameters of the synthetic-image generation process and in terms of the parameters of the histogram-mode seeking algorithm. Use a measure of performance from Exercise 10.2.

10.5. Write a program to perform a segmentation by a recursive histogram-directed spatial clustering.

10.6. Design and carry out empirical experiments that characterize the performance of a recursive histogram-directed spatial clustering in terms of the control parameters of the synthetic-image generation process and in terms of the parameters of the recursive histogram-directed spatial clustering algorithm. Use a measure of performance from Exercise 10.2.

10.7.   Write a program to perform a segmentation by a single-linkage region-growing algorithm.

10.8.   Design and carry out empirical experiments that characterize the performance of a single-linkage region growing in terms of the control parameters of the synthetic-image generation process and in terms of the parameters of the single-linkage region-growing algorithm. Use a measure of performance from Exercise 10.2.

10.9.   Write a program to perform a segmentation by a hybrid-linkage region-growing algorithm.

10.10. Design and carry out empirical experiments that characterize the performance of a hybrid-linkage region growing in terms of the control parameters of the synthetic-image generation process and in terms of the parameters of the hybrid-linkage region-growing algorithm. Use a measure of performance from Exercise 10.2.

■ Bibliography

Brice, C., and C. Fennema, "Scene Analysis Using Regions," *Artificial Intelligence,* Vol. 1, 1970, pp. 205–226.

Browning, J. D., and S. L. Tanimoto, "Segmentation of Pictures into Regions with a Tile by Tile Method," *Pattern Recognition,* Vol. 15, 1982, pp. 1–10.

Bryant, J., "On the Clustering of Multidimensional Pictorial Data," *Pattern Recognition,* Vol. 11, 1979, pp. 115–125.

Burt, P. J., T. H. Hong, and A. Rosenfeld, "Segmentation and Estimation of Image Region Properties through Cooperative Hierarchical Computation," *IEEE Transactions on Systems, Man, and Cybernetics,* Vol. SMC-11, 1981, pp. 802–809.

Chen, P. C., and T. Pavlidis, "Image Segmentation as an Estimation Problem," *Computer Graphics and Image Processing,* Vol. 12, 1980, pp. 153–172.

Chow, C. K., and T. Kaneko, "Boundary Detection of Radiographic Images by a Thresholding Method," in *Frontiers of Pattern Recogntion,* S. Wanatabe (ed.), Academic Press, New York, 1972, pp. 61–82.

Fu, K. S., and J. K. Mui, "A Survey on Image Segmentation," *Pattern Recognition,* Vol. 13, 1981, pp. 3–16.

Fukada, Y., "Spatial Clustering Procedures for Region Analysis," *Pattern Recognition,* Vol. 12, 1980, pp. 395–403.

Goldberg, M., and S. Shlien, "A Four-Dimensional Histogram Approach to the Clustering of LAND-SAT Data," *Machine Processing of Remotely Sensed Data,* IEEE CH 1218-7 MPRSD, Purdue University, West Lafayette, IN, 1977, pp. 250–259.

——, "A Clustering Scheme for Multispectral Images," *IEEE Transactions on Systems, Man, and Cybernetics,* Vol. SMC-8, 1978, pp. 86–92.

Gupta, J. N., et al., "Machine Boundary Finding and Sample Classification of Remotely Sensed Agricultural Data," *Machine Processing of Remotely Sensed Data,* IEEE 73 CHO 834-2GE, Purdue University, West Lafayette, IN, 1973, pp. 4B-25–4B-35.

Haralick, R. M., "Edge and Region Analysis for Digital Image Data," *Computer Graphics and Image Processing,* Vol. 12, 1980, pp. 60–73; also in *Image Modeling,* A. Rosenfeld (ed.), Academic Press, New York, 1981, pp. 171–184.

Haralick, R. M., "Zero-Crossing of Second Directional Derivative Edge Operator," *Proceedings of the Society of Photo-Optical Instrumentation Engineers Technical Symposium East,* Arlington, VA, Vol. 336, 1982.

——, "Digital Step Edges from Zero Crossing of Second Directional Derivative," *IEEE Transactions on Pattern Analysis and Machine Intelligence,* Vol. PAMI-6, 1984, pp. 58–68.

Haralick, R. M., and I. Dinstein, "A Spatial Clustering Procedure for Multi-Image Data," *IEEE Transactions on Circuits and Systems,* Vol. CAS-22, 1975, pp. 440–450.

Haralick, R. M., and G. L. Kelly, "Pattern Recognition with Measurement-Space and Spatial Clustering for Multiple Images," *Proceedings of the IEEE,* Vol. 57, 1969, pp. 654–665.

Horowitz, S. L., and T. Pavlidis, "Picture Segmentation by a Tree Traversal Algorithm," *Journal of the ACM,* Vol. 23, 1976, pp. 368–388.

Jain, R. C., "Segmentation of Frame Sequences Obtained by a Moving Observer," *IEEE Transactions on Pattern Analysis and Machine Intelligence,* Vol. PAMI-6, 1984, pp. 624–629.

Jain, R. C., W. N. Martin, and J. K. Aggarwal, "Extraction of Moving Object Images through Change Detection," *Proceedings of the Sixth International Joint Conference on Artificial Intelligence,* Tokyo, 1979, pp. 425–428.

Jarvis, R. A., and E. A. Patrick, "Clustering Using a Similarity Measure Based on Shared Near Neighbors," *IEEE Transactions on Computers,* Vol. C-22, 1973, pp. 1025–34.

Kanade, T., "Region Segmentation: Signal vs. Semantics," *Computer Graphics and Image Processing,* Vol. 13, 1980, pp. 279–297.

Kettig, R. L., and D. A. Landgrebe, "Computer Classification of Multispectral Image Data by Extraction and Classification of Homogeneous Objects," Laboratory for Application of Remote Sensing, LARS Information Note 050975, Purdue University, West Lafayette, IN, 1975.

Klinger, K., "Data Structures and Pattern Recognition," *Proceedings of the First International Joint Conference on Pattern Recognition,* Washington, D.C., 1973, pp. 497–498.

Kohler, R., "A Segmentation System Based on Thresholding," *Computer Graphics and Image Processing,* Vol. 15, 1981, pp. 319–338.

Leclerc, Y. G., "Constructing Simple Stable Descriptions of Image Partitioning," *International Journal of Computer Vision,* Vol. 3, 1989, pp. 73–102.

Levine, M. D., and J. Leemet, "A Method for Non-Purposive Picture Segmentation," *Proceedings of the Third International Joint Conference on Pattern Recognition,* San Diego, 1976, pp. 494–497.

Levine, M. D., and S. I. Shaheen, "A Modular Computer Vision System for Picture Segmentation and Interpretation," *IEEE Transactions on Pattern Analysis and Machine Intelligence,* Vol. PAMI-3, 1981, pp. 540–556.

Lumia, R., L. G. Shapiro, and O. Zemiga, "A New Connected Components Algorithm for Virtual Memory Computers," *Computer Vision, Graphics, and Image Processing,* Vol. 22, 1983, pp. 287–300.

Matsumoto, K., M. Naka, and H. Yanamoto, "A New Clustering Method for LANDSAT Images Using Local Maximums of a Multidimensional Histogram," *Machine Processing of Remotely Sensed Data,* IEEE CH 1637-8 MPRSD, Purdue University, West Lafayette, IN, 1981, pp. 321–325.

Milgram, D. L., "Region Extraction Using Convergent Evidence," *Computer Graphics and Image Processing,* Vol. 11, 1979, pp. 1–12.

Milgram, D. L., and M. Herman, "Clustering Edge Values for Threshold Selection," *Computer Graphics and Image Processing,* Vol. 10, 1979, pp. 272–280.

Milgram, D. L., and D. J. Kahl, "Recursive Region Extraction," *Computer Graphics and Image Processing,* Vol. 9, 1979, pp. 82–88.

Minor, L. G., and J. Sklansky, "The Detection and Segmentation of Blobs in Infrared Images," *IEEE Transactions on Systems, Man, and Cybernetics,* Vol. SMC-11, 1981, pp. 194–201.

Muerle, J., and D. Allen, "Experimental Evaluation of Techniques for Automatic Segmentation of Objects in a Complex Scene," in *Pictorial Pattern Recognition,* G. Cheng et al., (eds.), Thompson, Washington, DC, 1968, pp. 3–13.

Nagy, G., and J. Tolaba, "Nonsupervised Crop Classification through Airborne Multispectral Observations," *IBM Journal of Research and Development,* Vol. 16, 1972, pp. 138–153.

Narendra, P. M., and M. Goldberg, "A Non-Parametric Clustering Scheme, for LAND-SAT," *Pattern Recognition,* Vol. 9, 1977, pp. 207–215.

Nazif, A. M., and M. D. Levine, "Low-Level Image Segmentation: An Expert System," *IEEE Transactions on Pattern Analysis and Machine Intelligence,* Vol. PAMI-6, 1984, pp. 555–577.

Ohlander, R., K. Price, and D. R. Reddy, "Picture Segmentation Using a Recursive Region Splitting Method," *Computer Graphics and Image Processing,* Vol. 8, 1978, pp. 313–333.

Ohta, Y., T. Kanade, and T. Sakai, "Color Information for Region Segmentation," *Computer Graphics and Image Processing,* Vol. 13, 1980, pp. 222–241.

Panda, D. P., and A. Rosenfeld, "Image Segmentation by Pixel Classification in (Gray Level, Edge Value) Space," *IEEE Transactions on Computers,* Vol. C-27, 1978, pp. 875–879.

Pavlidis, T., "Segmentation of Pictures and Maps through Functional Approximation," *Computer Graphics and Image Processing,* Vol. 1, 1972, pp. 360–372.

Perkins, W. A., "Area Segmentation of Images Using Edge Points," *IEEE Transactions on Pattern Analysis and Machine Intelligence,* Vol. PAMI-2, 1980, pp. 8–15.

Pietikäinen, M., and A. Rosenfeld, "Image Segmentation by Texture Using Pyramid Node Linking," *IEEE Transactions on Systems, Man, and Cybernetics,* Vol. SMC-11, 1981, pp. 822–825.

Pong, T. C., et al., "Experiments in Segmentation Using a Facet Model Region Grower," *Computer Vision, Graphics, and Image Processing,* Vol. 25, 1984, pp. 1–23.

Riseman, E., and M. Arbib, "Segmentation of Static Scenes," *Computer Graphics and Image Processing,* Vol. 6, 1977, pp. 221–276.

Robertson, T. V., "Extraction and Classification of Objects in Multispectral Images," *Machine Processing of Remotely Sensed Data,* IEEE 73 CHO 837-2GE, Purdue University, West Lafayette, IN,, 1973, pp. 3B-27–3B-34.

Thompson, W. B., "Combining Motion and Contrast for Segmentation," *IEEE Transactions on Pattern Analysis and Machine Intelligence,* Vol. PAMI-2, 1980, pp. 543–549.

Wanatabe, S., and the CYBEST Group, "An Automated Apparatus for Cancer Prescreening: CYBEST," *Computer Graphics and Image Processing,* Vol. 3, 1974, pp. 350–358.

Weszka, J. S., "A Survey of Threshold Selection Techniques," *Computer Graphics and Image Processing,* Vol. 7, 1978, pp. 259–265.

Weszka, J. S., R. N. Nagel, and A. Rosenfeld, "A Threshold Selection Technique," *IEEE Transactions on Computers,* Vol. C-23, 1974, pp. 1322–26.

Weszka, J. S., and A. Rosenfeld, "Threshold Evaluation Techniques," *IEEE Transactions on Systems, Man, and Cybernetics,* Vol. SMC-8, 1978, pp. 622–629.

Yakimovsky, Y., "Boundary and Object Detection in Real World Images," *Journal of the ACM,* Vol. 23, 1976, pp. 599–618.

Young, T. Y., and T. W. Calvert, *Classification, Estimation, and Pattern Recognition,* Elsevior, New York, 1974.

Zucker, S., "Region Growing: Childhood and Adolescence," *Computer Graphics and Image Processing,* Vol. 5, 1976, pp. 382–399.

11 ARC EXTRACTION AND SEGMENTATION

11.1 Introduction

After edge labeling or image segmentation, sets or sequences of labeled or border pixel positions can be extracted by a grouping operation. Each set or sequence contains pixel positions that are considered to belong to the same curve. To set things up for matching, an analytic description of the curve must be determined by a suitable fitting operation. In this chapter we discuss techniques for extracting, from a segmented or labeled image, sequences of pixels that belong to the same curve. Given any such sequence of pixels, we show how to segment it into simple pieces and analytically fit a curve to the points in any piece.

A labeling operation such as edge detection labels each pixel as *edge* or *no edge*. If it is an edge, additional properties, such as edge direction, gradient magnitude, and edge contrast, may be associated with the pixel position. The next processing step is typically a grouping operation, in which edge pixels participating in the same region boundary are grouped together into a sequence. Then the boundary sequence can be segmented into simple pieces, and some analytic description of each boundary piece can be determined.

An image-segmentation operation groups together connected pixels with similar properties and labels each pixel with an index of the region of pixels to which it belongs. The next processing step here can be one of determining all the boundary pixels participating in the same region boundary, segmenting the boundary sequence into simple pieces, and determining some analytic description of each boundary piece suitable for some higher-level shape-matching operation. Ledley (1964) was one of the first researchers to develop such a technique.

11.2   Extracting Boundary Pixels from a Segmented Image

Once a set of regions has been determined by a procedure such as segmentation or connected components, the boundary of each region may be extracted. Boundary extraction can be done simply for small-sized images: Scan through the image and make a list of the first border pixel for each connected component. Then for each region, begin at the first border pixel and follow the border of the connected component around in a clockwise direction until the tracking reaches the first border pixel. For large-sized images, which may not be able to reside in memory, the simple border-tracking algorithm just outlined results in excessive I/O to the mass storage device on which the image resides.

In this section we describe an algorithm called *border,* which can extract the boundaries for all regions in one left-right, top-bottom scan through the image. *Border* inputs a symbolic image and outputs, for each region, a clockwise-ordered list of the coordinates of its border pixels. The algorithm is flexible in that it can be easily modified to select the borders of specified regions.

11.2.1   Concepts and Data Structures

The input image is a symbolic image whose pixel values denote region labels. It is assumed that there is one background label that designates those pixels in part of a possibly disconnected background region whose borders do not have to be found. Rather than tracing all around the border of a single region and then moving on to the next region, the border algorithm moves in a left-right, top-bottom scan down the image collecting chains of border pixels that form connected sections of the borders of regions. At any given time during execution of the algorithm, there is a set of *current regions* whose borders have been partially scanned but not yet output, a set of *past regions* that have been completely scanned and their borders output, and a set of *future regions* that have not yet been reached by the scan.

The data structures contain the chains of border pixels of the current regions. Since there may be a huge number of region labels in the symbolic image, but only at most 2 * *number_of_columns* may be active at once, a hash table can be used as the device to allow rapid access to the chains of a region, given the label of the region. When a region is completed and output, it is removed from the hash table. When a new region is encountered during the scan, it is added to the hash table. The hash table entry for a region points to a linked list of chains that have been formed so far for that region. Each chain is a linked list of pixel positions that can be grown from the beginning or the end.

11.2.2   Border-Tracking Algorithm

The border-tracking algorithm examines three rows of the symbolic image at a time: the current row being processed, the row above it, and the row below it. Two dummy rows of background pixels are appended to the image, one on top and one on the bottom, so that all rows can be treated alike. The algorithm is expressed in high-level pseudocode for an NLINES by NPIXELS symbolic image S as follows:

```
procedure border;
    for R:= 1 to NLINES do
      begin
        for C:= 1 to NPIXELS do
          begin
            LABEL:= S(R,C);
            if new_region(LABEL) then add (CURRENT,LABEL);
            NEIGHB:=neighbors(R,C,LABEL);
            T:= pixeltype(R,C,NEIGHB);
            if T == 'border'
            then for each pixel N in NEIGHB do
              begin
                CHAINSET:=chainlist(LABEL);
                NEWCHAIN:=true;
                for each chain X in CHAINSET while NEWCHAIN do
                  if N==rear(X)
                  then begin add(X,(R,C)); NEWCHAIN:= false end
                end for
                if NEWCHAIN
                then make_new_chain(CHAINSET,(R,C),LABEL)
              end
          end for
        end
      end for;
      for each region REG in CURRENT
        if complete(REG)
        then begin connect_chains(REG); output(REG); free(REG) end
      end for
    end
  end for
end border;
```

In this procedure, S is the name of the symbolic image; thus S(R,C) is the value (LABEL) of the current pixel being scanned. If this is a new label, it is added to the set CURRENT of current region labels. NEIGHB is the list of neighbors of pixel (R,C) that have the label LABEL. The function *pixeltype* looks at the values of (R,C) and its neighbors to decide whether (R,C) is a nonbackground border pixel. If so, the procedure searches for a chain of the region with the label LABEL that has a neighbor of (R,C) at its rear, and if it finds one, it appends (R,C) to the end of the chain by the procedure *add,* whose first argument is a chain and whose second argument is (R,C). If no neighbor of (R,C) is at the rear of a chain of this region, then a new chain is created containing (R,C) as its only element by the procedure *make_new_chain,* whose first argument is the set of chains to which a new chain

	1	2	3	4	5	6	7
1	0	0	0	0	0	0	0
2	0	0	0	0	2	2	0
3	0	1	1	1	2	2	0
4	0	1	1	1	2	2	0
5	0	1	1	1	2	2	0
6	0	0	0	0	2	2	0
7	0	0	0	0	0	0	0

(a) A symbolic image with two regions.

Region	Length	List
1	8	(3,2)(3,3)(3,4)(4,4)(5,4)(5,3)(5,2)(4,2)
2	10	(2,5)(2,6)(3,6)(4,6)(5,6)(6,6)(6,5)(5,5) (4,5)(3,5)

(b). The output of the border procedure
for the symbolic image.

Figure 11.1 Action of the border procedure on a symbolic image.

is being added. The new chain's sole element is the location (R,C), which is the second argument of the procedure. Its third argument is the label LABEL to be associated with the new chain.

After each row R is scanned, the chains of those current regions whose borders are now complete are merged into a single border chain, which is output. The hash table entries and list elements associated with those regions are then freed. Figure 11.1 shows a symbolic image and its output from the border procedure.

11.3   Linking One-Pixel-Wide Edges or Lines

The border-tracking algorithm in the previous section required as input a symbolic image denoting a set of regions. It tracked along the border of each region in parallel as it scanned the image line by line. Because of the assumption that each border bounded a closed region, there was never any point at which a border could be split into two or more segments. When the input is instead a symbolic edge (line) image with a value of 1 for edge (line) pixels and 0 for nonedge (nonline) pixels, the problem of tracking edge (line) segments is more complex. Here it is not necessary for edge pixels to bound closed regions, and the segments consist of connected edge (line) pixels that go from endpoint, corner, or junction to endpoint, corner, or junction with no intermediate junctions or corners. Figure 11.2 illustrates such a symbolic edge (line) image. Pixel (3,3) of the image is a *junction* pixel, where three different edge (line) segments meet. Pixel (5,3) is a corner pixel and may be considered a segment endpoint as well if the application requires ending segments at corners. An algorithm that tracks segments like these has to be concerned with

	1	2	3	4	5
1	1	0	0	0	1
2	0	1	0	1	0
3	0	0	1	0	0
4	0	0	1	0	0
5	0	0	1	1	1

Figure 11.2 Symbolic edge image containing a junction of three line segments at pixel (3,3) and a potential corner at pixel (5,3).

the following tasks:

1. Starting a new segment

2. Adding an interior pixel to a segment

3. Ending a segment

4. Finding a junction

5. Finding a corner

As in border tracking, efficient data structure manipulation is needed to manage the information at each step of the procedure. The data structures used are very similar to those used in the border algorithm. Instead of past, current, and future regions, there are past, current, and future segments. Segments are lists of edge points that represent straight or curved lines on the image. Current segments are kept in internal memory and accessed by a hash table. Finished segments are written out to a disk file and their space in the hash table freed. The main difference is the detection of junction points and the segments entering them from above or the left and the segments leaving them from below or the right. We will assume an extended neighborhood operator called *pixeltype* that determines whether a pixel is an isolated point, the starting point of a new segment, an interior pixel of an old segment, an ending point of an old segment, a junction, or a corner. If the pixel is an interior or endpoint of an old segment, the segment id of the old segment is also returned. If the pixel is a junction or a corner point, then a list of segment IDs of incoming segments and a list of pixels representing outgoing segments are returned. A procedure for tracking edges in a symbolic image is given below. Figure 11.3 gives the results of its application on the symbolic image of Fig. 11.2.

Segment ID	Length	List
1	3	(1,1)(2,2)(3,3)
2	3	(1,5)(2,4)(3,3)
3	3	(3,3)(4,3)(5,3)
4	3	(5,3)(5,4)(5,5)

Figure 11.3 Output of the *edge_track* procedure on the image of Fig. 11.2, assuming the point (5,3) is judged to be a corner point. If corner points are not used to terminate segments, then segement 3 would have length 5 and list [(3,3)(4,3)(5,3)(5,4)(5,5)].

```
procedure edge_track;
IDNEW := 0
for R := 1 to NLINES do
  for C := 1 to NPIXELS do
    begin
      NAME := address(R,C);
      NEIGHB := neighbors(R,C);
      T := pixeltype(R,C,NEIGHB,ID,INLIST,OUTLIST);
      case
        T = isolated point :
          next;
        T = start point of new segment:
          begin
            IDNEW := IDNEW + 1;
            make_new_segment(IDNEW,NAME)
          end;
        T = interior point of old segment :
          add(ID,NAME);
        T = end point of old segment :
          begin
            add(ID,NAME);
            output(ID);
            free(ID);
          end;
        T = junction or corner point:
          for each ID in INLIST do
            begin
              add(ID,NAME);
              output(ID);
              free(ID)
            end;
          for each pixel in OUTLIST do
            begin
              IDNEW := IDNEW + 1;
              make_new_segment(IDNEW,NAME)
            end;
      end case
    end
  end for
end for

end edge_track;
```

The exact details of keeping track of segment ids entering and leaving segments at a junction have been suppressed. This part of the procedure can be very simple and assume that every pixel adjacent to a junction pixel is part of a different segment. In this case, if the segments are more than one pixel wide, the algorithm will detect a large number of small segments that are really not new line segments at all. This can be avoided by applying the connected shrink operator discussed in Chapter 6 to the edge image. Another alternative would be to make the *pixeltype* operator even smarter. It can look at a larger neighborhood and use heuristics to decide whether this is just a thick part of the current segment or a new segment is starting. Often the application will dictate what these heuristics should be.

11.4   Edge and Line Linking Using Directional Information

The procedure *edge_track* described in the previous section linked one-pixel-wide edges that had no directional information associated with them. In this section we assume each pixel is marked to indicate whether it is an edge (line) or not, and if so, the angular direction of the edge (line) is associated with it. Edge (line) linking is a process by which labeled pixels that have similar enough directions can form connected chains and be identified as an arc segment that will have a good fit to a simple curvelike line.

The linking proceeds by scanning the labeled edge image in a top-down, left-right scan. If a labled pixel is encountered that has no previously encountered labeled neighbors, then it begins a new group with a group mean initialized as the direction of the edge or line, a number of pixels in the region initialized at N_0, and the scatter of the group initialized at $N_0 \sigma_0^2$, where N_0 and σ_0^2 are specified initial values. Then σ_0^2 can be considered as the a priori variance, before any data have been examined; N_0 can be considered as the weight of this a priori variance.

If the labeled pixel has a previously encountered labeled neighbor, then the statistically closest group to which these neighbors belong is identified. Because angle is a quantity that is modulo 360°, some care must be used in this determination. If γ is the mean angle for some group and θ is the angular direction for the given pixel, then the angular direction $\theta_{\min}$, which is the closest of $\theta, \theta + 360°$, and $\theta - 360°$ to γ, is defined in the following way:

$$\theta_{\min} = \begin{cases} \theta & \text{if } |\theta - \gamma| < |\theta^* - \gamma| \\ \theta^* & \text{otherwise} \end{cases}$$

where

$$\theta^* = \begin{cases} \theta + 360° & \text{if } \theta - \gamma < 0 \\ \theta - 360° & \text{otherwise} \end{cases}$$

If the group has N pixels and a scatter of S^2, then the statistical closeness of θ to γ can be measured by a t-statistic having $N - 1$ degrees of freedom

$$t = \frac{|\theta_{\min} - \gamma| / \sqrt{(N + 1)/N}}{\sqrt{S^2/N - 1}}$$

The given pixel is then added to that group having the smallest t-value, provided that $t < T_{\alpha, N-1}$, the α percentage point on the cumulative t-distribution with $N - 1$

degrees of freedom. If $t < T_{\alpha, N-1}$, the mean and scatter of the group are updated:

$$\gamma_{new} \leftarrow (N\gamma_{old} + \theta_{min})/(N+1)$$
$$S^2 \leftarrow S^2 + N(\gamma_{old} - \gamma_{new})^2 + (\theta_{min} - \gamma_{new})^2$$
$$N \leftarrow N + 1$$

$$\gamma_{old} \leftarrow \gamma_{new}$$

If there were two or more previously encountered labeled neighbors, then after the pixel is linked into its closest group, a test can be done to determine whether the two groups closest to the given pixel should be merged. This merging test is accomplished by another t-test. Suppose the group means are γ_1 and γ_2, the group scatters are S_1^2 and S_2^2, and the number of pixels in each group is N_1 and N_2, respectively. Define γ_{2min} by

$$\gamma_{2min} = \begin{cases} \gamma_2 & \text{if } |\gamma_2 - \gamma_1| < |\gamma_2^* - \gamma_1| \\ \gamma_2^* & \text{otherwise} \end{cases}$$

where

$$\gamma_2^* = \begin{cases} \gamma_2 + 360° & \text{if } \gamma_2 - \gamma_1 < 0 \\ \gamma_2 - 360° & \text{otherwise} \end{cases}$$

The t-statistic having $N_1 + N_2 - 2$ degrees of freedom is defined by

$$t = \frac{|\gamma_{2min} - \gamma_1|/\sqrt{\frac{1}{N_1} + \frac{1}{N_2}}}{\sqrt{(S_1^2 + S_2^2)/(N_1 + N_2 - 2)}}$$

If $t < T_{\alpha, N_1 + N_2 - 2}$, the two groups are merged, creating a new group having N pixels, scatter S^2, and mean γ, where

$$N = N_1 + N_2$$
$$\gamma = (\gamma_1 N_1 + \gamma_2 N_2)/N$$
$$S^2 = S_1^2 + S_2^2 + N_1(\gamma_1 - \gamma)^2 + N_2(\gamma_2 - \gamma)^2$$

11.5   Segmentation of Arcs into Simple Segments

The border-tracking and edge-linking algorithms we have discussed produce extracted digital arcs. An extracted digital arc is a sequence of row-column pairs in which the spatial coordinates of successive row-column pairs are close together. In fact, most often we would expect successive row-column pairs of an extracted digital arc to be digital 4-neighbors or digital 8-neighbors. However, in the development that follows, we need only the assumption of spatial closeness and not the assumption of 4-neighboring or 8-neighboring.

Arc segmentation is a process that partitions an extracted digital arc sequence into digital arc subsequences having the property that each digital arc subsequence is a maximal sequence that can fit a straight or curved line of a given type. The endpoints of the subsequences are called corner points or dominant points. The basis for the partitioning process is the identification of all locations (a) that have sufficiently high curvature (high change in tangent angle to change in arc length) and (b) that are enclosed by subsequences that can fit different straight lines or curves of a given type. Maximal subsequences that can fit a straight line are subsequences for which some measure of curvature is uniformly small. Maximal subsequences that can fit a curved-line segment are sequences for which some measure of curvature is uniformly high. The principal problem that must be handled by any arc segmentation technique is the determination of the appropriate region of support for any curvature calculation as well as the handling of spatial quantization and image noise, which perturbs point location, sometimes systematically.

Next we discuss a variety of techniques for segmenting digital arcs into simple segments. *Simple* here means either an arc segment that is a straight-line segment or one that is a curved-arc segment containing no straight-line segments. The techniques range from iterative endpoint fitting and splitting to using tangent angle deflection, prominence, or high curvature as the basis of the segmentation.

11.5.1 Iterative Endpoint Fit and Split

Ramer (1972) and Duda and Hart (1972) give the following iterative endpoint fit-and-split procedure to segment a digital arc sequence $S = <(r_1, c_1), \ldots, (r_N, c_N)>$ into subsequences that are sufficiently straight. It requires only one distance thresh-old d^*. Let $L = \{\binom{r}{c} | \alpha r + \beta c + \gamma = 0\}$, where $\alpha^2 + \beta^2 = 1$, be the line segment defined by the endpoints (r_1, c_1) and (r_N, c_N). For any point (r_n, c_n) let d_n be the distance between L and (r_n, c_n); $d_n = |\alpha r_n + \beta c_n + \gamma|$. Let m be any point for which $d_m = \max_n d_n$. If $d_m > d^*$, the sequence is split into two subsequences $S_1 = <(r_1, c_1), \ldots, (r_m, c_m)>$ and $S_2 = <(r_{m+1}, c_{m+1}), \ldots, (r_N, c_N)>$, and the procedure is recursively applied to S_1 and S_2. The splitting is shown in Fig. 11.4, and the technique is detailed in the procedure *endpoint_fit_and_split* whose arguments are $S = <(r_1, c_1), \ldots, (r_N, c_N)>$, the digital arc sequence; ϵ, the maximum

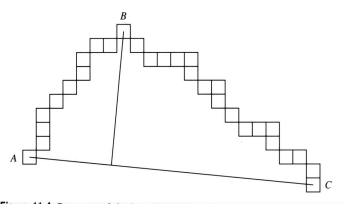

Figure 11.4 Geometry of the iterative endpoint fit and split. The pixel having the farthest distance to the line AC is the pixel B. The iterative endpoint fit and split segments the arc sequence at pixel B, creating two arc subsequences, each of which better fit a straight-line segment.

allowable error; *open,* an input list of the beginning and final indices for each of the segments (the *endpoint_fit_and_split* procedure will refine the position determined by open); *segmentlist,* the list of beginning and final indices for each of the resulting segments; and *sflag,* which has a value of 0 if *endpoint_fit_and_split* does not refine the input segmentation and a value of 1 if it does. The function *remove* removes the first element from the list specified by its argument and returns the first element as its value. The procedure *add* adds the item specified by its second argument to the end of the list specified by its first argument. The procedure *endpoint_line_fit* inputs the arc sequence S, the beginning and final indices b and f defining the subsequence of S being fit, a variable e_{max} in which to return the error of fit, and a variable k that marks the index of the point having the maximum distance to the line constructed between the points indexed by b and f.

```
procedure endpoint_fit_and_split(S,ε,open,segmentlist, sflag);
   sflag := 0;
   segmentlist := nil;
   while open ≠ nil do
      begin
         (b,f) := remove(open);
         endpoint_line_fit(S,b,f,e_max,k);
         if e_max > ε then
            begin
               sflag := 1;
               add(open,(b,k));
               add(open,(k+1,f))
            end
         else add(segmentlist,(b,f))
      end
   end endpoint_fit_and_split;
procedure endpoint_line_fit(S,b,f,e_max,k)
   d := √((r_f − r_b)² + (c_f − c_b)²);
   α := (c_f − c_b)/d;
   β := (r_b − r_f)/d;
   γ := (r_f c_b − r_b c_f)/d;
   for j := b to f do
      begin
      e_max := 0;
      e = |αr_j + βc_j + γ|;
      if e > e_max then
         begin
         e_max := e;
         k := j
         end
      end
   end for
   end endpoint_line_fit;
```

If the given digital arc sequence is obtained by tracing around a boundary of a region, the circular arc sequence must be initially split. Good candidate points for the split might be the two points farthest apart in any direction or the two points farthest apart in a vertical or horizontal direction. Once the circular arc sequence is split into two noncircular arc sequences, the iterative endpoint fit technique can be applied to each noncircular digital arc sequence. Han, Jang, and Foster (1989) note that if the arc sequence S is composed of two line segments, then a search among all points to determine $\max_n d_n$ is not necessary. A golden section search (Mangasarian, 1978) can compute the largest distance in a smaller number of operations.

11.5.2   Tangential Angle Deflection

Another approach to the segmentation of an arc sequence is to identify the locations where two line segments meet and form an angle. The exterior angle (see Fig. 11.5) between two line segments meeting at a common vertex is given by the change in angular orientation from the first line segment to the second. To measure the exterior angle at a place (r_n, c_n), where two line segments meet in a digital arc sequence $S = <(r_1, c_1), \ldots, (r_N, c_N)>$, it is not reasonable to use the line segments defined by $[(r_{n-1}, c_{n-1}), (r_n, c_n)]$ and $[(r_n, c_n), (r_{n+1}, c_{n+1})]$, because if successive points are really digital 4 or 8 neighbors, these line segments must have orientations at angles that are multiples of $45°$. Here we see that the spatial quantization effects at small distances can completely mask the correct line segment direction. This makes it imperative to use line segments defined by points that may not be immediate predecessors or successors in the arc sequence. The simplest way to obtain a larger arc neighborhood is to define the exterior angle at (r_n, c_n) by means of the line segments $[(r_{n-k}, c_{n-k}), (r_n, c_n)]$ and $[(r_n, c_n), (r_{n+k}, c_{n+k})]$ determined by the predecessor and successor k positions behind and k positions ahead of (r_n, c_n), for some $k > 1$. The cosine of the exterior angle is given by

$$\cos[\theta_n(k)] = \frac{a_n(k)'b_n(k)}{\|a_n(k)\|\,\|b_n(k)\|} \tag{11.1}$$

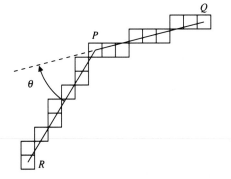

Figure 11.5 Geometry of the exterior angle formed by two line segments.

$$\text{where } a_n(k) = \begin{pmatrix} r_{n-k} - r_n \\ c_{n-k} - c_n \end{pmatrix}$$

$$\text{and } b_n(k) = \begin{pmatrix} r_n - r_{n+k} \\ c_n - c_{n+k} \end{pmatrix}$$

Rosenfeld and Johnston (1973) suggest associating with (r_n, c_n) the largest k_n satisfying $\cos \theta_n(m) > \cos \theta_n(m - 1) > \ldots > \cos \theta_n(k_n) \not> \cos \theta_n(k_n - 1)$, where m is the largest k to be considered. Rosenfeld and Johnston use $m = N/10$. Care must be used in selecting m since it must be no larger than the smallest number of points in a line segment of the arc sequence if the computed value $\cos \theta_n(k_n)$ is to have a proper geometric meaning.

Finally, we must recall that $\cos \theta_n(k_n)$ measures the exterior angle at (r_n, c_n) only if (r_n, c_n) is a place where two line segments meet. To judge whether (r_n, c_n) is indeed a place where two line segments meet, we can use the fact that at a place where two line segments meet, $\cos \theta_n(k_n)$ will be smaller (the angle will be larger) than the corresponding cosine values of the successor and predecessor positions. This motivates Rosenfeld and Johnston's criterion of deciding that (r_n, c_n) is a point at which two line segments meet if and only if

$$\cos \theta_n(k_n) < \cos \theta_i(k_i)$$

for all i satisfying $|n - i| \leq k_n/2$.

Davis (1977) discounts any local maximum in any extended neighborhood of size k for which there is some nearby point that has a significant exterior angle in some slightly smaller extended neighborhood. That is, (r_n, c_n) is the meeting place of two line segments if and only if

1. $\cos \theta_n(k) < \min\{\cos \theta_{n+j}(k) | \cos \theta_{n+j+\Delta n}(h) > t, k/2 \leq h < k, \ k \leq |\Delta n| \leq s(k), j = -k, \ldots, k\}$,
2. $\cos \theta_{n+\Delta n}(n) > t, \ k/2 \leq h < k, \ k \leq |\Delta n| \leq s(k)$.

where t is a threshold chosen so that points with exterior angles whose cosine is larger than t are considered to be part of straight-line segments, and $s(k)$ represents the maximum expected uncertainty in the position of an angle as a function of k, the size of its extended neighborhood.

Freeman and Davis (1977) and Freeman (1978) measure the prominence of a corner for each point (r_n, c_n) in an arc sequence. A point is a prominent corner point to the extent that:

1. There is a large extended neighborhood preceding (r_n, c_n) that has small curvature;
2. There is a large extended neighborhood succeeding (r_n, c_n) that has small curvature;
3. The extended neighborhood around (r_n, c_n) has large curvature.

They define the "curvature" δ_n^k as twice the mean over two adjacent angular differences of line segments defined by an extended neighborhood size of k. This is similar to Ledley (1964). So if

$$\theta_j(k) = \cos^{-1} \frac{a_j'(k)b_j(k)}{\|a_j(k)\|\|b_j(k)\|}$$

then

$$\delta_n^k = 2\left[\frac{[\theta_{n+1}(k) - \theta_n(k)] - [\theta_n(k) - \theta_{n-1}(k)]}{2}\right]$$

$$= \theta_{n+1}(k) - \theta_{n-1}(k)$$

The measure K_n of the prominence of the corner at (r_n, c_n) can be defined by

$$K_n = \sqrt{t_1 t_2} \sum_{i=n-k/2}^{n+k/2} \delta_i^k$$

where

$$t_1 = \max\{t \mid |\delta_{n-\nu}^k| < \Delta, \ k/2 \leq \nu \leq t\}$$
$$t_2 = \max\{t \mid |\delta_{n+\nu}^k| < \Delta, \ k/2 \leq \nu \leq t\}$$

and $\Delta = \tan^{-1}(1/(k-1))$. A point (r_n, c_n) is marked a corner point if

1. $|K_n| > |K_{n+j}|, \ -k/2 \leq j \leq k/2,$
2. $|K_n| > t.$

Shirai (1973) uses the following idea to associate an angle change at each interior point of an arc sequence. Let the digital arc sequence $S = < (r_1, c_1), \ldots, (r_N, c_N) >$. Let a positive integer $m > 1$ be given to specify the arc neighborhood size. For each n, $m + 1 \leq n \leq N - m$, the angle change δ_n at (r_n, c_n) is defined as the exterior angle between the line segment defined by the points (r_{n-m}, c_{n-m}) and (r_n, c_n) and the points (r_n, c_n) and (r_{n+m}, c_{n+m}). This is illustrated in Fig. 11.5. Each digital arc subsequence is then a maximally long subsequence of S in which successive points of the subsequence are successive points of S and where $\delta_n < \delta_{max}$ for each point (r_n, c_n) of the subsequence or where $\delta_n > \delta_{max}$ for each point (r_n, c_n) of the subsequence.

In a sequence $S = < (r_1, c_1), \ldots, (r_N, c_N) >$, the average exterior angle change is shown by

$$\frac{1}{N - 2m} \sum_{n=m+1}^{N-m} \delta_n$$

A sequence with N points has N/m mutually exclusive subsequences of length m each. Each pair of such successive subsequences has associated with it an angle change. There are $N/m - 1$ such angle changes. This motivates the quantity

$$\theta = \frac{N - m}{m} \frac{1}{N - 2m} \sum_{n=m+1}^{N-m} \delta_n \tag{11.2}$$

as a measure of the central angle spanned by the arc sequence.

A central angle of θ radians with an associated radius R produces a circular arc segment of length $L = \theta R$. The length (in units of pixel width) of an arc sequence S can be measured by

$$L = \sum_{n=1}^{N-1} \sqrt{(r_n - r_{n+1})^2 + (c_n - c_{n+1})^2}$$

This motivates the quantity

$$R = \frac{1}{\theta} \sum_{n=1}^{N-1} \sqrt{(r_n - r_{n+1})^2 + (c_n - c_{n+1})^2} \tag{11.3}$$

as an estimate of the radius associated with the arc.

The farthest distance d between a point on a circular arc having central angle θ and radius R and the chord connecting the endpoints of the arc is given by

$$d = R \left(1 - \cos \frac{\theta}{2} \right) \tag{11.4}$$

Using Eqs. (11.2) and (11.3) in Eq. (11.4) permits a chord-to-arc distance to be measured for any arc sequence.

To determine whether a digital arc subsequence is one that fits a straight or a curved line, the following classification scheme can be used. Let chord-to-arc distance thresholds d_* and $d^*, d_* < d^*$, be given and central angle θ^* be given. Then for any arc subsequence for which $\delta_n < \delta_{max}$ or $\delta_n > \delta_{max}$ for every point in the subsequence, the arc subsequence can be classified as a straight line if (1) $d < d_*$ or (2) $d < d^*$ and $\theta < \theta^*$. Otherwise it is classified as a curved line (Shirai, 1975).

Instead of using endpoints to define line segments, Pavlidis (1973), Davis (1977), and Anderson and Bezdek (1984) use a least-squares fit to determine a line. Anderson and Bezdek incorporate a least-squares fit of a fixed number m of points to segment an arc in the following way. They look for the first point in the arc sequence for which a least-squares straight-line fit is sufficiently good. This fit constitutes the baseline. Then they locate the following point p that can begin an m-point least-squares fit whose angular orientation is sufficiently different from the orientation of the baseline fit. The next breakpoint is the point q that can be no more than m points following p for which the local tangential deflection is a relative extremum. If there is no local extremum, q is m/c points following p. The local tangential deflection of a point v is measured by the angular orientation difference of the m-point least-squares fit preceding and following v.

Anderson and Bezdek (1984) derive the following computationally efficient means to determine the cosine of twice the tangential deflection angle arising from two least-squares line fits. For any digital arc sequence $S = < (r_1, c_1), \ldots, (r_N, c_N) >$, define the normalized scatter matrix A by

$$A = \frac{1}{S_{rr} + S_{cc}} \begin{pmatrix} S_{rr} & S_{rc} \\ S_{rc} & S_{cc} \end{pmatrix}$$

where

$$S_{rr} = \sum_{n=1}^{N} (r_n - \mu_r)^2$$

$$S_{rc} = \sum_{n=1}^{N} (r_n - \mu_r)(c_n - \mu_c)$$

$$S_{cc} = \sum_{n=1}^{N} (c_n - \mu_c)^2$$

$$\mu_r = \frac{1}{N} \sum_{n=1}^{N} r_n$$

$$\mu_c = \frac{1}{N} \sum_{n=1}^{N} c_n$$

Let

$$A = \begin{pmatrix} a_{11} & a_{12} \\ a_{21} & a_{22} \end{pmatrix} \quad \text{and} \quad B = \begin{pmatrix} b_{11} & b_{12} \\ b_{21} & b_{22} \end{pmatrix}$$

be the normalized scatter matrices for two arc subsequences, and let $\Delta\theta$ be the tangential deflection angle between the angular orientations of the least-squares fit to the arc subsequences. Then Anderson and Bezdek (1984) derive that

$$\cos 2\Delta\theta = \frac{(a_{22} - a_{11})(b_{22} - b_{11}) + 4a_{12}b_{12}}{\sqrt{(1 - 4|A|)(1 - 4|B|)}}$$

11.5.3 Uniform Bounded-Error Approximation

One way of viewing the arc segmentation problem is to segment the arc sequence into maximal pieces whose points deviate from a line-segment fit by no more than a given amount. It may be set up as an optimal uniform bounded-error approximation problem algorithm, as in the approach of Ichida and Kiyono (1975) or Montanari (1970). However, the optimal algorithms have excessive computational complexity. Here, we describe the approximation algorithm of Tomek (1974) and the split-and-merge algorithm of Pavlidis (1977a, 1977b). Both algorithms guarantee the bounded-error approximation. They are not optimal in the sense that the segments they determine may not be maximal-length segments. Other approaches include those of Williams (1978), Sklansky and Gonzalez (1979), Johnson and Uogt (1980), and Kurozumi and Davis (1982).

Tomek's technique, generalized to arcs, is as follows: At the beginning fitted point of any segment, determine the average tangent direction. Erect a line segment of length 2λ centered through the fitted point in a direction perpendicular to the average tangent direction, where λ is the specified bound. From the endpoints P and Q of this line segment, construct two maximal-length lines, which will eventually be close to parallel and between which the given arc is situated. The construction takes place by picking up the next point x of the arc sequence, computing the directions from P and Q to x, and keeping track, independently on each side, of those directions that point farthest away from the direction of the line on the opposite side. We call these directions the boundary directions. Initially these boundary directions actually point toward each other. As each successive point of the sequence is processed, one or both of these boundary directions change in a way that brings the directions closer to being parallel. Eventually a point is reached where these boundary directions no longer point toward each other, but away from each other. The first point at which this happens becomes the final point of the segment. The final fitted point of the segment is then computed as the intersection point of two lines, the first being the line passing through the beginning point in a direction of the average of the boundary directions and the second being the line passing through the final breakpoint of the segment in a direction perpendicular to the average of those directions that point farthest away from the directions of the line on the opposite side. This is illustrated in Fig. 11.6.

The procedure *segment_grow* details the algorithm. Its input arguments are $S = <(r_1, c_1,), \ldots, (r_N, c_N)>$, the digital arc sequence, and λ, the specified bound. It produces *segmentlist*, which is a list of beginning and final indices for the points in each segment. It calls a function *avg_tangent_direction*, which determines the average forward-looking tangent direction at a point having index b of arc sequence S. It also calls a function *linedir*, which, given two points, determines the direction cosines of the line passing through the two points.

procedure segment_grow (S,λ,segmentlist);

segmentlist := nil;
b := 1;
f := 2;
$(A_0, B_0) := (r_1, c_1)$;

while f<N **do**
    begin

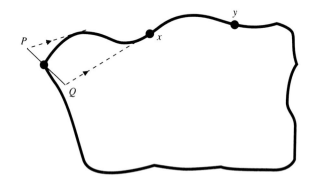

Figure 11.6 Geometry of Tomek's segmentation technique. At the time point x is being processed, the bounding directions emanating from P and Q are still pointing toward each other. However, at the time point y is processed, the bounding directions emanating from P and Q have become parallel and no longer point toward each other. The point y terminates the segment.

$$(t_r, t_c) := \text{avg\_tangent\_direction}(S, b);$$
$$(\alpha_0, \beta_0) := (A_0, B_0);$$
$$(\alpha_1, \beta_1) := (r_b, c_b) + \lambda(-t_c, t_r);$$
$$(\alpha_2, \beta_2) := (r_b, c_b) - \lambda(-t_c, t_r);$$
$$(u_1, v_1) := \text{linedir}((\alpha_1, \beta_1), (r_f, c_f));$$
$$(u_2, v_2) := \text{linedir}((\alpha_2, \beta_2), (r_f, c_f));$$

repeat
   begin
      $f := f+1;$
      $d := \text{dist}((\alpha_1, \beta_1) + (u_1, v_1), (\alpha_2, \beta_2) + (u_2, v_2));$
      $(g_1, h_1) := \text{linedir}((\alpha_1, \beta_1), (r_f, c_f));$
      $(g_2, h_2) := \text{linedir}((\alpha_2, \beta_2), (r_f, c_f));$
      if $\text{dist}((\alpha_1, \beta_1) + (g_1, h_1), (\alpha_2, \beta_2) + (u_2, v_2)) > d$
         then $(u_1, v_1) := (g_1, h_1);$
      if $\text{dist}((\alpha_1, \beta_1) + (u_1, v_1), (\alpha_2, \beta_2) + (g_2, h_2)) > d$
         then $(u_1, v_1) := (g_1, h_1);$
   end
   until $f = N$ or $\text{dist}((\alpha_1, \beta_1) + (u_1, v_1), (\alpha_2, \beta_2) + (u_2, v_2)) \geq 2\lambda;$

   $\text{push}(\text{segmentlist}, (b, f));$
   $b := f+1;$
   $(u_{avg}, v_{avg}) := (u_1 + u_2, v_1 + v_2)/\sqrt{(u_1 + u_2)^2 + (v_1 + v_2)^2};$
   $\epsilon := (r_f - \alpha_0)u_{avg} + (c_f - \beta_0)v_{avg};$
   $(A_0, B_0) := (\alpha_0, \beta_0) + \epsilon(u_{avg}, v_{avg})$
   end

end segment_grow;

11.5.4 Breakpoint Optimization

Once an initial segmentation of a digital arc sequence is obtained, there is an easy way to shift some of the breakpoints to produce a better arc segmentation (Pavlidis, 1973). The technique is simple. First shift the final point of any odd-numbered segment and the corresponding beginning point of the following even-numbered segment and test to see whether the maximum error of the two segments is reduced by the shift. If it is reduced, then keep the shifted breakpoint. Do the same on the final point of any even-numbered segment and the corresponding beginning point of the following odd-numbered segment.

Details are given in the procedure *move_break_point*, whose arguments are S, the digital arc sequence; *segmentlist,* a list of pairs (b,f) of the indices of the beginning and final points of each input segment; and *sflag,* which takes the value 0 if no breakpoints were moved and the value 1 if some breakpoints were moved. The function *length* returns a value that is the number of items in a list. The function *get_element* returns a value that is the *j*th element of the list specified by its first argument; *j* is its second argument. The procedure *put_element* puts its third argument in the jth position of the list specified by its first argument; j is its second argument.

```
procedure move_break_points(S,segmentlist,sflag);

sflag := 0;
flag = 1;
L = length(segmentlist);
while flag = 1 do
    begin
        flag = 0;
        for j := 1 to L-1 by 2 do
        adjust(S,j,segmentlist,flag);
        end for sflag := or(sflag,flag);
        for j := 2 to L by 2 do
            adjust(S,j,segmentlist,flag)
        end for sflag := or(sflag,flag);
    end
end move_break_points;
```

```
procedure adjust(S,j,segmentlist,flag)
```

$(b_j, f_j) := $ get_element(segmentlist,j);
$(b_{j+1}, f_{j+1}) := $ get_element(segmentlist,j+1);
$e_j := $ errornorm(S, b_j, f_j);
$e_{j+1} := $ errornorm(S, b_{j+1}, f_{j+1});
if $e_j > e_{j+1}$ **then**
   begin
      $d_j = $ errornorm($S, b_j, f_j - 1$);
      $d_{j+1} = $ errornorm($S, b_{j+1} - 1, f_{j+1}$);
      if $\max\{d_j, d_{j+1}\} < \max\{e_j, e_{j+1}\}$ **then**
         begin
            $f_j := f_j - 1$;
            $b_{j+1} := b_{j+1} - 1$;
            flag := 1
         end
   end
else
   begin
      $d_j = $ errornorm($S, b_j, f_j - 1$);
      $d_{j+1} = $ errornorm($S, b_{j+1}+1, f_{j+1}$);
      if $\max\{d_j, d_{j+1}\} < \max\{e_j, e_{j+1}\}$ **then**
         begin
            $f_j := f_j - 1$;
            $b_{j+1} := b_{j+1}+1$;
            flag=1
         end
   end;

put_element(segmentlist,j,(b_j,f_j));
put_element(segmentlist,j,(b_{j+1},f_{j+1}));
end adjust;

The procedure *adjust* actually performs the trial shifting of breakpoints. Each call to *adjust* either moves a breakpoint that reduces the error $\max\{e_j,e_{j+1}\}$ and leaves all the other errors the same or does not move a breakpoint and therefore leaves $\max\{e_j,e_{j+1}\}$ as well as all other errors alone. Therefore after each iteration through the while loop, either some breakpoint has been moved, in which case $\max\{e_1,\ldots,e_L\}$ is reduced and the while iterates, or no breakpoints have been moved, in which case the while terminates. So as the iteration proceeds, the sequence whose terms are the maximum resulting error constitute a nonincreasing sequence bounded below by 0. Therefore it must terminate. The termination, however, may be at a local minimum rather than at the global minimum.

11.5.5 Split and Merge

The *split_and_merge* paradigm for curves was introduced by Pavlidis and Horowitz (1974). The idea is simple. First split the arc into segments for which the error in each segment is sufficiently small. Then try to merge successive segments, providing any resulting merged segment has sufficiently small error. Then try to adjust the breakpoints to obtain a better segmentation. Do this repeatedly until all three steps produce no further change.

The *endpoint_fit_and_split* procedure of Section 11.5.1 can be used to accomplish the splitting, and the *move_break_points* procedure of Section 11.5.4 can be used for breakpoint adjustment. The procedure for successive segment merging is detailed below after the *arc_split_and_merge* procedure.

procedure arc_split_and_merge(S,ϵ_{max},segmentlist);

segmentlist := nil;
add(segmentlist,(1,N));

repeat
  begin
    endpoint_fit_and_split(S,ϵ_{max},segmentlist,segmentsplitlist,sflag1);
    endpoint_fit_and_merge(S,ϵ_{max},segmentsplitlist,segmentlist,sflag2);
    move_break_points(S,segmentlist,sflag3)
  end;
until sflag1=0 and sflag2=0 and sflag3=0
end arc_split_and_merge;

procedure endpoint_fit_and_merge(S,ϵ_{max},segmentlist,segmentmergelist,sflag);

segmentmergelist := nil;
(b_1,f_1) := remove(segmentlist);
sflag := 0;
while segmentlist $\neq$ nil **do**
  begin

```
    (b₂,f₂) := remove(segmentlist);
    endpoint_linefit_error(S,b₁,f₂,ε,k);
    if ε < εmax then
       begin
          add(segmentmergelist,(b₁,f₂));
          (b₁,f₁) := (b₁,f₂);
          sflag := 1
       end
    else
       begin
          add(segmentmergelist,(b₁,k));
          if k≠f₁ then sflag := 1;
          (b₁,f₂,) := (k+1,f₂)
       end
    end;
    if ε < εmax then
       add(segmentmergelist,(b₁,f₁))
    end endpoint_fit_and_merge;
```

11.5.6   Isodata Segmentation

A variant of the isodata-clustering algorithm can be used to segment an arc sequence into subsequences that fit a line. The basic idea of the iterative isodata line-fit clustering procedure is to determine the line-fit parameter for each cluster in a given partition. Then each point is assigned to the cluster whose line fit is closest to the point. The new clusters then constitute the partition for the next iteration. As before, $S = < (r_1,c_1),\dots,(r_N,c_N) >$; the first argument to the procedure *isodata_linefit* is the given digital arc sequence; the second argument is an initial partition. The outputs of the procedure are the final partition P, which is a partition of the points of S and the line-fitting parameters for each cluster in the partition. The triple (α,β,γ) designates three parallel arrays. The line-fit parameters for the kth cluster are $\alpha(k),\beta(k),\gamma(k)$, where $\alpha(k)r + \beta(k)c + \gamma(k) = 0$ is the line equation. The procedure calls the function *indexmindist*, which finds the index to that cluster whose line is closest to the given point that is its first argument. The internal variable P^q designates the partition produced on the qth iteration.

```
procedure isodata_linefit(S,Pᵒ,P,(α,β,γ));
   q:=0;
   repeat
      begin
         q:=q+1;
         (αq⁻¹,βq⁻¹,γq⁻¹) := linefit(Pq⁻¹);
         Pq:= nil;
         for i=1 to N do
            begin
               k:=indexmindist((rᵢ,cᵢ),(αq⁻¹,βq⁻¹,γq⁻¹));
```

$$P_k^q := \text{add}(P_k^q, (r_i, c_i));$$
   end
    end for
   end
until $P^{q-1} = P^q$;
$P = P^{q-1}$;
$(\alpha, \beta, \gamma) = (\alpha^{q-1}, \beta^{q-1}, \gamma^{q-1})$
end isodata_linefit

function indexmindist$((r,c),(\alpha,\beta,\gamma))$;

   d:=verylarge_number;
   for k=1 to K **do**
      begin
         dist:=$|\alpha(k)r + \beta(k)c + \gamma|$;
         if dist $<$ d **then**
            begin
               d:=dist;
               indexmindist := k
            end
      end
   end for
end indexmindist

The isodata segmentation as given in the procedure *isodata_linefit* puts together in the same cluster points from S that may be in two collinear segments. So a final pass through the ordered points in S must be made to determine the proper subsequences. If a point belongs to the same cluster as the previous point, then it is assigned to the same subsequence. But, if it belongs to a different cluster, it is assigned to a new subsequence.

11.5.7 Curvature

The geometric idea of curvature is simple. For a planar curve, the curvature at a point on the curve is the limit, as arc length change goes to zero, of the change in tangent angle divided by the change in arc length. Curvature has been long established to play an important role in shape perception (Attneave, 1954, 1957). Places of natural curve breaks are places of curvature maxima and minima. Places where curvature passes through zero are places where the local shape changes from convex to concave.

For this discussion we represent the curve parametrically as $[r(t), c(t)]$, $a < t < b$. For any t, the arc length $s(t)$ going from $[r(a), c(a)]$ to $[r(t), c(t)]$ is given by

$$s(t) = \int_a^t \sqrt{\left(\frac{dr(u)}{du}\right)^2 + \left(\frac{dc(u)}{du}\right)^2}\, du$$

Hence

$$\frac{ds}{dt}(t) = \sqrt{\left(\frac{dr(t)}{dt}\right)^2 + \left(\frac{dc(t)}{dt}\right)^2}$$

The unit length tangent vector T at $[r(t), c(t)]$ as measured clockwise from the column axis is given by

$$T = \begin{pmatrix} \dfrac{dr}{dt}(t) \\ \dfrac{dc}{dt}(t) \end{pmatrix} \dfrac{1}{\dfrac{ds}{dt}(t)}$$

The unit normal vector N at $[r(t), c(t)]$ is given by

$$T = \begin{pmatrix} \dfrac{-dc}{dt}(t) \\ \dfrac{dr}{dt}(t) \end{pmatrix} \dfrac{1}{\frac{ds}{dt}(t)}$$

The curvature κ is defined at a point of arc length s along the curve by

$$\kappa(s) = \lim_{\Delta s \to 0} \frac{\Delta \theta}{\Delta s}$$

where $\Delta \theta$ is the change in tangent angle produced by a change Δs of arc length. From this definition it follows that the curvature κ at $[r(t), c(t)]$ is computed by

$$\kappa(t) = \frac{\frac{dr}{dt}(t)\frac{d^2c}{dt^2}(t) - \frac{d^2r}{dt^2}(t)\frac{dc}{dt}(t)}{\left\{\left[\frac{dr}{dt}(t)\right]^2 + \left[\frac{dc}{dt}(t)\right]^2\right\}^{\frac{3}{2}}} \tag{11.5}$$

Given an arc sequence $S = <(r_1, c_1), \ldots, (r_N, c_N)>$, we can set up a normalized arc-length parametric representation by defining $S_r = <(s_1, r_1), \ldots, (s_N, r_N)>$ and $S_c = <(s_1, c_1), \ldots, (s_N, r_N)>$, where $s_1 = 0$ and

$$s_n = \frac{1}{s_N} \sum_{i=2}^{n} \sqrt{(r_i - r_{i-1})^2 + (c_i - c_{i-1})^2}. \tag{11.6}$$

Then a polynomial or spline least-squares fit for r as a function of s and c as a function of s can be computed, from which the curvature at s_n can be computed by Eq. (11.5).

The observed behavior of the curvature computed this way is often unsatisfactory because the required second derivatives can have excessive noise. A more stable approach is to find a way to use the largest arc length possible to estimate the tangent angle of a line fitted to the points on either side of the point having its curvature computed. The difference between the tangent angles of the line segments is the tangential deflection (as discussed in Section 11.5.2). The tangential deflection divided by the change in arc length across the given point is an estimate of curvature.

If the curvature is computed at (r_n, c_n), Anderson and Bezdek (1984) estimate Δs at (r_n, c_n) by $\sqrt{(r_n - r_{n+1})^2 + (c_n - c_{n+1})^2}$, just as we did in Eq. (11.6).

Perhaps a more accurate estimate of Δs at (r_n, c_n) can be computed by fitting a circular arc segment through (r_n, c_n) and (r_{n+1}, c_{n+1}), where the tangent angle (measured clockwise from the column axis) at (r_n, c_n) is given as θ_n and the tangent angle at (r_{n+1}, c_{n+1}) is given as θ_{n+1}. The geometry of this configuration is illustrated in Fig. 11.7. The parametric representation is then

$$r_n = a + R \sin t_n$$
$$c_n = b + R \cos t_n$$
$$r_{n+1} = a + R \sin t_{n+1}$$
$$c_{n+1} = b + R \cos t_{n+1}$$
$$\sin \phi_n = \cos t_n$$
$$\cos \phi_n = - \sin t_n$$
$$\sin \phi_{n+1} = \cos t_{n+1}$$
$$\cos \phi_{n+1} = - \sin t_{n+1}$$

From the last four relations it is apparent that $t_n = \phi_n - 90°$. Hence

$$r_n = a + R \sin(\phi_n - 90°) = a - R \cos \phi_n$$
$$c_n = b + R \cos(\phi_n - 90°) = b + R \sin \phi_n$$
$$r_{n+1} = a + R \sin(\phi_{n+1} - 90°) = a - R \cos \phi_{n+1}$$
$$c_{n+1} = b + R \cos(\phi_{n+1} - 90°) = b + R \cos \phi_{n+1}$$

This results in an overconstrained linear system

$$\begin{pmatrix} 1 & 0 & -\cos \phi_n \\ 0 & 1 & \sin \phi_n \\ 1 & 0 & -\cos \phi_{n+1} \\ 0 & 1 & \sin \phi_{n+1} \end{pmatrix} \begin{pmatrix} a \\ b \\ R \end{pmatrix} = \begin{pmatrix} r_n \\ c_n \\ r_{n+1} \\ c_{n+1} \end{pmatrix}$$

which can be solved in the least-squares sense for R. This produces

$$R = -\frac{(r_{n+1} - r_n)}{2}(\cos \phi_{n+1} - \cos \phi_n) + \frac{(c_{n+1} - c_n)}{2}(\sin \phi_{n+1} - \sin \phi_n) \qquad (11.7)$$

Curvature at (r_n, c_n) is then estimated by $1/R$.

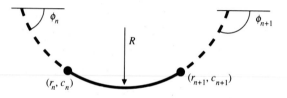

Figure 11.7 Geometry of the circular arc segment defined by two points (r_n, c_n) and (r_{n+1}, c_{n+1}) and their tangent directions ϕ_n and ϕ_{n+1}, respectively.

11.6   Hough Transform

The *Hough transform* (Hough, 1962; Duda and Hart, 1972) is a method for detecting straight lines and curves on gray level images. The method is given the family of curves being sought and produces the set of curves from that family that appears on the image. Stockman and Agrawala (1977) were the first to realize that the Hough transform is template matching. Rosenfeld (1969) describes an implementation that is almost always more efficient than the original Hough formulation. Here we describe the Hough transform technique and show how to apply it to finding straight-line segments and circular arcs in images. We will emphasize the O'Gorman and Clowes (1976) formulation. We then present a Bayesian approach to the Hough transform.

11.6.1   Hough Transform Technique

The Hough transform algorithm requires an accumulator array whose dimension corresponds to the number of unknown parameters in the equation of the family of curves being sought. For example, finding line segments using the equation $y = mx + b$ requires finding two parameters for each segment: m and b. The two dimensions of the accumulator array for this family would correspond to quantized values for m and for b.

Using an accumulator array A, the Hough procedure examines each pixel and its neighborhood in the image. It determines whether there is enough evidence of an edge at that pixel and if so, calculates the parameters of the specified curve that passes through this pixel. In the straight-line example with equation $y = mx + b$, it would estimate the m and the b of the line passing through the pixel being considered if the measure of edge strength (such as gradient) at that pixel were high enough. Once the parameters at a given pixel are estimated, they are quantized to corresponding values M and B and the accumulator $A(M, B)$ is incremented. Some schemes increment by one and some by the strength of the gradient at the pixel being processed. After all pixels have been processed, the accumulator array is searched for peaks. The peaks indicate the parameters of the most likely lines in the image.

Although the accumulator array tells us the parameters of the infinite lines (or curves), it does not tell us where the actual segments begin and end. To obtain this information, we can add a parallel structure called $PTLIST$. $PTLIST(M, B)$ contains a list of all the pixel positions that contributed to the sum in the accumulator $A(M, B)$. From these lists the actual segments can be determined.

This description of the Hough method is general; it omits the details needed for an implementation. We will now discuss in detail algorithms for straight-line and circle finding.

Finding Straight-Line Segments

The equation $y = mx + b$ for straight lines does not work for vertical lines. The equation $d = x \cos \theta + y \sin \theta$, where d is the perpendicular distance from the line to

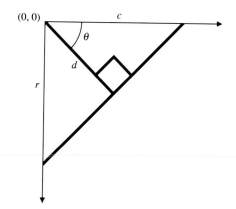

Figure 11.8 Parameters d and θ used in the equation $d = r \sin \theta + c \cos \theta$ of a straight line.

the origin and θ is the angle the perpendicular makes with the x-axis, was suggested in Duda and Hart (1972) and used by O'Gorman and Clowes (1976). We will use this form of the equation but convert to row (r) and column (c) coordinates. Thus our equation becomes

$$d = r \sin \theta + c \cos \theta$$

where d is the perpendicular distance from the line to the origin of the image (assumed to be at upper left), and θ is the angle this perpendicular makes with the c (column) axis. Figure 11.8 illustrates the parameters of the line segment. The accumulator A has subscripts that represent quantized values of d and θ. O'Gorman and Clowes quantized the values of d by 3s and θ by 10° increments in their experiments on gray level images of puppet objects. An accumulator array quantized in this fashion is illustrated in Fig. 11.9. The O'Gorman and Clowes algorithm for filling the accumulator A and parallel list array $PTLIST$ can be stated as follows:

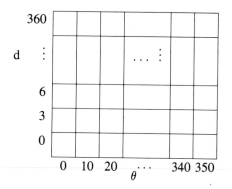

Figure 11.9 Accumulator array for finding straight-line segments in images of size 256×256.

```
procedure accumulate;
A := 0;
PTLIST := NIL;
for R := 1 to NLINES do
  for C := 1 to NPIXELS do
    begin
      DR := row_gradient(R,C);
      DC := col_gradient(R,C);
      GMAG := gradient(DR,DC);
      if GMAG > gradient_threshold
      then  begin
              THETA := atan2(DR,DC);
              THETAQ := quantize_angle(THETA);
              D := C*cos(THETAQ) + R*sin(THETAQ);
              DQ := quantize_distance(D);
              A(DQ,THETAQ) := A(DQ,THETAQ)+GMAG;
              PTLIST(DQ,THETAQ) := append(PTLIST(DQ,THETAQ),(R,C))
            end
    end
  end for
end for
end accumulate;
```

The algorithm is expressed in row-column space to be consistent with the other algorithms in the book. The functions *row_gradient* and *column_gradient* are neighborhood functions that estimate the row and column components of the gradient, and the function *gradient* combines the two to get the magnitude. The function *atan2* is the standard scientific library function that returns the angle in the correct quadrant given the row and column components of the gradient. We assume here that *atan2* returns a value between $0°$ and $359°$. Many implementations return the angle in radians, which would have to be converted to degrees. The actions of the procedure are illustrated in Fig. 11.10. Notice that with a 3×3 gradient operator, the lines are two pixels wide. Notice also that counts appear in other accumulators than the two correct ones.

Procedure *accumulate* is O'Gorman and Clowes's version of the Hough method and pretty much follows the Hough theory. Once the accumulator and list arrays are filled, though, there is no standard method for extracting the line segments. O'Gorman and Clowes presented an ad hoc procedure that illustrates some of the problems that come up in this phase of the line-segment extraction process. This procedure can be expressed as follows:

```
procedure find_lines;
V := pick_greatest_bin(A,DQ,THETAQ);
while V > value_threshold do
  begin
    list_of_points := reorder(PTLIST(DQ,THETAQ));
    for each point (R,C) in list_of_points do
```

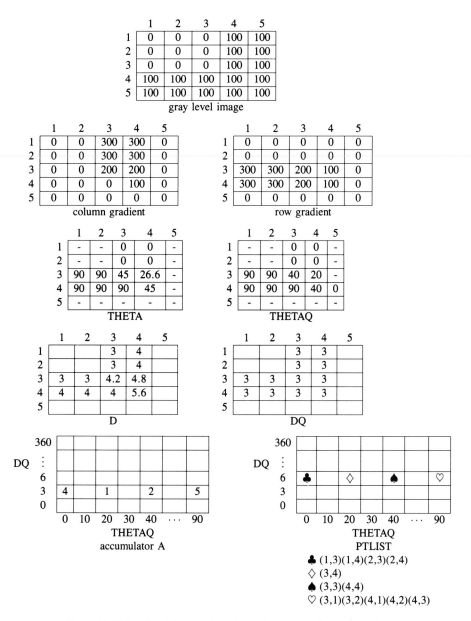

	1	2	3	4	5
1	0	0	0	100	100
2	0	0	0	100	100
3	0	0	0	100	100
4	100	100	100	100	100
5	100	100	100	100	100

gray level image

	1	2	3	4	5
1	0	0	300	300	0
2	0	0	300	300	0
3	0	0	200	200	0
4	0	0	0	100	0
5	0	0	0	0	0

column gradient

	1	2	3	4	5
1	0	0	0	0	0
2	0	0	0	0	0
3	300	300	200	100	0
4	300	300	200	100	0
5	0	0	0	0	0

row gradient

	1	2	3	4	5
1	-	-	0	0	-
2	-	-	0	0	-
3	90	90	45	26.6	-
4	90	90	90	45	-
5	-	-	-	-	-

THETA

	1	2	3	4	5
1	-	-	0	0	-
2	-	-	0	0	-
3	90	90	40	20	-
4	90	90	90	40	0
5	-	-	-	-	-

THETAQ

	1	2	3	4	5
1			3	4	
2			3	4	
3	3	3	4.2	4.8	
4	4	4	4	5.6	
5					

D

	1	2	3	4	5
1			3	3	
2			3	3	
3	3	3	3	3	
4	3	3	3	3	
5					

DQ

accumulator A

DQ	0	10	20	30	40	···	90
360							
:							
6							
3	4		1		2		5
0							

THETAQ

PTLIST

DQ	0	10	20	30	40	···	90
360							
:							
6	♣		◇		♠		♡
3							
0							

THETAQ

♣ (1,3)(1,4)(2,3)(2,4)
◇ (3,4)
♠ (3,3)(4,4)
♡ (3,1)(3,2)(4,1)(4,2)(4,3)

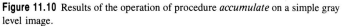

Figure 11.10 Results of the operation of procedure *accumulate* on a simple gray level image.

```
        for each neighbor (R',C') of (R,C) not in list_of_points do
          begin
            DPRIME := D(R',C');
            THETAPRIME := THETA(R',C');
            GRADPRIME := GRADIENT(R',C');
            if GRADPRIME > gradient_threshold
              and abs(THETAPRIME–THETA)≤ 10
            then  begin merge(PTLIST(DQ,THETAQ),PTLIST(DPRIME,
                                THETAPRIME));
                        set_to_zero(A,DPRIME,THETAPRIME)
                  end
          end
        end for
      end for
      final_list_of_points := PTLIST(DQ,THETAQ);
      create_segments(final_list_of_points);
      set_to_zero(A,DQ,THETAQ);
      V := pick_greatest_bin(A,DQ,THETAQ);
    end
  end while
end find_lines;
```

The function *pick_greatest_bin* returns the value in the largest accumulator while setting its last two parameters, DQ and THETAQ, to the quantized d and θ values for that bin. The *reorder function* orders the list of points in a bin by column coordinate for $\theta < 45$ or $\theta > 135$ and by row coordinate for $45 \le \theta \le 135$. The arrays D and THETA are expected to hold the quantized D and THETA values for a pixel that were computed during the accumulation. Similarly the array GRADIENT is expected to contain the computed gradient magnitude. These can be saved as intermediate images. The *merge* procedure merges the list of points from a neighbor of a pixel with the list of points for that pixel, keeping the spatial ordering. The *set_to_zero* procedure zeroes out an accumulator so that it will not be reused. Finally, the procedure *create_segments* goes through the final ordered set of points searching for gaps longer than one pixel. It creates and saves a set of line segments terminating at gaps. O'Gorman and Clowes use a least-squares procedure to fit lists of points to line segments.

Finding Circles

The Hough transform technique can be extended to circles and other parametrized curves. Kimme et al. (1975) develop a program for finding circles in chest x-rays. Like O'Gorman and Clowes, they use a gradient technique to reduce the dimension of the parameter space to be searched. The standard equation of a circle has three parameters. If (r,c) lies on a circle, then gradient (r,c) points to the center of that circle, as shown in Fig. 11.11. So if a point (r,c) is given, a radius d is selected, and the direction of the vector from (r,c) to the center is computed,

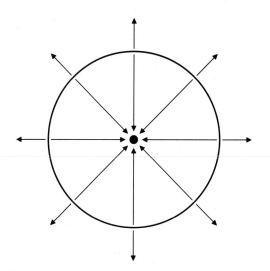

Figure 11.11 Direction of the gradient at the boundary points of a circle. The inward pointing gradients are the ones that will accumulate evidence for the center of the circle.

then the coordinates of the center can be found. The radius, d, the row-coordinate of the center, r_o, and the column-coordinate of the center, c_o, are the three parameters used to vote for circles in the Hough algorithm. Circles are represented by the equations

$$r = r_o + d \sin \theta$$
$$c = c_o + d \cos \theta$$

With these equations the accumulate algorithm for circles becomes

```
procedure accumulate_circles;
A := 0;
PTLIST := 0;
for R := 1 to NLINES do
   for C := 1 to NPIXELS do
      for each possible value D of d do
         begin
            THETA := compute_theta(R,C,D);
            R0 := R - D*cos(THETA);
            C0 := C - D*sin(THETA);
            A(R0,C0,D) := A(R0,C0,D)+1;
            PTLIST(R0,C0,D) := append(PTLIST(R0,C0,D),(R,C))
         end
      end for
   end for
end for
end accumulate_circles;
```

This procedure can easily be modified to take into account the gradient magnitude, like the procedure for line segments.

Extensions

The Hough transform method can be extended to any curve with analytic equation of the form $f(\mathbf{x}, \mathbf{a}) = 0$, where $\mathbf{x}$ denotes an image point and $\mathbf{a}$ is a vector of parameters. The procedure as expressed by Ballard and Brown (1982) is:

1. Initialize accumulator array $A(\mathbf{a})$ to zero.
2. For each edge pixel $\mathbf{x}$, compute all $\mathbf{a}$ such that $f(\mathbf{x}, \mathbf{a}) = 0$ and set A(**a**): = A(**a**)+1.
3. Local maxima in A correspond to curves of f in the image.

If there are m parameters in $\mathbf{a}$, each having M discrete values, then the time complexity is $O(M^{m-2})$.

The Hough transform method has been further generalized to arbitrary shapes specified by a sequence of boundary points (Ballard, 1981a). This is known as the *generalized Hough transform*.

Variations

A number of hybrid techniques exist that use some of the principles of the Hough transform. The Burns line finder (Burns, Hanson, and Riseman, 1986) was developed to find straight lines in complex images of outdoor scenes. The Burns method can be summarized as follows:

1. Compute the gradient magnitude and direction at each pixel.
2. For points with high enough gradient magnitude, assign two labels representing two different quantizations of the gradient direction. (For example, for eight bins, if the first quantization is 0 to 44, 45 to 90, 91 to 134, etc., then the second can be –22 to 22, 23 to 67, 68 to 112, etc.) The result is two symbolic images.
3. Find the connected components of each symbolic image and compute line length for each component.

    - Each pixel is a member of two components, one from each symbolic image.
    - Each pixel votes for its *longer* component.
    - Each component receives a count of pixels that voted for it.
    - The components (line segments) that receive the majority support are selected.

The Burns line finder takes advantage of two powerful algorithms: the Hough transform and the connected components algorithm. It attempts to get rid of the quantization problems that forced O'Gorman and Clowes to search neighboring bins by the use of two separate quantizations. In practice, it suffers from a problem that will affect any line finder that estimates angle based on a small neighborhood around a pixel: Diagonal digital lines are not straight. Diagonal lines are really a sequence of horizontal and vertical steps. If the angle detection technique uses too small a neighborhood, it will end up finding a lot of tiny horizontal and vertical segments instead of a long diagonal line. Thus in practice the Burns line finder and any other angle-based line finder can break up lines that a human would like to detect as a connected whole.

Boldt, Weiss, and Riseman (1989) attempt to solve this problem with a computational approach to the extraction of straight lines based on principles of perceptual organization. They define a straight line as a sequence of line segments satisfying the following conditions: (1) Consecutive pairs satisfy the relations of collinearity, proximity, and similarity of contrast; (2) the entire sequence has the least error locally among candidate groupings; and (3) the error for the best sequence is acceptably low. Their grouping process consists of three steps: linking, optimization, and replacement. Linking means finding pairs of line segments that satisfy the relational measures of orientation difference, contrast difference, relative overlap, lateral distance, and distance between endpoints. Linking is performed on a local area of the image and results in a graph structure. Optimization consists of searching the graph to find acceptable sequences of line segments. Replacement means manipulating the data structure to form new segments from several smaller ones. The algorithm has been applied to complex outdoor images and results in fewer, more meaningful line segments.

11.6.2 A Bayesian Approach to the Hough Transform

The Bayesian approach to the Hough transform described here applies to line detection using the parameterization $r \sin \theta + c \cos \theta = d$. We assume that some local operator has been applied to the image and at each pixel position (r, c) a vector $I(r, c)$ has been determined. $I(r, c)$ may contain only information relative to the existence of a line or edge pixel or it may contain additional information, such as line strength and orientation of a line passing through (r, c).

For any orientation angle θ and distance d, we define the set of pixels that can potentially participate in the line $r \sin \theta + c \cos \theta = d$ by

$$E(\theta, d) = \{(r, c) \, \epsilon \, R \times C \mid |r \sin \theta + c \cos \theta - d| \, < \, \delta\}$$

where δ is some fixed number related to a function of the resolution cell size. We refer to such a line segment as one with parameters (θ, d).

The Bayesian approach to the Hough transform computes for each quantized value of θ and d the conditional probability

$$P[\text{a line segment exists with parameters}(\theta, \, d) \mid I(r, c) : \, (r, c) \, \epsilon \, E(\theta, d)].$$

Now from the definition of conditional probability,

P[a line segment exists with parameters $(\theta, d) \mid I(r,c) : (r,c) \in E(\theta,d)$]

$$= P[I(r,c) : (r,c) \in E(\theta,d) \mid \text{a line segment exists with parameters } (\theta,d)] \tag{11.8}$$

$$\times \frac{P[\text{a line segment exists with parameters } (\theta,d)]}{P[I(r,c) : (r,c) \in E(\theta,d)]}$$

We henceforth denote the conditional probability

P[a line segment exists with parameters $(\theta,d) \mid I(r,c) : (r,c) \in E(\theta,d)$]

by $P[\theta, d \mid I(r,c) : (r,c) \in E(\theta,d)]$. We assume that the observations $\{I(r,c) : (r,c) \in E(\theta,d)\}$ are independent, conditioned on the line parameters. That is,

$$P[I(r,c) : (r,c) \in E(\theta,d) \mid \theta,d] = \prod_{(r,c) \in E(\theta,d)} P(I(r,c) \mid \theta,d) \tag{11.9}$$

Then

$$P[\theta,d \mid I(r,c) : (r,c) \in E(\theta,d)]$$

$$= \frac{P[I(r,c) : (r,c) \in E(\theta,d) \mid \theta,d] \, P(\theta,d)}{P[I(r,c) : (r,c) \in E(\theta,d)]} \tag{11.10}$$

$$= \frac{\left[\prod_{(r,c) \in E(\theta,d)} P[I(r,c) \mid \theta,d]\right] P(\theta,d)}{P[I(r,c) : (r,c) \in E(\theta,d) \mid \text{no line}]} \left[\frac{P[I(r,c) : (r,c) \in E(\theta,d) \mid \text{no line}]}{P[I(r,c) : (r,c) \in E(\theta,d)]}\right] \tag{11.11}$$

But the conditional distribution of the observations, given that there is no line, is, within a fairly good approximation, the unconditional distribution of the observations because the Prob(line) $\ll$ Prob(noline). That is, the right bracketed term of Eq. (11.11) is approximately one. Hence, Eq. (11.11) simplifies to

$$P[\theta,d \mid I(r,c) : (r,c) \in E(\theta,d)] = \frac{\left[\prod_{(r,c) \in E(\theta,d)} P[I(r,c) \mid \theta,d]\right] P(\theta,d)}{P[I(r,c) : (r,c) \in E(\theta,d) \mid \text{no line}]}$$

Conditioned on the state of no line existing, the observations are independent too. We therefore obtain from Eq. (11.11)

$$P[\theta,d \mid I(r,c) : (r,c) \in E(\theta,d)] = \left[\prod_{(r,c) \in E(\theta,d)} \frac{P[I(r,c) \mid \theta,d]}{P[I(r,c) \mid \text{no line}]}\right] P(\theta,d) \tag{11.12}$$

Upon taking logarithms of Eq. (11.12), there results

$\log P[\theta,d \mid I(r,c) : (r,c) \in E(\theta,d)]$

$$= \sum_{(r,c) \in E(\theta,d)} \log P[I(r,c) \mid \theta,d] + \log P(\theta,d) - \sum_{(r,c) \in E(\theta,d)} \log P[I(r,c) \mid \text{no line}] \tag{11.13}$$

Define the Hough transform $H(\theta,d)$ by

$$H(\theta,d) = \log \; P[\theta,d \mid I(r,c) : (r,c) \in E(\theta,d)]$$

In the original Hough methodology, $I(r,c)$ is just a binary number: $I(r,c)$ takes the value 0 if a local line detector determines that most likely no line is passing through pixel (r,c), and $I(r,c)$ takes the value 1 if the local line detector determines that most likely some line is passing through pixel (r,c). Specializing our result to this case, we obtain that if the local detector characteristics are

$$P[I(r,c) \mid \theta,d] = \begin{cases} q(\theta,d) & \text{if } I(r,c) = 1 \text{ and } (r,c) \in E(\theta,d) \\ 1 - q(\theta,d) & \text{if } I(r,c) = 0 \text{ and } (r,c) \in E(\theta,d) \end{cases}$$

and

$$P[I(r,c) \mid \text{no line}] = \begin{cases} w & \text{if } I(r,c) = 1 \\ 1 - w & \text{if } I(r,c) = 0 \end{cases}$$

where $q(\theta,d)$ is a specified parameter function related to the edge operator employed, then the Hough transform $H(\theta,d)$ takes the form

$$H(\theta,d) = \log \; P(\theta,d) + \sum_{\substack{(r,c)\in E(\theta,d) \\ I(r,c)=1}} \log \; q(\theta,d) + \sum_{\substack{(r,c)\in E(\theta,d) \\ I(r,c)=0}} \log \; [1 - q(\theta,d)]$$

$$- \sum_{\substack{(r,c)\in E(\theta,d) \\ I(r,c)=1}} \log \; w - \sum_{\substack{(r,c)\in E(\theta,d) \\ I(r,c)=0}} \log \; (1 - w)$$

$$= \log \; P(\theta,d) + \sum_{\substack{(r,c)\in E(\theta,d) \\ I(r,c)=1}} \log \frac{q(\theta,d)}{w} - \sum_{\substack{(r,c)\in E(\theta,d) \\ I(r,c)=0}} \log \frac{1 - w}{1 - q(\theta,d)}$$

$$= \log \; P(\theta,d) + \#\{(r,c)\in E(\theta,d) \mid I(r,c) = 1\} \log \frac{q(\theta,d)}{w}$$

$$+ \#\{(r,c)\in E(\theta,d) \mid I(r,c) = 0\} \log \frac{1 - q(\theta,d)}{1 - w} \quad (11.14)$$

This is closely related to the quantity

$$H_0(\theta,d) = \#\{(r,c) \in E(\theta,d) \mid I(r,c) = 1\} \quad (11.15)$$

which is what Hough described in his patent.

Since all real images are finite in size, we can see an immediate problem inherent in the original Hough transform given by Eq. (11.15). The finiteness of the image causes different numbers of pixels to be in the set $E(\theta,d)$, the set of all pixels on the line segment having parameters (θ,d). Thus all other things being equal, those parameter values (θ,d) having larger sets $E(\theta,d)$ are more likely to have higher counts for $H_0(\theta,d)$ than other parameter values when no line is present with parameter value (θ,d). This was noticed by Cohen and Toussaint (1977), who recommended adjusting the counts in $H_0(\theta,d)$ according to the size of $E(\theta,d)$.

However, the addition of the $\log \frac{1-q}{1-w}$ term of Eq. (11.14) naturally handles this problem, since if there is no line, even though there are potentially more terms, the terms will be negative rather than positive.

In the modified Hough transform of O'Gorman and Clowes described in the previous section, $I(r,c)$ can be represented by a three-dimensional vector, $I(r,c) = [(B(r,c),\ G(r,c),\ T(r,c)]$, the first component being a binary number indicating whether or not a line passes through the pixel at (r,c); the second component being the gradient, a measure of edge strength of a line boundary; and the third being the angle of the edge, which is also the angle of the line boundary. O'Gorman and Clowes use the angle $T(r,c)$ as an estimate for θ. The parameter d is then directly determined by $d = r \sin \theta + c \cos \theta$. Instead of incrementing by one to compute $H(\theta,d)$, O'Gorman and Clowes increment by the gradient $G(r,c)$. Specifically they define the modified Hough transform $H_1(\theta,d)$ by

$$H_1(\theta,d) = \sum_{\substack{(r,c) \in E(\theta,d) \\ T(r,c)=\theta \\ B(r,c)=1}} G(r,c) \tag{11.16}$$

To understand the relationship between Eq. (11.16) and the Hough transform as we have defined it, we rewrite Eq. (11.13) as

$$H(\theta,d) = \sum_{(r,c) \in E(\theta,d)} \log \frac{P[I(r,c)|\theta,d]}{P[I(r,c)|\text{no line }]} + \log P(\theta,d) \tag{11.17}$$

in which case we see that what should be summed is log likelihoods and not gradient strength. If a pixel (r,c) in $E(\theta,d)$ has an angle $T(r,c)$ very much different from θ, then the log likelihood will be small. The closer $T(r,c)$ is to θ, the larger the log likelihood will be. In the O'Gorman and Clowes Eq. (11.16), the pixels in the summation are restricted to only those in $E(\theta,d)$ for which $T(r,c) = \theta$ and for which $B(r,c) = 1$. In Eq. (11.17) we find that all pixels in $E(\theta,d)$ must be in the summation.

11.7   Line Fitting

Here we give a procedure for the least-squares fitting of a line to the observed noisy values. We derive expressions for the estimated parameters of the fitted line and their variances, as well as a variance expression for the orientation of the line. Because we need to differentiate between the observed noisy values and the values before random-noise perturbing, we adopt a notational change in this and the following sections. We denote the noisy observed values by $(\hat{r}_n, \hat{c}_n)$ and the unknown values before noise perturbation by (r_n, c_n).

Suppose that noisy observations $(\hat{r}_n, \hat{c}_n)$ of points (r_n, c_n) that lie on a line $\alpha r_n + \beta c_n + \gamma = 0$ are given. Our model for $(\hat{r}_n, \hat{c}_n)$ is

$$\begin{aligned} \hat{r}_n &= r_n + \xi_n \\ \hat{c}_n &= c_n + \eta_n \end{aligned} \tag{11.18}$$

where we assume that the random variables ξ_n and η_n are independent and identically distributed, having mean 0 and variance σ^2, and that they come from a distribution that is an even function. Hence

$$E[\xi_n] = E[\eta_n] = 0$$

$$V[\xi_n] = V[\eta_n] = \sigma^2$$

$$E[\xi_n \xi_j] = \begin{cases} \sigma^2 & n = j \\ 0 & \text{otherwise} \end{cases} \tag{11.19}$$

$$E[\eta_n \eta_j] = \begin{cases} \sigma^2 & n = j \\ 0 & \text{otherwise} \end{cases}$$

$$E[\eta_n \xi_j] = 0$$

Dorff and Gurland (1961) use a similar model for the noise, but they use the representation $c = mr + b$ instead of the more general representation $\alpha r + \beta c + \gamma = 0$. By way of notation we define the following moments

$$\mu_r = \frac{1}{N} \sum_{n=1}^{N} r_n$$

$$\mu_c = \frac{1}{N} \sum_{n=1}^{N} c_n$$

$$\mu_{rr} = \frac{1}{N} \sum_{n=1}^{N} (r_n - \mu_r)^2 \tag{11.20}$$

$$\mu_{rc} = \frac{1}{N} \sum_{n=1}^{N} (r_n - \mu_r)(c_n - \mu_c)$$

$$\mu_{cc} = \frac{1}{N} \sum_{n=1}^{N} (c_n - \mu_c)^2$$

which directly relate to the unknown parameters α, β, and γ of the line on which the points (r_n, c_n) lie. It is easy to determine that

$$\alpha \mu_r + \beta \mu_c = -\gamma$$
$$\alpha \mu_{rr} + \beta \mu_{rc} = 0$$
$$\alpha \mu_{rc} + \beta \mu_{cc} = 0$$

from which $\mu_{rc}^2 = \mu_{rr}\mu_{cc}$,

$$\alpha = \frac{\text{sign}(\mu_{rc})\mu_{cc}}{\sqrt{\mu_{rr} + \mu_{cc}}} = \frac{\mu_{rc}}{\sqrt{\mu_{rr}^2 + \mu_{cc}^2}}, \quad \text{and} \quad \beta = \frac{-\mu_{rr}}{\sqrt{\mu_{rr}^2 + \mu_{rc}^2}}$$

Now from the noisy observations $(\hat{r}_n, \hat{c}_n)$ we must estimate the parameters of the unknown line. To do this we employ the principle of minimizing the squared residuals under the constraint that $\hat{\alpha}^2 + \hat{\beta}^2 = 1$. Using the Lagrange multiplier form, we define

$$\epsilon^2 = \sum_{n=1}^{N} (\hat{\alpha}\hat{r}_n + \hat{\beta}\hat{c}_n + \hat{\gamma})^2 - \lambda(\hat{\alpha}^2 + \hat{\beta}^2 - 1)N \qquad (11.21)$$

Upon taking the partial derivative of ϵ^2 with respect to $\hat{\gamma}$ and setting the partial derivative to zero, we have

$$\frac{\partial \epsilon^2}{\partial \hat{\gamma}} = 2 \sum_{n=1}^{N} (\hat{\alpha}\hat{r}_n + \hat{\beta}\hat{c}_n + \hat{\gamma}) = 0$$

Letting

$$\hat{\mu}_r = \frac{1}{N} \sum_{n=1}^{N} \hat{r}_n \qquad \text{and} \qquad \hat{\mu}_c = \frac{1}{N} \sum_{n=1}^{N} \hat{c}_n$$

we can obtain

$$\hat{\gamma} = -(\hat{\alpha}\hat{\mu}_r + \hat{\beta}\hat{\mu}_c) \qquad (11.22)$$

Hence

$$\epsilon^2 = \sum_{n=1}^{N} \left[\hat{\alpha}(\hat{r}_n - \hat{\mu}_r) + \hat{\beta}(\hat{c}_n - \hat{\mu}_c) \right]^2 - \lambda(\hat{\alpha}^2 + \hat{\beta}^2 - 1)N$$

Continuing to take partial derviatives of ϵ^2 with respect to $\hat{\alpha}$ and $\hat{\beta}$, we obtain

$$\frac{\partial \epsilon^2}{\partial \hat{\alpha}} = \sum_{n=1}^{N} 2 \left[\hat{\alpha}(\hat{r}_n - \hat{\mu}_r) + \hat{\beta}(\hat{c}_n - \hat{\mu}_c) \right] (\hat{r}_n - \hat{\mu}_r) - \lambda(2\hat{\alpha})N = 0$$

$$\frac{\partial \epsilon^2}{\partial \hat{\beta}} = \sum_{n=1}^{N} 2 \left[\hat{\alpha}(\hat{r}_n - \hat{\mu}_r) + \hat{\beta}(\hat{c}_n - \hat{\mu}_c) \right] (\hat{c}_n - \hat{\mu}_c) - \lambda(2\hat{\beta})N = 0$$

Letting

$$\hat{\mu}_{rr} = \frac{1}{N-1} \sum_{n=1}^{N} (\hat{r}_n - \hat{\mu}_r)^2$$

$$\hat{\mu}_{cc} = \frac{1}{N-1} \sum_{n=1}^{N} (\hat{c}_n - \hat{\mu}_c)^2$$

$$\hat{\mu}_{rc} = \frac{1}{N-1} \sum_{n=1}^{N} (\hat{x} - \mu_r)(\hat{c}_n - \mu_c)$$

we obtain upon substitution

$$\begin{pmatrix} \hat{\mu}_{rr} & \hat{\mu}_{rc} \\ \hat{\mu}_{rc} & \hat{\mu}_{cc} \end{pmatrix} \begin{pmatrix} \hat{\alpha} \\ \hat{\beta} \end{pmatrix} = \lambda \begin{pmatrix} \hat{\alpha} \\ \hat{\beta} \end{pmatrix} \qquad (11.23)$$

So the sought-after $\begin{pmatrix} \hat{\alpha} \\ \hat{\beta} \end{pmatrix}$ must be an eigenvector of the sample covariance matrix. But which eigenvector? The one we want must minimize

$$\sum_{n=1}^{N} \left[\hat{\alpha}(\hat{r}_n - \hat{\mu}_r) + \hat{\beta}(\hat{c}_n - \hat{\mu}_c) \right]^2$$

$$= (N-1)(\hat{\alpha} \quad \hat{\beta}) \begin{pmatrix} \hat{\mu}_{rr} & \hat{\mu}_{rc} \\ \hat{\mu}_{rc} & \hat{\mu}_{cc} \end{pmatrix} \begin{pmatrix} \hat{\alpha} \\ \hat{\beta} \end{pmatrix}$$

$$= (N-1)(\hat{\alpha} \quad \hat{\beta}) \lambda \begin{pmatrix} \hat{\alpha} \\ \hat{\beta} \end{pmatrix} = (N-1)\lambda$$

Hence the eigenvector $\begin{pmatrix} \hat{\alpha} \\ \hat{\beta} \end{pmatrix}$ must correspond to that eigenvalue $\hat{\lambda}$ of the sample covariance matrix having the smallest eigenvalue.

Any eigenvalue λ must satisfy

$$\left[\begin{pmatrix} \hat{\mu}_{rr} & \hat{\mu}_{rc} \\ \hat{\mu}_{rc} & \hat{\mu}_{cc} \end{pmatrix} - \lambda \begin{pmatrix} 1 & 0 \\ 0 & 1 \end{pmatrix} \right] \begin{pmatrix} \hat{\alpha} \\ \hat{\beta} \end{pmatrix} = 0$$

and this means that the determinant

$$\begin{vmatrix} \hat{\mu}_{rr} - \lambda & \hat{\mu}_{rc} \\ \hat{\mu}_{rc} & \hat{\mu}_{cc} - \lambda \end{vmatrix} = 0$$

Therefore

$$\hat{\lambda} = \frac{(\hat{\mu}_{rr} + \hat{\mu}_{cc}) \pm \sqrt{(\hat{\mu}_{rr} + \hat{\mu}_{cc})^2 - 4(\hat{\mu}_{rr}\hat{\mu}_{cc} - \hat{\mu}_{rc}^2)}}{2}$$

$$= \frac{(\hat{\mu}_{rr} + \hat{\mu}_{cc}) \pm \sqrt{(\hat{\mu}_{rr} - \hat{\mu}_{cc})^2 + 4\hat{\mu}_{rc}^2}}{2} \tag{11.24}$$

The smaller eigenvalue corresponds to the minus sign. With $\hat{\lambda}$ determined, the corresponding unit length eigenvector can be determined.

$$\begin{pmatrix} \hat{\alpha} \\ \hat{\beta} \end{pmatrix} = \frac{1}{\sqrt{\hat{\mu}_{rc}^2 + (\lambda - \hat{\mu}_{rr})^2}} \begin{pmatrix} \hat{\mu}_{rc} \\ \lambda - \hat{\mu}_{rr} \end{pmatrix} = \frac{1}{\sqrt{\hat{\sigma}_{xy}^2 + (\hat{\mu}_{cc} - \lambda)^2}} \begin{pmatrix} \hat{\mu}_{cc} - \lambda \\ -\hat{\mu}_{rc} \end{pmatrix}$$

$$\tag{11.25}$$

11.7.1 Variance of the Fitted Parameters

The randomness of the observed data points in the noisy case leads to a randomness in the estimated parameters $\hat{\alpha}$ and $\hat{\beta}$. The question we now address is: How can the expected values of $\hat{\alpha}$ and $\hat{\beta}$ and the variances of $\hat{\alpha}$ and $\hat{\beta}$ be determined? We consider the case for $\hat{\alpha}$. From Eq. (11.25)

$$\hat{\alpha} = \frac{\hat{\mu}_{rc}}{\sqrt{\hat{\mu}_{rc}^2 + (\lambda - \hat{\mu}_{rr})^2}}$$

To find the expected value and variance of $\hat{\alpha}$, we need a way by which the expected value and variance of $\hat{\mu}_{rc}$ and $\hat{\lambda} - \hat{\mu}_{rr}$ can be related to $\hat{\alpha}$. We expand $\hat{\alpha}$ around the point $(\mu_{rc}, 0, \mu_{rr})$ in a first-order expansion. There results

$$
\hat{\alpha} = \frac{\mu_{rc}}{\sqrt{\mu_{rc}^2 + \mu_{rr}^2}} + (\hat{\mu}_{rc} - \mu_{rc})\frac{\mu_{rr}^2}{(\mu_{rc}^2 + \mu_{rr}^2)^{\frac{3}{2}}}
$$

$$
+ (\hat{\lambda} - 0)\frac{\mu_{rc}\mu_{rr}}{(\mu_{rc}^2 + \mu_{rr}^2)^{\frac{3}{2}}} + (\hat{\mu}_{rr} - \mu_{rr})\frac{-\mu_{rc}\mu_{rr}}{(\mu_{rc}^2 + \mu_{rr}^2)^{\frac{3}{2}}}
$$

Using the relation $\mu_{rc} = \text{sign}(\mu_{rc})\sigma_x\sigma_y$, which is true under our model, and noting that

$$
\alpha = \frac{\mu_{rc}}{\sqrt{\mu_{rc}^2 + \mu_{rr}^2}} \quad \text{and} \quad \beta = \frac{-\mu_{rr}}{\sqrt{\mu_{rc}^2 + \mu_{rr}^2}}
$$

we obtain

$$
\hat{\alpha} = \alpha + \frac{1}{\mu_{rr} + \mu_{cc}} \left[(\hat{\mu}_{rc} - \mu_{rc})(-\beta) + (\hat{\lambda} - \hat{\mu}_{rr} + \mu_{rr})\alpha \right] \tag{11.26}
$$

Then to determine $E[\hat{\alpha}]$ we simply take expectations on both sides of Eq. (11.26):

$$
E[\hat{\alpha}] = \alpha + \frac{1}{\mu_{rr} + \mu_{cc}} \left[-E(\hat{\mu}_{rc} - \mu_{rc})\beta + E(\hat{\lambda} - \hat{\mu}_{rr} + \mu_{rr})\alpha \right]
$$

To determine $V[\hat{\alpha}] = E\left[(\hat{\alpha} - \alpha)^2\right]$,

$$
E\left[(\hat{\alpha} - \alpha)^2\right] = \frac{1}{(\mu_{rr} + \mu_{cc})^2} E\left\{ \left[-(\hat{\mu}_{rc} - \mu_{rc})\beta + (\hat{\lambda} - \hat{\mu}_{rr} + \mu_{rr})\alpha \right]^2 \right\}
$$

To complete our calculation, we need expressions for $E[\hat{\mu}_{rc} - \mu_{rc}]$, $E[\hat{\lambda} - \hat{\mu}_{rr} + \mu_{rr}]$, $E[(\hat{\mu}_{rc} - \mu_{rc})^2]$, $E[(\hat{\lambda} - \hat{\mu}_{rr} + \mu_{rr})^2]$, and $E[(\hat{\mu}_{rc} - \mu_{rc})(\hat{\lambda} - \hat{\mu}_{rr} + \mu_{rr})]$. Some of these are tedious to calculate, so we leave the calculation for an exercise.

$$
E[\hat{\mu}_{rc} - \mu_{rc}] = 0
$$

$$
E[\hat{\lambda} - \hat{\mu}_{rr} + \mu_{rr}] = 0
$$

$$
E\left[(\hat{\mu}_{rc} - \mu_{rc})^2\right] = \frac{\sigma^2(\mu_{rr} + \mu_{cc} + \sigma^2)}{N - 1} \tag{11.27}
$$

$$
E\left[(\hat{\lambda} - \hat{\mu}_{rr} + \mu_{rr})^2\right] = \frac{4\sigma^2\mu_{rr}(\mu_{rr} + \mu_{cc} + \sigma^2)}{(N - 1)(\mu_{rr} + \mu_{cc})}
$$

$$
E\left[(\hat{\mu}_{rc} - \mu_{rc})(\hat{\lambda} - \hat{\mu}_{rr} + \mu_{rr})\right] = \frac{2\sigma^2(\mu_{rr} + \mu_{cc} + \sigma^2)}{(N - 1)}\alpha\beta
$$

Hence

$$E\left[(\hat{\alpha} - \alpha)^2\right] = \frac{1}{(\mu_{rr} + \mu_{cc})^2} \left\{\beta^2 E\left[(\hat{\mu}_{rc} - \mu_{rc})^2\right]\right.$$

$$\left. - 2\alpha\beta E\left[(\hat{\mu}_{rc} - \mu_{rc})(\hat{\lambda} - \hat{\mu}_{rr} + \mu_{rr})\right] + \alpha^2 E\left[(\hat{\lambda} - \hat{\mu}_{rr} + \mu_{rr})^2\right]\right\}$$

$$= \frac{1}{(\mu_{rr} + \mu_{rr})^2} \left\{\beta^2 \frac{\sigma^2(\mu_{rr} + \mu_{cc} + \sigma^2)}{N - 1}\right.$$

$$\left. - 4\alpha^2\beta^2 \frac{\sigma^2(\mu_{rr} + \mu_{cc} + \sigma^2)}{N - 1} + \alpha^2 \frac{4\sigma^2\mu_{rr}(\mu_{rr} + \mu_{cc} + \sigma^2)}{(N - 1)(\mu_{rr} + \mu_{cc})}\right\}$$

Using the fact that $\beta^2 = \frac{\mu_{rr}^2}{\mu_{rr}^2 + \mu_{cc}^2}$, we obtain

$$V[\hat{\alpha}] = \frac{\beta^2\sigma^2(\mu_{rr} + \mu_{cc} + \sigma^2)}{(N - 1)(\mu_{rr} + \mu_{cc})^2} \tag{11.28}$$

Using the relation

$$\hat{\beta} = \frac{-\hat{\mu}_{rc}}{\sqrt{\hat{\mu}_{rc} + (\hat{\mu}_{cc} - \hat{\lambda})^2}}$$

a symmetric calculation for $\hat{\beta}$ yields

$$\hat{\beta} = \beta + \frac{1}{\mu_{rr} + \mu_{cc}} \left[(\hat{\mu}_{rc} - \mu_{rc})(-\alpha) + (\hat{\lambda} - \hat{\mu}_{cc} + \mu_{cc})\beta\right] \tag{11.29}$$

from which

$$E\left[(\hat{\beta} - \beta)^2\right] = \frac{1}{(\mu_{rr} + \mu_{cc})^2} \left\{\alpha^2 \frac{\sigma^2(\mu_{rr} + \mu_{cc} + \sigma^2)}{N - 1}\right.$$

$$\left. - 4\alpha^2\beta^2 \frac{\sigma^2(\mu_{rr} + \mu_{cc} + \sigma^2)}{N - 1} + \frac{4\sigma^2\mu_{cc}\beta^2(\mu_{rr} + \mu_{cc} + \sigma^2)}{(N - 1)(\mu_{rr} + \mu_{cc})}\right\}$$

Therefore

$$V[\hat{\beta}] = \frac{\alpha^2\sigma^2(\mu_{rr} + \mu_{cc} + \sigma^2)}{(N - 1)(\mu_{rr} + \mu_{cc})^2} \tag{11.30}$$

From Eqs. (11.26) and (11.30) we can determine the covariance between $\hat{\alpha}$ and $\hat{\beta}$.

$$\text{Cov}(\hat{\alpha}, \hat{\beta}) = E[(\hat{\alpha} - \alpha)(\hat{\beta} - \beta)]$$

$$= \frac{1}{(\mu_{rr} + \mu_{cc})^2} E[\alpha\beta(\hat{\mu}_{rc} - \mu_{rc})^2 - \alpha^2(\hat{\mu}_{rc} - \mu_{rc})(\hat{\lambda} - \hat{\mu}_{rr} + \mu_{rr}) -$$

$$\beta^2(\hat{\mu}_{rc} - \mu_{rc})(\hat{\lambda} - \hat{\mu}_{cc} + \mu_{cc}) + \alpha\beta(\hat{\lambda} - \hat{\mu}_{rr} + \mu_{rr})(\hat{\lambda} - \hat{\mu}_{cc} + \mu_{cc})]$$

$$= \frac{-\alpha\beta\sigma^2(\mu_{rr} + \mu_{cc} + \sigma^2)}{(N - 1)(\mu_{rr} + \mu_{cc})^2} \tag{11.31}$$

To determine the variance of $\hat{\gamma}$, we recall from Eq. (11.22) that

$$\gamma = -(\alpha\mu_r + \beta\mu_c) \quad \text{and} \quad \hat{\gamma} = -(\hat{\alpha}\hat{\mu}_r + \hat{\beta}\hat{\mu}_c).$$

Hence

$$V[\hat{\gamma}] = E[(\hat{\gamma} - \gamma)^2]$$
$$= E\left[(-\hat{\alpha}(\mu_r + \bar{\xi}) - \hat{\beta}(\mu_c + \bar{\eta}) + \alpha\mu_r + \beta\mu_c)^2\right]$$

$$\text{where } \bar{\xi} = \frac{1}{N}\sum_{n=1}^{N}\xi_n$$

$$\bar{\eta} = \frac{1}{N}\sum_{n=1}^{N}\eta_n$$

and ξ_n and η_n constitute the random noise as given in Eq. (11.18). After some simplification and rearrangement,

$$V[\hat{\gamma}] = \mu_r^2 E[(\hat{\alpha} - \alpha)^2] + \mu_c^2 E\left[(\hat{\beta} - \beta)^2\right]$$
$$+ 2\mu_r\mu_c E\left[(\hat{\alpha} - \alpha)(\hat{\beta} - \beta)\right] + E\left[(\hat{\alpha}\bar{\xi} + \hat{\beta}\bar{\eta})^2\right]$$
$$+ 2\mu_r E\left[(\hat{\alpha} - \alpha)(\hat{\alpha}\bar{\xi} + \hat{\beta}\bar{\eta})\right] + 2\mu_c E\left[(\hat{\beta} - \beta)(\hat{\alpha}\bar{\xi} + \hat{\beta}\bar{\eta})\right]$$

As indicated in Exercise 11.5,

$$E\left[(\hat{\alpha}\bar{\xi} + \hat{\beta}\bar{\eta})^2\right] = \sigma^2\left(V[\hat{\alpha}] + V[\hat{\beta}] + 1\right)$$
$$E\left[(\hat{\alpha} - \alpha)(\hat{\alpha}\bar{\xi} + \hat{\beta}\bar{\eta})\right] = 0$$
$$E\left[(\hat{\beta} - \beta)(\hat{\alpha}\bar{\xi} + \hat{\beta}\bar{\eta})\right] = 0$$

Therefore

$$V[\hat{\gamma}] = \mu_r^2 V[\hat{\alpha}] + \mu_c^2 V[\hat{\beta}] + 2\mu_r\mu_c \text{Cov}(\hat{\alpha}, \hat{\beta})$$
$$+ \sigma^2\left(V[\hat{\alpha}] + V[\hat{\beta}] + 1\right)$$
$$= \sigma^2\left\{1 + \frac{(\mu_{rr} + \mu_{cc} + \sigma^2)}{(N-1)(\mu_{rr} + \mu_{cc})^2}[(\alpha\mu_c - \beta\mu_r)^2 + \sigma^2]\right\} \quad (11.32)$$

The covariance of $\hat{\alpha}$ and $\hat{\beta}$ is

$$\text{Cov}(\hat{\alpha}, \hat{\gamma}) = E\left[(\hat{\alpha} - \alpha)(\hat{\beta} - \beta)\right]$$
$$= E\left\{(\hat{\alpha} - \alpha)\left[-(\hat{\alpha} - \alpha)\mu_r - (\hat{\beta} - \beta)\mu_c - (\hat{\alpha}\bar{\xi} + \hat{\beta}\bar{\eta})\right]\right\}$$
$$= -\mu_r V[\hat{\alpha}] - \mu_c \text{Cov}(\hat{\alpha}, \hat{\beta})$$
$$= \beta(-\mu_r\beta + \mu_c\alpha)\frac{\sigma^2(\mu_{rr} + \mu_{cc} + \sigma^2)}{(N-1)(\mu_{rr} + \mu_{cc})^2} \quad (11.33)$$

Similarly,

$$\text{Cov}(\hat{\beta}, \hat{\gamma}) = \alpha(\mu_r \beta - \mu_c \alpha) \frac{\sigma^2(\mu_{rr} + \mu_{cc} + \sigma^2)}{(N-1)(\mu_{rr} + \mu_{cc})^2} \qquad (11.34)$$

The expression for $E\left[(\hat{\alpha} - \alpha)^2\right]$ and $E\left[(\hat{\beta} - \beta)^2\right]$ of Eqs. (11.28) and (11.30) can be used to generate an expression for the variance of the angle $\hat{\theta}$ defined by $\cos\hat{\theta} = \hat{\alpha}, \sin\hat{\theta} = \hat{\beta}$. A first-order expansion of $\cos\hat{\theta}$ around θ, where $\cos\theta = \alpha$, and a first-order expansion of $\sin\hat{\theta}$ around θ, where $\sin\theta = \beta$, give

$$\cos\hat{\theta} = \cos\theta + (\hat{\theta} - \theta)(-\sin\theta)$$

$$\sin\hat{\theta} = \sin\theta + (\hat{\theta} - \theta)\cos\theta$$

Using this approximation, we obtain

$$E\left[(\cos\hat{\theta} - \cos\theta)^2\right] + E\left[(\sin\hat{\theta} - \sin\theta)^2\right] \cong E\left[(\hat{\theta} - \theta)^2\right](\sin^2\theta + \cos^2\theta)$$
$$\cong E\left[(\hat{\theta} - \theta)^2\right]$$

Since

$$E\left[(\cos\hat{\theta} - \cos\theta)^2\right] + E\left[(\sin\hat{\theta} - \sin\theta)^2\right] \cong E\left[(\hat{\alpha} - \alpha)^2\right] + E\left[(\hat{\beta} - \beta)^2\right]$$

upon substituting there results

$$E\left[(\hat{\theta} - \theta)^2\right] = E\left[(\hat{\alpha} - \alpha)^2 + (\hat{\beta} - \beta)^2\right]$$

$$= \frac{\sigma^2(\mu_{rr} + \mu_{cc} + \sigma^2)(\alpha^2 + \beta^2)}{(N-1)(\mu_{rr} + \mu_{cc})^2}$$

$$= \frac{\sigma^2(\mu_{rr} + \mu_{cc} + \sigma^2)}{(N-1)(\mu_{rr} + \mu_{cc})^2} \qquad (11.35)$$

Finally, when $\sigma^2 < \mu_{rr} + \mu_{cc}$,

$$E\left[(\hat{\theta} - \theta)^2\right] = \frac{\sigma^2}{(\mu_{rr} + \mu_{cc})(N-1)}$$

11.7.2 Principal-Axis Curve Fit

Suppose that the curve to be fitted can be represented in the form

$$0 = f(r,c) = \sum_{k=1}^{K} \alpha_k f_k(r,c)$$

where the functions $f_k(r,c)$, $k = 1, \ldots, K$ are given and the unknown parameters

$\alpha_1, \ldots, \alpha_k$ satisfy the constraint

$$\sum_{k=1}^{K} \alpha_k^2 = 1$$

If the observed noisy points are $(\hat{r}_n, \hat{c}_n)$, $n = 1, \ldots, N$, a fit that minimizes $\sum_{n=1}^{N} f(r_n, c_n)^2$ can be determined by the principal-axis technique.

The objective function to be minimized is

$$\epsilon^2 = \sum_{n=1}^{N} f(\hat{r}_n, \hat{c}_n)^2 - \lambda(\sum_{k=1}^{K} \alpha_k^2 - 1)$$

$$= \sum_{n=1}^{N} \left[\sum_{k=1}^{K} \alpha_k f_k(r_n, c_n) \right]^2 - \lambda(\sum_{k=1}^{K} \alpha_k^2 - 1)$$

Taking partial derivatives of ϵ^2 with respect to each α_k results in the system

$$FF'\alpha = \lambda\alpha$$

where

$$F = \begin{pmatrix} f_1(\hat{r}_1, \hat{c}_1) & f_1(\hat{r}_2, \hat{c}_2) & \cdots & f_1(\hat{r}_n, \hat{c}_n) \\ f_2(\hat{r}_1, \hat{c}_1) & f_2(\hat{r}_2, \hat{c}_2) & \cdots & f_2(\hat{r}_n, \hat{c}_n) \\ \vdots & \vdots & & \vdots \\ f_K(\hat{r}_1, \hat{c}_1) & f_K(\hat{r}_2, \hat{c}_2) & \cdots & f_K(\hat{r}_n, \hat{c}_n) \end{pmatrix} \quad \text{and} \quad \alpha = \begin{pmatrix} \alpha_1 \\ \alpha_2 \\ \vdots \\ \alpha_k \end{pmatrix}$$

This means that α must be an eigenvector of FF'. To see which one, note that

$$\sum_{n=1}^{N} \left[\sum_{k=1}^{K} \alpha_k f_k(\hat{r}_n, \hat{c}_n) \right]^2 = \alpha'FF'\alpha$$

$$= \alpha'\lambda\alpha = \lambda$$

Hence α must be that eigenvector of FF' having the smallest eigenvalue.

The principal-axis curve fit is obviously a generalization of the line-fitting idea discussed at the beginning of Section 11.6. Simple curves such as conics may be fit with the principal-axis technique by taking $f_1(r, c) = 1, f_2(r, c) = r, f_3(r, c) = c, f_4(r, c) = r^2, f_5(r, c) = rc$, and $f_6(r, c) = c^2$. Bookstein (1979) gives a modification of this conic fitting that makes the fit invariant under rotation, translation, and change of scale. Instead of minimizing

$$\epsilon^2 = \sum_{n=1}^{N} \left(\sum_{k=1}^{6} \alpha_k f(\hat{r}_n, \hat{c}_n) \right)^2$$

subject to $\sum_{k=1}^{6} \alpha_k^2 = 1$, he minimizes ϵ^2 subject to $\alpha_4^2 + \frac{1}{2}\alpha_5^2 + \alpha_6^2 = 1$. However, as we shall see in the next section, the objective function that the original technique or Bookstein's modified technique minimizes is not the most appropriate one. Indeed, experience with the principal-axis technique has shown that the fit it provides to conics is often too eccentric, because the technique, in effect, gives too much influence to outlier points.

11.8   Region-of-Support Determination

Teh and Chin (1989) argue that the determination of the region of support for the calculation of the straight-line fits that are associated with tangential angle deflection or curvature are of primary importance. Techniques that use a fixed or nonadaptive region of support easily fail on curves that have segments of widely varying lengths. If the region of support is too large, fine features will be smoothed out. If the region of support is too small, many corner points or dominant points can be produced. Davis (1977), for example, gives instances where this happens.

Teh and Chin suggest that the appropriate region of support for a corner point is the largest symmetrically placed subsequence for which the chord joining the subsequence endpoints has maximal length. To prevent every point of a digital circle from being assigned a corner point, they add a second, alternative condition requiring that the ratio of the perpendicular distance between the point and the chord between the arc subsequences to the chord length be maximal. Formally, the region of support D_n for an observed point $(\hat{r}_n, \hat{c}_n)$ is given by

$$D_n = \{n - K, \ldots, n + K \mid \text{(a) } l_{n1} \leq l_{n2} \leq \ldots \leq l_{nK} \geq l_{nK+1}$$
$$\text{or (b) } \frac{d_{n1}}{l_{n1}} \leq \frac{d_{n2}}{l_{n2}} \leq \ldots \leq \frac{d_{nK}}{l_{nK}} \geq \frac{d_{nK+1}}{l_{nK+1}}\}$$

where

$$l_{nk} = \sqrt{(\hat{r}_{n-k} - \hat{r}_{n+k})^2 + (\hat{c}_{n-k} - \hat{c}_{n+k})^2}$$

and

$$d_{nk} = \max_{j=-k,\ldots,k} \sqrt{(\hat{r}_n - \hat{r}_{n+j})^2 + (\hat{c}_n - \hat{c}_{n+j})^2}$$

Teh and Chin (1988, 1989) give some experimental results demonstrating the efficacy of this way to determine the region of support, and they compare their results against some of the other techniques.

Another way to determine the region of support can be obtained from Eq. (11.35), the variance of the angle of the fitted line. At point $(\hat{r}_n, \hat{c}_n)$ of the arc sequence, the angle of the fitted line using points $(\hat{r}_{n-k}, \hat{c}_{n-k}), \ldots, (\hat{r}_n, \hat{c}_n)$ has variance

$V(n - k, n)$, where

$$V(i,j) = \frac{\sigma^2[\mu_{rr}(i,j) + \mu_{cc}(i,j) + \sigma^2]}{(j - i)[\mu_{rr}(i,j) + \mu_{cc}(i,j)]}$$

$$\mu_{rr}(i,j) = \frac{1}{j - i + 1} \sum_{k=i}^{j} [c_k - \mu_r(i,j)]^2$$

$$\mu_{cc}(i,j) = \frac{1}{j - i + 1} \sum_{k=i}^{j} [r_k - \mu_c(i,j)]^2$$

$$\mu_r(i,j) = \frac{1}{j - i + 1} \sum_{k=i}^{j} r_i$$

$$\mu_c(i,j) = \frac{1}{j - i + 1} \sum_{k=i}^{j} c_i$$

for $j > i$.

Likewise the angle of the fitted line using the noisy observed points $(\hat{r}_{n+1}, \hat{c}_{n+1})$, $\ldots, (\hat{r}_{n+k+1}, \hat{c}_{n+k+1})$ has variance $V(n + 1, n + 1 + k)$. The total variance around the endpoints $(\hat{r}_n, \hat{c}_n)$ and $(\hat{r}_{n+1}, \hat{c}_{n+1})$ is then $V(n - k, n) + V(n + 1, n + 1 + k)$. So long as the observed points $(\hat{r}_{n-k}, \hat{c}_{n-k}), \ldots, (\hat{r}_n, \hat{c}_n)$ are noisy observations of points lying on the same line and the observed points $(\hat{r}_{n+1}, \hat{c}_{n+1}), \ldots, (\hat{r}_{n+1+k}, \hat{c}_{n+1+k})$ are noisy observations of points lying on the same line, $V(n - k, n) + V(n + 1, n + 1 + k)$ will be decreasing as k increases. However, as soon as a point that is not a noisy observation of a point lying on the predecessor or successor line is included in either the predecessor sequence or the successor sequence, $V(n - k, n) + V(n + 1, n + 1 + k)$ increases. This motivates defining the region of support around the right endpoint $(\hat{r}_n, \hat{c}_n)$ by

$$\{n - k, \ldots, n \mid \hat{V}(n + 1 - k_o, n) + \hat{V}(n + 1, n + k_o) \geq \cdots$$
$$\geq \hat{V}(n + 1 + k, n) + \hat{V}(n + 1, n + k)$$
$$\leq \hat{V}(n + k, n) + \hat{V}(n + 1, n + k + 1)\}$$

and around the left endpoint $(\hat{r}_{n+1}, \hat{c}_{n+1})$ by

$$\{n + 1, \ldots, n + 1 + k \mid \hat{V}(n + 2 - k_o, n + 1) + \hat{V}(n + 1, n + k_o) \geq \cdots$$
$$\geq \hat{V}(n + 2 - k, n + 1) + \hat{V}(n + 1, n + k)$$
$$\leq \hat{V}(n + 1 - k, n + 1) + \hat{V}(n + 1, n + k + 1)\}$$

where $\hat{V}$ means V with the measured $\hat{\mu}_{rr}, \hat{\mu}_{rc}, \hat{\mu}_{cc}, \hat{\mu}_r, \hat{\mu}_c$ instead of the true values $\mu_{rr}, \mu_{rc}, \mu_{cc}, \mu_r, \mu_c$, and k_o is the given minimum number of points for a line fit.

It is possible for the right endpoint of the left line segment and the left endpoint of the right line segment to be identical. In this case, for each point n, the quantity to be minimized is $V(n - k, n) + V(n, n + k)$, where $k \geq k_o$. If the leftmost endpoint of the left segment and the rightmost endpoint of the right segment are approximately known, then the corner point can be located at index n, where n minimizes $v(n) = V(k_o, n) + V(n, N - k_o + 1)$, 1 is the index of the leftmost endpoint of the left segment, and N is the index of the rightmost endpoint of the right segment. However, if the minimizing n is not within $N/2$ of the middle of the sequence, there will be a bias to the result. The bias can be removed by limiting the segment with the greater number of points to be no more than three times the number of points in the smaller segment.

EXAMPLE 11.1

Table 11.1 lists a sequence of 24 row-column pairs of points on two noisy line segments meeting at a corner point of about $105°$. The digital curve defined by this sequence is shown in Fig. 11.12(a). Shown in Fig. 11.12(b) is the log of the variance v as a function of point index n, where $v(n) = V(k_o, n) + V(n, N - k_o + 1), k_o = 4$, and $N = 24$. Notice the sharp minimum that occurs at $n = 14$, the corner point.

Table 11.1   The points in an example digital arc sequence. r_n is the row number and c_n is the column number

n	r_n	c_n	n	r_n	c_n
1	10	10	13	17	22
2	11	11	14	17	24
3	12	12	15	17	26
4	12	13	16	16	26
5	12	14	17	15	27
6	12	15	18	14	27
7	13	16	19	13	28
8	14	17	20	12	29
9	14	18	21	11	31
10	14	19	22	10	31
11	15	20	23	9	32
12	16	21	24	8	32

11.9   Robust Line Fitting

We now consider a reformulation of the line-fitting problem that provides a fit insensitive to a few outlier points. First we give a least-squares formulation and then modify it to make it robust. Let the equation of the line be $\alpha r + \beta c + \gamma = 0$,

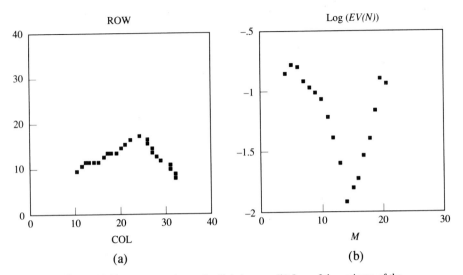

Figure 11.12 (a) Twenty-four point digital curve. (b) Log of the variance of the digital curve as a function of n, where $v(n) = V(k_o, n) + V(n, N - k_o + 1), k_o = 4$, and $N = 24$.

and let

$$A = \begin{pmatrix} r_1 & c_1 & 1 \\ r_2 & c_2 & 1 \\ & \vdots & \\ r_N & c_N & 1 \end{pmatrix}_{N \times 3}$$

$$p = (\alpha, \beta, \gamma)'$$

$$\epsilon = Ap$$

where ϵ is a fitting-error vector. Then, in the weighted least-squares sense, one way to formulate the problem is to find a vector p that minimizes the total weighted fitting error $\epsilon' P \epsilon$ subject to the condition that $\|p\| = 1$, where the weight matrix P is a diagonal matrix.

$$P = WW = \begin{pmatrix} w_1^2 & & \\ & \ddots & \\ & & w_N^2 \end{pmatrix}$$

If we know the uncertainty associated with each point (r_i, c_i), expressed as a variance σ_i^2, we can take $\frac{1}{\sigma_i^2}$ terms as the diagonal elements of the weight matrix P.

An iterative robust solution can be obtained to the line-fitting problem by having the weight matrix be computed iteratively from the previous iteration to best estimate the vector p. Let $P^k = W_k W_k$ be the weight matrix in the kth iteration, and let the singular-value decomposition of $W_k A$ be

$$W_k A = USV'$$

where

$$U = (u_1, \ldots, u_N)_{N \times N}$$

$$S = \begin{pmatrix} s_1 & 0 & 0 \\ 0 & s_2 & 0 \\ 0 & 0 & s_3 \\ 0 & 0 & 0 \\ & \vdots & \\ 0 & 0 & 0 \end{pmatrix}_{N \times 3}$$

$$V = (v_1, v_2, v_3)_{3 \times 3}$$

In the singular-value decomposition, both U and V are orthonormal matrices. Without loss of generality, we may assume that $s_1 \geq s_2 \geq s_3$. Then the total weighted fitting error becomes

$$\begin{aligned} \epsilon' P_k \epsilon &= p' A' P A p \\ &= p'(USV')'(USV')p \\ &= p'VS^2V'p \end{aligned}$$

This error has minimum value s_3^2 by taking $p = v_3$. For $p = v_3$, the weighted fitting error $W_k \epsilon$ can be expressed as

$$\begin{aligned} W_k \epsilon &= W_k A p \\ &= USV'v_3 \\ &= US \begin{pmatrix} 0 \\ 0 \\ 1 \end{pmatrix} \\ &= (u_1, \ldots, u_N) \begin{pmatrix} 0 \\ 0 \\ s_3 \\ 0 \\ \vdots \\ 0 \end{pmatrix} \\ &= s_3 u_3 \end{aligned}$$

and the total error is

$$\epsilon' P_k \epsilon = s_3^2$$

Now let U_2 be the $N \times (N - 2)$ matrix that consists of the columns 3 through

N of the matrix U, that is, $U_2 = (u_3, \ldots, u_N)$. Define the redundancy matrix $R = \{r_{ij}\} = U_2 U_2'$. Then

$$r_{ii} = \sum_{j=3}^{N} u_{ij}^2 \qquad \text{and}$$

$$\sum_{i=1}^{N} r_{ii} = \sum_{i=1}^{N} \sum_{j=3}^{N} u_{ij}^2$$

$$= \sum_{j=3}^{N} \sum_{i=1}^{N} u_{ij}^2$$

$$= \sum_{j=3}^{N} |u_j|^2$$

$$= N - 2$$

Let $e_i = \frac{\epsilon_i}{r_{ii}}$ and define the weight matrix in the $(k+1)$th iteration W_{k+1} as

$$W_{k+1} = \begin{pmatrix} w_1 & & \\ & \ddots & \\ & & w_N \end{pmatrix}$$

where

$$w_i = \begin{cases} \left[1 - \left(\frac{e_i}{cZ}\right)^2\right], & \text{if } \left(\frac{e_i}{cZ}\right)^2 < 1 \\ 0, & \text{otherwise} \end{cases}$$

and where c is a constant and Z is the median of $|e_i|$.

11.10   Least-Squares Curve Fitting

Suppose that a set of row-column positions $\{(\hat{r}_n, \hat{c}_n)\}_{n=1}^{N}$ has been determined by any of the arc extraction techniques. As in the case of fitting a line, the positions $(\hat{r}_n, \hat{c}_n)$, $n = 1, \ldots, N$ are assumed to be noisy observations of points coming from some curve $f(r, c, w) = 0$ whose parameter vector, w, must be estimated. That is,

$$\hat{r}_n = r_n + \xi_n$$

$$\hat{c}_n = c_n + \eta_n$$

where $f(r_n, c_n, w) = 0$. In this section we treat the problem of determining the free parameters w of the curve f that make the curve f a best fit, in the least-squares sense, to the given positions $(\hat{r}_n, \hat{c}_n)$, $n = 1, \ldots, N$. The problem we must solve, therefore, is to determine the parameter vector w and points (r_n, c_n), $n = 1, \ldots, N$ that lie on the curve and are closest to $(\hat{r}_n, \hat{c}_n)$, $n = 1, \ldots, N$, respectively.

Hence we seek w and (r_n, c_n), $n = 1, \ldots, N$, to minimize

$$\sum_{n=1}^{N} (r_n - \hat{r}_n)^2 + (c_n - \hat{c}_n)^2$$

subject to the constraint that $f(r_n, c_n, w) = 0$, $n = 1, \ldots, N$.

Note that this problem, which is to determine the parameters of the curve that minimize the sum of the squared distances between the noisy observed points and the curve, is not the same as the problem of determining the parameters w of the curve f that minimize

$$\sum_{n=1}^{N} f(r_n, c_n, w)^2$$

which can loosely be thought of as the fitting error.

The difference between the two formulations is illustrated geometrically in Fig. 11.13 for the simple case of the curve $y = x^2 - a$. The figure makes clear that it is necessary to determine how to calculate the closest point (r, c) on a fixed curve f to a given point (r_o, c_o). This problem is to determine a point (r, c) that minimizes $(r - r_o)^2 + (c - c_o)^2$, subject to the constraint $f(r, c) = 0$. Here, for the sake of brevity, we have suppressed the dependency on the parameter vector w. To solve the problem, we define $\epsilon^2 = (r - r_o)^2 + (c - c_o)^2 - 2\lambda f(r, c)$ to be the objective function. We take partial derivatives of ϵ^2 with respect to r, c, and λ and set these

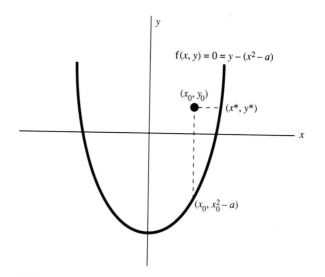

Figure 11.13 Difference between the distance $f(x_0, y_0)^2 = y_0 - (x_0^2 - a)$, which is the vertical distance between the point (x_0, y_0) and the point $(x_0, x_0^2 - a)$, which lies on the curve $y = x^2 - a$, and the distance $(x_0 - x^*)^2 + (y_0 - y^*)^2$, which is the shortest distance, taken over all directions, between the point (x_0, y_0) and the curve $y = x^2 - a$. Here (x^*, y^*) is the closest point on the curve to (x_0, y_0). Obviously one can be arbitrarily larger than the other.

partial derivatives to zero. This results in

$$\frac{\partial \epsilon^2}{\partial r} = 2(r - r_o) - 2\lambda \frac{\partial f}{\partial r}(r,c) = 0 \tag{11.36}$$

$$\frac{\partial \epsilon^2}{\partial c} = 2(c - c_o) - 2\lambda \frac{\partial f}{\partial c}(r,c) = 0 \tag{11.37}$$

$$\frac{\partial \epsilon^2}{\partial \lambda} = -2f(r,c) = 0 \tag{11.38}$$

From Eqs. (11.36) and (11.37) we can write the matrix equation

$$\begin{pmatrix} r - r_o \\ c - c_o \end{pmatrix} = \lambda \begin{pmatrix} \frac{\partial f}{\partial r}(r,c) \\ \frac{\partial f}{\partial c}(r,c) \end{pmatrix} \tag{11.39}$$

Expanding Eq. (11.38) in a Taylor series around (r_o, c_o) yields

$$0 = f(r,c) = f(r_o,c_o) + (r - r_o)\frac{\partial f}{\partial r}(r_o,c_o) + (c - c_o)\frac{\partial f}{\partial c}(r_o,c_o) \tag{11.40}$$

An approximate solution from Eqs. (11.39) and (11.40) is easily obtained. Assuming that the unknown (r,c) is close enough to (r_o,c_o) so that the partial derivatives of f do not change much around (r_o,c_o), we obtain that $\frac{\partial f}{\partial r}(r,c) = \frac{\partial f}{\partial r}(r_o,c_o)$ and $\frac{\partial f}{\partial c}(r,c) = \frac{\partial f}{\partial c}(r_o,c_o)$. In this case Eq. (11.39) becomes

$$\begin{pmatrix} r - r_o \\ c - c_o \end{pmatrix} = \lambda \begin{pmatrix} \frac{\partial f}{\partial r}(r_o,c_o) \\ \frac{\partial f}{\partial c}(r_o,c_o) \end{pmatrix} \tag{11.41}$$

Multiplying the left- and right-hand sides of Eq. (11.41) by $\left[\frac{\partial f}{\partial r}(r_o,c_o), \frac{\partial f}{\partial c}(r_o,c_o)\right]$, using Eq. (11.40), and solving for λ, we obtain

$$\lambda = \frac{-f(r_o,c_o)}{\frac{\partial f}{\partial r}(r_o,c_o)^2 + \frac{\partial f}{\partial c}(r_o,c_o)^2} \tag{11.42}$$

Substituting Eq. (11.42) into Eq. (11.39) and solving for (r,c) then results in

$$\begin{pmatrix} r \\ c \end{pmatrix} = \begin{pmatrix} r_o \\ c_o \end{pmatrix} - \frac{f(r_o,c_o)}{\frac{\partial f}{\partial r}(r_o,c_o)^2 + \frac{\partial f}{\partial c}(r_o,c_o)^2} \begin{pmatrix} \frac{\partial f}{\partial r}(r_o,c_o) \\ \frac{\partial f}{\partial c}(r_o,c_o) \end{pmatrix} \tag{11.43}$$

The distance d between (r,c) and (r_o,c_o) can then easily be computed from Eq. (11.43).

$$d = \sqrt{(r - r_o)^2 + (c - c_o)^2}$$

$$= \frac{|f(r_o,c_o)|}{\frac{\partial f}{\partial r}(r_o,c_o)^2 + \frac{\partial f}{\partial c}(r_o,c_o)^2} \sqrt{\frac{\partial f}{\partial r}(r_o,c_o)^2 + \frac{\partial f}{\partial c}(r_o,c_o)^2}$$

$$= \frac{|f(r_o,c_o)|}{\sqrt{\frac{\partial f}{\partial r}(r_o,c_o)^2 + \frac{\partial f}{\partial c}(r_o,c_o)^2}} \tag{11.44}$$

This relation (11.44) is exactly correct for any f that is a first-order polynomial.

From this approximate solution, Eq. (11.44), to the determination of the distance between a point and a curve, we can solve the original minimization problem, which is to determine the parameter vector w to minimize

$$\sum_{n=1}^{N} (r_n - \hat{r}_n)^2 + (c_n - \hat{c}_n)^2$$

subject to the constraint that $f(r_n, c_n, w) = 0$, $n = 1, \ldots, N$. With the use of Eq. (11.44), this problem then translates to finding the parameter vector w to minimize

$$\epsilon^2(w) = \sum_{n=1}^{N} \frac{f(\hat{r}_n, \hat{c}_n, w)^2}{\frac{\partial f}{\partial r}(\hat{r}_n, \hat{c}_n, w)^2 + \frac{\partial f}{\partial c}(\hat{r}_n, \hat{c}_n, w)^2} \tag{11.45}$$

a result obtained by Sampson (1982).

Analytic solutions do not necessarily exist for the determination of w for function f other than first-order polynomials in r and c. Therefore we treat this problem from the point of view of an iterative gradient descent solution.

11.10.1 Gradient Descent

To minimize a nonnegative function $\epsilon^2(w)$, we assume that some initial value w_o for w is available and we perform a search. Later we will discuss how reasonable initial values for w_o can be determined if the fit is to a circle or to a conic. For now, we just assume a w_o is given. Suppose that iterate w_t has been calculated. To determine the next iterate w_{t+1}, we represent w_{t+1} as a small perturbation on w_t.

$$w_{t+1} = w_t + \Delta w \tag{11.46}$$

Taking a first-order Taylor series expansion of ϵ^2 around w_t then produces

$$\epsilon^2(w_{t+1}) = \epsilon^2(w_t + \Delta w) = \epsilon^2(w_t) + \Delta w' \nabla \epsilon^2(w_t) \tag{11.47}$$

where ∇ is the gradient operator. Now to find the right Δw, consider the fact that $\Delta w' \nabla \epsilon^2(w_t)$ must be negative and smaller than $\epsilon^2(w_t)$ in magnitude.

This suggests that Δw should be in the negative gradient direction and should produce a change smaller than $\epsilon^2(w_t)$. Hence we take

$$\Delta w = -\beta \epsilon^2(w_t) \frac{\nabla \epsilon^2(w_t)}{\|\nabla \epsilon^2(w_t)\|^2 + \alpha^2} \tag{11.48}$$

The α^2 in the denominator assures us that as $\|\nabla \epsilon^2(w_t)\|^2$ becomes smaller than α^2, $\|\Delta w\|^2$ will also become small. The parameter β is some fraction, $0 \le \beta \le 1$, that can be a constant or a function of the iteration index or a function of $w + \Delta w, \epsilon^2$, and a tentative w_{t+1}. For example, $\beta = 0.5 \left(\frac{1+t}{t}\right)$ is one choice that for $t = 1$ produces $\beta = 1.0$ and for large t produces $\beta = 0.5$. The procedure *curvefit* details the iterative structure solution algorithm. Its input arguments are w_o, the initial guess;

ϵ^2, the function to be minimized; α, a small constant; β, the initial multiplicative constant for Δw; N, the number of iterations to perform; and w_f, the final answer. It calls a function *step* to determine the multiplicative constant for Δw.

procedure curvefit($w_0, \epsilon^2, \alpha, \beta, N, w_f$);

```
w_f := w_0;
for n = 1 to N do
   begin
```
$$\Delta w := -\beta \epsilon^2(w_f) \frac{\nabla \epsilon^2(w_f)}{\|\nabla \epsilon^2(w_f)\|^2 + \alpha^2};$$
$$w_f := w_f + \Delta w * \text{step}(w_f, \Delta w, \epsilon^2)$$
```
   end
end for

end curvefit;
```

The number of iterations can be reduced some by using a more sophisticated scheme for selecting the magnitude of Δw. Equation (11.48) can be used to select a trial size for Δw. Then the value of $\epsilon^2(w_{t+1}) = \epsilon^2(w_t + \Delta w)$ can be compared with $\epsilon^2(w_t)$. If $\epsilon^2(w_{t+1}) < \epsilon^2(w_t)$, a successful steepest-descent size has been determined. Now a small search of increasing step sizes may be done to determine whether there is a large step size that produces a smaller $\epsilon^2(w_{t+1})$. If so, we can use it. On the other hand, if $\epsilon^2(w_{t+1}) > \epsilon^2(w_t)$, the trial step size is too large. A smaller step size can surely produce an $\epsilon^2(w_{t+1})$ that can satisfy $\epsilon^2(w_{t+1}) < \epsilon^2(w_t)$. So in this case we can do a small search on reduced step sizes to find a sufficiently small step. The following function illustrates this idea.

```
function step (w_t, Δw, ε²);
   w_{t+1} := w_t + Δw;
   ε_p := ε²(w_{t+1});
   c := 1;
   if ε_p < ε²(w_t) then      k := 3
                    else      k := .333;
   for m := 1 to 5 do
      begin
         c := c * k;
         step := c;
         e := ε²(w_t + cΔw);
         if e < ε_p
            begin
               e_p := e;
               step := c
            end
         else break
      end
   end for

end step;
```

11.10.2   Newton Method

It is also possible to solve the minimization problem by a second-order iterative technique that typically requires fewer iterations to a solution than the steepest-descent method. Taking a second-order expansion of $\epsilon^2(w_t + \Delta w)$ around $\epsilon^2(w_t)$ results in

$$\epsilon^2(w_t + \Delta w) = \epsilon^2(w_t) + \Delta w' \nabla \epsilon^2(w_t) + \frac{1}{2}\Delta w' H \Delta w \qquad (11.49)$$

where $H = H(w_t)$, the Hessian of ϵ^2, is the matrix of second-order partial derivatives of ϵ^2 evaluated at w_t. To find the Δw that minimizes Eq. (11.49), take partial derivatives of Eq. (11.49) with respect to Δw, set the partial derivative to zero, and solve for Δw. This produces

$$\Delta w = -H^{-1}\nabla \epsilon^2 \qquad (11.50)$$

Here Δw is called the Newton direction. When H is positive definite, $w_t + \Delta w$ is the exact position to minimize Eq. (11.49).

The second-order method must be used with care since in situations where ϵ^2 is relatively flat, Δw could be very large, and although $w_t + \Delta w$ exactly minimizes $\epsilon^2(w_t) + \Delta w' \nabla \epsilon^2 + \frac{1}{2}\Delta w' H \Delta w$, there is no prior assurance that the second-order representation is accurate for long distances away from w_t. To guard against using potentially large Δw, at each iteration, a better Δw can be chosen from the Δw produced by steepest ascent and the Δw produced by the Newton technique.

Alternatively, one can solve the system

$$\Delta w = -(H + \lambda I)^{-1}\nabla \epsilon^2 \qquad (11.51)$$

instead of Eq. (11.50). When λ gets large, the direction that Eq. (11.51) produces is the negative gradient direction, and when λ gets close to zero, the direction that Eq. (11.51) produces is the Newton direction. Since ϵ^2 is the sum of N terms, it would not be unreasonable to consider using $\lambda = N$.

11.10.3   Second-Order Approximation to Curve Fitting

It is possible to obtain a more exact solution to the distance between a point and a curve than Eq. (11.44), but this involves determining the roots of a quadratic equation. Instead of approximating $(\frac{\partial f}{\partial r}, \frac{\partial f}{\partial c})$ by a zero-order expansion around (r_o, c_o), we approximate $(\frac{\partial f}{\partial r}, \frac{\partial f}{\partial c})$ by a first-order expansion around (r_o, c_o). This results in

$$\nabla f(r,c) = \nabla f(r_o, c_o) + F \begin{pmatrix} r - r_o \\ c - c_o \end{pmatrix} \qquad (11.52)$$

where

$$\nabla f = \begin{pmatrix} \frac{\partial f}{\partial r} \\ \frac{\partial f}{\partial c} \end{pmatrix} \quad \text{and} \quad F = \begin{pmatrix} \frac{\partial^2 f}{\partial r^2}(r_o, c_o) & \frac{\partial^2 f}{\partial r \partial c}(r_o, c_o) \\ \frac{\partial^2 f}{\partial r \partial c}(r_o, c_o) & \frac{\partial^2 f}{\partial c^2}(r_o, c_o) \end{pmatrix}$$

Substituting Eq. (11.52) into Eq. (11.39), we obtain

$$\begin{pmatrix} r - r_o \\ c - c_o \end{pmatrix} = \lambda \left[\nabla f(r_o, c_o) + F \begin{pmatrix} r - r_o \\ c - c_o \end{pmatrix} \right]$$

so that

$$\begin{pmatrix} r - r_o \\ c - c_o \end{pmatrix} = \lambda (I - \lambda F)^{-1} \nabla f(r_o, c_o) \tag{11.53}$$

From Eq. (11.40)

$$\nabla f(r_o, c_o)' \begin{pmatrix} r - r_o \\ c - c_o \end{pmatrix} = -f(r_o, c_o)$$

Hence

$$-f(r_o, c_o) = \lambda \nabla f(r_o, c_o)'(I - \lambda F)^{-1} \nabla f(r_o, c_o) \tag{11.54}$$

Writing Eq. (11.54) out, we have a quadratic polynomial in λ,

$$A\lambda^2 + B\lambda + C = 0 \tag{11.55}$$

where

$$A = \nabla f(r_o, c_o)' \begin{pmatrix} -\frac{\partial^2 f}{\partial c^2}(r_o, c_o) & \frac{\partial^2 f}{\partial r \partial c}(r_o, c_o) \\ \frac{\partial^2 f}{\partial r \partial c}(r_o, c_o) & -\frac{\partial^2 f}{\partial r^2}(r_o, c_o) \end{pmatrix} \nabla f(r_o, c_o)$$
$$+ f(r_o, c_o) \left(\frac{\partial^2 f}{\partial r^2}(r_o, c_o) \frac{\partial^2 f}{\partial c^2}(r_o, c_o) - \frac{\partial^2 f}{\partial r \partial c}(r_o, c_o)^2 \right)$$

$$B = \nabla f(r_o, c_o)' \nabla f(r_o, c_o) - f(r_o, c_o) \left(\frac{\partial^2 f}{\partial r^2}(r_o, c_o) + \frac{\partial^2 f}{\partial c^2}(r_o, c_o) \right)$$

$$C = f(r_o, c_o).$$

Once Eq. (11.55) is solved for λ, each of the two possible values can be substituted back into Eq. (11.53), and the squared distance d^2 to the curve is then determined by

$$d^2 = (r - r_o)^2 + (c - c_o)^2 = \lambda^2 \nabla f(r_o, c_o)'(I - \lambda F)^{-2} \nabla f(r_o, c_o)$$

The value of λ that produces the smaller value of d^2 is the root chosen, and the smaller value of d^2 is the desired squared distance.

11.10.4 Fitting to a Circle

In this section we apply the discussion of Section 11.10.3 to a circle. Then, since the difference between a point and a circle can be represented explicitly, we derive a specialized fitting technique for a circle. For comparison, we will discuss some other circle-fitting techniques that have appeared in the literature.

In the case of a circle, the parameter vector $w' = (a, b, R)$, where (a, b) is the center of the circle and R is its radius. Then the circle is represented by $f(r, c, w) = 0$.

$$f(r, c, w) = f(r, c, a, b, R) = (r - a)^2 + (c - b)^2 - R^2$$

and

$$\frac{\partial f}{\partial r} = 2(r - a) \quad \text{and} \quad \frac{\partial f}{\partial c} = 2(c - a)$$

By Eq. (11.45)

$$\epsilon^2(a, b, R) = \sum_{n=1}^{N} \frac{[(\hat{r}_n - a)^2 + (\hat{c}_n - b)^2 - R^2]^2}{4[(\hat{r}_n - a)^2 + (\hat{c}_n - b)^2]}$$

Approximate initial approximations for a, b, and R can be obtained from

$$a_o = \bar{r} = \frac{1}{N} \sum_{n=1}^{N} \hat{r}_n \tag{11.56}$$

$$b_o = \bar{c} = \frac{1}{N} \sum_{n=1}^{N} \hat{c}_n \tag{11.57}$$

$$R_o = \frac{1}{N} \sum_{n=1}^{N} \sqrt{(\hat{r}_n - a_o)^2 + (\hat{c}_n - b_o)^2} \tag{11.58}$$

The gradient of ϵ^2 to be used in calculating Δw is then

$$\nabla \epsilon^2 = \begin{pmatrix} \frac{\partial \epsilon^2}{\partial a} \\ \frac{\partial \epsilon^2}{\partial b} \\ \frac{\partial \epsilon^2}{\partial R} \end{pmatrix}$$

$$= \frac{1}{4} \sum_{n=1}^{N} \frac{f(\hat{r}_n, \hat{c}_n, a, b, R)}{[(\hat{r}_n - a)^2 + (\hat{c}_n - b)^2]^2}$$

$$\times \begin{pmatrix} \{-4[(\hat{r}_n - a)^2 + (\hat{c}_n - b)^2] + 2f(\hat{r}_n, \hat{c}_n, a, b, R)\}(\hat{r}_n - a) \\ \{-4[(\hat{r}_n - a)^2 + (\hat{c}_n - b)^2] + 2f(\hat{r}_n, \hat{c}_n, a, b, R)\}(\hat{c}_n - a) \\ -4[(\hat{r}_n - a)^2 + (\hat{r}_n - b)^2]R \end{pmatrix}.$$

The simple iteration algorithm is then given as shown below. The parameters r and c are vector arrays of the row and column coordinates of the N points to be fit. Parameters a, b, and R are the fitting parameters of the circle, which are computed by the procedure. The internal variable *number_of_iterations* will have to be around 200 or 300 for the iterative procedure to get close to the correct solution. This makes the procedure too slow to use in practice.

procedure circlefit1(r,c,N,α,β,a,b,R);
for $t := 1$ to *number_of_iterations* **do**
  begin
    $\epsilon^2 := 0$;
$$\nabla \epsilon^2 = \begin{pmatrix} 0 \\ 0 \\ 0 \end{pmatrix};$$
    for $n := 1$ to N **do**
      begin
        $d := (r(n) - a)^2 + (c(n) - b)^2$;
        $k := 1./d$;

$$f := d - R^2;$$

$$\nabla\epsilon^2 := \nabla\epsilon^2 + \begin{pmatrix} kf(r(n) - a)(-1 + 0.5(kf)^2) \\ kf(c(n) - b)(-1 + 0.5(kf)^2) \\ -kfR \end{pmatrix};$$

$$\epsilon^2 := \epsilon^2 + f * f * k$$

end

end for;

$$\epsilon^2 := 0.25 * \epsilon^2;$$

$$g := \frac{1}{|\nabla\epsilon^2| + \alpha^2};$$

$$\Delta w = \beta\epsilon^2 g \nabla\epsilon^2;$$

$$\begin{pmatrix} a \\ b \\ R \end{pmatrix} = \begin{pmatrix} a \\ b \\ R \end{pmatrix} + \Delta w * \text{step}\left(\begin{pmatrix} a \\ b \\ R \end{pmatrix}, \Delta w, \epsilon^2\right);$$

end

end for

end circlefit1;

Of course in the case of the circle, an exact function to be minimized can be worked out. The squared distance between a point (r_o, c_o) and a circle centered at (a, b) with radius R is $(\sqrt{(r_o - a)^2 + (c_o - b)^2} - R)^2$. The error to be minimized over N points is then

$$\epsilon^2 = \sum_{n=1}^{N}(\sqrt{(\hat{r}_n - a)^2 + (\hat{c}_n - b)^2} - R)^2 \tag{11.59}$$

from which

$$\nabla\epsilon = \begin{pmatrix} \frac{\partial\epsilon^2}{\partial a} \\ \frac{\partial\epsilon^2}{\partial b} \\ \frac{\partial\epsilon^2}{\partial R} \end{pmatrix} = \begin{pmatrix} -2\sum_{n=1}^{N}\left(1 - \frac{R}{\sqrt{(\hat{r}_n-a)^2+(\hat{c}_n-b)^2}}\right)(\hat{r}_n - a) \\ -2\sum_{n=1}^{N}\left(1 - \frac{R}{\sqrt{(\hat{r}_n-a)^2+(\hat{c}_n-b)^2}}\right)(\hat{c}_n - b) \\ -2\sum_{n=1}^{N}\left(\sqrt{(\hat{r}_n - a)^2 + (\hat{c}_n - b)^2} - R\right) \end{pmatrix} \tag{11.60}$$

The iterations can then proceed by substituting Eq. (11.60) into Eq. (11.48) and using Eq. (11.48) in Eq. (11.46) to produce the next value of $w = a, b, R$.

A faster and more tolerant iteration solution can be done by noticing that from $\frac{\partial\epsilon^2}{\partial R}$ of Eq. (11.60) an analytically computed value for R can be determined when $\frac{\partial\epsilon^2}{\partial R} = 0$.

$$R = \frac{1}{N}\sum_{n=1}^{N}\sqrt{(\hat{r}_n - a)^2 + (\hat{c}_n - b)^2} \tag{11.61}$$

If Eq. (11.61) is used, R becomes a function of the unknown (a, b) and

$$\nabla\epsilon = \begin{pmatrix} \frac{\partial^2\epsilon}{\partial a} \\ \frac{\partial^2\epsilon}{\partial b} \end{pmatrix} = -2\sum_{n=1}^{N}\left(1 - \frac{R}{\sqrt{(\hat{r}_n - a)^2 + (\hat{c}_n - b)^2}}\right)\begin{pmatrix} \hat{r}_n - a \\ \hat{c}_n - b \end{pmatrix}$$

$$+ \left[\sqrt{(\hat{r}_n - a)^2 + (\hat{c}_n - b)^2} - R\right]\begin{pmatrix} \frac{\partial R}{\partial a} \\ \frac{\partial R}{\partial b} \end{pmatrix} \tag{11.62}$$

where

$$\begin{pmatrix} \frac{\partial R}{\partial a} \\ \frac{\partial R}{\partial b} \end{pmatrix} = \frac{-1}{N} \sum_{n=1}^{N} \frac{1}{\sqrt{(\hat{r}_n - a)^2 + (\hat{c}_n - b)^2}} \begin{pmatrix} \hat{r}_n - a \\ \hat{c}_n - b \end{pmatrix}$$

Iterations can proceed by substituting Eq. (11.62) into Eq. (11.48) and Eq. (11.48) into Eq. (11.46) to produce the next value of $w = (a, b, R)$. Convergence is typically achieved after 20 iterations.

The procedure *circlefit* gives the pseudocode for these iterations. Its input is the row-column arrays r and c, each N long. It outputs the circle center (a, b) and radius R. It calls upon the function *epserr,* which, given the observed row-column points and a center estimate (a, b), determines the radius by Eq. (11.61) and then the error it returns by Eq. (11.59). It also calls upon the procedure *step,* which functions like the function *step* in Section 11.10.1 with natural modification to let it also output the radius and return the values of the updated center.

procedure circlefit(r,c,N,α,β,a,b,R)

```
a:=0;
b:=0;
for n=1 to N do
   begin
      a:=a+r(n);
      b:=b+c(n)
   end
end for
a:=a/N;
b:=b/N;
ε=epserr(r,c,N,a,b,radius);
for t=1 to 20 do
   for n=1 to N do
      d(n):=√((r(n) − a)² + (c(n) − b)²);
      drda:=0;
      drdb:=0;
      for i=1 to N bf do
         begin
            drda:=drda+(r(i)-a)/d(i);
            drdb:=drdb+(c(i)-b)/d(i)
         end
      end for
      drda:=-drda/N;
      drdb:=-drdb/N;
      at:=0;
      bt:=0;
      for n=1 to N do
         begin
            f:=1-radius/d(n);
```

```
              at:=at-2(f(r(n)-a)+(d(n)-radius)drda);
              bt:=bt-2(f(c(n)-b)+(d(n)-radius)drdb);
          end
      end for
      g :=1/(α² +at² +bt²);
      Δa := β * ε * g * at;
      Δb := β * ε * g * bt;
      step(a,b,Δa,Δb,ε,radius)
   end
  end for

end circlefit
```

EXAMPLE 11.2

The data given in Table 11.2 are noisy observed points from a 90° circular arc.
The estimated center for the circle is $(\hat{a}, \hat{b}) = (.1913, 10.2856)$, and the
estimated radius is $\hat{R} = 10.499$. The squared error

$$\epsilon^2 = \sum_{n=1}^{10} \left(\sqrt{(\hat{r}_n - a)^2 + (\hat{c}_n - b)^2} - R^2 \right)^2 = .3392$$

so that the estimated $\hat{\sigma}^2 = \sqrt{.3392/7} = .2201$.

Table 11.2   The points in a noisy 90° circular arc. $\hat{r}_n$ is the row number and $\hat{c}_n$
is the column number.

n	$\hat{r}_n$	$\hat{c}_n$
1	7.93535	17.15845
2	7.26935	18.43970
3	5.17017	19.61730
4	3.70451	19.83813
5	2.15564	20.73293
6	0.69466	20.86883
7	-1.14771	20.56556
8	-3.07478	20.03483
9	-5.17503	19.36585
10	-6.07584	18.91065

Robinson (1961) and Landau (1987) note that the desired values of $a, b,$ and R that minimize Eq. (11.59) are values of $a, b,$ and R that make $\nabla\epsilon$ of Eq. (11.60) zero. Therefore the simultaneous equations to be solved for $a, b,$ and R are Eq. (11.61) and

$$\sum_{n=1}^{N} \left[1 - \frac{R}{\sqrt{(\hat{r}_n - a)^2 + (\hat{c}_n - b)^2}} \right] (\hat{r}_n - a) = 0 \tag{11.63}$$

$$\sum_{n=1}^{N} \left[1 - \frac{R}{\sqrt{(\hat{r}_n - a)^2 + (\hat{c}_n - b)^2}} \right] (\hat{c}_n - b) = 0 \tag{11.64}$$

Landau rearranges Eqs. (11.63) and (11.64) to get

$$a = \bar{r} - \frac{R}{N} \sum_{n=1}^{N} \frac{\hat{r}_n - a}{\sqrt{(\hat{r}_n - a)^2 + (\hat{c}_n - b)^2}} \tag{11.65}$$

$$b = \bar{c} - \frac{R}{N} \sum_{n=1}^{N} \frac{\hat{c}_n - b}{\sqrt{(\hat{r}_n - a)^2 + (\hat{c}_n - b)^2}} \tag{11.66}$$

where $\bar{r}$ and $\bar{c}$ are given by Eqs. (11.56) and (11.57). He solves the simultaneous Eqs. (11.61), (11.65), and (11.66) iteratively. The initial values a_o and b_o for a and b are obtained from Eqs. (11.56) and (11.57). Once a center approximation (a_t, b_t) is calculated at iteration t, the iterations proceed by

$$R_{t+1} = \frac{1}{N} \sum_{n=1}^{N} \sqrt{(\hat{r}_n - a_t)^2 + (\hat{c}_n - b_t)^2}$$

$$a_{t+1} = \bar{r} - \frac{R_{t+1}}{N} \sum_{n=1}^{N} \frac{\hat{r}_n - a_t}{\sqrt{(\hat{r}_n - a_t)^2 + (\hat{c}_n - b_t)^2}} \tag{11.67}$$

$$a_{t+1} = \bar{c} - \frac{R_{t+1}}{N} \sum_{n=1}^{N} \frac{\hat{c}_n - b_t}{\sqrt{(\hat{r}_n - a_t)^2 + (\hat{c}_n + b_t)^2}}$$

Iterating the system of equations (11.67) to convergence is generally slow, requiring about 450 iterations.

Chernov and Ososkov (1984) claim a less computationally intensive approach that works when the relative noise perturbation is small compared with R. In this case

$$\left(\frac{\sqrt{(\hat{r}_n - a)^2 + (\hat{c}_n - b)^2} - R}{2R} \right)^2 \ll 1 \tag{11.68}$$

Hence

$$\epsilon^2 = \sum_{n=1}^{N} \left[\sqrt{(\hat{r}_n - a)^2 + (\hat{c}_n - b)^2} - R \right]^2$$

Now from Eq. (11.68),

$$\epsilon^2 = \sum_{n=1}^{N} \left[\sqrt{(\hat{r}_n - a)^2 + (\hat{c}_n - b)^2} - R \right]^2 \left[1 + \frac{\sqrt{(\hat{r}_n - a)^2 + (\hat{c}_n - b)^2} - R}{2R} \right]^2$$

$$= \frac{1}{4R^2} \sum_{n=1}^{N} \left[\sqrt{(\hat{r}_n - a)^2 + (\hat{c}_n - b)^2} - R \right]^2 \left[\sqrt{(\hat{r}_n - a)^2 + (\hat{c}_n - b)^2} + R \right]^2$$

$$= \sum_{n=1}^{N} \left[\frac{(\hat{r}_n - a)^2 + (\hat{c}_n - b)^2 - R^2}{2R} \right]^2$$

Define $r'_n = \hat{r}_n - \bar{r}$, $c'_n = \hat{c}_n - \bar{c}$, $a' = a - \bar{r}$, and $b' = b - \bar{r}$. Then

$$\epsilon^2 = \sum_{n=1}^{N} \left[\frac{(r'_n - a')^2 + (c'_n - b')^2 - R^2}{2R} \right]^2 \quad \text{and} \quad \sum_{n=1}^{N} r'_n = \sum_{n=1}^{N} c'_n = 0$$

Taking partial derivatives of ϵ^2 with respect to a', b', and R, setting these partial derivatives to zero, and using the fact that

$$\sum_{n=1}^{N} r'_n = \sum_{n=1}^{N} c'_n = 0$$

results in

$$Fa' + Hb' - \gamma a' = P \tag{11.69}$$

$$Ha' + Gb' - \gamma b' = Q \tag{11.70}$$

$$2Pa' + 2Qb' + \gamma^2 + \{2Pa' + 2Qb' - 2F(a')^2 - 2G(b')^2 - 4Ha'b' + 2[(a')^2 + (b')^2]\gamma\} = T \tag{11.71}$$

where

$$F = \frac{1}{N} \sum_{n=1}^{N} 3(r'_n)^2 + (c'_n)^2$$

$$G = \frac{1}{N} \sum_{n=1}^{N} (r'_n)^2 + 3(c'_n)^2$$

$$H = \frac{2}{N} \sum_{n=1}^{N} r'_n c'_n$$

$$P = \frac{1}{N} \sum_{n=1}^{N} r'_n [(r'_n)^2 + (c'_n)^2]$$

$$Q = \frac{1}{N} \sum_{n=1}^{N} c'_n [(r'_n)^2 + (c'_n)^2]$$

$$T = \frac{1}{N} \sum_{n=1}^{N} [(r'_n)^2 + (c'_n)^2]^2$$

and

$$\gamma = R^2 - (a')^2 - (b')^2$$

However, multiplying Eq. (11.69) by a' and Eq. (11.70) by b' and adding these together shows that the bracketed term in Eq. (11.71) is zero. Equation (11.71) then becomes

$$2Pa' + 2Qb' + \gamma^2 = T \tag{11.72}$$

Now Eqs. (11.69) and (11.70) can be used to determine an expression for a' and b' in terms of γ, and these expressions for a' and b' can be substituted back into Eq. (11.72). After rearranging, there results the fourth-order equation in γ

$$\gamma^4 + A\gamma^3 + B\gamma^2 + C\gamma + D = 0 \tag{11.73}$$

where

$$A = -F - G$$
$$B = FG - T - H^2$$
$$C = T(F + G) - 2(P^2 + Q^2)$$
$$D = T(H^2 - FG) + 2(P^2G + Q^2F) - 4PQH$$

Chernov and Ososkov solve Eq. (11.73) for the desired root by the iterative Newton method, beginning with the initial estimate

$$\gamma_o = \frac{1}{N}\sum_{n=1}^{N}(r_n^2 + c_n^2)$$

Bookstein (1979) gives the following regression procedure to fit a circle. He rewrites the circle equation

$$(r - a)^2 + (c - b)^2 = R^2$$

as follows:

$$2ra + 2cb - a^2 - b^2 + R^2 = r^2 + c^2$$

Letting $q = a^2 + b^2 - R^2$, he sets up the overconstrained linear system

$$\begin{pmatrix} 2\hat{r}_1 & 2\hat{c}_1 & 1 \\ 2\hat{r}_2 & 2\hat{c}_2 & 1 \\ \vdots & & \\ 2\hat{r}_n & 2\hat{c}_n & 1 \end{pmatrix} \begin{pmatrix} a \\ b \\ q \end{pmatrix} = \begin{pmatrix} \hat{r}_1^2 + \hat{c}_1^2 \\ \hat{r}_2^2 + \hat{c}_2^2 \\ \vdots \\ \hat{r}_n^2 + \hat{c}_n^2 \end{pmatrix} \tag{11.74}$$

which can be solved in the least-squares sense for (a, b, q). Then $R^2 = a^2 + b^2 + q$.

The least-squares solution for Eq. (11.74) minimizes the sum of the squared errors between the squared radius and the squared distance between the observed data points and the circle center:

$$e^2 = \sum_{n=1}^{N}[(\hat{r}_n - a)^2 + (\hat{c}_n - b)^2 - R^2]^2$$

The technique should be used with care, since it is easy for the numerical errors to influence the results unduly. For example, if Eq. (11.74) is solved by the normal equations,

$$\begin{pmatrix} a \\ b \\ q \end{pmatrix} = (A'A)^{-1} A' \begin{pmatrix} \hat{r}_1^2 + \hat{c}_1^2 \\ \vdots \\ \hat{r}_n^2 + \hat{c}_n^2 \end{pmatrix}$$

the roundoff error in the computation of $A'A$ can cause excessive inaccuracy. Therefore a singular-value decomposition technique must be used instead.

Finally, since $R^2 = a^2 + b^2 + q$, it is apparent that when the center (a,b) of a circle of radius 10 is in the bottom right corner of an image, $a^2 + b^2$ can easily be over 5×10^5 and q must be a large negative number just 100 larger than -5×10^5. Hence the computation for $R^2 = a^2 + b^2 + q$ will involve the subtraction of q, a large negative number, from $a^2 + b^2$, a large positive number, with the inherent loss of precision in the result.

Thomas and Chan (1989) also minimize

$$e^2 = \sum_{n=1}^{N} [(\hat{r}_n - a)^2 + (\hat{c}_n - b)^2 - R^2]^2$$

Taking partial derivatives of e^2 with respect to a, b, and R, setting them to zero, and rearranging results in

$$R^2 \sum_n \hat{r}_n = \sum_n \hat{r}_n^3 - 2a \sum_n \hat{r}_n^2 + a^2 \sum_n \hat{r}_n$$
$$+ \sum_n \hat{r}_n \hat{c}_n^2 - 2b \sum_n \hat{r}_n \hat{c}_n + b^2 \sum_n \hat{r}_n \quad (11.75)$$

$$R^2 \sum_n \hat{c}_n = \sum_n \hat{r}_n^2 \hat{c}_n - 2a \sum_n \hat{r}_n \hat{c}_n + a^2 \sum_n \hat{c}_n$$
$$+ \sum_n \hat{c}_n^3 - 2b \sum_n \hat{c}_n^2 + b^2 \sum_n \hat{c}_n \quad (11.76)$$

$$NR^2 = \sum_n \hat{r}_n^2 - 2a \sum_n \hat{r}_n + Na^2 + \sum_n \hat{c}_n^2 - 2b \sum_n \hat{c}_n + Nb^2 \quad (11.77)$$

The a^2 and b^2 terms can be eliminated. Multiply Eq. (11.75) by N and subtract from it Eq. (11.77) multiplied by $\sum_n \hat{r}_n$. Multiply Eq. (11.76) by N and subtract it from Eq. (11.77) multiplied by $\sum_n \hat{c}_n$. The resulting linear system is Eq. (11.78).

$$\begin{pmatrix} d & e \\ e & f \end{pmatrix} \begin{pmatrix} a \\ b \end{pmatrix} = \begin{pmatrix} g \\ h \end{pmatrix} \quad (11.78)$$

where

$$d = 2 \left[\left(\sum_n \hat{r}_n^2 \right)^2 - N \sum_n \hat{r}_n^2 \right]$$

$$e = 2 \left[\sum_n \hat{r}_n \sum_n \hat{c}_n - N \sum_n \hat{r}_n \hat{c}_n \right]$$

$$f = 2\left[\left(\sum_n \hat{c}_n\right)^2 - N\sum_n \hat{c}_n^2\right]$$

$$g = \sum_n \hat{r}_n^2 \sum_n \hat{r}_n - N\sum_n \hat{r}_n^3 + \sum_n \hat{r}_n \sum_n \hat{c}_n^2 - N\sum_n \hat{r}_n \hat{c}_n^2$$

$$h = \sum_n \hat{c}_n^2 \sum_n \hat{c}_n - N\sum_n \hat{c}_n^3 + \sum_n \hat{r}_n^2 \sum_n \hat{c}_n - N\sum_n \hat{r}_n^2 \hat{c}_n$$

Solve Eq. (11.78) for a and b and then substitute into Eq. (11.77) to obtain R^2.

11.10.5 Variance of the Fitted Parameters

We suppose that the noisy observations $(\hat{r}_n, \hat{c}_n)$ are of points (r_n, c_n) that lie on the circle $(r_n - a)^2 + (c_n - b)^2 = R^2$. As in the case of the line fitting, our model for $(\hat{r}_n, \hat{c}_n)$ is

$$\hat{r}_n = r_n + \xi_n \tag{11.79}$$
$$\hat{c}_n = c_n + \eta_n$$

where we assume that the random variables ξ_n and η_n are independent and identically distributed, having mean 0 and variance σ^2. Hence

$$E[\xi_n] = E[\eta_n] = 0$$
$$V[\xi_n] = \nu[\eta_n] = \sigma^2$$
$$E[\xi_n\xi_j] = \begin{cases} \sigma^2 & n = j \\ 0 & \text{otherwise} \end{cases} \tag{11.80}$$
$$E[\eta_n\eta_j] = \begin{cases} \sigma^2 & n = j \\ 0 & \text{otherwise} \end{cases}$$
$$E[\xi_n\eta_j] = 0$$

The least estimates $\hat{a}, \hat{b}, \hat{R}$ for a, b, R minimize

$$\epsilon^2(\hat{a}, \hat{b}, \hat{R}) = \sum_{n=1}^N \left[\sqrt{(\hat{r}_n - \hat{a})^2 + (\hat{c}_n - \hat{b})^2} - \hat{R}\right]^2$$

Hence they must satisfy $g_1(\hat{a}, \hat{b}, \hat{R}) = g_2(\hat{a}, \hat{b}, \hat{R}) = g_2(\hat{a}, \hat{b}, \hat{R}) = 0$, where

$$g_1(\hat{a}, \hat{b}, \hat{R}) = \sum_{n=1}^N \left[1 - \frac{\hat{R}}{\sqrt{(\hat{r}_n - \hat{a})^2 + (\hat{c}_n - \hat{b})^2}}\right](\hat{r}_n - \hat{a})$$

$$g_2(\hat{a}, \hat{b}, \hat{R}) = \sum_{n=1}^N \left[1 - \frac{\hat{R}}{\sqrt{(\hat{r}_n - \hat{a})^2 + (\hat{c}_n - \hat{b})^2}}\right](\hat{c}_n - \hat{b}) \tag{11.81}$$

$$g_3(\hat{a}, \hat{b}, \hat{R}) = \sum_{n=1}^N \sqrt{(\hat{r}_n - \hat{a})^2 + (\hat{c}_n - \hat{b})^2} - N\hat{R}$$

Of course the unknown true values a, b, R also satisfy $g_1(a,b,R) = g_2(a,b,R) = g_3(a,b,R) = 0$. Assuming that the noise is sufficiently small so that a first-order expansion of g_1, g_2, and g_3 around (a,b,R) is accurate, we may compute the variances of the estimates $\hat{a}, \hat{b}, \hat{R}$. Let $\Delta a, \Delta b$, and ΔR satisfy

$$
\begin{aligned}
\hat{a} &= a + \Delta a \\
\hat{b} &= b + \Delta b \\
\hat{R} &= R + \Delta R
\end{aligned}
\tag{11.82}
$$

Then

$$
\begin{aligned}
g_i[\hat{a}, \hat{b}, \hat{R}, (\hat{r}_1, \hat{c}_1), \ldots, (\hat{r}_N, \hat{c}_N)] &= g_i[a, b, R, (r_1, c_1), \ldots, (r_N, c_N)] + \\
&\quad \Delta a \frac{\delta g_i}{\delta a}[a, b, R, (r_1, c_1), \ldots, (r_N, c_N)] + \\
&\quad \Delta b \frac{\delta g_i}{\delta b}[a, b, R, (r_1, c_1), \ldots, (r_N, c_N)] + \\
&\quad \Delta R \frac{\delta g_i}{\delta R}[a, b, R, (r_1, c_1), \ldots, (r_N, c_N)] + \\
&\quad \sum_{n=1}^{N} \xi_n \frac{\delta g_i}{\delta r_n}[a, b, R, (r_1, c_1), \ldots, (r_N, c_N)] + \\
&\quad \sum_{n=1}^{N} \eta_n \frac{\delta g_i}{\delta c_n}[a, b, R, (r_1, c_1), \ldots, (r_N, c_N)] \\
&\qquad\qquad\qquad\qquad\qquad\qquad\qquad\qquad i = 1, 2, 3
\end{aligned}
$$

But $g_i[\hat{a}, \hat{b}, \hat{R}, (\hat{r}_1, \hat{c}_1), \ldots, (\hat{r}_N, \hat{c}_N)] = g_i[a, b, R, (r_1, c_1), \ldots, (r_N, c_N)] = 0$, so that

$$
-\begin{pmatrix} \frac{\delta g_1}{\delta a} & \frac{\delta g_1}{\delta b} & \frac{\delta g_1}{\delta R} \\ \frac{\delta g_2}{\delta a} & \frac{\delta g_2}{\delta b} & \frac{\delta g_2}{\delta R} \\ \frac{\delta g_3}{\delta a} & \frac{\delta g_3}{\delta b} & \frac{\delta g_3}{\delta R} \end{pmatrix} \begin{pmatrix} \Delta a \\ \Delta b \\ \Delta R \end{pmatrix} = \begin{pmatrix} \frac{\delta g_1}{\delta r_1} & \cdots & \frac{\delta g_1}{\delta r_N} & \frac{\delta g_1}{\delta c_1} & \cdots & \frac{\delta g_1}{\delta c_N} \\ \frac{\delta g_2}{\delta r_1} & \cdots & \frac{\delta g_2}{\delta r_N} & \frac{\delta g_2}{\delta c_1} & \cdots & \frac{\delta g_2}{\delta c_N} \\ \frac{\delta g_3}{\delta r_1} & \cdots & \frac{\delta g_3}{\delta r_N} & \frac{\delta g_3}{\delta c_1} & \cdots & \frac{\delta g_3}{\delta c_N} \end{pmatrix} \begin{pmatrix} \xi_1 \\ \vdots \\ \xi_N \\ \eta_n \\ \vdots \\ \eta_n \end{pmatrix}
$$

or

$$
-J_1 \begin{pmatrix} \Delta a \\ \Delta b \\ \Delta R \end{pmatrix} = J_2 \begin{pmatrix} \xi_1 \\ \vdots \\ \xi_N \\ \eta_1 \\ \vdots \\ \eta_N \end{pmatrix}
$$

Solving for $(\Delta a, \Delta b, \Delta R)$, we obtain

$$\begin{pmatrix} \Delta a \\ \Delta b \\ \Delta R \end{pmatrix} = -J_1^{-1}J_2 \begin{pmatrix} \xi_1 \\ \vdots \\ \xi_N \\ \eta_1 \\ \vdots \\ \eta_N \end{pmatrix}$$

By the system of equations (11.82) the covariance matrix for $\hat{a}, \hat{b}, \hat{R}$ is identical to the covariance matrix of $\Delta a, \Delta b, \Delta R$. By the equal-variance and no-correlation assumption of Eq. (11.80), we obtain that the covariance matrix for $\Delta a, \Delta b,$ and ΔR is given by

$$E\left[\begin{pmatrix} \Delta a \\ \Delta b \\ \Delta R \end{pmatrix} (\Delta a\ \Delta b\ \Delta R)\right] = \sigma^2 J_1^{-1} J_2 J_2' J_1'^{-1} \tag{11.83}$$

In the case when g_1, g_2, g_3 are defined by Eq. (11.81),

$$J_1 = \frac{1}{R^2}\begin{pmatrix} \sum_{n=1}^{N}(r_n - a)^2 & \sum_{n=1}^{N}(r_n - a)(c_n - b) & \sum_{n=1}^{N}(r_n - a)R \\ & \sum_{n=1}^{N}(c_n - b)^2 & \sum_{n=1}^{N}(c_n - b)R \\ & & NR^2 \end{pmatrix}$$

$$J_2 = \frac{1}{R^2}\begin{pmatrix} (r_1 - a)^2 \ldots (r_N - a)^2 & (r_1 - a)(c_1 - b) \ldots (r_N - a)(c_N - b) \\ (r_1 - a)(c_1 - b) \ldots (r_N - b)(c_N - b) & (c_1 - b)^2 \ldots (c_N - b)^2 \\ (r_1 - a)R \ldots (r_N - a)R & (c_1 - b)R \ldots (c_N - b)R \end{pmatrix}$$

Since $(r_n - a)^2 + (c_n - b)^2 = R^2$ for $n = 1, \ldots, N$, $J_2 J_2'$ must then satisfy $J_2 J_2' = J_1$. In this case the covariance matrix simplifies to

$$E\left[\begin{pmatrix} \Delta a \\ \Delta b \\ \Delta R \end{pmatrix} (\Delta a\quad \Delta b\quad \Delta R)\right] = \sigma^2 J_1^{-1} \tag{11.84}$$

To estimate the covariance matrix for $(\Delta a, \Delta b, \Delta R)$, we use estimates $\hat{\sigma}^2$ and $\hat{J}_1$ in Eq. (11.84) for σ^2 and J, respectively. $\hat{J}_1$ is J_1 with the observed values $(\hat{r}_1, \hat{c}_1), \ldots, (\hat{r}_N, \hat{c}_N)$ and the inferred values $\hat{a}, \hat{b}, \hat{R}$ in place of the unknown but true values $[(r_1, c_1), \ldots, (r_N, c_N), a, b, R]$.

Finally, we work out the expected value of ϵ^2 assuming the error is computed by using the true values for $a, b,$ and R. This expectation is directly related to σ^2.

$$E[\epsilon^2] = E\left[\sum_{n=1}^{N}\left(\sqrt{(\hat{r}_n - a)^2 + (\hat{c}_n - b)^2} - R\right)^2\right]$$

$$= \sum_{n=1}^{N} E\left[\left(\sqrt{(r_n - a)^2 + 2\xi(r_n - a) + \xi_n^2 + (c_n - b)^2 + 2\eta_n(c_n - b) + \eta_n^2} - R\right)^2\right]$$

$$= \sum_{n=1}^{N} E\left[\left(R\sqrt{1 + \Delta_n} - R\right)^2\right] \tag{11.85}$$

where

$$\Delta_n = \frac{2\xi_n(r_n - a) + \xi_n^2 + 2\eta_n(c_n - b) + \eta_n^2}{R^2} \tag{11.86}$$

Then by squaring the argument of the expectation and simplifying, we obtain

$$E[\epsilon^2] = R^2 \sum_{n=1}^{N} E\left[(1 + \Delta_n) - 2\sqrt{1 + \Delta_n} + 1\right]$$

$$= R^2 \sum_{n=1}^{N} E\left[2 + \Delta_n - 2\sqrt{1 + \Delta_n}\right]$$

Assuming the variance of the noise is small compared with R^2, so that $|\Delta_n| \ll 1$, we may expand $\sqrt{1 + \Delta_n}$ in a Taylor series to obtain

$$\sqrt{1 + \Delta_n} = 1 + \frac{\Delta_n}{2} - \frac{\Delta_n^2}{8}$$

Hence

$$E[\epsilon^2] = R^2 \sum_{n=1}^{N} E\left[2 + \Delta_n - 2\left(1 + \frac{\Delta_n}{2} - \frac{\Delta_n^2}{8}\right)\right]$$

$$= \frac{R^2}{4} \sum_{n=1}^{N} E[\Delta_n^2] \tag{11.87}$$

Now, using Eq. (11.86) and assuming that $E[\xi_n^3] = E[\eta_n^3] = 0$, we determine that

$$E[\Delta_n^2] = \frac{4\sigma^2}{R^2} + \frac{2(\sigma^4 + \mu_4)}{R^4} \tag{11.88}$$

where $\mu_4 = E[\xi_n^4] = E[\eta_n^4]$.

If the noise is Gaussian, then $\mu_4 = 3\sigma^4$. In this case Eq. (11.88) becomes

$$E[\Delta_n^2] = \frac{4\sigma^2}{R^2} + \frac{8\sigma^4}{R^4} = \frac{4\sigma^2}{R^2}\left(1 + \frac{2\sigma^2}{R^2}\right) \tag{11.89}$$

Substituting Eq. (11.89) into Eq. (11.87), we obtain

$$E[\epsilon^2] = \frac{R^2}{4} \sum_{n=1}^{N} \frac{4\sigma^2}{R^2}\left(1 + \frac{2\sigma^2}{R^2}\right)$$

$$= N\sigma^2\left(1 + \frac{2\sigma^2}{R^2}\right) \tag{11.90}$$

Therefore when $\sigma^2 \ll R^2$,

$$E[\epsilon^2] = N\sigma^2$$

which suggests $\hat{\sigma}^2 = \epsilon^2/N$ as an estimator for σ^2. Since in actual practice a, b, and R are estimated as those values that minimize ϵ^2, we must use

$$\hat{\sigma}^2 = \frac{\epsilon^2}{(N - 3)} \tag{11.91}$$

as the estimator for σ^2.

The analysis we have just done to determine the expected value of ϵ^2 is also useful for establishing the expected value of the estimator $\hat{R}$, which is actually slightly biased. To make our analysis easier, we assume N is large enough so that the difference between $\hat{a}$ and a and $\hat{b}$ and b is negligible. In this case

$$\hat{R} = \frac{1}{N} \sum_{n=1}^{N} \sqrt{(\hat{r}_n - \hat{a})^2 + (\hat{c}_n - \hat{b})^2}$$

$$\approx \frac{1}{N} \sum_{n=1}^{N} \sqrt{(\hat{r}_n - a)^2 + (\hat{c}_n - b)^2} = \frac{R}{N} \sum_{n=1}^{N} \sqrt{1 + \Delta_n}$$

$$\approx \frac{R}{N} \sum_{n=1}^{N} \left(1 + \frac{\Delta_n}{2}\right) = R + \frac{R}{2N} \sum_{n=1}^{N} \Delta_n$$

Hence $E[\hat{R}] \approx R + \frac{R}{2N} \sum_{n=1}^{N} E[\Delta_n]$. But from Eq. (11.86) $E[\Delta_n] = \frac{2\sigma^2}{R^2}$, so that $E[\hat{R}] \approx R + \frac{\sigma^2}{R}$.

Berman (1989) observes that the least-squares solutions $\hat{a}, \hat{b}$, and $\hat{R}$ to the sum of the squared error of Eq. (11.59) are biased. As we have done, he shows that the asymptotic bias of R is about σ^2/R, where σ^2 is the Gaussian variance of the additive noise that perturbs the true (r_n, c_n) to produce the observed $(\hat{r}_n, \hat{c}_n)$. The biases of $\hat{a}$ and $\hat{b}$ tend to be negligible in most cases. Other statistical analyses of the circle-fitting model can be found in Berman and Griffiths (1985), Berman (1983), Berman and Culpin (1986), and Anderson (1981).

11.10.6 Fitting to a Conic

In the case of the conic, the parameter vector $w' = (a, b, A, B, C)$ and

$$f(r, c, w) = f(r, c, a, b, A, B, C) = A(r - a)^2 + 2B(r - a)(c - b) + C(c - b)^2 - 1.$$

Then

$$\frac{\partial f}{\partial r} = 2A(r - a) + 2B(c - b)$$

$$\frac{\partial f}{\partial c} = 2B(r - a) + 2C(c - b)$$

Hence by Eq. (11.45)

$$\epsilon^2 = \frac{1}{4} \sum_{n=1}^{N} \frac{[A(\hat{r}_n - a)^2 + 2B(\hat{r}_n - a)(\hat{c}_n - b) + C(\hat{c}_n - b)^2 - 1]^2}{[A(\hat{r}_n - a) + B(\hat{c}_n - b)]^2 + [B(\hat{r}_n - a) + C(\hat{c}_n - b)]^2} \tag{11.92}$$

The gradient of ϵ^2 to be used to determine Δw by Eq. (11.48) is then given by

$$
\nabla \epsilon^2 = \begin{pmatrix} \frac{\partial \epsilon^2}{\partial a} \\ \frac{\partial \epsilon^2}{\partial b} \\ \frac{\partial \epsilon^2}{\partial A} \\ \frac{\partial \epsilon^2}{\partial B} \\ \frac{\partial \epsilon^2}{\partial C} \end{pmatrix}
$$

$$
= \frac{1}{2} \sum_{n=1}^{N} d_n f_n \left\{ \begin{pmatrix} -2g_n \\ -2h_n \\ (\hat{r}_n - a)^2 \\ 2(\hat{r}_n - a)(\hat{c}_n - b) \\ (\hat{c}_n - b)^2 \end{pmatrix} = d_n f_n \begin{pmatrix} -Ag_n - Bh_n \\ -Bg_n - Ch_n \\ g_n(\hat{r}_n - a) \\ g_n(\hat{c}_n - b) + h_n(\hat{r}_n - a) \\ h_n(\hat{c}_n - b) \end{pmatrix} \right\}
$$

where

$$
\begin{aligned}
g_n &= A(\hat{r}_n - a) + B(\hat{c}_n - b) \\
h_n &= B(\hat{r}_n - a) + C(\hat{c}_n - b) \\
d_n &= 1/(g_n^2 + h_n^2) \\
f_n &= A(\hat{r}_n - a)^2 + 2B(\hat{r}_n - a)(\hat{c}_n - b) + C(\hat{c}_n - b)^2
\end{aligned}
$$

To determine initial values for the parameters, we can proceed by using the principal-axis curve-fit procedure of Section 11.7.2.

Sampson (1982) gives an iterative refinement method to find the conic parameters to minimize Eq. (11.92). Pavlidis (1983) has a good discussion on fitting curves with conic splines.

11.10.7   Fitting to an Ellipse

Probably the most common conic fitting done is the fit to an ellipse. If the conic is known to be an ellipse, there is an additional constraint on the relationships between A, B, and C that must be imposed: $B^2 < AC$.

We describe here a way of implicitly incorporating this constraint in the fitting procedure by working with a different set of parameters. Instead of representing the ellipse with a functional form,

$$
\begin{pmatrix} r - a \\ c - b \end{pmatrix}' \begin{pmatrix} A & B \\ B & C \end{pmatrix} \begin{pmatrix} r - a \\ c - b \end{pmatrix} = 1, \text{ where the matrix form } \begin{pmatrix} A & B \\ B & C \end{pmatrix}
$$

is not constrained and therefore could be negative definite, we represent

$$
\begin{pmatrix} A & B \\ B & C \end{pmatrix}
$$

by a matrix product guaranteed to be positive semidefinite:

$$
\begin{aligned}
\begin{pmatrix} A & B \\ B & C \end{pmatrix} &= \begin{pmatrix} d & e \\ 0 & f \end{pmatrix}' \begin{pmatrix} d & e \\ 0 & f \end{pmatrix} \\
&= \begin{pmatrix} d^2 & de \\ de & e^+ f^2 \end{pmatrix}
\end{aligned}
$$

It is clear from this relation that for any values d, e, and f, the matrix

$$\begin{pmatrix} d^2 & de \\ de & e^2 + f^2 \end{pmatrix}$$

is positive definite. Conversely, for any positive definite matrix $\begin{pmatrix} A & B \\ B & C \end{pmatrix}$, there exist values of d, e, and f such that

$$\begin{pmatrix} A & B \\ B & C \end{pmatrix} = \begin{pmatrix} d^2 & de \\ de & e^2 + f^2 \end{pmatrix}$$

One set of relations from A, B, C to d, e, f is given by

$$d = \sqrt{A}$$

$$e = \frac{B}{d}$$

$$f = \sqrt{C - e^2}$$

This means that we can set up the fitting problem with the free parameters d, e, f. With this perspective we define the functions to be minimized by

$$\epsilon^2 = \frac{1}{4} \sum_{n=1}^{N} \frac{[d^2(r_n - a)^2 + 2de(r_n - a)(c_n - b) + (e^2 + f^2)(c_n - b)^2 - 1]^2}{[d^2(r_n - a) + de(c_n - b)]^2 + [de(r_n - a) + (e^2 + f^2)(c_n - b)]^2}$$

and proceed as before.

To determine an initial estimate for the parameters a, b, A, B, C, we can use the relationships between the first- and second-order moments of the observed points and the parameters a, b, A, B, C. Hence using the relation developed in Appendix A on ellipses, we have

$$a = \frac{1}{N} \sum_{n=1}^{N} \hat{r}_n$$

$$b = \frac{1}{N} \sum_{n=1}^{N} \hat{c}_n$$

$$\begin{pmatrix} A & B \\ B & C \end{pmatrix} = \frac{1}{(\hat{\mu}_{rr}\hat{\mu}_{cc} - \hat{\mu}_{rc}^2)} \begin{pmatrix} \hat{\mu}_{cc} & -\hat{\mu}_{rc} \\ -\hat{\mu}_{rc} & \hat{\mu}_{rr} \end{pmatrix}$$

where

$$\hat{\mu}_{rr} = \frac{1}{N} \sum_{n=1}^{N} (\hat{r}_n - a)^2$$

$$\hat{\mu}_{rc} = \frac{1}{N} \sum_{n=1}^{N} (\hat{r}_n - a)(\hat{c}_n - b)$$

$$\hat{\mu}_{cc} = \frac{1}{N} \sum_{n=1}^{N} (\hat{c}_n - b)^2$$

Proffitt (1982) uses a discrete Fourier transform technique for fitting ellipses. Wang, Hanson, and Riseman (1988) give a short discussion on extracting ellipses from images.

11.10.8 Bayesian Fitting

The equal-weight least-squares fit discussed in the previous section is suitable when all the observed data points are noisy observations of points that lie on a curve of interest. That is, they satisfy the curve-fitting model. However, if there are some observed data points that are not noisy observations of points that lie on the curve of interest, then the simple least-squares fitting model is incorrect. Indeed a data point that should not be included in a fit, but is, can have an arbitrarily large effect in throwing off an estimated parameter value; for this reason a more robust approach should be considered. In this section we give a Bayesian approach for fitting under the conditions that some of the observed data points may be points having nothing to do with the curve being fit.

To set up this framework, we need to write expressions for the probability density of observing a noisy data point (r, c) that comes from a curve $f(r, c, w) = 0$. Using a model that the random perturbations are normal and the simple expressions of Eq. (11.39) are derived for the distance between a point and a curve, we can write

$$P(r, c \mid w) = \frac{1}{\sqrt{2\pi}\sigma} e^{\frac{1}{2}\frac{f(r,c,w)^2}{\sigma^2 |\nabla|^2}}$$

where $(\nabla f)' = \left(\frac{\partial f}{\partial r}, \frac{\partial f}{\partial c}\right)$. Also, we need the probability density of observing a data point (r, c), given that it does not come from the curve being fit. In this case we will assume that (r, c) comes from a uniform distribution over an area of $\frac{1}{\epsilon}$ centered at $(0,0)$. Hence

$$P(r, c \mid \text{ not from curve}) = \epsilon$$

Finally, we need the probability q that an observed data point comes from the curve of interest, and for each observation (r_n, c_n) we define a random variable y_n, where $y_n = 1$ if (r_n, c_n) comes from the curve and $y_n = 0$ if (r_n, c_n) does not come from the curve. Hence $P(y_n = 1) = q$ and $P(y_n = 0) = 1 - q$. Then

$$P[w \mid (r_1, c_1), \ldots, (r_N, c_N)] = \frac{P[(r_1, c_1), \ldots, (r_N, c_N) \mid w]}{P[(r_1, c_1), \ldots, (r_N, c_N)]} P(w)$$

$$= \frac{\sum_{y_1=0}^{1}, \ldots, \sum_{y_N=0}^{1} P[(r_1, c_1), y_1, \ldots, (r_N, c_N), y_N \mid w]}{P[(r_1, c_1), \ldots, (r_N, c_N)]} P(w)$$

$$\geq \frac{P[(r_1, c_1), y_1, \ldots, (r_N, c_N), y_N \mid w]}{P[(r_1, c_1), \ldots, (r_N, c_N)]} P(w) \quad \text{for every } (y_1, \ldots, y_N)$$

Assuming the data points are independently conditioned on w and that $P(y_n|w) = P(y_n)$, we obtain

$$P[(r_1,c_1),y_1,\ldots,(r_N,c_N),y_N|w] = \prod_{n=1}^{N} P[(r_n,c_n),y_n|w]$$

$$= \prod_{n=1}^{N} P[(r_n,c_n)|w,y_n)]P(y_n|w)$$

$$= \prod_{n=1}^{N} \begin{cases} P[(r_n,c_n)|w,y_n]q & \text{if } y_n = 1 \\ \epsilon(1-q) & \text{if } y_n = 0 \end{cases}$$

Hence a lower bound $P[w|(r_1,c_1),\ldots,(r_N,c_N)]$ is given by

$$P[w|(r_1,c_1),\ldots,(r_N,c_N)] \geq \frac{\displaystyle\prod_{n=1}^{N} \begin{cases} P(r_n,c_n|w)q & \text{if } y_n = 1 \\ \epsilon(1-q) & \text{if } y_n = 0 \end{cases}}{P[(r_1,c_1),\ldots,(r_N,c_N)]}P(w)$$

This lower bound motivates the following fitting procedure:

1. For L iterations, iterate by selecting at each iteration K observations, with a reasonable spread, from the set of N observations and do a least-squares fit to estimate an initial w_o.

2. Determine which points to take. At iteration t, w_t is defined. Define y_n^t by

$$y_n^t = \begin{cases} 1 & \text{if } P[(r_n,c_n)|w_t]q > \epsilon(1-q) \\ 0 & \text{otherwise} \end{cases}$$

3. Determine probability P_t. Define P_t by

$$P_t = P(w_t)\prod_{n=1}^{N} \begin{cases} P[(r_n,c_n)|w_t]q & \text{if } y_n^t = 1 \\ \epsilon(1-q) & \text{if } y_n^t = 0 \end{cases}$$

4. Having hypothesized which points come from the curve and which points do not come from the curve, determine w_{t+1} by maximizing

$$P(w_{t+1})\prod_{\substack{n=1 \\ y_n^t=1}}^{N} P[(r_n,c_n)|w_{t+1}]$$

5. Iterate so long as $P_{t+1} > P_t$ and $t < number\_of\_iterations$.

6. From the L iterations, select the resulting w yielding the largest P.

11.10.9 Uniform Error Estimation

If all the points in the observed arc are reliable (deviations from their true values are small), uniform error estimation may be appropriate. We will set the problem up by using a parametric representation of the curve to be estimated. Suppose the unknown curve can be parametrically represented as

$$r(s) = \sum_{m=1}^{M} \alpha_m \phi_m(s)$$

$$c(s) = \sum_{m=1}^{M} \beta_m \phi_m(s)$$

where s is arc length, $\phi_1, \ldots, \phi_M$ are given basis functions, and $\alpha_1, \ldots, \alpha_M$ and $\beta_1, \ldots, \beta_M$ are the unknown coefficients. The observed arc sequences $S = < (r_1, c_1), \ldots, (r_N, c_N) >$ can be put into parametric form by defining $S_r = < (s_1, r_1), \ldots, (s_N, r_N) >$ and $S_c = < (s_1, c_1), \ldots, (s_N, c_N) >$, where $s_1 = 0$ and

$$s_n = \sqrt{\sum_{i=2}^{n} (r_i - r_{i-1})^2 + (c_i - c_{i-1})^2}, \quad n = 1, \ldots, N$$

The uniform error estimation for $\alpha_1, \ldots, \alpha_M$, $\beta_1, \ldots, \beta_M$ seeks to minimize

$$e = \max_n \left\{ \left| \sum_{m=1}^{M} \alpha_m \phi_m(s_n) - r_n \right|, \left| \sum_{m=1}^{M} \beta_m \phi_m(s_n) - c_n \right| \right\} \qquad (11.93)$$

This is equivalent to finding $\alpha_1, \ldots, \alpha_M$ to minimize

$$e_r = \max_n \left| \sum_{m=1}^{M} \alpha_m \phi_m(s_n) - r_n \right| \qquad (11.94)$$

and finding $\beta_1, \ldots, \beta_M$ to minimize

$$e_c = \max_n \left| \sum_{m=1}^{M} \beta_m \phi_m(s_n) - c_n \right| \qquad (11.95)$$

Each of these problems can be solved as a linear programming problem. To see how to represent the problem, consider Eq. (11.94), which implies

$$-e_r \leq \sum_{m=1}^{M} \alpha_m \phi_m(s_n) - r_n \leq e_r, \quad n = 1, \ldots, N \qquad (11.96)$$

The inequalities of Eq. (11.96) imply

$$e_r + \sum_{m=1}^{M} \alpha_m \phi_m(s_n) \geq r_n$$

$$e_r - \sum_{m=1}^{M} \alpha_m \phi_m(s_n) \geq -r_n, \quad n = 1, \ldots, N \qquad (11.97)$$

The linear programming problem is to find $(e_r, \alpha_1, \ldots, \alpha_M)$ to minimize e_r subject to the constraint system

$$
\begin{pmatrix}
1 & \phi_1(s_1) & \cdots & \phi_m(s_1) \\
  & \vdots & & \\
1 & \phi_n(s_N) & \cdots & \phi_M(s_N) \\
1 & -\phi_1(s_1) & \cdots & -\phi_M(s_N) \\
  & \vdots & & \\
1 & \phi_1(s_N) & \cdots & -\phi_M(s_N)
\end{pmatrix}
\begin{pmatrix}
e_r \\ \alpha_1 \\ \vdots \\ \alpha_M
\end{pmatrix}
\geq
\begin{pmatrix}
r_1 \\ \vdots \\ r_N \\ -r_1 \\ \vdots \\ -r_N
\end{pmatrix}
$$

The solution to Eq. (11.95) can be likewise obtained as the solution to a linear programming problem.

Exercises

11.1. Show that if A is a 2×2 matrix, then for any λ,

$$
(I - \lambda A)^{-1} = \frac{I - \lambda A^{-1} |A|}{1 - \lambda \text{ trace } A + \lambda^2 |A|}
$$

11.2. Suppose x and y are angles expressed in degrees in the range $0°$ to $360°$. Prove that the following procedure determines a y^* that is equal to y modulo $360°$ such that

$$
|x - y^*| = \min_{\substack{u \\ u=y \bmod 360}} |x - u|
$$

$d = x - y$;
if $d > 0$ then $u = y + 360°$
else $u = y - 360°$;
$e = x - u$;
if $|d| < |e|$ then $y^* = y$
else $y^* = u$;

11.3. Refer to Eq. (11.27) of Section 11.7.1. Show that

$$
E[\hat{\mu}_{rc} - \mu_{rc}] = 0
$$

$$
E[\hat{\lambda} - \hat{\mu}_{rr} + \mu_{rr}] = 0
$$

$$
E\left[(\hat{\mu}_{rc} - \mu_{rc})^2\right] = \frac{\sigma^2(\mu_{rr} + \mu_{cc} + \sigma^2)}{N - 1}
$$

$$
E\left[(\hat{\lambda} - \hat{\mu}_{rr} + \mu_{rr})^2\right] = \frac{4\sigma^2 \mu_{rr}(\mu_{rr} + \mu_{cc} + \sigma^2)}{(N - 1)(\mu_{rr} + \mu_{cc})}
$$

$$
E\left[(\hat{\mu}_{rc} - \mu_{rc})(\hat{\lambda} - \hat{\mu}_{rr} + \mu_{rr})\right] = \frac{2\sigma^2(\mu_{rr} + \mu_{cc} + \sigma^2)}{(N - 1)} \alpha\beta
$$

11.4. Suppose that in the line-fit model of Eq. (11.18),

$$E[\xi_n] = E[\eta_n] = 0$$

$$E[\xi_n \xi_j] = \begin{cases} \sigma_n^2 & n = j \\ 0 & \text{otherwise} \end{cases}$$

$$E[\eta_n \eta_j] = \begin{cases} \sigma_n^2 & n = j \\ 0 & \text{otherwise} \end{cases}$$

$$E[\xi_n \eta_j] = 0$$

Show that

$$V[\hat{\alpha}] = \beta^2 \frac{(\mu_{rr} + \mu_{cc} + N/W)}{\tilde{W}(\mu_{rr} + \mu_{cc})^2}$$

and

$$V[\hat{\beta}] = \alpha^2 \frac{(\mu_{rr} + \mu_{cc} + N/W)}{\tilde{W}(\mu_{rr} + \mu_{cc})^2}$$

where

$$W = \sum_{n=1}^{N} \frac{1}{\sigma_n^2}$$

and

$$\tilde{W} = \frac{N-1}{N} W$$

11.5. Refer to Eq. (11.32). Show that

$$E\left[(\hat{\alpha}\bar{\xi} + \hat{\beta}\bar{\eta})^2\right] = \sigma^2(V[\hat{\alpha}] + V[\hat{\beta}] + 1)$$

$$E\left[(\hat{\alpha} - \alpha)(\hat{\alpha}\bar{\xi} + \hat{\beta}\bar{\eta})\right] = 0$$

$$E\left[(\hat{\beta} - \beta)(\hat{\alpha}\bar{\xi} + \hat{\beta}\bar{\eta})\right] = 0$$

11.6. Show that the point (r, c) on the line $\alpha r + \beta c + \gamma$ closest to a given point (r_0, c_0) is given by

$$\begin{pmatrix} r \\ c \end{pmatrix} = \begin{pmatrix} r_0 \\ c_0 \end{pmatrix} - (\alpha r_0 + \beta c_0 + \gamma) \begin{pmatrix} \alpha \\ \beta \end{pmatrix}$$

11.7. A matrix A is skew symmetric if and only if $A' = -A$. Show that if A and B are symmetric matrices, then $AB - BA$ is skew symmetric. Then show that if A is any 2×2 skew symmetric matrix and R is a 2×2 rotation matrix, then $A = RAR'$. Finally, show that if A and B are 2×2 matrices and $T_A' A T_A = \Omega_A$ and $T_B' B T_B = \Omega_B$, where T_A and T_B are rotation matrices and

$$\Omega_A = \begin{pmatrix} \lambda_{A_{large}} & 0 \\ 0 & \lambda_{A_{small}} \end{pmatrix} \quad \text{and} \quad \Omega_B = \begin{pmatrix} \lambda_{B_{large}} & 0 \\ 0 & \lambda_{B_{small}} \end{pmatrix}$$

then

$$AB - BA = M - M'$$

where

$$m_{12} = \lambda_{A_{large}} (\lambda_{B_{large}} - \lambda_{B_{small}}) \sin \Delta\theta \cos \Delta\theta$$

$$m_{21} = \lambda_{A_{small}} (\lambda_{B_{large}} - \lambda_{B_{small}}) \sin \Delta\theta \cos \Delta\theta$$

and $\Delta\theta$ is the difference between the angular orientation of the eigenvectors of A and B having the largest eigenvalues, and therefore

$$m_{12} - m_{21} = \frac{1}{2}\sqrt{1 - 4|A|}\sqrt{1 - 4|B|} \sin 2\Delta\theta$$

This is the basis of the Anderson and Bezdek (1984) procedure for determining tangential deflection.

11.8. Show that the point (r,c) on the circle $(r - a)^2 + (c - b)^2 = R^2$ closest to a given point (r_0, c_0) is given by

$$\begin{pmatrix} r \\ c \end{pmatrix} = \begin{pmatrix} a \\ b \end{pmatrix} + R \begin{pmatrix} r_0 - a \\ c_0 - b \end{pmatrix} / \sqrt{(r_0 - a)^2 + (c_0 - b)^2}$$

11.9. For the given observed points that are noisy observations of a 90° circular arc, determine the circle center and radius by three of the techniques discussed in Section 11.10.4.

n	$\hat{r}_n$	$\hat{c}_n$
1	7.93535	17.15845
2	7.26935	18.43970
3	5.17017	19.61730
4	3.70451	19.83813
5	2.15564	20.73293
6	0.69466	20.86883
7	-1.14771	20.56556
8	-3.07478	20.03483
9	-5.17503	19.36585
10	-6.07584	18.91065

The circle center is $(a, b) = (14.9027, 44.8558)$ and the radius is 9.2441. The ϵ^2 is .4368, so that an estimate of the noise variance is $\hat{\sigma}^2 = .2497$.

11.10. Let an ellipse $A(r - a)^2 + B(r - a)(c - b) + D(c - b)^2 = 1$ and a point (r_0, c_0) be given. Show that the point (r,c) on the ellipse that intersects the line segment determined (r_0, c_0) and (a, b) is given by

$$\begin{pmatrix} r \\ c \end{pmatrix} = \begin{pmatrix} r_0 - a \\ c_0 - b \end{pmatrix} \frac{1}{\sqrt{A(r_0 - a)^2 + B(r_0 - a)(c_0 - b) + D(c_0 - b)^2}}$$

Then determine a bound for the difference between the distance between (r_0, c_0) and (r, c) and the distance between (r_0, c_0) and the closest point on the ellipse to (r_0, c_0).

11.11. The template-matching approach to the Hough transform is to go through each angle θ and each distance d and determine the set of pixel positions interacting with the line $E(\theta, d)$. To determine the Hough value $H(\theta, d)$, perform the summation

$$H(\theta, d) + \sum_{(r,c) \in E(\theta, d)} I(r, c)$$

where $I(r, c)$ is the binary image having a value of 1 if the pixel (r, c) takes the value 1 and 0 otherwise. Show that the computational complexity of this approach is

$$C_o = \sum_{\theta} \sum_{d} \#E(\theta, d)$$

11.12. A second approach to the Hough transform is to go through each pixel position (r, c) on the image. If $I(r, c) = 0$, go on to the next pixel. If $I(r, c) = 1$, then determine d as a function of θ by

$$d = r \sin \theta + c \cos \theta$$

In the Hough space, each pair $(\theta, d(\theta))$ is incremented by one. Show that the computational complexity of this procedure is

$$\#R \times C + \#\{(r, c) | I(r, c) = 1\} \times \text{number of quantized values for } \theta$$

11.13. Write a program to generate a correlated Gaussian noise sequence of given length N. Use a standard Gaussian pseudo-random number generator with a given noise standard deviation to generate a sequence of length $N + 2K$. Then correlate the noise by averaging with a filter of length $2K + 1$. The averaging filter can be a box filter or can be a Gaussian filter where the standard deviation σ of the Gaussian filter is related to K by $3\sigma = K$.

11.14. Write a program to generate a noisy digital straight-line segment given the expected value (a, b) of the first point [(a, b) does not necessarily lie on the integer grid], the counterclockwise angle θ that the line segment makes with the column axis, and the length L of the line segment. From L, the number N of points on the noisy digital straight line can be determined by $N = \max L \cos \theta, L \sin \theta$. If $< m_1, \ldots, m_N >$ is the noisy correlated noise sequence generated in Exercise 11.13, the noisy digital line sequence is $< (r_i, c_i) : i = 1, \ldots, N >$ where

$$\left. \begin{array}{l} r_i = [a + i \tan \theta + m_i] \\ c_i = [b + i] \end{array} \right\} \quad \text{if } \cos \theta \geq \sin \theta$$

and

$$\left. \begin{array}{l} r_i = [a + i] \\ c_i = [b + i \cot \theta + m_i] \end{array} \right\} \quad \text{if } \cos \theta < \sin \theta$$

and where [ ] designates rounding the nearest integer.

11.15. Write a program to generate a pair of connected noisy digital line segments each of a given length L in the following way. Given (a, b) the expected value of the first point of the first line segment, and the noise standard deviation of the Gaussian pseudo-random number generator, choose the orientation of the line at random. The last point of the generated first line segment becomes the first point of the second line segment. The second line segment is generated at a given angle θ with respect to the first line segment and for the same length L.

11.16. Write a program that inputs a noisy sequence of digital points and detects a corner by any method discussed in this chapter.

11.17. Do an experiment to determine the performance of the corner detector programmed in Example 11.16. The experimental protocol is as follows: For each of the chosen values for line length L, included angle θ and noise standard deviation σ, generate 200 noisy digital sequences $C_1, \ldots, C_{200}$ of a connected pair of line segments (see

Example 11.15). Apply the corner detection algorithm to each of the 200 sequences. Let (s_i, t_i) be the true corner location associated with C_i. For each detected corner (p, q) on C_i, compute Dist$[(s_i, t_i), (p, q)]$, the distance from true corner (s_i, t_i). If this distance is less than D, consider that the true corner is detected by the corner detection algorithm. Otherwise (p, q) is considered as a false alarm. The fraction of misdetections p_m and the fraction of false alarms p_f can be estimated from the following numbers $f_{00}, f_{01}, f_{10}, f_{11}$ where

$$f_{10} = \#\{(s_i, t_i) | \text{Dist}((s_i, t_i), (p, q)) \geq D$$

$$\text{for all detected corner points } (p, q) \text{ on curve } C_i\}$$

$$f_{11} = \#\{(s_i, t_i) | \text{for some detected corner point } (p, q)$$

$$\text{on some curve } C_i, \text{Dist}((s_i, t_i), (p, q)) < D\}$$

$$f_{01} = \#\{(p, q) | \text{for some } C_i, (p, q) \text{ is detected as a corner}$$

$$\text{point on } C_i \text{ and Dist}((s_i, t_i), (p, q)) \geq D\}$$

$$f_{00} = 400N - f_{11} - f_{10} - f_{01}$$

$$p_m = \frac{f_{10}}{f_{10} + f_{11}}$$

$$p_f = \frac{f_{01}}{f_{00} + f_{01}}$$

For the detected corner points, which are close to a true corner point, we can compute the average and variance of the distance between the detected corner point and the true corner point. Operating curves plotting p_m against p_f can be obtained by varying threshold D holding all other parameters constant. Chosen values of parameters N, θ, and σ can be

$$N \text{ at } 8, 10, 15, 20, 30, 40, 50, 100$$

$$\theta \text{ at } 15°, 30°, 60°, 90°, 120°, 150°, 165°$$

$$\sigma \text{ at } 0, .5, 1, 1.5, 2.0$$

■ Bibliography

Alagar, V. S., and L. H. Thiel, "Algorithms for Detecting M-Dimensional Objects in N-Dimensional Spaces," *IEEE Transactions on Pattern Analysis and Machine Intelligence,* Vol. PAMI-3, 1981, pp. 245–256.

Amir, I., "Algorithm for Finding the Center of Circular Fiducials," *Computer Vision, Graphics, and Image Processing,* Vol. 49, 1990, pp. 398–406.

Anderson, D. A., "The Circular Structural Model," *Journal of the Royal Statistical Society, B,* Vol. 43, 1981, pp. 131–141.

Anderson, I. M., and J. C. Bezdek, "Curvature and Tangential Deflection of Discrete Arcs: A Theory Based on the Commutator of Scatter Matrix Pairs and Its Application to Vertex Detection in Planar Shape Data," *IEEE Transactions on Pattern Analysis and Machine Intelligence,* Vol. PAMI-6, 1984, pp. 27–40.

Angell, I., and J. Barber, "An Algorithm for Fitting Circles and Ellipses to Megalithic Stone Rings," *Science and Archaeology,* Vol. 20, 1977, pp. 11–16.

Attneave, F., "Some Informal Aspects of Visual Perception," *Psychological Review,* Vol. 61, 1954, pp. 183–193.

——, "Physical Determinants of the Judged Complexity of Shapes," *Journal of Experimental Psychology,* Vol. 53, 1957, pp. 221–227.

Ballard, D. H., "Generalizing the Hough Transform to Detect Arbitrary Shapes," *Pattern Recognition,* Vol. 13, 1981a, pp. 111–122.

——, "Parameter Networks: Towards a Theory of Low-Level Vision," *Seventh International Joint Conference on Artificial Intelligence,* Vancouver, BC, 1981b, pp. 1068–78.

Ballard, D. H., and C. M. Brown, *Computer Vision,* Prentice-Hall, Englewood Cliffs, NJ, 1982.

Ballard, D. H., and D. Sabbah, "On Shapes," *Seventh International Joint Conference on Artificial Intelligence,* 1981, Vancouver, BC, pp. 607–612.

——, "Viewer Independent Shape Recognition," *IEEE Transactions on Pattern Analysis and Machine Intelligence,* Vol. PAMI-5, 1983, pp. 653–660.

Baruch, O., and M. H. Loew, "Segmentation of Two-Dimensional Boundaries Using the Chain Code," *Pattern Recognition,* Vol. 21, 1988, pp. 581–589.

Bellman, R., "On the Approximation of Curves by Line Segments Using Dynamic Programming," *Communications of the ACM,* Vol. 4, 1961, p. 284.

Berman, M., "Estimating the Parameters of a Circle When Angular Differences Are Known," *Applied Statistics,* Vol. 32, 1983, pp. 1–6.

——, "Large Sample Bias in Least Squares Estimators of a Circular Arc Center and Its Radius," *Computer Vision, Graphics, and Image Processing,* Vol. 45, 1989, pp. 126–128.

Berman, M., and D. Culpin, "The Statistical Behaviour of Some Least Squares Estimators of the Centre and Radius of a Circle," *Journal of the Royal Statistical Society, B,* Vol. 48, 1986, pp. 183–196.

Berman, M., and D. Griffiths, "Incorporating Angular Information into Models for Stone Circle Data," *Applied Statistics,* Vol. 34, 1985, pp. 237–245.

Beus, H. L., and S. S. H. Tiu, "An Improved Corner Detection Algorithm Based on Chain-Coded Plane Curves," *Pattern Recognition,* Vol. 20, 1987, pp. 291–296.

Beylkin, G., "Discrete Radon Transform," *IEEE Transactions on Acoustics, Speech, and Signal Processing,* Vol. ASSP-35, 1987, pp. 162–172.

Bezdek, J. C., and I. M. Anderson, "An Application of the c-Varieties Clustering Algorithms to Polygonal Curve Fitting," *IEEE Transactions on Systems, Man, and Cybernetics,* Vol. SMC-15, 1985, pp. 637–641.

Bixler, J. P., L. T. Watson, and J. P. Sanford, "Spline-Based Recognition of Straight Lines and Curves in Engineering Line Drawings," *Image and Vision Computing,* Vol. 6, 1988, pp. 262–269.

Boldt, M., R. Weiss, and E. Riseman, "Token-Based Extraction of Straight Lines," *IEEE Transactions on Systems, Man, and Cybernetics,* Vol. 19, 1989, pp. 1581–94.

Bookstein, F. L., "Fitting Conic Sections to Scattered Data," *Computer Graphics and Image Processing,* Vol. 9, 1979, pp. 56–71.

Brown, C. M., "Inherent Bias and Noise in the Hough Transform," *IEEE Transactions on Pattern Analysis and Machine Intelligence,* Vol. PAMI-5, 1983, pp. 493–505.

Bruckstein, A. M., and A. N. Netravali, "On Minimal Energy Trajectories," *Computer Vision, Graphics, and Image Processing,* Vol. 49, 1990, pp. 283–296.

Burns, J. R., A. R. Hanson, and E. M Riseman, "Extracting Straight Lines," *IEEE Transactions on Pattern Analysis and Machine Intelligence,* Vol. PAMI-8, 1986, pp. 425–455.

Cantoni, A., "Optimal Curve-Fitting with Piecewise Linear Functions," *IEEE Transactions on Computers,* Vol. C-20, 1971, pp. 59–67.

Casasent, D., and R. Krishnapuram, "Curved Object Location by Hough Transformations and Inversions," *Pattern Recognition,* Vol. 20, 1987, pp. 181–188.

Chernov, N. I., and G. A. Ososkov, "Effective Algorithms for Circle Fitting," *Computer Physics Communications,* Vol. 33, 1984, pp. 329–333.

Cohen, M., and G. T. Toussaint, "On the Detection of Structures in Noisy Pictures," *Pattern Recognition,* Vol. 9, 1977, pp. 95–98.

Conker, R. S., "A Dual Plane Variation of the Hough Transform for Detecting Non-Concentric Circles of Different Radii," *Computer Vision, Graphics, and Image Processing,* Vol. 43, 1988, pp. 115–132.

Connelly, S., and A. Rosenfeld, "A Pyramid Algorithm for Fast Curve Extraction," *Computer Vision, Graphics, and Image Processing,* Vol. 49, 1990, pp. 332–345.

Cooper, D. B., and N. Yalabik, "On the Computational Cost of Approximating and Recognizing Noise-Perturbed Straight Lines and Quadratic Arcs in the Plane," *IEEE Transactions on Computers,* Vol. C-25, 1976, pp. 1020–32.

Davies, E. R., "Image Space Transforms for Detecting Straight Edges in Industrial Images," *Pattern Recognition Letters,* Vol. 4, 1986, pp. 185–192.

Davis, L. S., "Understanding Shape: Angles and Sides," *IEEE Transactions on Computers,* Vol. C-26, 1977, pp. 236–242.

——, "Hierarchical Generalized Hough Transforms and Line-Segment Based Generalized Hough Transforms," *Pattern Recognition,* Vol. 15, 1982, pp. 277–285.

Deans, S. R., "Hough Transform from the Radon Transform," *IEEE Transactions on Pattern Analysis and Machine Intelligence,* Vol. PAMI-3, 1981, pp. 185–188.

Dorff, M., and J. Gurland, "Estimation of the Parameters of a Linear Functional Relation," *Journal of the Royal Statistical Society, B,* Vol. 23, 1961, pp. 160–170.

Duda, R. O., and P. E. Hart, "Use of the Hough Transformation to Detect Lines and Curves in Pictures," *Communications of the ACM,* Vol. 15, 1972, pp. 11–15.

Dudani, S. A., and A. L. Luk, "Locating Straight-Line Edge Segments on Outdoor Scenes," *Pattern Recognition,* Vol. 10, 1978, pp. 145–157.

Dunham, J. G., "Optimum Uniform Piecewise Linear Approximation of Planar Curves," *IEEE Transactions on Pattern Analysis and Machine Intelligence,* Vol. PAMI-8, 1986, pp. 67–75.

Dyer, C. R., "Gauge Inspection Using Hough Transforms," *IEEE Transactions on Pattern Analysis and Machine Intelligence,* Vol. PAMI-5, 1983, pp. 621–623.

Fahn, C. S., J. F. Wang, and J. Y. Lee, "An Adaptive Reduction Procedure for the Piecewise Linear Approximation of Digitized Curves," *IEEE Transactions on Pattern Analysis and Machine Intelligence,* Vol. 11, 1989, pp. 967–973.

Fischer, M. A., and R. C. Bolles, "Perceptual Organization and Curve Partitioning," *IEEE Transactions on Pattern Analysis and Machine Intelligence,* Vol. PAMI-8, 1986, pp. 100–105.

Freeman, H., "Shape Description via the Use of Critical Points," *Pattern Recognition,* Vol. 10, 1978, pp. 159–166.

Freeman, H., and L. S. Davis, "A Corner-Finding Algorithm for Chain-Coded Curves," *IEEE Transactions on Computers,* Vol. C-26, 1977, pp. 297–303.

Gerig, G., "Linking Image-Space and Accumulator-Space: A New Approach for Object Recognition," *First International Conference on Computer Vision,* London, 1987, pp. 112–117.

Grimson, W. E. L., and D. P. Huttenlocher, "On the Sensitivity of the Hough Transform for Object Recognition," *Second International Conference on Computer Vision,* Tampa, FL, 1988, pp. 700–706.

Han, M., D. Jang, and J. Foster, "Identification of Cornerpoints of Two-Dimensional Images Using a Line Search Method," *Pattern Recognition*, Vol. 22, 1989, pp. 13–20.

Hough, P. V. C., "A Method and Means for Recognizing Complex Patterns," U.S. Patent No. 3,069,654, 1962.

Huang, K. Y., et al., "Image Processing of Seismographs: (A) Hough Transformation for the Detection of Seismic Patterns; (B) Thinning Processing in the Seismogram," *Pattern Recognition*, Vol. 18, 1985, pp. 429–440.

Hunt, D. J., L. W. Nolte, and W. H. Ruedger, "Performance of the Hough Transform and Its Relationship to Statistical Signal Detection Theory," *Computer Vision, Graphics, and Image Processing*, Vol. 43, 1988, pp. 221–238.

Ichida, K., and T. Kiyono, "Segmentation of Planar Curve," *Electronics and Communications in Japan*, Vol. 58-d, 1975, pp. 689–696.

Illingworth, J., and J. Kittler, "The Adaptive Hough Transform," *IEEE Transactions on Pattern Analysis and Machine Intelligence*, Vol. PAMI-9, 1987, pp. 690–698.

——, "A Survey of the Hough Transform," *Computer Vision, Graphics, and Image Processing*, Vol. 44, 1988, pp. 87–116.

Jain, A. N., and D. B. Krig, "A Robust Hough Technique for Machine Vision," *Vision '86*, Detroit, 1986, pp. 4-75–4-87.

——, "A Robust Hough Transform Technique," *Vision*, Vol. 4, 1987, pp. 1–5.

Johnson, H. H., and A. Uogt, "A Geometric Method for Approximating Convex Arc," *SIAM Journal of Applied Math*, Vol. 38, 1980, pp. 317–325.

Kamgar-Parsi, B., and N. S. Netanyahu, "A Nonparametric Method for Fitting a Straight Line to a Noisy Image," *IEEE Transactions on Pattern Analysis and Machine Intelligence*, Vol. 11, 1989, pp. 998–1001.

Kashyap, R. L., and B. J. Oommen, "Scale Preserving Smoothing of Polygons," *IEEE Transactions on Pattern Analysis and Machine Intelligence*, Vol. PAMI-5, 1983, pp. 667–671.

Kawai, S., "A Boundary Curve Criterion," *Computer Graphics and Image Processing*, Vol. 11, 1979, pp. 281–289.

Kelley, R., and P. Gouin, "Vision Algorithm for Finding Holes," *Intelligent Robots and Computer Vision*, SPIE Vol. 521, 1984, pp. 74–79.

Kimme, C., D. Ballard, and J. Sklansky, "Finding Circles by an Array of Accumulators," *Communications of the ACM*, Vol. 18, 1975, pp. 120–122.

Krishnapuram, R., and D. Casasent, "Hough Space Transformations for Discrimination and Distortion Estimation," *Computer Vision, Graphics, and Image Processing*, Vol. 38, 1987, pp. 299–316.

Kurozumi, Y., and W. A. Davis, "Polygonal Approximation by the Minimax Method," *Computer Graphics and Image Processing*, Vol. 19, 1982, pp. 248–264.

Landau, U. M., "Estimation of a Circular Arc Center and Its Radius," *Computer Vision, Graphics, and Image Processing*, Vol. 38, 1987, pp. 317–326.

Langridge, D. J., "On the Computation of Shape," in *Frontiers in Pattern Recognition*, S. Watanabe (ed.), Academic Press, New York, 1972.

——, "Curve Encoding and the Detection of Discontinuities," *Computer Graphics and Image Processing*, Vol. 20, 1982, pp. 58–71.

Ledley, R. S., "High-Speed Automatic Analysis of Biomedical Pictures," *Science*, Vol. 146, 1964, pp. 216–223.

Li, H. F., D. Pao, and R. Jayakumar, "Improvements and Systolic Implementation of the Hough Transformation for Straight Line Detection," *Pattern Recognition*, Vol. 22, 1989, pp. 697–706.

Lowe, D. G., "Organization of Smooth Image Curves," *Proceedings of the Second International Conference on Computer Vision,* Tampa, FL, 1988, pp. 558–567.

Ma, S. D, and X. Chen, "Hough Transform Using Slope and Curvature as Local Properties to Detect Arbitrary 2D Shapes," *Ninth International Conference on Pattern Recognition,* Rome, 1988, pp. 511–513.

Maitre, H., "Contribution to the Prediction of Performances of the Hough Transform," *IEEE Transactions on Pattern Analysis and Machine Intelligence,* Vol. PAMI-8, 1986, pp. 669–674.

Mangasarian, O. L., "Nonlinear Programming," *Handbook of Operation Research,* Moder and Elmoghraby (Eds.). Van Nostrand Reinhold Company, New York, 1978, pp. 245–268.

McClure, D. E., "Nonlinear Segmented Function Approximation and Analysis of Line Patterns," *Quarterly of Applied Mathematics,* Vol. 33, 1975, pp. 1–37.

McClure, D. E., and R. A. Vitale, "Polygonal Approximation of Plane Convex Bodies," *Journal of Mathematical Analysis and Applications,* Vol. 51, 1975, pp. 326–358.

Medioni, G., and Y. Yasumoto, "Corner Detection and Curve Representation Using Cubic *B*-Splines," *Computer Vision, Graphics, and Image Processing,* Vol. 39, 1987, pp. 267–278.

Mokhtarian, F., "Evolution Properties of Space Curves," *Proceedings of the Second International Conference on Computer Vision,* Tampa, FL, 1988, pp. 100–105.

Montanari, A., "A Note on Minimal Length Polygonal Approximation to a Digitized Contour," *Communications of the ACM,* Vol. 13, 1970, pp. 41–47.

Murakami, K., H. Koshimizu, and K. Hasegawa, "An Algorithm to Extract Convex Hull on $\theta - \rho$ Hough Transform Space," *Ninth International Conference on Pattern Recognition,* Rome, 1988, pp. 500–503.

Nakagawa, Y., and A. Rosenfeld, "A Note on Polygonal and Elliptical Approximation of Mechanical Parts," *Pattern Recognition,* Vol. 11, 1979, pp. 133–142.

O'Gorman, F., and M. B. Clowes, "Finding Picture Edges through Collinearity of Feature Points," *IEEE Transactions on Computers,* Vol. C-25, 1976, pp. 449–454.

O'Rourke, J., "Dynamically Quantized Spaces for Focusing the Hough Transform," *Seventh International Joint Conference on Artificial Intelligence,* Vancouver, BC, 1981, pp. 737–739.

O'Rourke, J., and K. R. Sloan, Jr., "Dynamic Quantization: Two Adaptive Data Structures for Multidimensional Spaces," *IEEE Transactions on Pattern Analysis and Machine Intelligence,* Vol. PAMI-6, 1984, pp. 266–280.

Parent, P., and S. W. Zucker, "Trace Inference, Curvature Consistency, and Curve Detection," *IEEE Transactions on Pattern Analysis and Machine Intelligence,* Vol. 11, 1989, pp. 823–839.

Pavlidis, T., "Waveform Segmentation through Functional Approximation," *IEEE Transactions on Computers,* Vol. C-22, 1973, pp. 689–697.

——, "Polygonal Approximations by Newton's Method," *IEEE Transactions on Computers,* Vol. C-26, 1977a, pp. 800–807.

Pavlidis, T., *Structural Pattern Recognition,* Springer-Verlag, Berlin, 1977b.

——, "Curve Fitting with Conic Splines," *ACM Transactions on Graphics,* Vol. 2, 1983, pp. 1–31.

Pavlidis, T., and S. L. Horowitz, "Segmentation of Plane Curves," *IEEE Transactions on Computers,* Vol. C-23, 1974, pp. 860–870.

Petkovic, D., W. Niblack, and M. Flickner, "Projection-Based High Accuracy Measurement of Straight Line Edges," *Machine Vision and Applications,* Vol. 1, 1988, pp. 183–199.

Pham, B., "Conic B-Splines for Curve Fitting: A Unifying Approach," *Computer Vision, Graphics, and Image Processing,* Vol. 45, 1989, pp. 117–125.

Phillips, T. Y., and A. Rosenfeld, "A Method of Curve Partitioning Using Arc-Chord Distance," *Pattern Recognition Letters,* Vol. 5, 1987, pp. 285–288.

———, "An ISODATA Algorithm for Straight Line Fitting," *Pattern Recognition Letters,* Vol. 7, 1988, pp. 291–297.

Porrill, J., "Fitting Ellipses and Predicting Confidence Envelopes Using a Bias Corrected Kalman Filter," *Image and Vision Computing,* Vol. 8, 1990, pp. 37–41.

Proffitt, D., "The Measurement of Circularity and Ellipticity on a Digital Grid," *Pattern Recognition,* Vol. 15, 1982, pp. 383–387.

Ramer, U., "An Iterative Procedure for the Polygonal Approximation of Plane Curves," *Computer Graphics and Image Processing,* Vol. 1, 1972, pp. 244–256.

Risse, T., "Hough Transform for Line Recognition: Complexity of Evidence Accumulation and Cluster Detection," *Computer Vision, Graphics, and Image Processing,* Vol. 46, 1989, pp. 327–345.

Robergé, J., "A Data Reduction Algorithm for Planar Curves," *Computer Vision, Graphics, and Image Processing,* Vol. 29, 1985, pp. 168–195.

Robinson, S. M., "Fitting Spheres by the Method of Least Squares," *Communications of the ACM,* 1961, p. 491.

Ronse, C., "A Bibliography on Digital and Computational Convexity," *IEEE Transactions on Pattern Analysis and Machine Intelligence,* Vol. 11, 1989, pp. 181–190.

Rosenfeld, A., *Picture Processing by Computer*, Academic Press, New York, 1969.

Rosenfeld, A., and E. Johnston, "Angle Detection on Digital Curves," *IEEE Transactions on Computers,* Vol. C-22, 1973, pp. 875–878.

Rosenfeld, A., J. Ornelas, Jr., and Y. Hung, "Hough Transform Algorithms for Mesh-Connected SIMD Parallel Processors," *Computer Vision, Graphics, and Image Processing,* Vol. 41, 1988, pp. 293–305.

Rutkowski, W. S., "Shape Segmentation Using Arc/Chord Properties," *Computer Vision and Image Processing,* Vol. 17, 1981, pp. 114–129.

Sampson, R. D., "Fitting Conic Section to 'Very Scattered' Data: An Iterative Refinement of the Bookstein Algorithm," *Computer Graphics and Image Processing,* Vol. 18, 1982, pp. 97–108.

Sankar, P. V., and C. U. Sharma, "A Parallel Procedure for the Detection of Dominant Points on a Digital Curve," *Computer Vision and Image Processing,* Vol. 7, 1978, pp. 403–412.

Shapiro, S. D., "Feature Space Transforms for Curve Detection," *Pattern Recognition,* Vol. 10, 1978a, pp. 129–143.

———, "Properties of Transforms for the Detection of Curves in Noisy Pictures," *Computer Graphics and Image Processing,* Vol. 8, 1978b, pp. 219–236.

Shapiro, S. D., "Use of the Hough Transform for Image Data Compression," *Pattern Recognition,* Vol. 12, 1980, pp. 333–337.

Shapiro, S. D., and A. Iannino, "Geometric Constructions for Predicting Hough Transform Performance," *IEEE Transactions on Pattern Analysis and Machine Intelligence,* Vol. PAMI-1, 1979, pp. 310–317.

Shibata, T., and W. Frei, "Hough Transform for Target Detection in Infrared Imagery," *Techniques and Applications of Image Understanding,* SPIE Vol. 281, 1981, pp. 105–109.

Shirai, Y., "A Context Sensitive Line Finder for Recognition of Polyhedra," *Artificial Intelligence,* Vol. 4, 1973, pp. 95–119.

——, "Edge Finding, Segmentation of Edges and Recognition of Complex Objects," *Fourth International Joint Conference on Artificial Intelligence,* Los Altos, CA, 1975, pp. 674–681.

Silberberg, T. M., L. Davis, and D. Harwood, "An Iterative Hough Procedure for Three-Dimensional Object Recognition," *Pattern Recognition,* Vol. 17, 1984, pp. 621–629.

Sklansky, J., "On the Hough Technique for Curve Detection," *IEEE Transactions on Computers,* Vol. C-27, 1978, pp. 923–926.

Sklansky, J., and V. Gonzalez, "Fast Polygonal Approximation of Digitized Curves," *Pattern Recognition and Image Processing Conference,* Chicago, 1979, pp. 604–609.

Slgale, J. R., and J.K. Dixon, "Finding a Good Figure That Approximately Passes through Given Points," *Pattern Recognition,* Vol. 12, 1980, pp. 319–326.

——, "Freedom Descriptions: A Way to Find Figures That Approximate Given Points," *Pattern Recognition,* Vol. 17, 1984, pp. 631–636.

Stephens, R. S., "Real-Time 3D Object Tracking," *Image and Vision Computing,* Vol. 8, 1990, pp. 91–96.

Stockman, G., "Object Recognition and Localization via Pose Clustering," *Computer Vision, Graphics, and Image Processing,* Vol. 40, 1987, pp. 361–387.

Stockman, G. C., and A. K. Agrawala, "Equivalence of Hough Curve Detection to Template Matching," *Communications of the ACM,* Vol. 20, 1977, pp. 820–822.

Stone, H., "Approximation of Curves by Line Segments," *Mathematical Computation,* Vol. 15, 1961, pp. 40–47.

Svalbe, I. D., "Natural Representations for Straight Lines and the Hough Transform on Discrete Arrays," *IEEE Transactions on Pattern Analysis and Machine Intelligence,* Vol. 11, 1989, pp. 941–950.

Teh, C. H., and R. T. Chin, "A Scale-Independent Dominant Point Detection Algorithm," *IEEE Computer Society Conference on Computer Vision and Pattern Recognition,* Ann Arbor, MI, 1988, pp. 229–234.

——, "On the Detection of Dominant Points on Digital Curves," *IEEE Transactions on Pattern Analysis and Machine Intelligence,* Vol. 11, 1989, pp. 859–872.

Thomas, S. M., and Y. T. Chan, "A Simple Approach for the Estimation of Circular Arc Center and Its Radius," *Computer Vision, Graphics, and Image Processing,* Vol. 45, 1989, pp. 362–370.

Thrift, P. R., and S. M. Dunn, "Approximating Point-Set Images by Line Segments Using a Variation of the Hough Transform," *Computer Vision, Graphics, and Image Processing,* Vol. 21, 1983, pp. 383–394.

Tomek, I., "Two Algorithms for Piecewise-Linear Continuous Approximation of Functions of One Variable," *IEEE Transactions on Computers,* Vol. C-23, 1974, pp. 445–448.

Tsuji, S., and F. Matsumoto, "Detection of Elliptic and Linear Edges by Searching Two Parameter Spaces," *International Joint Conference on Artificial Intelligence,* Cambridge, MA, 1977, pp. 700–705.

——, "Detection of Ellipses by a Modified Hough Transformation," *IEEE Transactions on Computers,* Vol. C-27, 1978, pp. 777–781.

Turney, J. L., T. N. Mudge, and R. A. Volz, "Recognizing Partially Hidden Objects," *Intelligent Robots and Computer Vision,* SPIE Vol. 521, 1984, pp. 108–113.

van Veen, T. M., and F. C. A. Groen, "Discretization Errors in the Hough Transform," *Pattern Recognition,* Vol. 14, 1981, pp. 137–145.

Wall, K., and P. E. Danielsson, "A New Method for Polygonal Approximation of Digitized Curves," *Third Scandinavian Conference on Image Analysis,* Copenhagen, 1983, pp. 60–66.

———, "A Fast Sequential Method for Polygonal Approximation of Digitized Curves," *Computer Vision, Graphics, and Image Processing,* Vol. 28, 1984, pp. 220–227.

Wang, R., A. R. Hanson, and E. M. Riseman, "Fast Extraction of Ellipses," *Proceedings of the Ninth International Conference on Pattern Recognition,* Rome, 1988, pp. 508–510.

Wechsler, H., and J. Sklansky, "Finding the Rib Cage in Chest Radiographs," *Pattern Recognition,* Vol. 9, 1977, pp. 21–30.

Weiss, I., "3D Shape Representation by Contours," *Computer Vision, Graphics, and Image Processing,* Vol. 41, 1988, pp. 80–100.

Williams, C. M., "An Efficient Algorithm for the Piecewise Linear Approximation of Planar Curves," *Computer Graphics and Image Processing,* Vol. 8, 1978, p. 286–293.

Wójcik, Z. M., "Method of Contour Recognition," *Digital Systems for Industrial Automation,* Vol. 2, 1983, pp. 63–83.

Wu, L. D., "A Piecewise Linear Approximation Based on a Statistical Model," *IEEE Transactions on Pattern Analysis and Machine Intelligence,* Vol. PAMI-6, 1984, pp. 41–45.

Wu, X., and J. Rokne, "On Properties of Discretized Convex Curves," *IEEE Transactions on Pattern Analysis and Machine Intelligence,* Vol. 11, 1989, pp. 217–223.

Yang, M. C. K., et al., "Automatic Curve Fitting with Quadratic B-Spline Functions and Its Applications to Computer-Assisted Animation," *Computer Vision, Graphics, and Image Processing,* Vol. 33, 1986, pp. 346–363.

Yuen, H. K., et al., "Comparative Study of Hough Transform Methods for Circle Finding," *Image and Vision Computing,* Vol. 8, 1990, pp. 71–77.

Yuen, H. K., J. Illingworth, and J. Kittler, "Detecting Partially Occluded Ellipses Using the Hough Transform," *Image and Vision Computing,* Vol. 7, 1989, pp. 31–37.

Zucker, S. V., et al., "The Organization of Curve Detection: Coarse Tangent Fields and Fine Spline Coverings," *Proceedings of the Second International Conference on Computer Vision,* Tampa, FL, 1988, pp. 568–577.

APPENDIX A

A.1 Properties of an Ellipse

In this appendix we review several properties relevant to the use of the ellipse as a single-shape approximation to a simple, compact two-dimensional region. The most interesting properties of the ellipse are its center position, the orientation of its major axis, and the lengths of its major and minor axes. The easily computed properties are its first moments, its extremal points, and its second central moments. The appropriately normalized first moments define the center of the ellipse. Determining its orientation and the lengths of its major and minor axes from its extremal points or from its second moments can be done. The required algebra and analytic geometry are developed in this appendix.

Sections A.2 and A.3 discuss the analytic geometry of the arbitrary ellipse. Sections A.4 through A.6 derive the equation for the supporting lines tangent to the ellipse and the relationship between the extremal points of the ellipse and the orientation of the major axis and the lengths of the major and minor axes. Section A.7 derives the second central moments of the ellipse and the relationship between the second central moments and the orientation of the major axis and the lengths of the major and minor axes.

A.2 Analytic Geometry of the Ellipse

We can understand an ellipse in an arbitrary position in terms of the operations transforming a unit diameter circle centered at origin to an ellipse having a specified major axis length, minor axis length, orientation, and position. Let u be a two-dimensional vector representing the row and column positions of a point, that is, $u = \binom{r}{c}$. The unit diameter circle (radius $= \frac{1}{2}$) centered at origin is given by the equation

$$u'u = \frac{1}{4} \tag{A.1}$$

The graph of all points satisfying this equation is shown in Fig. A.1.

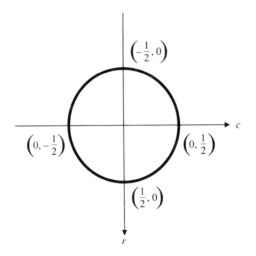

Figure A.1 Graph of $u'u = \frac{1}{4}$, where $u = \binom{r}{c}$.

Suppose the specified ellipse has major axis length $d_1 > 0$ and minor axis length $d_2 > 0$. To obtain this, we scale the row and column axes by d_1 and d_2. This means that one unit length in the current row axis must correspond to a length of d_1 units in the scaled row axis. Similarly, one unit length in the current column axis must correspond to a length of d_2 units in the scaled column axis. Hence, to convert the coordinates u of the current axes to the coordinates v of the scaled axes, we must multiply by the diagonal matrix

$$D = \begin{pmatrix} d_1 & 0 \\ 0 & d_2 \end{pmatrix} \tag{A.2}$$

That is,

$$v = Du \tag{A.3}$$

To determine the equation of the unit diameter circle in the scaled coordinate system, we solve Eq. (A.3) for u and substitute this expression into Eq. (A.1). From Eq. (A.3)

$$u = D^{-1}v \tag{A.4}$$

Substituting this into Eq. (A.1), we obtain the equation of an ellipse

$$v'D^{-2}v = \frac{1}{4} \tag{A.5}$$

The graph of all points satisfying this equation is shown in Fig. A.2.

Next we must rotate the coordinate system. The old row-column axis system is to be at a counterclockwise rotation of θ from the new rotated row-column axis system. Hence $\binom{1}{0}$ of the old coordinate system corresponds to $\binom{\cos\theta}{\sin\theta}$ in the new coordinate system, and $\binom{0}{1}$ of the old coordinate system corresponds to $\binom{-\sin\theta}{\cos\theta}$ of the new coordinate system. The rotation matrix R relating old to new must satisfy

$$\begin{pmatrix} 1 & 0 \\ 0 & 1 \end{pmatrix}_{new} = R \begin{pmatrix} \cos\theta & -\sin\theta \\ \sin\theta & \cos\theta \end{pmatrix}_{old} \tag{A.6}$$

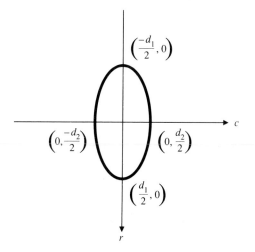

Figure A.2 Graph of $v'D^{-2}v = \frac{1}{4}$, where $v = \binom{r}{c}$.

Hence

$$R = \begin{pmatrix} \cos\theta & \sin\theta \\ -\sin\theta & \cos\theta \end{pmatrix} \tag{A.7}$$

and if w represents the new coordinates,

$$v = Rw \tag{A.8}$$

Substituting Rw for v in Eq. (A.5) results in

$$w'R'D^{-2}Rw = \frac{1}{4} \tag{A.9}$$

The graph of all points satisfying Eq. (A.9) is shown in Fig. A.3.

Finally, we want to express the rotated ellipse of Eq. (A.9) in a new translated coordinate system. Row 0 of the old coordinate system corresponds to row r_0 of the new translated coordinate system. Column 0 of the old coordinate system corresponds to column c_0 of the new translated coordinate system. Hence the translation vector x_c relating old coordinates w to new coordinates x must satisfy

$$x = w + x_c \tag{A.10}$$

where $x_c = \binom{r_0}{c_0}$.

Solving Eq. (A.10) for w and substituting into Eq. (A.9) results in

$$(x - x_c)'[R'(4D^{-2})R](x - x_c) = 1 \tag{A.11}$$

The graph of all points satisfying Eq. (A.11) is shown in Fig. A.4. Substituting the matrix A for the matrix $R'(4D^{-2})R$ in Eq. (A.11) results in

$$(x - x_c)'A(x - x_c) = 1 \tag{A.12}$$

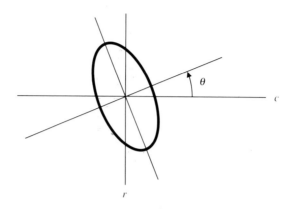

Figure A.3 Graph of $w'R'D^{-2}Rw = \frac{1}{4}$, where $R' = \begin{pmatrix} \cos\theta & \sin\theta \\ -\sin\theta & \cos\theta \end{pmatrix}$ and $w = \begin{pmatrix} r \\ c \end{pmatrix}$ (expressed in the original coordinate system).

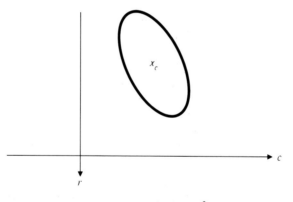

Figure A.4 Graph of $(x - x_c)'[R'(4D^{-2})R](x - x_c) = 1$.

which is the equation of an ellipse centered at x_c. The matrix A must be real symmetric, and since the diagonal entries of D are positive, A must be positive definite.

A.3   Orientation and Axis Length

Given an equation in the form of Eq. (A.12), we can determine the orientation of the ellipse as well as the lengths of the major and minor axes from the matrix A. In this section we show how. All that we need to do is determine the eigenvalues and eigenvectors of A. Let T be an orthonormal matrix whose columns are the eigenvectors of A, and let Λ be the diagonal matrix of corresponding eigenvalues. Then by definition of eigenvector and eigenvalue

$$AT = T\Lambda \tag{A.13}$$

Since T is orthornormal, $T^{-1} = T'$, and multiplying both sides of Eq. (A.13) by T' results in

$$A = T\Lambda T' \tag{A.14}$$

Here we will demonstrate that identifying T' with R and identifying $4D^{-2}$ with Λ produces the transformation we seek.

$$R = T' \tag{A.15}$$
$$D = 2\Lambda^{-1/2} \tag{A.16}$$

We begin by showing how Eq. (A.12) of the arbitrary ellipse centered at x_c can be easily obtained from the general second-order equation

$$x'Bx + t'x = k \tag{A.17}$$

of an ellipse by determining the translation x_c that will annihilate the first-order term $t'x$. We obtain that the center x_c of the ellipse is given by

$$x_c = -\frac{1}{2}B^{-1}t \tag{A.18}$$

since in this case

$$(x - x_c)'B(x - x_c) - x_c'Bx_c = x'Bx + t'x = k \tag{A.19}$$

Now

$$(x - x_c)'B(x - x_c) = k + x_c'Bx_c \tag{A.20}$$

so we take

$$A = \frac{B}{k + x_c'Bx_c} \tag{A.21}$$

to obtain Eq. (A.12).

Having transformed the general second-order equation to the canonic equation

$$(x - x_c)'A(x - x_c) = 1$$

of an ellipse, we now want to determine the orientation and length of the axes of the ellipse. To do this we need to determine the eigenvalues and eigenvectors of A. If $v = \binom{v_1}{v_2}$ is an eigenvector of

$$A = \begin{pmatrix} d & e \\ e & f \end{pmatrix}$$

with corresponding eigenvalue λ, then

$$Av = \lambda v \tag{A.22}$$

or

$$(A - \lambda I)v = 0$$

The only way for every row of $A - \lambda I$ to be orthogonal to a nonzero length vector v is for $A - \lambda I$ to be singular. Hence the determinant of $A \lambda - I$ must be equal to zero.

$$|A - \lambda I| = 0 \tag{A.23}$$

or

$$\begin{vmatrix} d - \lambda & e \\ e & f - \lambda \end{vmatrix} = 0$$

Multiplying out the determinant, we obtain the quadratic equation

$$\lambda^2 - (d + f)\lambda + df - e^2 = 0 \tag{A.24}$$

Solving this equation for the eigenvalues results in

$$\lambda = \frac{d + f \pm \sqrt{(d - f)^2 + 4e^2}}{2} \tag{A.25}$$

In the case of an ellipse, $d + f > 0$, since A must be positive definite (i.e., $\lambda > 0$). Hence the larger eigenvalue will be

$$\lambda_{large} = \frac{d + f + \sqrt{(d - f)^2 + 4e^2}}{2} \tag{A.26}$$

and the smaller eigenvalue will be

$$\lambda_{small} = \frac{d + f - \sqrt{(d - f)^2 + 4e^2}}{2} \tag{A.27}$$

For λ_{small}, the eigenvector $v = \binom{v_1}{v_2}$ must satisfy

$$\begin{pmatrix} d & e \\ e & f \end{pmatrix} \begin{pmatrix} v_1 \\ v_2 \end{pmatrix} = \frac{d + f - \sqrt{(d - f)^2 + 4e^2}}{2} \begin{pmatrix} v_1 \\ v_2 \end{pmatrix} \tag{A.28}$$

Hence

$$\begin{pmatrix} v_1 \\ v_2 \end{pmatrix} = \frac{1}{N_1} \begin{bmatrix} f - d + \sqrt{(f - d)^2 + 4e^2} \\ -2e \end{bmatrix} \tag{A.29}$$

where $N_1 = \sqrt{[(f - d) + \sqrt{(f - d)^2 + 4e^2}]^2 + 4e^2}$

If $d > f$, a more numerically stable form that replaces a subtraction by an addition can be obtained by multiplying both components by $f - d - \sqrt{(f - d)^2 + 4e^2}$ and then simplifying. There results

$$\begin{pmatrix} v_1 \\ v_2 \end{pmatrix} = \frac{1}{N_2} \begin{bmatrix} -2e \\ (d - f) + \sqrt{(d - f)^2 + 4e^2} \end{bmatrix} \tag{A.30}$$

where $N_2 = \sqrt{\left[(d - f) + \sqrt{(d - f)^2 + 4e^2}\right]^2 + 4e^2}$

For λ_{large}, the eigenvector $v = \begin{pmatrix} v_1 \\ v_2 \end{pmatrix}$ must satisfy

$$\begin{pmatrix} d & e \\ e & f \end{pmatrix} \begin{pmatrix} v_1 \\ v_2 \end{pmatrix} = \frac{d + f + \sqrt{(d - f)^2 + 4e^2}}{2} \begin{pmatrix} v_1 \\ v_2 \end{pmatrix} \tag{A.31}$$

Hence

$$\begin{pmatrix} v_1 \\ v_2 \end{pmatrix} = \frac{1}{N_1} \left[f - d + \frac{2e}{\sqrt{(f - d)^2 + 4e^2}} \right] \tag{A.32}$$

If $d > f$, a more numerically stable form is

$$\begin{pmatrix} v_1 \\ v_2 \end{pmatrix} = \frac{1}{N_2} \left[\frac{d - f + \sqrt{(d - f)^2 + 4e^2}}{2e} \right] \tag{A.33}$$

We will want to reference the orientation of the major axis of the ellipse relative to the column axis. The smaller eigenvalue relates to the major axis. This implies that when we set up the diagonal matrix whose diagonal entries are the eigenvalues of A, we will want the larger eigenvalue in the (row, row) position and the smaller eigenvalue in the (column, column) position. Thus the diagonal matrix Λ containing the eigenvalues is given by

$$\Lambda = \begin{pmatrix} \lambda_{large} & 0 \\ 0 & \lambda_{small} \end{pmatrix}$$

$$= \begin{pmatrix} \frac{d + f + \sqrt{(d - f)^2 + 4e^2}}{2} & 0 \\ 0 & \frac{d + f - \sqrt{(d - f)^2 + 4e^2}}{2} \end{pmatrix} \tag{A.34}$$

By Eq. (A.16), the major axis has length $2/\sqrt{\lambda_{small}}$ and the minor axis has length $2/\sqrt{\lambda_{large}}$. Hence

$$\text{Major axis length} = \frac{2\sqrt{2}}{\sqrt{(d + f) - \sqrt{(d - f)^2 + 4e^2}}} \tag{A.35}$$

and

$$\text{Minor axis length} = \frac{2\sqrt{2}}{\sqrt{(d + f) + \sqrt{(d - f)^2 + 4e^2}}} \tag{A.36}$$

The determinant 1 matrix T whose columns are the unit normed eigenvectors of A corresponding to the eigenvalue matrix Λ is given as follows: If $f > d$,

$$T = \frac{1}{N_1} \begin{pmatrix} 2e & -\left[f - d + \sqrt{(f - d)^2 + 4e^2} \right] \\ f - d + \sqrt{(f - d)^2 + 4e^2} & 2e \end{pmatrix} \tag{A.37}$$

If $f \leq d$, the determinant 1 matrix T whose columns are the unit normed eigenvectors of A is given by

$$T = \frac{1}{N_2} \begin{bmatrix} \dfrac{d - f + \sqrt{(d - f)^2 + 4e^2}}{2e} & \dfrac{-2e}{d - f + \sqrt{(d - f)^2 + 4e^2}} \end{bmatrix}$$
(A.38)

Since by Eq. (A.15) the rotation matrix R is related to T by $R = T'$, if $f > d$, we have

$$\cos \theta = 2e/N_1$$

$$\sin \theta = \left[f - d + \sqrt{(f - d)^2 + 4e^2} \right] /N_1 \qquad \text{(A.39)}$$

or

$$\theta = \tan^{-1} \frac{f - d + \sqrt{(f - d)^2 + 4e^2}}{2e}$$

If $f \le d$, we have

$$\cos \theta = \frac{d - f + \sqrt{(d - f)^2 + 4e^2}}{N_1}$$

$$\sin \theta = 2e/N_1 \qquad \text{(A.40)}$$

or

$$\theta = \tan^{-1} \frac{2e}{d - f + \sqrt{(d - f)^2 + 4e^2}}$$

The orientation angle θ can actually be determined in a computationally simpler manner than indicated in Eq. (A.39) and (A.40). Recall that

$$\tan 2\theta = \frac{2 \tan \theta}{1 - \tan^2 \theta} \qquad \text{(A.41)}$$

Hence, if we are careful not to perform any operation that would change the sign in the numerator or denominator of Eq. (A.41), then if $f > d$, from Eq. (A.39) we obtain

$$\tan 2\theta = \frac{2e}{d - f}$$

or

$$\theta = \frac{1}{2} \tan^{-1} \frac{2e}{d - f} \qquad \text{(A.42)}$$

If $f \le d$, from Eq. (A.40) we obtain

$$\tan 2\theta = \frac{2e}{d - f}$$

or

$$\theta = \frac{1}{2} \tan^{-1} \frac{2e}{d - f} \qquad \text{(A.43)}$$

EXAMPLE A.1

Consider the ellipse $4r^2 + 2\sqrt{3}\,rc + 2c^2 = 1$. In matrix form the ellipse satisfies

$$(r \quad c)\begin{pmatrix} 4 & \sqrt{3} \\ \sqrt{3} & 2 \end{pmatrix}\begin{pmatrix} r \\ c \end{pmatrix} = 1$$

By Eq. (A.35)

$$\text{Major axis length} = \frac{2\sqrt{2}}{\sqrt{6}-4} = 2$$

By Eq. (A.36)

$$\text{Minor axis length} = \frac{2\sqrt{2}}{\sqrt{6}+4} = \frac{2}{\sqrt{5}}$$

By Eq. (A.38) the matrix whose columns are the eigenvectors of

$$\begin{pmatrix} 4 & \sqrt{3} \\ \sqrt{3} & 2 \end{pmatrix}$$

is given by

$$\frac{1}{\sqrt{48}}\begin{pmatrix} 6 & -2\sqrt{3} \\ 2\sqrt{3} & 6 \end{pmatrix} = \begin{pmatrix} \sqrt{3}/2 & -1/2 \\ 1/2 & \sqrt{3}/2 \end{pmatrix}$$

By Eq. (A.40) the major axis orientation, taken counterclockwise with respect to the column axis, satisfies

$$\theta = \tan^{-1}\frac{1/2}{\sqrt{3}/2} = 30°$$

or, by Eq. (A.43), we have

$$\theta = \frac{1}{2}\tan^{-1}\frac{2\sqrt{3}}{(4-2)}$$

$$= \frac{1}{2}\,60° = 30°$$

A.4   Tangent Lines and Extremal Points

Without loss of generality, we will assume that the ellipse is centered at the origin. Its equation is

$$x'Ax = 1 \tag{A.44}$$

An outward vector normal to the ellipse at x is given by partially differentiating the vector function $x'Ax$ with respect to x to obtain the vector $2Ax$. Hence the outward unit vector h at any point x_0 that is on the ellipse and therefore satisfies Eq. (A.44) is given by

$$h = \frac{Ax_0}{||Ax_0||} \tag{A.45}$$

The line orthogonal to a vector h and passing through a given point x_0 is

$$h'(x - x_0) = 0 \tag{A.46}$$

From Eqs. (A.45) and (A.46) we can obtain the equation of the tangent line at a point x_0 on the ellipse:

$$x_0'A(x - x_0) = 0 \tag{A.47}$$

Now suppose that, instead of the preceding situation, a unit vector h is given and we want to determine any point x_0 on the ellipse such that h is normal to the tangent line at x_0. In this case the unknown point x_0 satisfies Eq. (A.44)

$$x_0'Ax_0 = 1 \tag{A.48}$$

and h satisfies Eq. (A.45). From Eq. (A.45) we have

$$x_0 = A^{-1}h||Ax_0|| \tag{A.49}$$

Substituting the expression for x_0 from Eq. (A.49) into Eq. (A.48), we obtain

$$(A^{-1}h||Ax_0||)'A(A^{-1}h||Ax_0||) = 1 \tag{A.50}$$

from which

$$||Ax_0|| = \frac{1}{\sqrt{h'A^{-1}h}} \tag{A.51}$$

Finally, substituting the expression for $||Ax_0||$ from Eq. (A.51) into Eq. (A.49), we obtain

$$x_0 = \frac{A^{-1}h}{\sqrt{h'A^{-1}h}} \tag{A.52}$$

Thus, given the outward normal unit vector h, the tangent line normal to h passes through the point x_0 on the ellipse given by Eq. (A.52). Furthermore, by substituting the expression from Eq. (A.52) for x_0 into Eq. (A.46) and simplifying, we find that the equation of the tangent line is given by

$$h'x = \sqrt{h'A^{-1}h} \tag{A.53}$$

A.5   Extremal Points

Extremal points of an ellipse are those points in which one coordinate takes the largest or smallest value possible from among all the points on the ellipse. (Fig. A.5)

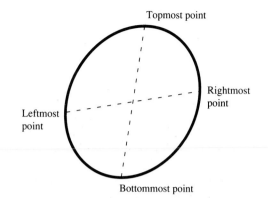

Figure A.5 An ellipse and its extremal points.

An ellipse will have four distinct extremal points corresponding precisely to those points on the ellipse having outward normal vectors

$$\begin{pmatrix} 0 \\ 1 \end{pmatrix} \begin{pmatrix} 0 \\ -1 \end{pmatrix} \begin{pmatrix} 1 \\ 0 \end{pmatrix} \text{ and } \begin{pmatrix} -1 \\ 0 \end{pmatrix}$$

These correspond to tangent lines that are the rightmost vertical, leftmost vertical, bottommost horizontal, and topmost horizontal tangent lines in the row-column coordinate system.

To determine the extremal points, we need only substitute these unit normal vectors into Eq. (A.52) and evaluate.

EXAMPLE A.2

Consider the ellipse defined by $x'Ax = 1$, where $A = \frac{1}{11} \begin{pmatrix} 3 & -1 \\ -1 & 4 \end{pmatrix}$. Then

$$A^{-1} = \begin{pmatrix} 4 & 1 \\ 1 & 3 \end{pmatrix}$$

$$\begin{pmatrix} 4 & 1 \\ 1 & 3 \end{pmatrix} \begin{pmatrix} 1 \\ 0 \end{pmatrix} = \begin{pmatrix} 4 \\ 1 \end{pmatrix} \text{ and } \sqrt{(1\ 0) \begin{pmatrix} 4 & 1 \\ 1 & 3 \end{pmatrix} \begin{pmatrix} 1 \\ 0 \end{pmatrix}} = 2$$

The extremal point corresponding to $\begin{pmatrix} 1 \\ 0 \end{pmatrix}$ is then $\frac{1}{2} \begin{pmatrix} 4 \\ 1 \end{pmatrix}$.

$$\begin{pmatrix} 4 & 1 \\ 1 & 3 \end{pmatrix} \begin{pmatrix} -1 \\ 0 \end{pmatrix} = \begin{pmatrix} -4 \\ -1 \end{pmatrix} \text{ and } \sqrt{(-1\ 0) \begin{pmatrix} 4 & 1 \\ 1 & 3 \end{pmatrix} \begin{pmatrix} -1 \\ 0 \end{pmatrix}} = 2$$

The extremal point corresponding to $\begin{pmatrix} -1 \\ 0 \end{pmatrix}$ is $\frac{1}{2} \begin{pmatrix} -4 \\ -2 \end{pmatrix}$.

$$\begin{pmatrix} 4 & 1 \\ 1 & 3 \end{pmatrix} \begin{pmatrix} 0 \\ 1 \end{pmatrix} = \begin{pmatrix} 1 \\ 3 \end{pmatrix} \text{ and } \sqrt{(0 \ 1) \begin{pmatrix} 4 & 1 \\ 1 & 3 \end{pmatrix} \begin{pmatrix} 0 \\ 1 \end{pmatrix}} = \sqrt{3}$$

The extremal point corresponding to $\begin{pmatrix} 0 \\ 1 \end{pmatrix}$ is $\frac{1}{\sqrt{3}} \begin{pmatrix} 1 \\ 3 \end{pmatrix}$.

$$\begin{pmatrix} 4 & 1 \\ 1 & 3 \end{pmatrix} \begin{pmatrix} 0 \\ -1 \end{pmatrix} = \begin{pmatrix} -1 \\ -3 \end{pmatrix} \text{ and } \sqrt{(0 \ 1) \begin{pmatrix} 4 & 1 \\ 1 & 3 \end{pmatrix} \begin{pmatrix} 0 \\ -1 \end{pmatrix}} = \sqrt{3}$$

The extremal point corresponding to $\begin{pmatrix} 0 \\ -1 \end{pmatrix}$ is $\frac{1}{\sqrt{3}} \begin{pmatrix} -1 \\ -3 \end{pmatrix}$.

A.6   From Extremal Points to Characterization of the Ellipse

In Section A.2 we showed how the orientation and size characteristics of the ellipse are contained in the matrix A of Eq. (A.12). In this section we show how to derive an expression for each entry of A from the four extremal points. As before, we assume A has the form

$$A = \begin{pmatrix} d & e \\ e & f \end{pmatrix}$$

Then from Eq. (A.52) the extremal points

$$\begin{pmatrix} r_1 \\ c_1 \end{pmatrix} \begin{pmatrix} r_2 \\ c_2 \end{pmatrix} \begin{pmatrix} r_3 \\ c_3 \end{pmatrix} \text{ and } \begin{pmatrix} r_4 \\ c_4 \end{pmatrix}$$

corresponding to unit normal directions

$$\begin{pmatrix} 0 \\ 1 \end{pmatrix} \begin{pmatrix} 0 \\ -1 \end{pmatrix} \begin{pmatrix} 1 \\ 0 \end{pmatrix} \text{ and } \begin{pmatrix} -1 \\ 0 \end{pmatrix}$$

satisfy

$$\begin{pmatrix} r_1 \\ c_1 \end{pmatrix} = \begin{pmatrix} -e \\ d \end{pmatrix} \frac{1}{\sqrt{d(df - e^2)}} \qquad \text{(rightmost)} \qquad (A.54)$$

$$\begin{pmatrix} r_2 \\ c_2 \end{pmatrix} = \begin{pmatrix} e \\ -d \end{pmatrix} \frac{1}{\sqrt{d(df - e^2)}} \qquad \text{(leftmost)} \qquad (A.55)$$

$$\begin{pmatrix} r_3 \\ c_3 \end{pmatrix} = \begin{pmatrix} f \\ -e \end{pmatrix} \frac{1}{\sqrt{d(df - e^2)}} \qquad \text{(bottommost)} \qquad (A.56)$$

$$\begin{pmatrix} r_4 \\ c_4 \end{pmatrix} = \begin{pmatrix} -f \\ e \end{pmatrix} \frac{1}{\sqrt{f(df - e^2)}} \qquad \text{(topmost)} \qquad (A.57)$$

For a translated ellipse, each extremal point would have added to it the coordinates of the ellipse center. This suggests that a translation invariant extremal feature can be obtained by the difference between opposite pairs of extremal points. Define

$$\begin{pmatrix} r_5 \\ c_5 \end{pmatrix} = \begin{pmatrix} r_1 \\ c_1 \end{pmatrix} - \begin{pmatrix} r_2 \\ c_2 \end{pmatrix} = \frac{2}{\sqrt{d(df - e^2)}} \begin{pmatrix} -e \\ d \end{pmatrix} \tag{A.58}$$

$$\begin{pmatrix} r_6 \\ c_6 \end{pmatrix} = \begin{pmatrix} r_3 \\ c_3 \end{pmatrix} - \begin{pmatrix} r_4 \\ c_4 \end{pmatrix} = \frac{2}{\sqrt{f(df - e^2)}} \begin{pmatrix} f \\ -e \end{pmatrix} \tag{A.59}$$

There are two cases to consider. Either $r_5 = c_6 = 0$ or not. If $r_5 = c_6 = 0$, then $e = 0$. If $r_6 > c_5$, then the orientation angle is $90°$, the length of the major axis is r_6, and the length of the minor axis is c_5. If $r_6 \leq c_5$, then the orientation angle is $0°$, the length of the major axis is c_5, and the length of the minor axis is r_6.

If $r_5 \neq 0$ and $c_6 \neq 0$, then we can determine an expression for $\frac{f-d}{e}$ in terms of r_5, r_6, c_5, and c_6. It is simply

$$\frac{c_5}{r_5} - \frac{r_6}{c_6} = \frac{f - d}{e}$$

If $\frac{c_5}{r_5} - \frac{r_6}{c_6} > 0$, we can use Eq. (A.39) to compute the orientation angle θ.

$$\theta = \tan^{-1} \left[\frac{1}{2} \left(\frac{f - d}{e} + \sqrt{\left(\frac{f - d}{e} \right)^2 + 4} \right) \right]$$

$$= \tan^{-1} \left\{ \frac{1}{2} \left[\left(\frac{c_5}{r_5} - \frac{r_6}{c_6} \right) + \sqrt{\left(\frac{c_5}{r_5} - \frac{r_6}{c_6} \right)^2 + 4} \right] \right\} \tag{A.60}$$

If $\frac{c_5}{r_5} - \frac{r_6}{c_6} < 0$, we can use the more numerically stable Eq. (A.30).

$$\theta = \tan^{-1} \left[2 \frac{1}{-\left(\frac{f-d}{e} \right) + \sqrt{\left(\frac{f-d}{e} \right)^2 + 4}} \right]$$

$$= \tan^{-1} \left[\frac{2}{\left(\frac{c_5}{r_5} - \frac{r_6}{c_6} \right) + \sqrt{\left(\frac{c_5}{r_5} - \frac{r_6}{c_6} \right)^2 + 4}} \right] \tag{A.61}$$

From Eq. (A.35) the eigenvalues of A are given by

$$\lambda = \frac{|e|}{2} \left\{ \left| \frac{d + f}{e} \right| \pm \sqrt{\left(\frac{f - d}{e} \right)^2 + 4} \right\} \tag{A.62}$$

An expression for $\frac{d+f}{e}$ in terms of r_5, c_5, r_6, and c_6 is

$$\frac{d + f}{e} = -\left(\frac{c_5}{r_5} + \frac{r_6}{c_6} \right)$$

To determine an expression for e, note that

$$r_5c_6 = \frac{4e^2}{\sqrt{fd}\,(df - e^2)}$$

and

$$r_6c_5 = \frac{4\sqrt{fd}}{(df - e^2)}$$

Hence

$$\frac{r_5c_6}{r_6c_5} = \frac{e^2}{fd}$$

and

$$r_6c_5 - r_5c_6 = \frac{4}{\sqrt{fd}}$$

Putting these two together, we can obtain

$$\frac{4\sqrt{\frac{r_5c_6}{r_6c_5}}}{r_6c_5 - r_5c_6} = |e| \tag{A.63}$$

Hence, if we put Eq. (A.60) into (A.59), we will find that the eigenvalues of A are given by

$$\lambda = \frac{2\sqrt{\frac{r_5c_6}{r_6c_5}}}{r_6c_5 - r_5c_6} \left\{ \left| \frac{c_5}{r_5} + \frac{r_6}{c_6} \right| \pm \sqrt{\left(\frac{c_5}{r_5} - \frac{r_6}{c_6} \right)^2 + 4} \right\} \tag{A.64}$$

The smaller eigenvalue λ_{small} takes the minus sign and the larger eigenvalue λ_{large} takes the plus sign. The axis lengths are then given by

$$\text{Major axis length} = \sqrt{\frac{4}{\lambda_{small}}} \tag{A.65}$$

$$\text{Minor axis length} = \sqrt{\frac{4}{\lambda_{large}}} \tag{A.66}$$

EXAMPLE A.3

We consider again the ellipse $4r^2 + 2\sqrt{3}rc + 2c^2 = 1$. The points where the lines tangent to the ellipse have normal directions

$$\begin{pmatrix} 0 \\ 1 \end{pmatrix} \begin{pmatrix} 0 \\ -1 \end{pmatrix} \begin{pmatrix} 1 \\ 0 \end{pmatrix} \quad \text{and} \quad \begin{pmatrix} -1 \\ 0 \end{pmatrix}$$

are given by Eqs. (A.54) through (A.57). We have

$$\begin{pmatrix} r_1 \\ c_1 \end{pmatrix} = \frac{1}{\sqrt{20}} \begin{pmatrix} -\sqrt{3} \\ 4 \end{pmatrix}$$

$$\begin{pmatrix} r_2 \\ c_2 \end{pmatrix} = \frac{1}{\sqrt{20}} \begin{pmatrix} \sqrt{3} \\ 4 \end{pmatrix}$$

$$\begin{pmatrix} r_3 \\ c_3 \end{pmatrix} = \frac{1}{\sqrt{10}} \begin{pmatrix} 2 \\ -\sqrt{3} \end{pmatrix}$$

$$\begin{pmatrix} r_4 \\ c_4 \end{pmatrix} = \frac{1}{\sqrt{10}} \begin{pmatrix} -2 \\ \sqrt{3} \end{pmatrix}$$

Now by Eqs. (A.58) and (A.59)

$$\begin{pmatrix} r_5 \\ c_5 \end{pmatrix} = \frac{2}{\sqrt{20}} \begin{pmatrix} -\sqrt{3} \\ 4 \end{pmatrix}$$

$$\begin{pmatrix} r_6 \\ c_6 \end{pmatrix} = \frac{2}{\sqrt{10}} \begin{pmatrix} 2 \\ -\sqrt{3} \end{pmatrix}$$

Hence

$$\frac{c_5}{r_5} - \frac{r_6}{c_6} = \frac{4}{-\sqrt{3}} - \frac{2}{-\sqrt{3}} = \frac{-2}{\sqrt{3}}$$

We can compute the orientation angle θ of the major axis by Eq. (A.59).

$$\theta = \tan^{-1} \left[\frac{2}{\frac{2}{\sqrt{3}} + \sqrt{\left(\frac{2}{\sqrt{3}}\right)^2 + 4}} \right]$$

$$= \tan^{-1} \frac{1}{\sqrt{3}} = 30°$$

From Eq. (A.68) the eigenvalues of A satisfy

$$\lambda = \frac{2\sqrt{\frac{3}{8}}}{20/\sqrt{200}} \left\{ \frac{6}{\sqrt{3}} \pm \sqrt{\frac{16}{3}} \right\}$$

$$= 5.1$$

Hence by Eqs. (A.65) and (A.66)

$$\text{Major axis length} = \sqrt{\frac{4}{1}} = 2$$

and

$$\text{Minor axis length} = \sqrt{\frac{4}{5}} = \frac{2}{\sqrt{5}}$$

A.7   Moments of an Ellipse

In this section we derive the formulas for the area and second moments of the ellipse

$$\begin{pmatrix} r \\ c \end{pmatrix}' A \begin{pmatrix} r \\ c \end{pmatrix} = 1$$

where

$$A = \begin{pmatrix} d & e \\ e & f \end{pmatrix}$$

A.7.1   Area

Equations (A.56) and (A.57) determine the leftmost and rightmost column coordinates for the ellipse of Eq. (A.67). The points of an ellipse having fixed column coordinates c will have the row coordinates run between

$$\frac{-2ec - \sqrt{(2ec)^2 - 4d(fc^2 - 1)}}{2d}$$

and

$$\frac{-2ec + \sqrt{(2ec)^2 - 4d(fc^2 - 1)}}{2d}$$

Hence the area of the ellipse is given by

$$\text{Area} = \int_{c = \frac{-d}{\sqrt{d(df - e^2)}}}^{\frac{d}{\sqrt{d(df - e^2)}}} \int_{r = \frac{-2ec - \sqrt{(2ec)^2 - 4d(fc^2 - 1)}}{2d}}^{\frac{-2ec + \sqrt{(2ec)^2 - 4d(fc^2 - 1)}}{2d}} dr \; dc$$

$$= \frac{2}{\sqrt{d}} \int_{\frac{-1}{\sqrt{\frac{dt - e^2}{d}}}}^{\frac{1}{\sqrt{\frac{dt - e^2}{d}}}} \sqrt{1 - \left(\frac{df - e^2}{d}\right)} \; c^2 \; dc$$

Let

$$x = \sqrt{\frac{df - e^2}{d}} \; c$$

Then

$$\text{Area} = \frac{2}{\sqrt{df - e^2}} \int_{-1}^{1} \sqrt{1 - x^2} \; dx$$

Now, making another substitution of variables, let $\sin \theta = x$. Then

$$\text{Area} = \frac{2}{\sqrt{df - e^2}} \int_{-\pi/2}^{\pi/2} \cos^2\theta \; d\theta$$

$$= \frac{2}{\sqrt{df - e^2}} \frac{\pi}{2} = \frac{\pi}{\sqrt{df - e^2}} \tag{A.67}$$

A.7.2 Second Moments

Proceeding in a similar manner to the area integration, we define the unnormalized second column moment M_{cc} by

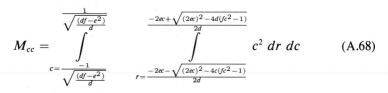

$$M_{cc} = \int_{c=-\frac{1}{\sqrt{\frac{(df-e^2)}{d}}}}^{\frac{1}{\sqrt{\frac{(df-e^2)}{d}}}} \int_{r=\frac{-2ec-\sqrt{(2ec)^2-4c(fc^2-1)}}{2d}}^{\frac{-2ec+\sqrt{(2ec)^2-4d(fc^2-1)}}{2d}} c^2 \, dr \, dc \qquad \text{(A.68)}$$

After the same substitution

$$x = \sqrt{\frac{df-e^2}{d}} \, c$$

and some simplification, we have

$$M_{cc} = \frac{2d}{(df-e^2)^{3/2}} \int_{-1}^{1} x^2 \sqrt{1-x^2} \, dx$$

Finally, making the substitution $\sin\theta = x$, we obtain

$$M_{cc} = \frac{2d}{(df-e^2)^{3/2}} \int_{-\pi/2}^{\pi/2} \sin^2\theta \cos^2\theta \, d\theta$$

$$= \frac{2d}{(df-e^2)^{3/2}} \frac{\pi}{8}$$

$$= \frac{\pi d}{4(df-e^2)^{3/2}} \qquad \text{(A.69)}$$

The normalized second column moment μ_{cc} is defined by

$$\mu_{cc} = \frac{M_{cc}}{\text{area}} = \frac{d}{4(df-e^2)} \qquad \text{(A.70)}$$

An exactly similar derivation results in

$$\mu_{rr} = \frac{M_{rr}}{\text{area}} = \frac{f}{4(df-e^2)} \qquad \text{(A.71)}$$

The unnormalized mixed second moment M_{rc} is defined by

$$M_{rc} = \int_{c=-\frac{1}{\sqrt{\frac{(df-e^2)}{d}}}}^{\frac{1}{\sqrt{\frac{(df-e^2)}{d}}}} \int_{r=\frac{-2ec-\sqrt{(2ec)^2-4d(fc^2-1)}}{2d}}^{\frac{-2ec+\sqrt{(2ec)^2-4d(fc^2-1)}}{2d}} rc \, dr \, dc \qquad \text{(A.72)}$$

Performing the row integration and simplifying, we obtain

$$M_{rc} = \int_{-\frac{1}{\sqrt{\frac{df-e^2}{d}}}}^{\frac{1}{\sqrt{\frac{df-e^2}{d}}}} \frac{-2e}{d^{3/2}}\, c^2 \sqrt{1 - \left(\frac{df-e^2}{d}\right) c^2}\; dc$$

After making the substitution $x = \sqrt{\frac{(df-e^2)}{d}}\, c$ and simplifying, we have

$$M_{rc} = \frac{-2e}{(df - e^2)^{3/2}} \int_{-1}^{1} x^2 \sqrt{1 - x^2}\; dx$$

Finally, making the substitution $x = \sin\theta$, we obtain

$$M_{rc} = \frac{-2e}{(df - e^2)^{3/2}} \int_{-\pi/2}^{\pi/2} \sin^2\theta \cos^2\theta\; d\theta$$

$$= \frac{-2e}{(df - e^2)^{3/2}} \frac{\pi}{8}$$

$$= \frac{-\pi e}{4(df - e^2)^{3/2}} \tag{A.73}$$

The normalized second mixed moment is defined by

$$\mu_{rc} = \frac{M_{rc}}{\text{area}} = \frac{-e}{4(df - e^2)} \tag{A.74}$$

A.7.3   Second Moments and the Properties of the Ellipse

The ellipse centered at (r_0, c_0) satisfies

$$\begin{pmatrix} r - r_0 \\ c - c_0 \end{pmatrix}' A \begin{pmatrix} r - r_0 \\ c - c_0 \end{pmatrix} = 1$$

There is an immediate relationship between the matrix

$$A = \begin{pmatrix} d & e \\ e & f \end{pmatrix}$$

and the matrix of normalized second moments. From Eqs. (A.72), (A.73), and

(A.74) we have

$$\begin{pmatrix} \mu_{rr} & \mu_{rc} \\ \mu_{rc} & \mu_{cc} \end{pmatrix} = \frac{1}{4(df - e^2)} \begin{pmatrix} f & -e \\ -e & d \end{pmatrix} \tag{A.75}$$

$$= \frac{1}{4} \begin{pmatrix} d & e \\ e & f \end{pmatrix}^{-1}$$

$$= \frac{1}{4} A^{-1}$$

Hence

$$A = \frac{1}{4} \begin{pmatrix} \mu_{rr} & \mu_{rc} \\ \mu_{rc} & \mu_{cc} \end{pmatrix}^{-1} \quad \text{or}$$

$$\begin{pmatrix} d & e \\ e & f \end{pmatrix} = \frac{1}{4(\mu_{rr}\mu_{cc} - \mu_{rc}^2)} \begin{pmatrix} \mu_{cc} & -\mu_{rc} \\ -\mu_{rc} & \mu_{rr} \end{pmatrix} \tag{A.76}$$

This means that once the center position (r_0, c_0) of the ellipse is known, the set of points constituting the ellipse or equivalently, the equation of the ellipse can be determined from Eq. (A.76).

Having the values of d, e, and f from Eq. (A.76), we can substitute these back into Eqs. (A.35) and (A.36) to determine the lengths of the major and minor axes. From Eq. (A.35) we have

$$\text{Major axis length} = \frac{4\sqrt{2}\sqrt{\mu_{rr}\mu_{cc} - \mu_{rc}^2}}{\sqrt{\mu_{cc} + \mu_{rr} - \sqrt{(\mu_{cc} - \mu_{rr})^2 + 4\mu_{rc}^2}}} \tag{A.77}$$

One of the potentially numerically unstable subtractions in Eq. (A.77) can be eliminated by multiplying both numerator and denominator by

$$\sqrt{\mu_{cc} + \mu_{rr} + \sqrt{(\mu_{cc} - \mu_{rr})^2 + 4\mu_{rc}^2}}$$

and simplifying. This results in

$$\text{Major axis length} = 2\sqrt{2}\sqrt{\mu_{cc} + \mu_{rr} + \sqrt{(\mu_{cc} - \mu_{rr})^2 + 4\mu_{rc}^2}} \tag{A.78}$$

Substituting the values of d, e, and f into Eq. (A.36) to determine the minor axis length, we have

$$\text{Minor axis length} = \frac{4\sqrt{2}\sqrt{\mu_{rr}\mu_{cc} - \mu_{rc}^2}}{\sqrt{\mu_{cc} + \mu_{rr} + \sqrt{(\mu_{cc} - \mu_{rr})^2 + 4\mu_{rc}^2}}} \tag{A.79}$$

Equation (A.79) can be reexpressed in a manner similar to the major axis length Eq. (A.78). This results in

$$\text{Minor axis length} = 2\sqrt{2}\sqrt{\mu_{cc} + \mu_{rr} - \sqrt{(\mu_{cc} - \mu_{rr})^2 + 4\mu_{rc}^2}} \tag{A.80}$$

The counterclockwise orientation of the major axis relative to the column axis can be determined by using Eqs. (A.39) or (A.40). If $\mu_{rr} > \mu_{cc}$, we use Eq. (A.39) to obtain

$$\theta = \tan^{-1} \frac{\mu_{rr} - \mu_{cc} + \sqrt{(\mu_{rr} - \mu_{cc})^2 + 4\mu_{rc}^2}}{-2\mu_{rc}} \tag{A.81}$$

If $\mu_{rr} \leq \mu_{cc}$, we use Eq. (A.40) to obtain

$$\theta = \tan^{-1} \frac{-2\mu_{rc}}{(\mu_{cc} - \mu_{rr}) + \sqrt{(\mu_{cc} - \mu_{rr})^2 + 4\mu_{rc}^2}} \tag{A.82}$$

EXAMPLE A.4

We continue with an example ellipse

$$(r \quad c) \begin{pmatrix} 4 & \sqrt{3} \\ \sqrt{3} & 2 \end{pmatrix} \begin{pmatrix} r \\ c \end{pmatrix} = 1$$

By Eqs. (A.72), (A.73), and (A.76), we have

$$\begin{pmatrix} \mu_{rr} & \mu_{rc} \\ \mu_{rc} & \mu_{cc} \end{pmatrix} = \frac{1}{4(8-3)} \begin{pmatrix} 2 & -\sqrt{3} \\ -\sqrt{3} & 4 \end{pmatrix}$$

By Eq. (A.80) the major axis length satisfies

$$\text{Major axis length} = \frac{2\sqrt{6 + \sqrt{4 + 12}}}{\sqrt{20}}$$

$$= \sqrt{2}$$

By Eq. (A.82) the minor axis length satisfies

$$\text{Minor axis length} = \frac{2\sqrt{6 - \sqrt{4 + 12}}}{\sqrt{20}}$$

$$= \frac{2}{\sqrt{10}}$$

Since $\mu_{cc} > \mu_{rr}$, we use Eq. (A.84) to obtain the clockwise orientation of the major axis of the ellipse with respect to the column axis.

$$\theta = \tan^{-1} \frac{-2(-\sqrt{3})}{(4-2) + \sqrt{4 + 12}}$$

$$= 30°$$

B APPENDIX B

B.1 Linear Algebra Background

In this appendix we review some basic facts about linear algebra, orthogonal projections, and least-squares approximations. We demonstrate why the solution of a least-squares problem in the discrete setting has an interpretation as the determination of an orthogonal projection in a function space. All of this is standard in numerical analysis and approximation theory. Detailed proofs can be found in the textbooks found in the bibliography; Shampine and Gordon, 1975, is the most advanced. For concreteness, we think of a *vector* as being an N-tuple of real numbers, although a vector in the general context may be a function or even a matrix, depending on the vector space under consideration. We assume the concepts of linear independence, basis, and spanning are already understood.

Let E denote the real numbers, E^N be N-dimensional Euclidean space (all N-tuples of real numbers), L be a finite dimensional real vector space, and M a subspace of L. An *inner product* (also known as a *positive definite hermitian form*) on L is a function that assigns to every pair of vectors $x, y \in L$ a real number $< x, y >$ such that

1. $< x, y > = < y, x >$ for all $x, y \in L$;
2. $< \alpha x, y > = \alpha < y, x >$ for all $x, y \in L, \alpha \in E$;
3. $< x + w, y > = < x, y > + < w, y >$ for all $x, y, w \in L$;
4. $< x, x > \; > 0$ for all $x \neq 0$ in L.

For $L = E^N$, the standard inner product is $< x, y > = x'y$. The inner product with respect to a positive definite symmetric matrix A is $< x, y > = x'Ay$. An inner product $< x, y >$ always leads to a norm on L defined by

$$\|x\| = \sqrt{< x, x >} \tag{B.1}$$

659

For $L = E^N$ where the norm is induced by the symmetric positive definite matrix A of the inner product, we will write

$$\|x\|_A = \sqrt{<x,x>} = \sqrt{x'Ax} \tag{B.2}$$

A norm has properties
1. $\|x\| \geq 0$ with equality if and only if $x = 0$;
2. $\|\alpha x\| = \|\alpha\| \|x\|$ for all $x \in L$, $\alpha \in E$;
3. $\|x + y\| \leq \|x\| + \|y\|$ for all $x, y \in L$.

Not every norm arises from some inner product, but those that do have nicer properties.

Vectors $u, v \in L$ are *orthogonal* if $<u,v>= 0$. A set of vectors $\{u_1, \ldots, u_k\}$ is *orthonormal* if

$$<u_i, u_j >= \delta_{ij} = \begin{cases} 1, i = j \\ 0, i \neq j \end{cases} \tag{B.3}$$

A vector $v \in L$ is orthogonal to the subspace M if $<v,x>= 0$ for all $x \in M$. The orthogonal complement of M, denoted by $M^{\perp}$, is the set of all vectors orthogonal to M:

$$M^{\perp} = \{x \in L | <x,w >= 0 \text{ for all } w \in M\} \tag{B.4}$$

It follows from these definitions that every vector $x \in L$ has a unique representation of the form

$$x = u + v, \quad u \in M, \quad v \in M^{\perp}$$

This is sometimes expressed by saying L is the direct sum of M and $M^{\perp}$, denoted $L = M \oplus M^{\perp}$. Note that u and v are unique and $<u,v>= 0$. The vector u is called the *orthogonal projection* of x onto M.

To see that x can be represented in the form $x = u + v$ and that the representation $x = u + v$ is unique, let $b_1, \ldots, b_I$ be an orthonormal basis for M and let $b_{I+1}, \ldots, b_N$ extend this orthonormal basis to the entirety of L. Since $b_{I+1}, \ldots, b_N$ is orthonormal to b_i, $i = 1, \ldots, I$, $b_{I+1}, \ldots, b_N$ constitutes an orthonormal basis for $M^{\perp}$.

Now since $b_1, \ldots, b_N$ is a basis for L, we can uniquely represent any $x \in L$ by $x = \sum_{n=1}^{N} \alpha_n b_n$. The scalar coefficients of this representation are easily determined by taking inner products.

$$<x,b_m> = \left\langle \sum_{n=1}^{N} \alpha_n b_n, b_m \right\rangle$$
$$= \sum_{n=1}^{N} \langle \alpha_n b_n, b_m \rangle$$
$$= \sum_{n=1}^{N} \alpha_n \langle b_n, b_m \rangle$$
$$= \alpha_m \tag{B.5}$$

since $b_1, \ldots, b_N$ are orthonormal. Finally, notice that

$$x = \sum_{n=1}^{N} \alpha_n b_n = \sum_{n=1}^{I} \alpha_n b_n + \sum_{n=I+1}^{N} \alpha_n b_n \tag{B.6}$$

Since $b_1, \ldots, b_I$ is a basis for M and $b_{I+1}, \ldots, b_N$ is a basis for $M^\perp$ by taking $u = \sum_{n=1}^{I} \alpha_n b_n$ and $v = \sum_{n=I+1}^{N} \alpha_n b_n$, the representation and its uniqueness of $x = u + v$, where $u \in M$ and $v \in M^\perp$, are shown.

Next we want to show that if $x = u + v$, where $u \in M$ and $v \in M^\perp$, the map $x \to u$ defines a linear operator. Let

$$y = u_y + v_y \qquad \text{where} \quad u_y \in M, \ v_y \in M^\perp$$
$$z = u_z + v_z \qquad \text{where} \quad u_z \in M, \ v_z \in M^\perp \tag{B.7}$$

Let α and β be scalars. Suppose that

$$\alpha y + \beta z = u + v \quad \text{where} \quad u \in M \text{ and } v \in M^\perp$$

Consider

$$\alpha y + \beta z = \alpha(u_y + v_y) + \beta(u_z + v_z)$$
$$= (\alpha u_y + \beta u_z) + (\alpha v_y + \beta v_z) \tag{B.8}$$

Since $u_y, \ u_z \in M$ and $v_y, \ v_z \in M^\perp$,

$$\alpha u_y + \beta u_z \in M \quad \text{and} \quad \alpha v_y + \beta v_z \in M^\perp \tag{B.9}$$

But the representation of $\alpha y + \beta z$ in terms of its projections in M and $M^\perp$ is unique. Hence $u = \alpha u_y + \beta u_z$ and $v = \alpha v_y + \beta v_z$. This means that if $x = u + v$ where $u \in M$ and $v \in M^\perp$, the map $x \to u$ defines a linear operator.

Furthermore, this linear operator is symmetric and idempotent. Let the name of this linear operator be P. The definition for P to be symmetric is that $< Py, z > = < y, Pz >$ for all $y, z \in L$. The definition for P to be idempotent is that $P(Py) = Py$ for all $y \in L$. To see that P is symmetric and idempotent, let y and $z \in L$ have representation

$$y = u_y + v_y$$
$$z = u_z + v_z \tag{B.10}$$

where $u_y, \ u_z \in M$ and $v_y, \ v_z \in M^\perp$. Then

$$< Py, z > = < P(u_y + v_y), u_z + v_z >$$
$$= < u_y, u_z + v_z >$$
$$= < u_y, u_z > + < u_y, v_z >$$
$$= < u_y, u_z >$$
$$= < u_y, u_z > + < v_y, u_z >$$
$$= < u_y + v_y, u_z >$$
$$= < u_y + v_y, P(u_z + v_z) >$$
$$= < y, Pz >$$
$$P(Py) = P[P(u_y + v_y)]$$
$$= P(u_y)$$
$$= P(u_y + v_y)$$
$$= Py \tag{B.11}$$

It also follows that any linear symmetric idempotent operator P defined on L is an orthogonal projection onto the subspace M, which is defined as the range of P.

When $L = E^N$, a matrix P is an orthogonal projection operator with respect to the norm induced by the symmetric positive definite matrix A of the inner product if and only if $PA = (PA)'$ (symmetric) and $PP = P$ (idempotent). Orthogonal projection operators are intimately related to least-squares problems.

Let P be the projection operator onto the subspace M, and $f \in L$. Let $f = u + v, u \in M, v \in M^{\perp}$. Then there is a unique closest point in M to f, namely, $u = Pf$, and the distance from f to M is $\|v\|$. In other words, the approximation problem

$$\min \|y - f\|, \qquad y \in M \tag{B.12}$$

has the unique solution $u = Pf$, and the minimum is $\|v\| = \|(I - P)f\|$.

For $L = E^N$ and $< x, y > = x'Ay$, projection operators have an explicit representation. Let $b_1, \ldots, b_I$ be a basis for a subspace M of L and $B = (b_1, \ldots, b_I)$. Then the projection operator P onto M is given by $P = B(B'AB)^{-1}B'A$. This is easily seen by direct calculation.

$$\begin{aligned} PP &= [B(B'AB)^{-1}B'A][B(B'AB)^{-1}B'A] \\ &= B(B'AB)^{-1}(B'AB)(B'AB)^{-1}B'A \\ &= B(B'AB)^{-1}B'A = P \end{aligned} \tag{B.13}$$

Also, P is symmetric,

$$\begin{aligned} < Px, y > &= (Px)'Ay = x'P'Ay \\ &= x'[B(B'AB)^{-1}B'A]'Ay \\ &= x'AB(B'AB)^{-1}B'Ay \\ &= < x, Py > \end{aligned} \tag{B.14}$$

The explicit representation is convenient for theoretical purposes, but serious roundoff error due to possible ill conditioning of $B'AB$ sometimes makes it computationally impractical. However, if the columns of B are othonormal with respect to the norm induced by positive definite symmetric matrix A, then $B'AB = I$ is perfectly conditioned and there are no numerical difficulties. In this case the orthogonal projection operator P is simply given by $P = BB'A$.

The orthogonal projection of x onto M has a particularly simple representation in terms of the orthonormal basis $b_1, \ldots, b_I$ of M with respect to the norm induced by the symmetric positive definite matrix A.

$$\begin{aligned} Px &= BB'Ax \\ &= \begin{pmatrix} b_1 \\ \vdots \\ b_I \end{pmatrix} \begin{pmatrix} < b_1, x > \\ \vdots \\ < b_I, x > \end{pmatrix} \\ &= \sum_{i=1}^{I} < b_i, x > b_i \end{aligned} \tag{B.15}$$

This says that the orthogonal projection of x onto M is given as a linear combination of an orthonormal basis $b_1, \ldots, b_I$ of M, where the coefficient associated with basis b_i is just the inner product of b_i with x. These coefficients are sometimes known as the generalized *Fourier coefficients*.

In this case the orthogonal projection P is given by

$$P = BB'A$$

$$Px = BB'Ax$$

$$= B \begin{pmatrix} b'_1 \\ \vdots \\ b'_I \end{pmatrix} Ax$$

$$= B \begin{pmatrix} <b_1, x> \\ \vdots \\ <b_I, x> \end{pmatrix}$$

$$= (b_1, \ldots, b_I) \begin{pmatrix} <b_1, x> \\ \vdots \\ <b_I, x> \end{pmatrix}$$

$$= \sum_{i=1}^{I} <b_i, x> b_i \tag{B.16}$$

B.2 Discrete Least Squares Understood in Terms of Orthogonal Projection

In this section we illustrate that the problem of discrete least squares fitting a set $\{(x_i, y_i); i = 1, \ldots, K\}$ of points whose N-dimensional x-coordinates constitute the independent variables and whose y-coordinate is the dependent variable, with respect to a set of functions $\{f_n(x); n = 1, \ldots, N\}$, is exactly the same problem as taking the orthogonal projection of the vector

$$y = \begin{pmatrix} y_1 \\ \vdots \\ y_K \end{pmatrix} \tag{B.17}$$

onto the space spanned by the set of vectors

$$\left\{ \begin{pmatrix} f_n(x_1) \\ \vdots \\ f_n(x_K) \end{pmatrix} \middle| n = 1, \ldots, N \right\} \tag{B.18}$$

It is assumed that $N < K$ and that the functions $f_n(x)$ are independent with respect to the points x_i. This means that

$$\sum_{i=1}^{N} \alpha_i f_i(x_k) = 0 \tag{B.19}$$

for $k = 1, \ldots, K$ implies $\alpha_1 = \ldots = \alpha_N = 0$.

Imagine the data points (x_i, y_i) as lying on the graph of some function $g(x)$, and let L be a vector space (of functions) containing, among others, g and $f_1, \ldots, f_n$. Let A be a $K \times K$ symmetric positive definite matrix. Define an inner product on the vector space of functions L by

$$< h, k >= \begin{pmatrix} h(x_1) \\ \vdots \\ h(x_K) \end{pmatrix}' A \begin{pmatrix} k(x_1) \\ \vdots \\ k(x_K) \end{pmatrix} \tag{B.20}$$

(actually this may only be a positive *semidefinite* hermitian form, but this technical subtlety is irrelevant for our purposes). The problem of finding the best approximation f to g by a linear combination of $f_1, \ldots f_N$ with respect to this inner product can be solved by considering

$$\|g - \hat{f}\|^2 = < g - \hat{f}, g - \hat{f} >$$

$$= \left\langle \begin{pmatrix} y_1 \\ \vdots \\ y_K \end{pmatrix} - \begin{pmatrix} \hat{f}(x_1) \\ \vdots \\ \hat{f}(x_K) \end{pmatrix}, \begin{pmatrix} y_1 \\ \vdots \\ y_K \end{pmatrix} - \begin{pmatrix} \hat{f}(x_1) \\ \vdots \\ \hat{f}(x_K) \end{pmatrix} \right\rangle$$

$$= \left\| \begin{pmatrix} y_1 \\ \vdots \\ y_K \end{pmatrix} - \begin{pmatrix} \hat{f}(x_1) \\ \vdots \\ \hat{f}(x_K) \end{pmatrix} \right\|_A^2 \tag{B.21}$$

Hence the $\hat{f} \in M$, where M is the subspace of L spanned by $\{f_1, \ldots, f_N\}$, which minimizes $\|g - \hat{f}\|^2$, will be that $\hat{f}$ having values $\hat{f}(x_1), \ldots, \hat{f}(x_K)$ at the given points $x_1, \ldots, x_K$ satisfying that

$$\begin{pmatrix} \hat{f}(x_1) \\ \vdots \\ \hat{f}(x_K) \end{pmatrix}$$

is the orthogonal projection of

$$\begin{pmatrix} y_1 \\ \vdots \\ y_K \end{pmatrix}$$

onto the subspace spanned by

$$\left\{ \begin{pmatrix} f_1(x_1) \\ \vdots \\ f_1(x_K) \end{pmatrix}, \ldots, \begin{pmatrix} f_N(x_1) \\ \vdots \\ f_N(x_K) \end{pmatrix} \right\}$$

Such an $\hat{f}$ is called the best discrete least-squares approximation to g. It follows from what we have already developed about the representation for orthogonal projection operators that

$$
\begin{pmatrix} \hat{f}(x_1) \\ \vdots \\ \hat{f}(x_K) \end{pmatrix} = B(B'AB)^{-1}B'A \begin{pmatrix} y_1 \\ \vdots \\ y_n \end{pmatrix} \tag{B.22}
$$

where

$$
B = \begin{pmatrix} f_1(x_1) & \cdots & f_N(x_1) \\ \vdots & & \vdots \\ f_1(x_K) & \cdots & f_N(x_K) \end{pmatrix}. \tag{B.23}
$$

Now if we define the $N \times 1$ coefficient vector $\alpha = \begin{pmatrix} \alpha_1 \\ \vdots \\ \alpha_N \end{pmatrix}$ by

$$
\alpha = (B'AB)^{-1}B'A \begin{pmatrix} y_1 \\ \vdots \\ y_K \end{pmatrix} \tag{B.24}
$$

then the discrete fit equation is

$$
\begin{pmatrix} \hat{f}(x_1) \\ \vdots \\ \hat{f}(x_K) \end{pmatrix} = B\alpha = \sum_{n=1}^{N} \alpha_n \begin{pmatrix} f_n(x_1) \\ \vdots \\ f_n(x_K) \end{pmatrix} \tag{B.25}
$$

But as the fit was originally posed in the function space M, we also have

$$
\hat{f} = \sum_{n=1}^{N} \alpha_n f_n \tag{B.26}
$$

Here $\hat{f}$ is the best-fit function in the subspace of functions M.

■ Bibliography

de Boor, C., *A Practical Guide to Splines,* Springer–Verlag, New York, 1978.

Cheney, E. W., *Introduction to Approximation Theory,* McGraw–Hill, New York, 1966.

Dahlquist, G., and A. Bjorck, *Numerical Methods,* Prentice Hall, Englewood Cliffs, NJ, 1974.

Isaacson, E., and H. B. Keller, *Analysis of Numerical Methods,* Wiley, New York, 1966.

Shampine, L. F., and M. K. Gordon, *Computer Solution of Ordinary Differential Equations: The Initial Value Problem,* W. H. Freeman, San Francisco, 1975.

C EXPERIMENTAL PROTOCOL

Controlled experiments are an important component of computer vision, for the controlled experiment demonstrates that the algorithm, designed by the computer-vision researcher, recognizes, locates, and measures what it is designed to do from image data. A properly designed scientific experiment provides evidence to accept or reject the hypothesis that the algorithm performs to a specified accuracy level. To properly set up such an experiment, in a way that it can be repeated and the evidence verified by another researcher, you must pay considerable attention to experimental protocol.

The experimental protocol states the quantity to be measured, the accuracy to which it is to be measured, and the population of scenes/images on which the vision algorithm is to be applied. Then the protocol must give the experimental design and the data analysis plan.

The experimental design describes how a suitably random, independent, and representative set of images from the specified population is to be sampled, generated, or acquired. If, for example, the population includes a range of sizes for the object of interest or if the object of interest can appear in a variety of situations, then the sampling mechanism must assume that a reasonable number of images are sampled with the object appearing in each of the different sizes or appearing with sizes and orientations throughout its permissible range.

Similarly, if the object to be recognized or measured can appear in a variety of different lighting conditions that create a similar variety in shadowing, then the sampling must assure that images are acquired with the lighting and shadowing varying throughout their permissible range. In general, the essential variation of the images in the population can be described by some number, say N variables. If the N variables $X_1, \ldots, X_N$, having to do with kind of lighting, light position, object position, object orientation, undesired object occlusion, environmental clutter, distortion, noise, etc., have respective range sets $R_1, \ldots, R_N$, then the sampling design must assure that images sample the domain $R_1 \times R_2 \times \ldots \times R_N$ in a representative way. The domain $R_1 \times R_2 \times \ldots \times R_N$ is an infinitesimal fraction of the number of possibilities in $R_1 \times R_2 \times \ldots \times R_N$. This suggests that the experimental design may have to make judicious use of a latin-square layout. If there are some free parameters that must be set in the vision algorithm, then these parameters can as well be part of the N-variables.

The experiments must then be carried out for each image in the sample. Suppose there are M different measurements $\hat{y}_1, \ldots, \hat{y}_M$ made on each image. These variables would be a subset of the N variables, which might describe the images in the population of interest. There will be a difference between the true values $y_1, \ldots, y_M$ of the measured quantities and the measured values themselves. The accuracy criterion must state how the comparison between the true values and the measured values will be evaluated. Finally, the experimental data analysis plan must state how the hypothesis that the algorithm meets the specified requirement will be tested. It indicates how the observed data (the true values and the corresponding measured values) will be analyzed. The plan must be supported by theoretically developed statistical analysis, which shows that an experiment carried out according to the experimental design and analyzed according to the data analysis plan will produce a statistical test itself having a given accuracy. That is, since the entire population was only sampled, the sampling fluctuation will introduce random fluctuation in the test results. For some fraction of experiments carried out according to the protocol the hypothesis to be tested will be accepted but the algorithm, in fact, if it were tried on the complete population of image variations, would not meet the specified requirements; for some fraction of experiments carried out according to the protocol, the hypothesis to be tested will be rejected, but the algorithm, if in fact it were tried on the complete population of image variations, would meet the specified requirements. The specified size of these errors of false acceptance and missed acceptance will dictate the number of images to be in the sample. This relation between sample size and false acceptance rate and missed acceptance rate of the test for the hypothesis must be determined on the basis of statistical theory. One would certainly expect that the sample size would be large enough so that these error rates would be below 20%.

For example, if the error rate of vision algorithm is less than 1/1,000, then in order to be about 85% sure that the performance meets specification, 10,000 tests should be run. If the vision algorithm performs incorrectly 9 or fewer times, then we can assert that with 85% probability, the vision algorithm meets specification (Haralick, 1989).

■ Bibliography

Haralick, R. M., "Performance Assessment of Near Perfect Machines," *Machine Vision and Applications,* Vol. 2, No. 1, 1989, 1–16.

INDEX